W
Africa

Cabo Verde (p74)

Mauritania (p261)

Mali (p257)

Niger (p274)

Senegal (p312)

The Gambia (p163)

Guinea-Bissau (p232)

Guinea (p217)

Burkina Faso (p56)

Benin (p38)

Nigeria (p278)

Sierra Leone (p340)

Côte d'Ivoire (p133)

Ghana (p183)

Cameroon (p105)

Liberia (p244)

Togo (p356)

São Tomé & Príncipe (p298)

Equatorial Guinea (p149)

WITHDRAWN

Anthony Ham

Stuart Butler, Michael Grosberg, Nana Luckham,
Vesna Maric, Helen Ranger, Caroline Sieg, Helena Smith,
Regis St Louis, Paul Stiles

Contents

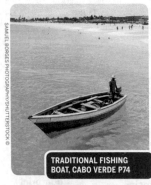

TRADITIONAL FISHING
BOAT, CABO VERDE P74

TUAREG MAN, MALI P257

Contents

ON THE ROAD

JT PLATT/SHUTTERSTOCK ©

Contents

UNDERSTAND

SURVIVAL GUIDE

SPECIAL FEATURES

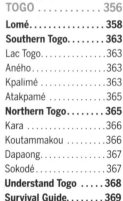

CHIMP, RIVER GAMBIA
NATIONAL PARK P177

Welcome to West Africa

West Africa has cachet and soul. Home to African landscapes of our imaginations and inhabited by an astonishing diversity of traditional peoples, this is Africa as it once was.

African Landscapes

From the Sahara to tropical rainforests, from volcanic outcrops to stony depressions in the desert's heart, West Africa is an extraordinary sweep of iconic African terrain. There are many West African views that will define your journey: an oasis-like clearing in the heart of a rainforest; a gloriously deserted arc of sand along a gloriously deserted coastline; and improbably shaped rocky outcrops in the heart of the Sahel. And through it all run two of Africa's longest rivers, the Congo and the Niger.

African Peoples

The mosaic of peoples who inhabit West Africa is one of the region's most beguiling characteristics. The sheer number of peoples who call the region home will take your breath away. Drawing in a little nearer, you'll discover that traditions survive in West Africa like nowhere else on the continent, revealing themselves in fabulous festivals, irresistible music and the mysterious world of masks and secret societies. These are peoples whose histories are epic and whose daily struggles are similarly so. West Africa is in-your-face, full-volume Lagos or the quiet solitude of an indigo-clad nomad – not to mention everything in between.

A Musical Soundtrack

West Africa's musical tradition is one of extraordinary depth and richness. Youssou N'Dour, Tinariwen and other musicians may have been 'discovered' in recent decades, but the region's music is so much more than mere performance. The *griots* of ancient African empires bestowed upon West Africa's musicians the gift of storytelling as much as the power to entertain. They do both exceptionally well and their ability to make you dance or learn something new about the region may just rank among your most memorable travel experiences.

Secret Wildlife

You wouldn't come to West Africa looking for an East African–style safari. If you did, you'd be disappointed, unless, of course, you head for the wildlife-rich national parks of Gabon and Republic of Congo; there are few finer places to see gorillas on the planet. Elsewhere there's more to West Africa's wildlife than initially meets the eye (which may not be much) if you know where to look, including elephants, primates, big cats, pygmy hippos and some of the world's best birdwatching. And unlike East or Southern Africa, you're likely to have whatever you find all to yourself.

Why I Love West Africa

By Anthony Ham, Writer

On my first journey into West Africa, I felt like I was visiting another planet, and I loved it. It was the cooling sand beneath my feet as I shared a campfire with Tuareg nomads in the Sahara, or a dawn glimpse of paradise at a bend in the river deep in the Cameroonian rainforest. It was dancing the night away in the bars of Bamako or Dakar, or the silence of the Sahelian night. And no matter how many times I return, I never lose that sense of having wandered into some kind of otherworldly African fairy tale.

For more about our writers, see p504

For more about our writers, see p504

Above: Grande Mosquée, Bobo-Dioulasso, Burkina Faso (p63)

West Africa

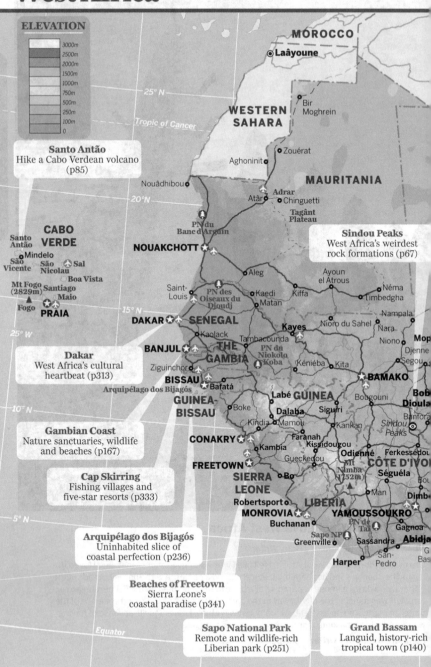

0   0
(N)   ───────────────── 1000 km
      ───────────────── 500 miles

Kpalimé
Lush highlands
ripe for hiking (p363)

Atakora Region
Stunning highlands and
cultural mix (p49)

Adrar

Sabha
LIBYA

denni

Bordj-
Mokhtar

Djado

ALGERIA

Séguédine

hnâchîch

Tessalit

Réserve Naturell
Nationale de l'Aïr
et du Ténéré

ouane

Aïr Massif

Bilma

MALI

Anéfis

Iferouâne
Arlit   **Aïr Mountains**

Ténéré Desert

buktu
nbouctou)

Bourem

Sahara

Timia

NIGER

CHAD

Niger

Adrar des
Ifôghas

In-Gall

Agadez

dam

Gao

Ménaka

Tillia

Aderbissinat

uentza

Ansongo

Réserve
d'Ansongo-
Ménaka

Tahoua
Birni
N'konni

Tanout

Ring Road
Cameroon's forgotten
rainforest villages (p121)

iagara

Djibo
Dori

Maradi

Zinder

Diffa

Lake
Chad

N'DJAMÉNA

Kaya

Dosso

Sokoto

Gashua

OUAGADOUGOU

PN du W
(Benin)
Gaya

Katsina
Gusau

Hadejia-Nguru
Wetlands

Maiduguri

PN de
Waza

URKINA FASO

Malanville

Kano

Potiskum

Mandara
Mountains

Maroua

Pô

Dapaong

Kandi

Kamuku
WR

Kontagora

Jos Plateau

Bauchi

Biu
Gombe

Bolgatanga   **BENIN**

Natitingou

Kaduna

Jos

Garoua

Wa

Djougou

Parakou

ABUJA

Yankari NP

Moundou

ole NP   Tamale

GHANA

Sokodé

NIGERIA

TOGO

Ilorin

Oshogbo

Lokoja

Makurdi

Gembu

CAMEROON

N'Gaoundéré

Techiman   Atakpamé

Lake Volta

Kpalimé

Abomey

Ibadan

PORTO-NOVO

Benin
City

Ogoja

PN du
Faro

Kumasi   Ouidah

Ho

Lagos

Cotonou

Onitsha Bamenda

Bamenda Mountains

Foumban

Bertoua

Elmina

LOMÉ

Warri

Korup NP

Aba

Mt Cameroon
(4095m)

Kenzou

P

Sekondi   **ACCRA**

Cape
Coast

Port Harcourt   **Calabar**

Buea

Douala

Abong
Mbang

MALABO

Edéa   **YAOUNDÉ**

Ghana's Slave Coast
Evocative coastal
e forts and castles (p197)

Calabar
River port and
rich biodiversity (p291)

EQUATORIAL   CONGO

Ebolowa

SÃO TOMÉ & PRINCIPE

Monte
Mitra   **GUINEA**

SÃO TOMÉ

LIBREVILLE   **GABON**

Baía das Agulhas
Tropical Atlantic Ocean
perfection (p307)

Port-
Gentil

Ureca
Dense rainforest and
stirring wildlife (p154)

0°   5°E   Annobón

West Africa's
Top 17

Cap Skirring, Senegal

1 Take a pirogue (traditional canoe; pictured) from busy fishing village Elinkine and hop over to Île de Karabane; a French trading station in the 19th century, it still boasts a Breton-style church with ancient pews, and you can sip palm wine on the island's peaceful beaches. Check into a room with a view of the waves gently lapping at the sand or, better yet, venture out on a fishing or kayaking expedition from Cap Skirring (p333), followed by a dose of live music and dancing barefoot with abandon under a star-filled sky.

Gambian Coast

2 Gambia's Atlantic Coast is peppered with oodles of flashy resorts and the country may be one of Africa's smallest, but it's amazing how much it crams into such a small space. Birdwatching and wildlife are definite highlights among numerous options, but nothing beats drifting past river islands and exploring superb nature sanctuaries such as Bijilo Forest Park (p167), where you can observe monkeys, including the vervet (pictured), monitor lizards and more than 100 bird species.

BSIP/GETTY IMAGES ©

LIDIA FOTOGRAFIE/SHUTTERSTOCK ©

Ghana's Slave Coast

3 No matter how well versed you are with the history of the slave trade, nothing can prepare you for the experience of visiting Ghana's slave forts. Standing in the damp dungeons or being shut in the pitch-black punishment cells will chill your blood, and the wreaths and messages left by those whose forebears went through the ordeal are poignant. Cape Coast Castle (pictured; p197) is one of the largest and best-preserved forts but there are many smaller ones along the coast too, which tell the same sorry tale.

Mole National Park, Ghana

4 West Africa has nothing to match East and Southern Africa's national parks but it does have more wildlife than many imagine. Mole (p208) is a prime example of this stunning diversity. Famed for the large herds of elephant that wander the saffron savannah, the park is also home to antelopes (pictured), warthogs, monkeys, crocodiles and thousands of birds, all of which you'll be able to see at a fraction of the cost of a 'traditional' safari.

Ring Road, Cameroon

5 Deep in Cameroon's northwest, the so-called Ring Road (p121) is a grassland area of unparalleled natural beauty, boasting rushing chocolate-coloured rivers, soaring hilltops, lush forests and small, traditional *fondoms* (kingdoms ruled by traditional chiefs known as *fons*) where foreigners are rarely seen. The area is great for hiking, though it's best explored with your own wheels, as local public transport is extremely infrequent. Be aware that the 'ring road' itself is most of the time little more than a dirt track – don't attempt to come here in the rainy season!

Sindou Peaks, Burkina Faso

6 Nature's work of art, the otherworldly rock formations of Sindou Peaks (p67) are a sight to behold. Cast against the darkening sky of a brewing storm or the lush paddy fields of the plains below, they are one of Burkina's great signature landscapes. Trekking is the best way to explore this natural wonder, although there will be plenty of wonderful photo opportunities on the drive there. Local guides organise sunrise breakfasts at a particularly scenic spot, an experience that will likely be the highlight of your trip.

Freetown Beaches, Sierra Leone

7 Freetown's long peninsula is lined with sun-drenched beaches (p347) that you'll find hard to leave. Begin with the famous River No 2 for calm, clear waters and up-river mangrove trips – and when the high tide hits, boat across to Tokeh Beach, whose forest-backed sweep of fine white sand is probably the most spectacular of them all. Then there's surfing at Bureh Beach and wine-fuelled lobster dinners at Sussex Beach, while John Obey Beach and Black Johnson Beach will take you far off the beaten track.

DE AGOSTINI/GETTY IMAGES ©

Atakora Region, Benin

8 Northwestern Benin is dominated by the rugged landscapes of the Atakora mountains (p49). There's a lot to love about this area: the captivating culture and traditions of the animist Betamaribé people, the eye-catching architecture of the *tata somba* houses (round-tiered huts), and utterly beautiful hills that offer plenty of breathtaking pan-oramas. It's still a secretive world with a peculiar appeal, and it begs exploration. You can base yourself in Natitingou or, even better, stay in villages. Elder smoking a pipe

Santo Antão, Cabo Verde

9 From long lonely walks through lush valleys to strenuous treks along craggy peaks and remote ravines, the dramatic is-land of Santo Antão (p85) is a hiker's paradise. Set aside at least three full days; first tackle its clas-sic hikes, like the sharp descent along the cobbled path from the Cova crater to Paúl valley, and then set out to explore the island's uncharted western sec-tion. Get a good map, stock up on local advice and hire a guide for the more de-manding treks.

Kpalimé, Togo

10 Itchy feet? Con-sider exploring the Kpalimé area (p365), which offers lots of hiking opportunities amid stun-ning scenery. With its lush forested hills, numerous waterfalls and profusion of butterflies, it is a walking heaven and possibly West Africa's premier hiking terrain. Good news: most walks are suitable for all levels of fitness. Tackle Mt Agou (986m) or Mt Klouto (710m) with a knowledge-able local guide, who'll give you the lowdown on local fauna and flora and show you the highlights. Boy hold-ing a locust

Dakar, Senegal

11 Hit West Africa's trendiest nightlife venues and swing your hips to *mbalax*, the mix of Cuban beats and traditional drumming that forms the heart and soul of the Senegalese music scene. Relax at the beach (pictured) and feast on fresh-off-the-boat seafood, or explore the workshops of Senegal's artists at the Village des Arts (p313). Finally, climb up one of Dakar's 'breasts' to contemplate the controversial, socialist-style African Renaissance monument and take in sweeping views across the city.

Arquipélago dos Bijagós, Guinea-Bissau

12 Like Atlantis or Treasure Island, the Bijagós (p236) is such a magical archipelago that you might wonder if it's fictional. Its 88 islands fall away from the mainland in an ocean-imposed constellation that would take light years to navigate. With two or three weeks on your hands, you could start in Bubaque or Bolama. From there, you might head to Orango to spot the salty sea hippos, or throw your luggage into a speedboat and make for the luxury lodges on Kere or Rubane.

Grand Bassam, Côte d'Ivoire

13 Arty Grand Bassam (p140) is everything its neighbour Abidjan is not: gentle, quiet and unassuming. Yet it's teeming with creative endeavours, from local street-art initiatives to wild horseback rides on the golden sands. It makes an easy weekend trip from the economic capital – only 40 minutes away by car, you'll have plenty of time to take in the old French architecture, art market and cosy terrace restaurants. Woman at mask stall

Sapo National Park, Liberia

14 For years, Liberia's Sapo National Park (p251) – baked between skinny red roads and clandestine gold mines – was off-limits to travellers. Now its towering trees, rare flora and unusual inhabitants – like the secretive pygmy hippo and the duiker (pictured) – are ready to be discovered. But that doesn't mean a trip to Sapo is easy. Prepare to tackle Liberia's bumpiest roads on the 12-hour drive there, where you'll have to bed down beneath the stars until plans to build an ecolodge come to fruition.

BLUEGREEN PICTURES/ALAMY STOCK PHOTO ©

SETH LAZAR/ALAMY STOCK PHOTO ©

Baía das Agulhas, São Tomé & Príncipe

15 The magnificent Baía das Agulhas (Bay of Spires; p307) on Príncipe is easily the top sight in the country. As you travel across the bay by boat, the postcard view of the island's world-class skyline slowly unfolds. This includes a series of phonolite towers, huge peaks of raw volcanic rock dripping with jungle and steaming in the mist. You almost expect to hear the primordial roar of a T-Rex at any moment. It's a glorious spot, and there's ample reason why this could just be Africa's next big ecotourism destination.

Ureca, Equatorial Guinea

16 Perched on the southern tip of Bioko Island, Ureca (p154) is the jewel in the crown of Equatorial Guinea. This tiny village is one of the wettest places on earth. It is surrounded by the dense rainforest of Bioko Sur that teems with animals including the rare red colobus monkey, there's a fabulous array of birds, waterfalls cascade down caldera walls, and four species of marine turtles come to lay their eggs on its pristine black-sand beaches between September and April. Aerial view of rainforest, Bioko Island

Calabar, Nigeria

17 Located in green and gorgeous Cross River State, Calabar (p291) is the antidote to Nigeria's customary clamour. Its proximity to the extraordinary biodiversity of the Cameroon–Nigeria border region finds expression in one of the most innovative conservation projects in West Africa. Put it all together and it's the kind of place that you'll leave with a backpack full of memories that trump just about every stereotype about Nigeria. Market stall holder

Need to Know

For more information, see Survival Guide (p439)

Currency
West African CFA franc (eight countries), Central African CFA franc (four countries) and nine other currencies

Mobile Phones
Local SIM cards widely available, compatible with. European and Australian phones.

Money
Cash is king. Don't bring anything except euros in former French, Portuguese or Spanish colonies, while US dollars are preferred in Anglophone countries.

Time
All GMT/UTC except Cabo Verde (one hour behind) and Benin, Cameroon, Equatorial Guinea, Gabon, Niger, Nigeria and Republic of Congo (one hour ahead)

Visas
The general rule for West Africa is to get your visas before leaving home. They're rarely issued at land borders and only occasionally at airports.

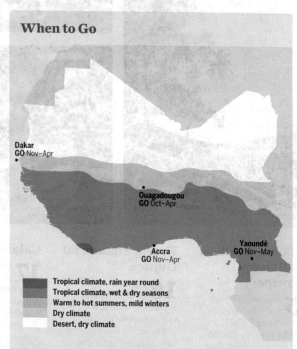

When to Go

Dakar
GO Nov–Apr

Ouagadougou
GO Oct–Apr

Accra
GO Nov–Apr

Yaoundé
GO Nov–May

- Tropical climate, rain year round
- Tropical climate, wet & dry seasons
- Warm to hot summers, mild winters
- Dry climate
- Desert, dry climate

High Season
(Nov–Mar)

➡ Generally cooler temperatures and dry weather make getting around easy.

➡ Atlantic Coast beaches packed with European sunbathers from December to March.

➡ December and January are prime time for trekking.

Shoulder
(Apr–May)

➡ Temperatures begin to rise across the Sahel.

➡ May can be unbearably hot in the Sahara; dry season begins in the tropical south.

➡ Rains can arrive in May and humidity is very high along the coast.

Low Season
(Jun–Oct)

➡ High humidity and heavy rains in coastal countries; many roads are impassable.

➡ Many wildlife reserves in the north are closed to visitors.

➡ Extreme temperatures in the Sahara and Sahel, but dry conditions in the tropical south.

Useful Websites

Lonely Planet (www.lonelyplanet.com) Destination information, hotel bookings, traveller forum and more.

Travel Africa (www.travelafricamag.com) Excellent print magazine on Africa; articles on West Africa thinly scattered.

Sahara Overland (www.sahara-overland.com) The best practical guide for travellers to the Sahara, with useful forums, route information and book reviews.

Africa Geographic (www.africageographic.com) Nature-focused Africa online mag with good wildlife and birdwatching content.

BBC News (www.bbcnews.com/africa) Good for up-to-the-minute news from Africa.

Ecowas (www.ecowas.int) The official site of the Economic Community of West African States (Ecowas), with a few useful links.

Important Numbers

Emergency numbers differ from one country to the next. Some have a general emergency number, others have separate numbers for police, fire and ambulance services. See individual country chapters for important numbers.

Currencies

Benin, Burkina Faso, Côte d'Ivoire, Guinea-Bissau, Mali, Niger, Senegal and Togo West African CFA

Cameroon, Equatorial Guinea Central African CFA

Cabo Verde escudo; CVE

The Gambia dalasi; D

Ghana cedi; C

Guinea Guinean franc; GF

Liberia Liberian dollar; L$

Mauritania ouguiya; UM

Nigeria naira; N

São Tomé & Príncipe dobra; Db

Sierra Leone Leone; Le

Daily Costs

Budget: Less than US$75

➡ Dorm bed: US$10

➡ Double room in budget hotel: up to US$50

➡ Main course in cheap local restaurant: less than US$5

Midrange: US$75–200

➡ Double room in midrange hotel: US$50–150

➡ Main course in midrange restaurant: US$5–10

➡ Long-distance bus rides: from US$15

Top end: More than US$200

➡ Double room in top-end hotel: more than US$150

➡ Car hire: at least US$100 per day and sometimes more, plus petrol

Arriving in West Africa

Murtala Muhammed International Airport (p454; Lagos, Nigeria) No public transport from the international terminal; licensed airport taxis (N6000) can be booked from the arrivals hall; get a local to meet you.

Léopold Sédar Senghor International Airport (p454; Dakar, Senegal) No public transport; taxis outside arrivals hall cost CFA5000 to the city centre.

Kotoka International Airport (p454; Accra, Ghana) A taxi from the airport to the city centre should cost no more than C30.

Getting Around

Air Major capitals are reasonably well connected by flights within West Africa; other smaller capitals may require inconvenient connections. Royal Air Maroc connects most major cities with Casablanca.

Bus & Bush Taxi Often the only option in rural areas, bush taxis in varying stages of disrepair leave when full; buses connect major cities with those of neighbouring countries.

Car Reasonable road infrastructure connects major cities; roads deteriorate elsewhere, and are sometimes impassable after rains; car-rental prices are comparable to those in Europe.

Train Trains operate in Benin, Burkina Faso, Cameroon, the Republic of Congo, Côte d'Ivoire, Gabon, Ghana, Mali, Mauritania, Nigeria, Senegal and Togo. International services connect Dakar with Bamako, and Ouagadougou with Abidjan.

For much more on **getting around**, see p457

If You Like...

Wildlife

West Africa is an underrated wildlife destination and its little-known national parks host more African mega-fauna than they do tourists. They can be difficult to reach, but worth it for sheer isolation.

São Tomé & Príncipe Ecotourism heaven offering fabulous marine-mammal experiences, including turtles, whales and dolphins. (p298)

Monte Alen National Park, Equatorial Guinea Gorillas, chimpanzees, mandrills and bush elephants. (p158)

Mole National Park, Ghana Almost 100 mammal species, savannah and good for elephants. (p208)

Parc National de la Pendjari, Benin Big cats and elephants in one of West Africa's best parks. (p50)

Parc National de Niokolo-Koba, Senegal Elephants, crocs and hippos, with river tours and an accessible waterhole. (p331)

Tiwai Island Wildlife Sanctuary, Sierra Leone Rare pygmy hippos and plenty of primate species. (p351)

Réserve de Nazinga, Burkina Faso Some of the best elephant-watching in West Africa. (p68)

Beaches

From Senegal to Cameroon, the West African coast includes some of the continent's most pristine stretches of sand. Whether you opt for a popular resort or a palm-fringed beach all to yourself, it's all here.

Isla Corisco, Equatorial Guinea Beaches here are the stuff of dreams: pure white sands, swaying palms and azure sea. (p157)

Ilhéu das Rolas, São Tomé & Príncipe A world unto itself, with blowholes, sea caves, snorkelling, hiking and some beautiful beaches. (p305)

Praia Banana, São Tomé & Príncipe This picture-perfect, banana-shaped tropical beach has golden sands and swaying palms. (p307)

Praia de Santa Mónica, Cabo Verde Bask in the aquamarine waters of Boa Vista's stunning southern coastline. (p94)

Akwidaa & Cape Three Points, Ghana Sweeping beaches, trips through plantations and mangroves, and, in season, turtles nesting in the sand. (p203)

Varela, Guinea-Bissau Wide, beautiful and with few visitors; some days you can see all the way to Senegal. (p238)

Cap Skirring, Senegal The coastal jewel of Casamance, with some of Senegal's loveliest beaches. (p333)

Robertsport, Liberia A cult classic for surfers and a world-class beach destination in waiting. (p250)

Route des Pêches, Benin Chill out on the endless beaches along the Beninese coast. (p44)

Untouched Landscapes

West Africa's wilderness areas rank among the continent's best-kept secrets, including the offshore archipelagos of Guinea-Bissau and rainforests from Sierra Leone to Cameroon.

Arquipélago dos Bijagós, Guinea-Bissau One of the world's most beautiful chains of offshore islands, with endangered wildlife. (p236)

Reserva Natural de Rio Campo, Equatorial Guinea Hippos swim in the river estuary in this deserted nature reserve. (p156)

Parc National de Campo-Ma'an, Cameroon A precursor to the vast rainforests of Central Africa. (p20)

Sindou Peaks, Burkina Faso Rock formations in southwestern Burkina that might just be the most beautiful place in the Sahel. (p67)

Outamba-Kilimi National Park, Sierra Leone Remote savannah interspersed with dense rainforest. (p350)

Siné-Saloum Delta, Senegal Splendid network of mangroves best explored in a wooden canoe. (p325)

Sapo National Park, Liberia Primary rainforest rich in wildlife and far from well-trodden trails. (p251)

Hiking

West Africa's trekking trails take you beyond the stereotypes and deep into an extraordinary human and natural landscape.

Sindou Peaks, Burkina Faso Otherworldly rock formations and intriguing cultural backdrop in Burkina's southwest. (p67)

Kpalimé, Togo Outstanding hiking amid lush, forested hills in the heart of coffee country. (p365)

Mt Cameroon Two- to three-day hike to the summit of West Africa's highest peak. (p116)

Santo Antão, Cabo Verde Spectacular canyons, cloud-soaked peaks and vertigo-inspiring drops – what more could you need? (p85)

Amedzofe, Ghana Fabulous, little-known trails with a waterfall in Ghana's east. (p194)

Pico de São Tomé, São Tomé & Príncipe This impressive peak (2024m) is São Tomé's signature climb and a wonderful two-day adventure. (p306)

PLAN YOUR TRIP IF YOU LIKE...

Top: Resort on Ilhéu das Rolas (p305), São Tomé
Bottom: Hippo, Parc National de Niokolo-Koba (p331), Senegal

Month by Month

January

West Africa's high season (except in the tropical south), with cooler, dry weather and many fine festivals; watch for the arrival of dust-laden harmattan winds late in the north and sea turtles in the south.

✿ Voodoo Festival

Held on 10 January across Benin; the celebrations in the voodoo heartland around Ouidah are the largest and most exuberant.

☆ Festival Sur Le Niger

Mali's premier music festival (www.festivalsegou.org) draws a cast of world-renowned local and international musicians to the Niger riverbank in Ségou in late January or early February. Check the security situation before travelling.

32 Race of Hope

In late January/early February Cameroonian and international athletes gather for the Race of Hope to the summit of Mt Cameroon, West Africa's highest peak.

February

February is high season in the north; book accommodation well in advance. The relatively cool, dry weather makes for good hiking. Last chance for bearable temperatures in the Sahel and to see sea turtles down south.

✿ Carnival

West Africa's former Portuguese colonies celebrate Carnival (sometimes spelt Carnaval) with infectious zeal. Bissau – with its Latin-style street festival of masks, parties and parades – or Cabo Verde are the places to be, while Porto Novo in Benin also gets into the spirit. Sometimes in January, sometimes March.

✿ Fêtes des Masques

Held in the villages around Man in western Côte d'Ivoire, the region's most significant mask festival brings together a great variety of masks and dances from the area.

☆ Fespaco

Africa's premier film festival is held in February/March in Ouagadougou in Burkina Faso in odd years. Cinemas across the city screen African films, and there's a prestigious awards ceremony. (p57)

March

March can be a bit hit or miss, although it's still generally considered high season. Temperatures are warming up, the harmattan winds are usually blowing in the Sahel and it's raining in the south.

✿ Mardi Gras

During the Mardi Gras, held 40 days before Easter, Cabo Verde can feel like Rio. It's a sexy, spectacular carnival-type celebration with street parades, especially in Mindelo. (p89)

April

By now, much of the Sahel and Sahara are too

hot for comfort and the harmattan is a staple throughout the month. The humidity along the coast and hinterland is starting to get uncomfortable and in the region's south the rains set in.

☆ Jazz à Ouaga

An established fixture on West Africa's musical circuit, this fine festival traverses jazz, Afrobeat, soul and blues with some respected regional names in attendance. (p57)

May

Unbearably hot in the Sahara, unbearably humid elsewhere – it's invariably a relief when the rains arrive. Down south, Gabon and surrounds should be starting to dry out. Few festivals enliven the month, but Dakar hosts a notable exception.

☆ Dak'Art Biennale

In even years in May, Dakar hosts the Dak'Art Biennale, easily West Africa's premier arts festival. In addition to the main exhibitions, some fabulous fringe stuff happens. (p317)

☆ Saint-Louis Jazz Festival

Hands-down the most internationally renowned festival in West Africa, attracting major jazz performers to this sexy, Unesco Heritage–designated colonial town. (p329)

☆ Roots International Festival

The biennial Roots International Festival celebrates the culture of The Gambia and its slaving history with music workshops, carnival parades and performances by local ethnic groups in late May and early June.

June

There are few reasons to visit the region at this time with the rains well and truly underway. The exceptions are Equatorial Guinea, Gabon, Republic of Congo and São Tomé & Príncipe, where the dry season is only just beginning.

July

Rain is heavy south of the Sahara, but the festivals are aimed at a local audience. This is the dry season and the best time to go hiking or venture out into the forests of tropical West Africa, from Equatorial Guinea south.

☆ Bakatue Festival

On the first Tuesday in July, Elmina (Ghana) hosts the colourful Bakatue Festival, a joyous harvest thanksgiving feast. One of its highlights is watching the priest in the harbour waters casting a net to lift a ban on fishing in the lagoon.

☆ Dagomba Fire Festival

In the heat of Tamale in Ghana, the Dagomba Fire Festival commemorates the local legend whereby a chief was overjoyed to find his missing son asleep under a tree. Angry that the tree had hidden his son, he punished it by having it burnt.

☆ Wrestling Festival

In Togo's north, watch out for Evala, the coming-of-age and wrestling festival in the Kabyé region around Kara.

August

Europeans flock to Cabo Verde, Senegal and The Gambia; book months in advance. Elsewhere, the rains and humidity make this a difficult time for travelling, except in the far south when it's a good time to see wildlife.

☆ Festival de Música

Every August, Mindelo's Festival de Música in Cabo Verde attracts musicians of all styles from around the islands and way beyond. It's wonderful fun, with a three-day extravaganza of singing, dancing and partying.

☆ Panafest

Ghana's Cape Coast hosts the biennial Pan-African Historical Theatre Festival (Panafest; digitalvalleygh. com/panafestghana.org), with a focus on African contemporary and traditional arts, including music, dance, fashion and theatre. Its centrepiece is a moving candlelit emancipation ceremony to honour African slaves.

☆ Osun Festival

With nary a tourist in sight, the Osun Festival takes place in Oshogbo, 86km northeast of Ibadan in Nigeria, on the last Friday in August. It has music, dancing and sacrifices, and is a highlight of the Yoruba cultural and spiritual year. (p290)

September

The rains should be easing off in the north. It's a lovely time to visit the south (watch for whales off Gabon), although the dry season is drawing to a close.

⭐ Fetu Afahye Festival

Cape Coast's Fetu Afahye Festival is a raucous celebration on the first Saturday of September. The main ritual event is the slaughter of a cow for the gods.

⭐ La Cure Salée

Niger's world-famous annual celebration by Fula herders features a male beauty contest and camel races, near In-Gall. It's in the first half of September but, like most Saharan festivals, it depends on the prevailing security situation.

⭐ Kano Durbar & Tabaski

West Africa's most colourful Tabaski celebrations are those in Kano where there are cavalry processions and high ceremony. Tabaski, which takes place 69 days after Ramadan, is widely celebrated in Muslim areas, especially Niger and Cameroon, where the celebrations in Foumban are

unmissable. Check security before travelling.

⭐ Adae Kese Festival

Coinciding with the yam harvest season, the Adae Kese Festival in Ghana celebrates the glorious Ashanti past and involves ritual purifications of the ancestral burial shrines.

October

October can be a good month for travelling in the region – clear, post-rain skies make for good visibility and the high-season crowds have yet to arrive. Rains are possible in the south but October's good for Congo's northern parks.

☆ Salon International de l'Artisanat de Ouagadougou

In even-numbered years Ouagadougou hosts the Salon International de l'Artisanat de Ouagadougou, which attracts artisans and vendors from all over Africa. (p57)

☆ Felabration

The week-long celebration of Afrobeat-legend Fela Kuti in Lagos takes place around the great man's birthday on 15 October. Concerts, theatre pieces and exhibitions, culminating in a free gig at the New Afrika Shrine. (p284)

November

High season has just begun but the early part of the month can be surprisingly quiet. Night-time temperatures in desert regions can drop close to zero. It can be rainy in the south but watch for sea turtles in Gabon and Equatorial Guinea.

⭐ Fête de l'Abissa

Close to Abidjan in Côte d'Ivoire, Grand Bassam hosts the Fête de l'Abissa in October/November. Over the course of a week, the N'Zima people honour their dead and exorcise evil spirits with big street parties and men in drag.

December

High season is very much underway in the coastal belt immediately south of the Sahara, and you should make accommodation bookings months in advance; beach areas are particularly busy with sun-starved Europeans. Weather is mild and dry.

⭐ Igue Festival

Also called the Ewere Festival, this colourful seven-day festival in Benin City, Nigeria, in the first half of the month, showcases traditional dances, mock battles and a procession to the palace to reaffirm local loyalty to the *oba* (king).

Itineraries

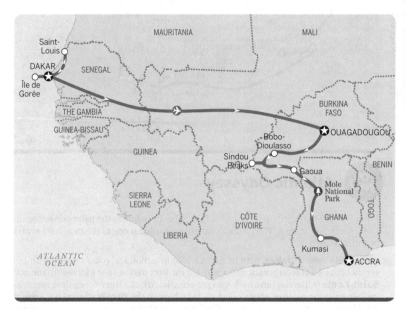

 Best of the West

West Africa's heartland takes in a beguiling mix of the region's dry-as-dust Sahel and its tropical coast. By following this route you'll get a taste for all that's good about the region.

If you're wondering why Francophone Africa gets under the skin, begin in cosmopolitan **Dakar** to sample the outstanding Musée Théodore Monod by day and the city's vibrant nightlife after dark. After excursions to the World Heritage–listed architecture of **Saint-Louis** and offshore to tranquil **Île de Gorée** (three days in total), fly to **Ouagadougou** (or Ouaga to its friends) in Burkina Faso. Ouaga has excellent places to stay and eat, as well as a happening cultural scene, and is worth a full day and night at least. Take a bus to languid **Bobo-Dioulasso** to hang out for a couple of days and then continue on to the otherworldly **Sindou Peaks**, one of West Africa's most remarkable landscapes, for two days' hiking. Travel through **Gaoua** in the heart of Lobi country then cross into northern Ghana for some of West Africa's best wildlife-watching at **Mole National Park**. Depending on how long you linger, there should be just enough time to stop off in **Kumasi** to absorb a little Ashanti culture en route to buzzing **Accra**.

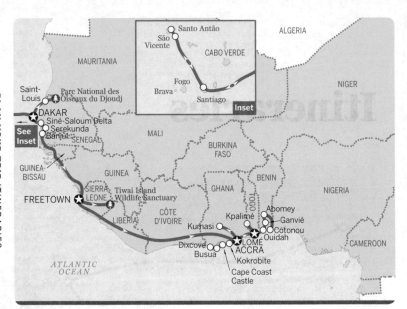

6 WEEKS Atlantic Odyssey

From Senegal to Benin, from the cusp of the Sahel in Dakar to the palm-fringed semi-tropics around Cotonou, West Africa's Atlantic coastline is one of the most varied and beautiful in Africa.

Senegal's capital **Dakar**, with its African sophistication and role as regional air hub, serves both as a starting point and a base for the first part of your journey. To the north, **Saint-Louis** is like stepping back into pre-colonial Africa. Other Senegalese excursions include enjoying some of Africa's best birdwatching in the **Parc National des Oiseaux du Djoudj** and drifting through the **Siné-Saloum Delta**. You could easily spend a week or more exploring it all, before returning to Dakar to fly to the islands of Cabo Verde. With their soulful musical soundtrack, unspoilt beaches, mountainous interior and laid-back locals, **Santiago**, **São Vicente** and **Santo Antão** are particularly beautiful and worth at least a week of your time. Returning to Dakar, head south to The Gambia, which may be small, but its beaches, especially those around **Serekunda**, make a good (English-speaking) rest stop for taking time out from the African road. From sleepy **Banjul**, consider flying to **Freetown** in Sierra Leone – the nearby beaches are beautiful and utterly undeveloped. Attractions such as **Tiwai Island Wildlife Sanctuary**, with its fabulous wildlife concentrations, should not be missed.

With three weeks under your belt, you could continue along the coast through Liberia and Côte d'Ivoire, but most travellers fly over them to agreeable **Accra** in Ghana. From there, excursions to the old coastal forts, **Cape Coast Castle** and stunning beaches at **Kokrobite**, **Busua** and **Dixcove** won't disappoint. Don't fail to detour north to **Kumasi** in the Ashanti heartland. After a week to 10 days in Ghana, there's plenty of onward transport to the fascinating markets and fine museum of **Lomé**, and don't miss an inland hiking detour around **Kpalimé**. Not far away is Benin, with **Ouidah**, the evocative former slaving port and home of voodoo, the history-rich town of **Abomey** and the stilt villages of **Ganvié** filling up your final week. **Cotonou** has all the steamy appeal of the tropics and is a fine place to rest at journey's end.

Top: Fontainhas, Santo Antão (p85), Cabo Verde

Bottom: Voodoo festival (p46), Benin

DAN KITWOOD/GETTY IMAGES ©

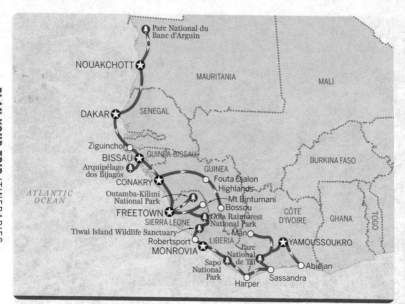

Unknown West Africa

4 WEEKS

These West African trails are some of the least travelled by tourists on earth. If having a beach all to yourself while sea turtles come ashore or venturing into the frontiers of African travel is your idea of a great trip, read on.

Begin in **Nouakchott**, the dry-as-dust capital of Mauritania, which has a wonderful fish market and a palpable sense of lying somewhere close to the end of the earth. An excursion north takes you along one of the planet's most deserted coastlines to the birdwatcher's paradise of **Parc National du Banc d'Arguin**. Three or four days after beginning your trip, head south via **Dakar** to catch the ferry to **Ziguinchor**, capital of Casamance, home to fine beaches, labyrinthine river systems and lush forests. Return to Dakar, then fly to **Bissau**, Guinea-Bissau's village-like capital. The **Arquipélago dos Bijagós** is isolated, rich in wildlife and like nowhere else on the coast – it could just be West Africa's most pristine slice of paradise.

With around 10 days behind you, you might just be ready for Guinea. **Conakry**, at once sassy and muscular, is worth experiencing for some of the region's best live music, before you truly drop off the map by tracking chimps at **Bossou** and trekking the **Fouta Djalon Highlands**.

After four or five days in Guinea, your next stop is Sierra Leone. Linger in **Freetown** and the nearby beaches, head inland to remote **Mt Bintumani** and the unknown gems of **Outamba-Kilimi National Park** and **Gola Rainforest National Park**. On your way to Liberia, stop at **Tiwai Island Wildlife Sanctuary**. Begin your Liberian sojourn in **Monrovia** and don't miss **Sapo National Park**, the beaches of **Robertsport** and soulful **Harper**. Both Sierra Leone and Liberia should fill at least a week.

From Harper, it's a short hop across the border into Côte d'Ivoire and **Sassandra**, a glorious fishing village with great beaches. Security permitting, head north to the rainforests of chimpanzee-rich **Parc National de Taï**, then on to **Man** in the heart of Dan country. From there, make your way to **Yamoussoukro** and its improbable basilica. Considering where you've been, the end of the road at **Abidjan** will feel like visiting another planet.

Top: Rustic shelter
on Ilha de Bubaque
(p236), Guinea-Bissau

Bottom: Fisherman on
the beach at Freetown
(p341), Sierra Leone

Top: Bom Bom Resort (p308), Príncipe, São Tomé & Príncipe

Bottom: Street scene, Douala (p113), Cameroon

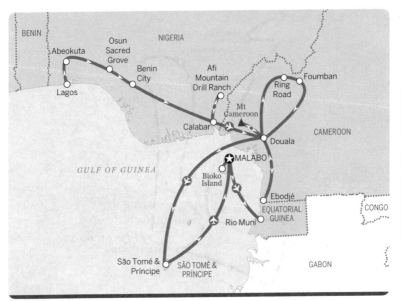

Gulf of Guinea

From Nigeria to the Republic of Congo, this route traverses West Africa's tropical southeast. It takes in frenetic urban Lagos, West Africa's tallest mountain, the pristine natural environment of São Tomé & Príncipe, and the world-class national parks of Equatorial Guinea.

Most visitors will encounter nothing but warmth and humour in their interactions with Nigerians. **Lagos** may be in-your-face, high-volume and logistically confronting, but it's also Africa's most energetic city, awash with a pulsating nightlife, clamorous markets and a resurgent arts scene. Historic **Abeokuta**, with its Yoruba shrines and sacred rock, **Osun Sacred Grove** and the Oba's Palace in **Benin City** are worthwhile stopovers en route to **Calabar** and its old colonial buildings, fish market and lovely setting. Close to Calabar, don't miss **Afi Mountain Drill Ranch**. Count on 10 days in Nigeria.

From here fly east to **Douala** in Cameroon. After longish detours to see the sea turtles at **Ebodjé** and to climb **Mt Cameroon**, West Africa's highest peak, head for Bamenda, gateway to the villages of the **Ring Road**, a deeply traditional part of Cameroon; Bafut is one of our favourite villages in the region. Later, head for **Foumban** for a slice of traditional West Africa, and a fascinating vision of the town's ancient and still-active sultanate. A week in Cameroon should give you a taste of the country's riches.

Return to Douala then fly out to **São Tomé & Príncipe**, one of West Africa's most beautiful destinations and an emerging ecotourism hot spot. From São Tomé, fly into **Malabo** in Equatorial Guinea, obtain a tourist permit and set out to see the colonial architecture, rainforest and wildlife on **Bioko Island**, and the fabulous beaches and national parks on the mainland at **Rio Muni**.

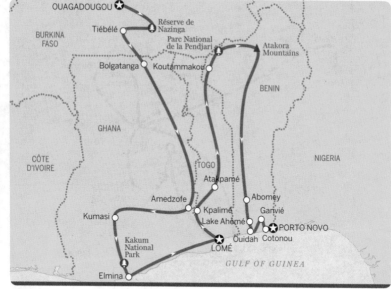

Burkina Faso, Ghana, Togo & Benin

The four countries covered in this meandering route from Ouagadougou to Cotonou are West Africa in microcosm, and there's a perfect mix of wildlife, architecture, culture and beach indulgence to entice even the most jaded of travellers.

Begin in cool **Ouagadougou**, the Burkinabé capital, then head south for two of the region's most rewarding destinations – the elephant-rich **Réserve de Nazinga**, and **Tiébélé**, with its beautifully painted traditional houses. Cross into Ghana and do some craft shopping in **Bolgatanga**. While you're in the north, and after five days on the road, spend some time exploring **Amedzofe** and the jungly Avatime Hills where the hiking is outstanding; Tafi Atome and Tafi Abuipe with their ecotourism possibilities; and glorious Wli Falls.

As you make your way towards the coast, visit the Kejetia Market in **Kumasi** – West Africa's biggest – and the rainforest experience of **Kakum National Park**, with its canopy walk and great birdwatching. Charming **Elmina** is a lovely base for exploring the slave-era castles of Ghana's Cape Coast. After 10 days to two weeks in Ghana, cross into Togo.

Begin your Togolese time in the fascinating melting pot of **Lomé**, Togo's capital. On your way north, **Kpalimé** and **Atakpamé** are worth sampling as you head towards that gem of northern Togo, **Koutammakou**, one of West Africa's least-known treasures, with remote clay-and-straw fortresses set amid stunning scenery.

Cross the border into northern Benin and make for Natitingou, gateway to the spectacular **Atakora Mountains** and wildlife-rich **Parc National de la Pendjari**, home to West Africa's last big population of lions, as well as other wildlife. It doesn't take long to return to the coast, but stop off in **Abomey** on your way to sexy Cotonou, a good base for excursions to **Ganvié** and the beaches of the Route des Pêches, as well as the voodoo strongholds of **Lake Ahémé** and **Ouidah**. **Porto Novo** is Cotonou's tranquil alter ego, with superb architecture, good museums and a palpable tropical languor. **Cotonou** itself is one of West Africa's coolest cities and it's well connected by air to the rest of the region.

Countries at a Glance

It's difficult to generalise about West Africa's 19 countries but some common themes do dominate travellers' experiences here. Stunning and varied landscapes are found across the region, from mountains and the Sahara to rainforests and palm-fringed beaches. This is also one of the most diverse and intriguing mixes of cultures on earth, while wildlife can be another big draw. Few travellers include Mali and Niger in their itineraries these days so our coverage for these countries is limited.

Benin

Culture
Beaches
Wildlife

For culture buffs, Benin impresses with its Afro-Brazilian heritage, voodoo traditions, stilt villages around Lake Nohoué and fascinating Somba culture in the northwest. The palm-fringed coastline has lovely beaches, while the Parc National de la Pendjari is a magnet for wildlife-lovers.

p38

Burkina Faso

Culture
Landscapes
Peoples

Burkina is a dream destination in Africa: the food is good, the music fabulous, the landscapes stunning and the people delightful. Despite this wealth of assets, it remains relatively low-key, which makes it all the more attractive.

p56

Cabo Verde

Landscapes
Beaches
Music

A set of spectacular Atlantic islands, Cabo Verde is a world of its own. Come for dramatic hikes through mountains, forests and volcanoes, miles of pristine sand beaches and the islands' soulful music.

p74

Cameroon

**Culture
Scenery
Beaches**

With West Africa's highest peak, the glorious landscape of the Ring Road and some of Africa's most accessible traditional cultures, Cameroon is for scenery and culture lovers. Kribi and Limbe vie for the title of Cameroon's best beach.

p105

Côte d'Ivoire

**Culture
Beaches
Landscapes**

Speed through sleek Abidjan, stopping for a bite of *poisson braisé* and a cold local beer. Explore some of West Africa's last remaining rainforest before lazing on the peroxide-blonde sands of Assinie.

p133

Equatorial Guinea

**Wildlife
Rainforest
Beaches**

Bioko Island has capital Malabo's Spanish heritage and the rainforests of the south with its apes, marine turtles and birds. The mainland, Rio Muni, is home to EG's largest city, Bata, as well as undiscovered forests and untouched beaches.

p149

The Gambia

**Birdwatching
Landscapes
Beaches**

Beyond the glittering resort towns, The Gambia offers nature reserves, pretty beaches and decadent ecolodges where you can see new birdlife every day and fall asleep in a jungle hammock built for two.

p163

Ghana

**History
Wildlife
Peoples**

West Africa's rising star is among the most exciting places to be in Africa right now: see history, both in the making and long gone. Attractions range from hiking and wildlife viewing to cultural tours and partying.

p183

Guinea

**Landscapes
Culture
Wildlife**

Guinea is one of West Africa's most adventurous destinations, with many rewards for the intrepid: remote and dramatic landscapes, a dynamic music scene and some of Africa's least-known wildlife possibilities.

p217

Guinea-Bissau

Islands
Wildlife
Landscapes

West Africa's roughest gem, Guinea-Bissau is where you can kick off your shoes beneath scarlet sunsets, sip cool juice infused with magic, knock back oysters sweet as the sea and weave between hippo-inhabited islands in the otherwordly Arquipélago dos Bijagós.

p232

Liberia

Culture
Landscapes
Music

Liberia is postcard-perfect sands and swaths of rainforest, a soundtrack of birdsong, hip-co (music of Liberian vernacular) tracks and the playful beat of Liberian English. Discover its pretty ecolodges, secret surf spots and haunting architecture.

p244

Mali

Landscapes
Culture
Music

Mali is passing through troubled times and much of the country remains off-limits. But it has a mother lode of African music, the land here is rugged and beautiful, and the mosaic of cultures provides endless interest.

p257

Mauritania

National Parks
Desert
Birdwatching

Mauritania is a country of big horizons – leave Nouak-chott, the dusty capital, to soak up the coast's bird-rich Banc d'Arguin and Diawling national parks. And if the security situation improves, revel in the wide vistas of the true Saharan oases of the Adrar region.

p261

Niger

Landscapes
Architecture
Culture

Niger has dropped off travellers' radars as it's off-limits due to serious security issues, but this vast land that straddles the Sahara, Sahel and beyond has a splendid river, diverse ethnic groups and, in Aga-dez, a glorious, mud-built old town.

p274

Nigeria

Culture
Landscapes
Peoples

Nigeria is West Africa's cultural powerhouse, a brash, sassy, complicated melting pot of fascinating peoples arrayed across a land that spans the full range of African landscapes, from the sultry rainforests of the south to the semi-deserts of the north.

p278

São Tomé & Príncipe

Islands
Hiking
Wildlife

This Atlantic Ocean jewel glitters with islands of rare beauty, plenty of birdlife and marine mammals, and some of West Africa's quietest and most rewarding hiking trails. It's an ecotourism hot spot and the region's real destination to watch.

p298

Senegal

National Parks
Culture
Birdwatching

From snazzy, sophisticated Dakar and its endless live-music beats and urban grit to the Unesco-designated colonial architecture of sultry Saint-Louis and the water gently lapping while you float though the mangrove-lined Siné-Saloum Delta, Senegal captivates.

p312

Sierra Leone

Food
Wildlife
Landscapes

Peel back the mountainous curtains of Sierra Leone and discover a country that has it all, from chimpanzees to sea turtles, spicy chop to lobster suppers, and velvety beaches to rocky peaks.

p340

Togo

Hiking
Rural Landscapes
Beaches

Very few travellers know that Togo's beaches are thick with white sand (but no crowds) or that its rugged interior is rife with hiking opportunities. It's also easy to arrange a village stay and learn about local culture.

p356

On the Road

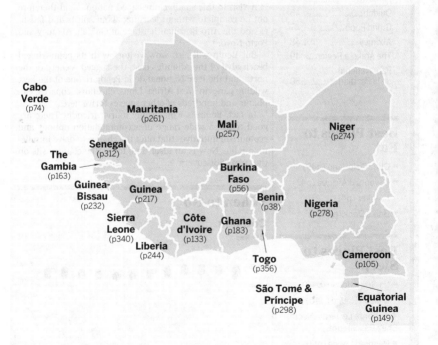

Benin

☑ 229 / POP 9.6 MILLION

Best Places to Eat

➜ Chez Delphano (p49)
➜ Saveurs d'Afrique (p47)
➜ L'Atelier (p41)
➜ Bab's Dock (p44)

Best Places to Sleep

➜ La Guesthouse (p40)
➜ Maison Rouge (p40)
➜ Auberge Le Jardin Secret – Chez Pascal (p46)
➜ Pendjari Lodge (p50)
➜ Hôtel Chez Théo (p48)

Why Go?

The birthplace of voodoo and a pivotal platform of the slave trade for nearly three centuries, Benin is steeped in a rich and complex history still very much in evidence today.

A visit to this small, club-shaped nation could therefore not be complete without learning about spirits and fetishes and the Afro-Brazilian heritage of Ouidah, Abomey and Porto Novo,

But Benin will also wow visitors with its palm-fringed beach idyll of the Atlantic coast, the rugged scenery of the north and the Parc National de la Pendjari, one of the best wildlife parks in West Africa. Lions, cheetahs, leopards, elephants and hundreds of other species thrive here.

In fact, Benin is wonderfully tourist friendly. There are good roads, a wide range of accommodation options and ecotourism initiatives that offer the chance to delve into Beninese life. Now is an ideal time to go: the country sits on the cusp of discovery.

When to Go

Cotonou

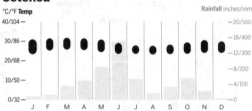

Nov–Feb
Warm and dry. Wildlife-watching at its prime. Ouidah Voodoo Festival in January.

Mar–May The hottest period, after the harmattan lifts. Some rains in the south.

Jun–Oct Usually wet and uncomfortably humid; dry spell mid-July to mid-September in the south.

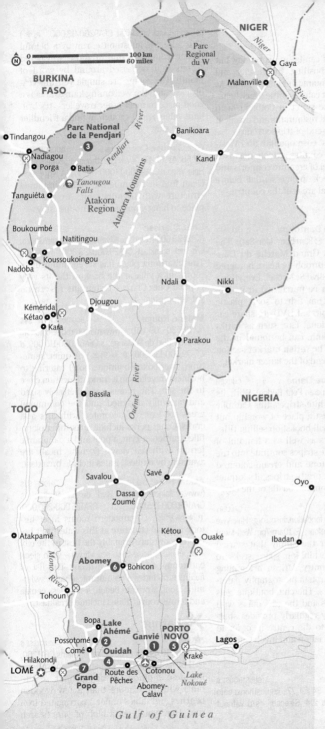

Benin Highlights

1 Ganvié (p45) Spending a night at this lakeside stilt village while while peering out over sublime lake life.

2 Lake Ahémé (p48) Learning traditional fishing techniques and taking a dip at lake's shores.

3 Parc National de la Pendjari (p50) Spotting lions, cheetahs, elephants and more in one of West Africa's best wildlife parks.

4 Zinzou Foundation Museum (p46) Pondering contemporary African Art at this remarkable museum.

5 Porto Novo (p44) Discovering Benin's mellow capital, with its Afro-Brazilian heritage.

6 Abomey (p48) Visiting the ruined palaces and temples of the kings of Dahomey.

7 Grand Popo (p47) Putting your bags down at this lovely beach town and relaxing on Benin's beautiful palm-fringed coast.

COTONOU

📱 21 / POP 970,000

Cotonou is Benin's capital in everything but name: a vibrant, bustling, full-on city, and very much the economic engine of Benin. As a first port of call, it can be a little overwhelming, but life can be sweet in Cotonou, with good nightlife, great restaurants and excellent shopping (ideal for end-of-trip souvenirs).

It's also the most cosmopolitan and Western place in the country, which means a slightly higher level of creature comforts and a good place to stock up on essentials before venturing into rural areas of the country.

◉ Sights

Grand Marché de Dantokpa   MARKET
(north of Jonquet; ⊘ 8am-5pm Mon-Sat) The seemingly endless Grand Marché du Dantokpa is Cotonou's throbbing heart, bordered by the lagoon and Blvd St Michel. Everything under the sun can be purchased in its labyrinthine lanes, from fish to soap, plastic sandals to goats, pirated DVDs to spare car parts. More traditional fare, such as batiks and Dutch wax cloth, can be found in the market building. The **fetish market** section is at the northern end of the larger market.

Cathedral de Notre Dame   CHURCH
(Ave Clozel, by the Ancien Pont Bridge) With its vibrant red and white stripes, this Catholic cathedral is not just a place of worship but also home to a small bookshop selling titles by regional writers as well as a handful of academic texts. The stripes continue into the inside with sandstone and cream-coloured arches. Beyond its pretty stripes, it's a quiet and cool escape from the bustle of the city.

Fondation Zinsou   GALLERY
(📱 21 30 99 92; www.fondationzinsou.org; Haie Vive District, near the Carrefour; ⊘ 10am-7pm Wed-Mon) **FREE** Named after the family that started it, this fantastic exhibition space seeks to promote contemporary African art among Beninese people through photography, paintings and sculptures. The chic boutique sells beautiful art books and the cafe offers wi-fi access. The gallery regularly provides shuttles from schools to the centre in order to promote art appreciation and involvement.

⌁ Sleeping

★ **La Guesthouse**   GUESTHOUSE $
(📱 99 36 80 09, 67 34 64 77; laguesthousecotonou@gmail.com; Rue 214, Sikécodji; s/d without

bathroom incl breakfast CFA9200/13,000; ℗ 🛜) This adorable guesthouse, run by a helpful French couple, is one of those whispered secrets that is passed around by word of mouth. The rooms are simple yet impeccably clean and the welcoming lounge area is a good place to meet other travellers. It's brilliant value, and it's tough to find a friendlier place to stay.

Guesthouse Cocotiers   GUESTHOUSE $
(📱 66 41 61 17; www.guesthouse-cocotiers.com; Haie Vive; r CFA9000-17,000; ℗ 🛜) A squeaky-clean find in a simple but well-maintained structure with friendly staff. An excellent place to hang your hat for a no-fuss stay.

Chez Clarisse   GUESTHOUSE $$
(📱 21 30 60 14; clarishot@yahoo.com; Camp Guézo; s/d incl breakfast CFA29,000/33,000; ❄🛜📺) This charming place has seven immaculate rooms in a villa at the back of the its very popular Chez Clarisse restaurant. It's central yet very quiet.

Maison Rouge   BOUTIQUE HOTEL $$$
(📱 21 30 09 01; www.maison-rouge-cotonou.com; off Blvd de la Marina; s CFA65,000-110,000, d CFA79,000-135,000; ℗❄🛜📺) A quiet, sometimes overlooked boutique hotel catering to business travellers in a tranquil location close to the sea. The rooms are generously sized and tastefully designed, and the communal areas are expertly decorated with arts and crafts. Other perks include a soothing plant-filled garden, a gym, a pool and a panoramic terrace with sea views. Evening meals are available by request. Rates include breakfast.

Azalai Hotel de la Plage   HOTEL $$$
(www.azalaihotels.com; Blvd de la Marina; s CFA109,000-185,000, d CFA125,000-200,000; ℗❄@🛜📺) Ultramodern rooms meet historic colonial structure at this waterfront hotel. Its rooms are arguably the best in the city – especially those with sea views – with sleek bathrooms and attractive decor. The list of facilities includes a restaurant, a bar, a swimming pool, a private beach, a business centre and tennis courts. Rates include breakfast.

✗ Eating

★ **Maman Aimé**   BENINESE $
(📱 97 64 16 49; off Pl de Bulgarie; mains CFA1200; ⊘ 11.30am-10pm) This is a super atmospheric Beninese *maquis* (rustic open-air restaurant) with little more than a few wooden benches and tables under a corrugated iron roof. Here you'll get a blob of *pâte* (starch

staple, often made from millet, corn, plantains, manioc or yams) and ladle of sauce for next to nothin'. And yes, you'll eat with your fingers. There's no signboard; it's in a *von* (alleyway) off Pl de Bulgarie.

Chez Maman Bénin   AFRICAN $
(☑21 32 33 38; Rue 201A; meals CFA1000-3000; ⊙11.30am-11pm) This long-standing no-frills canteen off Blvd St Michel has a large selection of West African dishes. There's no decor except for a couple of blaring TVs showing the latest football action.

⭐**Chez Clarisse**   FRENCH $$
(☑21 30 60 14; Camp Guézo; mains CFA3000-15,000; ⊙8am-10pm) This small French restaurant, in a pretty residential area next to the US embassy, is a perennial favourite that churns out excellent French and local specialties, such as fish with moyo sauce, as well as pancakes and sandwiches.

⭐**L'Atelier**   FRENCH $$$
(☑21 30 17 04; Cadjéhoun; mains CFA8000-19,000; ⊙11am-11pm Mon-Sat) Considered by some connoisseurs to be one of the most refined restaurants in town, with excellent French and fusion cuisine, and an ambience that's as optimal for business lunches as it is for a romantic evening out.

🍷 Drinking & Nightlife

Haie Vive is a lively, safe area by night, with many of the city's best bars and restaurants. There are also plenty of unpretentious bars and *buvettes* (small cafes that double as drinking places) in the Jonquet area and around Stade de l'Amitié.

⭐**Buvette**   BAR
(Carrefour de Cadjéhoun; ⊙3pm or 4pm-late) This place with no name is brilliant for sundowners. Tables spill out of nowhere as soon as darkness falls and there is often live music.

⭐**Le Livingstone**   BAR
(☑21 30 27 58; Haie Vive; ⊙11am-late) One of the most atmospheric spots for a drink is the terrace of this pub in Haie Vive, which serves as one of the biggest expat hangouts in town.

🛍 Shopping

**Centre de Promotion
de l'Artisanat**   ARTS & CRAFTS
(Blvd St Michel; ⊙9am-6pm) Here you'll find woodcarvings, bronzes, batiks, leather goods, jewellery and appliqué banners.

ℹ ARRIVING IN COTONOU

Upon arrival at Aéroport International de Cotonou Cadjéhoun (p54), porters wearing blue uniforms will surround you. It's best to pay one for safe transfer of your luggage and a seamless transfer (past the aggressive touts and rampant thieves) to the taxi stand (tip them about CFA1500 to CFA2000). Taxis are the best way to get to the the city and cost around CFA3000 to CFA6000 to the centre (depending on your negotiating skills).

ℹ Information

DANGERS & ANNOYANCES

The biggest danger in Cotonou is the traffic – the reckless *zemi-johns* (or *zems*, motorcycle taxis) in particular. They're unavoidable, however, so always make sure that the driver agrees to drive slowly *(aller doucement)* before hopping on.

The Jonquet, the beach and the port area all have their fair share of undesirables: don't walk alone at night and watch your bag at traffic lights if you're on a *zem*.

INTERNET ACCESS

Ave Clozel, Blvd Steinmetz and Rue des Cheminots have the most internet cafes.

Cyber Océane (☑21 30 69 41; Haie Vive; per hr CFA500; ⊙9am-10pm)

Star Navigation (☑21 31 81 28; off Blvd Steinmetz; per hr CFA700; ⊙8am-10pm) Perhaps country's fastest internet connections.

MEDICAL SERVICES

There are numerous pharmacies around town.

Pharmacie Jonquet (☑21 31 20 80; Rue des Cheminots; ⊙24hr) Open seven days a week.

Polyclinique les Cocotiers (☑21 30 14 20; Rue 373, Cadjéhoun) A private clinic at Carrefour de Cadjéhoun; also has a dentist.

MONEY

All banks change cash. There are plenty of ATMs, most of which accept Visa.

Banque Atlantique (Blvd St Michel; ⊙8am-5pm Mon-Fri, 9am-12.30pm Sat) Temperamental MasterCard and Visa ATM.

Trinity Forex (Bureau de Change Forex Bureau; ☑21 31 79 38; Ave van Vollenhoven; ⊙8am-6.30pm Mon-Fri, 8am-2pm Sat) Changes US dollars, euros, Swiss francs and British pounds.

POST

Main Post Office (off Ave Clozel; ⊙7am-7pm Mon-Fri, 8am-11.30am Sat)

Cotonou

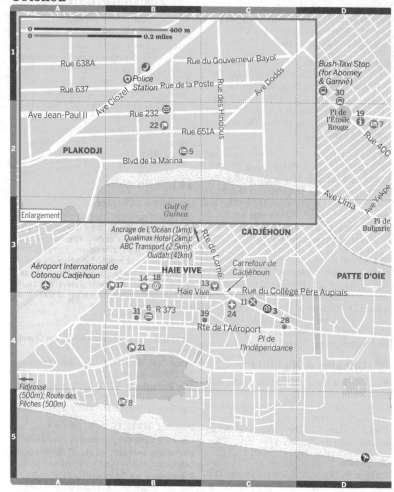

TELEPHONE

Telecom (OPT) Building (Ave Clozel; ⊙7.30am-7pm Mon-Sat, 9am-1pm Sun) You can make overseas telephone calls and send faxes.

TOURIST INFORMATION

Direction du Tourisme et de l'Hôtellerie (⊡21 32 68 24; Pl de l'Étoile Rouge; ⊙8am-12.30pm & 3-6.30pm Mon-Fri) Inconveniently located out of the city centre, behind Pharmacie de l'Étoile Rouge; of limited use.

🔓 Getting There & Away

BUSH TAXI & BUS

Cotonou has a confusingly large number of stations for minibuses, buses and bush taxis. It's easiest to ask a taxi or a *zemi-john* to take you to the right one.

Gare Jonquet (Rue des Cheminots), just west of Blvd Steinmetz, services western destinations such as Grand Popo (CFA4000, two hours).

Bush taxis for Porto Novo (CFA500 to CFA700, 45 minutes) leave from **Gare du Dantokpa** (Ave de la Paix) at the new bridge; those to Calavi-Kpota (for Ganvié; CFA500, 25 minutes),

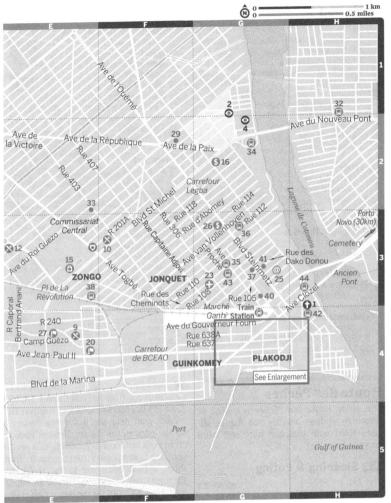

Ouidah (CFA1000) and Abomey (CFA3100, two hours) leave **north of Stade de l'Amitié**. **Gare Missébo** (Ave van Vollenhoven) services Abomey (CFA2500).

For more-distant destinations, such as Natitingou, take the bus. The most reliable company at the time of writing was **ATT** (☑ 95 95 34 18; Pl de l'Étoile Rouge), with daily services for Natitingou (CFA85600).

There are also additional national and international services with **ABC Transport** (☑ 66 56 45 15; Stade de l'Amitié), **Cross Country International** (☑ 66 99 92 41; Ave du Nouveau Pont), **Rimbo-RTV** (☑ 95 23 24 82; Zongo), **STIF** (☑ 97

98 11 80; off Ave Clozel), **TCV** (☑ 97 60 39 68; Rue 108) and **UTB** (☑ 95 42 71 20; Ave Clozel).

❶ Getting Around

A *zemi-john* will whiz you around town for CFA100 to CFA500, depending on the distance.

Fares in shared taxis are CFA150 to CFA400.

SOUTHERN BENIN

Benin's south is an enticing but intriguing mix of heavenly shores, lush lagoons and momentous history.

Cotonou

Route des Pêches

The sandy Route des Pêches is a land of seemingly endless beaches and fishing villages filled with thatched huts and palm groves.

🛌 Sleeping & Eating

Tichani　　　　　　　　　　　　GUESTHOUSE $
(☑ 97 88 65 60; off Rte des Pêches; r with fan/air-con incl breakfast CFA12,000/18,000; 🛜) This well-run guesthouse scores high points with its location – it's only 300m away from the beach in a peaceful area. The six sun-soaked rooms are neat and tidy, the flower-filled garden is a great spot to decompress and the views of the sea from the rooftop terrace are nothing short of charming. Meals can be arranged (from CFA3000).

Wado　　　　　　　　　　　　　SEAFOOD $$
(☑ 97 68 53 18; Rte des Pêches; mains CFA3500-3900, seafood platters CFA27,000; ☺ lunch & dinner Sat & Sun) This eatery overlooking the beach has garnered high praise for its ultra-fresh fish and seafood platters.

★ Bab's Dock　　　　　　　EUROPEAN, BAR $$$
(☑ 97 97 01 00; off Rte des Pêches; CFA3000-7000; ☺ 10am-8pm Sat, Sun & bank holidays) This hidden gem near the Route des Pêches is on the edge of the lagoon. Food is European in style but local in production. A secure car park is signposted from the route; from there, a boat takes you to the restaurant through thick mangrove. There's an admission fee (CFA2500) for the day, which covers the car park and boat trip.

ⓘ Getting There & Away

The best way to reach this area is by taxi. From Cotonou centre it costs around CFA500 to CFA600. From Ouidah, expect to pay CFA100 to CFA300.

Porto Novo

POP 262,000

Nestling on the shores of Lake Nokoué, Porto Novo is Benin's unlikely capital. Its leafy streets, wonderful colonial architecture, unperturbed pace and interesting museums are in striking contrast to full-on Cotonou.

DON'T MISS

GANVIÉ

The main attraction in Ganvié is the **stilt village**, where roughly 24,000 Tofinu people live in bamboo huts on stilts. The village extends several kilometres out on Lake Nokoué.

This stilt village was created to protect the Tofinu people from slave hunters. It has become part of their culture and way of life. The teetering houses, schools, churches and other structures form a ramshackle village. The villagers live almost exclusively from fishing.

The best way to get to Ganvié is via Cotonou. Take a taxi from Pl de l'Étoile Rouge or Stade de l'Amitié to Calavi-Kpota (CFA700, 25 minutes). The embarkation point is 800m downhill (take a *zem*). If you opt for a tour, head to the people standing at the tour counters at Stade de l'Amitié. Return fares to Ganvié in a regular/motorised pirogue are CFA9000/11,500 per person, or CFA6300/8200 each for two to four people, including tour and pirogue transport. Prices generally include a circuit of the village with stop-offs. The trip takes about 2½ hours. You can also hire a guide.

The Portuguese named the city after Porto when they established a slave-trading post here in the 16th century.

○ Sights

★ Centre Songhai
GARDENS

(☑ 20 24 68 81; www.songhai.org; Rte de Pobè; guided tours CFA500; ◷ guided tours 8.30am, 10.30am, noon, 3.30pm & 5pm Mon-Sat) The Centre Songhai is a major research, teaching and production centre in sustainable farming. There are one-hour guided tours to visit the plantations and workshops. You can also buy the centre's produce – anything from fresh quail eggs to biscuits and preserves. Songhai is about 1km north of town. Every *zem* knows where it is.

Musée Honmé
MUSEUM

(☑ 20 21 35 66; Rue Toffa; CFA1000; ◷ 9am-noon & 3.30-6pm) This museum is housed in the walled palace of King Toffa, who signed the first treaty with the French in 1863. It focuses on the *alounloun* musical instrument, a long piece with a sliding metal ring, the key element in the local Porto Novo *adjogan* music. The museum traces the instrument's symbolism as a sound that echoed the king's strength.

Musée Ethnographique de Porto Novo
MUSEUM

(☑ 20 21 25 54; Ave 6; CFA1000; ◷ 9am-6pm, closed 1 May & 1 Jan) Housed in a pretty colonial building, this museum is well worth a gander. The top floor is organised thematically around birth, life and death, with everything from costumes to carved drums. Downstairs there's an impressive display of ceremonial masks.

🍴 Sleeping & Eating

Centre Songhai
HOTEL **$**

(☑ 20 24 68 81; www.songhai.org; Rte de Pobè; r with fan CFA5500-7500, with air-con CFA12,500-15,500, ste CFA30,000-50,000; ⚹❄@🛜) Built to accommodate its numerous visitors, the 70 rooms at Centre Songhai are spartan but clean. Fan rooms have a shower cubicle but shared toilets; the more-expensive air-con rooms have a private bathroom (with hot water) but are still very good value. The centre has two good restaurants: a cheap African open-air *maquis* (mains CFA1200) and a more upmarket restaurant (mains CFA2500 to CFA3500).

Hôtel Beaurivage
HOTEL **$$**

(☑ 20 21 23 99; Blvd Lagunaire; r CFA15,500-25,500; ❄) Tired but spacious rooms (and new beds, finally!) with the town's best lagoon views and a wonderful terrace bar and restaurant. Even if you don't sleep here, you should definitely come for sundowners.

Java Promo
AFRICAN, FRENCH **$**

(☑ 66 96 68 78; Pl du Gouvernement; meals CFA1600-4200; ◷ 8am-9pm) No one seems to remember a time before Java Promo. Hidden behind the aquamarine shutters of a crumbling colonial building and shielded from the sun by a big *paillote* (straw awning), this is a popular haunt for an omelette at brekkie or rustic European meals for lunch.

ⓘ Information

Porto Novo has several banks with ATMs that accept Visa.

Bank of Africa (Ave Liotard; ◷ 8am-4pm Mon-Fri) Changes money.

County Hospital De L'ouémé (☑ 97 09 25 14)

Tourist Office (☑ 97 02 52 29; www.porto-novo.org; Pl Bayol; ⊙ 9am-1pm & 3-6pm Mon-Fri) Has a few brochures and can help with finding guides. Near the cathedral.

❶ Getting There & Away

Plenty of minibuses and bush taxis leave for Cotonou (minibus/bush taxi CFA6500/900, 45 minutes) from Carrefour Catchi and in front of Ouando mosque. To Abomey from Porto Novo is CFA3800. ATT buses that ply the Cotonou–Natitingou route also stop in front of Ouando mosque (CFA7900 for Natitingou) and at the Gare Routière.

For Nigeria, you can get a taxi to the border point in Kraké (CFA900, 30 minutes), but you'll have to change there to go on to Lagos.

Ouidah

POP 86,500

Ouidah is a relaxed and relatively prosperous beach town with sweeping expanses of golden sand to laze upon. It's also a must-see for anyone interested in voodoo (it's considered the voodoo capital of Benin), Benin's history of slavery or its Brazilian heritage. From the 17th to the late 19th centuries, captured countrymen from across West Africa left Ouidah for the Americas.

DON'T MISS

VOODOO DAY

Vodou (voodoo) got its current name in Haiti and Cuba, where the religion arrived with Fon and Ewe slaves from the Dahomey Kingdom and mixed with Catholicism. It means 'the hidden' or 'the mystery'. Traditional priests are consulted for their power to communicate with particular spirits and seek intercession with them. This communication is achieved through spirit possession and ritual that often involves a gift or 'sacrifice' of palm wine, chickens or goats.

Voodoo was formally recognised as a religion by the Beninese authorities in February 1996. Since then, 10 January, Voodoo Day, has been a bank holiday, with celebrations all over the country. Those in Ouidah, voodoo's historic centre, are among the best and most colourful, with endless singing, dancing, beating of drums and drinking.

⊙ Sights

★ **Zinzou Foundation Museum** MUSEUM
(☑ 21 34 11 54; http://fondationzinsou.org; Rue des Missions; ⊙ 9am-7pm Wed-Sun, 1-7pm Tue) FREE
This museum of contemporary African art, housed in a stunning 1920s Afro-Brazilian villa, displays paintings and sculptures as well as light, video and sound installations. It's a classy affair, run by the Zinzou foundation out of Cotonou, a respectable organisation with a strong history of supporting Beninese artists. Most guides speak at least passable English.

Route des Esclaves MEMORIAL
(Route of the Slaves; museum CFA1200; ⊙ museum 10am-5pm) The Route of the Slaves includes the slave auction plaza, the Tree of Forgetfulness (where slaves were branded with their owners' symbols and, to make them forget where they came from, forced to walk around the tree in circles) and the Tree of Return, another tree the slaves often circled with the belief that their souls would return home after death. There is a poignant memorial on the beach, **Gate of No Return**, with a bas-relief depicting slaves in chains.

Musée d'Histoire de Ouidah MUSEUM
(☑ 21 34 10 21; www.museeouidah.org; Rue van Vollenhoven; CFA1000; ⊙ 8am-12.30pm & 3-6pm Mon-Fri, 9am-6pm Sat & Sun) Ouidah's main site is its Musée d'Histoire de Ouidah, housed in the beautiful Fortaleza São João Batista, a Portuguese fort built in 1721. It retraces the town's slave-trading history and explores the links between Benin, Brazil and the Caribbean.

Python Temple TEMPLE
(off Rue F Colombani; admission CFA1000, photos CFA5000; ⊙ 9am-6.30pm) Those interested in voodoo could visit the python temple, home to some 60 sleepy snakes. The guide explains some of the beliefs and ceremonies associated with the temple.

🛏 Sleeping

★ **Auberge Le Jardin Secret – Chez Pascal** GUESTHOUSE $
(☑ 96 66 90 14; www.lejardinsecretouidah.net; near Radio Kpassé; r CFA12,000-15,000; ⓟ) An atmosphere of dreamlike tranquility wafts over this well-organised guesthouse tucked away in a side *von* in a quiet neighbourhood. The neatly tended garden has places to lounge; the six rooms, though not luxurious are crisp

and spruce; and there's an on-site restaurant (meals from CFA2500). Bike hire is available.

Casa Del Papa RESORT $$$
(☑95 95 39 04; www.casadelpapa.com; Ouidah Plage; d incl breakfast CFA37,500-68,000; P ✳ ☒) Squeezed between the ocean and the lagoon, Casa Del Papa is the closest thing to an exclusive resort you'll find on the coast. It features a host of facilities and amenities, including three pools, a volleyball court, two bars and a restaurant overlooking the beach. There are numerous activities on offer as well as excursions across the lagoon and to nearby villages.

✕ Eating

Restaurant d'Amicale AFRICAN $
(by the Catholic church; mains CFA1000-3000; ☺10am-11.30pm) This colourful, friendly spot serves a mix of sandwiches and pizzas, fresh salads and *attiéké* (a dish from Côte d'Ivoire made with cassava, beans, fish, plantains and pasta). It's a spacious spot with shaded tables and an interior with fans so strong they'll quickly cool your food down.

Côté Pêche SEAFOOD $$
(☑96 82 27 03, 97 46 43 79; Rte des Esclaves; mains CFA3400-4500; ☺7.30am-9pm) Fish lovers, you'll find nirvana here: Côté Pêche has a wide assortment of fish delivered daily from the harbour, including barracuda and grouper. The menu also features meat dishes, pasta, salads and sandwiches. The owners have three rooms for rent (CFA7000). It's at the beginning of Rte des Esclaves.

ℹ Information

Continental Bank Bénin (☑21 34 14 32; Pl du Marché; ☺8.30am-noon & 3-6pm Mon-Fri) Changes cash.

Tourist Office (☑21 19 35 11, 97 87 80 93; ouidah_tourisme@yahoo.fr; ☺8.30am-6.30pm) Has various brochures and can arrange cultural tours. Ask for Modeste Zinsou. Near the post office.

UBA The only bank with an ATM (Visa only).

ℹ Getting There & Away

Ouidah is 42km west of Cotonou. From Carrefour Gbena, north of town, you can catch shared taxis to Cotonou (CFA1200, one hour), Grand Popo (CFA1700, one hour) and the Hilakondji border (CFA1800, 1½ hours).

ADJARA

Adjara is famous for its market, one of the most colourful in Benin. Held every fourth day, it's stocked with fetishes, grigri charms, unique blue-and-white tie-dyed cloth, some of the best pottery in Benin, and tam-tams and other musical instruments. You'll also see blacksmiths at work.

Chez Houssou (Adjara; mains CFA1500; ☺11am-3pm) is an unpretentious *maquis* (open-air restaurant), with no more than a couple of wooden benches, famous for one thing and one thing only: *porc grillé sauce sang* (grilled pork cooked in a blood sauce). Houssou cuts morsels of pork, puts them in a mudbrick oven, then serves them on a small plate – it can't get more authentic than that.

From Porto Novo, a *zem* ride shouldn't cost more than CFA900.

Grand Popo
POP 9000

Grand Popo is a wonderful beach town in which to spend a few tranquil days. The village has plenty going on at the weekend, when Cotonou residents come to decompress.

On the main road through the village, **Villa Karo** (☑94 20 31 20; ☺gallery 8am-noon & 4-6pm Mon-Fri, 8-11am Sat) is a small gallery with great exhibitions focusing on local art.

Run by two local guides, **GG Tours** (☑95 85 74 40; Azango Maison) organises excursions on the Mono River or to the Bouche du Roy, where the river meets the ocean. Trips on the river last about two hours (CFA6000 per person). Trips to the Bouche du Roy cost CFA50,000: you need a motorised boat, which fits up to eight people; the trip lasts about six hours.

🛏 Sleeping & Eating

★**Saveurs d'Afrique** BUNGALOW $
(☑66 69 69 80, 97 89 28 19; www.saveursdafrique.net; bungalows CFA17,000; P) Looking for a night at some place extra-special? Make a beeline for this lovely property, the pride and joy of affable Mathieu Yélomé, a young Beninese chef. The six units borrow from

African traditional designs and are embellished with various artistic touches.

Food is a big thing here; the range of daily specials (around CFA600) on offer – mostly French-influenced dishes prepared with local ingredients – is well priced and filled with subtle flavours. Near the beach.

Lion Bar
GUESTHOUSE $

(☑95 42 05 17; kabla_gildas@yahoo.fr; campsite per person CFA5500, r without bathroom CFA5000-7000) Down a track from the main street, you'll easily find this reggae land by following Bob Marley's languorous beats. It's the hideout of choice for Cotonou's expat beatniks, and oozes peace and love: cocktails flow at all hours of the day and night, rooms are spartan yet funky and the shared facilities surprisingly clean.

Awalé Plage
RESORT $$

(☑22 43 01 17; www.hotel-benin-awaleplage.com; Rte du Togo; r CFA37,000, bungalows with fan/air-con CFA27,500/32,500; P❉🖨☃) A great place to recharge the batteries, Awalé Plage's most notable features are its excellent service, beachfront setting, beautiful gardens awash with tropical trees, large swimming pool and well-maintained bungalows. There is an excellent beach bar and the on-site restaurant (mains CFA2600 to CFA6500) prepares delectable French-inspired dishes with a tropical twist.

Auberge de Grand Popo
HOTEL $$

(☑22 43 00 47; www.voyageurbenin.com; d CFA17,500-28,000; P) Right by the beach, this place oozes colonial charm and serves divine cuisine in its attractive terrace restaurant (menus CFA8500).

ⓘ Getting There & Away

From Cotonou, take a bush taxi from Gare Jonquet, Stade de l'Amitié or Pl de l'Étoile Rouge (CFA3500, two hours) and have it drop you off at the Grand Popo junction on the main coastal highway, 20km east of the Togo border crossing at Hilakondji. The beach and village are 3.5km off the main road and are easily accessible via *zemi-john* (CFA280).

Possotomé & Lake Ahémé

The fertile shores of Lake Ahémé are a wonderful place to spend a few days, particularly around lively Possotomé, the area's biggest village. It's possible to swim in the lake, which makes for a great way to cool down, or explore the area's wildlife.

Activities

Learn traditional fishing techniques, meet craftspeople at work or go on a fascinating two-hour botanic journey to hear about local plants and their medicinal properties. There are half a dozen thematic circuits to choose from (from two hours to day trips, CFA4800 to CFA17,000), all run by delightful local guides.

Eco-Bénin
ADVENTURE SPORTS

(www.ecobenin.org) Various trips and excursions are offered by this local tour operator.

🛏 Sleeping & Eating

Gîte de Possotomé
GUESTHOUSE $

(☑67 19 58 37, 94 38 80 34; www.ecobenin.org; s without bathroom CFA5700-6000, d without bathroom CFA7000-8500, s/d CFA9500/15,000; P🖨) Embedded in a manicured tropical garden, this well-run venture has eight impeccable rooms with salubrious bathrooms. It's not on the lakeshore, but the congenial atmosphere more than makes up for this. The ethos here is laid-back, ecological and activity-oriented – various tours can be arranged.

Hôtel Chez Théo
RESORT $$

(☑96 44 47 88, 95 05 53 15; www.chez-theo.com; r CFA18,000-23,000, bungalows CFA36,000; P❉🖨) In a stunning lakeside location, Chez Théo is guaranteed to help you switch to 'relax' mode. A path through a garden bursting with all sorts of exotic trees leads to a great bar-restaurant (mains from CFA4200) on a stilt platform with cracking views. Rooms are far from fancy but are kept scrupulously clean. All kinds of tours can be organised.

ⓘ Getting There & Away

Taxis that ply the Cotonou–Hilakondji (or Comé) route will generally drop you off at the Comé turn-off (CFA2700), from where the only option to Possotomé is a *zemi-john* (CFA1500).

Abomey
POP 124,500

If you're looking to immerse yourself in ancient Beninese history, one of the best places to start is Abomey. The name is mythical, and not without reason: Abomey, 144km northwest of Cotonou, was the capital of the fierce Dahomey kingdom and a force colonial powers had to reckon with for centuries. Its winding lanes dotted with palaces and temples, Abomey is shrouded with a palpable historical aura and filled with character.

🅞 Sights

Musée Historique d'Abomey   MUSEUM
(☑22 50 03 14; www.epa-prema.net/abomey; adult/child   CFA1500/1000;   ⊘9am-6pm) Abomey's main and seriously impressive attraction (and a World Heritage site since 1985), this sprawling museum is housed in two palaces, those of the ancient kings Ghézo and Glélé. The museum displays royal thrones and tapestries, human skulls that were once used as musical instruments, fetish items and Ghézo's throne, mounted on four real skulls of vanquished enemies.

🛏 Sleeping & Eating

A La Lune – Chez Monique   GUESTHOUSE $
(☑22 50 01 68; north of Rond-Point de la Préfecture; r CFA7600-9200; 🅿) You'll love the exotic garden, complete with antelopes, crocodiles, tortoises, monkeys, flower bushes and huge wood carvings. Accommodation-wise, it's a bit less overwhelming, with no-frills, yet spacious, rooms. The on-site restaurant is average; opt for a contemplative drink in the garden instead.

Auberge d'Abomey   GUESTHOUSE $$
(☑97 89 87 25, 95 82 80 28; www.voyageurbenin. com; Rond-Point de la Préfecture; s/d with fan CFA13,500/15,000, with air-con CFA19,000/25,500; ❄) This reliable option off the main roundabout is a small, rustic hotel with a colonial feel and just a handful of spare rooms. It gets high marks from travellers for its relaxing garden full of mango trees and its on-site restaurant (menus from CFA8500). Staff can organise various excursions.

★Chez Delphano   BENINESE $
(☑93 64 02 40; mains CFA800-1900; ⊘8am-10pm) This delightful *maquis* is a winner. Marguerite prepares exquisite Beninese cuisine in a jovial atmosphere. She also prepares crêpes in the morning, with freshly ground coffee and a mountain of fruit. Yum! Chez Delphano is north of Rond-Point de la Préfecture.

ℹ Information

Tourist Office (☑94 14 67 30, 95 79 09 45; near the Rond-Point de la Préfecture.; ⊘9am-1pm & 3-6pm Mon-Fri, 9am-4pm Sat) Has some interesting brochures and can provide informa-

THE ROUTE OF KINGS

The tourist office runs excellent cultural tours focusing on Abomey's rich architectural heritage. They last about two hours and cost CFA3000 per person (not including *zem* rental). There are some 10 sites to be seen, all of which have an air of faded majesty about their crumbling walls. Highlights include Palais Akaba, Place de Goho, Palais Ghézo, Palais de Glélé, Temple Hwemu, Temple Zéwa and Palais Agonglo – the best-kept of Abomey's nine palaces.

tion about Abomey's main sights. It also keeps a list of accredited guides (some of whom speak English) and can arrange guided tours.

ℹ Getting There & Away

Plenty of bush taxis depart from Cotonou (CFA3800, three hours), sometimes with a connection at Bohicon. *Zemi-johns* (CFA1200) frequently run between Abomey and Bohicon.

Most **Confort Lines** (☑21 32 58 15) and **Inter City Lines** (☑21 00 85 54) buses (between Cotonou and Natitingou) stop in Bohicon on the way, but be sure to verify this with the driver.

NORTHERN BENIN

Northern Benin's arid, mountainous landscape is a world away from the south's beaches and lagoons but all the more attractive for it. It's all about the natural heritage, with one fantastic wildlife park and a mountain range. It is also ethnically more diverse than the south, and Islam is the main religion.

The Atakora Region

This fantastic trekking destination is famous for its scrubby, rugged and rocky mountain range full of red *piste* (rough track), bucolic corn fields and huge baobab trees, as well as lively markets where *tchoukoutou* (sorghum beer) flows. It's also home to Parc National de la Pendjari, one of West Africa's most respected wildlife parks.

🏃 Activities

Perle de l'Atakora   WALKING
(Pearl of the Atakora; ☑97 44 28 61; www.eco benin.org/koussoukoingou)   Ecotourism

> ### ⓘ CROSSING INTO TOGO
>
> If you cross into Togo from Boukoumbé, make sure you get your passport stamped at the *gendarmerie* (police station) at Boukoumbé as there is no border checkpoint.

association Perle de l'Atakora offers guided walks around Koussoukoingou (CFA2000 to CFA3500 for 2½ to 3½ hours) taking in local sights such as the famous *tata* houses (fort-like huts with clay turrets and thatched spires). You can arrange to spend the night at a *tata* (CFA8000 per person including breakfast and dinner, without bathroom).

🛏 Sleeping

Ecolodge La Perle de l'Atakora
GUESTHOUSE $

(📝67 46 78 01, 97 35 02 86; www.ecobenin.org; Koussoukoingou; r without bathroom CFA8000; ℗) We can't think of a better place for immersion in local culture. This modernish *tata* house features five rooms that are tidy, functional and well priced, and a well-scrubbed ablution block. Hearty meals too. It's run by Ecobenin, which offers high-quality ecotours in the area. Bikes are also available. Rooms include breakfast and dinner.

Tata Touristique Koubetti Victor
GUESTHOUSE $

(📝97 35 29 24, 94 68 75 49; Boukombé; r without bathroom CFA6000; ℗🛜) This is a wonderfully laid-back Boukombé haven, with a leafy courtyard, a chilled-out ambience and tasty meals. Rooms occupy a large *tata* house. It's basic but clean and high on character. Joséphine and her daughter Valérie can organise village visits, cultural tours and dance classes. Pick-ups from Natitingou can also be arranged.

ⓘ Getting There & Away

It's best to get to the Atakora with your own transport, but a few bush taxis do ply the dusty trail between Nati, Koussoukoingou and Boukoumbé (CFA2500, roughly two hours), where you can cross into Togo. Otherwise, *zemi-johns* (about CFA7000, three hours) will take you, but be prepared for a dusty and tiring ride.

Parc National de la Pendjari

Set amid the majestic landscape of the Atakora's rugged cliffs and wooded savannah, this 2750-sq-km park (Pendjari National Park; www.pendjari.net; 1/2/3 days per person CFA10,000/20,000/25,000, per vehicle CFA3000, 'A' guides per day CFA10,000; ⊘6am-5pm) is home to lions, cheetahs, leopards, elephants, baboons, hippos, myriad birds (it's estimated 300 to 350 varieties live here) and countless antelope – it's undoubtedly one of the West Africa's top wildlife destinations.

🏃 Activities

With big cats, elephants, antelope, hippos and other iconic wildlife, the park is ripe for wildlife viewing. The best viewing time for sighting animals is near the end of the dry season (November to February), when animals start to hover around waterholes. To maximise your chances, use an accredited grade 'A' guide. The list of accredited guides can be found on the park's website, at park entrances and in Nati's better hotels. The 'A' guides have the most in-depth knowledge and several years of experience in the park, and they can be trusted to handle the terrain and conduct a tour that is both informative and safe.

🛏 Sleeping

★Pendjari Lodge
LODGE $$

(📝in France 336 68 42 73 43; www.pendjari-lodge.com; tents CFA34,000-37,000; ⊘Nov-Jul; ℗🛜) A lovely place in a beautiful setting on a small hill (views!), Pendjari Lodge mixes old-style safari ambience with nouveau bush chic. It sports a handful of luxury, semipermanent tents and a large dining area and lounge with wooden decks overlooking a valley. One quibble: the menu (set menus from CFA6000) is a bit limited but does the trick after a hot day out and about.

Hôtel de la Pendjari
HOTEL $$

(📝23 82 11 24; http://hoteltatasomba.5web5.com; r CFA27,000-30,000; ⊘Dec-May; ℗❄🖢) Although it's starting to fray around the edges, this establishment offers spacious, utilitarian rooms with good bedding, and its location at the heart of the park is hard to beat. If you're watching your money, opt for the spartan bungalows. There's an on-site restaurant (meals CFA6500) and bar with decent Beninese fare and cold-ish beers.

UNDERSTAND BENIN

Benin Today

Benin is one of the more stable countries in West Africa, although things are not all that rosy. The current president, Patrice Talon, has been in office since 2016. He has pledged to overhaul and reform the current constitution, improve relations with France, reduce the maximum presidential term to five years and reduce internal government corruption. He inherits a country with a recent history of corruption scandals and a distrustful public, with the majority living below the poverty line.

History

More than 350 years ago the area now known as Benin was split into numerous principalities. Akaba of Abomey conquered his neighbouring ruler Dan and called the new kingdom Dan-Homey, later shortened to Dahomey by French colonisers. By 1727, Dahomey spread from Abomey down to Ouidah and Cotonou and into parts of modern Togo. The kingdoms of Nikki, Djougou and Parakou were still powerful in the north, as was the Kingdom of Toffa in Porto-Novo.

Each king pledged to leave his successor more land than he inherited, achieved by waging war with his neighbours. They grew rich by selling slaves to the European traders, notably the Portuguese, who established trading posts in Porto Novo, Ouidah and along the coast. For more than a century, an average of 10,000 slaves per year were shipped to the Americas. Southern Dahomey was dubbed the Slave Coast.

Following colonisation by the French, great progress was made in education, and many Dahomeyans were employed as government advisers throughout French West Africa.

Independence & le Folklore

When Dahomey became independent in 1960, other former French colonies started deporting their Dahomeyan populations. Back home without work, they were the root of a highly unstable political situation. Three years after independence, following the example of neighbouring Togo, the Dahomeyan military staged a coup.

During the next decade Dahomey saw four military coups, nine changes of government and five changes of constitution: what the Dahomeyans called, in jest, *le folklore*.

Revolution

In 1972 a group of officers led by Lieutenant Colonel Mathieu Kérékou seized power in a coup, then embraced Marxist-Leninist ideology and aligned the country with superpowers such as China. To emphasise the break from the past, Kérékou changed the flag and renamed the country Benin. He informed his people of the change by radio on 13 November 1975.

The government established Marxist infrastructure, which included implementing collective farms. However, the economy became a shambles, and there were ethnic tensions between the president, a Natitingou-born northerner, and the Yoruba population in the south. There were six attempted coups in one year alone.

In December 1989, as a condition of French financial support, Kérékou ditched Marxism and held a conference to draft a new constitution. The delegates engineered a coup, forming a new cabinet under Nicéphore Soglo.

Soglo won the first free multiparty elections, held in March 1991, but his autocracy, nepotism and austere economic measures – following the devaluation of the CFA franc – came under fire. Kérékou was voted back into power in March 1996. Kérékou's second and final five-year term in office finished with the presidential elections in March 2006, bringing an end to his 33 years at the top.

People of Benin

There is an array of different ethnic groups within Benin's narrow borders, although three of them account for nearly 60% of the population: Fon, Adja and Yoruba. The Adja people live near the border of Benin and Togo and are primarily farmers. The Fon and the Yoruba both migrated from Nigeria and occupy the southern and mideastern zones of Benin.

The Bariba and the Betamaribé, who make up 9% and 8% of the population respectively, live in the northern half of the country and have traditionally been very

THE SOMBA

Commonly referred to as the Somba, the Betamaribé people are concentrated to the southwest of Natitingou in the plains of Boukoumbé on the Togo border. What's most fascinating about the Betamaribé is their *tata somba* houses – fort-like huts with clay turrets and thatched spires. The ground floor of a house is mostly reserved for livestock. A stepladder leads from the kitchen to the roof terrace, where there are sleeping quarters and grain stores.

The Betamaribé's principal religion is animism – as seen in the rags and bottles they hang from the trees. Once famous for their nudity, they began wearing clothes in the 1970s.

protective of their cultures and distant towards southern people.

The nomadic Fula (also called Fulani or Peul), found widely across West Africa, live primarily in the north and comprise 6% of the population.

Despite the underlying tensions between the southern and northern regions, the various groups live in relative harmony and have intermarried.

Religion

Some 40% of the population is Christian and 25% Muslim, but most people practise voodoo, whatever their religion. The practice mixed with Catholicism in the Americas, to where the Dahomeyan slaves took it and their Afro-Brazilian descendants brought it back. Christian missionaries also won over Dahomeyans by fusing their creed with voodoo.

The Arts

Under the Dahomeyan kings, richly coloured appliqué banners were used to depict the rulers' past and present glories. With their bright, cloth-cut figures, the banners are still being made, particularly in Abomey.

Benin has a substantial Afro-Brazilian architectural heritage, best preserved in Porto Novo and Ouidah – there are plenty of hidden gems to seek out in the streets. The Lake Nokoué stilt villages, especially Ganvié, and

the *tata somba* houses around Natitingou, are remarkable examples of traditional architecture.

The *cire perdue* (lost wax) method used to make the famous Benin bronzes originates from Benin City, which lies in present-day Nigeria. However, the method spread west and the figures can be bought throughout Benin itself.

If you're into music, you'll love Angélique Kidjo, a major international star and Benin's most famous recording artist. Born in Ouidah in 1960 to a choreographer and a musician with Portuguese and English ancestry, Kidjo is a world musician in the true, boundary-busting sense of the phrase. Her music is inspired by the links between Africa and Latin America and the fusion of cultures. Check out www.kidjo.com for more information about her career. Other well-known Beninese artists include Gnonnas Pedro, Nel Oliver and Yelouassi Adolphe, and the bands Orchestre Poly-Rythmo and Disc Afrique.

Food & Drink

Beninese grub is unquestionably among the best in West Africa and is very similar to Togolese food, the main differences being the names: *fufu* (a starchy staple from ground plantain or cassava) is generally called *igname pilé* here, and *djenkoumé* (a savoury cornmeal and tomato cake) is called *pâte rouge,* for example. In southern Benin, fish is a highlight of local cuisine. It's usually barracuda, dorado or grouper, and is usually served grilled or fried.

Environment

Sandwiched between Nigeria and Togo, Benin is 700km long and 120km across in the south, widening to about 300km in the north. Most of the coastal plain is a sand bar that blocks the seaward flow of several rivers. As a result, there are lagoons a few kilometres inland all along the coast, which is being eroded by the strong ocean currents. Inland is a densely forested plateau and, in the far northwest, the Atakora Mountains.

Wildlife thrives in Parc National de la Pendjari, with elephants and several feline species.

Deforestation and desertification are major issues because of the logging of valuable wood, such as teak.

SURVIVAL GUIDE

 Directory A–Z

ACCOMMODATION

Benin has accommodation to suit every budget
– from beach resorts to guesthouses. Swanky
hotels are confined to Cotonou and, to a lesser
extent, Ouidah and Natitingou. Most have restaurants and bars, offer wi-fi service and have
air-con.

DANGERS & ANNOYANCES

⇒ Cotonou has its fair share of traffic accidents
and muggings, so be careful. In Ouidah, avoid
the roads to and along the coast at any time
of day.

⇒ Children, and sometimes also adults, will
shout 'Yovo! Yovo!' (meaning 'white person') ad
nauseam. It's normally harmless, but tiresome.

⇒ The beaches along the coast are not safe for
swimming because of strong currents. Stick to
hotel swimming pools or the lagoon.

EMBASSIES & CONSULATES

British Community Liaison Officer (☑ 21
30 32 65; www.fco.gov.uk; Haie Vive, Cotonou; ⊘ 10am-4pm Mon-Fri) Officially, British
nationals must deal with the British Deputy
High Commission in Lagos (Nigeria). However,
the Community Liaison Officer for the British
community in Benin, based at the English International School, can be of some help.

French Embassy (☑ 21 36 55 33; www.amba-
france-bj.org; Ave Jean-Paul II; ⊘ 11am-4pm
Mon-Thu)

German Embassy (☑ 21 31 29 67; www.coto
nou.diplo.de; Ave Jean-Paul II)

Ghanaian Embassy (☑ 21 30 07 46; off Blvd de
la Marina, Cotonou)

Nigerian Embassy (☑ 21 31 56 65; off Blvd de
la Marina, Cotonou)

US Embassy (☑ 21 30 06 50; cotonou.usem
bassy.gov; Rue Caporal Bernard Anani)

EMERGENCY & IMPORTANT NUMBERS

Benin's country code	☑ 229
Police	☑ 117
Ambulance	☑ 112
Fire	☑ 118

GAY & LESBIAN TRAVELLERS

While homosexuality is technically legal in Benin,
it is a conservative country and gay and lesbian
travellers should avoid making their sexual orientation known.

ⓘ SLEEPING PRICE RANGES

The following price ranges refer to a
double room with bathroom and air-con.

$ less than CFA16,000

$$ CFA16,000–40,000

$$$ more than CFA40,000

INTERNET ACCESS

In towns and cities, complimentary wi-fi is
available in almost every midrange and top-end
hotel.

Internet cafes are plentiful in towns and cities.
Connection speeds vary from pretty good to
acceptable.

MONEY

The currency in Benin is the West African CFA
franc. The best foreign currency to carry is euros, which are easily exchanged at banks, hotels
or bureaux de change.

Exchange Rates

Australia	A$1	CFA452
Canada	C$1	CFA440
Europe	€1	CFA656
Japan	¥100	CFA538
New Zealand	NZ$1	CFA415
United Kingdom	£1	CFA774
United States	US$	CFA600

For current exchange rates, see www.xe.com.

Tipping

Tipping is generally not necessary except at
upmarket restaurants, where around 10% extra
should be given for good service.

OPENING HOURS

Banks 8am to 12.30pm and 3pm to 6.30pm
Monday to Friday, 9am to 1pm Saturday. Some
banks are open through lunchtime.

Bars Late morning until the last customers
leave (late); nightclubs generally go from 10pm
into the wee hours.

Restaurants Lunch 11.30am to 2.30pm, dinner
6.30pm to 10.30pm.

Shops & businesses 8am to noon and 3pm to
7pm Monday to Saturday.

PUBLIC HOLIDAYS

In addition to Muslim holidays, Benin celebrates
the following days:

New Year's Day 1 January

Vodoun 10 January

Easter Monday March/April

Labour Day 1 May

Ascension Thursday May

Pentecost Monday May

Independence Day 1 August

Assumption 15 August

Armed Forces Day 26 October

All Saints' Day 1 November

Christmas 25 December

TELEPHONE

Depending on which mobile network you use at home, your phone may or may not work while in Benin – ask your mobile network provider. However, local mobile phone coverage is excellent and fairly cheap. Local networks include Moov and MTN. You can buy a local SIM card (CFA1500). Top-up vouchers are readily available.

TOURIST INFORMATION

There are tourist offices in Cotonou, Abomey, Ouidah and Porto Novo. The **Benin Tourism** (www.benin-tourisme.com) website is another source of information.

VISAS

Local authorities have done a couple of U-turns on visa policies in recent years, with the latest turn meaning that visas were not obtainable at the border or upon arrival at the airport. Be sure to get your visa from a Beninese embassy before travelling. Allow €50 for a one-month single-entry visa.

Visa des Pays de l'Entente (p451) are not available in Benin.

For onward travel, the following embassies deliver visas:

Burkina Faso No diplomatic representation in Benin – contact the French consulate.

Niger The embassy in Cotonou issues 30-day visas. They cost CFA23,500 and you'll need two photos. Allow three to four working days. You cannot get visas at the border.

Nigeria The Nigerian embassy only issues transit visas to travellers with a Nigerian embassy in their home country (there is no need to contact the embassy in your home country beforehand). You need two photos, along with photocopies of your passport and, if you have one, your ticket for onward travel from Nigeria. Fees vary according to nationality. Visas are normally issued on the same day.

Togo Seven-day visas (CFA10,000) are issued at the border. If crossing the border at Nadoba (coming from Boukombé), head to Kara where the Direction Régionale de la Documentation Nationale issues 30-day multiple-entry visas (CFA10,000, four photos).

WOMEN TRAVELLERS

Beninese men can give women travellers a lot of unwanted attention. Particularly unnerving are military and other officials using their power to get more of your company than is strictly necessary. Always stay polite but firm and make sure you have a good 'husband story'.

ⓘ Getting There & Away

AIR

The **Aéroport International de Cotonou Cadjéhoun** (www.aeroport-cotonou.com) is Benin's main gateway.

The main international carriers are **Air France** (www.airfrance.com; Rte de l'Aéroport), **Royal Air Maroc** (☑ 21 30 86 04; www.royalairmaroc.com; Rte de l'Aéroport), **Brussels Airlines** (☑ 21 30 16 82; www.brusselsairlines.com; Rte de l'Aéroport) and **Ethiopian Airlines** (☑ 21 32 71 61; www.flyethiopian.com; Rue 403), which offer direct flights to France, Morocco, Belgium and Ethiopia respectively, and connecting flights to the rest of the world.

Other major airlines include **Asky** (☑ 21 32 54 18; www.flyasky.com; Ave de la Paix), which flies to major capitals in West and Central Africa via Lomé; **South African Airways** (www.flysaa.com; Blvd Steinmetz), which flies to Johannesburg (South Africa); **Kenya Airways** (☑ 21 31 63 71; www.kenya-airways.com; Blvd Steinmetz), which flies to Nairobi (Kenya) and Ouagadougou (Burkina Faso); **Air Burkina** (www.air-burkina.com; Rte de l'Aéroport), which serves Ouagadougou (Burkina Faso) and Abidjan (Côte d'Ivoire); and

Senegal Airlines (🖉 21 31 76 51; www.sene-galairlines.aero; Ave Steinmetz), which flies to Dakar (Senegal) and Abidjan (Côte d'Ivoire). All airlines have offices in Cotonou.

LAND
Burkina Faso

From Tanguiéta in northwestern Benin, you can find bush taxis to Nadiagou, on the Burkina side of the border north of Porga, from where you can find services to Ouagadougou. There's also a daily bus from Tanguiéta to Ouagadougou.

TCV (p43) bus services go two times a week between Cotonou and Bobo Dioulasso via Ouagadougou (CFA19,000, 18 hours).

Niger

From Malanville in northeastern Benin, a *zemijohn* (motorcycle taxi) or shared taxi can take you across the Niger River to Gaya in Niger.

From Cotonou, Rimbo-RTV (p43) has daily services to Niamey (CFA24,000, 18 hours).

Nigeria

ABC Transport (p43) operates a daily Lagos–Accra bus service, which stops in Cotonou (CFA12,000 to CFA14,000, four hours). Add another CFA6000 for the *convoyeur* (the middleman who'll handle and facilitate formalities at the border).

There are no direct taxis to Lagos from Porto Novo, so you'll have to change at the Kraké–Seme border (CFA1000, 30 minutes). Make sure you have some naira to pay for your journey on the other side.

Togo

Cotonou and Lomé are connected by frequent bush taxis (CFA6500, three hours), which regularly leave the Gare Jonquet in Cotonou for Lomé. Alternatively, pick up a taxi to the border point at Hilakondji and grab another taxi on the Togolese side of the border.

Various bus companies, including STIF (p43), **CTS** (🖉 99 27 83 32; Blvd du 13 Janvier (Blvd Circulaire)) and UTB (p43), also regularly service the Cotonou–Lomé–Accra–Abidjan route (CFA5000 for Lomé, four hours).

Other crossings are at Kétao–Ouaké, on the Kara–Djougou road, and between Nadoba in Togo and Boukoumbé in Benin along a good track. The latter crossing takes you through spectacular countryside but has little public transport except on Wednesdays, Nadoba market day.

🛈 Getting Around

BUS
Buses are the most reliable and comfortable way to get around, especially between cities in southern Benin and Natitingou to the north.

ATT (p43) and Confort Lines (p49) buses are better maintained and more reliable than those of other companies. They also have air-con.

Buses almost always operate with guaranteed seating and fixed departure times; arrive early or book the day before to ensure you have a seat on your preferred service.

CAR & MOTORCYCLE
Roads are in relatively good condition throughout Benin except the Cotonou–Bohicon road, which is appalling. It has been scheduled for resurfacing for years, but little progress has been made.

Hiring a car with a driver is a good option if you're short on time. Travel agencies and tour operators in Cotonou can organise 4WD hire for about CFA50,000 per day (with driver). For a regular vehicle, you'll pay about CFA20,000 per day. Fuel is extra.

If you're driving, you need an International Driving Permit.

A litre of petrol cost around CFA600 at the time of research. Petrol stations are easy to find throughout the country.

LOCAL TRANSPORT
Bush Taxi

Bush taxis, generally beaten-up old vehicles, cover outlying communities that large buses don't serve, but also run between major towns and cities. There is sometimes a surcharge for luggage. Most leave from the *gares routières*; morning is the best time to find them.

Zemi-Johns

The omnipresence of *zems* (*zemi-johns;* motorbike taxis) has translated into the near disappearance of car taxis for short journeys. While they are by far the fastest and most convenient way of getting around, they are dangerous: most drive like lunatics and helmets are not available.

Zem drivers wear numbered yellow shirts in Cotonou (various colours in other towns). Hail them just as you would a taxi, and be sure to agree on a price before the journey. The typical fare is from CFA200 to CFA350 for trips within a town. They are also an easy way to get to remote villages where public transport is infrequent.

Burkina Faso

📞 226 / POP 18.5 MILLION

Best Places to Eat

➡ La Canne d'Or (p65)
➡ Le Calypso (p66)
➡ Maquis Aboussouan (p60)
➡ Le Verdoyant (p61)
➡ Chez Haregua (p61)

Best Places to Sleep

➡ Villa Bobo (p63)
➡ Auberge Kunkolo (p67)
➡ Le Calypso (p66)
➡ Les Jardins de Koulouba (p57)
➡ Ranch de Nazinga (p66)

Why Go?

Burkina should be on everyone's travel list – it may not have many big-ticket attractions, but the warmth of its welcome and the friendliness of the Burkinabé people is unique. Wherever you go you'll be greeted with a memorable *bonne arrivée* ('welcome') and a handshake.

There's also the lively cultural scene. The capital, Ouagadougou, and Bobo-Dioulasso, Burkina's two largest and gloriously named cities, are famous for their musical traditions and beautiful handicrafts. Throw in Fespaco, Africa's premier film festival (held in Ouaga every odd-numbered year), and there's enough to engage your mind and senses for a couple of weeks or so.

Tourism infrastructure is fairly limited, but the true gems of Burkina Faso are in the remoter areas, outside of the cities: the enchanting beauty of the landscapes – from rolling savannah and surprising geology to the mesmerising painted houses at Tiébélé – and the unique culture and genuine hospitality of the Burkinabé.

When to Go
Ouagadougou

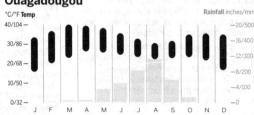

| **Jan–Mar** Perfect wildlife-viewing time; dusty harmattan winds can produce hazy skies. | **Apr–Sep** Hot season (April to May) best avoided; rainy season (June to September) difficult for transport. | **Oct–Dec** A lovely time of year, with green landscapes and pleasant temperatures. |

OUAGADOUGOU

POP 1.4 MILLION

Ouaga, as it's affectionately dubbed, is a thriving, eclectic arts hub, with dance and concert venues, live bands, theatre companies, a busy festival schedule and beautiful handicrafts. Its streets are a busy, dusty mix of concrete and red roads, thousands of mopeds, street-peddlers and general, exuberant life that more than makes up for the capital's lack of major sights.

◎ Sights

Moro-Naba Palace PALACE
(Ave Moro-Naba) FREE On Fridays at 7am the Moro-Naba of Ouagadougou – emperor of the Mossi and the most powerful traditional chief in Burkina Faso – presides over the **Moro-Naba Ceremony** at the palace. It's a formal ritual that lasts only about 15 minutes. Travellers are welcome to attend, but photos are not permitted.

National Museum MUSEUM
(☑25 39 19 34; Blvd Charles de Gaulle; CFA1000; ◎9am-12.30pm & 3-5.30pm Tue-Sat) The national museum, almost 4km east of the city centre, has displays of the various masks, ancestral statues and traditional costumes of Burkina Faso's major ethnic groups.

Musée de la Musique MUSEUM
(Ave d'Oubritenga; CFA1000; ◎9am-4pm Tue-Sat, by appt Sun) You don't need to be into music to enjoy this excellent museum: the Burkinabé live and breathe music and a visit to the museum serves as a great introduction to Burkinabé culture. The new building is a traditional adobe structure that gives the place a special atmosphere in which to soak up local music history.

✸ Festivals & Events

Fespaco FILM
(Festival Pan-Africain du Cinéma de Ouagadougou; www.fespaco.bf; ◎Feb-Mar) Going strong since 1969, this world-renowned biennial festival (held in odd-numbered years) sees African films competing for the prestigious Étalon d'Or de Yennenga – Fespaco's equivalent of the Oscars.

Jazz à Ouaga MUSIC
(www.jazz-ouaga.org; ◎Apr-May) A well-established music festival bringing out the Afrobeat, soul and blues influence in jazz.

SIAO ART
(Salon International de l'Artisanat de Ouagadougou; www.siao.bf; Blvd des Tensoba; ◎Oct) Biennial trade fair (held in even-numbered years) of reference for the arts and crafts sector in Africa – and a godsend for gem-hunting visitors.

⊟ Sleeping

★Les Jardins de Koulouba GUESTHOUSE $
(☑25 30 25 81; www.jardins-koulouba.fr; r with air-con CFA25,000, with fan & without bathroom CFA15,000; ✻ 🛜 ≋) A wonderfully decorated patio and a lush tropical garden, African art, spacious rooms, a fantastic location, a pool and a relaxed vibe make this lovely guesthouse one of the best in Ouaga.

★Le Pavillon Vert HOSTEL $
(☑25 31 06 11; www.hotel-pavillonvert.com; Ave de la Liberté; s/d with fan CFA12,500/13,500, with air-con CFA17,000/18,000, with fan & without bathroom CFA8000/8500; ✻ 🛜) The stalwart 'PV' is the best backpackers' spot in Ouaga. It has competitive prices, a lively bar and restaurant, a gorgeous plant-filled garden and an assortment of well-kept rooms for all budgets. It's run by the same management as the excellent Couleurs d'Afrique (p62) travel agency and the **Hotel de la Liberte** (☑25 33 23 63; www.hotel-liberte.com; Avenue de la Liberté; s/d CFA17,500/20,000; ✻ 🛜).

Villa Yiri Suma GUESTHOUSE $
(☑25 30 54 82; www.yirisuma.com; 428 Ave du Petit Maurice Yameogo; d CFA21,000-28,000; ✻ 🛜) Yiri Suma is all about art: Lucien, the owner, is passionate about African art and likes nothing better than to share his passion with guests via displaying contemporary Burkinabé works in the courtyard. The villa regularly houses exhibitions and cultural events, and the five spotless rooms enjoy their own contemporary decor and unique works.

Chez Giuliana GUESTHOUSE $
(☑25 36 33 97; www.chezgiuliana.com; Rue Lamine Gueye, Quartier 1200 Logements; s/d without bathroom CFA16,000/20,000, with bathroom CFA20,000/24,000; ✻ 🛜) This bustling Italian guesthouse is a perennial favourite among aid workers: the welcome is as colourful as the rooms and the roof terrace is simply awesome for sundowners. It's about 3km outside the centre, near the Maternité Sainte Camille hospital. Rates include breakfast.

Auberge Le Karité Bleu B&B $$
(☑25 36 90 46; www.karitebleu.com; 214 Blvd de l'Onatel, Zone du Bois; d CFA28,000-47,000; ✻ 🛜) In a residential neighbourhood, this adorable B&B offers eight spiffy rooms decorated

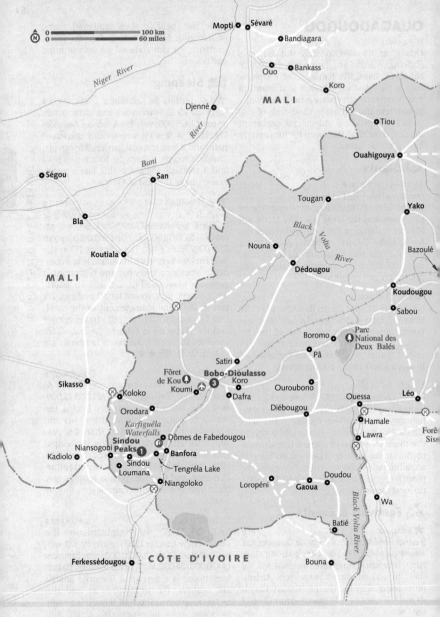

Burkina Faso Highlights

1 Sindou Peaks (p67)
Wandering amid other-worldly rock formations and Burkina's lush landscapes.

2 Cour Royale (p68)
Marvelling over the meaning and originality of Kassena houses at Tiébélé.

3 Live music (p62)
Sipping beers to the sound of Bobo-Dioulasso's fantastic musicians.

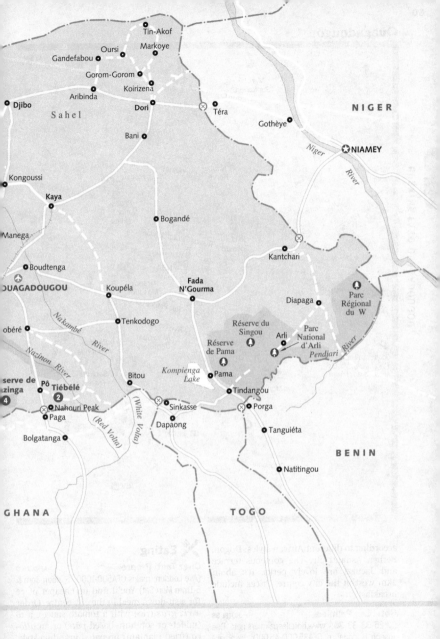

NIGER

Tin-Akof
Markoye
Oursi
Gandefabou
Gorom-Gorom
Koirizena
Aribinda
Djibo
Dori
Téra
S a h e l
Gothèye
NIAMEY
Niger
Bani
River
Kongoussi
Kaya
Manega
Bogandé
Boudtenga
Kantchari
OUAGADOUGOU
Koupéla
Fada
N'Gourma
Diapaga
Parc
Régional
du W
Nakambé
Tenkodogo
Réserve du
Singou
Parc
River
oberé
Réserve
de Pama
Arli
National
d'Arli
Nazinon River
Pendjari
River
serve de
azinga
Bitou
Kompienga
Lake
Pama
4
Pô
Tiébélé
2
Nahouri Peak
Tindangou
Paga
Sinkasse
Porga
(White Volta)
Dapaong
Tanguiéta
Bolgatanga
(Red Volta)
BENIN
Natitingou
GHANA
TOGO

4 Réserve de Nazinga
(p68) Coming face-to-face
with the elephants, alligators
and antelope at Burkina's
favourite national park.

5 Festivals (p57) Joining
in one of the fabulous
Ouagadougou festivals and
soaking up the atmosphere.

BURKINA FASO OUAGADOUGOU

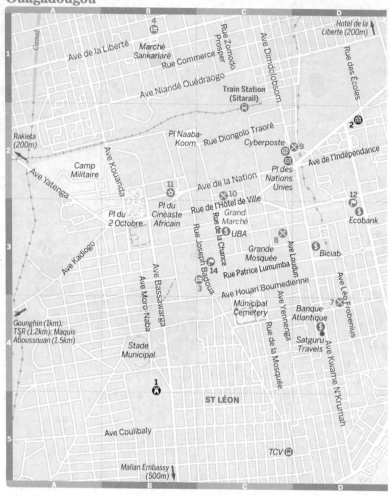

according to different African styles: Dogon, Berber, Ashanti etc. The gorgeous terrace and Jacuzzi are lovely perks. It's about 2km west of the city centre. Prices include breakfast.

Hôtel Les Palmiers
HOTEL **$$**

(☑ 25 33 33 30; www.hotellespalmiers.net; Rue Joseph Badoua; d CFA35,000-45,000; ❄️🛜🏊) Les Palmiers is an oasis blending African touches with European levels of comfort. The rooms are arranged around a leafy compound and embellished with local decorations. The garden, pool and terrace provide the finishing touches.

🍴 Eating

Chez Tanti Propre
AFRICAN **$**

(Ave Loudun; mains CFA500-1000; ☺ noon-3pm & 6-11pm Mon-Sat) You'll find no cheaper place for a sit-down meal in the city centre. Order a *riz gras* (rice with a tomato sauce), a *tô* (millet- or sorghum-based *pâte*) or an *alloco* (fried plantain) prepared grandma-style. Perfect for a quick bite at lunchtime.

★ Maquis Aboussouan
AFRICAN **$$**

(☑ 25 34 27 20; Rue Simon Compaoré; mains CFA2500-5000; ☺ 11am-11pm Tue-Sun; ❄️) This upmarket *maquis* (rustic, open-air restau-

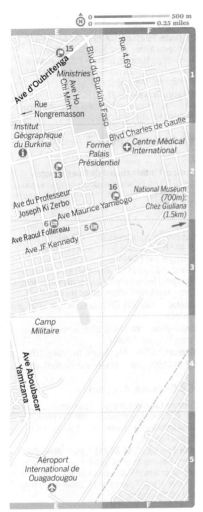

Ouagadougou

◎ Sights

🛏 Sleeping

🍴 Eating

◎ Entertainment

ℹ Information

Espace Gondwana   FUSION $$
(☎ 50 36 11 24; www.africartisanat.com; Rue du Dr Balla Moussa Traoré, Zone du Bois; mains CFA4000-9000; ⊗ 6-11pm; ❀🛜) Espace Gondwana sports sensational decor, with four dining rooms richly adorned with masks and traditional furniture. The food impresses, too, with an imaginative menu that runs the gamut from frogs' legs and fish dishes to grilled meats and salads.

L'Eau Vive   FRENCH $$
(Rue de l'Hôtel de Ville; mains CFA2000-7000; ⊗ noon-2.30pm & 7-10pm; ❀🛜) This Ouagadougou institution is run by an order of nuns and promises an air-conditioned haven from the clamour outside; there's also a garden dining area out the back. French staples are served, and 'Ave Maria' is sung at 9.30pm every night. There is a sister (excuse the pun) restaurant in Bobo (p65).

★ Chez Haregua   ETHIOPIAN $$$
(☎ 25 50 52 38; chezharegua@gmail.com; Ave Léo Frobenus; mains CFA6000-10,000; ❀) If you want to give your taste buds a sensuous treat, go for this Ethiopian choice – the excellent *alicha doro* (turmeric chicken) is served with the traditional, pancake-like *injera* bread and eaten by hand. The staff is super-friendly and the service excellent. Highly recommended.

rant) is the place to enjoy Burkinabé and Ivoirian staples such as *poulet kedjenou* (slow-cooked chicken with peppers and tomatoes) or *attiéké* (grated cassava). The ample, lively courtyard is filled with regular locals and is great for soaking up the atmosphere.

★ Le Verdoyant   PIZZA, ITALIAN $$
(☎ 25 31 54 07; Ave Dimdolobsom; mains CFA4000-6000; ⊗ noon-2.30pm & 6.30-11pm Thu-Tue) A favourite haunt of expats, the ultracentral Le Verdoyant is famous for its pasta, wood-fired pizzas and ice creams. Note that the mosquitoes are ferocious at night.

☆ Entertainment

Institut Français ARTS CENTRE

(Ave de la Nation) The French cultural centre has one of the best line-ups of Burkinabé and West African musicians, theatre directors, cinema and visual artists.

🔒 Shopping

★Village Artisanal
de Ouaga GIFTS & SOUVENIRS

(☑25 37 14 83; Blvd Tengsoba; ⊙7am-7pm) A government-run cooperative with a wide range of crafts, ideal for souvenir-shopping without the hard sell. If you're not a fan of bargaining to death and want to find real local handicrafts, this is the place to go. Note that Blvd Tengsoba is also known as Blvd Circulaire.

ℹ Information

DANGERS & ANNOYANCES

Ouagadougou is one of the safer cities in the region, but avoid walking around alone at night. Bag snatching is a problem – don't carry valuables with you.

INTERNET ACCESS

Cyberposte (off Ave de la Nation; per hr CFA500; ⊙8am-8pm Mon-Sat) Also offers printing and scanning services.

MEDICAL SERVICES

Centre Médical International (☑70 20 00 00, 50 30 66 07; Rue Nazi Boni, Koulouba; ⊙24hr) In the Koulouba neighbourhood, west of the centre.

MONEY

There are numerous banks around town, most with ATM.

Banque Atlantique (Ave Kwame N'Krumah; ⊙9am-2pm)

Biciab (Ave Kwame N'Krumah; ⊙7-11am & 3.30-5pm Mon-Fri) Efficient exchange office with a Biciab ATM (Visa only). There are also two other Bicicab ATMs in the centre, at Ave Yennenga and Ave Loudun.

Ecobank (Rue Maurice Bishop; ⊙7-11am & 3.30-5pm)

UBA (Rue de la Chance; ⊙9am-2pm)

TOURIST INFORMATION

Institut Géographique du Burkina (Ave de l'Indépendance) Maps and general info on the country are available here.

TRAVEL AGENCIES

Couleurs d'Afrique (☑25 31 06 11; www.couleurs-afrique.com; Ave de l'Olympisme,

Gounghin) Offers circuits in Burkina and neighbouring countries. Highly recommended.

L'Agence Tourisme (☑25 31 84 43; www.agence-tourisme.com; Hôtel les Palmiers, Rue Joseph Badoua, Burkina Faso) Excellent tour operator, with many years' experience in Burkina and West Africa.

Satguru Travels (☑25 30 16 52; cpshewkani@satguruun.com; Ave Kwame N'Krumah) Recommended for buying airline tickets.

ℹ Getting There & Away

AIR

Aéroport International de Ouagadougou (☑25 30 65 15; www.aeroport-ouagadougou. com) The taxi ride from the centre costs about CFA3000.

BUS

Buses from companies such as **Rakieta** (☑25 31 40 56; www.transport-rakieta.com; Ave Yatenga) and **TCV** (Transport Confort Voyageurs; ☑25 30 14 12; www.tcv-sa.com; Rue de la Mosquée) leave from the bus companies' depots (every taxi knows where to find them).

Banfora CFA8500, 6½ hours, six daily, TCV and Rakieta

Bobo-Dioulasso CFA7000, five hours, seven daily, TCV and Rakieta

Gaoua CFA7000, four hours, five daily, TCV

Pô CFA2500, 2½ hours, four daily, Rakieta

ℹ Getting Around

Shared taxis (beaten-up old green cars) cost a flat CFA300; flag them anywhere in town. They tend to follow set routes, often to/from the Grand Marché.

Allo Taxi (☑25 34 34 35) A good alternative if you happen to be in a street without much traffic or would like to be picked up at a certain time or place. Taxis must be booked and they run on the meter.

THE SOUTHWEST

Southwestern Burkina Faso ticks all the right boxes, with a heavy mix of natural and cultural sights vying for your attention.

Bobo-Dioulasso

POP 490,000

Bobo-Dioulasso – or Bobo, as it's widely known – may be Burkina Faso's second-largest city, but it has small-town charm. Its tree-lined streets exude a languid, semitropical atmosphere that makes it a favourite rest stop for travellers.

You'll have plenty to do during the day in and around the city – hire a moped to see the surrounding sights – but save some energy for night time to enjoy Bobo's thriving live-music scene and excellent restaurants.

⊙ Sights

Grande Mosquée
MOSQUE

(CFA1000) Built in 1893, this mosque is an outstanding example of Sahel-style mud architecture, with conical towers and wooden struts (which both support the structure and act as scaffolding during replastering efforts). Visits take you inside the building and onto the roof terrace, where you'll get a different perspective of the towers.

Koro
VILLAGE

(CFA1000) Perched on the hillside, Koro's houses – built amid rock formations – are unique in the area, and there are fine panoramic views over the countryside from the top of the village. Koro is 13km east of Bobo, off the main Ouagadougou road.

Kibidwé
AREA

(CFA1000) Bobo's historical centre is a thriving neighbourhood. Little has changed over the centuries in terms of organisation: Muslims, *griots* (traditional musicians, storytellers or praise singers), blacksmiths and 'nobles' (farmers) still live in their respective quarters but happily trade services and drink at the same *chopolo* (millet beer) bars.

Guided tours are not official, but unavoidable in practice – allow CFA2000 to CFA3000. They offer a great insight into local life, although the compulsory stops at craft shops are tedious.

Grand Marché
MARKET

(Rue du Commerce, Harndalaye) Bobo-Dioulasso's centrepiece, the expansive Grand Marché, is hugely enjoyable and atmospheric, and a wonderful (and largely hassle-free) place to experience a typical African city market. The market spills over onto the surrounding streets in a chaos of mopeds, wandering traders and general clamour, which together provide a lively counterpoint to Bobo's otherwise tranquil streets.

Koumi
VILLAGE

(CFA1000) The village of Koumi, on the Bobo–Orodara road (6km south of Kou), is well-known for its ochre-coloured adobe houses. Villagers run informative guided

FÊTE DES MASQUES

In the Bobo-Dioulasso region, whenever there's a major funeral, it's accompanied by a late-night *fête des masques* (festival of masks).

Masked men dance to an orchestra of flute-like instruments and narrow drums beaten with curved canes. Each dancer, representing a different spirit, performs in turn – leaping, waving sticks and looking for evil spirits that might prevent the deceased from going to paradise.

As the celebrations continue, dancers become increasingly wild, performing acrobatic feats and waving their heads backwards and forwards until they catch someone and strike them. The victim, however, must not complain.

tours (CFA1000) touching on animist beliefs, architecture and local life.

🛏 Sleeping

★ Villa Rose
GUESTHOUSE $

(☑ 20 97 67 58; www.villarosebobodioulasso.com; Ave Philiippe Zinda Kaboré, Koko; s/d with fan CFA13,000/14,000, with air-con CFA16,500/17,500; ❄ 🛜) This lovely guesthouse, run by Dutch-Burkinabé couple Franca and Moctar, sits in the leafy neighbourhood of Koko, east of the centre, just off the main street. The fourteen rooms are impeccable, combining a minimalist decor and Burkinabé arts and crafts. The massive courtyard garden is the hotel's centrepiece, and a beautiful place to relax.

★ Villa Bobo
B&B $

(☑ 20 98 54 16; www.villabobo.com; No 292 Rue 35, Secteur 4, Koko; s/d with fan CFA12,000/15,000, with air-con CFA16,500/19,000; P ❄ 🛜 ⏹) With its four zealously maintained rooms, prim bathrooms, atmospheric veranda, colourful garden and pool, Villa Bobo is a delight. Xavier, the French owner, speaks English and can arrange excursions in the area, and you can hire scooters (CFA5000 per day).

Entente Hôtel
HOTEL $

(☑ 20 97 12 05; sopresbobo@yahoo.fr; Rue du Commerce; s/d with fan CFA9300/12,600, s/d/tr with air-con CFA12,300/20,600/27,900; ❄ 🛜) One of the few central establishments in Bobo, Entente has clean, tidy rooms. The fan rooms are rather small for the price, but there is

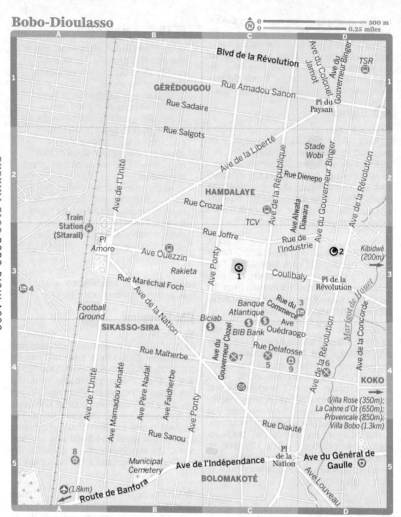

plenty of space to hang out in the pleasant courtyard.

Les 2 Palmiers HOTEL $$
(📞20 97 27 59; www.hotelles2palmiers.com; off Rue Malherbe; d CFA37,500-41,500; ❇️🛜) In a quiet street, this excellent option gets an A+ for its spotless rooms embellished with African crafts. The on-site restaurant is hailed as one of the best in Bobo.

✕ Eating

Restaurant Dankin AFRICAN $
(📞20 98 28 42; Rue Malherbe; mains CFA1000-4000; ⏰7am-3pm & 6-11pm; 🛜) Sister restau-

rant to Mandé, Dankin serves a loyal base of local customers, who come for the simple West African dishes – *riz gras* or *riz arachide* (rice with a peanut sauce) – delicious fresh juices and Brakina beer. The atmosphere is always lively, and the service jovial.

Mandé AFRICAN $
(Ave de la Révolution; mains CFA1000-4000; ⏰7am-3pm & 6-11pm; ❇️🛜) With an open-air terrace, great prices and a wide-ranging menu specialising in African dishes, Mandé is an excellent deal. If you just eat *riz sauce* (rice with sauce) or couscous and drink tamarind juice, you'll be well fed for around

Bobo-Dioulasso

CFA1500. Its owners also run nearby Restaurant Dankin.

⭐**La Canne d'Or**　　　　　　FUSION **$$**
(🔊20 98 15 96; Ave Philippe Zinda Kaboré; mains CFA4000-6000; ⊙11.30am-2.30pm & 6.30-10pm Tue-Sun) This villa-style eatery, with its African decor and riot of fairy lights, serves French fare with an African twist. House faves include frogs' legs and a great grill selection (kebabs, steak, Nile perch etc). Service is stellar.

L'Eau Vive　　　　　　　　FRENCH **$$**
(Rue Delafosse; mains CFA2500-6000; ⊙noon-2.30pm & 6.30-10pm Mon-Sat; ❄🛜) L'Eau Vive offers imaginative French cooking and a varied menu. Try the fresh mango juice – it's absolutely delightful. It's the sister venue of the restaurant of the same name in Ouagadougou, and is also run by nuns.

🍷 Drinking & Entertainment

Provencale　　　　　　　　　　CLUB
(Ave Phililppe Zinda Kaboré, Koko; ⊙11am-late) Come and shake your stuff to *coupé-décalé* (Ivoirian beats) and other Afro-beats at the funky Provencale. The Sunday matinée is particularly popular.

Le Bois d'Ébène　　　　　　LIVE MUSIC
(Ave de l'Unité; ⊙noon-late) One of the best venues in town for live music. Local bands come to play Afrobeat and there's always lots of dancing. Concerts held Thursday to Sunday.

Shopping

⭐**Gafreh**　　　　FASHION & ACCESSORIES
(www.gafreh.org; Rue Delafosse; ⊙7am-7pm Mon-Sat) This brilliant initiative, a women's coop-

erative, recycles the millions of black sachets handed out with purchases across Burkina into chic handbags, wallets and other accessories. Check out their factory outlet in Koko: ask someone at this location to take you there for the full range of their products.

❶ Information

Most banks are in the centre, and have ATMs.
Banque Atlantique (Ave de la République; ⊙8.30am-5.30pm)
BIB Bank (Ave Ouédraogo; ⊙9am-2pm)
Biciab (Ave Ouédraogo; ⊙9am-2pm)
Main Post Office (Ave de la Republique; ⊙9am-4pm)

❶ Getting There & Away

Bus services, such as those of **Rakieta** (🔊20 97 18 91; www.transport-rakieta.com; Ave Ouezzin), **TCV** (Transport Confort Voyageurs; 🔊20 97 75 75; www.tcv-sa.com; Rue Crozat) and **TSR** (Transport Sana Rasmane; 🔊25 34 25 24; Blvd de la Revolution), leave from each company's depot.

Banfora CFA1500, 1½ hours, eight daily, TCV and Rakieta
Gaoua CFA5000, 2½ hours, two to three daily, TSR
Ouagadougou CFA7000, five hours, seven daily, TCV and Rakieta

❶ Getting Around

Standard taxi fare for a shared cab ride in town is CFA300.

Ismael Sawadogo (🔊76 45 85 71) is a delightful and very reliable taxi driver (as well as a professional storyteller!). He can arrange anything from early morning pick-ups for bus services to day trips around Bobo.

Banfora

POP 76,000
Banfora is a sleepy town in its eponymous region, one of the most beautiful areas in Burkina Faso. It makes an ideal base for exploring the lush surrounding countryside: scaling up the magnificent Dômes de Fabedougou and taking a dip in the Karfiguéla Falls are experiences that are bound to stay with you for years, and a boat ride on Tengréla Lake is the perfect way to spot hippos.

The town itself has a lively **Sunday market**, with plenty of goods from nearby Côte d'Ivoire – heaps of bananas, pineapples and great ceramics and textiles.

LA MARE AUX POISSONS SACRÉS & KORO

The sacred fish pond of **Dafra**, around 6km southeast of Bobo, is an important animist site: local people come here to solicit spirits by sacrificing chickens and feeding them to the fish. It is a fairly grisly sight, with chicken bones and feathers everywhere; the 30-minute walk from the nearest parking spot to the pond is truly stunning, however, with arresting rock formations and gorgeous savannah landscapes. A taxi there and back from Bobo-Dioulasso will cost around CFA10,000 (be aware that the track is atrocious).

You can easily follow on from Dafra to the village of Koro (p63) for some beautiful views of the area.

◉ Sights & Activities

Dômes de Fabedougou   LANDMARK
(CFA1000) These limestone formations were sculpted into quirky domelike shapes over millennia by water and erosion – an arresting sight. They're found 3km north of the Karfiguéla Waterfalls (off the N2 road to Bobo). Don't miss it.

Karfiguéla Waterfalls   WATERFALL
(Cascades de Karfiguéla; CFA1000) The Karfiguéla Waterfalls, where you can take a dip in the lovely natural pools on the upper section, are at their best during and just after the rainy season. Unfortunately, the dirt tracks leading to the falls via a magnificent avenue of mango trees can be impassable at these times. But if the track is open (you'll have to ask around), it's worth the journey. The site is some 11km northwest of Banfora.

Tengréla Lake   WILDLIFE, CANOEING
(CFA2000) Just 7km west of Banfora, Tengréla Lake is home to a variety of birdlife; if you're lucky, you'll even see hippos (especially from January to April). The admission price includes a guided pirogue (traditional canoe) trip.

🛏 Sleeping & Eating

★ Le Calypso   LODGE $
(☑70 74 14 83, 20 91 02 29; famille_houitte@ yahoo.fr; Rte de Bobo-Dioulasso; r with fan/air-con CFA9500/16,000; ❋🛜) Le Calypso's lovely rooms combine traditional adobe architecture with modern comforts and impeccable

cleanliness. The huts are arranged around a beautiful garden. It's about 1km outside of town on the road to Bobo.

Campement Farafina   HUT $
(☑26 24 46 21; http://farafinaclub.free.fr; Tengréla Lake; huts without bathroom CFA4000) Want to laze a few days at Tengréla Lake? Park your backpack here – it's a five-minute walk from the lake. Facilities are very basic (bucket shower, mud huts without fan) but the owner, Solo, is an adept musician and a fantastic host.

Hôtel La Canne à Sucre   HOTEL $$
(☑20 91 01 07; www.banfora.com; off Rue de la Poste; d with fan from CFA8500, with air-con CFA15,000-35,000, 4-bed apt CFA49,000; ❋🛜🏊) Beautiful rooms are kitted out with African woodcarvings and cloth and the leafy garden feels like heaven after a tiring day. The apartments (located across the road) are ideal for groups and have exclusive use of the pool. The restaurant is the fanciest in town, and perfect for a treat (mains CFA3000 to CFA5000).

McDonald   BURGERS, AFRICAN $
(off Rue de la Préfecture; mains CFA1500-3000; ⊙11am-10pm Thu-Tue) This cool den off the main drag boasts an inviting covered terrace and a vividly decorated interior. It churns out a good range of satisfying dishes, including its famous *hamburger frites* (burger with fries) and the standard West African staples.

★ Le Calypso   EUROPEAN, AFRICAN $$
(☑20 91 02 29; off Rue de la Poste; mains around CFA3000; ⊙11.30am-11pm; 🛜) Run by the same jovial Franco-Burkinabé family as Le Calypso hotel, this popular restaurant is a wonderful place for tasty, slow-cooked fish, marinated steak and pizzas. The homemade juices are highly recommended.

ℹ Information

There are Visa ATMs at **Banque Atlantique** (Rte de la Côte d'Ivoire) and **Ecobank** (Rte de la Côte d'Ivoire).

ℹ Getting There & Away

Rakieta (☑20 91 03 81; www.transport-rakieta.com; Rue de la Poste) and **TCV** (Transport Confort Voyageurs; ☑75 79 13 08; www.tcv-sa.com; Rue de la Poste) have regular departures for Bobo-Dioulasso (CFA1500, 1½ hours, eight daily) and Ouaga (CFA8500, 6½ hours, six daily), and one daily service each to Bouaké in Côte d'Ivoire (CFA11,500, 10 hours).

The road to Gaoua is in bad condition and is serviced only by taxi-brousse (bush taxi; CFA5000, four to five hours). Pick them up at the **gare routière** (bus station; Rte de Bobo-Dioulasso). Otherwise go by bus via Bobo.

Sindou Peaks

Sindou Peaks (Pics de Sindou; CFA1000) are one of Burkina's most unforgettable sights. Millions of years ago, these brown, sandy cones were underwater, and they've been shaped by the elements ever since. It's a great place for light hiking and exploring the different formations. A sunrise and a breakfast here promise a magical experience.

🏃 Activities

Association Djiguiya   HIKING
(☎76 08 46 60; www.djiguiya.org; Sindou) Run by the brilliant Tiémoko Ouattara, this organisation promotes responsible travel and offers a range of services to travellers: anything from half-day walks, moped and cycling tours to cultural activities, homestays and even multi-day treks in Sénoufo country, featuring a sunrise breakfast among the Sindou Peaks.

🛏 Sleeping

Campement Soutrala   HUT $
(☎76 08 46 60; Sindou; huts without bathroom CFA5000) In Sindou, and run by Association Djiguiya (p67), this friendly *campement* (guesthouse) has basic huts with open-air showers; they also have electricity. Meals must be ordered two hours in advance (mains CFA600 to CFA6000). It's a good base if you'd like to spend time in the area rather than visit on a day trip from Banfora.

ℹ Getting There & Away

There are a few taxis-brousses (bush taxis) plying the asphalted road between Sindou and Banfora every day. Consider chartering a taxi for the day (CFA25,000).

Coming from Banfora, the main gateway is located about 1km before the entrance to the town of Sindou.

Gaoua & Lobi Country

The small town of Gaoua (population 31,000) is a good base for exploring Lobi country, an area that's culturally distinct from the traditions found in the rest of the country. There's a vibrant **Sunday market**, but the town's unique selling point is

its excellent ethnological museum, Musée de Poni.

◉ Sights

Musée de Poni   MUSEUM
(www.musee-gaoua.gov.bf; Gaoua; CFA2000; ⊙8am-12.30pm & 3-6pm Tue-Sun) This excellent ethnological museum contains full-scale reproductions of Lobi and Gan compounds, as well as a wide range of photographs and artefacts. The guides really know their stuff, too; Golane Oumar is particularly recommended.

🛏 Sleeping & Eating

Hôtel Hala   HOTEL $
(☎20 90 01 21; www.hotelhala.com; Gaoua; s/d with fan CFA13,000/15,000, with air-con CFA23,000/27,500; ❄ ☎) This is, all told, Gaoua's best option; service is glacial and the rooms are nothing to write home about but the compound is very pleasant. It has a handy location between town and the bus station and the wi-fi works. It also has the only decent restaurant in town, serving grilled meat and a few Lebanese specials (mains CFA2000 to CFA5000).

Maison Madeleine Père   GUESTHOUSE $
(☎20 90 03 41; Gaoua; s/d CFA6000/8000) Run by nuns, this quiet establishment in a monastery southwest of the city centre has impeccable rooms in pretty grounds. The biggest downsides are that it doesn't serve meals and that it's a bit out of the way. To find it, ask in the centre of town; most people will know it.

Le Flamboyant   AFRICAN $
(Gaoua; mains CFA800-2000; ⊙10am-10pm) One of the town's better *maquis*, right in the centre of town; expect the usual rice or *tô* (millet- or sorghum-based *pâte*) with sauce.

ℹ Information

For internet, head to the women-run **Association Pour la Promotion Féminine de Gaoua** (Gaoua; ⊙7.30am-6pm Mon-Fri) in the centre of Gaoua. Also, Hôtel Hala has wi-fi, which you can use in the bar/restaurant.

There are a couple of ATMs (Visa only) in town.

ℹ Getting There & Around

The *gare routière* is 2km out of town. You'll find bus services to Bobo-Dioulasso (CFA5000, 2½ hours, two to three daily) and Ouagadougou (CFA7000, four hours, five daily).

Direct services to Banfora are by taxi-brousse only (CFA5000, four to five hours); it's best to go to Bobo and find onward connections.

To get around Lobi country, charter a taxi in Gaoua; prices should start around CFA25,000, depending on how far you want to go.

THE SOUTH

The beauty of southern Burkina is a highlight of any trip to the country; it's also one of Burkina's most accessible corners.

Réserve de Nazinga

The 97,000-hectare Réserve de Nazinga (☑ 72 66 47 95; CFA10,000, vehicle entry CFA1000, guide fee CFA5000; ☺ 6am-6pm), about 40km southwest of Pô near the Ghanaian border, has become a highlight on many a wildlife-lover's itinerary, with antelope, monkeys, warthogs, crocodiles and plenty of birds. Elephants are the stars of the show. The best time to see them is December to April, though your chances are pretty good year-round.

At the heart of Nazinga, Ranch de Nazinga (☑ 72 66 47 95; nazingaranch@yahoo.fr; r CFA10,000, bungalows CFA25,000) has an exceptional location right by the reserve's biggest watering hole. Accommodation is a little lacklustre but the restaurant churns out tasty meals (mains CFA1000 to CFA3000) and the setting is unrivalled – you'll see animals regularly roaming among the bungalows.

You will need your own vehicle to access the reserve and go on wildlife drives. The travel agencies in Ouaga are your best bet.

Tiébélé & Kassena Country

Set in the heart of the green and low-lying Kassena country, Tiébélé, 40km east of Pô on a dirt track, is famous for its *sukhala* – colourful, windowless traditional houses. Painted by women in geometrical patterns of red, black and white guinea-fowl feathers, the houses offer an antidote to the monochrome mudbrick villages found elsewhere in Burkina Faso.

More than 450 people live in Tiébélé's royal court, the Cour Royale (Tiébélé; CFA2000, guide fee CFA3000; ☺ 8am-5.30pm), a large compound of typical *sukhalas*, or traditional painted houses. Children live with their grandparents in octagonal huts, couples live in rectangular huts and single people in round ones. Painting is generally done in February/March, after the harvest. Each drawing, whether geometrical or illustrative, has a meaning (fertility, afterlife, wisdom etc).

At nearly 800m, the cone-shape Nahouri Peak (CFA1000) is the tallest structure for miles around: the steep climb to its summit guarantees 360 degrees of uninterrupted savannah views. You'll have to hire a guide (CFA500) from Nahouri village, at the foot of the peak. The drive from Tiébélé will take one to 1½ hours (depending on the season), on a rough road.

Auberge Kunkolo (☑ 50 36 97 38, 76 53 44 55; Tiébélé; huts without bathroom CFA5000), a lovely guesthouse with impeccable Kassena-style huts and beautiful garden, is the best place to stay in the area, and one of Burkina's most atmospheric settings. Simple huts with fans and outdoor showers make up the accommodation, but the starlit skies above are magical. It's just 200m from the

---

LOBI TRADITIONS

Lobi traditions are some of the best preserved in West Africa. For travellers, the most obvious is the architecture of rural Lobi homes. The mudbrick compounds are rectangular and walls have only small slits for windows, for defensive purposes. In the old days, polygamous men built a bedroom for each of their wives.

The Lobi are also known for their cultural rituals. For example, the *dyoro* initiation rites, which take place every seven years, are still widely observed. As part of this important rite of passage, young men and women are tested on their stamina and skills; they also learn about sexual mores, the clan's history and the dos and don'ts of their culture.

The best way to explore Lobi heritage is to hire a guide in Gaoua (ask at Hôtel Hala). Visits will take in villages such as Sansana and Doudou, where you can admire different architectural styles and crafts (pottery, basket-weaving, sculpture). Doudou is famed for its artisanal gold-mining, which is the prerogative of women, and its market (held every five days).

chief's compound in Tiébélé. Simple meals (CFA1000) are also served.

❶ Getting There & Away

There is one direct bus from Ouaga to Tiébélé (and back) on Tuesdays, Fridays and Sundays (CFA3000, 3½ hours).

If you don't have your own vehicle, you can easily rent mopeds in Tiébélé for CFA4000 to CFA6000 per day.

UNDERSTAND BURKINA FASO

Burkina Faso Today

In November 2015 former prime minister Roch Marc Christian Kaboré, a French-educated banker who identifies as a social democrat, became president. His platform aimed to reduce youth unemployment and to improve education and health care, with free health care provided for children under six.

But Burkina's relative stability was profoundly shaken in January 2016, when Islamist militants attacked a hotel and cafe in Ouagadougou. Twenty-nine people died, several of them foreigners. This has affected the rate of visitors to the country, leading to closures of businesses dependent on tourism.

Burkina ranks 181st out of 187 countries on the UN's Human Development Index. The economy remains overly reliant on cotton exports, and a recent gold rush – which has seen a huge increase in illegal mining – has increased the country's exposure to market fluctuations. Socially, Burkina's biggest challenges are to improve access to education (the child literacy rate remains under 30%) and address chronic food insecurity.

History

The Mossi & the French

Little is known about Burkina Faso's early history, though archaeological finds suggest that the country was populated as far back as the Stone Age. Its modern history starts with the Mossi peoples (now almost half of Burkina Faso's population), who moved westward from settlements near the Niger River in the 13th century; they founded their first kingdom in what is now Ouagadougou. Three more Mossi states were subsequently established in other parts of the country, all paying homage to Ouagadougou, the strongest. The government of each of the Mossi states was highly organised, with ministers, courts and a cavalry known for its devastating attacks against the Muslim empires in Mali.

During the colonial scramble for Africa in the second half of the 19th century, the French exploited rivalries between the different Mossi kingdoms and established their sway over the region. At first the former Mossi states were assimilated into the Colonie du Haut Sénégal-Niger. Then, in 1919, the area was hived off for administrative expedience as a separate colony, Haute Volta (Upper Volta).

Thomas Sankara

World War II brought about profound changes in France's relationship with its colonies. The Mossi, like numerous other people in Africa, started challenging the colonial hegemony. The Upper Volta became a state in 1947; in 1956, France agreed to give its colonies their own governments, with independence quickly following in 1960.

Following independence, dreams of freedom and prosperity quickly evaporated. Between 1960 and 1983, the country experienced six coups and counter-coups and the economy stagnated. Then in 1983, Captain Thomas Sankara, an ambitious young left-wing military star, seized power.

Over the next four years 'Thom Sank' (as he was popularly known) recast the country. He changed its name to Burkina Faso (meaning 'Land of the Incorruptible'), restructured the economy to promote self-reliance in rural areas and tackled corruption with rare zeal. He was ahead of his time, promoting women's rights and standing up against Western paradigms on aid and development. But his authoritarian grip on power and intolerance towards those who didn't share his ideals were to be his downfall: in late 1987 a group of junior officers seized power and Sankara was killed.

The Compaoré Years

The new junta was headed by Captain Blaise Compaoré, Sankara's former friend and co-revolutionary. In late 1991 Compaoré was elected president. But as the sole candidate – with low voter turnout and the assassination of Clément Ouédraogo, the leading opposition figure, a couple of weeks later – his legitimacy remained weak.

In a bid to mark a clear break with Sankara, Compaoré immediately orchestrated a U-turn on the economy, overturning nationalisation and bringing the country back to the IMF fold. He was reelected three times, in 1998, 2005 and 2010, each time with more than 80% of the vote. In July 2013, thousands of demonstrators took to the streets over plans to create a senate; they continued to demonstrate into the following year in opposition to possible plans by President Compaoré to extend his rule. The revolt culminated with a mass uprising in October 2014, driving Compaoré out of office and leading to the establishment of a provisional government.

People of Burkina Faso

Burkina Faso, which occupies an area about half the size of France, is extremely diverse, with its 18.5 million people scattered among some 60 ethnic groups. The largest of these is the Mossi, who are primarily concentrated in the central plateau area.

Important groups in the south include the Bobo, Senoufo, Lobi and Gourounsi. In the Sahel areas of the north are the Hausa, Fula, Bella and Tuareg.

Religion

An old local joke says that 50% of Burkinabés are Muslim, 50% are Christian – and 100% are animist. In reality, the actual percentages for Islam and Christianity are about 60% and 23%, respectively, but most people do retain traditional beliefs.

The remaining are animists, who have not been converted or adopted Christianity or Islam. This traditional religion attributes a living soul to plants, inanimate objects and natural phenomena, and involves ritual sacrifice of animals (such as chickens or cattle) to ancestors.

The Arts

Burkina Faso has a vibrant contemporary arts and crafts scene: painting, sculpture, woodcarving, bronze and brass metalwork and textiles are all represented. Artistic works are exhibited in Ouagadougou's galleries, cultural centres and collective workshops.

The Burkinabés live and breathe music: it's the mainstay of traditional celebrations, with djembe (drum), balafon (a kind of xylophone) and flute the main instruments. Modern musicians draw on traditional influences from home and the rest of the continent, especially Mali, Congo and Côte d'Ivoire, as well as Jamaican reggae, jazz, rock and rap.

Burkina Faso also has a thriving film industry that receives considerable stimulation from the biennial Fespaco film festival (p57). Two Burkinabé filmmakers who have won prizes and developed international reputations are Idrissa Ouédraogo, who won the 1990 Grand Prix at Cannes for *Tilä*, and Gaston Kaboré, whose film *Buud Yam* was the 1997 winner of the Étalon d'Or.

Food & Drink

Burkinabé food is largely influenced by Senegalese and Ivoirian cuisines. Sauces, especially *arachide* (peanut) or *graine* (a hot sauce made with palm nuts), are the mainstay and are always served with a starch, usually rice (called *riz sauce* or *riz gras*) or the Burkinabé staple, *tô*, a millet- or sorghum-based *pâte* (a pounded, dough-like substance). The Ivoirian *attiéké* (grated cassava), *aloco* (plantain fried with chilli in palm oil) and *kedjenou* (simmered chicken or fish with vegetables) are also commonly found.

Grilled dishes of chicken, mutton, beef, guinea fowl, fish (especially Nile perch, known locally as *capitaine*) and agouti (a large rodent) also feature on the menu. In the Sahel, couscous is widely available.

Castel, Flag, Brakina, Beaufort and So.b.bra are popular and palatable brands of beer; more adventurous – and potent – is *dolo* (millet beer). Locally produced juices include *bissap* (hibiscus), *gingembre* (ginger), tamarind and mango; soft drinks are available everywhere, too.

Lafi is the most reliable brand of bottled water. Avoid the water sold in small plastic bags, since it's often tap water.

Environment

Landlocked Burkina Faso's terrain ranges from the harsh desert and semidesert of the north to the woodland and savannah of the green southwest. Around Banfora, rainfall is heavier and forests thrive alongside irrigated sugar-cane and rice fields; it's here that most of Burkina Faso's meagre 13% of arable land is found. The country's dominant feature, however, is the vast central laterite plateau of the Sahel, where hardy trees and bushes thrive.

Burkina's former name, Haute Volta (Upper Volta), referred to its three major rivers – the Black, White and Red Voltas, known today as the Mouhoun, Nakambé and Nazinon Rivers. All flow south into the world's second-largest artificial lake, Lake Volta, in Ghana.

SURVIVAL GUIDE

ℹ Directory A–Z

ACCOMMODATION
Ouagadougou, Bobo-Dioulasso and Banfora have a good range of accommodation, including charming B&Bs. In more remote areas, *campements* (basic mud huts with bucket showers and no electricity) are usually the only option but can be very atmospheric.

DANGERS & ANNOYANCES
Burkina Faso is one of the safest countries in West Africa. Crime isn't unknown, particularly around big markets and *gares routières* (transport stations), but it's usually confined to petty theft and pickpocketing. Wear a money belt and don't flash cash or valuables in public. Solo women might get some hassle, but a simple *bonne journée* ('have a good day') should suffice in warding off unwanted attention.

EMBASSIES & CONSULATES
The following embassies are based in Ouagadougou:
Canadian Embassy (☎ 25 31 18 94; www.canadainternational.gc.ca/burkinafaso; 316 Ave du Professeur Joseph Ki Zerbo; ⊗8.30am-noon Mon-Fri & 2-4pm Mon-Thu) Also offers diplomatic help to Australian citizens.
French Embassy (☎ 25 49 66 66; www.ambafrance-bf.org; Ave du Trésor; ⊗8-11.30am Mon, Wed & Thu)
German Embassy (☎ 25 30 67 31; www.ouagadougou.diplo.de; Rue Joseph Badoua; ⊗9-11am Mon-Fri)
Ghanaian Embassy (☎ 25 30 76 35; embagna@fasonet.bf; Ave d'Oubritenga; ⊗8am-2pm)
Ivoirian Embassy (☎ 25 31 82 28; cnr Ave Maurice Yameogo & Ave du Burkina Faso)
US Embassy (☎ 25 49 53 00; http://ouagadougou.usembassy.gov; Rue 15.873, Secteur 15, Ouagadougou; ⊗7.30am-5pm Mon-Thu, to 12.30pm Fri)

British citizens should contact the **British High Commission** (☎ 030-2213250; www.ukinghana.fco.gov.uk; Julius Nyerere Link, off Gamel Abdul Nasser Ave; ⊗9.30-11.30am Mon-Thu, 8.30-10.30am Fri) in Accra, Ghana.

EMERGENCY & IMPORTANT NUMBERS

Ambulance	☎112
Burkina Faso's country code	☎226
Fire	☎18
International access code	☎00
Police	☎17

GAY & LESBIAN TRAVELLERS
Homosexuality is not illegal in Burkina Faso, but any sexual behaviour that goes against 'good morals' is punishable by law. Local attitudes are highly conservative and utmost discretion is advisable. Public displays of affection between same-sex (and even opposite-sex) couples should be avoided. There are no openly gay or lesbian bars or clubs in Burkina.

INTERNET ACCESS
Wi-fi is available in most midrange and top-end hotels and restaurants in towns and cities. Internet cafes are plentiful there, too – the post office is usually a good bet – but nonexistent in more remote areas.

MONEY
ATMs There are numerous Visa ATMs in every city; the only bank to accept MasterCard is

ⓘ EATING PRICE RANGES

The following price ranges refer to the cost of a main dish.

$ less than CFA3000

$$ CFA3000–6000

$$$ more than CFA6000

Banque Atlantique (in Ouaga, Bobo and Banfora only).

Cash Burkina Faso uses the West African franc (CFA). The bank notes come in 500, 1000, 2000, 5000 and 10,000; coins are split into 1, 5, 10, 25, 50, 100, 200, 250 and 500 francs.

Changing money The best foreign currency to carry is euros, which are easily exchanged at any bank, hotel or bureau de change.

Credit cards Payments by credit card are rarely accepted and are subject to a 5% surcharge.

Tipping There are no strict rules about tipping in Burkina Faso. Tipping in a *maquis* (rustic restaurant), or if you've bargained a taxi fare, is not done. More upmarket restaurants are accustomed to receiving tips, though it remains very much at your discretion.

Exchange Rates

Australia	A$1	CFA452
Canada	C$1	CFA440
Europe	€1	CFA656
Japan	¥100	CFA538
NZ	NZ$1	CFA415
UK	UK£1	CFA774
US	US$1	CFA600

For current exchange rates, see www.xe.com.

OPENING HOURS

Banks Typically open 9am to 2pm, Monday to Friday.

Bars & clubs Normally open from late morning until the last customers leave (late); nightclubs generally open from 9pm into the wee hours.

Restaurants Lunch is served from 11.30am to 2.30pm, dinner 6.30pm to 10.30pm.

Shops & businesses Usually 8am to noon and 3pm to 6pm, Monday to Friday, as well as 9am to 1pm on Saturday.

POST

Sonapost is Burkina's national postal service. The main **post office** (Ave de la Liberte; ⊙7.30am–noon & 3.30-5pm Mon-Fri, 8am-noon Sat) branch in Ouagadougou is on Avenue de la Liberté.

PUBLIC HOLIDAYS

Burkina Faso also celebrates Islamic holidays, including **Eid al-Fitr** and **Eid al-Adha**, the dates of which change each year.

New Year's Day 1 January

Revolution Day 3 January

Women's Day 8 March

Easter Monday March/April

Labour Day 1 May

Ascension Day 40 days after Easter

National Day 5 August

Assumption 15 August

All Saints' Day 1 November

Republic Day 11 December

Christmas Day 25 December

TELEPHONE

➡ Landline phone numbers here start with 2, while mobile numbers begin with 7.

➡ Telephone cards for international calls are expensive; using a VoIP service (such as Skype) is a better bet.

TOURIST INFORMATION

Couleurs d'Afrique (p62) In the Ouagadougou neighbourhood of Gounghin.

L'Agence Tourisme (p62) In Hôtel les Palmiers, Ouagadougou.

ⓘ Getting There & Away

AIR

Tiny **Aéroport International de Ouagadougou** (p62) is Burkina's main gateway.

The main international carriers are **Air France** (www.airfrance.com) and **Royal Air Maroc** (www.royalairmaroc.com), which offer direct flights to France and Morocco and connecting flights to the rest of the world.

Air Burkina (www.air-burkina.com), the national carrier, flies to Paris (France) as well as regional destinations including Accra (Ghana), Abidjan (Côte d'Ivoire), Bamako (Mali), Cotonou (Benin), Dakar (Senegal) and Lomé (Togo).

LAND
Benin

TSR (p65) has a twice-weekly bus service from Ouagadougou to Cotonou (CFA21,000, 24 hours), while TCV has a weekly departure (on Sunday).

The alternative is to take a bus to Fada N'Gourma (CFA4500, five hours), where taxis-brousses and minibuses wait for customers – sometimes all day, as transport to the border (CFA4000) is scarce and fills up slowly.

Côte d'Ivoire

Sitarail (☑25 31 07 39) passenger-train services between Burkina Faso and Côte d'Ivoire

DESTINATION	FARE (CFA)	DURATION (HR)	FREQUENCY	COMPANY	DEPARTS
Abidjan (Côte d'Ivoire)	27,000	36	daily	TCV, Rakieta	Ouagadougou
Bamako (Mali)	17,000	17	daily	TCV	Bobo
Bouaké (Côte d'Ivoire)	17,000	20	daily	TCV, Rakieta	Bobo
Cotonou (Benin)	21,000	24	twice weekly	TCV, TSR	Ouagadougou
Kumasi (Ghana)	10,000	11	daily	TCV	Ouagadougou
Lagos (Nigeria)	38,000	36	weekly	TCV	Ouagadougou
Lomé (Togo)	18,000	24	twice weekly	TCV, TSR	Ouagadougou
Niamey (Niger)	11,000	8-10	daily	TCV	Ouagadougou

(three weekly) have resumed, but it's a long, tiring journey to Abidjan (at least 36 hours, possibly more). Get an update while in Bobo before setting off.

TCV has a daily bus service to Bouaké from Bobo-Dioulasso (CFA17,000, 20 hours) and Abidjan (CFA27,000, 36 hours). You can also take one of Rakieta's two daily buses from Banfora (CFA900, one hour) to Niangoloko, from where onward transport may be possible.

Ghana

TCV has a daily service from Ouagadougou to Kumasi (CFA10,000, 11 hours).

The other frequently used border crossing is at Hamale (Ghana), near Ouessa in the southwest of Burkina Faso. Coming from Ghana, you may have to stay at Hamale's cheap hotel and catch a bus to Bobo-Dioulasso the next morning. From Bobo-Dioulasso, Rakieta has two buses per day (at 8am and 2.30pm) to Hamale (CFA4500) that pass through Banfora en route.

Mali

Almost every bus company in Bobo-Dioulasso offers a daily service to Bamako (CFA17,000, 17 hours).

Niger

TCV operates a daily bus service between Ouagadougou and Niamey, via Fada N'Gourma (CFA11,000, eight to 10 hours).

Togo

TSR has twice-weekly bus services from Ouagadougou to Lomé (CFA18,000, 24 hours), while TCV has weekly departures.

❶ Getting Around

AIR

Air Burkina (www.air-burkina.com) has two flights per week between Ouagadougou and Bobo-Dioulasso (CFA55,000).

BUS

Buses are the most reliable and comfortable way to get around the country. They almost always operate with guaranteed seating and fixed departure times; arrive early or book the day before to ensure you have a seat on your preferred service.

TCV (p62) and **Rakieta** (p62) buses are better maintained and more reliable than those of other companies; they also have air-con.

TAXIS-BROUSSES

Taxis-brousses (bush taxis) are generally beaten-up old vehicles that cover routes to outlying communities that large buses don't serve. Most leave from the *gares routières* (bus stations); morning is the best time to find them. There are more-or-less fixed prices, starting from CFA1000, that local people share. You can bargain if you're hiring one alone.

CAR & MOTORCYCLE

Travel agencies in Ouagadougou can organise 4WD rental (with a driver) for about CFA60,000 per day.

In rural areas, mopeds are ideal on unsealed roads and readily available for CFA5000 per day (not including fuel).

TRAIN

There are **Sitarail** (p72) trains between Ouaga and Bobo, but they can take up to 10 hours and are highly unreliable.

Cabo Verde

📞 238 / POP 553,000

Best Places to Eat

➡ Casa Cafe Mindelo (p83)
➡ Maracujá (p77)
➡ Caleta (p86)
➡ Fado Crioula (p95)
➡ Pipi's (p90)

Best Places to Sleep

➡ Aldeia Manga (p87)
➡ Jardim do Vinho (p76)
➡ Kira's (p81)
➡ Migrante Guesthouse (p95)

Why Go?

Jutting up from the Atlantic, some 500km west of Senegal, this stunning island chain has a captivating blend of mountains, beaches and peaceful seaside villages. On Santo Antão, craggy peaks hide piercing green valleys of flowers and sugar cane, ideal for epic hikes. São Vicente is home to the cultural capital of the islands, Mindelo, which throbs with bars and music clubs. On Sal and Maio, undulating windswept dunes merge with indigo-blue seas on unspoilt beaches of powdery white sand. Meanwhile, far-flung Fogo and Brava in the southwest offer their own enchantments, from surreal volcanic landscapes, to sparkling bays framed by towering peaks. Throw in the constant beat of music that Cabo Verde is famed for and the renowned *morabeza* (Creole for hospitality) of its people and you'll see why many have come – and never left.

When to Go
Santiago

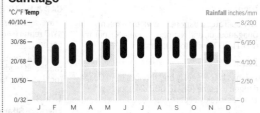

Aug–Oct So-called rainy season; very hot, and weeks can go by without a downpour.

Dec–Apr Best time for surfing. Whale watching February to May.

Jun–Oct Turtle-watching season.

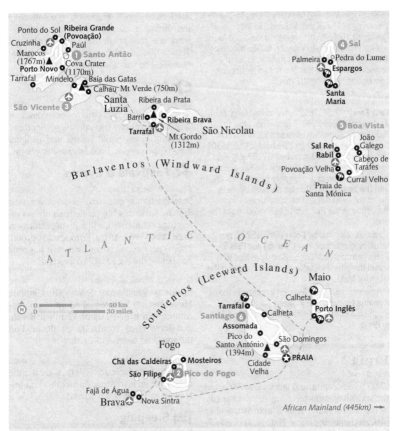

Cabo Verde Highlights

1 Santo Antão (p85)
Hiking the misty pine-clad ridges, the sheer canyons and the verdant valleys of Cabo Verde's most spectacular island.

2 Pico do Fogo (p90)
Admiring the views from the summit of the country's only active volcano, a stunning, cinder-clad, 2829m-high peak.

3 São Vicente (p80)
Following the melodic sounds of *morna* and *coladeira* to festive, open-air spots scattered around this music-loving seaside town.

4 Sal (p91) Riding the giant waves off lovely white-sand beaches in one of the finest destinations in the archipelago for windsurfing.

5 Boa Vista (p94)
Relaxing on the beach and feasting on delicious seafood at this wondrously laid-back island.

6 Santiago (p75)
Exploring the colonial ruins of the picturesque Cidade Velha followed by seaside drinks and dancing in nearby Praia.

SANTIAGO

POP 266,000

Santiago, the largest island of the archipelago and the first to be settled, has a little bit of all the other islands. It has the sandy beaches, the desert plains, the verdant valleys and the mountainous interior as well as the cap-

ital, Praia. All this makes it a worthy stop on your Cabo Verdean rambles.

ℹ Getting There & Away

AIR

Praia's airport is, together with Sal's, the main air hub for the islands. **TACV** (Rua Serpa Pinto;

⊙ 8am-5pm Mon-Fri) has daily flights to Boa Vista, Fogo (São Filipe), Sal and São Vicente (Mindelo), three flights weekly to Maio and four weekly (via Sal or São Vicente) to São Nicolau. **TAP** (☑ 2615826; www.flytap.com; Praia International Airport) has one to two flights daily connecting Lisbon with Praia.

BOAT

Fast Ferry (☑ 2617552; www.cvfastferry.com; Av Andrade Corvo 35; ⊙ 8am-6pm Mon-Fri, 8.30am-12.30pm Sat) departs Praia several times per week for Fogo (3½ hours, CVE3350) and on to Brava (40 minutes, CVE3750). Fast Ferry also goes to São Vicente via São Nicolau, but these run irregularly (only twice a month), and the boats can often be delayed by many hours (or even days). Purchase tickets from the office in the Platô (city centre) or from the port.

Ferries operated by **Polar** (☑ 2615223; polarp@cvtelecom.cv; Rua Candido dos Reis 6A, Praia; return CVE3800; ⊙ 8am-2pm Mon-Fri) travel three times weekly between Praia and the island of Maio.

A general source of ferry information is the **Agencia Nacional de Viagens** (☑ 2603100; Rua Serpa Pinto 58; ⊙ 8am-3.30pm Mon-Fri) in Praia.

Praia

POP 134,000

Cabo Verde's capital and largest city, Praia, has the sprawling suburbs of any developing city. In the centre, standing on a large fortress-like plateau (hence the name Platô) and overlooking the ocean, is an attractive old quarter with enough to keep you occupied for a day.

⊙ Sights

During your ambles around the multihued streets of the old Platô quarter, be sure to spend some time ferreting around the small food market (⊙ 8am-5pm).

Farol Dona Maria Pia   LIGHTHOUSE

(Rua do Mar; lighthouse CVE100, grounds free; ⊙ 9am-7pm Mon-Sat) Built in 1881 and named after a Portuguese queen, this wind-battered lighthouse provides a scenic vantage point for views across the coastline.

Sala-Museu Amilcar Cabral   MUSEUM

(Rua Dr Julio Abreu; ⊙ 9am-noon & 3-6pm) FREE This small museum and foundation is dedicated to preserving the memory of freedom fighter Amilcar Cabral (1924–73). Photographs and other memorabilia shed light on one of West Africa's great visionaries. An

intellectual, poet, engineer, revolutionary and diplomat, Cabral helped lead an independence movement for Cabo Verde and Guinea-Bissau, ultimately sacrificing his own life – he was assassinated in 1973.

☞ Tours

CaboNed   HIKING

(☑ 9210488; www.caboned.com; excursions from CVE3200) Great day-trip options on Santiago, including hikes, photo safaris and explorations of the interior. Book by email or phone.

✵ Festivals & Events

Atlantic Music Expo   MUSIC

(www.atlanticmusicexpo.com; ⊙ Apr) Over four days in April, this big music bash always offers a good time, with a line-up of performers from Cabo Verde, Africa, Europe and beyond. There's also a good street market. It happens just before the big Kriol Jazz Festival.

Gamboa Music Festival   MUSIC

(www.festivalgamboa.com; ⊙ May) The Gamboa Music Festival features a line-up of up-and-coming bands and DJs on Gamboa Beach, and draws huge crowds. It's usually held on the weekend nearest to 19 May.

Kriol Jazz Festival   MUSIC

(www.krioljazzfestival.com; ⊙ Apr) A great time to be in town is in April, during this jazz festival spread over two weekends.

🛏 Sleeping

Residencial Sol Atlántico   GUESTHOUSE $

(☑ 2612872; Praça Alexandre Albuquérque 13; s/d CVE3220/4440, without bathroom CVE2520/3740; ❄) This long-standing *residencial* (guesthouse) has 15 old-fashioned rooms with starched white sheets, blue furniture and TVs. Rooms fronting the square catch the wi-fi signal. Look for the unmarked entrance between a bank and an optician. Head in and up the stairs.

★ Jardim do Vinho   B&B $$

(☑ 2624760; www.ojardimdovinho.com; Rua Carlos Veiga 17, Achada de Santo António; s/d CVE4300/5600, without bathroom CVE3200/4500; ⊙ closed Sep; 🛜) This French-run guesthouse offers a warm welcome in a converted home in a peaceful corner of Achada de Santo António. The five rooms are pleasantly set with hardwood floors, sizeable windows and colourful textiles or artwork on the walls. The small leafy courtyard is a fine spot for an evening drink. Great local tips for exploring the island.

Praia Confort
HOTEL $$

(🖉 2600200; praiaconfort@gmail.com; Av Amilcar Cabral 11; s/d CVE4830/6000; ❄ 🛜) In a great location overlooking Platô's main plaza, this comfy guesthouse has attractively furnished rooms with a modern aesthetic. Several rooms have balconies with fine views over the city.

Hotel Santa Maria
HOTEL $$

(🖉 2614337; www.facebook.com/hotelsantamariacaboverde; Av 5 de Julho; s/d from CVE4500/6300; ❄ 🛜) The position of this friendly hotel, right in the heart of all the action in the Platô, is tops. The rooms are clean and well-equipped. The brightest overlook the front street; those in the back are quieter, but a little dark. You can also arrange tours around the island.

Hotel Oásis Atlântico Praiamar
HOTEL $$$

(🖉 2608440; www.oasisatlantico.com; Prainha; r from CVE14,000; 🅿 ❄ @ 🛜 ≋) On a breezy bluff pointing out to sea is this glossy Praia address. Though similar to business-class hotels around the world, the spacious rooms are comfortable with a touch of class. Some come with garden views; others overlook the ocean.

🍴 Eating

Mirage
CAFE $

(Av Jorge Barbosa, Quebra-Canela; mains around CVE500; ⊙ 9.30am-1.30am; 🛜) For dining and drinking with a view, Mirage serves up pizzas, sandwiches, salads and cocktails from the open-air terrace at Praia Shopping.

Pão Quente de Cabo Verde
BAKERY, CAFE $

(Av Andrade Corvo; mains CVE150-400; ⊙ 6.30am-9.30pm) Famed for its pastries, the ever-popular Pão Quente also serves up hot sandwiches, pastas, salads, savoury tarts, omelettes and other light fare. The coffee is best avoided.

★ Maracujá
FUSION $$

(🖉 9138854; Rua 19 de Maio, Chã d'Areia; mains CVE550-950; ⊙ 10am-11pm Tue-Sun) Inés, who spent 40 years in France, brings a touch of Europe to her cooking in this cheery cafe across the road from Gamboa beach. Market-fresh ingredients play a starring role in zesty salads, grilled octopus, seafood spaghetti, and crepes with seasonal vegetables. Great daily lunch specials (around CVE450).

Churrasqueira Dragoeiro
BARBECUE $$

(🖉 2624767; Rua da UCCLA; mains CVE600-1200; ⊙ noon-5pm & 6.30pm-1am) Follow the scent of fresh barbecue and the wafts of smoke pluming overhead at this famous, open-sided grill-house in Achada de Santo António. It's a very casual spot that draws a mix of locals and tourists, who chatter away over drinks and sizzling plates of char-grilled chicken, tuna or pork skewers.

Sofia Café
CAFE $$

(Praça 11 Maio 31; tapas CVE600-1000; ⊙ 7am-11pm; 🛜) This pleasant cafe-restaurant in Platô has outdoor tables on the square and a good selection of small sharing plates, including marinated octopus, grilled shrimp and yucca with steak. There's free wi-fi, decent drink options and heartier lunch specials that change daily (CVE900).

🍷 Drinking & Nightlife

Freedom
BAR

(🖉 2614454; Praia de Gamboa, Chã d'Areia; ⊙ 11am-2am Tue-Sun) Overlooking scruffy Gamboa beach, this buzzing eating and drinking spot draws a festive crowd, particularly on Thursday through Saturday nights when there's live music (from 9pm or 10pm). The outdoor tables on the deck are a fine spot for a sundowner. Good menu too (mains CVE400 to CVE900), with seafood, grilled meats, vegetarian spaghetti and lots of snacks.

Kebra Cabana
BAR

(Quebra-Canela beach; ⊙ 10am-2am) Cool beach bar with a hipster crowd, loungey tunes, live music on Friday nights and good food to boot – crepes, sandwiches, burgers and grilled seafood (mains CVE400 to 1100).

★ Entertainment

Quintal da Música
LIVE MUSIC

(🖉 2611679; www.facebook.com/quintaldamusica; Av Amilcar Cabral; ⊙ 8am-midnight Mon-Sat) For the best local music, head to this Platô restaurant, which showcases live acts every night except Sunday. Traditional sounds abound, from *morna* and *coladeira* to *batuko* and *funaná*. Reserve ahead.

ℹ Information

INTERNET ACCESS

Internet cafes are scarce, but the two main squares in the Platô (Praça Alexandre Albuquérque and Praça 11 Maio) have free wi-fi.

MONEY

There are ATMs throughout the city, especially around Praça Alexandre Albuquérque.

Praia

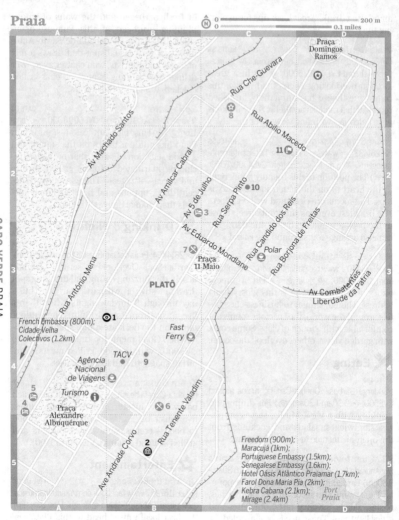

N 0 ——————————— 200 m
0 ——————————— 0.1 miles

Praça Domingos Ramos

Rua Che-Guevara

Rua Abílio Macedo

Av Machado Santos

Av Amílcar Cabral

Av 5 de Julho

Rua Serpa Pinto

Rua Candido dos Reis

Rua Polar

Rua Borjona de Freitas

Av Eduardo Mondlane

Praça 11 Maio

PLATÔ

Av Combatentes Liberdade da Pátria

Rua António Mena

French Embassy (800m);
Cidade Velha;
Colectivos (1.2km)

Fast Ferry

TACV

Agência Nacional de Viágens

Turismo

Praça Alexandre Albuquérque

Rua Tenente Valadim

Ave Andrade Corvo

Freedom (900m);
Maracujá (1km);
Portuguese Embassy (1.5km);
Senegalese Embassy (1.6km);
Hotel Oásis Atlântico Praiamar (1.7km);
Farol Dona Maria Pia (2km);
Kebra Cabana (2.1km);
Mirage (2.4km)

Port Praia

POST

The main post office is three blocks east of the main square, Praça Alexandre Albuquerque.

TOURIST INFORMATION

Turismo (Praça Alexandre Albuquerque; ⊙9am-6pm Mon-Fri, to 1pm Sat) This tourist information kiosk is on the northeast corner of the Praça Alexandre Albuquerque in the Platô, but it was none too helpful when we passed through.

TRAVEL AGENCIES

Girassol Tours (☎2614178; www.girassol.cv; Rua Serpo Pinto 46; ⊙8am-6pm Mon-Fri, to noon Sat) Travel agency that sells plane tickets, offers tours of Santiago and car rental.

❶ Getting There & Around

A taxi from the airport to Platô (5km) costs around CVE1000. There's no regular bus service.

Small Transcor buses connect Platô with all sections of the city; short journeys cost from CVE50. Destinations are marked on the windshields.

Cream-coloured taxis are plentiful, inexpensive and easy to spot – you can go from Platô to Achada de Santo António, for example, for about CVE200. Note that fares go up after 8pm. You

Praia

can rent a taxi for the day for an island tour for around CVE9000.

It is best to move around Praia by taxi at night, no matter what the distance, as crime has been on the rise, especially in Achada de Santo António.

Cidade Velha

Dramatically situated on the sea, 15km from Praia, Cidade Velha (literally 'Old City') gained Unesco World Heritage status less than a decade ago as the first European settlement in the tropics. Founded in 1462 as Ribeira Grande, the city became wealthy as a station for the transatlantic slave trade. Raids by pirates – including a particularly destructive visit from Sir Francis Drake in 1585 – eventually forced the Portuguese to move shop to Praia.

Remains from its heyday include the ruins of the **cathedral**, constructed in 1693, and the *pelourinho* (pillory) on the town square where enslaved captives were chained up and displayed. Most impressive is the town's position between the sea and the mouth of a canyon that, thanks to irrigation, remains green even in the driest months.

⊙ Sights

São Francisco
Monastery & Church   MONASTERY, CHURCH
Complete with Gothic portals and walls covered in *azulejo* tiles, this once imposing monastery is worth a look, and is reached

along a marked trail that leads up from the lush valley. The church is often locked, though you can peer through metal grates for a look inside.

Fortaleza Real de São Filipe   FORTRESS
(CVE500; ⊙8am-6pm) For sweeping views, take the curving trail up to this dramatic cliff-side fort built in 1593. A 15-minute film in English and Portuguese gives an overview of the history of the fort and Cidade Velha.

🍴 Sleeping & Eating

Kama Ku Kafé   GUESTHOUSE $
(📞9151674; fernando@caboverdesantiago.net; Estrada de acesso a Cidade Velha; s/d from CVE3300/4600; ⚹🛜) A very welcoming family-run spot in the Cidade Velha, this place has clean, bright, but simply furnished rooms, the best of which have sea views. It also offers excursions around the island. It's on the main road just before the centre, less than a 10-minute walk from the *pelourinho*.

Restaurante Pelourinho   SEAFOOD $$
(mains CVE800-1400; ⊙9am-9pm) Serves some of the best grilled seafood in town, with tables set on an open-sided thatched roof terrace overlooking the crashing waves. The dish of the day is a bargain (CVE400).

ℹ Information

For area info, visit the **turismo** (⊙9am-3pm) near the centre of town, just past the *pelourinho*, and near the waterfront.

ℹ Getting There & Away

Cidade Velha Colectivos in Praia leave from opposite a Shell station and near the Terra Branca Market, north of Achada Santo António and return regularly until 7pm (CVE80 to CVE100, 30 minutes). Taxis charge about CVE4000 for a return trip, including up to four hours to visit the sights.

Rui Vaz
POP 1100
This mountain village is home to a great inn and restaurant, and is a good base for hikes into the surrounding mountains. The drive from the nearby town of São Domingos is spectacular, along a curvy country road up into the mountains, with a stellar panorama at the top.

The hilltop **Quinta da Montanha** (📞2685002; quintamontanha@cvtelecom.cv; s/d

CVE4830/6000; ☎) has pleasant if a little chintzy rooms, most with terraces and gorgeous views of the surrounding mountains. The restaurant itself is worth a drive, for delicious food prepared with local ingredients, including veggies from the garden. On weekends it's a buffet (CVE1700); otherwise mains are around CVE900.

Alugueres (share taxis) go to Rui Vaz (CVE200) from Sucupira Market in Praia regularly, and return through late afternoon. It's possible to hire a taxi to drive you for CVE2000.

Tarrafal

POP 7400

With a small but fine white-sand beach and cooling breezes, Tarrafal is a favourite getaway from Praia, some 70km to the southeast. The town itself has a pleasant, hibiscus-lined main square. The beach is short but lovely and the surrounding area offers plenty of attractions. For water sports, including boat and snorkel rental, head to Pizzeria Alto Mira. Word of warning: the walk to the lighthouse is popular (takes about two hours), but it's best to go with a trustworthy local guide, as muggings have been reported.

Tarrafal Residence (☑ 2662060; tarrafal residence@gmail.com; Ribeira do Coquiero; s CVE4000-4300, d CVE5500-6000; ❊☎) is a great spot with 10 contemporary and colourful rooms, all equipped with fridges and TVs, and many showcasing ocean views. Some rooms have balconies.

Tarrafal Tourist Information (☉ 8am-6pm Mon-Sat) offers excellent info on outdoor activities, lodging and nearby attractions from a kiosk on the main square in Tarrafal.

Minibuses from Praia (CVE500, two hours) depart from Sucupira Market; service is most frequent early in the morning, from about 6.30am. From Tarrafal, minibuses leave from the western end of the central park, till about 6pm.

SÃO VICENTE

POP 79,400

Small, stark and undulating, the island of São Vicente would be fairly forgettable were it not for the beautiful Mediterranean town of Mindelo, Cabo Verde's prettiest city and home to one of Africa's most raucous festivals.

For a break from the city, Mt Verde (750m), the island's highest peak and only touch of green, is an easy day's hike and offers panoramic views.

There are also windy but fine beaches at Baía das Gatas, Calhau and Salamansa. The lovely bay off the latter offers windsurfing and kitesurfing classes – look for the Kitesurf Cabo Verde (☑ 9871954; ola@kitesurfcaboverde.com; ☉ 10am-6pm) beach shack (two-hour windsurfing and kitesurfing classes €60 to €80).

Another popular weekend escape is Baía das Gatas, 12km from Mindelo, where you can swim in natural pools and dine in beachfront restaurants. Near the airport is the quaint fishing village of São Pedro, with a pretty beach and harbour.

❶ Getting There & Around

TACV (☑ 2608260; www.flytacv.com) has one to two flights daily to and from Praia, one daily to Sal, two weekly to São Nicolau (and four weekly via Sal), and one weekly to Lisbon (plus four weekly via Praia). **TAP** (www.flytap.com) has four weekly flights to/from Lisbon. Taxis to and from the **Cesária Évora Airport** (www.asa.cv) cost CVE1000.

Daily ferries connect Mindelo to neighbouring Santo Antão. For service to other islands, including Praia, Sal and São Nicolau, check at the ferry port, a short walk from Mindelo downtown; note that departures are sporadic (roughly once every two weeks) and crossings long.

The most convenient way around the island is by taxi or *aluguer* from Mindelo. Note that *aluguer* services are irregular on weekdays and can involve long waits.

Mindelo

POP 72,000

Set around a moon-shaped port and ringed by barren mountains, Mindelo is Cabo Verde's answer to the Riviera, complete with cobblestone streets, candy-coloured colonial buildings and yachts bobbing in a peaceful harbour. Around a bend is the country's deepest industrial port, which in the late 19th century was a key coaling station for British ships and remains the source of the city's relative prosperity.

Mindelo has long been the country's cultural centre, producing more than its share of poets and musicians, including the late Cesária Évora, and it's still a fine place to hear *morna* while downing some *grogue* (a rum-like drink). Savvy locals, plus a steady flow of travellers, support a number of cool bistros and bars.

⊙ Sights

Mindelo is a city to savour, taste and experience. Its colonial heart is centred on Rua da Libertad d'Africa, also known as Rua de Lisboa, which runs from the oceanfront to **Palácio do Povo** (Av Baltazar Lopes da Silva; CVE200; ⊙9am-1pm & 3-6pm Tue-Sat) and its semi-permanent exhibition dedicated to Cesária Évora.

Heading about 1km north via the coastal road, Avenida Marginal, you'll reach **Prainha Laginha**, the pleasant town beach. It may be ringed by industrial-looking silos, but its waters are clean and crystal clear.

Museu do Mar   MUSEUM
(Av Marginal; CVE100; ⊙9am-6pm Mon-Fri, 9.30am-12.30pm Sat) Inside the Torre de Belém, Mindelo's most intriguing museum gives an overview of São Vicente's history, from the island's role in the triangular trade to whaling in the late 19th century. Displays from shipwrecks reveal intriguing finds like 200-year-old bottles of port wine (still sealed) and massive elephant tusks (a jaw-dropping 820 tusks were logged on the 1743 wreck of the *Princess Louisa*).

Fish Market   MARKET
(Av Marginal; ⊙7am-3pm) The city's photogenic fish market lies just beyond Torre de Belém, with a jetty right behind it where fishermen unload their daily catch.

Mercado Municipal   MARKET
(Rua da Libertad d'Africa; ⊙8am-6pm Mon-Sat) The restored two-storey food market from 1784 is a great place to see sweet-talking vendors hawking local produce and medicinal herbs.

🏃 Activities

Dive Tribe   DIVING
(☑9829498; www.dive-tribe.com; Av Marginal; 1 dive with equipment €55, open-water course €420) This professionally run outfit offers a wide range of diving packages around São Vicente. There are over 50 dive sites in the area, including wreck-diving opportunities. It offers instruction for beginners as well. It's located below Dokas restaurant just south of the port.

Sabura Adventures   ADVENTURE SPORTS
(☑9775681; www.sabura-adventures.com; Av Marginal) Based out of the restaurant Nautilus, this outfit offers surf lessons (two hours €48)

and gear hire (body boards, surf boards, stand-up paddleboards). It also offers horse riding (per hour €35) and snorkelling trips (per person €30).

🎊 Festivals & Events

Baía das Gatas Festival   MUSIC
(⊙Aug) The Baía das Gatas Festival attracts musicians of all styles from around the islands and beyond. Held at the Baía das Gatas over the August full moon, it's a three-day extravaganza of singing, dancing and partying.

Creole Carnival   CARNIVAL
(⊙Feb or Mar) Mindelo puts on the sexiest Mardi Gras this side of Río: Creole Carnival, with its colourful street parades. It happens in the build-up to Ash Wednesday – usually February (early March in 2018).

Mindelact Festival   THEATRE
(www.mindelact.org; ⊙Sep) A festival that brings theatre to the streets, squares and cultural centres of Mindelo.

🛏 Sleeping

Simabo   HOSTEL **$**
(☑2312465; www.simabo.org; Av Rendall Leite 13; r per person CVE1500) 🐾 A top choice for animal lovers, Italian-run Simabo is a budget-friendly guesthouse and rescue shelter for abandoned dogs and cats. Lodging is clean but simple, with shared (cold-water) facilities for its four rooms. There's ample opportunity to interact with the four-legged residents. Opportunities for volunteers too.

★Kira's   BOUTIQUE HOTEL **$$**
(☑2300274; www.kirashotel.com; Rua de Argélia 24; s CVE7400-9600, d CVE9100-11,300; ❄) In a pretty yellow building near Praça Amilcar Cabral, Kira's earns rave reviews for its well-equipped, handsomely furnished rooms and kind-hearted multilingual staff. Each of the cheerfully painted guestrooms is named after an island – forest-green Santo Antão evokes its lush peaks, while powder-blue Maio calls to mind its gently lapping seas.

★Casa Colonial   GUESTHOUSE **$$**
(☑9995350; www.casacolonial.info; Rua 24 de Setembro; s/d CVE7200/8300; ☎❄) A boutique British-owned guesthouse on a quiet street, Casa Colonial sits inside a beautifully restored colonial building with a fresh green coat of paint and white wooden shutters. Rooms are spacious with tall ceilings, dark

Mindelo

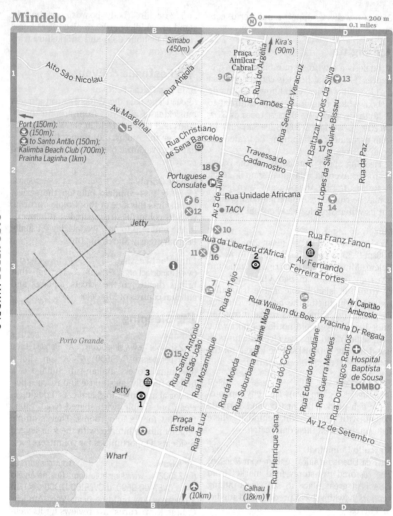

wood floors and period details. Perks include a small patio with a plunge pool where breakfast is served, and free wi-fi.

Casa Café Mindelo
GUESTHOUSE $$

(☑ 2313735; www.casacafemindelo.com; Rua Governador Calheiros 6; s/d from CVE4500/6600; 🛜) Above the restaurant of the same name, you'll find charming, simply furnished rooms, the best of which have sparkling views over the bay. It's set in a 19th-century building in a great central location. Breakfast, served in the restaurant, is a highlight.

Prassa
BOUTIQUE HOTEL $$$

(☑ 2300809; www.prassa3hotel.com; Praça Amilcar Cabral 3; s/d from CVE8700/9900; ✳🛜) This boutique hotel has bright, attractively set rooms with eye-catching wallpaper, suede furniture, shag carpets and a chic, ultra-modern vibe. It has a good restaurant and tapas bar on the ground floor.

🍴 Eating

La Pergola
CAFETERIA $$

(Rua Santo António, Alliance Française; mains CVE550-700; ⊙ 8am-7pm Mon-Fri, 8am-2pm Sat; 🛜🍴) This cosy cafe, under a straw roof in-

Mindelo

⊙ Sights
1 Fish Market B4
2 Mercado Municipal C3
3 Museu do Mar...B4
4 Palácio do Povo D3

⊙ Activities, Courses & Tours
5 Dive Tribe...B2
6 Sabura Adventures...............................B2

⊙ Sleeping
7 Casa Café Mindelo C3
8 Casa Colonial...D3
9 Prassa C1

⊙ Eating
Casa Cafe Mindelo ....(see 7)
10 Chave d'Ouro..C3
11 La Pergola C3
12 Nautilus B2

⊙ Drinking & Nightlife
13 Jazzy Bird D1
14 ZeroPointArt...D2

⊙ Entertainment
15 Casa da Morna B4

⊙ Information
16 Banco Comercial do Atlântico C3
17 Barracuda Tours D2
18 Caixa Económica C2

side the courtyard of the Alliance Française, has delicious salads, pastas and mixed seafood plates, plus tempting cakes and pastries. It's also a fine anytime spot for coffee or a glass of Fogo wine.

Chave d'Ouro SEAFOOD $$
(☑2327050; Av 5 de Julho; mains CVE450-900; ⊙noon-3pm & 7-11pm) This old-fashioned 2nd-floor restaurant hasn't changed in decades. The menu has good-value classics *such as cachupa* (beans and corn mixed with fish or meat) and *feijoada* (bean stew with pork or seafood; both CVE450), and there's live music at Sunday dinners in summer.

Nautilus INTERNATIONAL $$
(Av Marginal; mains CVE650-1650; ⊙9am-2am; ☎) Near the waterfront, Nautilus has an open-air courtyard with a sizzling grill where you can get tasty plates of char-grilled tuna, grouper, octopus, chicken and filet mignon, along with *cachupa, arroz de marisco* (seafood rice) and other hits. The daily lunch special is a deal at CVE490. There's live music Friday through Sunday nights.

Kalimba Beach Club INTERNATIONAL $$
(Av Marginal; mains CVE350-1000; ⊙10am-1am) Out on Prainha Laginha, a 15-minute walk from the centre, Kalimba is a great spot for a sundowner. The open-sided deck perched over the sand offers fine views of the turquoise waters and Mt Cara beyond. Aside from drinks, the mostly foreign crowd stops in for sandwiches, burgers, lasagne, and plates of calamari and other seafood.

★**Casa Cafe Mindelo** BISTRO $$$
(☑2313735; www.casacafemindelo.com; Rua Governador Calheiros 6; mains CVE1300-2500, lunch specials CVE400-500; ⊙7am-11pm) Near the waterfront, this buzzing place serves up some of the best cooking in town amid chunky wooden tables and industrial light fixtures, with traditional artwork adorning the walls. The chalkboard menu lists changing specials like pasta with lobster, mussels in white wine, and Portuguese-style seafood stew, and there's live music nightly (from 8pm).

🍷 Drinking & Nightlife

ZeroPointArt WINE BAR
(☑2312525; www.zeropointart.org; Rua Unidade Africana 62; ⊙10am-12.30pm & 6pm-midnight Mon, Wed & Thu, 8pm-2am Fri & Sat, 8pm-midnight Sun) Gallery space downstairs and a chilled wine bar upstairs, with lots of contemporary artwork, dark ambient lighting and cool music. A good place for a low-key night out, over wine and tapas-style snacks. It has live music and other events (like film screenings) from time to time. Stop in to see what's on.

Jazzy Bird BAR
(Av Baltazar Lopes da Silva; ⊙6pm-1am Mon-Sat) Known to locals as Vou, after the friendly owner, this cool little basement bar plastered with old jazz posters attracts an older crowd. Big-name local musicians play jazz late on Friday nights.

☆ Entertainment

Casa da Morna LIVE MUSIC
(Av Marginal; ⊙8.30-11pm Fri & Sat) On the waterfront, this breezy top-floor restaurant draws a good mix of talent to its live concerts on Friday and Saturday nights. It has a tropical vibe and the usual array of seafood dishes (mains CVE850 to CVE1100).

ⓘ Information

There's free wi-fi on Praça Amilcar Cabral, although the signal is finicky.

CABO VERDE MINDELO

MINDELO'S MARDI GRAS

There's nothing like Mindelo's Mardi Gras (usually in February) anywhere else in Africa. Taking the best African beats and mixing it up with a healthy dose of Latin style and Brazilian sex appeal, the result is a sultry, raunchy party you'll never forget. Preparations begin several months in advance, and on Sunday you can see the various groups practising for the procession. The saucy costumes, however, are worn only on Mardi Gras Tuesday. The weekend just prior to this sees a number of lesser processions and street parties, while on the Monday afternoon the whole city goes crazy as a huge street party takes place and people dress up in 'lesser costumes'. The Tuesday itself is a much more organised affair and after the procession has wound around the city a couple of times everyone seems to magically disappear.

If you want to be a part of it, plan accordingly, as all flights and accommodation are booked up way in advance. If you can't make it to Mindelo then head to São Nicolau (p98), which puts on a fabulous and utterly nontouristy affair around the same time. Fogo (p89) puts on a pretty good show as well.

MEDICAL SERVICES

Hospital Baptista de Sousa (☑ 2311879; Rua Domingos Ramos)

MONEY

The city centre has several banks with ATMs. There's also a handy ATM at the port.

Banco Comercial do Atlântico (Rua da Liberdad d'Africa)

Caixa Económica (Av 5 de Julho)

POLICE

Police Station (Av Marginal) Near the fish market.

POST

Post Office (Rua Cristiano Barcelos; ⊘ 9am-4pm Mon-Fri) Near the main plaza.

TOURIST INFORMATION

Tourist Info (☑ 9110016; www.cabocontact.com; ⊘ 8.30am-12.30pm & 2.30-6.30pm Mon-Fri, 9am-1pm Sat) This kiosk near the harbour offers info on attractions on São Vicente and beyond, and books a variety of activities, excursions and tours. São Vicente maps available for CVE220.

TRAVEL AGENCIES

Barracuda Tours (☑ 2325591; www.barracuda tours.com; Av Baltazar Lopes da Silva 54; ⊘ 8am-12.30pm & 2.30-6pm Mon-Fri, 9am-1pm Sat) A full-service travel agency that can book flights, car rentals, accommodation and tours.

❶ Getting There & Around

Mindelo has flight connections to the islands of Santiago and Sal, and a daily ferry to Santo Antão. **TACV** (www.flytacv.com; Av 5 de Julho) has an office in the town centre.

The most convenient way around the island is by taxi from Mindelo, including trips to Monte Verde (CVE1000), Calhau (CVE1200), Baía das Gatas (CVE1000) and Salamansa (CVE1000).

Official taxis are generally safe and easy to find in Mindelo. In the city centre, expect to pay CVE150 to CVE170 for a ride. After 8pm, the fare goes up to CVE200. *Alugueres* (minivans) to Baia das Gatas (CVE100), Salamansa (CVE100) and Calhau (CVE150) leave from Praça Estrela in the morning (around 10am) and afternoon (around 4pm) when full. Note that service is irregular on weekdays and can involve long waits.

Calhau

POP 1200

Some of the island's best beaches are at Calhau, 18km southeast of Mindelo. It's all but deserted during the week, but comes alive at the weekend. Calhau is also the best gateway for boat trips to the uninhabited island of Santa Luzia across the way, with its blissfully empty beaches.

In a blue-and-white building behind the beach, Hamburg (☑ 2329309; mains CVE600-1100; ⊘ 9am-10pm) serves up satisfying grilled seafood and changing daily specials such as *feijoada*, seafood rice and pork skewers. It has a pleasant front patio.

❶ Getting There & Away

A boat trip from Calhau to Santa Luzia with one of the local fishermen, which takes about 1½ hours each way, typically costs CVE15,000 round-trip (for up to four people). The man to look for among the fishermen is Alcides, who speaks a little English and can make arrangements.

Taxis and *alugueres* run between Mindelo and Calhau.

SANTO ANTÃO

POP 47,500

For many people the main reason for visiting Cabo Verde is the spectacular island of Santo Antão. This dizzyingly vertical isle, ruptured with canyons, gorges and valleys, offers some of the most amazing hiking in West Africa. The second-largest island in the archipelago, it is the only one that puts the verde in Cabo Verde. As you approach from São Vicente by ferry, you wouldn't guess how green it is, as the south side looks barren and harsh. But the northeast of the island, the most populated corner and the most popular with hikers, receives enough regular moisture for forests of pine trees to dominate the hilltops and tropical plants to flourish in the steamy valleys. See the northeast first, before heading for the untravelled western reaches of Santo Antão, with its mighty mountains and a nascent tourism industry.

❶ Getting There & Away

Currently, two ferry companies offer daily services between Mindelo and Porto Novo in Santo Antão. The *Mar d'Canal* leaves Mindelo at 8am, returning at 10am. It leaves Mindelo again at 3pm (except on Sunday, when there's only the morning departure), returning at 5pm. The *Inter-Ilhas* has a similar schedule, leaving an hour earlier (departing Mindelo at 7am and 2pm, returning at 9am and 4pm). The trip on either boat costs CVE800 and lasts just under one hour. Buy tickets 30 minutes before departure (or the day before) at the ferry-dock offices on both islands.

❶ Getting Around

If you want to see a lot of the island in a single day, your best bet is to hire your own *aluguer*, though expect to pay around CVE9000 for a full day around the east side of the island. Alternatively, you can join locals on an *aluguer* headed towards Ribeira Grande and Ponta do Sol (CVE500, 45 minutes). Note that *alugueres* use the new faster coastal road; if you want to travel along the scenic mountain road, be prepared to negotiate with the driver and dish out extra. If you want to explore the west of the island, you may want to overnight in Porto Novo to get an early start.

Porto Novo

POP 9400

Arriving by ferry, the grubby port town of Porto Novo will be your first impression of Santo Antão. Don't worry; things rapidly improve!

⬛ Sleeping

Residencial Antilhas   GUESTHOUSE $
(☑ 2221193; residencialantilhas@hotmail.com; d CVE2020-3220) A short stroll from the ferry terminal, Antilhas has a mix of decent rooms, all with private bathrooms. The best and priciest have balconies with views of the harbour.

Santantao Art Resort   RESORT $$
(☑ 2222675; www.santantaoresort.com; s/d from CVE6100/7800; ❄@🛜🏊) The upscale Santantao Art Resort to the south of town has balconied rooms, a range of facilities and a small tropical garden.

❶ Getting There & Away

After exiting the ferry terminal, colectivos (shared minivans) run to Ribeira Grande and Ponta do Sol (CVE500, one hour).

Ponta do Sol

POP 2200

Ponta do Sol feels like the end of the world, which in many ways it is: it sits where the road ends, literally. The sense of raw power here, with monstrous Atlantic waves and sheer cliffs reaching for the clouds leaves you feeling in awe of nature. It has a burgeoning guesthouse scene and a few decent eateries, and its pretty cobblestone centre makes a fine base for clifftop walks along the coast.

⬛ Sleeping

Casa D-Mar   GUESTHOUSE $
(☑ 2251390; casadmar.caboverde@gmail.com; Rua Maria Violante; s/d 3850/4950, without bathroom CVE2750/3630; 🛜) This delightful five-room guesthouse offers comfortably furnished rooms and a lovely terrace with sea views, not to mention a warm welcome provided by the young French–Cabo Verdean couple who run the place. Two rooms have private bathrooms and ocean views (one room also has a balcony).

Hotel Blue Bell   HOTEL $
(☑ 2251310; www.newbluebell.com; s/d from CVE3500/4800; ❄@🛜) The closest the town has to a real hotel, the Blue Bell is on the main square and has friendly service and sparsely furnished rooms with a splash of colour on one wall. The best rooms have small sea-facing balconies and catch cool breezes. Note that it often hosts tour groups.

Kasa Tambla B&B
GUESTHOUSE $$

(☑2251526; www.kasatambla.com; s/d/tr from CVE4400/4700/5400, ste from CVE5400; 🛜) One of the best lodging options in town, Kasa Tambla has handsomely appointed rooms, each with a bright colour scheme and high-quality fixtures. The best rooms open onto a shared balcony with views over the water. It's just up from the oceanfront, fronted by a tropical patio, which is a great afternoon or evening spot for relaxing over drinks.

✖️ Eating

★ Caleta
SEAFOOD $$

(☑2251561; mains CVE800-1300; ⏲11.30am-2.30pm & 6-10.30pm) A bistro-like restaurant with sidewalk tables on the waterfront, Caleta has a French owner who conjures up a mix of European and Cabo Verdean specialities using prime local products. Start with the fried-goat-cheese cakes or sweet-potato soup and move on to risotto with seafood, sautéed king prawns or grilled pork chops. Often has live music (from 8pm).

Cantinho do Gato Preto
INTERNATIONAL $$

(☑2251539; mains CVE800-1100; ⏲11am-2pm & 6.30-11pm) A popular spot along the main road leading to the oceanfront from the square, this eatery mixes international classics and some local faves. Its small patio hosts live music on Wednesday and Sunday evenings (from 6.30pm to 10.30pm).

ℹ️ Information

There's free (slow) wi-fi on the main square.

ℹ️ Getting There & Away

Colectivos meet the ferries at Porto Novo and provide shared transport to Ponta do Sol (CVE500, one hour). A taxi here from the dock is about CVE4000.

Ribeira Grande

The municipal region of Ribeira Grande occupies the island's northeastern section. Officially Ponta do Sol belongs to Ribeira Grande, although it's a world of its own. The region's urban centre is the unseemly town of Ribeira Grande, known by its old name of Povoação.

Beyond the town are gorgeous valleys and mountains, and a couple of adorable towns worth taking in. These include Chã da Igreja, a sweet little place surrounded by mountains and sugarcane plantations, and centred on a main plaza with a church.

🛏️ Sleeping & Eating

Sonafish
GUESTHOUSE $

(☑2261027; Cruzinha; s/d with breakfast & dinner CVE2500/5000) This guesthouse-restaurant has rooms in a blue-and-white building on a rock right above the ocean. Three rooms have ocean views, and only one has a private bathroom.

Kasa da Igreja
GUESTHOUSE $$

(☑9789090; kasa-d-igreja@hotmail.com; s/d CVE4000/6500, tent s/d CVE2500/4000; 🛜) Located just north of the small village of Chã da Igreja (heading towards the coast), this French-run charmer has four attractive rooms (the best with ocean views) and four well-appointed safari tents, all set amid abundant greenery and mountain views. There are great walks nearby, seasonal vegetable gardens (put to good use in Mimi's cooking) and plenty of tips on island exploring.

Casa no Caminho
GUESTHOUSE $$

(☑9531072; http://hausamweg.com; d for 1 night/subsequent nights €60/50) North of Chã da Igreja, the German-run Casa no Caminho consists of three attractive bungalows, all with fine views. The pleasant garden is strung with hammocks, and the friendly owners are a fount of knowledge about the region. Meals are available (breakfast for €5, dinner for €8).

Pedracin Village
INN $$

(☑2242020; s/d/tr from CVE4000/6100/7900; 🅿️❄️🛜🏊) This series of delightfully set stone cottages sits above the hamlet of Boca de Coruja, 12km from Ribeira Grande. They are set around a lush hillside garden connected by cobblestone paths. There's a swimming pool, a restaurant and free wi-fi in the public areas.

ℹ️ Getting There & Away

Colectivos cost CVE600 between Chã da Igreja and Porto Novo and operate around ferry times (early morning and afternoon).

Paúl

Located southeast of Ribeira Grande is the municipality of Paúl, home to its pretty main town of Vila das Pombas and, stretching be-

DON'T MISS

HIKING SANTO ANTÃO

Dramatic canyons, cloud-soaked peaks and vertigo-inspiring drops all help to make Santo Antão a hiker's paradise. Walks here cover all ranges of abilities, from gentle hour-long valley hikes to strenuous ascents only for the fittest. If you're intending to do some serious hiking, get hold of the Goldstadt Wanderkarte hiking map. You may also consider hiring a local guide; prices depend on the hike and whether the guide speaks English, but rates are about CVE4000.

Many of the hikes begin or end on the trans-island road. From here you can hitch a ride on a passing *aluguer* (minibus), or arrange for a taxi to wait for you ahead of time.

The classic hike is from the Cova crater (1170m), with its fascinating patchwork of farms, down to the stunning Valé do Paúl. The steep downhill route, which can get dangerously slippery, passes through lush mountainside, verdant stands of bananas and fields of sugarcane, all the way down to the string of villages that line the country road leading to the coastal town of Vila das Pombas.

An easier hike is along the coastal track from Ponta do Sol to Fontainhas. This hour-long walk takes you along a narrow path carved out of the cliff face, which in places is really high and steep. At the end, the village of Fontainhas clings like a spider to a little ridge high above its fertile valley and a small, rocky cove. From Fontainhas, you can continue the marvellous clifftop walk all the way to Cruzinha (another four hours).

hind the coast, the dreamy valley that winds up into the heart of the island.

Thousands of people live in villages and hamlets that dot this idyllic valley, known for its lush and fertile land. Flowers and fruit trees are everywhere – from breadfruit to bananas and bougainvilleas – as are sugarcane fields; Paúl is famed for its potent *grogue*. A scenic country road leads from Vila das Pombas up the valley, passing the villages of Eito, Passagem, Lombinho, Chã João Vaz and Cabo de Ribeira, where the road ends. A steep cobblestone footpath leads from Cabo de Ribeira to Cova, an extinct volcanic crater, whose floor is a patchwork of farms and lush greenery.

🛏 Sleeping

Chez Sandro   GUESTHOUSE $
(☎9812478; http://chezsandro.com; Chã de Manuel dos Santos; s/d/tr/q CVE2800/3900/5600/6700; @) The last lodging option up the valley from Vila das Pombas is Chez Sandro, a hostel-like guesthouse run by a Frenchman and his Cabo Verdean wife. It has computer use (for a fee), hot water in the mornings and free laundry after three days. Downstairs is a cosy bar-restaurant with 25 different kinds of local liqueur, homemade ice cream and good food (mains CVE560 to CVE800).

★Casa Cavoquinho   GUESTHOUSE $$
(☎2232065; www.cavoquinho.com; r CVE5400-6300; ☎) In the last roadside village (Chã de Manuel dos Santos) up the valley road

from Vila das Pombas is this adorable Spanish-run option housed in an orange building nestled on a hillside, with four spruced-up doubles with private bathrooms, pine floors and hot water. There's a terrace with dazzling valley views and deck chairs, a snack bar and free wi-fi.

★Aldeia Manga   LODGE $$
(☎2231880; www.aldeia-manga.com; Lombo Comprido; s/d bungalow CVE4900/6400, house with kitchen from CVE8400; ☎☀) Inland, on a hillside away from the main road, is the charming Aldeia Manga, which has four two-person adobe bungalows (cold water only) and a big house for families, with soft pine furnishings and solar-heated showers. It has a garden with lounge chairs and a small natural pool with jaw-dropping valley views. Meals are available and there's free wi-fi in the public area.

Residencial Chez Hujo   GUESTHOUSE $$
(☎3522000, mobile 9232515; jbeaudancaboverde1@gmail.com; d/tw CVE5000/6000; ☎) The recently opened Chez Hujo has 12 brightly painted rooms, all with quality mattresses, windows overlooking greenery and private hot-water bathrooms (heated by solar panels). Hosts give a warm welcome, help organise excursions and spread a fine breakfast with fresh fruits and other local products. A restaurant is in the works.

✗ Eating

O Curral
HEALTH FOOD $

(☑2231213; mains CVE250-650; ⊙10am-6pm Mon-Sat, 11am-5pm Sun) Along the road in the tiny settlement of Chã João Vaz is O Curral, known to locals as Alfred's, a straw-roofed restaurant, farm shop and *grogue* distillery run by an Austrian who's been living in the valley for decades.

❶ Getting There & Away

Colectivos meet the ferries and provide shared transport to destinations around Paúl (CVE500, 45 minutes).

Vila das Pombas
POP 1200

The main centre of Paúl is this pretty strip of pastel houses along the ocean. There's nothing much to do here except wander, ponder the waves and plot your next day exploring the island at one of the laid-back restaurants in town.

◉ Sights

Trapiche Ildo Benrós
DISTILLERY

(CVE100; ⊙6am-7pm) At Trapiche Ildo Benrós, *grogue* is made using the 400-year-old *trapiche* (a machine for juicing sugarcane). Sample drinks such as passion-fruit caipirinha under tall almond trees, as a veritable zoo of animals roams around. Look for a small green-and-white sign for Trapiche Ildo Benrós along the coastal road.

⌷ Sleeping

Residencial Familiar Takrida
GUESTHOUSE $

(☑2231129; damiaosilvacv@hotmail.com; s/d CVE2500/3000) Takrida is a friendly, family-run option that makes guests feel right at home. It has six rooms (three with sea views) and books up, so reserve ahead. It's tucked down a side street, a short stroll from the waterfront.

Aldeia Jerome
GUESTHOUSE $

(☑2232173; www.aldeiajerome.it.gg; s/d/ste CVE3300/4000/6000; ☞) This lovely garden hideaway with rooms and suites in two buildings is tucked away from the coastal strip along a footpath through banana and mango trees. All are clean, colourful and cosy, and equipped with fans and fridges. Ask for a room with a garden view. Breakfast is served on the top-floor terrace, plus there's wi-fi (for a fee) on the garden patio.

Hotel Paul Mar
HOTEL $$

(☑2232300; st.hotelpaulmar@gmail.com; Rua Agostinho Neto; s/d CVE5020/6560; ❋☞) This seafront hotel has contemporary spick-and-span rooms with all the trimmings, such as air-con, safes, free wi-fi (in the reception area) and verandas. Sea-view rooms have balconies perched right over the ocean.

✗ Eating

Pizzeria Ti Lello
PIZZA $

(mains CVE500-800; ⊙7-10pm) This Italian-run spot with a covered patio churns out the island's best pizzas as well as a decent lasagne. It's a short walk away from the coastal strip, opposite Aldeia Jerome.

Casa Maracujá
SEAFOOD $$

(☑2231000; mains CVE800-1400; ⊙9am-midnight; ☞) This charming open-air rooftop eatery with mountain views serves up some of the island's best cooking, with delicious, locally sourced ingredients prepared with care. Start off with grilled goat cheese or fish carpaccio before moving on to grilled tuna, pork stew or seafood rice.

Atelier
CAFE $$

(mains CVE700-1400; ⊙11am-late) This artsy hideaway behind Hotel Paul Mar is the local hipster hang-out. Run by a young musician and his wife, it serves yummy snacks, traditional dishes and herb teas in the small interior or on the large terrace outside. There's live music on weekends, often featuring up-and-coming musicians.

❶ Getting There & Away

Colectivos meet the ferries at Porto Novo and provide shared transport to Villa das Pombas (CVE500, 40 minutes).

Tarrafal
POP 900

Lost in the burning desert beige of the west coast, the sleepy little oasis of Tarrafal, set along a beach of inky-black sand, is a delightful place to rest, unwind and do nothing more strenuous than flip the pages of a book. The high cliffs here shelter the beach from the worst of the winds.

The **Pensão Mar Tranquilidade** (☑2276012; www.martranquilidade.com; s/d CVE2500/4200, d with full board CVE6900) offers lovely stone-and-thatch cottages as well as good meals and all kinds of activities.

ⓘ Getting There & Away

The journey to Tarrafal is long and bumpy (two to three hours), and sometimes the road is washed out in the rainy season. *Alugueres* (CVE700 to CVE1000) normally leave Porto Novo every morning except Sunday after the ferry disgorges its passengers. Have something soft to sit on (a jumper or two), as the bench seats are hard. Taxis charge a hefty CVE10,000 one way; to find them, head to the bar of Residencial Antilhas (p85) in Porto Novo.

FOGO

POP 38,000

Whether you're being tossed and turned in the heavy seas during the boat ride from Praia or thrown about by unpredictable winds and turbulence in the small prop plane, the drama of Fogo begins long before you set foot on this island's volcanic soils. The island of Fire (Fogo translates as fire) consists of a single, giant black volcano, at 2829m Cabo Verde's highest peak, which dominates every view and every waking moment. It burst back to life with a large eruption in late 2014.

Life here isn't just about macho tectonic movements, though: the island is encircled by a scenic, cobbled road, punctuated by hamlets with lava-black houses. São Filipe is easily one of the most attractive towns in the archipelago and can be used as a base for great hikes and pretty drives around the island's eastern side to the small town of Mosteiros, past terraced hillsides yielding mild Arabica coffee.

TACV (☑ 2608260; www.flytacv.com) has one to two daily flights to/from Praia, which last 30 minutes. A taxi from the airport into São Filipe (2km) costs CVE300. Boats arrive at the port 3km from town (taxis charge CVE400). The port looks like a giant construction site.

São Filipe

POP 23,000

Set commandingly atop the cliffs like the nest of a seabird, São Filipe is a town of grace, charm, immaculate Portuguese houses, and plazas full of flowers and sleepy benches. Below, at the base of the cliffs, lies a beach of jet-black sand and evil, dumping waves; beyond, tantalising on the horizon, squats the island of Brava. All this makes São Filipe one of the most compelling and charming towns in Cabo Verde. Note that strong currents make the town beach unsafe for swimming, especially in winter.

◉ Sights

Casa da Memoria   MUSEUM
(☑ 2812765; www.casadamemoria.com.cv; Praça da Igreja; donations accepted; ⊙ 10am-noon Wed-Fri or by appt) **FREE** Set in an 1820s house, this delightful little cultural space illustrates what life was like in Fogo over the past two centuries, via a collection of ceramics, photographs, decorative objects and household items. The pretty courtyard sometimes hosts film screenings, discussion groups and other events.

Baía da Salinas   BEACH
Join the locals at the lovely Baía da Salinas. Protected by strange volcanic rock formations, the beach is 19km to the north of São Filipe on the route to Mosteiros.

Dja'r Fogo   GALLERY
(☑ 9919713; djarfogo-agnelo@hotmail.com; ⊙ 9am-12.30pm & 3-6pm Mon-Fri, 9am-12.30pm Sat) A must-stop for visitors interested in history, culture and coffee, Dja'r Fogo is run by a local artist who splits his time between Lisbon, Paris and Fogo. It serves as art gallery, cafe, information point and launch pad for informal trips around the island. It's also the best place to taste artisanal Fogo coffee; the owner's family has had a coffee plantation since 1874, and six generations later, he still roasts and packages it into neat little cotton bags.

✦ Festivals & Events

Nhô São Filipe   CULTURAL
(⊙ 1 May) The town celebrates Nhô São Filipe, its yearly citywide festival.

Mardi Gras   CARNIVAL
(⊙ Feb or Mar) São Filipe hosts a lively Mardi Gras celebration.

⛌ Sleeping

Pousada Belavista   GUESTHOUSE $
(☑ 2811734; www.bela-vista.net; s/d from CVE2800/3800; ❈ ☞) An understated, impeccably run hotel built around an old colonial home and a new adjacent building. Rooms, some with ocean views, are well furnished if a little stuffy, and breakfasts are hearty. Balcony rooms are brightest, though a little noisy.

Colonial Guest House   GUESTHOUSE $$
(☑ 9914566; Rua do Câmara Municipal; s/d from CVE6100/9100; ☞ ❈) This gorgeously

CABO VERDE CHÃ DAS CALDEIRAS

renovated colonial mansion facing the ocean houses the town's nicest place to stay. Run by a Danish–Cabo Verdean couple, it has rooms with antique furniture and wooden floors; some have terraces with ocean views. On the downside, some rooms lack bathrooms (though every room has its own private bathroom in the corridor).

Tortuga B&B GUESTHOUSE **$$**
(☑ 9941512; www.tortuga-fogo.eu; s/d CVE4500/6100) This heavenly little beach hideaway is a 10-minute drive or a 30-minute walk along the beach from town. The live-in Italian owners take good care of their guests, who stay in one of four stylish rooms with an earthy look or the straw bungalow in the garden. Think hammocks between palm trees, the sound of crashing waves, a beach at your doorstep...

Casa Beiramar GUESTHOUSE **$$**
(☑ 2813485; www.cabo-verde.ch; Praça Igreja; s CVE3500-4500, d CVE5900-6500, tr CVE7900-9000) In a colonial building opposite the main church, Beiramar has a handful of simply furnished rooms. The upstairs rooms are quite spacious and open onto a lovely terrace with an ocean view. There's a pleasant courtyard, where breakfast is served, and dinners and drinks are also available upon request.

✖ Eating

Maria Augusta Bakery BAKERY **$**
(Praça Igreja; snacks from CVE20; ⊘ 7am-7pm Mon-Sat, to noon Sun) The friendly Maria Augusta churns out delicious bread and pastries from the giant wood-burning oven inside what looks like a garage. Look for an orange building on the edge of the sea near the church. Stock up on *pudim de queijo* (sweet goat-cheese tarts*)*, coconut biscuits and marmalade-filled doughnuts.

★ Pipi's INTERNATIONAL **$$**
(☑ 2814156; Rua do Câmara Municipal; ⊘ 11am-3pm & 6-11pm Mon-Sat, 6-11pm Sun) Overlooking a small plaza, Pipi's fires up some of the best cooking in Fogo. Senegalese-style *maffé* (a peanut-sauce) with grilled tuna or chicken is first-rate, along with fish stew and spaghetti with shrimp. It's all served in an inviting space decorated with West African carvings and tapestries. There's also lighter fare like crepes, sandwiches and pumpkin ice cream.

Calerom CABO VERDEAN **$$**
(☑ 2813267; mains CVE800-1400; ⊘ noon-11pm Mon-Fri, to late Sat) Calerom's open-air courtyard makes a laid-back setting for grilled meat and seafood dishes. It draws locals on game days – note the murals of Messi and Ronaldo adorning the walls – as well as on Saturday nights, when there's live music from 10.30pm onward.

Tortuga SEAFOOD **$$**
(☑ 9941512; www.tortuga-fogo.eu; 3-course dinner CVE1800, lunch mains CVE700-1000; ⊘ noon-2pm & 7.30-10pm) For a special meal, make dinner reservations at Tortuga B&B, where Italian owner Roberto cooks up innovative seafood dishes based on his father's old recipes, prepared using local ingredients and homemade products; wash it all down with the top-quality aged *grogue* from Brava.

Tropical Club SEAFOOD **$$**
(☑ 2811188; mains CVE750-1600; ⊘ 8am-11pm) Just up from the main square, this cheerful restaurant with a palm-shaded terrace has an extensive menu of mainly seafood dishes; try the delicious Fogo-style tuna. On Friday nights it has a *tocatina* (live traditional music performance), which starts around 9pm.

ℹ Information

The main plaza has free wi-fi, although with spotty signal. There are several banks with ATMs around the centre.

Qualitur (☑ 2811089; www.qualitur.cv; Praça 4 de Setembro; ⊘ 8am-1pm & 2-5pm Mon-Fri, 8am-noon Sat) This well-run outfit offers island tours and trekking excursions, books plane and ferry tickets and can arrange hire cars. Its most popular outing is a full-day excursion to Chã das Caldeiras, visiting the settlement still rebuilding after the 2014 eruption. Ask for English-speaking Fátima, who has a wealth of information on the island.

Zebra Travel (☑ 9194566; www.zebratravel.net; Rua do Câmara Municipal; ⊘ 8am-5pm Mon-Fri, 9am-noon Sat) Based out of Colonial Guest House, Zebra Travel offers guided volcano climbs and day trips to the crater.

Chã das Caldeiras

The conical 2829m-high Pico do Fogo volcano, shrouded in black cinder, rises dramatically out of the floor of an ancient crater known as Chã das Caldeiras ('Chã'). Bound by a half-circle of precipitous cliffs, Chã was born when, sometime in the last 100,000 years, some 300 cubic km of the island collapsed and slid into the sea to the east. The main cone has been inactive for more than 200 years, though there have been regular eruptions in Chã. The latest, in 2014–15, devastated the villages of Portela and Bangaeira. Today, a new settlement is rising atop the ashes of half-buried houses, but no one refers to it by either of the old village names. Instead, most people call the new village simply (and somewhat confusingly since it's also the name of the surrounding area) Chã das Caldeiras.

◎ Sights

Chã Vinho do Fogo WINERY
(☑2821533; agrocoopcha@gmail.com) Located a few kilometres outside the village of Chã das Caldeiras (en route to São Filipe), this state-of-the-art winery is a recent rebuild of the original, which was destroyed by the eruption of 2014–15. Vines are actually grown in the volcanic ash of the crater. Stop in for tastings. There's also a new guesthouse here.

🛏 Sleeping

Casa Alcindo & Laetitia GUESTHOUSE $
(☑9921409; alcindo6@gmail.com; Chã das Caldeiras; s/d CVE2500/3500) This is a delightful guesthouse run by a French–Cabo Verdean couple, with fine views over the crater floor. Alcindo is one of the top guides in the area.

Casa Lavra Cicilio GUESTHOUSE $
(☑9882127; casadelavrafogo@hotmail.com; Chã das Caldeiras; s/d/tr CVE2500/3500/4200) A pretty spot with lime and lavender trim, Casa Lavra Cicilio has rooms set around a small lava-rock courtyard. Good meals (CVE800) available upon request. It's well-located in the centre, about 300m from the entrance to the village.

Casa Marisa II GUESTHOUSE $
(☑5308440; s/d/tr CVE3000/4600/5900) About 1km before reaching the village, this German–Cabo Verdean-run guesthouse has pleasant rooms set around a lava-stone-filled courtyard. It also has a good restaurant with outdoor seating, which is a favourite of day-tripping groups passing through the area.

☆ Entertainment

Casa Ramiro LIVE MUSIC
(Chã das Caldeiras; ⊙noon-11pm) If you're staying overnight, don't miss the nightly performance (around 6pm) at Casa Ramiro, a grocery store where you can try local goat cheese and homemade manecon wine. Ramiro and his children, neighbours and friends all perform live music.

❶ Getting There & Away

Colectivos run from São Filipe (near the market) to Chã das Caldeiras; these depart in the afternoon and return the following morning around 6am (confirm return times wherever you lodge for the night). Fare for the two-hour ride is CVE1000.

You can also get here on a tour offered by Qualitur (p88) and Zebra Travel (p90). These don't allow much time to wander around Chã, however.

SAL

POP 26,000

Though flat, desolate and overdeveloped, Sal boasts more tourists than any other island. They fall into three categories: the package-holiday crowd, hard-core windsurfers and those in transit to more interesting islands. If you don't mind the heavy tourist crowds, Sal has a fine restaurant scene, plenty of nightlife and some lovely beaches where you can unwind and enjoy some water sports.

The largest town is Espargos, right next to the international airport, but most people stay near the pretty beach in Santa Maria, 18km to the south.

◎ Sights

The great attraction is the surreal, lunarlike **Pedra do Lume** (CVE550; ⊙9am-5.45pm), an ancient volcano, where seawater is transformed into shimmering salt beds. You can see the old salt extraction machinery of the 1805 plant; float in the medicinal salt water; have a massage, salt scrub or mud treatment at the small Salinas Relax spa; and have a meal at the restaurant.

Other points of interest include the fish market in **Palmeira**, the gorgeous **Igrejinha beach** at the far eastern end of Santa Maria and the **Buracona** natural swimming pool (time your visit for noon to see the Blue Eye, a natural light effect in a small underground pool).

❶ Getting There & Away

The airport has an ATM, a bureau de change, free (but rarely working) wi-fi and a tourist info booth. **TACV** (☑2411305; www.flytacv.com) has several flights daily to/from Praia, five weekly to

São Vicente, five weekly to Boa Vista and three weekly to São Nicolau.

There are currently no regular inter-island ferries at Sal. The port is at Palmeira, about 4km northwest of Espargos.

❶ Getting Around

Minibuses ply the road between Santa Maria and Espargos (CVE100, 25 minutes); all stop on the main road just in front of the airport. Taxis from the airport to Santa Maria charge CVE1000 during the day and CVE1200 at night.

Santa Maria

POP 6400

The star of the show is the beach: a sublime strip of gentle sand and ever-so-blue waters with world-class windsurfing and lots of fun-in-the-sun activities. Beyond the shoreline, there aren't many attractions, though Santa Maria is the best place to arrange excursions to other parts of the island. While sleepy during the day, the town comes to life at night, with buzzing open-air eateries and bars lining the inland streets parallel to the beach.

🏃 Activities

You can't get bored in Santa Maria, where the accent is on water sports. There are a number of centres and schools, which cover anything from scuba diving, kitesurfing and snorkelling to windsurfing and sailing. Other activities include shark-watching jaunts, turtle-watching (www.sostartarugas.org), horseback riding and island tours with a 4WD.

Manta Diving Center   DIVING
(🎯 2421540; www.mantadivingcenter.cv) Located on the grounds of the beachfront Hotel Belorizonte, this multilingual outfit receives high marks for its professionalism and excellent range of dives.

Yoga Cabo Verde   YOGA
(Rua 15 de Agosto; per class CVE1000; ⊘ Mon-Fri) A much-loved yoga spot that offers one-hour morning classes (Monday, Wednesday and Friday) and afternoon classes from Monday to Friday. English-speaking instructors offer a mix of Hatha and Vinyasa styles, including several beginner classes and others for more advanced practitioners.

Angulo Cabo Verde   WATER SPORTS
(🎯 2421580; www.angulocaboverde.com; Praia António de Sousa) The hippest water-sports centre and beach hang-out is Angulo Cabo Verde,

1km from the centre, east of the pier. It offers kitesurfing lessons, equipment rentals and food (mains CVE800 to CVE1400) served on a wooden deck with parasols and loungers.

Orca Dive Club   DIVING
(🎯 9819287; www.orca-diveclubs.com) Offers a wide range of dives, including wreck diving, wall diving and even cave diving. The outfit suffered a devastating fire in 2016, and was continuing to operate with the help of other dive operators.

Surf Zone   SURFING
(🎯 9978804; www.surfcaboverde.com) Based out of the Morabeza Hotel Beach Club, Surf Zone rents gear and offers lessons for surfing, kitesurfing, windsurfing and stand-up paddleboarding.

🛏 Sleeping

⭐ **Sakaroulé B&B**   GUESTHOUSE $
(🎯 2421682; www.sakaroulecaboverde.com; Rua a Tras; s/d/tr CVE3400/4200/5300; 🛜) In a very local neighbourhood 500m from the beach, Sal's most atmospheric B&B has stylish rooms that come in different sizes and pretty colours, and with African decor touches. The multilingual staff can set up you up with tours and activities. Sakaroulé is a top choice away from the tourist buzz, with a friendly, earthy and hip vibe.

Porta do Vento   GUESTHOUSE $$
(🎯 2422121; portadovento@gmail.com; Ave João de Deus Maximiano; s/d from CVE4900/6100; 🛜) This well-run Italian-owned guesthouse has 15 clean, comfortable rooms – all with fridges, tile floors and elderly TVs. Some rooms are rather spacious with balconies (though no view). It's away from the noise and bustle, being 700m north (straight inland) of the beach. There's a decent restaurant on site. Wi-fi is pricey (CVE550 per hour).

Les Alizés   HOTEL $$
(🎯 2421446; www.pensao-les-alizes.com; Rua 1 de Junho; s/d CVE5400/7000; @🛜) Right at the heart of town, the French-owned Les Alizés, has a mix of comfortable rooms with all the mod cons (flat-screen TVs, in-room fridges) but stiff mattresses. The best rooms have ceramic tile floors and French doors opening onto a small balcony.

Hotel Morabeza   HOTEL $$$
(🎯 2421020; www.hotelmorabeza.com; s/d CVE15,000/23,000, with sea view CVE19,000/26,000; ❄@🛜🏊) Fronting a lively patch of beach,

this grande dame of a beach hotel was the very first on the strip. Over 40 years later, it's still a great choice, with well-appointed rooms facing the beach or the gardens, several restaurants, two pools and lots of activities.

✕ Eating

★ Cape Fruit
CAFE $

(☑9822205; Rua 15 de Agosto; mains CVE400-800; ⊙8am-8pm Thu-Tue; 🛜🍴) Just inland and a few blocks east of the beach, Cape Fruit serves creative salads, hummus and grilled veggie sandwiches and fresh tropical fruit juices. The setting evokes laid-back island life, with upcycled furniture scattered around an outdoor patio that's partially shaded by thatched awnings.

Giramondo
ICE CREAM $

(Rua 1 de Junho; s/d/tr scoop CVE150/250/350; ⊙8am-1am) The island's best gelato draws big crowds most nights. There's outdoor seating in front, perfect for snacking on a cone of lemon, pistachio and strawberry while taking in the passing people parade. Giramondo also runs a good-value bistro next door.

Cafe Criolo
CABO VERDEAN $

(mains CVE600-900; ⊙8am-10pm Mon-Sat; 🖻) The least touristy, most down-home place to eat in town, this low-key eatery with a streetside veranda serves delicious homemade food, such as *cachupa* (preorder it), fish stews and tuna steaks. The lunch specials at CVE450 are a deal.

Tam Tam
CAFE $

(mains CVE450-900; ⊙10am-11pm) This friendly cafe with outdoor seating has earned many fans for its tasty, reasonably priced dishes and friendly service. Stop in early for French toast, omelettes and other breakfast fare (served till 1pm) or later on for pulled-pork sandwiches, sweet-potato fries and grilled tuna salad.

D'Angela
SEAFOOD $$

(mains CVE700-1800; ⊙10.30am-11.30pm) The oceanfront terrace is the highlight of this simple, always-buzzing restaurant that dishes out reliably good seafood fare. Live music makes it even livelier on Friday and Saturday evenings, and at lunchtime on Sundays.

🍷 Drinking & Nightlife

Ocean Cafe
BAR

(☑2421895; www.oceancafe.com; Rua 15 de Agosto; ⊙noon-1am; 🛜) For a lively scene, it's hard to top this festive drinking and eating space

one block up from the beach. There's live music most nights, and DJs heat things up on weekends. The food is also quite good, with thin-crust pizzas, fish and chips, burgers and other pub fare.

Londres
CAFE, BAR

(⊙8am-11pm Wed-Mon; 🛜) Run by a couple of friendly English expats, Londres offers a winning combination of tapas plates (calamari, Spanish-style meatballs, zucchini carpaccio) and a good drink selection, with live music three nights a week. Currently, you can catch Cabo Verdean singers on Wednesday, Friday and Sunday, from 8pm onward.

Sal Beach Club
BAR

(⊙8am-midnight; 🛜) Buzzing beachfront spot with live music on weekends, free wi-fi, a big TV screen, and plenty of snacks when hunger strikes – fish and chips, burgers, pastas and wraps.

ℹ️ Information

There are several banks with ATMs (although they tend to run out of cash on weekends).

Info Kiosk (☑9592030; ⊙9am-4pm Mon-Sat) Near the Hotel Nhá Terra and the beach, this info kiosk is a good spot to book outdoor activities like boat trips, turtle-watching, horseback riding and island tours.

ℹ️ Getting There & Away

Taxis between Santa Maria and the airport cost around CVE1000 during the day and CVE1200 at night. Plenty of minibuses ply the road between Espargos and Santa Maria (CVE100), and all stop on the main road in front of the airport. To catch it airport-bound in Santa Maria, you'll find minibuses lined up behind Hotel Nhá Terra.

ℹ️ Getting Around

One-day island tours are a popular way to take in all the sights. If you prefer to explore at your own pace, you can hire vehicles from **Hotel Nhá Terra** (☑2421109; nhaterra@hotmail.com; Rua 1 de Junho;) – prices start at €50 per day.

Espargos

POP 17,200

Located near both the airport and the ferry dock, Espargos – the island's capital – is a small, dusty workaday town that feels more like the real Cabo Verde than touristy Santa Maria.

On the square, Sivy (Praça 12 de Setembro; mains CVE500-1200; ⊙11am-midnight) is a good old-fashioned cafe-bar that serves simple meals and drinks.

There are a several banks with ATMs around Praça 19 de Setembro.

Fares on the plentiful minibuses between Espargos and Santa Maria are CVE100.

BOA VISTA

POP 12,000

With its feathery lines of peachy dunes, stark plains and scanty oases, the island of Boa Vista looks as if a chunk of the Sahara somehow broke off the side of Africa and floated out to the middle of the Atlantic. Though the island offers some fantastic if wind-blown beaches, incredible windsurfing, the pretty little town of Sal Rei and an ever-increasing number of resorts and hotels, it's this desert interior that is the best reason for venturing out here. Be ready for some rough off-roading, as most of Boa Vista's roads are treacherous.

◉ Sights

In addition to attractions such as the Praia de Estoril and Centro de Artes e Cultura, there is the long and beautiful Praia de Santa Mónica on the island's southern coast, as well as the beaches of Curralinho and Varandinha. It's worth whizzing through the village of Povoaçao Velha, the Viana Desert – great to visit on a full-moon night; Migrante Guesthouse offers tours – and the oasis town of Rabil.

While you can't take in all these sights in one day, two days is more than enough to see the entire island. Several agencies in town offer excursions, including Sabura Center (☑ 2511933; saburacenter@ymail.com; Sal Rei; half-/full-day tour per person from €25/37).

Praia de Estoril   BEACH
A short stroll south of the Sal Rei town centre, this lovely beach has turquoise waters and white sands, making it a fine setting for a day out. A handful of beach bars serve up seafood, snacks and plenty of drinks, with tables and lounge chairs on the sand. Several places here hire out gear – stand-up paddleboards, surfboards, kayaks – and give lessons in surfing, kitesurfing, windsurfing and sailing.

Centro de Artes e Cultura   ARTS CENTRE
(☑ 2519690; Sal Rei; ⊙ 9am-5pm Mon-Fri) This new arts centre hosts a wide range of events,

from art and photography exhibitions to African craft and jewellery shows. There's also a 350-seat theatre that hosts concerts and dance performances. The centre is a 10-minute walk northeast (inland) from Sal Rei's main plaza.

Santa Maria   SHIPWRECK
An eerie sight is the wreck of the *Santa Maria*, a rusting hulk laid out on a stormy stretch of beach to the north of Sal Rei along Costa de Boa Esperança. While this makes a decent half-day walk, it's better not to attempt it as there have been muggings on this route; take a taxi or visit it as part of an island tour instead.

Curral Velho   RUINS
The spooky village of Curral Velho was abandoned due to near-endless drought. You can wander amid the crumbling ruins of the old buildings, then head down to the nearby beach, a gorgeous stretch of pristine shoreline.

Morro Negro   LIGHTHOUSE
The Morro Negro lighthouse, standing atop a 150m-high cape, is Cabo Verde's most easterly point. The views are spectacular.

⚡ Activities

Naturalia   WILDLIFE WATCHING
(☑ 2511558; www.naturaliaecotours.com; Largo Santa Isabel) Turtles come to Boa Vista in massive numbers in order to lay eggs. Several agencies on the island offer turtle-watching tours in season (July to October), but Naturalia is the best and most environmentally sensitive; tours cost €50 per person and typically depart around 7.30pm, returning around 1am.

Naturalia also offers whale-watching excursions (€65 per person for a half day) between February and May when humpback whales travel the waters off Cabo Verde, and birdwatching tours for €50 (there are 24 species on Boa Vista). It also arranges snorkelling trips to Baía das Gatas, where you swim among rich coral and nurse sharks.

Submarine Dive Center   WATER SPORTS
(☑ 9924865; atilros@gmail.com; 2hr hire for surfboards/kayaks/stand-up paddleboards €30/50/50; ⊙ 9am-5.30pm) A highly experienced outfitter, Submarine Dive Center provides equipment, dives for experienced folk (€70 with equipment) and crash courses for novices (€120). You can also rent kayaks, surfboards and stand-up paddleboards, and

arrange lessons in surfing, windsurfing and kitesurfing. A good restaurant and a beach bar are also here.

🛌 Sleeping

La Boaventura   HOSTEL $
(☑9509167; www.laboaventura.com; Av dos Pescadores, Sal Rei; dm €10, r €25-55; 🛜) La Boaventura has simply furnished dorms and guestrooms – all with private bathrooms and some with sea views – set around a vine-fringed courtyard. The real draw, though, is the low-lit cafe/lounge (festooned with Tibetan prayer flags, a small aquarium and a mini disco ball), where you can meet other travellers or use wi-fi over drinks. Book well ahead at this popular French-owned place.

⭐Migrante Guesthouse   GUESTHOUSE $$
(☑2511143; www.migrante-guesthouse.com; Av Amilcar Cabral, Sal Rei; s/d from CVE7700/9900; 🛜) The gorgeous Migrante has four rooms set around a courtyard of mustard yellow and bougainvillea pink, with a giant palm tree. Each room has dark-wood floors, big soft beds and black-and-white portraits hanging on the icy white walls, which give an arty feel. The downstairs cafe is lovely too. Rates include airport transfers.

Spinguera Eco Lodge   LODGE $$$
(☑2511941; www.spinguera.com; s/d CVE17,000/26,000; 🅿🛜) 🌿 Boa Vista's most magical hideaway is an abandoned fishing village converted into a stunning eco-lodge by the Italian artist owner. Inside white-washed cottages, stylish and minimalist rooms showcase reclaimed wood and clay floors, and ocean views. The restaurant serves delectable food and there's a walkway down to your own little beach. A stay here is a splurge but a worthy one.

Spinguera Eco Lodge is located about 18km northeast of Sal Rei.

🍴 Eating

⭐Beramar   FUSION $$
(☑9746514; Av dos Pescadores, Sal Rei; small/large plates CVE600/1100; ⊗noon-2pm & 7-10pm Mon-Fri, 7-10pm Sun, closed May-Sep) Under the helm of a talented Milanese chef, Beramar showcases high-quality local ingredients with creative accents in its dishes, which are ideal for sharing. Think crunchy risotto with goat cheese, pork ribs with lentil and apple, wahoo curry and char-grilled vegetables. It's near the waterfront, a couple blocks south of Sal Rei's plaza.

Blue Marlin   SEAFOOD $$
(Sal Rei; mains CVE800-1300; ⊗noon-3pm & 7-10pm) On Sal Rei's main square, this matchbox-sized restaurant with checked tablecloths and graffiti-covered walls serves some of the island's best seafood. Start off with an appetiser of smoked fish or grilled goat cheese, then opt for grilled tuna or seafood pasta. Good Portuguese wines by the glass. Book in advance.

Grill Luar   SEAFOOD $$
(☑9953653; Rua da Cruz, Sal Rei; mains CVE900-1300; ⊗7-10pm Mon-Sat) A short walk west of Sal Rei's main square, this attractive top-floor restaurant has a pretty view of the harbour and serves up a decent selection of grilled fish and meat plates, plus pastas, sautéed shrimp and octopus. The seafood rice is a standout.

⭐Fado Crioula   FUSION $$$
(☑9314703; www.facebook.com/FadoCrioula8; Sal Rei; mains around CVE1400; ⊗9am-10pm Mon-Thu, to 11pm Sun; 🛜) This creative, art-filled space serves up market-fresh fare that changes daily: expect delightful salads, creative appetisers and a fresh-grilled fish of the day. Fado Crioula hosts jam sessions, film screenings, art exhibitions, language exchanges and other events throughout the month. It's set on a breezy perch, with views over the coastline.

Chandinho   ITALIAN $$$
(☑9910360; Rua Santa Barbara, Sal Rei; mains CVE1100-2200; ⊗7-10.30pm Mon-Sat) An elegant spot that specialises in hot stone cooking – flavourful meat, fish or vegetables grilled up at your tableside. Large grilled prawns, grouper stew and seafood spaghetti are among the other Italian-accented hits. Finish off with chocolate soufflé for dessert. Reserve ahead.

🍷 Drinking & Nightlife

Caffè del Porto   CAFE
(Sal Rei; ⊗noon-10pm) Near the Sal Rei waterfront, a few blocks from the plaza, this place with outdoor tables makes a fine spot for a sundowner. You can also order food (seafood, pizza, kebabs), watch televised football matches and catch live music from time to time.

Wakan Bar   CAFE
(Sal Rei; ⊗1-11pm Mon-Sat) Adorable little blue-and-white shack with a boat shape, right by the fishing boats on Praia de Diante.

CABO VERDE BOA VISTA

Expect no less than 70 cocktail varieties, nice snacks, good Italian coffee and good happy-hour specials.

ℹ️ Information

The plaza has free wi-fi. There are several banks with ATMs around the plaza.

ℹ️ Getting There & Around

TACV (📞 2412401; www.flytacv.com) has six weekly flights to Praia (one hour) and five weekly to Sal (15 minutes). Irregular ferries sail to/from Boa Vista, Praia and Sal, but they are so sporadic you may lose many days waiting for one.

Alugueres (from CVE200) ply the island's roads, but they're scarce. Taxis are readily available; the short hop from the airport to Sal Rei costs CVE700.

Bikes and scooters are available from **Let's Go** (📞 29773000; Av 4 de Julho, Sal Rei; ⊙10am-12.30pm & 4-6pm Mon-Sat), located on the main road, before reaching the plaza.

OTHER ISLANDS

Brava

POP 6500

Except for the occasional car that braves the cobblestone roads, the island of Brava seems to reside firmly in the 19th century. Its terraced hillsides are farmed with the aid of mules and life moves at a pace that would make a sloth sleepy. Its mountainous interior is breathtaking and the coastline dramatic, though thanks to its distance from anywhere else and infrequent, erratic travel connections, the island receives little foreign tourism. You will see fancy mansions dotted around the island; these are built by US returnees – Brava's population has left in droves for US shores, but some come back to build their lifelong dream.

🛏️ Sleeping

⭐ **Kaza di Zaza** BUNGALOW $
(📞 9820785; www.kazadizaza.com; Fajã d'Agua; bungalow CVE2500-4000; 🌐) An idyllic base on the island, Kaza di Zaza has one stylish guest apartment and two small self-contained bungalows, which are a bit rustic but undeniably charming. All three have small terraces with pretty views over the bay. It's run by a Dutch couple, who also whip up tasty din-

ners (CVE900) and make a brilliant bottle of passion-fruit wine.

Pensão Paulo GUESTHOUSE $
(📞 2851312; Nova Sintra; s/d CVE2720/3440) One block from the main plaza in Nova Sintra, this good-value option has 20 rooms, clean and comfortably furnished; the best open onto a shared balcony with views of the mountains.

Hotel Djabraba's Eco-Lodge GUESTHOUSE $
(http://hoteldjabrabasecolodge.jimdo.com; Nova Sintra; s/d/tr CVE2720/3440/4500) Perched on a hill just outside the centre of Nova Sintra, this friendly Italian-owned spot has attractive rooms with fine views over the island. Good meals available upon request.

Sol na Baia GUESTHOUSE $$
(📞 9897902; www.solnabaia.cv; Fajã d'Agua; r CVE7000; 🌐) One of the most attractive places to stay in Brava, Sol na Baia offers a handful of tastefully appointed rooms (some with balconies), French-inspired meals and a delightful garden. Artwork adorns the house, with many paintings by the acclaimed artist-owner José Andrade. It's set on the lovely waterfront in Fajã d'Agua.

🍴 Eating

O Poeta CABO VERDEAN $$
(Nova Sintra; mains CVE700-1200; ⊙11am-9pm) On the main street leading up from Nova Sintra's square, this restaurant with a terrace serves decent fish and meat dishes off a picture menu. There's occasional live music.

Vila Luanda CABO VERDEAN $$
(Nova Sintra; mains CVE500-900; ⊙8am-7pm) Two blocks from Nova Sintra's main square, this casual place serves up some of the best meals in town, with changing daily specials – like oven-baked chicken, *feijoada* and grilled fish of the day. Grab a seat at one of the outdoor tables and watch village life drift slowly past.

ℹ️ Getting There & Away

There are no flights to Brava, but there is a reliable ferry operated by **Cabo Verde Fast Ferry** (📞 2617552; www.cvfastferry.com). It operates a solid boat that runs between Praia, Fogo and Brava several times a week. Schedules change often, so it's best to consult the website for the latest. The journey from Fogo to Brava lasts 50 minutes and costs CVE1550; from Praia to Fogo it's about four hours and costs CVE3350 (if heading to Brava, a one-way ticket is CVE3750).

Note that the ferry from Fogo departs from the port outside São Filipe, which looks like a giant construction site.

ℹ Getting Around

Alugueres ply the road between Nossa Senhora do Monte, Nova Sintra and the ferry port. Most prices are around CVE100 to CVE150 per person for a ride, though the trip from the ferry port to Nova Sintra is CVE300 per person. You can find a car and driver for a full-day tour of the island for as little as CVE4000 – ask around among the *aluguer* drivers. To get to Fajã, *alugueres* charge about CVE2000. Plan ahead if you have a morning boat, as transport can be scarce. One of the best drivers on the island is the delightful **Carlos Correia** (🖉 9781934; carloscorreia08@hotmail.com), who speaks perfect English.

Maio

POP 6500

Glittering like a white crystal in a sea of turquoise, Maio is an island of squeaky-clean beaches where days drift slowly by in a haze of sunshine and long conversations. Aside from the pretty, if slightly overdeveloped, main town of Porto Inglês (also known as Vila do Maio), the sleepy fishing village of Calheta 11km to the north and the many beaches, the only other 'attraction' is the scrubby acacia-dotted interior with its string of 13 villages. But for the traveller after something a little different, Maio is begging you to leave your footprints on its gorgeous beaches.

🏃 Activities

Aquanautic   WATER SPORTS
(🖉 9955701; Praia Bitxe Rotxa, Porto Inglês; paddleboards/kayaks per hr CVE1500/700, surfboard/bicycle per half-day CVE2500/700; ⊙9am-6pm Tue-Sun) This beach shack hires out all the essentials for a sunny day's outing, including stand-up paddleboards, surfboards, sea kayaks, body boards, bicycles and more. You can also hire a boat here.

🛏 Sleeping

★Kaza Tropikal   GUESTHOUSE $
(🖉 9594151; www.tropikalmaio.com; 169 Rua Jaime Mota, Porto Inglês; s/d CVE2300/2800) Just back from the main street in Porto Inglês and a short stroll from the beach, Kaza Tropikal has four bright, simply furnished rooms that open onto a shared balcony. There's also a roof terrace with sparkling sea views. The

HIKING ON BRAVA

From the tiny capital of Nova Sintra ('Vila') atop a little plateau there are some short but lovely hikes: eastward down to the ghost village of Vinagre via Santa Barbara and westward to Cova Joana and then on to Nossa Senhora do Monte or Lima Doce, both nearby.

Another highlight includes the 1½-hour walk to the mountainside hamlet of Baleia from the village of Mato Grande, 4km from Nova Sintra. The scenic village of Fajã de Agua on the northwestern coast is set dramatically between a rocky cove and impressive cliffs. It's great to hike down to the village, along a sharp 7km descent with stunning views.

kind-hearted French–New Zealand couple who run the place have a wealth of island information, and also operate the beach bar of the same name.

Hotel Marilu   HOTEL $
(🖉 2551198; Rua 24 de Setembre, Porto Inglês; s/d/ste CVE2900/4400/5500; ❄) Offers very clean rooms with quality mattresses and all the mod cons in a central location near the church. Some rooms open onto shared balconies, and the suites have excellent sea views.

Big Game   GUESTHOUSE $$
(🖉 9710593; www.biggamemaio.com; Av Amilcar Cabral, Porto Inglês; s/d from CVE4100/5600; ❄) A popular Italian-run spot with small but well-equipped rooms adorned with colourful, childlike murals and small balconies. It sits above one of the best restaurants in town (mains CVE600 to CVE900). It's on the main road in Porto Inglês, a short walk from the beach.

Torre Sabina   GUESTHOUSE $$
(🖉 2561299; www.inseltraum.biz; Calheta; d CVE6620) Run by a German couple, Torre Sabina consists of one amazing double room with panoramic ocean vistas inside a funky tower right on Baixona beach in Calheta. There's also a handsomely appointed suite with a chapel-like design. Gardens surround the place, and there's a kayak you can use for free. Delicious breakfast is included and dinners are available on request.

✗ Eating

Bar Tropikal
SEAFOOD $

(☑ 5977268; www.tropikalmaio.com; Praia Bitxe Rotxa, Porto Inglês; mains CVE400-800; ⊙ 8.30am-11pm Tue-Sun) One of Maio's best-loved destinations, this beachfront spot serves a good range of food, including daily fish and chicken specials, plus pastas, pizza, burgers and snacks. There's a great sunset happy hour. Don't miss the Saturday night *tocatina*, which starts at 9pm.

Tutti Frutti
ITALIAN, SEAFOOD $$

(☑ 9702535; Av Amilcar Cabral, Porto Inglês; mains CVE750-1300; ⊙ noon-10pm) Serves up excellent seafood and Italian cooking on the main drag in Porto Inglês. Stop in to reserve one of the outdoor tables for dinner. Brenda, who runs the place, is a kind-hearted soul and a talented chef.

Wolf Djarmai
INTERNATIONAL $$

(Porto Inglês; mains CVE600-900; ⊙ 8am-11pm Mon-Sat) Cabo Verdean and European food is dished out at this funky spot inside a blue container fronted with a tree-shaded terrace, just up from the main square behind the church.

❶ Getting There & Around

TACV (☑ 2608260; www.flytacv.com) has three flights weekly to/from Praia (10 minutes). The transfer into town costs CVE300. The ferry company **Polar** (p76) sails three times a week between Praia on Santiago and Maio.

For island tours, contact **Bemvindo** (☑ 9959713; bemvindomaio@gmail.com), one of the island's most trustworthy drivers. He charges around CVE6000 to CVE7000 for an island tour. Infrequent colectivos run between Vila do Maio and Calheta when full (CVE120).

São Nicolau

POP 13,400

São Nicolau hides its secrets well. First impressions are of a desolate and barren island, but hidden among the three ridges that dominate all views are lush green valleys and soaring peaks that rise up to Mt Gordo (1312m), the island's highest peak.

Near the mouth of the fertile Fajã Valley lies Ribeira Brava, the island's capital. Long Cabo Verde's religious centre, it was built inland to protect its treasures from pirates. Its narrow, hillside streets and tiled roofs are reminiscent of 17th-century Portugal. Ribeira Brava's Carnival celebration in February or March is second only to Mindelo's.

✺ Festivals & Events

Carnival
PARADE

São Nicolau's pre-Lenten bash features wild costumes, dancing, and late-night revelry. It happens on the days preceding Ash Wednesday. Plan ahead if you want to attend, as flights book up weeks in advance.

⊨ Sleeping

Pensão Residencial Jardim
PENSION $

(☑ 2351117; pensaoresidencialjardim@hotmail.com; s/d CVE3200/4100) Located on a hill with breathtaking views that overlook Ribeira Brava, this spotless *pensão* (pension) has quaint, comfortable rooms and a very good rooftop restaurant (mains around CVE800; order ahead).

Edificio Magico
APARTMENT $$

(☑ 2361941; www.edificiomagico.com; Tarrafal, São Nicolau; apt from CVE5500) Overlooking the beach, this friendly Italian-owned spot in Tarrafal has a great location and tidy, simply furnished rooms. The staff whips up delicious breakfasts.

❶ Getting There & Away

TACV (www.flytacv.com) has three flights a week to Sal and two weekly to São Vicente. The airport is 5km southeast of Ribeira Brava (CVE500 by taxi). Ferry transport is infrequent, with boats operated by **Cabo Verde Fast Ferry** (www.cvfastferry.com) calling in just twice a month while travelling between Praia and São Vicente. The ferries dock at Tarrafal.

❶ Getting Around

You can go to Ribeira Brava by minibus (CVE500) or taxi (around CVE3200) from the unbeautiful town of Tarrafal, the island's port. A great option is to get off halfway at Cachaço and hike down through the Fajã Valley to Ribeira Brava. The trail up to Mt Gordo also goes through Cachaço, passing through a protected pine forest before reaching the summit.

UNDERSTAND CABO VERDE

Cabo Verde Today

Cabo Verde is one of West Africa's most stable nations, both politically and economically. In many areas, it tops the charts in comparison to other parts of Africa – and the developing world. It has a high literacy rate of 88% (and over 97% among school-age children), an active and relatively free press, a declining poverty rate and one of the highest living standards in West Africa. In fact, a little over a decade ago, it became one of the few countries to 'graduate' out of its ranking among the world's 50 least developed nations according to the UN. This in spite of a lack of natural resources – and even adequate water supplies – is impressive. Today, tourism, which accounts for over 25% of GDP, is helping to fuel the growth. Though the global financial crisis of 2008-9 had an impact, GDP growth has been on the rise in the last few years, and is expected to reach 4% in 2017 – a healthy figure, though still below the boom years before the global crisis.

In 2016, Cabo Verde re-elected its popular president, Jorge Carlos Fonseca, to a second term. Despite the nation's solid economic performance, big challenges remain: namely taming the public debt (over 115% of GDP), lowering the unemployment rate (over 12%) and grappling with crumbling infrastructure spread over nine inhabited islands.

History

Slavery, Drought & Neglect

When Portuguese mariners discovered the archipelago in 1456, the islands that would become known as Cabo Verde were uninhabited but fertile enough to attract the first group of settlers six years later. They founded Ribeira Grande (now Cidade Velha), the first European town in the tropics, on the island of Santiago. To work the land, settlers almost immediately began to import slaves from the West African coast. The islands' remote yet strategic position made them a perfect clearing house and victualling station for the transatlantic slave trade.

Cabo Verde's first recorded drought occurred in 1747; from that date droughts became ever more common and, in the century from 1773, three droughts killed some 100,000 people. This cycle lasted well into the 20th century. At the same time, the island's economic clout fell as Britain, France and the Netherlands challenged Portugal's control over the slave trade. As a result, Lisbon invested little in Cabo Verde. To escape hunger, many men left the islands, principally to work as hired hands on American whaling ships. Even today, Cabo Verdean communities along the New England coast in the US rival the population of Cabo Verde itself.

Independence from Portugal

Cabo Verde's mostly mixed-race population tended to fare better than fellow Africans in other Portuguese colonies. Beginning in the mid-19th century, a privileged few received an education, many going on to help administer mainland colonies. By independence, 25% of the population could read (compared with 5% in Guinea-Bissau).

In 1956, Cabo Verdean intellectual Amilcar Cabral (born in Guinea-Bissau) founded the Marxist-inspired Partido Africano da Independência da Guiné e Cabo Verde (PAIGC), later renamed the Partido Africano da Independência de Cabo Verde (PAICV).

As other European powers were relinquishing their colonies, Portugal's right-wing dictator, António de Oliveira Salazar, propped up his regime with dreams of colonial greatness. From the early 1960s, one of Africa's longest wars of independence ensued. However, most of the fighting took place in Guinea-Bissau rather than Cabo Verde, and indeed many middle-class Cabo Verdeans remained lukewarm about independence.

Eventually, Portugal's war became an international scandal and led to a nonviolent end to its dictatorship in 1974, with Cabo Verde gaining full independence a year later.

Cabo Verde Since Independence

On gaining power, the PAICV created a one-party state but also instituted a remarkably successful health and education program. Drought and food-aid dependence remained a serious issue in a country that produces only about 20% of its food supply.

By the late 1980s there were increasing calls for a multiparty democracy, and in 1990 the PAICV acquiesced, allowing lawyer Carlos Veiga to found the Movimento para a Democracia (MpD). With a centre-right policy of political and economic liberalisation, the MpD swept to power in the 1991 elections. Privatisation and foreign investment – especially in tourism – brought only slow results, however, and in 2001 the PAICV reclaimed power and Pedro Pires became president.

Culture

Cabo Verde boasts by far the highest GDP per capita (US$3900) in West Africa. The country's literacy rate of 88% is also the highest in the region. Virtually all children of primary-school age attend school, though attendance at secondary schools is considerably lower. Opportunities for pursuing higher education have improved markedly in the past decade. The islands have some 10 post-secondary educational institutes, with several key universities in Praia and Mindelo.

People

Based on the UN's *Africa Human Development Report 2012*, Cabo Verde comes out on top in West Africa. From 1975 to 2016, life expectancy leapt from 46 years to 73 years, far higher than the sub-Saharan African average. The country also has one of the lowest population-growth rates in the region. It's the only country in West Africa with a population of primarily mixed European and African descent. About 40% of the population lives on Santiago – mainly around the capital, Praia. The rest live largely in small towns clustered in the agriculturally productive valleys. As tourism grows, so do the once-tiny populations of arid Sal, Boa Vista and Maio, all of which have seen an influx of foreign residents.

Religion

The vast majority of Cabo Verdeans are Roman Catholic. Evangelical Protestantism is making inroads thanks to the influence of Cabo Verdean expats returning from the US. Traces of African animism remain in the beliefs of even devout Christians.

Music

Much of Cabo Verdean music evolved as a form of protest against slavery and other types of oppression. Today, two kinds of song dominate traditional Cabo Verdean music: *mornas* and *coladeiras*, both built on the sounds of stringed instruments like the fiddle and guitar. As the name suggests, *mornas* (melodic, melancholic music) are mournful songs of *sodade* – an unquenchable longing, often for home. With faster, more upbeat rhythms, *coladeiras*, in contrast, tend to be romantic love songs or else more active expressions of protest. Another popular style is *funaná*, built on fast-paced, Latin-influenced rhythms and underpinned by the accordion. The most African of music and dance styles is *batuko*, with lots of drumming and call-and-response chanting.

Cesária Évora was hands-down the most famous practitioner of *morna* and *coladeiras*. Contemporary musicians to look for include the ensemble groups Simentera and Ferro Gaita, and singers Maria de Barros and Sara Tavares.

Environment

Cabo Verde consists of 10 major islands (nine of them inhabited) and five islets, all of volcanic origin. All are arid or semiarid, but the mountainous islands of Brava, Santiago, Fogo, Santo Antão and São Nicolau – all with peaks over 1000m – catch enough moisture to support grasslands as well as fairly intensive agriculture. Still, only 20% of the total land mass is arable. Maio, Boa Vista and Sal are flatter and almost entirely arid, with long, sandy beaches and desert-like interiors.

Cabo Verde has less fauna than just about anywhere in Africa. Birdlife is a little richer (around 75 species), and includes a good number of endemics (38 species). The frigate bird and the extremely rare razo lark are much sought after by twitchers.

Humpback whales breed in these waters; the peak is March and April. Five endangered species of turtle visit the islands on their way across the Atlantic. Cabo Verde also has the world's third-largest loggerhead turtle nesting population. Nesting takes place from June to October.

SURVIVAL GUIDE

❶ Directory A–Z

ACCOMMODATION

By West African standards, accommodation is expensive in Cabo Verde, especially on Sal and Boa Vista, and in Praia, where prices are around 30% higher than in the rest of the country.

Camping

There are no campsites in Cabo Verde, but camping on remote beaches, and on Santa Luzia, is possible and generally safe (except on Sal, Boa Vista and Santiago).

ACTIVITIES

The main draws in Cabo Verde are windsurfing, kitesurfing, scuba diving and deep-sea fishing on Sal and Boa Vista.

There is trekking in the mountains of São Nicolau, Brava, Fogo and especially Santo Antão. Conditions are generally good throughout the year, though things can get treacherous during the rainiest months of July to September.

Diving

Diving in Cabo Verde is well known for the diversity of species that can be seen, plus a few wrecks; dolphins, whales, sharks and rays are all occasionally seen. Because of currents, not all sites are suitable for beginners or inexperienced divers. The best months are from March to November; Sal and Boa Vista are the best-organised places in which to dive.

Water Sports

Windsurfing and kiteboarding conditions are among the best in the world on Sal, Boa Vista and lesser-known Maio. Ponta Preta on Sal is a world-famous break. The best months are between mid-November and mid-May (particularly January to March, when winds are strong and constant).

Surfing is growing in popularity on Sal and Santiago, though the waves are inconsistent.

CHILDREN

Travel in Cabo Verde can be a great experience for kids. There are gorgeous beaches for fun days in the sun, eerie volcanic landscapes and great walks (including short rambles) amid lush valleys and towering peaks. Plus, locals are apt to lavish attention on young ones.

Logistics of moving around the archipelago can be challenging, so it's wise to plan well – and not to pack in too much travel. Pick one, two or three islands and allow plenty of down time to enjoy the slow pace of Cabo Verdean life.

Travelling with infants and very young children will present the biggest challenges, as baby seats are a rarity for vehicle hire, and high chairs and changing facilities are uncommon. A sturdy pram is essential for sometimes treacherous cobblestone streets and sandy paths.

A few key destinations for kids:

➡ **Sal** Best selection of Western-style restaurants, ample beach activities, resort-style accommodation.

➡ **Boa Vista** Laid-back, walkable centre near pretty beaches. Easy day trips to desert-like interior, an abandoned seaside village and deserted beaches.

➡ **Maio** Play on the beaches with village kids, good local and Italian restaurants.

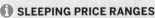

ℹ SLEEPING PRICE RANGES

The following price ranges refer to a double room with bathroom:

$ less than CVE4500

$$ CVE4500-9000

$$$ more than CVE9000

Additionally, São Vicente and Santo Antão make a fine combination, as do Fogo and Brava. Inter-island ferries connect these island pairs on scenic boat rides that last under an hour.

DANGERS & ANNOYANCES

Violent crime is a threat in Praia, where it's highly advisable to take taxis at night, no matter where and how far you're going. Take caution in Mindelo, too, where pickpocketing and muggings are not uncommon.

Some hiking trails have become sites of banditry in recent years, as on Boa Vista and around Tarrafal on Santiago; always ask locals before you set out.

The rest of Cabo Verde is very safe, though petty crime like pickpocketing is always a possibility.

EMBASSIES & CONSULATES

French Embassy (☑ 2604535; www.amba-france-cv.org; Quartier de Prainha, Praia; ⊙ 8am-5.30pm Mon-Thu, to 1pm Fri)

Portuguese Consulate (☑ 2323130; Av 5 de Julho; ⊙ 8.30-11.30am Mon-Fri)

Portuguese Embassy (☑ 2626097; www.praia.embaixadaportugal.mne.pt; Av da OUA, Achada de Santo António; ⊙ 9am-1pm & 3-6pm Mon-Fri)

Senegalese Embassy (☑ 2615621; www.gouv.sn; Rua Dr Manuel Duarte)

US Embassy (☑ 2608900; praia.usembassy.gov; Rua Abilio Macedo 6; ⊙ 8am-5pm Mon-Fri)

EMERGENCY & IMPORTANT NUMBERS

Cabo Verde's country code	☑ 238
Fire	☑ 112
Medical assistance	☑ 112
Police	☑ 112

FOOD

While Cabo Verdean cuisine may include Portuguese niceties such as imported olives and Alentejo wines, it's built on a firm African base, with *milho* (corn) and *feijão* (beans) the ubiquitous staples. Thanks to the large number of Italian tourists and expats, good pizza and pasta dishes are available in even the most out-of-the-way places.

❶ EATING PRICE RANGES

The following price ranges refer to a main course:

$ less than CVE700

$$ CVE700-1200

$$$ more than CVE1200

The Basics

Cabo Verde has a mix of humble family-run eateries and more polished restaurants in tourist destinations. At the most popular restaurants it's best to reserve ahead, especially during peak season (November to March).

→ **Restaurants** Offer a wide mix of dining options including seafood, European fare and local specialities.

→ **Cafes** Good place for snacks and drinks; some offer daily lunch specials.

→ **Hotels & Guesthouses** Sometimes the only place to get a meal in rural areas.

GAY & LESBIAN TRAVELLERS

Cabo Verde has less of the homophobia and open discrimination encountered in other parts of West Africa. Homosexual acts were decriminalised in 2004, and although the LGBT community is largely underground, the islands are fairly tolerant. The most gay-friendly destinations in the archipelago are Santa Maria (Sal) and Mindelo (São Vicente). Mindelo even hosts an annual Gay Pride parade (late June), which first kicked off in 2013.

INTERNET ACCESS

Internet cafes are a rare breed in a country with a growing number of smartphone users, but the main town squares on all major islands in Cabo Verde have free wi-fi. Note that some hotels, even the upscale ones, charge for wi-fi.

❶ PRACTICALITIES

Electricity Voltage is 220V with European-style twin-pronged plugs.

Newspapers *A Semana* (www.asemana .publ.cv), *A Nação* (www.anacao.cv) and *Expresso das Ilhas* (www.expresso dasilhas.sapo.cv) are the weekly newspapers.

Radio & TV Mostly limited to Portugal's, with Portuguese and Brazilian shows as well as Cabo Verde news.

Weights & measures The metric system is used.

MONEY

Most banks change travellers cheques and cash (except the West African CFA), and have ATMs. Credit cards are not widely accepted.

ATMs

Most accept bank cards and Visa, but tthe daily withdrawal limit is CVE20,000.

Cash

The unit of currency is the Cabo Verde escudo (CVE), divided into 100 centavos. It is a stable currency, pegged to the euro. Most businesses also accept euros.

Credit Cards

Not widely accepted (Visa preferable). Even where accepted, there's typically a 3% to 5% commission for credit-card payments.

Exchange Rates

Australia	A$1	CVE76
Canada	C$1	CVE74
Europe	€1	CVE110
Japan	¥100	CVE91
New Zealand	NZ$1	CVE70
UK	UK£1	CVE131
USA	US$	CVE104

Tipping

It's common to tip at restaurants, typically around 5% to 10% of the bill.

OPENING HOURS

Note that for hours posted on shop windows, days are often numbered according to the Portuguese system from 1° to 7° (1° is Sunday, 7° is Saturday).

Banks From 8am to 3pm Monday to Friday.

Businesses Generally 8am to noon and 3pm to 6pm Monday to Friday, and 8am to noon or 1pm Saturday.

Restaurants Mostly open from around noon to 3pm and 7pm to 10pm.

POST

The postal service is cheap, reliable and reasonably quick. Correios (post offices) are generally open 8am to 3pm Monday to Friday, with additional Saturday morning hours in Praia and Mindelo.

PUBLIC HOLIDAYS

New Year's Day 1 January

National Heroes' Day 20 January

Labour Day 1 May

Independence Day 5 July

Assumption Day 15 August

All Saints' Day 1 November

CABO VERDE DIRECTORY A–Z

Immaculate Conception 8 December
Christmas Day 25 December

TELEPHONE

Every number for a fixed telephone line in Cabo Verde has seven digits; all landlines start with '2'. No area code is necessary.

Don't expect to rely on public telephones. Most are gone or don't work.

Mobile Phones

Mobile-phone reception is excellent, and numbers are seven digits long.

If bringing a phone from home with roaming facilities, it will connect automatically.

Local SIM cards (from CVE100) are available at all mobile phone offices and will work with unlocked phones, as is credit to use data on a smartphone. Credit is available in multiples of CVE100, and start at CVE100.

TOURIST INFORMATION

Do your planning in advance of your trip to Cabo Verde. On the islands, tourist information is limited. Mindelo (São Vicente), Santa Maria (Sal) and Tarrafal (Santiago) all have helpful info kiosks. Elsewhere, the best source of information is often the guesthouse where you stay. You can get an overview of the islands at the country's tourism website, www.turismo.cv.

VISAS

The one-month tourist visa for Cabo Verde is available on arrival at the airports and at the ports of Praia and Sal. The €25 fee is payable in euros only – it helps to bring the exact money.

Visa Extensions

Technically, there's a fine of CVE15,000 if you let your Cabo Verdean visa expire; in reality, if you're only a little over nobody is likely to care.

For an extension you need, in theory, to fill in a form, supply a photo and lodge the application at the **Direcção de Emigração e Fronteiras** (☑ 2611845; Rua Serpa Pinto, Praia; ☉ 9am-4pm Mon-Fri); in reality, staff members here are likely to be highly confused if you turn up requesting an extension!

VOLUNTEERING

It's helpful to have some Portuguese or better yet Crioulo (Creole) skills before approaching volunteer organisations. **SOS Tartarugas** (www.sostartarugas.org) accepts volunteers for conservation programs on Sal, Boa Vista and Maio.

A few other organizations that occasionally list volunteer opportunities in Cabo Verde include the following:

Frontier (www.frontier.ac.uk)
Idealist (www.idealist.org)
Worldwide Volunteering (http://worldwidevolunteering.org)

ℹ Getting There & Away

Most international flights land on Sal or Santiago, though there are also international flights arriving in Boa Vista and São Vicente.

AIR

International flights arrive at the following airports:

Aeroporto Internacional Amílcar Cabral, Sal (www.asa.cv/aeroportos/aeroporto-internacional-amilcar-cabral)

Aeroporto Internacional da Praia Nelson Mandela, Santiago (www.asa.cv/aeroportos/aeroporto-da-praia)

Aeroporto Internacional da Boa Vista Aristides Pereira, Boa Vista (www.asa.cv/aeroportos/aeroporto-da-boavista)

Aeroporto Internacional Césaria Évora, São Vicente (www.asa.cv/aeroportos/aeroporto-internacional-cesaria-evora)

TACV (https://flytacv.com) is the national carrier of Cabo Verde and connects the islands with Lisbon (Portugal), Dakar (Senegal), Bissau (Guinea-Bissau), Providence (USA), Amsterdam, Fortaleza (Brazil) and Paris. TACV also offers inter-island flights.

Other airlines include TAP (p76) and the various charter airlines that fly to Sal and Boa Vista from the UK, Germany and Italy.

ℹ Getting Around

AIR

TACV (https://flytacv.com) serves seven of the nine inhabited islands of Cabo Verde, except Brava and Santo Antão. You can purchase tickets at travel agents or online, and it's wise

---

ℹ ARRIVING IN CABO VERDE

Aeroporto Internacional Amílcar Cabral (Sal) Taxis charge CVE1000 to CVE1200 for the 30-minute trip into Santa Maria. If you're travelling light, you can catch a colectivo by walking five minutes out to the main highway and flagging one down.

Aeroporto Internacional da Praia Nelson Mandela (Santiago) A taxi to Praia costs CVE1000 for the 30-minute trip.

Aeroporto Internacional da Boa Vista Aristides Pereira (Boa Vista) A taxi into Sal Rei costs about CVE600 and takes about 15 minutes.

Aeroporto Internacional Césaria Évora (São Vicente) A taxi costs CVE1000 for the 30-minute journey.

to book in advance as flights can fill up in peak season.

Inter-island flights are generally not expensive. Sample one-way fares with tax include the following:

FLIGHT	COST (CVE)	TIME	FREQUENCY
Praia to São Vicente	5100-8600	55min	1-2 daily
Praia to Maio	4500-5100	20min	2 weekly
São Vicente to Sal	5100-8600	50min	5 weekly
Sal to Boa Vista	4300-5500	30min	5 weekly

Newly launched at time of research, **Binter Canarias** (www.bintercanarias.com) offers inter-island flights around Cabo Verde. Early plans were to connect Santiago, São Vicente and Sal, though eventually the airline intends to fly to all seven islands that have operational airports.

BOAT

The only reliable scheduled ferry services in Cabo Verde are between Praia, Brava and Fogo; Praia and Maio; and Mindelo (São Vicente) and Santo Antão. There's less frequent service (twice monthly) from Praia to São Vicente via São Nicolau.

Seas can be rough and the crossings rocky, especially during winter months.

There are cafes on board the bigger boats, but it's always a good idea to bring a reserve of water and snacks.

CAR & MOTORCYCLE

You can rent cars on many Cabo Verdean islands, but the only three that make the expense worth it are Santiago, Boa Vista and possibly Fogo. Cars cost from CVE5000 per day, including tax and insurance.

Consider a 4WD, especially on Boa Vista, as conditions are rough once you get off the few main roads.

MINIBUS

Ranging from comfortable vans to pick-up trucks with narrow wooden benches, minibuses – known as colectivos or *alugueres* – provide connections between even relatively small towns on most islands.

TAXIS

Taxis are generally plentiful in Cabo Verde, with round-town fares rarely topping CVE300. Airport runs and excursions are more costly.

Cameroon

🕿 237 / POP 24.4 MILLION

Best Places to Eat

➜ Saga African Restaurant (p115)

➜ Iya (p116)

➜ La Fourchette (p115)

➜ La Paillote (p109)

Best Places to Sleep

➜ Foyer du Marin (p113)

➜ Bird Watchers' Club (p117)

➜ Hotel Ilomba (p124)

➜ Hotel Akwa Palace (p114)

Why Go?

Cameroon is Africa's throbbing heart, a crazed, sultry mosaic of active volcanoes, white-sand beaches, thick rainforest and magnificent parched landscapes broken up by the bizarre rock formations of the Sahel. With both Francophone and Anglophone regions, not to mention some 250 local languages, the country is a vast ethnic and linguistic jigsaw, yet one that, in contrast to so many of its neighbours, enjoys a great deal of stability.

With reasonable road infrastructure, travel is a lot easier here than in many parts of Africa. Still, you'll miss none of those indicators that you're in the middle of this fascinating continent: everyone seems to be carrying something on their heads, *makossa* music sets the rhythm, the street smells like roasting plantains and African bliss is just a piece of grilled fish and a sweating beer away.

When to Go
Yaoundé

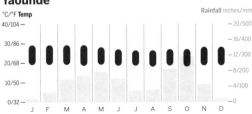

Nov–Feb High season; dry but not too hot.

Mar & Oct Light rains in the grasslands in March. In the north temperatures can reach 40°C.

Apr–Oct Intense rainfall; road travel is slow, muddy and at times impossible.

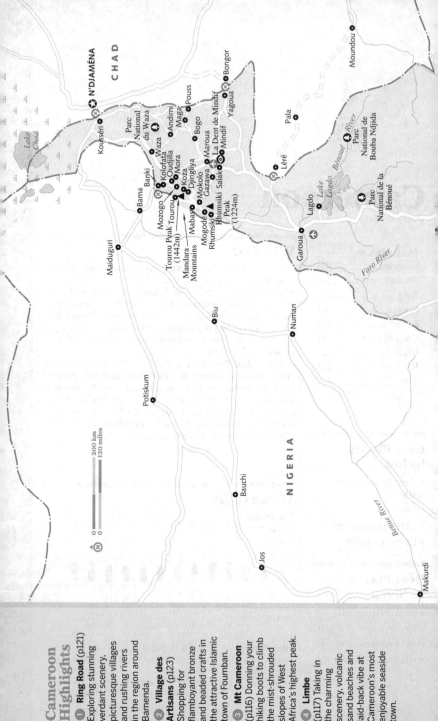

Cameroon Highlights

1 Ring Road (p121)
Exploring stunning verdant scenery, picturesque villages and rushing rivers in the region around Bamenda.

2 Village des Artisans (p123)
Shopping for flamboyant bronze and beaded crafts in the attractive Islamic town of Foumban.

3 Mt Cameroon (p116) Donning your hiking boots to climb the mist-shrouded slopes of West Africa's highest peak.

4 Limbe (p17) Taking in the charming scenery, volcanic sand beaches and laid-back vibe at Cameroon's most enjoyable seaside town.

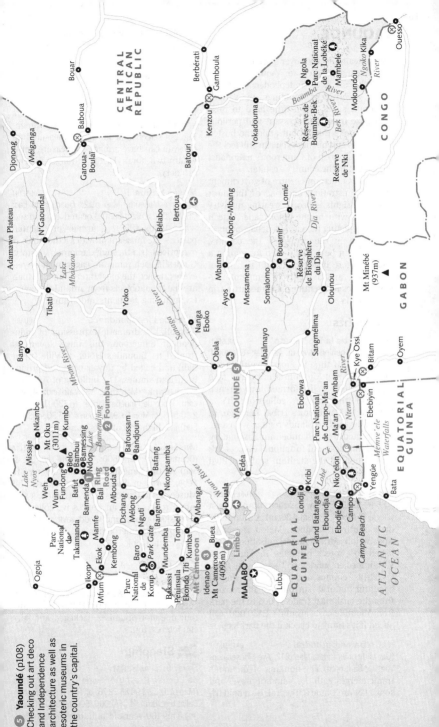

5 Yaoundé (p108)
Checking out art deco
and independence
architecture as well as
esoteric museums in
the country's capital.

YAOUNDÉ

POP 3 MILLION

Dramatically spread over seven hills, the rapidly expanding city of Yaoundé features a host of art deco, independence-era and 1970s government buildings in various exuberant styles. It's a little hard to raise your gaze from the incessant and perilous traffic to take this in, but amid the busted pavements and hustlers you can still feel the confident flourish of Cameroon's nationalist movement in the country's capital.

This is Cameroon's centre of government and administration, and one of the most attractive sights is people wearing ministry uniforms, with bright tailor-made African fabrics depicting the various departments.

Located in the centre of the country, Yaoundé can be a useful stop for getting a visa or before heading off into the rest of Cameroon, and a relatively temperate climate makes it a gentler place to start a trip than Douala.

◉ Sights

★ **Musée de la Blackitude** MUSEUM
(Map p112; behind Blvd du 20 Mai; CFA2000; ◷ 9am-6pm) If time is short, give the overpriced National Museum a miss, and take a passionately well-informed tour (French only) of this private collection. It's a homage to Cameroon's tribal heritage, in particular the Grasslands region, with a reconstructed royal chamber and fascinating sacred, musical and functional objects. It's tucked behind the stadium seats on Blvd du 20 Mai.

★ **Mefou National Park** NATURE RESERVE
(☑ 6 99 51 30 73; www.apeactionafrica.org; Metet village; CFA7500; ◷ 9am-4.30pm) A 45-minute drive south of Yaoundé, Mefou is run by Ape Action Africa, an organisation established to protect primates in Cameroon. Well-informed guides will show you gorillas, drills, chimps and mandrills living in beautiful natural surrounds, all rescued from the bushmeat trade. A taxi to the park from Yaoundé costs around CFA50,000; call ahead if it's rainy to check if the park's open.

Nôtre Dame Cathedral CATHEDRAL
(Our Lady of Victories; Map p112; Ave Monseigneur Vogt; ◷ 8am-6pm) The honking of Yaoundé's traffic merges with the sound of prayer and song at Nôtre Dame Cathedral. It's a bold triangular building, consecrated in 1955, with a stunning Afrocentric mosaic above the altar.

Marché Central MARKET
(Map p112; Ave Ahidjo; ◷ 7am-7pm Wed-Mon, 1pm-7pm Tue) The market is housed in a dramatic brutalist building in central Yaoundé, with towering floors of fabric and garment sellers and a bank of tailors. It can feel overwhelming, but select some fabric, get measured up and you can have a made-to-measure outfit within two hours. Factor in longer for embroidery.

Musée National MUSEUM
(National Museum; Map p112; Quartier du Lac; CFA10,000; ◷ 9am-6pm) Located in a grand white 1930s villa – a former presidential palace – the museum provides a thorough, if overpriced, trip through Cameroon's history. Guides in each room are eager to show you every artefact, the most interesting of which are the tribal objects from around the country, including garments and drums.

Place de l'Indépendance SQUARE
(Map p112) A dramatic expression of independent Cameroon, this huge square is fronted by Yaoundé's Hôtel de Ville (town hall) and edged by flower beds and proudly African statues. The building of **Afriland First Bank** (Map p112; www.afrilandfirstbank. com; Place de l'Indépendance; ◷ 7.30-11.45am & 2.30-5.45pm Mon-Fri, 9am-noon & 4-5.30pm Sat & Sun) is a highlight of the square.

Musée d'Art Camerounais MUSEUM
(Quartier Fébé; CFA1500; ◷ 3-6pm Thu, Sat & Sun) At the Benedictine monastery on Mt Fébé, north of Yaoundé's city centre, the Musée d'Art Camerounais has three exhibition rooms with an impressive collection of masks, bronze- and woodwork and other examples of Cameroonian art. The chapel is also worth a look.

☞ Tours

Safar Tours TOURS
(Map p112; www.safartours.com; Blvd du 20 Mai; ◷ 9am-6pm) Located at the Hilton Hotel, this tour operator organises packaged and special interest tours.

🛏 Sleeping

Foyer International de l'Église Presbytérienne HOSTEL $
(Map p110; ☑ 2 99 85 23 76; off Rue Joseph Essono Balla; tent/dm/s/d CFA2000/5000/8000/10,000; ℗) This 100-year-old building has two fair-

ly uninviting private rooms and two eight-bed dorms, all of which share the same very basic bathrooms. Campers can set up their own tents in the garden where there's a bonfire pit. From the main road, walk to the right of the water towers, and it's in the second brick house on your left.

Ideal Hotel   HOTEL $

(Map p110; ☎ 2 22 66 95 37; idealhotel72@yahoo.fr; Carrefour Nlongkak; d CFA8000-10,000, apt CFA15,000; P) Rooms here are decent enough for the low price, though there's no hot water and rooms are fan cooled. Balconies in some make up for a general lack of light (plus you get Yaoundé smog for free). If you're visa-hunting, this is well located for embassies.

Central Hotel   HOTEL $$

(Map p112; ☎ 2 22 22 65 98; Quartier des Ministères; d CFA32,000; P ❋) Central indeed, but miraculously tucked away from Yaoundé traffic in a spacious courtyard garden in the ministerial district. Rooms are threadbare but clean with large balconies: this old-fashioned and modestly welcoming place is one of the city's best bargains. Have something to eat or sink a beer at the pavilion restaurant opposite.

Prestige Hotel   HOTEL $$

(Map p110; ☎ 2 22 31 82 52; Ave Charles Atangana; d CFA22,000; ❋ 🛜) This sprawling and rather raucous hotel has good-value rooms and is handily located for buses from Yaoundé to Douala. Rooms are on the small side, but they're fairly clean and secure, and many have balconies. There's a popular bar and restaurant on the site, too, but also lots of traffic noise.

Tou'ngou Hotel   HOTEL $$

(Map p110; ☎ 2 22 20 10 25; www.toungouhotel.com; Rue Onembele Nkou; s/d/ste incl breakfast CFA23,000/30,000/45,000; P ❋ 🛜) One of Yaoundé's better-value midrange hotels, the Tou'ngou is a relatively smart and popular option. The rooms are comfortable and clean, the location is central and there's a good restaurant with a dramatic terrace view. It's best to book ahead.

Merina Hotel   HOTEL $$$

(Map p112; ☎ 6 55 09 94 98; hotelmerina@cameroun-plus.com; Ave Ahidjo; s & d CFA38,000-45,000; P ❋ 🛜 🏊) Located right in the heart of Yaoundé, the smart Merina has a fancy orchid-strewn lobby, modern and comfortable rooms and good service. Other perks include a free airport-shuttle service and small pool.

 Eating

Around Carrefours Bastos and Nlongkak there are grills serving brochettes (kebabs) throughout the day. On Place de l'Indépendance, you can get delicious grilled fish with chilli or peanut sauce from CFA1000. Yaoundé excels at bustling patisseries, and there are several decent eating places.

Calafatas   PATISSERIE $

(Map p112; ☎ 2 22 23 17 29; www.calafatas.com; Rue de Nachtigal; baked goods CFA200-2000) Concealed in a synthetic wooden cabin but founded way back in 1935, this is Yaoundé's best bakery, selling scrumptious madeleines, palmiers and croissants.

Le Sintra   INTERNATIONAL $

(Map p112; Ave Kennedy; dishes CFA3000-5000; ⊙ 6am-11pm Mon-Sat) With a friendly welcome, a faint whiff of colonial atmosphere and a pleasant screened terrace in the heart of Yaoundé, La Sintra does a full breakfast menu, Italian and Cameroonian cuisine, as well as delicious French dishes such as *crevettes à la provençale* (shrimps cooked in garlic).

Patisserie Select Plus   BAKERY $

(Map p112; Ave Monseigneur Vogt; baked goods CFA200-1500; ⊙ 24hr) This bustling bakery near Yaoundé's cathedral sells a delicious line of freshly baked croissants, *beignets* (pastries) and sandwiches which you can consume at stand-up tables by the window. Other treats include pizzas, burgers and coffee to go.

Le Biniou   CRÊPES $

(Map p112; ☎ 6 99 50 31 68; off Pl de l'Indépendance; pancakes CFA3800; ⊙ 10am-midnight Mon-Fri & Sun) Well located near the Afriland First Bank (p108), in a gated enclosure with a terrace enclosed by greenery. Sweet and savoury pancakes are a speciality, as well as Cameroonian meat and fish dishes.

★ La Paillote   VIETNAMESE $$

(Map p110; Rue Joseph Essono Balla; mains CFA3500-6000; ⊙ noon-2pm & 7-10pm; ❋ 🍴) This stylish Vietnamese restaurant has a charming shaded terrace and a smart dining room inside, both of which attract a loyal crowd of Yaoundé expats. The dishes are delicious and service is excellent. The iced coffee and spring rolls are a treat.

Istanbul   TURKISH $$

(Map p110; Rue Joseph Mballa Eloumden; mains CFA4500; ⊙ 8am-11pm; ❋ 🍴) Fresh and

Yaoundé

MAP KEY / LOCATIONS

- Pharmacie Bastos (A1)
- Canadian Embassy (400m) (B1)
- Routière d'Etoudi (3km) (D1)
- 12 — Rue 1805 (B1)
- 13 — (C1)
- Rue 1816 (C1)
- 11 — (C1)
- Rue 1815 (C1)
- Rue de l'URSS (B1)
- Carrefour Bastos (B2)
- 6 — (A2)
- Blvd de l'URSS (B2)
- 5 — (B2)
- 10 — (B2)
- Rue Joseph Mballa Eloumden (B2)
- 15 — (B2)
- Rue 1810 (C2)
- Rue 1863 (C2)
- 9 — (D2)
- BASTOS (C2)
- NLONGKAK (D2)
- Rue Mbono (C2)
- Rue Marcus Etoundi (C3)
- Rue Albert Ateba Ebé (C3)
- DJOUNGOLO (D3)
- Rue Fouda Ngono (A2)
- Rue Zoégo Fou da Ngono (B3)
- 2 — Carrefour Nlongkak (C3)
- 4 — (D3)
- Rue Onembele Nkou (C3)
- Water Towers (C3)
- Pl Etoa-Meki (D3)
- Ave du 27 Août (A3)
- 1 — (D3)
- ETOA-MEKI (D4)
- Rue Joseph Essono Balla (D4)
- Rue Hayabou Hammoa (A4)
- Rue Sabastien Essomba (B4)
- Rue Briqueterie (B4)
- MESSA (A4)
- 8 — (C4)
- 14 — (C4)
- Ave Charles de Gaulle (C4)
- SGBC Bank (C4)
- Rue Djoungolo (C4)
- Rue Frédéric Foe (C4)
- 7 — (D4)
- BRIQUETERIE (B4)
- Ave Konrad Adenauer (C4)
- Rue du Cercle Municipal (C5)
- Ave Churchill (C4)
- Polyclinique André Fouda (350m) (D4)
- ELIG ESSONO (D5)
- Gare Voyageurs (Central Train Station) (D5)
- Blvd Manga Bell (B5)
- Samba (B5)
- Rue de Narvik (C5)
- Ave de l'Indépendance (C5)
- Rue Paul Martin (A6)
- QUARTIER DU LAC (B6)
- Rue Mpondo Akwa (B6)
- Ave Foch (C5)
- Rond-Point du Blvd 20 Mai (B6)
- CENTRE VILLE (C6)
- Ave Marchand (Ave des Ministères) (B6)
- Blvd du 20 Mai (C6)
- Ave Ahidjo (C6)
- Ave Kennedy (D6)
- Ave Monseigneur Vogt (D6)
- Place Melen (A6)
- MELEN (A6)
- Mvog-Betsi Zoo (1.5km) (A6)
- Blvd Réunification (A7)
- PLATEAU D'ATEMENGUE (A7)
- See Central Yaounde Map (p112) (B7)
- Pl Ahmadou Ahidjo (C7)
- French Embassy (1.9km) (B7)
- 3 — (C7)
- Central Voyages (800m); Guaranti Express (800m); Nsimalen (18km) (D7)

Scale: 0 — 500 m / 0 — 0.25 miles

Yaoundé

🛏 Sleeping
1 Foyer International de l'Église
    Presbytérienne.................................D3
2 Ideal Hotel..C3
3 Prestige Hotel....................................D7
4 Tou'ngou Hotel..................................D3

🍴 Eating
5 Chez Wou..B2
6 Istanbul B1
7 La Paillote D4

ℹ Information
8 British High Commission C4
9 Central African Republic Embassy D1
10 Chadian Embassy B2
11 Congolese Embassy C1
12 Equatorial Guinean Embassy C1
13 Gabonese Embassy C1
14 German Consulate.............................. C4
15 Nigerian Embassy...............................B2

well-prepared Turkish food is served up swiftly at this smart terrace restaurant (with an even smarter inside dining room complete with white tablecloths and silver service). Takeaway is available.

Chez Wou   CHINESE **$$**
(Map p110; Rue Joseph Mballa Eloumden; mains from CFA4500; ☺noon-3.30pm & 6-11pm) One of Yaoundé's older Chinese restaurants, this one has nice tables set under a wide porch, and a comprehensive menu. It's good if you're ready for a change from Cameroonian food: try the ginger-and-garlic prawns.

☆ Entertainment

★Institut Français   ARTS CENTRE
(Map p112; ☑ 2 22 22 09 44; www.ifcameroun.com/category/yaounde; 140 Ave du Président Ahmadou Ahidjo; ☺8.30am-1pm & 3-6pm Mon-Fri plus evening events; ☎) With a hip, graffitied exterior and a culturally buzzing interior, this is a relaxed spot to catch a film or music event, see an exhibition or have a drink or food at the in-house Café de France. There's a good library of French titles to browse.

ℹ Information

DANGERS & ANNOYANCES
Western visitors in Yaoundé are conspicuous, and muggings happen, though you'll be the object of lots of friendly attention, too. Daytime is generally fine, but take taxis at night and be

particularly wary around the Marché Central and tourist hotels.

INTERNET ACCESS
Your best bet for internet in Yaoundé is the smarter hotels and restaurants for a wireless connection. Try also **Cometé Internet** (Map p112; Rue de Narvik; ☺8pm-6pm).

MEDICAL SERVICES
Pharmacie Bastos (Map p110; ☑ 2 22 20 65 55; Carrefour Bastos; ☺8am-6pm) Well-stocked pharmacy.

Polyclinique André Fouda (☑ 2 22 23 30 38; Route De Ngousso; ☺8am-6pm) For medical emergencies; in Elig Essono, southeast of Carrefour Nlongkak.

MONEY
There are ATMs at most of the major banks in Yaoundé. As always in Cameroon, travellers cheques are problematic to change in banks – try the banks around the cathedral.

Bicec Bank (Map p112; Ave Ahidjo; ☺8am-3.30pm Mon-Fri) Has an ATM.

Express Exchange (Map p112; Ave Kennedy; ☺8.30pm-6pm Mon-Sat) For money changing.

SCB (Map p112; near Place Ahmadou Ahidjo; ☺8.30am-3.30pm Mon-Fri) Money exchange and ATM.

SGBC Bank (Map p110; Ave Charles de Gaulle; ☺8am–3.30pm Mon–Fri) Has an ATM.

Standard Chartered Bank (Map p112; Ave de l'Indépendance; ☺8am–3pm Mon–Fri) Has an ATM.

POST
Central Post Office (Map p112; Pl Ahmadou Ahidjo; ☺7.30am-3.30pm Mon-Fri, 7.30am-noon Sat)

ℹ Getting There & Away

AIR
Yaoundé's airport is Yaoundé Nsimalen International Airport, although far more international services go to and from Douala. Internal flights with **Camair-Co** (☑ 2 33 50 55 00; www.camair-co.cm) connect Yaoundé to Douala daily (CFA45,000, 45 minutes) and other cities.

BUS
There are buses between Yaoundé and all major cities in Cameroon. Buses leave from their companies' offices, spread out on the outskirts of town. For Douala (CFA3000 to CFA6000, three to four hours, three to five daily), **Central Voyages** (☑ 2 22 30 39 94; Carrefour Coron, Mvog-Mbi; ☺6am-10pm) and **Guaranti Express** (☑ 6 77 08 41 08; Blvd de l'Oua, Quartier Nsam; ☺6am-10pm) are recommended. Guaranti Express is also recommended for travel to

Central Yaoundé

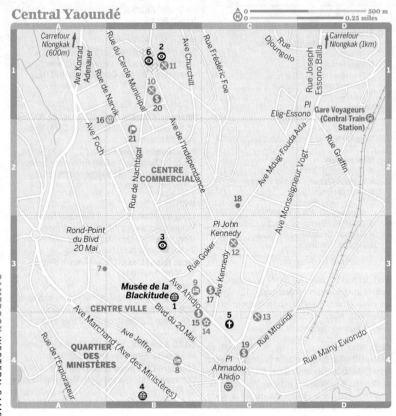

Limbe (CFA5000, five hours, three to four daily), Bamenda (CFA5000, six hours, two daily), Bafoussam (CFA2500, three hours, two daily) and Kumba (CFA4000, four hours, two daily).

Otherwise, all agency and nonagency buses for Kribi, Bertoua, Batouri, Ebolowa, Limbe and Buea depart from Blvd de l'Ocam, about 3km south of Pl Ahmadou Ahidjo (direct taxi drivers to Agences de Mvan; fare is around CFA1000).

Transport to Bafoussam, Bamenda and points north departs from Gare Routière d'Etoudi, 5km north of Centre Ville. Taxi fare there costs around CFA1500.

TRAIN

There are also two daily services between Yaoundé and Douala (1st/2nd class CFA9000/3600), though these are used much less frequently, as buses are cheaper, faster and more convenient. A major derailment in 2016 caused many deaths, so travel on the service can't be recommended at this time.

❶ Getting Around

Shared taxis and *moto-taxis* (motorbike taxis) are the only public-transport option in Yaoundé. Fares are CFA200 per place for short- to medium-length rides. A private taxi to Nsimalen airport from central Yaoundé should cost CFA4000 to CFA6000 (40 minutes).

WESTERN CAMEROON

Imagine Africa: wormy red tracks and vegetation so intensely green you can almost taste the colour. This image comes alive in Western Cameroon. The country's economic heart intermittently beats in Douala, and from here it's a short hop to the haze and laze of beach towns like Limbe and the savannah-carpeted slopes of the magnificent Mountain of Thunder – Mt Cameroon. In the Anglophone northwest you can slip between sunburnt green hills while exploring a patchwork of secret societies, traditional chiefdoms and some of the country's best arts and crafts, particularly the wooden masks that are so often associated with this continent.

Douala

POP 2.9 MILLION

Sticky and frenetic, Douala isn't as bad as some say, but it's not likely to be your first choice for a honeymoon, either. By any measurement but political power this is Cameroon's main city. It's the primary air hub and a leading business centre with a major port, and the result is a chaotic hodgepodge. There is some charm in the street life and battered Independence architecture, though, and here you can set your finger on Cameroon's pulse.

◎ Sights

Espace Doual'art　　　　　MUSEUM
(www.doualart.org; Pl du Gouvernement, Bonanjo; ◎9am-7pm Mon-Sat) FREE Well worth dropping into if you're nearby in Douala, this contemporary art space hosts changing displays of work from all over Cameroon and the rest of Africa. There's a cafe here too, and it's a good introduction to the city's small art scene.

◎ Sleeping

Centre d'Accueil Missionaire　　HOSTEL $
(Procure; ☎2 33 42 27 97; aprocure@yahoo.fr; Rue Franqueville; s CFA10,000, without shower CFA8000, d/tr CFA14,000/18,000; ⓟ❄🛜🏊) Praise be to this Catholic mission in Douala, with its clean if basic upstairs rooms, pleasant veranda and lovely pool. A convenient laundry service and an excellent location seal the deal. You'll be woken by the harmonious sound of hymns from the mission church.

★Foyer du Marin　　　　GUESTHOUSE $$
(☎2 33 42 27 94; Rue Gallieni; s/d/apt CFA27,000/30,000/45,000; ⓟ❄@🏊) Definitely the best-value accommodation in Douala, the German Seaman's Mission is a literal oasis of tranquillity in the city centre. It's set in a gorgeous garden with a pool and terrific views towards the port, the rooms are comfortable and spacious, and the restaurant (p114) serves up delicious poolside food all day long. Book ahead.

Hotel Majestic　　　　　　HOTEL $$
(☎2 33 42 87 34; ngatcherv1@yahoo.fr; Blvd de la Liberté; d CFA25,000; ❄🛜) You can expect quite a bit of noise at this otherwise good-value hotel; as well as the traffic on Douala's main avenue outside, there's an incredibly loud music shop downstairs blaring out pop music all day. That said, rooms are clean and comfortable, each coming with a fridge, TV and modern bathroom.

Hotel Beausejour Mirabel　　HOTEL $$
(☎6 50 60 62 57; www.beausejour-mirabel.com; Rue Joffre; d CFA30,000-60,000; ❄🛜) Centrally located and with very friendly staff, the Beausejour was once quite a smart place, as evidenced by its impressive facade and former rooftop pool. It's fallen on less glamorous times, but the rooms have balconies and are clean and spacious, while downstairs there's wi-fi and a good on-site restaurant, making it one of Douala's best midrange options.

CAMEROON DOUALA

Douala

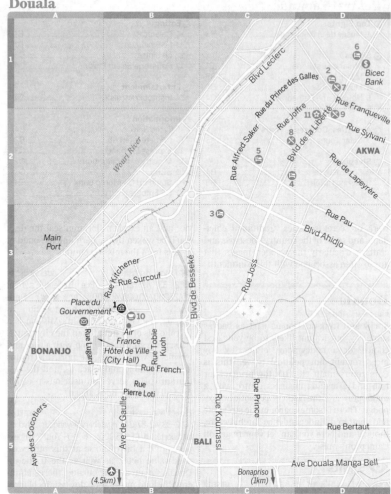

CAMEROON DOUALA

Hotel Akwa Palace　　　LUXURY HOTEL **$$$**
(☑ 2 33 42 26 01; www.hotel-akwa-palace.
com; Blvd de la Liberté; d CFA120,000-180,000;
🅿✳@🛜🏊) If money's not a concern then
this is still the best choice in town, if for
nothing else than its superb location in the
heart of things in Douala. Rooms are plush
and stylish, staff are helpful, and the vast
swimming pool in the back garden is the
best place to forget the chaos outside. The
marble- and wood-lined lobby is a good
place for a cool drink.

🍴 Eating

Zepol　　　BAKERY, EATERY **$**
(Blvd de la Liberté; baked goods CFA500-4000;
⊙24hr) The best and most stylish takeaway
patisserie and *boulangerie* (bakery) in town,
founded 1968. The wood-lined interior is
decorated with carnival masks. There's also
a small supermarket here.

Foyer du Marin　　　EUROPEAN **$$**
(☑2 33 42 27 94; Rue Gallieni; mains CFA4000-
8000; ⊙8am-10pm) It's worth making a detour for the nightly grill at this hotel; great
kebabs, steaks, chicken, seafood dishes and

decked out, with an open-air area at the front and a cool glass-fronted dining room behind.

★**La Fourchette** INTERNATIONAL $$$
(🖉 2 33 43 26 11; Rue Franqueville; mains CFA7000-18,000; ⊙ noon-11pm Mon-Sat) A smart and tasteful option, La Fourchette's menu is out of this world if you're used to the more normal Cameroonian choice of chicken or fish. Here you'll find steak tartare, grilled zebu fillet, goat's-cheese ravioli and stuffed crab, with prices to match. Service is charmingly formal, you should dress to impress and booking ahead is a good idea.

🍸 Drinking & Nightlife

Douala has a lively nightlife scene, though much of it can be inaccessible to visitors without local contacts. The areas of Bonapriso, Bonanjo and Akwa contain the most bars and clubs.

Café des Palabres CAFE
(Pl du Gouvernement; mains around CFA8000; ⊙ 7.30am-11pm Mon-Sat; 🖙) Housed inside a 1905 colonial German residence, this charming cafe-restaurant on Bonanjo's main square has a great garden terrace perfect for an evening drink, as well as a cool interior with a full menu and an intellectual vibe. Literary types might like to know this building was identified as 'la Pagode' in Céline's *Journey to the End of the Night*.

---

juicy German sausage are all well prepared, and served up by the friendly staff at poolside tables under thatched rondavels. This is also a great drinking spot, with fresh fruit juice as well as beers.

Saga African Restaurant AFRICAN $$
(Blvd de la Liberté; mains CFA4000-7000; ⊙ noon-11pm) Atmospheric and upmarket, the Saga offers an interesting mix of African dishes with some local classics, such as *ndole* (a dish made with bitter leaves similar to spinach and flavoured with smoked fish), plus pizza, Chinese and pasta dishes. It's nicely

CAMEROON DOUALA

☆ Entertainment

Institut Français   ARTS CENTRE
(☑ 6 79 26 33 51; www.ifcameroun.com/category/
douala; Blvd de la Liberté; ⊙ 8am-6pm Mon-Sat,
plus evening events) A popular creative space
for theatre, dance, movies, debates and
workshops. It also runs a Nuit Blanche program, and dance and music festivals. Get a
drink or a coffee here, and eat at the Café
de France.

🛍 Shopping

★ Marché des Fleurs   MARKET
(Rue Dominique Savio, Bonapriso, entrance opposite
Star Land Hotel; ⊙ 9am-4pm) A huge, atmospheric complex of roofed stalls selling crafts
from around Cameroon, but mainly the
grasslands region. You can buy wonderful
masks, baskets, jewellery, batik clothes and
tablecloths. On the airport-road side of the
market, large ornamental garden plants are
sold in glorious profusion, with cut-flower
bouquets lining the Star Land Hotel side.

ℹ Information

Muggings happen: if you'd rather be safe than
sorry, after dark it's recommended to take a taxi.
Leave valuables in a safe place, and be extra
careful around nightspots.

For changing money, try the banks along Blvd
de la Liberté, such as **Bicec** (Blvd de la Liberté;
⊙ 8am–5pm Mon–Fri), or Rue Joss; most have
ATMs.

The **Central Post Office** (⊙ 7.30am–5pm
Mon–Fri) is on Rue joss.

ℹ Getting There & Away

Douala has an **international airport** (☑ 2 33 42
35 77; 10km west of Douala) with links to cities
in Cameroon, around the region and to Europe.
There's an **Air France office** (1 Pl du Gouvernement; ⊙ 8am-12.30pm & 3-6pm Mon-Fri, 8am-
noon Sat) in town.

Arriving from Limbe by bus, ask to be dropped
at Rompoint, which is fairly central.

Buses to Yaoundé (CFA3000 to CFA6000,
three to four hours) depart throughout the day
from agency offices along Blvd de l'Unité such as
Guaranti Express (Blvd de la Liberté; ⊙ 6am-
10pm). For buses to Kribi (CFA2000, three
hours, four to five daily) use **Centrale Voyages**
(Blvd Ahidjo; ⊙ 6am-10pm).

For other destinations, use the sprawling **Gare
Routière Bonabéri** (15km north of Douala, Bonabéri). There are at least five departures daily
for destinations including Limbe (CFA3000,
1½ hours), Bamenda (CFA4500, seven hours),

Bafoussam (CFA3500, five hours) and Foumban
(CFA3500, six hours).

ℹ Getting Around

The main ways of getting around Douala are
shared taxis and *moto-taxi*, of which there are
thousands; they are both cheaper than taxis
(CFA100 to CFA200 per short ride). Charter taxis
from central Douala to Bonabéri (30 minutes)
generally charge CFA3000. A taxi to the airport
costs CFA3000 (20 minutes).

Buea

POP 95,000

Basically built into the side of Mt Cameroon, Buea (pronounced *boy*-ah) has a hill
station's coolness, especially compared to
sticky Limbe. If you're going up the mountain, you're inevitably coming to this little
university town.

The **Mount Cameroon Intercommunal
Ecotourism Board** (Mount CEO; ☑ 2 33 32 20
38; www.facebook.com/mountceo; Buea Market;
⊙ 7.30am-5pm Mon-Fri, 7.30am-1pm Sat & Sun)
provides respected mountain guides for the
climb up Mt Cameroon. Its goal is to promote ecotourism and biodiversity conservation. The office also has a small shop selling
locally produced handicrafts.

🛏 Sleeping

Paramount Hotel   HOTEL $
(☑ 2 33 32 20 74; Molyko Rd; s/d/tr CFA7000/
9000/11,000; 🅿) This is one of the better
places to sleep in Buea. The large and pretty
rooms come with TV and are a nice respite
from the mountain. To get here, turn left off
the main road from town and continue some
way up the hill and you'll find the hotel on
your right.

Presbyterian Mission   GUESTHOUSE $
(☑ 2 33 32 23 36; Market Rd; campsites
CFA1000, s/d CFA4000/6000, without bathroom
CFA3000/5000; 🅿) This church mission is
set in attractive gardens and has comfy and
spotless rooms, a tidy communal sitting
room and cooking facilities. It's up the hill
from Buea's police station.

🍴 Eating

★ Iya   FUSION $$
(☑ 6 65 00 10 00; www.iyabuea.com; former Alli-
ance Franco, Grand Stand; mains CFA3000-6500;
⊙ 11am-11pm Mon-Sat; 🅿 ❄ 🛜) A rarity in Cam-
eroon: a stylish restaurant with warm atten-

tive service. The minimal interior has white walls brightened with feathered hats and geometric basketwork from the northwest highlands. The menu is also traditional with a contemporary twist, featuring imaginative reinterpretations of Cameroonian standards. *Ndole* and *kati-kati* (marinated chicken) never looked – or tasted – this good.

ℹ Information

Conveniently, Buea's **Express Exchange** (Molyko Rd) will exchange euros, US dollars and travellers cheques.

ℹ Getting There & Away

From Buea's frenetic bus station at Mile 17, there are regular departures for Limbe (CFA800, 25 minutes), and points north.

Limbe

POP 88,000

Limbe is a charming place, blessed with a fabulous natural position between the rainforest-swathed foothills of Mt Cameroon and the dramatic Atlantic coastline. Popular with both foreign and Cameroonian tourists, this is a great spot to chill out on the beach for a few days before heading elsewhere.

◉ Sights

The best of Limbe's beaches are north of town and known by their distance from Limbe. Our favourite is at the village of Batoké at Mile 6, from where the lava flows of one of Mt Cameroon's eruptions are still visible. Head to Bota Road for a shared taxi to the beaches (from CFA500).

Unfortunately, Down Beach in the heart of Limbe is strewn with rubbish.

Botanical Gardens   GARDENS
(Botanic Garden Rd; admission CFA2000, camera CFA2000, guide CFA2000; ⊙8am-6pm) Limbe's Botanical Gardens, the second oldest in Africa, are the home of, among others, cinnamon, nutmeg, mango, ancient cycads and an unnamed tree that locals describe as 'African Viagra'. There's a small visitors centre and an area with Commonwealth War Graves. Guides aren't required but are recommended as labelling is minimal. Bring bug repellant.

Limbe Wildlife Centre   ZOO
(www.limbewildlife.org; Bota Rd; CFA3000; ⊙9am-4pm; 📷) Many zoos in Africa are depressing places, but the Limbe Wildlife Centre is a

shining exception. It houses rescued chimpanzees, gorillas, drills and other primates in large enclosures, with lots of interesting information about local conservation issues. Staff are well informed, and are heavily involved in community education.

🏃 Activities

Bimbia Rainforest & Mangrove Trail   WALKING
(☑2 77 33 70 14; bbcnaturetrail@yahoo.com; local development fee CFA5000, guide CFA3000) An hour south of Limbe, this trail runs through the only coastal lowland rainforest remaining between Douala and Limbe. An experienced guide will take you on day tours through some rather lovely submerged woods, birdwatching areas and old slave-trading sites. It's CFA15,000 for a taxi-brousse (bush taxi) from Limbe; the trip is cheapest done in a group.

🛏 Sleeping

Victoria Guest House   GUESTHOUSE $
(☑2 2 22 81 62 45; off Makangal St; d CFA9000, with air-con CFA12,000-16,000; 🅿❄) The best-value budget place in town, the Victoria has clean and well-maintained rooms on the hill above Limbe's main restaurant strip: follow the path up behind the King William Hotel. Nearly all rooms have air-con, but there are a couple of cheaper fan-cooled variants.

★ Bird Watchers' Club   GUESTHOUSE $$
(☑2 6 96 83 81 88, 6 75 73 40 86; Limbe Botanical Gardens; d incl breakfast CFA28,000; 🅿) This charmingly secluded and gently welcoming spot on a rocky promontory overlooks the sea. With just two rooms it's a good idea to call ahead and book. You'll be rewarded with spacious accommodation and a great restaurant with superb sea views. Arriving by taxi, steer the driver to Miramar – Bird Watchers' is just up the road.

Hotel Seme Beach   RESORT $$
(☑2 6 77 93 45 50; www.semebeach.com; Mile 11, Rte d'Idenau, Bakingili; r incl breakfast CFA25,000-35,000, ste incl breakfast CFA50,000-100,000; 🅿❄🛜🏊) Not in Limbe itself, but 18km beyond along the rain-lashed coast, this is a good choice if you want to enjoy the beach and creature comforts. The location is gorgeous, with full frontage onto the beach and views of Equatorial Guinea rising in the distance, while touches such as a freshwater swimming pool and a spa make for great relaxation.

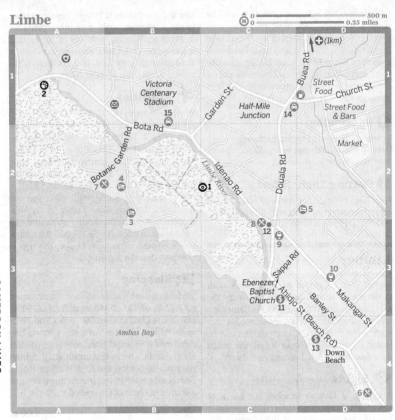

Limbe

⊙ Sights
1 Botanical Gardens C2
2 Limbe Wildlife Centre A1

🛏 Sleeping
3 Bird Watchers' Club B2
4 Park Hotel Miramar B2
5 Victoria Guest House D2

🍽 Eating
6 Grilled Fish Stalls D4
7 Hot Spot A2
8 Le Moulin C3

🍸 Drinking & Nightlife
9 Bamboo Lounge C3
10 Ocean Blu D3

ℹ Information
11 Bicec Bank C3
12 Flora Travel & Tours C3
13 SGBC Bank D4

ℹ Transport
14 Shared Taxis C1
15 Shared Taxis B1

Park Hotel Miramar　　　　　　　HOTEL **$$**
(📞 2 33 33 29 41; Botanic Garden Rd; d incl break-
fast CFA20,500; 🅿❄🛜🏊) While this place
has certainly seen better days, its location on
a wave-kissed cliff backed by screaming jun-
gle is unbeatable. Accommodation is in cute,
if rather dark, *boukarous* (self-contained
circular, thatched-mud huts) that abut a res-
taurant and a decent-sized swimming pool.
Book ahead.

✖ Eating

Hot Spot   INTERNATIONAL **$**
(Limbe Botanical Gardens; mains CFA3000-4000; ⊘7.30am-11pm) With hands down the best location in town, overlooking the dramatic coastline and Park Hotel Miramar, this place offers a fairly standard selection of meat grills, shrimp, fish and chicken dishes. The friendly staff, outdoor seating and views make it, though. Get there via the dirt road to the hotels through the gardens and take the middle path after the bridge.

Le Moulin   INTERNATIONAL **$**
(Idenao Rd; mains CFA2000-3000; ⊘10am-10pm) Right on the roundabout in the thick of things, Le Moulin is the best eating option in Limbe's town centre. The menu encompasses *ndole,* chicken and beef dishes served up with fresh vegetables, plantains or rice.

Grilled Fish Stalls   SEAFOOD **$**
(Down Beach; dishes from CFA1000; ⊘7am-10pm) You'll find this cluster of open-air grills with attached seating where the fishing boats haul up on Limbe's main beach. Soak up your beer with something from the sea that was probably happily unaware it would be your dinner a few minutes before you ordered it.

❢ Drinking & Nightlife

Ocean Blu   CLUB
(Makangal St; ⊘10pm–6am) An excellent place to cut loose in Limbe, this is a young vibrant club playing street music, R&B and soul. A lot of posing from funkily dressed locals occurs before the dancing starts around midnight.

Bamboo Lounge   BAR
(📞6 79 77 92 39; Makangal St, Down Beach; ⊘7pm–7am) Attractively screened with bamboo, this is an upbeat bar hosting DJ nights and live music nights. It serves beers, whiskies and spirits plus barbecued meat and fish dishes.

❶ Information

Limbe's Ahidjo St has several ATMs; try **Bicec** (Ahidjo St; ⊘8am-3.30pm Mon-Fri) or **SGBC** (Ahidjo St; ⊘8am-4pm Mon-Fri). You'll find the **police station** (opposite Botanic Gardens; ⊘24hr) at the western end of Limbe; the **post office** (Bota Rd; ⊘7.30am-4pm Mon-Sat) is out near the Botanical Gardens.

 Flora Travel & Tours (📞2 33 33 35 82; www.floratraveltours.com; opposite Total Down-

beach; ⊘8am-5pm Mon-Fri) can arrange local tours, hotels and trips up Mt Cameroon.

❶ Getting There & Away

The main motor park (bus station) is Mile 4, about 6km out of town; shared taxis leave from Douala Rd near the petrol station (around CFA500, 15 minutes). Minibuses and taxis-brousses leave approximately hourly to Buea (CFA800, 25 minutes) and Douala (CFA1500, 70 minutes). From Mile 2, take a bus heading to Yaoundé (CFA5000, five hours, 4-5 daily).

 Ferries should travel every Monday and Thursday from Limbe to Calabar in Nigeria (1st/2nd class CFA35,000/45,000, four hours), departing at 2am and returning on Tuesday and Friday at 7am. At the time of writing though, the service was not operating due to problems with the boat. Take your own food and water if you make it on-board.

Bamenda

POP 275,000

The capital of Northwest Province, Bamenda, is a dusty sprawl that tumbles down a hill at an altitude of more than 1000m. With plenty of traveller amenities, it's a good jumping-off point for exploring the Ring Road (p121) circuit. The colonial Upstation district is the cooler, more residential area of town, while downtown is frenetic and commercial. If you're coming from Douala, you'll see some impressive views of town as you descend the hill. Bamenda has also traditionally been a centre of political opposition to President Biya; rival party the Social Democratic Front (SDF) was founded here.

▦ Sleeping

Baptist Mission Resthouse   GUESTHOUSE **$**
(📞2 75 45 83 39; Finance Junction; dm/s/d CFA4000/9000/13,000, apt CFA50,000; 🅿🛜) This compound on the main road into Bamenda's centre has a bunch of well-maintained rooms, all fan cooled and with mosquito nets and hot water, though some are a little on the small side and rather mildewy. There's a communal kitchen and it's secure and welcoming.

International Hotel   HOTEL **$**
(📞2 76 06 70 18; off Commercial Ave; s/d CFA16,000; ❄) Right in the middle of town and convenient for buses, this budget place charges extra for hot water and air-con. Rooms are modern, clean and have reasonable bathrooms as well as balconies

Bamenda

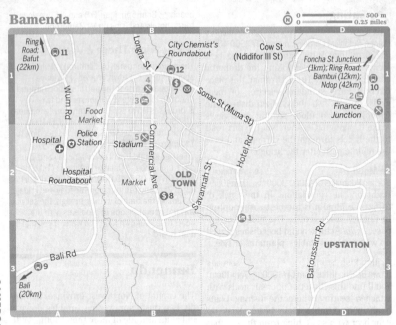

Bamenda

offering sweeping views over, er, 'scenic' Bamenda.

Ayaba　　　　　　　　　　　　　　HOTEL $$
(☎ 2 33 02 59 32; Rte N 6, just north of the Catholic University; r CFA30,000; ※ ⊛) A concrete government-run place in Bamenda with a bold exterior, now in need of renovation. But the restaurant is decent, the staff are friendly and the views from the terrace dramatic.

There are tennis courts, too, if you need some exercise.

🍴 Eating

Dreamland Restaurant　　　　　AFRICAN $
(Commercial Ave; mains CFA1500-3500; ⊙ 7am-11pm) Bamenda's Dreamland doesn't look like much from the outside, but inside it's a well-set-out establishment with a large menu. There's a daily lunchtime buffet (CFA3500 per person) and a choice of grills, salads, fish and soups the rest of the time.

Super Class Restaurant　　　　AFRICAN $
(near Finance Junction; mains CFA3000; ⊙ 7.30am-8pm) This cute little shack in Nkwen Nkwen, Bamenda, with red tablecloths and friendly service, serves up simple Cameroonian fare such as fried chicken and plantains or meat grills with rice.

Pres Cafe　　　　　　　　　　　　CAFE $
(Commercial Ave, next to the British Council library)
🌿 Bamenda's Pres Cafe offers rare finds in Cameroon: good local coffee including cappuccino, fresh salads, carrot cake and a wide range of natural juices. It's located by the excellent Fairtrade PresCraft gift shop which sells bronzes, baskets, carvings and jewellery at fixed prices.

ℹ Information

Express Exchange (City Chemist's Roundabout; ⊘8am–4pm Mon–Fri) Changes travellers cheques as well as US dollars cash.

Hospital (Wum Rd; ⊘24hr) There's a centrally located hospital for medical emergencies.

Police Station (Wum Rd; ⊘24hr) Emergency police assistance.

Post Office (Sonac Street; ⊘8am–3.30pm Mon–Fri) Send your postcards from here.

SGBC Bank (Commercial Ave, Old Town; ⊘7.30–3pm Mon–Fri) ATM.

ℹ Getting There & Away

Most agency offices with buses for destinations to the south are on Sonac St in Bamenda, or try **Vatican Express** (Muna St; ⊘6am-10pm). Destinations include Yaoundé (CFA5000, six hours, four to five daily), Douala (CFA4500, seven hours, four to five daily) and Bafoussam (CFA1500, 90 minutes, six daily). **Nkwen Motor Park** (south end of Nkwen Street; ⊘6am-10pm) has transport to the eastern stretch of the Ring Road, including Ndop (CFA1200, 90 minutes, three daily) and Kumbo (CFA3000, five hours, two to three daily). The west Ring Road is served by **Ntarikon Motor Park** (Wum Rd; ⊘6am-10pm), which runs minibuses to Wum (CFA3000, six hours). Bali and Mamfe transport departs from the **Bali Motor Park** (Bali Rd, 1km south of the centre; ⊘6am-10pm).

The Ring Road

Cameroon's northwest highlands bear the pretty name 'Grassfields', an appellation too pleasant to really capture the look of this landscape. These aren't gentle fields; they're green and yellow valleys, tall grass, red earth and sharp mountains. Clouds of mist rise, with the wood smoke and dung smoke that mark the villages speckled on this deceptively inviting – but hard and rugged – terrain.

The 367km Ring Road runs a circle around the Grassfields, and if it were in better shape it'd be one of Cameroon's great scenic drives. As it is, get your butt ready for some bumpy, red-earth roads. The pay-off? Mountains dolloped with lakes, cattle loping into the hills and one of the greatest concentrations of fondoms (traditional kingdoms) in Cameroon.

It's worth considering, too, the more manageable small Ring Road route, linking Bamenda, Bafut, Wum, Weh, Fundong, Belo and Bambui. This will take one to two days.

◉ Sights

Fon's Palace   PALACE

(Bafut; palace CFA1000, camera CFA1500, museum CFA2000; ⊘10am-4pm Mon-Sat) Just north of Bamenda is the large Tikar community of Bafut, traditionally the most powerful of the Grassfields kingdoms. The *fon*'s (local chief's) palace here is home to the representative of a 700-year-old dynasty and is a fascinating insight into Cameroon's traditional culture.

🏃 Activities

Hiking, cycling and camping are all options for the Ring Road, but always ask the permission of the local chief, and bring some gifts (whisky is a good idea).

ℹ Getting There & Away

Transport links along the Ring Road are extremely slow, crowded and irregular, with minibuses usually leaving very early in the morning. Roads are poor throughout. If you plan to drive this incredibly challenging road, hire a 4WD and don't even think about it in the rainy season.

It's essential to take travel advice in Bamenda before setting out.

Bafoussam

POP 240,000

The Bamiléké stronghold of Bafoussam is haphazardly built on agriculture money and a refined sense of chaos. But despite its heavy traffic and uninspiring appearance, the town is friendly and has adequate amenities, and you'll have to pass through it on the way to more-enticing Foumban.

🛏 Sleeping & Eating

Hotel Altitel   HOTEL $$

(🕿2 33 44 51 11; www.hotelaltitel.net; Route de Bamenda; d CFA23,000-33,000, ste CFA50,000; P🅿❄🛜) Despite the grim brutalist exterior, this is a clean and friendly choice with pleasant en-suite rooms and a good restaurant.

Residence Sare   HOTEL $$

(🕿2 33 44 25 99; Route de Bamenda; d CFA12,500-28,000; ❄🛜) On the road towards Bamenda, this hotel is a solid midrange option, with accommodation in green rondavels in a pleasant garden.

Boulangerie La Paix   BAKERY $

(Rte de Foumban; pastries from CFA150; ⊘8am-10pm) This bakery sells good bread and

RING ROAD ROUTE

Starting from Bamenda and heading east, you pass Sabga Hill, which rises powerfully above Ndop, then Bamessing, with a handicraft centre and pottery workshop. After that you reach Kumbo, dominated by its Catholic cathedral and *fon*'s (traditional chief's) palace. It's a good place to base yourself, with a nice market. From there you go north to Nkambe and on to Missaje if the road permits.

The road from Missaje to We is just a dirt track and in the rainy season you won't find it; the bridges here are in an ongoing state of collapse. Some travellers continue on foot, sometimes with help from Fula herdsmen. It can take a couple of days to get to We, so bring supplies.

If you hike from Missaje to We, you'll pass Lake Nyos, a volcanic lake that was the site of a natural gas eruption in 1986, which resulted in around 1700 deaths. Continuing south you reach Wum, the biggest town on the west side of the Ring Road. South of Wum the road passes the Metchum Falls, where most shared-taxi drivers will stop to let you take a quick peek or photo.

The last town on the Ring Road (or the first, if you're heading clockwise) is Bafut, traditionally the strongest of the region's kingdoms. The Fon's Palace (p121) is a highlight of the Ring Road and includes a tour of the compound where the *fon*'s large family lives.

sticky sweet treats in the morning, and is a handy general food shop the rest of the day.

❶ Getting There & Away

Minibuses from Bafoussam to Foumban (CFA800 to CFA1000, one hour, three to four per day) depart from near Carrefour Total, along with shared taxis. Bus agents for Yaoundé (CFA2500 to CFA3000, three hours) and Douala (CFA4000, five hours) have offices along the main road south of the town centre. Transport to Bamenda (CFA1500, 1½ hours) leaves every couple of hours from the Bamenda road, north of the town centre (CFA150 in a shared taxi).

Foumban

POP 92,000

Foumban has a deep tradition of home-grown arts and its traditional monarchy centred around a sultan, who resides in a palace. The town is plopped architecturally and conceptually between West and North Africa, as if the Sahel and its sharp music, bright robes and Islam – this is the city with most Muslims in the south – were slowly creeping into the eastern corner of Cameroon's West Province.

◉ Sights

The Grand Marché (⊘8am-5pm Sat) is a warren of narrow stalls and alleys, which are great fun to explore; the paths eventually lead to where the Grande Mosquée faces the palace.

★ Palais Royal   PALACE
(Sultan's Palace; http://palaisdesroisbamoun. com/; Rue du Palais; admission CFA2000, camera CFA2000; ⊘9am-6pm) The must-see attraction is the sultan's palace, home to the 19th sultan of the Bamoun dynasty. It has a fascinating, well-organised museum providing great historical insight into the region. At the time of writing, the treasures were being transferred to a startling new building symbolically shaped as a serpent and a spider; the palace itself will remain open to visitors.

Constructed in the early 20th century and modelled on German colonial architecture, the palace was built by the remarkable Sultan Njoya, who invented a corn-grinding machine, a script for the Bamun language, and a religion which fused Christianity and Islam. He had 681 wives, which made him well qualified to write his own version of the *Kama Sutra* (look out for it in the museum shop).

Museum artefacts include a ancient feathered cloak worn only for the initiation of each sultan, beaded buffalo masks sported by members of secret societies, documents written using Sultan Njoya's script and a drinking horn made from the skull of one of his enemies.

The palace sits opposite the market and main mosque, the minaret of which can be climbed as part of the palace tour. Palace entrance includes a visit to a nearby ceremonial drum housed in a bamboo hut: it's a huge creation topped with animal hides and carved with a double-headed serpent.

⚔️ Festivals & Events

Nguon tribal festival
CULTURAL

(⊙Dec, every 2 years) A biennial week-long harvest festival which dates back around 600 years; Bamoun culture is celebrated with dance and masquerades.

Tabaski
RELIGIOUS

Every year at Tabaski, the Islamic holiday of Eid al-Adha, Foumban attracts thousands of pilgrims for an extraordinary blend of Muslim and traditional Bamoun ceremonies, with the sultan playing a key role, parading in his white Cadillac and on horseback. It culminates with horse racing through the town, drumming and dancing.

🛏️ Sleeping

Hotel Complexe Adi
HOTEL $

(📋2 76 07 95 07; Rue de l'Hotel Beau Regarde; d CFA6000) Look for the giant voodoo statue of a man studded by nails to find Adi's entrance. While the rooms here are clean, they're smallish and very basic (just a bed and a small bathroom), and the bar downstairs gets pretty loud. If there are no rooms available here, try the similar Hotel Beau Regard across the road.

⭐Hotel Pekassa de Karché
HOTEL $$

(📋2 33 26 29 35; hotelpekassadekarche@yahoo.fr; Rte de Bafoussam; s/d without air-con CFA10,000/15,000, d with air-con & balcony CFA25,000, ste CFA40,000; P ❄ @) This friendly hotel decorated with local crafts and fronted by bronze statues is by far the best choice in Foumban. Just 200m from the royal palace, it makes for a pleasant change from the norm in Cameroonian hotels, with smart, clean rooms, well-informed staff and good security. There's a decent on-site restaurant, too (mains CFA2500 to CFA4000).

🍴 Eating

Bars, beer and grilled meat are abundant; Foumban's main street has several cafes, and the hotel restaurants are dependable.

La Saveur
AFRICAN $

(📋2 99 95 00 69; main CFA1500) An easy-to-miss upstairs restaurant (near the market on the road to the Catholic mission) with blue-green walls, a mosaic tiled floor, plastic flowers on the tables and bargain food,

including a selection of village cuisine: Senegalese rice, *ndole* and *njapche* (another type of green).

🛍️ Shopping

⭐Village des Artisans
ARTS & CRAFTS

(Rue des Artisans; ⊙10am-2.30pm) South of town, the Village des Artisans seems to produce more handicrafts than the rest of Cameroon combined. Get ready for some bargaining and banter – it's well worth it to explore the fine crafts from this wonderfully artistic region. Feathered hats and beaded staffs are among the collectable items.

ℹ️ Information

CPAC bank (⊙8am-5pm Mon-Fri), south of Foumban's market, may change euros if you're lucky, but it's best to change money in Bafoussam.

Don't wander Foumban at night, not least because of perilous pavements and lack of street lighting.

ℹ️ Getting There & Away

There are a three to four direct daily buses from Foumban to Yaoundé (CFA3500, five hours) and Douala (CFA3500, six hours); otherwise head for Bafoussam (CFA800 to CFA1000, one hour, four daily) and change there. Bus-agency offices are on the west side of town, about 3km from the Grande Marché (CFA150 in a shared taxi).

Transport between Foumban and Kumbo (CFA3000, around six hours) runs year-round, with journey times varying according to the rains. Although the road is very, very poor, it's easily one of the most beautiful in the country, skirting along the edge of the spectacular Mbam Massif.

Bandjoun

POP 25,000

The otherwise unremarkable country town of Bandjoun has a remarkable attraction in the form of a huge traditional *chefferie* (chief's compound), its pillars adorned with striking carvings by local artisans.

⦿ Sights

⭐Chefferie
HISTORIC BUILDING

(Chief's Compound; www.museumcam.org; just south of Bandjoun; CFA2000; ⊙10am-5pm) Approached via a ceremonial gate, the compound is centred on a hugely impressive bamboo building, its conical thatched roof supported by wooden pillars carved with figures from secret societies, former chiefs, dancers, musicians and even the World Cup–winning Cameroon football team. The interior is out of bounds, but the visitor centre to the left offers an informative tour.

Bandjoun Station ARTS CENTRE
(☑ 6 93 53 79 50; http://bandjounstation.com; BP 52; ⊙10am-6pm) FREE Dramatically decorated with mosaics, this arts centre and workshop boldly announces itself. The centre supports the work of local contemporary artists.

🛏 Sleeping & Eating

Centre Climatique de Bandjoun HOTEL $$
(☑ 2 33 44 67 50; Route National 4; r CFA25,000-35,000; ☞) This weirdly named country hotel is on the Bafoussam road, where rooms in tin-roofed huts offer TV and wi-fi. There's also a decent restaurant.

ⓘ Getting There & Away

Bandjoun is located 3km south of Bafoussam. Your best option for onward travel is to take a shared taxi to Bafoussam (CFA500, 20 minutes), which is a hub for buses.

SOUTHERN CAMEROON

Southern Cameroon is largely taken up by thick jungle, and there are few large towns or other population centres. However, the coastline is by far Cameroon's best: head to Kribi for great scenery and a relaxed vibe, and continue further down the coast to indulge in a spot of beach exploration and ecotourism in Parc National de Campo-Ma'an.

Kribi

POP 64,000
Kribi is home to Cameroon's best beaches: the sand is fine, the water crystal clear, fresh fish is on the menu and cold beer on tap; there are times when Africa hugs you.

However, the biggest port in West Africa has just opened to the north of town, and it remains to be seen what impact this will have on the beaches and forested surroundings of the town.

◉ Sights

Chutes de la Lobé WATERFALL
(8km south of Kribi) The Chutes de la Lobé are an impressive set of waterfalls that empty

directly into the sea – it's a beautiful sight. Take a *moto-taxi* (CFA500), or make a trip with Urbain Mandoua, who can arrange a lunch of sole, shrimps and plantains on the beach. The beach itself is idyllic, with log seats and hammocks under the trees.

⌲ Tours

Urbain Mandoua OUTDOORS
(☑ 6 96 20 13 53; urbmand@yahoo.fr) Urbain organises trips in a motorised canoe up the rapidly flowing river from the Chutes de la Lobé to a Pygmy settlement, past a dense tangle of mangrove, bamboo and palms. Bear in mind that some of the Pygmies may not want to meet you, but you can view their huts, shrimp baskets and animal traps.

Wear long-sleeved shirts, trousers and closed shoes, and take mosquito repellent.

🛏 Sleeping

Hotel Panoramique HOTEL $
(☑ 6 70 59 59 48; hotel panoramique@yahoo. fr; Rue du Marché; r CFA6000-15,000; ☀) This semi-sprawling compound feels like a down-at-heels villa evolved into a low-rent flophouse. Some rooms are good value, but at the cheapest end you're in an ugly annexe with the dust and roaches.

★**Indaba** GUESTHOUSE $$
(☑ 6 96 52 24 39; http://freeland-kribi.blogspot. co.uk; d CFA30,000-40,000) Indaba offers delightful *boukarous* in a lush garden with banana palms and ferns. There are also four (cheaper) rooms with mosquito nets in the guesthouse itself. There's no pool, but you're a stroll away from the beach. The owners will organise trips to the waterfall, fishing villages and national parks for you.

★**Hotel Ilomba** HOTEL $$
(☑ 6 99 91 29 23; www.hotelilomba.com; Rte de Campo; d CFA40,000, ste CFA130,000; 🅿️✳@ 🛜🏊) South of Kribi, this is the loveliest and most relaxing hotel in the area. Rooms are in *boukarous*, all well furnished and tastefully decorated. It's also just a short walk to the Chutes de la Lobé and right on a beautiful stretch of beach. The restaurant serves shrimp cooked in coconut milk and other treats.

Les Gîtes de Kribi GUESTHOUSE $$
(☑ 6 75 08 08 45; www.kribiholidays.com; Rte de Campo; r CFA35,000, gîte CFA60,000; 🅿️✳🛜🏊) Ideal for families, the *gîtes* (self-contained

cottages) here are of varying sizes, but all are well equipped and have their own small kitchens. There are also normal rooms in the main building for those not *en famille*. Across the road, a charming beach restaurant serves up fresh fish in high season.

⭐ **Auberge du Phare** GUESTHOUSE $$$
(☑ 6 75 64 04 64; off Rte de Campo; d CFA50,000-110,000; P ❄ 🛜 🏊) Located immediately south of Kribi, this great place has white-washed terraced rooms splashed with bright colours opening onto the palm-edged pool and beach. Its seafront restaurant is excellent. Turn right on the beach and after 100m you'll see the eponymous 1904 *phare* (lighthouse).

🍴 Eating

Fish Market SEAFOOD $
(meals from CFA1000; ⊙10am-5pm Wed & Sat) This market at Kribi's marina grills the day's catch over coals. From crab and lobster to massive barracuda, you'd be hard-pressed to find a better and tastier selection of seafood anywhere in Cameroon.

❶ Getting There & Away

Bus agencies have offices on Rue du Marché in the centre of Kribi. Nonagency transport leaves from the main *gare routière* (bus station). Buses for Douala (CFA1800 to CFA2000, three hours) leave throughout the day, along with transport to Campo (CFA2000, three hours) and Yaoundé (CFA3000, 3½ hours).

Ebolowa

POP 74,000

Ebolowa, capital of Cameroon's Ntem district, is a bustling place built on cocoa wealth, and a possible stopping point en route between Yaoundé and Equatorial Guinea or Gabon. Its main attraction is the artificial Municipal Lake in the centre of town, where there's also a large market.

The basic **Hotel Âne Rouge** (☑ 2 22 28 34 38; Place Ans 2000; s/d CFA6000/10,000) has a few en-suite rooms with fans, and a pleasant terrace.

The **Florence Hotel** (☑ 2 22 28 44 04; www.florencehotelebolowa.com; BP 1097; d CFA50,000; P 🛜 🏊) is not cheap and not hugely glamorous, but it is the best option in Ebolowa, and it has a generator to cope with the frequent electricity outages. There's a pool, and the restaurant is the best eating in town.

❶ Getting There & Away

During the dry season there's at least one vehicle daily along the rough road between Ebolowa and Kribi (CFA4000, four hours). There are also many buses daily to Yaoundé (CFA3000, three hours). Several vehicles depart in the morning for Ambam (CFA1000, one hour), from where you can find transport towards Ebebiyin (Equatorial Guinea) or Bitam (Gabon).

Campo

POP 10,000

Taking the road to here from Kribi is half Campo's attraction – it's a hard but rewarding slog through immense rainforest, past Pygmy villages, and with views out to the ocean and fire-spouting petrol platforms shimmering in the west.

For travellers, Campo mainly serves as a jumping-off point for visiting wildlife-rich Parc National de Campo Ma'an, as well as the sea-turtle conservation project in nearby Ebodjé.

Campo is the last Cameroonian town before the Equatorial Guinea border (which theoretically is open, though in practice even with a visa you're unlikely to be allowed to enter EG).

Parc National de Campo-Ma'an (CFA5000, vehicle CFA2000, local guide CFA10,000) comprises 7700 sq km of protected biodiverse rainforest, sheltering many wonderful plants and animals, including buffaloes, forest elephants, leopards, gorillas and mandrills. The park is being developed by World Wildlife Fund (WWF) as an ecotourism destination, with canopy walks and river trips available. Because of the difficulty of spotting shy forest animals it's much better to visit with a guide.

Pay your park fee and book a guide at the park HQ in Campo, and aim to get to the park as early as possible.

Auberge Bon Course (☑ 2 74 51 18 83; Campo; CFA5000) is scruffy accommodation with simple meals and very friendly faces – it's found at the Bon Course Supermarché at the main junction in Campo.

❶ Getting There & Away

There are daily minibuses between Campo and Kribi (CFA1500, three hours), which also stop at Ebodjé (45 minutes). *Moto-taxis* to Campo Beach (for Equatorial Guinea) cost CFA500 and take 20 minutes. Taxis to Ebodjé (45 minutes) cost CFA500.

CAMEROON EBOLOWA

Ebodjé

POP 30,000

Ebodjé, a small fishing village 25km north of Campo, is worth a trip to see the sea-turtle conservation project and eco-tourism site.

KUDU Cameroun (☑ 2 96 22 08 29; per person CFA12,000) offers fantastic turtle walks, where visitors are taken out at night to spot egg-laying turtles. There's no guarantee you'll see any, though some groups see as many as six. Even if you don't see any turtles, the beach is gorgeous, pristine and better than anything in Kribi.

The total fee includes accommodation in a local home, village development fee, meal and tour. A proportion of fees helps locals, many of whom have been trained as guides. For between CFA8000 and CFA115,000 you can arrange local river trips and cultural evenings.

Remember to bring your own water or filter, mosquito net and sleeping sheets as well as good walking shoes.

Taxis between Campo and Ebodjé (45 minutes) cost CFA500.

EASTERN CAMEROON

Cameroon's remote east is wild and untamed. Populated by Baka people but seldom visited by travellers, it's very much a destination for those with plenty of time and the stamina to back up an appetite for adventure. There's little infrastructure and travel throughout is slow and rugged, with dense green forest and red-laterite earth roads. The rainforest national parks are the main attraction, along with routes into the Central African Republic and Congo.

Bertoua

POP 218,000

The capital of East Province, administrative hub Bertoua is also a genuine boom town, born of logging and gold-mining. It hasn't got much to excite visitors, but you will find all the facilities lacking elsewhere in the region, including banks and sealed roads. The town has lost its role as a stepping-off spot en route to the Central African Republic because of instability there, but you may just wind up here, at the transition point between Cameroon's forest and grasslands.

🛏 Sleeping

Hotel Mansa   HOTEL $$

(☑ 2 22 03 92 00; D 30, 1km north of Bertoua; CFA25,000-37,500; P ✲ ✲) Bertoua's best hotel comes complete with an artificial lake, satellite TV and a tennis court. It's definitely worth a splurge if you've been lost in the forest.

❶ Getting There & Away

Buses to Yaoundé (CFA5000, seven hours, two to three daily), Bélabo (for the train; CFA1000, one hour, four daily) and Garoua-Boulaï (CFA400, four hours, four daily), leave from the *gare routière* near the market.

UNDERSTAND CAMEROON

Cameroon Today

Having re-elected presidential strongman Paul Biya in a contentious yet, broadly speaking, free election in 2011, Cameroon has gained a reputation as a relatively stable country. Biya's current seven-year term ends in 2018, with growing pressure on him to stand aside and end his 35-year (and counting) rule. Meanwhile, in the beleaguered north of the country, Cameroonian villagers are struggling to host huge numbers of Nigerian refugees on the run from the Boko Haram insurgency.

For most people though, corruption remains Cameroon's major issue. Paying bribes can be the only way to open a business or access government services and school places. The international anticorruption organisation, Transparency International, consistently ranks Cameroon among the world's most corrupt countries. Until this issue is addressed and genuine political openness permitted, Cameroon will inevitably continue to limp along.

The most spoken-about person in the country is first lady Chantal Biya, who has taken on the mantle of an African Princess Diana. Her love of haute couture, spectacular 'banana' hairdos and high-profile charity work mean she is a staple in the national press.

History

Parts of what is now Cameroon were divided and ceded between European countries throughout the colonial era until the modern boundaries were established in 1961, creating a part-Anglophone but majority Francophone nation.

Colonialism to Independence

Portuguese explorers first sailed up the Wouri River in 1472, and named it Rio dos Camarões (River of Prawns). Soon after, Fula pastoral nomads from what is now Nigeria began to migrate overland from the north, forcing the indigenous forest peoples southwards. The Fula migration took on added urgency in the early 17th century as they fled Dutch, Portuguese and British slave traders.

British influence was curtailed in 1884 when Germany signed a treaty with the chiefdoms of Douala and central Bamiléké Plateau. After WWI the German protectorate of Kamerun was carved up between France and Great Britain.

Local revolts in French-controlled Cameroon in the 1950s were suppressed, but the pan-African momentum for throwing off the shackles of colonial rule soon took hold. Self-government was granted in French Cameroon in 1958, quickly followed by independence on 1 January 1960.

Uniting Cameroon

Ahmadou Ahidjo, leader of one of the independence parties, became president of new-ly independent French Cameroon, a position he was to hold until his resignation in 1982. Ahidjo ensured his longevity through the cultivation of expedient alliances, brutal repression and wily regional favouritism.

In October 1961 a UN-sponsored referendum in British-mandated northwestern Cameroon split the country in two, with the area around Bamenda opting to join the federal state of Cameroon and the remainder joining Nigeria. In June 1972, the federal structure of two Cameroons (previously French and British) was replaced by the centralised United Republic of Cameroon – a move that is resented to this day by Anglophone Cameroonians, who feel that, as the minority, they have become second-class citizens.

The Biya Era

In 1982 Ahidjo's hand-picked successor, Paul Biya, distanced himself from his former mentor, but adopted many of Ahidjo's repressive measures, clamping down hard on calls for multiparty democracy. Diversions such as the national football team's stunning performance in the 1990 FIFA World Cup bought him time, but Biya was forced eventually to legalise 25 opposition parties. The first multiparty elections in 25 years were held in 1992 and saw the Cameroonian Democratic People's Movement, led by Biya, hang on to power with the support

CAMEROON HISTORY

THE BAKA PEOPLE OF SOUTHEAST CAMEROON

With few roads, dense forest and sparse settlements, the southeast of Cameroon is hard for visitors to access. But the area is not empty of human life: it is home to the Baka people, popularly known as Pygmies. These hunter-gatherers maintain a traditional lifestyle in their forest environment, and are notably small, growing to be no taller than 150cm (4ft 11in).

The population of Baka people in the region is hard to estimate, but it is thought to be up to 30,000. The Baka are accomplished hunters, moving with quiet agility through the forest to fell animals such as elephants and antelope with their crossbows and spears. They also collect honey; women fish using wicker baskets, and also gather wild fruit, insects and roots. Baka traditionally wear loin cloths made from beaten bark, and use plant-life to create medicine and poison arrows.

The Baka are semi-nomadic, leaving their rounded leaf-and-branch huts in order to hunt in bands of 20 to 100. They worship spirits of the forest, evoking them in masquerade and dance. Their polyphonic song is akin to yodelling, using sounds rather than words, and women 'drum' river water, slapping it in syncopated rhythms.

Threats to the Baka include the armed poachers involved in the illegal wildlife trade, mining, logging and the transformation of forest into farmland. Their territories are being encroached on, and the way of life is consequently being eroded. You can visit Baka in Cameroon on small-scale tours, though these may well you leave you wondering what the benefit is to you or them.

WILDLIFE IN SOUTHEAST CAMEROON

With some perseverance it may be possible to visit Cameroon's southeast to explore the wonderful forest wildlife: Lobéké National Park near the (currently unstable) Central African Republic border can be reached either in a 4WD via Bertoua or by chartered plane. The park is rich in animal life, including chimps, forest elephants, red forest buffaloes, leopards and lowland gorillas, plus 215 types of butterflies and more than 300 bird species.

of minority parties. International observers alleged widespread vote-rigging and intimidation; such allegations were repeated in elections in 1999, 2004 and, most recently, in 2011. The next election is set for 2018, amid suppressed dissatisfaction with Biya's long reign.

Culture

It's hard to pigeonhole more than 250 distinct ethnolinguistic groups divided by colonial languages, Christianity and Islam and an urban-rural split into one identity. The Cameroonian psyche is, ultimately, anything and everything African – diversity is the key.

There's a distinct cultural and political gap between the Francophone and Anglophone parts of Cameroon, albeit one felt predominantly by the Anglophone minority, who complain of discrimination in the workplace and in education (two of the country's eight universities lecture in French only).

A few characteristics do seem shared across Cameroon's divides. Traditional social structures dominate life. Local chiefs (known as *fon* in the west or *lamido* in the north) wield considerable influence; when you are travelling in places that don't receive many tourists, it's polite to announce your presence to them.

Many Cameroonians demonstrate a half-laconic, half-angry sense of frustration with the way their country is run. They are aware that while Cameroon is doing well compared with its neighbours, it could be immeasurably better off if corruption didn't curtail so much potential. Mixed in with this frustration is a resignation ('such is life'),

expressed as serenity in good times but simmering rage in bad times.

Meanwhile, the arrival of Chinese immigrants in great numbers – especially in Yaoundé and Douala – is bringing a dash of multiculturalism to this already incredibly multi-ethnic society.

Arts

Cameroon has produced a few of the region's most celebrated artists: in literature, Mongo Beti deals with the legacies of colonialism; musically, jazz-funk saxophonist Manu Dibango is the country's brightest star.

Woodcarving makes up a significant proportion of traditional arts and crafts. The northwestern highlands are known for their carved masks. These are often representations of animals, and it's believed that the wearers of the masks can transform themselves and take on the animal's characteristics and powers. Cameroon also has some highly detailed bronze- and brasswork, particularly in Tikar areas north and east of Foumban. The areas around Bali and Bamessing (both near Bamenda), and Foumban, are rich in high-quality clay, and some of Cameroon's finest ceramic work originates here, as well as intricate beadwork.

Sport

Cameroon exploded onto the world's sporting consciousness at the 1990 FIFA World Cup when the national football team, the Indomitable Lions, became the first African side to reach the quarter finals. Football is truly the national obsession. Every other Cameroonian male seems to own a copy of the team's strip; go into any bar and there'll be a match playing on the TV. The country has qualified for the World Cup seven times, amid wild celebrations, and has been garlanded with five Africa Cup of Nations titles, most recently in 2017.

Food & Drink

Cameroonian cuisine is straightforward and satisfying. The staple dish is some variety of peppery sauce served with starch – usually rice, pasta or *fufu* (mashed yam, corn, plantain or couscous). One of the most popular sauces is *ndole,* made with bitter leaves similar to spinach and flavoured with smoked fish. Grilled meat and fish are eaten in huge quantities, and huge fresh *gambas* (prawns) are a particular delight.

Environment

Cameroon is geographically diverse. The south is a low-lying coastal plain covered by swaths of equatorial rainforest extending east towards the Congo Basin. Heading north, the sparsely populated Adamawa Plateau divides the country in two. To the plateau's north, the country begins to dry out into a rolling landscape dotted with rocky escarpments that are fringed to the west by the barren Mandara Mountains. That range represents the northern extent of a volcanic chain, now a natural border with Nigeria down to the Atlantic coast, often punctuated by stunning crater lakes. One active volcano remains in Mt Cameroon, at 4095m the highest peak in West Africa.

There is a range of wildlife found in Cameroon, although more exotic species are in remote areas. Elephants stomp and crocodiles glide through the southern and eastern jungles. Of note are several rare primate species, including the Cross River gorilla, mainland drill monkey, chimpanzees and Preuss's red colobus.

Bushmeat (from African wild animals) has traditionally been big business in Cameroon. While there have been crackdowns on the trade both here and abroad (African expats are some of its main consumers), it has not been entirely stamped out.

SURVIVAL GUIDE

❶ Directory A–Z

ACCOMMODATION

Cameroon has a reasonable range of accommodation options, from simple *auberges* (hostels) and dorm beds in religious missions to luxury hotels. Expect to pay around CFA15,000 for a decent single room with bathroom and fan. Most hotels quote prices per room – genuine single and twin rooms are the exception rather than the norm. Rather than seasonal rates, most hotels in Kribi and Limbe generally charge more during holidays and weekends.

ACTIVITIES

Hiking is a big drawcard in Cameroon. The two most popular hiking regions are Mt Cameroon (near the coast) and the Mandara Mountains (in the north), the latter currently out of bounds for

security reasons. The Ring Road near Bamenda also offers great hiking possibilities, but you'll need to be self-sufficient here.

CHILDREN

Children will undoubtedly be welcomed with open arms in Cameroon, though you will not find baby-change facilities, and pushing prams on the busted pavements is likely to be a challenge. You often see Cameroonian children on buses, but bear in mind that these are crowded, often hot, and loo breaks are few and far between.

Limbe Wildlife Centre (p117) Get your little ones up close to drill monkeys and other primates, saved from the bushmeat trade.

Mefou National Park (p108) More appealing rescued primates, including gorillas.

Kribi's beaches (p124) Sun, sea and sand on the southwest coast of the country.

DANGERS & ANNOYANCES

➡ Douala and Yaoundé both have reputations for petty crime, especially in the crowded central areas.

➡ Scams and official corruption are a way of life in Cameroon; keep your guard up and maintain a sense of humour.

➡ It's theoretically a legal requirement to carry your passport with you at all times. In practice, the police rarely target travellers.

➡ Roads pose a risk, with plenty of badly maintained vehicles driven at punishing speeds.

➡ The north of Cameroon is out of bounds following Boko Haram's insurgency; check your government's travel advisory for up-to-date information.

EMBASSIES & CONSULATES

A number of embassies and consulates are located in Yaoundé. Australians and New Zealanders should contact the Canadian High Commission in case of an emergency.

ⓘ BEST ACTIVITIES

Mt Cameroon (p83) From hilltop Buea take the three-day hike up this imposing volcano.

Parc National de Campo-Ma'an (p125) Enjoy canopy walks and river trips.

Chutes de la Lobé (p124) Take the plunge where these wide waterfalls join the sea.

British High Commission (Map p110; ☎2 22 22 07 96; bhc.yaounde@fco.gov.uk; Ave Churchill; ☺8am-4pm Mon-Fri)

Canadian Embassy (☎2 22 50 39 00; Les Colonnades Building, New Bastos; ☺8.30am-2pm Mon-Fri)

Central African Republic Embassy (Map p110; ☎2 22 20 51 55; Rue 1863, Bastos; ☺8.30am-3pm Mon-Fri)

Chadian Embassy (Map p110; ☎2 22 60 88 24; Rue Joseph Mballa Eloumden, Bastos; ☺8am-2pm Mon-Fri)

Congolese Embassy (Map p110; ☎2 22 20 51 03; Blvd de l'URSS, Bld 1782, Bastos; ☺8.30pm-3pm Mon-Fri)

Equatorial Guinean Embassy (Map p110; ☎2 22 21 08 04; Rue 1805, Bastos; ☺9pm-3pm Mon-Fri)

French Embassy (☎2 22 22 79 00; Rue Joseph Atemengué, near Pl de la Réunification; ☺8.30am-4pm Mon-Fri)

Gabonese Embassy (Map p110; ☎2 22 20 29 66; Rue 1816, Bastos; ☺8am-4pm Mon-Fri)

German Consulate (Map p110; ☎6 90 69 63 62; Ave Charles de Gaulle, Centre Ville; ☺8.30am-2pm Mon-Fri)

Nigerian Embassy (Map p110; ☎2 22 21 35 09; Rue Joseph Mballa Eloumden, Bastos; ☺8.30am-3pm Mon-Fri)

US Embassy (Map p112; ☎2 22 20 15 00; Ave Rosa Parks, Centre Ville; ☺7.30am–5pm Mon-Thu, 7.30am-12.30pm Fri)

EMERGENCY & IMPORTANT NUMBERS

Emergencies facilities are severely limited in Cameroon, and these numbers really only apply in big cities. In rural areas, you have to rely on local help.

Cameroon's country code	☎237
Fire	☎112
Medical assistance	☎112
Police	☎112

GAY & LESBIAN TRAVELLERS

Homosexuality is illegal in Cameroon and prosecutions have taken place. Sadly it is inadvisable for gay couples to openly express their sexuality.

INTERNET ACCESS

Internet access can be found in any Cameroonian town of a reasonable size. Connections range from OK to awful, and costs average CFA300 to CFA600 per hour. Fancy hotels are the best bet.

MONEY

The currency is the Central African franc (CFA), pegged to both the West African franc and the euro (at an unchanging rate of CFA655.957). Cash is king, especially in remote regions – bring plenty of euros or US dollars.

ATMs

All Cameroonian towns now have ATMs, tied to the Visa network. It's a good idea to withdraw money during bank hours, as cards can become stuck in the machines and need to be extracted. Banks won't generally offer cash advances on credit cards. Western Union has branches throughout Cameroon for international money transfers.

Banks regularly refuse to change travellers cheques, and charge around 5% commission when they do.

Changing Money

Moneychangers on the street in Douala and Yaoundé will change money at good rates and without taxes or commission, but there's always an element of risk to such transactions. Express Exchange moneychangers change US dollars as cash; there are branches in many towns across the country.

Exchange Rates

Australia	A$1	CFA452
Canada	C$1	CFA440
Europe	€1	CFA656
Japan	¥100	CFA538
New Zealand	NZ$1	CFA415
UK	UK£1	CFA774
US	US$1	CFA600

For current exchange rates, see www.xe.com

Tipping

Hotels Tip CFA1000 or so for help with bags.

Restaurants For decent service, 10% is customary.

Taxis Tips are not expected, but add one for good service.

OPENING HOURS

Banks From 7.30am or 8am to 3.30pm Monday to Friday.

Businesses From 7.30am or 8am until 6pm or 6.30pm Monday to Friday, generally with a one-to two-hour break sometime between noon and 3pm. Most are also open from 8am to 1pm (sometimes later) on Saturday.

Government offices From 7.30am to 3.30pm Monday to Friday.

POST

International post is fairly reliable for letters, but international couriers should be preferred for packages – there are branches in all large towns.

PUBLIC HOLIDAYS

New Year's Day 1 January
Youth Day 11 February
Easter March/April
Labour Day 1 May
National Day 20 May
Assumption Day 15 August
Christmas Day 25 December

Islamic holidays are also observed throughout Cameroon; dates change yearly for these.

TELEPHONE

Cameroon's country code is 237. For international calls out, dial 00 then the relevant country code.

All Cameroonian telephone numbers have nine digits. Mobile numbers begin with 7, 8 or 9. There are no city area codes in Cameroon – all landline numbers begin with a 2 or 3.

Mobile Phones

It's easy to buy a SIM card for an unlocked mobile phone to make local calls while in Cameroon. MTN and Orange are the main national networks.

TOURIST INFORMATION

Formal tourist information is not readily available in Cameroon, though there are some useful small independent agencies and cooperatives which we've listed in the relevant location.

VISAS

Applications in Europe and the US will require a confirmed flight ticket, a letter of invitation authorised by the Cameroonian police, yellow-fever vaccination certificate and proof of funds (minimum £1000/US$1250). A standard visa is valid for three months.

Visa Extensions

You can obtain visa extensions at Cameroon's **Ministry of Immigration** (Map p112; 2 22 22 24 13; Ave Mdug-Fouda Ada; ☺8am-4pm Mon-Fri) in Yaoundé, where one photo plus CFA15,000 is required.

ℹ **PRACTICALITIES**

Electricity Cameroon's electricity supply is 220V and plugs are mostly of the European two-round-pin variety. You'll find a few three-pin sockets in English-speaking areas.

Newspapers The *Cameroon Tribune* is the government-owned bilingual paper, which appears daily in French and weekly in English. The weekly bilingual *Le Messager* is the main independent newspaper.

Radio Most broadcast programming is government run and in French, through Cameroon Radio-TV Corporation (CRTV). TVs at top-end hotels often have CNN or French news stations.

Weights & measures Cameroon uses the metric system.

Visas for Onward Travel

Visas available in Yaoundé for neighbouring African countries include the following:

Central African Republic A one-month visa costs FA55,000 and takes 48 hours to process.

Congo A 15-day visa costs CFA50,000, three months costs CFA100,000. A local invitation is required and processing takes 48 hours.

Equatorial Guinea Does not generally issue visas to nonresidents or people with an Equatorial Guinean embassy in their home country.

Gabon A one-month visa costs CFA50,000; unlike at many Gabonese embassies, a hotel reservation is not required at the Cameroonian office.

Nigeria In Yaoundé, a one-month visa costs CFA45,000 to CFA60,000 and takes 48 hours to process, and you'll need a local invitation.

ℹ **Getting There & Away**

AIR

The national carrier of Cameroon is Camair-Co (p111), which flies to Libreville (Gabon), N'Djaména (Chad), Brazzaville (Congo), Lagos (Nigeria), Abidjan (Ivory Coast), Cotonou (Benin), Kinshasa (DRC) and Paris.

Airports & Airlines

Both Yaoundé (p111) and Douala (p116) have international airports linking Cameroon to major cities in Africa and Europe.

Both are served by Camair-Co (p111) for internal and regional African flights, and by Air France (p116).

ℹ️ ARRIVING IN CAMEROON

Douala International Airport (p116)
Take a licensed taxi to your accommodation. They will be waiting to meet incoming flights but are unmetered, so ask the fee before getting in (around CFA4000, 30 minutes).

Yaoundé Nsimalen International Airport Take a licensed taxi to the centre (around CFA5000, 40 minutes).

LAND

Cameroon's borders with neighbouring countries are open, but the border with Congo is sometimes closed, so check in advance. While the border with Equatorial Guinea is theoretically open, in practice you're likely to be refused entry at the land border, even with a visa.

It is not currently safe to travel from Cameroon to Central African Republic or Chad.

Equatorial Guinea

The main border crossings into Equatorial Guinea and Gabon are a few kilometres from each other, and are both accessible from Ambam in Cameroon. The road splits here, with the westerly route heading for Ebebiyin and Bata (Equatorial Guinea).

The Cameroon–Equatorial Guinea border at Campo is normally closed.

Nigeria

The main crossing point is Ekok, west of Mamfe, where you access Mfum for shared taxis to Calabar (treacherous in the rainy season). The crossing at Banki in the extreme north is inadvisable due to security issues.

SEA

A twice-weekly ferry sails from Limbe (Cameroon) to Calabar (Nigeria) on Monday and Thursday, and in the opposite direction every Tuesday and Friday. Boats are dangerous and not recommended; indeed at the time of writing the service wasn't functioning.

ℹ️ Getting Around

AIR

Internal flights in Cameroon are operated by Camair-Co (p111) and connect Douala and Yaoundé

to Maroua and Garoua. The hop between Yaoundé and Douala (45 minutes) costs around CFA45,000 one way.

The north and east of Cameroon were inaccessible due to security issues at time of writing, but when operational flights from Douala or Yaoundé to Maroua or Garoua (around 1½ hours) cost around CFA125,000 one way.

BUS

Agences de voyages (agency buses, running from depots also called *agences*) run along all major and many minor routes in Cameroon. Prices are low and fixed, and on some bus lines you can even reserve a seat. From Yaoundé to Douala it costs anywhere between CFA3000 and CFA6000, depending on the class of bus you take: so-called VIP services have air-conditioning and aren't quite so cramped. However, some drivers are extremely reckless, and bus accidents occur all too frequently.

Taxis-brousses (bush taxis, which are shared private vehicles) are also popular, especially to some more remote destinations.

Note that, while they might be called *agences*, *gares routières* (bus stations) and sometimes motor parks, these are really glorified car parks for buses, that operate all day and far into the night.

CAR & MOTORCYCLE

Driving in Cameroon is feasible, with mainly decent roads and little police harassment, though the driving all around you is hair-raising. You can hire cars in all large towns, but there's more choice in Douala and Yaoundé. Car hire is very expensive, however, partly because you'll need a 4WD for most itineraries: this becomes essential in the rainy season. In Douala, try Avis in the Hotel Akwa Palace (p114).

A better option is to hire a car and an experienced local driver, who can negotiate road blocks and potholes on your behalf. Ask at your hotel for suggestions, and expect to pay around CFA100,000 for a full day, including petrol.

TRAIN

Cameroon's rail system (Camrail) operates three main lines: Yaoundé to N'Gaoundéré; Yaoundé to Douala; and Douala to Kumba. In 2016 a tragic derailment between Douala and Yaoundé killed 70 passengers and injured many more. Check locally about the current state of train safety.

Côte d'Ivoire

🎵 225 / POP 23.4 MILLION

Best Places to Eat

➡ Bushman Café (p137)

➡ Le Mechoui (p137)

➡ Le Nandjelet (p137)

➡ Aboussouan (p137)

➡ Allocodrome (p137)

Best Places to Sleep

➡ Bushman Café (p134)

➡ Koral Beach Hotel (p141)

➡ La Licorne (p134)

➡ Touraco Ecotel (p144)

➡ Le Wafou (p135)

Why Go?

Côte d'Ivoire is a stunner, shingled with starfish-studded sands, palm-tree forests and roads so orange they resemble strips of bronzing powder. This is a true tropical paradise, and a country that is striding towards economic progress – it's a nation that is fast modernising its lifestyle and culture, but managing to do so without losing its identity.

In the south, the Parc National de Taï hides secrets, species and nut-cracking chimps under the boughs of its trees, while the peaks and valleys of Man offer a highland climate, fresh air and fantastic hiking opportunities through tropical forests.

The beach resorts of low-key Assinie and arty Grand Bassam were made for weekend retreats from Abidjan, the capital in all but name, where lagoons wind their way between skyscrapers and cathedral spires pierce the blue heavens.

When to Go
Abidjan

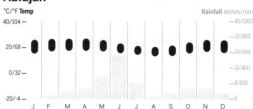

Nov–May Dry season and best time to visit; beaches are best during this time.

May–Jul Rainy season in the south, along with October to November.

Oct–Jun Best time for hiking in the north. Parc National de Taï is best outside wet season.

ABIDJAN

20, 21, 22, 23 / POP 4.5 MILLION

Côte d'Ivoire's economic engine is strapped between lagoons and waterways, overlooking the crested waves of the Atlantic. At first glimpse, you wonder if these shiny skyscrapers can really be West Africa, but once you walk around Abidjan's neighbourhoods, local life comes alive and the city's vibrant tropical mood is revealed.

Abidjan is a challenging city to move around – it's vast and connected by mini-motorways – and you'll have to get in the swing of hailing taxis, negotiating fares and buzzing down the busy roads in order to get from one spot to another. But each neighbourhood's distinct feel gives you an insight into the vast scope of Abidjan's character and contradiction; it's quite common for sharp luxury to exist right next to painful poverty.

Make sure to dip into the markets, street-food stops, art galleries and sleek bars.

◉ Sights

★ Galerie Cécile Fakhoury   GALLERY
(Map p136; 22-446677; www.cecilefakhoury.com; Boulevard Latrille, Cocody; ⊙10am-7pm Tue-Sun) FREE An absolute trove of African contemporary art, this cubical, 600-sq-metre gallery features the best of the continent's artists, from sculpture and painting to photography. Check the website for individual exhibitions or just explore what's on at the time. A real gem of a place.

Hôtel Ivoire   HISTORIC BUILDING
(Map p136; 22-482626; www.sofitel.com; Blvd Hassan II, Blokosso) Every middle-class Abidjani holds a dear memory of Hôtel Ivoire. Built in 1963 by Israeli architect Moshe Mayer, it was *the* place in town to go ice skating and see a movie (the cinema still stands, though the ice rink, unfortunately, does not). Even if you don't stay here, it's worth visiting this hotel for its unique retro African decor.

La Pyramide   NOTABLE BUILDING
(Map p138; cnr Ave Franchet d'Esperey & Blvd Botreau-Roussel) Some of the buildings of Le Plateau are as breathtaking up close as from a distance. La Pyramide, designed by the Italian architect Rinaldo Olivieri and built between 1970 and 1973, was the first daring structure and is considered a highlight of African modernism in architecture. A concrete pyramid striped horizontally with balconies, it rests upon a gigantic cubic pillar, lifting itself over the city's skyline.

Marché de Cocody   MARKET
(Map p136; Blvd de France; ⊙9am-4pm) The super lively Marché de Cocody is a labyrinth of stalls that offer every type of souvenir you can possibly imagine, including wooden sculptures and dishes, antiques, jewellery and traditional decorations. Bargain hard.

Cathedrale St Paul   CHURCH
(Map p136; Blvd Angoulvant, Le Plateau; ⊙8am-7pm) FREE Designed by Italian architect Aldo Spiritom, the Cathedrale St Paul is a bold and innovative modern cathedral. The stained glass is as warm and rich as that inside the Yamoussoukro basilica (p143).

Musée National   MUSEUM
(Map p136; Blvd Nangui Abrogoua, Le Plateau; CFA2000; ⊙9am-5pm Tue-Sat) The national museum houses a dusty but interesting collection of traditional art and craftwork, including wooden statues and masks, pottery, ivory and bronze.

🛏 Sleeping

La Nouvelle Pergola   HOTEL $
(Map p136; 21-753501; www.hotelnouvellepergola.com; Blvd de Marseille, cnr Rue Pierre et Marie Curie, Zone 4; d CFA30,000; P❄@🛜🏊) For reasonable rooms on a budget, La Nouvelle Pergola is an OK bet. There are over 130 rooms in this complex, which includes a pool, a nightclub and wi-fi – though it has none of Côte d'Ivoire's traditional charms.

★ Bushman Café   BOUTIQUE HOTEL $$
(88-358508; Riviera 4, Ciad, Cocody; r from CFA60,000; ❄🏊) French-Ivoirian couple Alain and Pascale run this fusion of hotel and restaurant, which offers impeccable style, local art and artists, the most exquisite decor, lush rooms and gourmet food. Every corner of this three-storey townhouse is spoken for with antiques and art collected by Alain, who also commissioned Ivoirian artists to adorn the walls.

★ La Licorne   BOUTIQUE HOTEL $$
(Map p136; 22-410730; Rue des Jardins, Deux Plateaux Vallons; r CFA65,000-90,000; P❄@🏊) La Licorne is a pretty boutique hotel run by a friendly French family. Rooms are individually decorated, and there's wi-fi, a bar, a hot tub, a book exchange and a decent restaurant.

Le Griffon   BOUTIQUE HOTEL $$
(Map p136; 22-416622; Rue des Jardins, Deux Plateaux Vallons; r CFA45,000-75,000; ❄@🛜🏊) This boutique hotel offers beautifully deco-

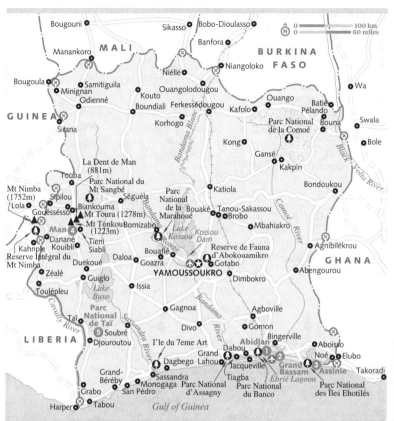

Côte d'Ivoire Highlights

1 Abidjan (p134) Dining on creative Ivoirian dishes, exploring contemporary African art and swaying to the sweet sounds of *coupé-decalé* music in the shadow of the stunning skyline.

2 Grand Bassam (p140) Enjoying the relaxed beach vibe and exploring the

dilapidating colonial past of Côte d'Ivoire.

3 Assinie (p141) Lazing in a pirogue while watching surfers slide to shore, then tucking into fresh seafood under the stars.

4 Man (p143) Hiking to the point where three West

African countries converge and feasting on the green fields below.

5 Parc National de Taï (p144) Exploring the dense rainforest, home to a colony of nut-cracking chimps, and seeing some of the most stunning natural life in Africa.

rated rooms, complete with Ivoirian art and coffee-table books. With friendly staff, great food, wi-fi and a hot tub in the backyard, it's a gem.

⭐ **Le Wafou** BOUTIQUE HOTEL $$$
(☑ 21-256201; www.lewafou.com; Blvd de Marseille, Zone 4; r CFA58,000-110,000, ste CFA150,000-225,000; 🅿 ❄ 🛜 🏊) If the Flintstones won the lottery and moved to West Africa, they'd live

somewhere like this. Set in large grounds, Le Wafou's gorgeous bungalows take cues from traditional Dogon villages in neighbouring Mali. At night you can enjoy great food and wine poolside. A hit with kids, too.

Le Pullman HOTEL $$$
(Map p138; ☑ 20-302020; www.sofitel.com; Rue Abdoulaye Fadiga, Le Plateau; r from CFA120,000; 🅿 ❄ @ 🛜 🏊) A good, upmarket chain hotel.

Abidjan

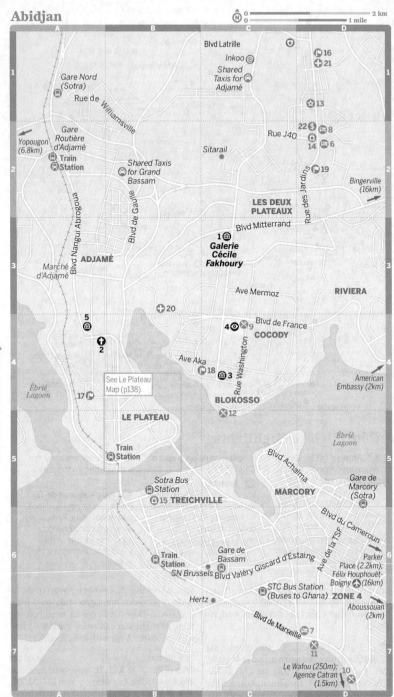

0 ————————— 2 km
0 ————————— 1 mile

Blvd Latrille

Inkoo

Shared Taxis for Adjamé

16
21

Gare Nord (Sotra)

Rue de Williamsville

13

Yopougon (6.8km)

Gare Routière d'Adjamé

Train Station

Shared Taxis for Grand Bassam

Sitarail

Rue J40

22 8
14 6

19

Bingerville (16km)

LES DEUX PLATEAUX

Rue des Jardins

Blvd Mitterrand

1
Galerie Cécile Fakhoury

Marché d'Adjamé

Blvd Nangui Abrogoua

Blvd de Gaulle

ADJAMÉ

Ave Mermoz

RIVIERA

5

2

20

4 9 Blvd de France COCODY

Ave Aka

18 3

Rue Washington

BLOKOSSO

12

American Embassy (2km)

Ébrié Lagoon

17

See Le Plateau Map (p138)

LE PLATEAU

Train Station

Ébrié Lagoon

Blvd Achalma

Gare de Marcory (Sotra)

MARCORY

Sotra Bus Station

15 TREICHVILLE

Train Station

Gare de Bassam

SN Brussels Blvd Valéry Giscard d'Estaing

Hertz

STC Bus Station (Buses to Ghana)

Blvd du Cameroun

Ave de la TSF

Parker Place (2.2km); Félix Houphouët-Boigny (16km)

ZONE 4

Aboussouan (2km)

Blvd de Marseille

7

11

Le Wafou (250m); Agence Catran (1.5km)

10

Abidjan

Plush rooms come equipped with wi-fi and everything you could possibly need.

 Eating

★ **Le Nandjelet** AFRICAN $
(Map p136; Blokosso; mains from CFA2000; ☺ dinner) Tucked away in Blokosso (opposite the cemetery), this enchanting local spot offers good *kedjenou* (slowly simmered chicken or fish with peppers and tomatoes) and Ivoirian *escargot* (snails). Make a beeline for one of the outdoor tables on the edge of the lagoon – they offer a breathtaking panorama of the Abidjan skyline. Mind that on weekends the music gets very loud.

Mille Maquis AFRICAN $
(Map p138; Place de la République) An excellent local strip of *maquis* (rustic open-air restaurants) serving Ivoirian dishes in a jolly, lively atmosphere.

Allocodrome AFRICAN $
(Map p136; Rue Washington, Cocody; mains around CFA2000; ☺ noon-3pm & 7-11pm) Brochettes (kebabs), beer and beats: this fantastic outdoor spot, with dozens of vendors grilling meats, sizzles until late. Once you arrive you'll be swarmed by different vendors – choose one and surrender to the vibe.

★ **Le Mechoui** LEBANESE $$
(Map p136; ☑ 21-246893; inside the Athletic Club, Blvd de Marseille, Zone 4; meze from CFA4000; ☺ noon-3pm & 7-11pm) In an elegant setting that overlooks the lagoon, Le Mechoui serves fantastic Lebanese food. All the ingredients are fresh, the taste is top-notch,

and the choice of the meze is simultaneously authentic and imaginative. Try the lamb tartare, tangy tabbouleh and the classic, creamy hummus – and a serving of hot Lebanese bread. Run by a local Lebanese family.

★ **Bushman Café** AFRICAN $$$
(☑ 88-358508; Riviera 4; mains from CFA10,000) This rooftop terrace restaurant is number-one for gastronomic delights in Abidjan, drawing locals from across the city to come and dine under the stars. The menu is simple and focused on local flavour, and it's perfect. Try the delicate and fresh fish tartare, or the excellent grilled meat. Properly brewed Ivoirian coffee is served here, too. Do not miss.

★ **Aboussouan** AFRICAN $$$
(☑ 21-241309; Blvd Giscard-D'Estaing, Treichville; mains from CFA8000; ☺ noon-3pm & 7-11pm Tue-Sat; ✤) Take Côte d'Ivoire's best *maquis* dishes, ask top chefs to prepare them and add fine, innovative touches – that's Aboussouan. Foodie heaven, and there's an excellent wine list too.

Le Marlin Bleu SEAFOOD $$$
(Map p136; ☑ 21-259727; Blvd de Marseille, Zone 4; mains from CFA15,000) An upmarket, yachting-orientated seafood restaurant (ignore the hotel!) that has fresh fish and luxurious seafood offerings. Popular with the expats. In a kind of compound off Blvd de Marseille.

🍷 **Drinking & Entertainment**

If there is a city in West Africa to party in, it's Abidjan. There are plenty of parties,

CÔTE D'IVOIRE ABIDJAN

Le Plateau

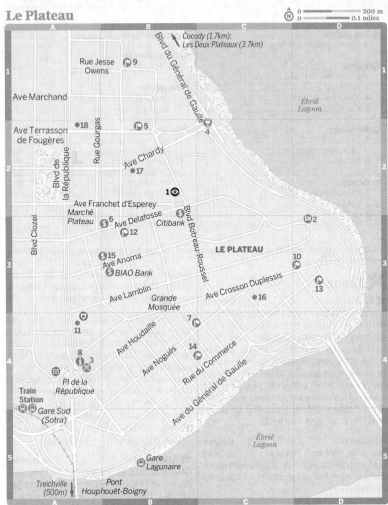

N 0 ————————— 200 m
   0 ————————— 0.1 miles

Cocody (1.7km);
Les Deux Plateaux (3.7km)

Rue Jesse Owens

Ave Marchand

Ave Terrasson de Fougères

Rue Gourgas

Blvd du Général de Gaulle

Ébrié Lagoon

Ave Chardy

Blvd de la République

Ave Franchet d'Esperey

Marché Plateau

Ave Delafosse

Citibank

Blvd Clozel

Ave Anoma

BIAO Bank

Blvd Botreau-Roussel

LE PLATEAU

Ave Lamblin

Grande Mosquée

Ave Crosson Duplessis

Ave Houdaille

Ave Noguès

Rue du Commerce

Pl de la République

Train Station

Gare Sud (Sotra)

Ave du Général de Gaulle

Ébrié Lagoon

Gare Lagunaire

Treichville (500m)

Pont Houphouët-Boigny

COTE D'IVOIRE ABIDJAN

---

from ordinary *maquis* dancing to sleek DJ parties on rooftops. Note that a lot of the nightclub scene caters to wealthy Ivoirians and expats.

Bushman Café
ROOFTOP BAR

(☑88-358508; www.facebook.com/africaisafrica; Riviera 4) A wide range of cocktails means you can spend hours choosing between passionfruit cocktails or something with a tamarind twist. There's great music here, and DJ parties, too – check their Facebook page for what's coming up.

Life Star
CLUB

(Map p138; ☑49-202020; Ave Chardy, Le Plateau; ⊙11pm-6am) A fancy club that attracts wealthy Ivoirians and well-off expats, and anyone who's anyone in Abidjan.

Parker Place
LIVE MUSIC

(☑05-373459; Rue Paul Langevin, Zone 4; ⊙Tue-Sun) This is Abidjan's most famous reggae bar – Alpha Blondy and Tiken Jah Fakoly played here before they were famous. The bar is still going strong and welcomes live acts most Thursday, Friday and Saturday nights (there's usually a cover charge).

Le Plateau

L'Acoustic LIVE MUSIC
(Map p136; Rue des Jardins, Deux Plateaux) L'Acoustic's stage has held the feet of everyone from hip female vocalists to jazz and big-band ensembles. The place attracts an arty, musical crowd. There's a restaurant for late-night dinners.

🛍 Shopping

Marché de Treichville MARKET
(Map p136; Ave Victor Blaka) The Marché de Treichville is an ugly, Chinese-built building, but inside it's African to the core and incredibly well stocked, from food to household products and secondhand clothing. There is little you can't find here.

Galerie d'Arts Pluriels ARTS & CRAFTS
(Map p136; ☑22-411506; Centre Commercial Municipal, Rue des Jardins, Deux Plateaux) This fantastic art gallery and shop is run by an Ivoirian art historian. You can view and buy paintings, sculptures and jewellery from all over the continent.

ℹ Information

INTERNET ACCESS

Most hotels, and a growing number of restaurants and bars, offer wi-fi.
Inkoo (Map p136; ☑21-247065; Cap Sud Centre Commercial & Gallerie Sococé, Rue K 125, Deux Plateaux; per 30min CFA500; ⊙9am-8pm) Has speedy connections, a printing centre, phone booths, faxes and scanners.

MEDICAL SERVICES

PISAM (Polyclinique Internationale St Anne-Marie; Map p136; ☑22-483131; www.pisam.ci; Ave Joseph Blohorn, off Blvd de la Corniche, Cocody) Recommended by UN staff. Has a 24-hour intensive care unit.
Polyclinique des Deux Plateaux (Map p136; ☑22-413334, 22-414621; www.polycliniquedes2plateaux.com; Rue du Commissariat du 30e Arrondisement, Deux Plateaux) Has good medical services.

The US embassy publishes a list of recommended practitioners on its website at http://abidjan.usembassy.gov.

MONEY

Euros and dollars can be changed at main branches of banks in Le Plateau. **SGBCI** (Map p138; Ave Anoma, Le Plateau) and **Bicici** (Map p138; Ave Delafosse, Le Plateau) have ATMs that accept Visa, MasterCard and Maestro.

The following banks all have Visa ATMs:
BIAO Bank (Map p138; Ave Anoma, Le Plateau)
Citibank (Map p138; Ave Delafosse, Le Plateau)
SGBCI Bank (Map p136; Rue des Jardins, Deux Plateaux)

POLICE

POST

La Poste (Map p138; Place de la République, Le Plateau; ⊙7.30am-noon & 2.30-4pm Mon-Fri) Has Western Union service and poste restante.

ℹ ARRIVING IN ABIDJAN

Félix Houphouët-Boigny International Airport (p140) There is no public transport to or from the airport. A taxi to/from Abidjan can cost around CFA5000 to CFA6000, depending on your bargaining skills.

Côte d'Ivoire Tourisme (Map p138; ☑20-251600, 20-251610; Place de la République, Le Plateau; ☺7.30am-noon & 2.30-4pm Mon-Fri) There's a good map on the wall and the helpful staff will happily shower you with brochures.

❶ Getting There & Away

Félix Houphouët-Boigny International Airport (Port Bouet Airport; www.aeria-ci.com; Port-Bouët) Takes all of the international air traffic.

Gare de Bassam (Map p136; cnr Rue B4 & Blvd Valéry Giscard d'Estaing, Zone 2B) South of Treichville. Bush taxis and minibuses for destinations east along the coast, such as Grand Bassam, Aboisso and Elubo (at the Ghanaian border), stop here.

Gare Routière d'Adjamé (Map p136; Ave 13, Adjamé) The main bus station is located some 4km north of Le Plateau, and is quite chaotic. Most UTB and Sotra buses and bush taxis leave from here, and there's frequent transport to all major towns.

Other bus stations here include the following:

Gare de Marcory (Sotra) (Map p136; Rue du Taureau, Marcory)

Gare Lagunaire (Map p138; Ave du General de Gaulle, Le Plateau)

Gare Nord (Sotra) (Map p136; Autoroute d'Abobo, Williamsville)

Gare Sud (Sotra) (Map p138; Blvd de la Paix, Le Plateau)

Sotra Bus Station (Map p136; ☑21-757100; www.sotra.ci; Ave Christiani, Treichville)

STC Bus Station (Map p136; Rue des Carrossiers, Zone 3) For buses to Ghana.

❶ Getting Around

Woro-woro (shared taxis) cost between CFA300 and CFA800, depending on the length of the journey, and vary in colour according to their function. The yellow taxis work like minibuses, going from one designated spot to another across town; they're usually shared, and do not drop people off to individual destinations.

The red taxis are usually hired just by you (unless you choose to share) and will take you pretty much anywhere within Abidjan. A short hop in a cab from Le Plateau to Zone 4 costs around CFA2000.

Shared Taxis for Adjamé (Map p136; Rue K57, Deux Plateaux)

Shared Taxis for Grand Bassam (Map p136; Adjamé)

THE EASTERN BEACHES

Grand Bassam
☑21

Arty and bathed in faded glory, beachside Bassam was Côte d'Ivoire's French colonial capital until a yellow-fever epidemic broke out in 1896, prompting the French to move their capital to Bingerville. The town, named a Unesco World Heritage Site in 2012, had a glittery image as the top resort in the country until a March 2016 terrorist attack, claimed by al-Qaeda, killed 16 people, many of them foreigners. The town is now safe, but the attack caused a slump in the local tourism industry and Grand Bassam is working hard to recover its flair.

The city is laid out on a long spit of land, with a quiet lagoon on one side and the turbulent Atlantic Ocean on the other. Weekenders fill the beach and enjoy the sun and the sand, but swimming is not advised due to the strong currents – people drown every year, especially tourists.

◉ Sights & Activities

Palais de Justice　　　　　NOTABLE BUILDING
(Blvd Treich-Laplene) The Palais de Justice should be your first stop on a walk through town. Built in 1910, it was in this building that members of Côte d'Ivoire's PDCI-RDA political group – that of the country's first president, Félix Houphouët-Boigny – were arrested by the French authorities in 1949, in the struggle that preceded the country's independence.

Nick Amon's Art Gallery　　　　GALLERY
(Blvd Treich-Laplene) One of Côte d'Ivoire's most respected contemporary artists, Amon will greet you with paint-splattered clothing and a warm smile. His canvases start at around CFA50,000; profits go to an organisation that offers art classes to street kids.

Canoeing　　　　　CANOEING
You can take to the waters on a dugout-canoe trip to see traditional crab fishers, mangroves and birdlife. You can make arrangements with local boatmen.

✪ Festivals & Events

Fête de l'Abissa　　　　RELIGIOUS
(☺Oct or Nov) This week-long ceremony honouring the dead offers a great opportunity to witness local traditions.

Grand Bassam

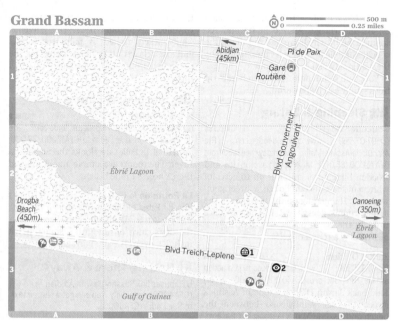

Abidjan (45km)

Pl de Paix

Gare Routière

Blvd Gouverneur Angoulvant

Ébrié Lagoon

Drogba Beach (450m)

Canoeing (350m)

Ébrié Lagoon

Blvd Treich-Leplene

Gulf of Guinea

🛏 Sleeping & Eating

Hôtel Boblin la Mer HOTEL **$**
(☎21-301418; Blvd Treich-Laplene; r with air-con CFA20,000-30,000; P❄🎧) Breezy and sunwashed, Boblin la Mer is easily the best value in Bassam. The rooms are decorated with masks and woodcarvings, and breakfast is served on the beach.

★Koral Beach Hotel HOTEL **$$**
(☎07-239212; koralbeach@yahoo.fr; Blvd Gouverneur Angoulvant/Blvd Treich-Laplene; d from CFA30,000; P❄🎧🛏🍴) Run by the wonderful and energetic Cheryl, the KBH has been redecorated to perfection – it's all African wood sculptures and white, pristine walls. The rooms are equally elegant and stylish, with ample beds and featuring local art. The

hotel restaurant is good – you can dine overlooking the beach and watching the sunset.

La Madrague HOTEL **$$**
(☎21-301564; www.hotellamadrague.com; Blvd Treich-Laplene; d CFA25,000-40,000; ❄🎧🛏) La Madrague taps into Grand Bassam's spirit with its smart, lovingly decorated rooms. There's local art on the walls and Ivoirian cloth swaddling the luxurious beds.

Drogba Beach AFRICAN **$$**
(Blvd Treich-Leplene; mains from CFA3000) A nice and simple *maquis* on the beach, popular with local families at the weekends. Rustic Ivoirian food is served at the simple wooden terrace.

ℹ Getting There & Away

Woro-woro (CFA700, 40 minutes) leave from Abidjan's Gare de Bassam. In Bassam, the **gare routière** (bus station) is beside the Place de Paix roundabout, north of the lagoon.

Assinie

☎21 / POP 16,720

Quiet little Assinie tugs at the heartstrings of overlanders, washed-up surfers and rich weekenders from Abidjan who run their quad bikes up and down its peroxide-blonde beach. It's actually a triumvirate of villages: Assinie village, Assinie Mafia and Assouindé, all of which are laid out along the beaches and flow into each other, unified by their uniquely holiday atmosphere.

You can swim here, but watch the rip tides – they can be powerful.

🛏 Sleeping & Eating

Coucoue Lodge BUNGALOW $$
(📞07-077769; www.coucoue-lodge.com; Rte Assouindé-Assinie-Mafia; d weekday/weekend from CFA75,000/85,000; 🅿️❄️🛜🏊) Colourful and wooden bungalows spill out on to acres of white sand at Coucoue Lodge, a sweet getaway spot. If lounging on the beach or in the luxury rooms doesn't cut it, you can slice through the ocean on jet skis, rent inflatables or play a round of golf.

Jardin D'Eden BUNGALOW $$
(📞07-135300; www.facebook.com/jardineden assinie; Rue 30; s/d CFA40,000/55,000; ❄️🛜) Laid-back Jardin D'Eden is one of Assinie's sweetest spots, sandwiched between the beach and Assinie Mafia. A good bet for a relaxed weekend away with friends, with nice Ivoirian food on offer and cool, calm, clean, comfortable rooms.

Le Voile Rouge AFRICAN $$
(📞58-722971; Assinie Mafia; mains from CFA6000; ⏲noon-3pm & 6-11pm) A fantastic little place on the waterfront in Assinie Mafia, serving up Ivoirian specialities such as chicken *kedjenou* (slowly simmered chicken or fish with peppers and tomatoes) and grilled prawns. You can swim off the little wooden pier in the afternoons when the tide comes in.

ℹ Getting There & Away

Coming from Grand Bassam or Abidjan, take a *woro-woro* to Samo (CFA2000, 45 minutes). From here you can pick up another car to Assouindé, 15 minutes away. Once there, the rest of the area is accessible by pirogue (traditional canoe) or *woro-woro*.

THE WEST COAST

Sassandra
📞 34 / POP 72,220

Sassandra, a low-key beach resort in the far western corner of Côte d'Ivoire, may be a little dog-eared these days but there's something endearing – and enduring – here, for travellers keep going back. The gorgeous sandy beach backed by palm-tree forests and the relaxed atmosphere make for the perfect environment for a couple of days of utter rest.

🛏 Sleeping & Eating

Hôtel le Pollet HOTEL $
(📞34-720578; http://lepolletuk.jimdo.com; Rte du Palais de Justice; ⏲r/ste CFA17,000/38,000; ❄️) Hôtel le Pollet overlooks the Sassandra River. The rooms are simple and clean, and there's access to the beach.

La Route de la Cuisine SEAFOOD $
(Rte du Palais de Justice; mains from CFA1000; ⏲noon-3pm & 7-11pm) The chef here throws the day's catch on the grill – sometimes it includes swordfish and barracuda.

ℹ Getting There & Away

UTB buses link Sassandra with Abidjan (CFA4000) once daily. You can get a shared taxi to San Pédro (CFA3000).

San Pédro
📞 34 / POP 631,155

Framed by a strip of soft white sand on one side, and the distant shadows of the fertile Parc National de Taï (p144) on the other, a stop in San Pédro promises a sweet marriage of beach life and forest treks.

West of San Pedro are the balmy beaches of Grand-Béréby. It's also the best place to overnight if you're heading overland into Liberia via Tabou and Harper.

🛏 Sleeping & Eating

Le Cannelle HOTEL $
(📞34-710539; Blvd Houphouët-Boigny; r CFA25,000; ❄️🛜) Overlooking the waters and with simple and clean rooms, Le Canelle also has a decent restaurant on the beach.

Les Jardins d'Ivoire HOTEL $
(📞34-713186; Blvd Houphouët-Boigny, Quartier Balmer; r CFA26,000; 🅿️❄️🏊) Located in the Balmer area of town, Les Jardins d'Ivoire has a pretty garden, a swimming pool and clean, smart rooms.

ℹ Getting There & Away

UTB buses link San Pédro with Abidjan (CFA5000) once daily. *Woro-woro* go to Grand-

Béréby (CFA2500) and east to Sassandra (CFA3000).

For Harper, just across the Liberian border, you can take a shared taxi to Tabou (about CFA4000), then continue on by a combination of road and boat; note that it's not worth attempting in the rainy season.

THE CENTRE

Yamoussoukro

📋 30 / POP 281,070

Yamoussoukro (or Yamkro, as it's affectionately dubbed) isn't exactly its country's cultural epicentre, but it is worth a stop here, if only to marvel at the oddity of the capital that was built on the site of former President Félix Houphouët-Boigny's ancestral village. Its basilica, a near-replica of the Vatican's Basilica di San Pietro, is a marvel, its gigantic dome hovering on the flat horizon like a mirage.

The **tourist office** (📋 30-640814; Ave Houphouët-Boigny; ⊙ 8am-noon & 3-6pm Mon-Fri) arranges Baoulé dancing performances in nearby villages.

⊙ Sights

Presidential Palace   NOTABLE BUILDING

The presidential palace, where Houphouët-Boigny is now buried, can only be seen from afar, but visitors come to see the **sacred crocodiles** that live in the lake on its southern side. The keeper tosses them some meat around 5pm, touching off an impressive feeding frenzy. Otherwise, the dozens of sleepy reptiles laze away while curious onlookers take photos. But keep your distance: in 2012, a veteran keeper was killed by one of the creatures.

Basilica   CHURCH

(Basilique Notre-Dame de la Paix; Rte de Daloa; CFA2000; ⊙ 8am-noon & 2-5.30pm Mon-Sat, 2-5pm Sun) Yamoussoukro's spectacular basilica will leave you wide-eyed. Based on the Basilica of St Peter in the Vatican and designed by Lebanese architect Pierre Fakhoury, it was constructed between 1985 and 1989, with Italian marble and 7000 sq metres of French stained glass specially imported to build it. The nave is a luminous harmony of columns, with a flamboyant altar taking centre stage. There are well-informed English-speaking guides on duty

who will take you around the dome and the grounds.

🛏 Sleeping & Eating

Le Brennus   HOTEL $

(📋 59-127737; www.lebrennus.com; Rte d'Abidjan; r/ste CFA30,000/70,000; 🅿 ❄ 🛜) A good hotel in the centre of town, with simple and clean rooms and efficient service.

Hôtel Président   HOTEL $$

(📋 30-646464; www.hotelpresident.ci; Rte d'Abidjan; s/d/ste US$65/80/150; ❄ 🖭) Yamoussoukro's signature hotel, imposing but faded – the rooms are old, but still swish. There's an 18-hole **golf course**, as well as three restaurants (including a panoramic eatery on the 14th floor), four bars and a nightclub.

A La Bella Pizza   PIZZA $

(Ave Houphouët-Boigny; mains CFA3500-5000; ⊙ noon-3pm & 6-11pm) Serves great pastas, crêpes and local fare, as well as its namesake pizzas.

Maquis le Jardin   AFRICAN $$

(mains CFA3000-5000; ⊙ noon-3pm & 7-11pm) More upmarket and expensive than the other *maquis* clustered by the lake – the excellent food here makes it worthwhile.

❶ Getting There & Away

MTT and UTB, whose bus stations are south of town, run buses frequently to Abidjan (CFA4500, 1½ hours); UTB also runs frequently to Bouaké (CFA3800, two hours) and once daily to Man (CFA5000, five hours) and San Pédro (CFA6000, five hours).

THE NORTH

Man

📋 33 / POP 188,700

The green, green peaks and valleys of Man are nothing short of magical. Here the air is cooler, the food lighter and the landscapes muddier than in the south. And it's perfect hiking territory. The town itself is a grid of busy streets filled with vendors.

⊙ Sights & Activities

Silacoro   VILLAGE

This celebrated village is famous for its stilt dancing. It's found 110km north of Man.

La Cascade
WATERFALL

(CFA400) The area around Man is known for La Cascade, a crashing waterfall 5km from town that hydrates a bamboo forest. You walk a pretty paved path to reach it. Locals come here to swim and visitors are welcome to join in.

★ Le Dent de Man
HIKING

(guide fee CFA3000) 'The Man's Tooth' sticks out like, well, a tooth, northeast of town. A hike up this steep mountain (881m) starts in the village of Zoguale (where you can find a guide), 4km from Man, running through coffee, cocoa and banana plantations. The final stretch requires some serious leg work. Allow at least four hours for the round trip. Bring snacks.

Mt Tonkoui
HIKING

(guide fee CFA3000) At 1223m, Mt Tonkoui is the second-highest peak in Côte d'Ivoire. The views from the summit are breathtaking and extend to Liberia and Guinea, even during the dusty harmattan winds. The route begins about 18km from Man. You can ask for a guide at your hotel.

🛏 Sleeping & Eating

Hôtel Amointrin
HOTEL $

(📞 33-792670; Rte du Lycée Professionnel; r standard/superior CFA15,000/16,000; ❄) Hôtel Amointrin is probably Man's smartest hotel; the rooms come with hot water and pretty views out over the mountains.

Hôtel Leveneur
HOTEL $

(📞 33-791776; Rue de l'Hôtel Leveneur; r CFA12,000; ❄) The centrally located Hôtel Leveneur has the dishevelled backpacker thing down to a T, though we suspect it's not deliberate.

Maquis Flamboyant
AFRICAN $

(Rte du Lycée Professionnel; CFA1500) You can find great *attiéké* (grated cassava) – a slightly bitter, couscous-like dish – and brochettes (grilled meat or fish cubes) in this low-key eatery.

Pâtisserie la Brioche
BAKERY $

(Rue du Commerce; croissants CFA240) A fine place for breakfast or morning coffee.

🛍 Shopping

Tankari Gallery
ARTS & CRAFTS

(Ave du President Alassane Ouattara; ⊙9am-4pm) You can find West African woodwork here, such as dishes, masks and small wooden sculptures. There is also jewellery and textiles.

ℹ Getting There & Away

You can reach Abidjan by *woro-woro* (CFA8000, seven hours) or UTB bus (CFA7000, eight hours).

Taxis for N'zérékoré in Guinea run via Sipilou (CFA3000, three hours).

PARC NATIONAL DE TAÏ

There are many places in West Africa that could be dubbed one of the region's 'best-kept secrets', but perhaps none so as much as Taï (📞 34-722299; www.parcnationaltai.com) FREE, a 5000-sq-km reserve of rainforest so dense that scientists are only just beginning to discover the wealth of flora and fauna that lies within.

Parc National de Taï is one of West Africa's last areas of primary rainforest, and has been a World Heritage Site since 1982. The park is mostly known for its chimpanzees, who famously use tools in their daily activities, but the general wealth of the flora and fauna inside the park is incredible. Besides forest elephants and buffalo, there are at least eleven types of primates, 250 species of birds and 1300 species of plants, more than 50 of which are endemic to the region.

🏃 Activities

Visitors can take forest hikes with local rangers, visiting Hana river, Buya lake and Mt Niénokoué, where you can stop at the primate research base famous for its nut-cracking chimps.

The Wild Chimpanzee Foundation (www.wildchimps.org) is a great source of information on chimp life.

🛏 Sleeping & Eating

Touraco Ecotel
HUT $

(📞 34-722299; www.parcnationaltai.com; huts from CFA10,000) This eco-camp has a mix of thatch-topped round huts with no more than a bed inside them, and a restaurant on the edge of a forest clearing. There are outdoor toilets and showers. You can stay here and explore the park's offerings with the excellent local rangers. Ring ahead.

Auberge Beau Séjour
GUESTHOUSE

(📞 47-971453; Taï; r with fan/air-con CFA6000/12,000; 🅿❄) Simple, clean and minimally furnished rooms in Taï town that are perfect for an overnight stay before you hit the park. There's air-con and en suite bathrooms.

Le Plein Air   AFRICAN $
(☑ 47-701637; mains CFA2000-2500) A simple *maquis* (open-air restaurant) in Taï town. You can get the usual grilled chicken or fish with *aloco* (ripe bananas fried with chilli in palm oil) and *attiéké* (grated cassava) or rice with a sauce in a peaceful local setting.

❶ Getting There & Away

Taï is 213km from San Pédro; it's about a three-hour drive outside the rainy season. If you have your own vehicle, hit the road until you reach the village of Djouroutou, on the west side of the park.

You can also reach Djouroutou from San Pédro via **shuttle** (☑ 34-722299; CFA4000), but it will take longer and you may have to change cars.

UNDERSTAND CÔTE D'IVOIRE

Côte d'Ivoire Today

After the long-delayed presidential elections, Alassane Ouattara took power in 2010. His predecessor, Laurent Gbagbo, had to be forcibly removed from office after refusing to accept defeat. The ensuing violence left 3000 people dead and 500,000 displaced. In November 2011 Gbagbo was extradited to The Hague and charged with war crimes.

Ouattara won a second five-year term in 2015. Economically, Côte d'Ivoire has been one of the best-performing African countries since Ouattara was elected: its GDP grew at an average rate of 8.5% per year between 2012 and 2015.

But while the economy booms, politics remain shaky. Côte d'Ivoire suffered a terrorist attack in March 2016, when an armed group, allegedly Islamist fundamentalists, killed 16 people – both local and foreign – in a beachside resort in Grand Bassam. This has affected tourism, with many hotel owners in Grand Bassam complaining of a dramatic drop in revenue.

January 2017 saw more political instability in the form of military mutiny. Soldiers seized Bouaké and kidnapped the country's defence minister for a short time; there was mild unrest in Abidjan, too. Since the mutiny was reported to be about soldiers' pay, President Ouattara promised salary increases and fired the army and police chiefs,

leading the soldiers to withdraw to their barracks.

It is said that many of the soldiers who took part in the mutiny are former rebels who were integrated into the army when Ouattara took power, and that this episode reflects the wider dissatisfaction of the chunk of the population – among them teachers and civil servants – who feel left out of the country's economic boom.

History

After decades of stability, Côte d'Ivoire's troubles began in September 2002, when troops from the north gained control of much of the country. A truce was short-lived and fighting resumed. France sent in troops to maintain the ceasefire boundaries; meanwhile, tensions from Liberia's war began to spill over the border.

In March 2004 one of numerous peace deals was signed, and Guillaume Soro, formerly the secretary of the New Forces rebel coalition, was named prime minister. UN peacekeepers arrived, but on 4 November President Laurent Gbagbo broke the ceasefire and bombed rebel strongholds, including Bouaké. Two days later, jets struck a French military base, killing nine French peacekeepers. In retaliation, the French destroyed much of the Ivoirian air force's fleet. Government soldiers clashed with peacekeepers, while most French citizens fled, and dozens of Ivoirians died.

A UN resolution backed the president's bid to stay in office until fair elections could be held. In April 2007 French peacekeepers began a staged pull back from the military buffer zone, to be replaced gradually by mixed brigades of government and rebel troops. Gbagbo declared the end of the war and the two sides moved to dismantle the military buffer zone.

In June that year a rocket attack on Prime Minister Soro's plane killed four of his aides, shaking the peace process further. Protests over rising food costs spread through the country. The elections were finally held in 2010.

Arts & Crafts

The definitive Ivoirian craft is Korhogo cloth, a coarse cotton painted with geometrical designs and fantastical animals. Also prized are Dan masks from the Man region, and

Senoufo wooden statues, masks and traditional musical instruments from the northeast. A fantastic range of contemporary arts can be explored in Abidjan's Galerie Cécile Fakhoury (p134).

Environment

Côte d'Ivoire used to be covered in dense rainforest, but most of it was cleared during the agricultural boom, and what remains today is under attack from outlawed logging and farming practices.

The country is the world's largest cocoa producer, though much of the production takes place illegally – inside the rainforests, where land is cleared and eventually becomes barren. It is estimated that about 80 percent of the country's forests have disappeared since the 1970s.

Several peaks in the west rise more than 1000m, and a coastal lagoon with a unique ecosystem stretches 300km west from the Ghanaian border. The north is dry scrubland.

SURVIVAL GUIDE

 Directory A–Z

ACCOMMODATION

Accommodation in Abidjan is expensive and not always good value for money. Elsewhere in the country, you'll find better deals, but standards of comfort are generally lower.

ACTIVITIES

Several spots on the coast, most notably Assinie and Dagbego, have decent surfing. Côte d'Ivoire also has a lot to offer birdwatchers, particularly during the (European) winter migration season from December to March. For hiking, head to Man or the beautiful Parc National de Taï.

 SLEEPING PRICE RANGES

The following price ranges refer to a double room with bathroom during high season. Breakfast is not included in the price unless noted.

$ less than CFA30,000

$$ CFA30,000–90,000

$$$ more than CFA90,000

DANGERS & ANNOYANCES

➡ Abidjan and other parts of the south are now entirely safe to visit.

➡ Avoid Bouaké: it's prone to outbreaks of political and military violence.

➡ If you're heading to the border with Liberia, check with locals first: tensions flare sporadically.

➡ Take care when walking at night – it's unwise to walk alone outside of well-populated areas.

➡ Beware of riding in cars without a seatbelt, and in general, if driving – there is a high rate of motor accidents here.

➡ People drown in the fierce currents and ripping undertow of the Atlantic every year – often strong, overly confident swimmers. Don't swim anywhere the locals won't.

EMBASSIES & CONSULATES

The following embassies are in Abidjan.

Belgian Embassy (Map p138; ✆ 20-210088, 20-219434; http://cotedivoire.diplomatie. belgium.be; 4th fl, Immeuble Alliance, Ave Terrasson des Fougères 01, Le Plateau; ⊙ 8-11am Mon-Thu) Also assists Dutch nationals.

Burkinabé Embassy (Map p136; ✆ 20-211501; Ave Terrasson de Fougères, Le Plateau; ⊙ 8amnoon Mon-Fri) Also has a consulate in Bouaké.

Canadian Embassy (Map p138; ✆ 20-300700; www.canadainternational.gc.ca/cotedivoire; Immeuble Trade Centre, 23 Ave Noguès, Le Plateau; ⊙ 7.30am-12.30pm & 1.30-4.30pm Mon-Thu, 7.30am-1pm Fri) Also assists Australian nationals.

French Embassy (Map p138; ✆ 20-207500; www.ambafrance-ci.org; 17 Rue Lecoeur, Le Plateau; ⊙ 8am-4pm Mon-Fri)

German Embassy (Map p136; ✆ 22-442030; www.abidjan.diplo.de; 39 Blvd Hassan II, Cocody; ⊙ 9am-noon & 2-4pm Mon-Thu, 9amnoon Fri)

Ghanaian Embassy (Map p136; ✆ 22-410288; www.ghanaembassy-ci.org; Rue J95, Deux Plateaux; ⊙ 8.30am-12.30pm & 2-4pm Mon-Fri)

Guinean Embassy (Map p138; ✆ 20-222520; 3rd fl, Immeuble Crosson Duplessis, Ave Crosson Duplessis, Le Plateau; ⊙ 8am-noon Mon-Fri)

Liberian Embassy (Map p138; ✆ 20-324636; Immeuble Taleb, Ave Delafosse, Le Plateau; ⊙ 8am-noon Mon-Thu)

Malian Embassy (Map p138; ✆ 20-311570; Maison du Mali, Rue du Commerce, Le Plateau; ⊙ 8am-4pm Mon-Fri)

Senegalese Embassy (Map p138; ✆ 20-332876; Immeuble Nabil, off Rue du Commerce, Le Plateau; ⊙ 8am-2pm Mon-Fri)

EMERGENCY & IMPORTANT NUMBERS

Côte d'Ivoire's country code	225
International access code	00
Police	111
Fire	180
Medecins Urgence (ambulance)	07-082626
SOS Medecins (ambulance)	185

GAY & LESBIAN TRAVELLERS
Same-sex relations are not a crime in Côte d'Ivoire, but there are no legal protections for sexual minorities. Although there are several LGBT organisations (one of them suffered a mob attack in 2014), and a relatively good LGBT scene for the region, there are regular reports of violence based on sexual orientation. Caution and discretion are well advised in public.

INTERNET ACCESS
Abidjan, and the south, have wi-fi in midrange and upmarket establishments. It's rare to find wi-fi in the north.

MONEY
ATMs are available in the bigger cities, but take cash if you're going anywhere more remote. Credit cards are accepted in top-end establishments.

ATMs
Visa ATMs are widespread in Abidjan, Grand Bassam, Yamoussoukro and major towns. Most SGBCI branches have ATMs that accept Visa, MasterCard and sometimes Maestro. There are no banks in Assinie but there is a branch of SGB-CI (with an ATM) in Grand Bassam.

Exchange Rates

Australia	A$1	CFA452
Canada	C$1	CFA440
Europe	€1	CFA656
Japan	¥100	CFA538
NZ	NZ$1	CFA415
UK	UK£1	CFA774
US	US$1	CFA600

For current exchange rates, see www.xe.com.

Tipping
Guesthouses You can tip around CFA500 if the service was very good.

Hotels Tipping the cleaning staff is at your discretion, but if you're very happy with the job they did, anything up to CFA1500 is reasonable.

EATING PRICE RANGES

The following price ranges refer to a main course.

$ less than CFA3000
$$ CFA3000–6000
$$$ more than CFA6000

Tours Beyond the guided tour price, if your guide has been excellent, tip them from CFA500 to CFA1000.

Taxi Since you'll mostly have to bargain down the price, tipping is not expected.

OPENING HOURS
Banks 8am to 11.30am and 2.30pm to 4.30pm Monday to Friday
Bars noon to 11pm
Cafes 9am to 6pm
Clubs 11pm to 4am
Government offices 7.30am to 5.30pm Monday to Friday (with breaks for lunch)
Restaurants noon to 3pm (lunch) and 7pm to 11pm (dinner)
Shops 8am to 6pm

POST
La Poste is the country's main postal service. The main **La Poste** branch is in Abidjan (p139).

PUBLIC HOLIDAYS
New Year's Day 1 January
Labour Day 1 May
Independence Day 7 August
Fête de la Paix 15 November
Christmas 25 December

TELEPHONE
If you have a GSM mobile phone, you can buy SIM cards from CFA2500. Street stalls also sell

---

PRACTICALITIES

Electricity The power supply is 220V. Plugs are of the European two-round-pin variety.

Newspapers Among the nearly 20 daily newspapers, all in French, Soirinfo, 24 Heures and L'Intelligent d'Abidjan steer an independent course. Gbich! is a satirical paper.

Radio Jam (99.3FM) and Radio Nostalgie (101.1FM) play hit music. The BBC World Service broadcasts some programs in English on 94.3FM.

top-up vouchers from CFA550. Calls generally cost between CFA25 and CFA150 per minute.

The Orange network is reliable and accessible in most parts of the country, even some rural areas, although it can be expensive.

TOURIST INFORMATION

Côte d'Ivoire Tourisme (p140) in Abidjan has helpful staff.

VISAS

Everyone except Ecowas (Economic Community of West African States) nationals must arrange a visa in advance.

Visas can be extended at **La Sureté Nationale** (Map p138; ☑ 20-320289; www.diplomatie.gouv.ci; Police de l'Air et des Frontières, Immeuble Douane, Blvd de la République, Le Plateau; ⊘ 8am-noon & 3-5pm Mon-Fri) in Abidjan.

Visas for Onward Travel

If you want to travel to several countries in the area, consider the Visa de l'Entente, which allows entry to Côte d'Ivoire, Benin, Burkina Faso, Niger and Togo. This multiple-entry visa is valid for two months and costs €120. Apply for it at the **Beninese Embassy** (Map p136; ☑ 22-414413, 22-414414; www.ambassadebeninci.com; 09 BP 283, Cocody II; ⊘ 8-11am Mon-Thu) in Abidjan.

❶ Getting There & Away

AIR

Félix Houphouët-Boigny (p140) is Côte d'Ivoire's swish international airport, complete with wi-fi access.

Airlines that service Côte d'Ivoire include:

Air France (AF; Map p138; ☑ 20-202424; www.airfrance.com; Immeuble Kharrat, Rue Noguès, Le Plateau)

Air Ivoire (VU; Map p138; ☑ 20-251400, 20-251561; www.airivoire.com; Immeuble Le République, Place de la République, Le Plateau)

Ethiopian Airlines (ET; Map p138; ☑ 20-215284; www.flyethiopian.com; Ave Chardy, Le Plateau)

Kenya Airways (KQ; Map p138; ☑ 20-320767; www.kenya-airways.com; Immeuble Jeceda, Blvd de la République, Le Plateau)

SN Brussels (SN; Map p136; ☑ 27-232345; www.flysn.com; off Blvd Valéry Giscard d'Estaing, Treichville)

South African Airways (SA; Map p138; ☑ 20-218280; www.flysaa.com; Immeuble Jeceda, Blvd de la République, Le Plateau)

LAND

Burkina Faso Passenger train services (at least 36 hours, three times a week) run between Abidjan and Ouagadougou in Burkina Faso. Contact **Sitarail** (Map p136; ☑ 20-208000, 20-210245).

Ghana It will take you about three hours to reach the crossing at Noé from Abidjan. Note that the border shuts at 6pm promptly, accompanied by a fancy flag ceremony.

Guinea The most frequently travelled route to Guinea is between Man and N'zérékoré, either through Danané and Nzo or Biankouma and Sipilou. The Liberia–Guinea border closes at 6pm each day.

Liberia Minibuses and shared taxis make the quick hop from Danané to the border at Gbé-Nda. A bus takes this route from Abidjan to Monrovia (two days) several times a week. From Monrovia, plan on about three days to cross through Guinea and board a bus for Abidjan.

Mali Buses and shared taxis run from Abidjan, Yamoussoukro and Bouaké to Bamako, usually via Ferkessédougou, and Sikasso in Mali. The Mali–Côte d'Ivoire border closes at 6pm each day.

❶ Getting Around

AIR

Air Ivoire offers internal flights throughout the country, but prices can be high.

BUS

The country's large, relatively modern buses are around the same price and are significantly more comfortable than bush taxis or minibuses.

CAR & MOTORCYCLE

You can hire cars from **Hertz** (Map p136; ☑ 21-253706; www.hertz.com; 19 Rue Thomas Edison, Marcory Zone 4C) in Abidjan. Road conditions can be bad, and Ivoirian driving is atrocious, so exercise extreme caution when on the road.

LOCAL TRANSPORT

Shared taxis (ageing Peugeots or covered pick-ups, known as *bâchés*) and **minibuses** cover major towns and outlying communities not served by the large buses. They leave at all hours of the day, but only when full, so long waits may be required.

TRAIN

Sitarail offers the romantically named *Bélier* and *Gazelle* trains linking Abidjan with Ferkessédougou (CFA12,000, daily).

Equatorial Guinea

🎵 240 / POP 1,862,158

Best Places to Eat

➡ L'Atelier (p153)
➡ La Ferme Beach (p155)
➡ La Luna Complex (p153)

Best Places to Sleep

➡ Magno Suites (p150)
➡ Apart-Hotel Impala (p150)
➡ Hotel Finisterre San Pedro (p155)

Why Go?

This is the land of primates with painted faces, soft clouds of butterflies and insects so colourful they belong in the realm of fiction. Yes, Equatorial Guinea has something of a reputation, with a history of failed coups, allegations of corruption, trafficked bushmeat and buckets of oil, but there is plenty to bring you to this country's beautiful black-and-white shores.

The capital, Malabo, boasts fascinating colonial architecture alongside sleek oil company high-rises, yet retains its African flavour with colourful markets and a bustling port. Though the country is currently dripping in oil wealth, many people's taps run dry. Poverty permeates ordinary life, making a trip to Malabo at once hedonistic and heartbreaking.

Beyond Malabo, on Bioko Island, are volcanic views, fishing villages, rainforests full of endangered primates, vibrant birdlife and shores of nesting sea turtles. On the mainland, Rio Mu i's white beaches, forest paths and jungle-scapes await.

When to Go
Malabo

Jun–Aug Dry season on the mainland, Rio Muni; more comfortable to travel and roads easier to navigate.

Dec–Feb Bioko Island's dry season, although it can rain at any time.

Nov–Feb Turtles comes ashore to lay their eggs at Ureca and in the Reserva Natural de Rio Campo.

BIOKO ISLAND

Bioko Island, rather curiously, sits off the coast of Cameroon rather than the mainland of Equatorial Guinea, and is home to the capital, Malabo. The northern third of the island, Bioko Norte, has a number of small villages along the coast but the further south you go towards Bioko Sur, the thicker the rainforest becomes and stately ceiba trees dot the landscape.

Surrounded by beautiful beaches with either black volcanic or white sands, Bioko has rainforests, woodland, savannah and one volcanic peak, Pico Basile (3012m), usually covered in cloud. While the capital can keep you occupied for a few days, it is worth exploring the southern regions of the island, easily visited on a day trip. Ureca in the far south is the jewel in the crown. Four types of turtles visit from November to February to lay their eggs on the beaches here, and the dense forest around the Luba Crater is home to the primates for which Equatorial Guinea is so well known.

Malabo

POP 439,070

Malabo is a city of sharp contrasts. To the east is the port and the old city with its splendid cathedral and some interesting colonial architecture. To the west, the city positively gleams with upmarket suburbs sporting elegant villas, smart hotels, government ministries and embassies.

In the heart of it all, the city centre has wide boulevards and modern buildings including a shopping mall featuring upmarket tenants and an array of restaurants and hotels.

Sights

★Catedrál de Santa Isabel CATHEDRAL

(Ave de la Independencia/Calle de 12 Octubre) On the west side of the Plaza de España, this gracious, recently restored apricot-hued building is the most beautiful in the country. The architect, Llairadó Luis Segarra, had some input from Antonio Gaudí. Construction began in 1887 and it was consecrated in 1916. The style is Gothic Revival and it is flanked by two 40m-high towers and has three naves.

Equatoguinean Cultural Centre NOTABLE BUILDING

(Centro Cultural Ecuatoguineano; ☎222 110 450, 333 091 032; ccegmalabo@hotmail.com; Ave de la Independencia; ⊙9am-10.30pm Mon-Fri) A bright yellow building on the main street, this centre is a lovely colonial building with large windows. It has a central atrium that serves as a performance area and gallery, and is worth visiting to see if there's anything cultural planned during your visit. There are always lots of young people about, using the free wi-fi.

Tours

Ruta 47 TOURS

(☎222 019 786; www.visitguineaecuatorial.com; Hotel Yoly, Calle 3 de Agosto; ⊙8am-6pm) The personable and highly professional Ángel Vañó is a mine of information on Equatorial Guinea. He organises trips (and visa applications) throughout the country.

Sleeping

Internet Hostal HOTEL $

(☎222 126 653; www.facebook.com/Internet-Hostal-548468751952667; Ave de las Naciones Unidas; d CFA20,000, with wi-fi CFA25,000; ❄📶) One of the cheapest options in town, this hotel has large, quiet rooms and is in an excellent location. However, the bathrooms are rather grubby, shower-over-the-toilet affairs. The owner only speaks Chinese so making a reservation in advance is difficult.

Hotel Yoly & Hermanos HOTEL $$

(☎333 091 895; www.hotelyolyhermanos.com; d CFA46,000; ❄📶) Hotel Yoly is a good mid-range hotel: the rooms are pleasant and have a fridge, and bathrooms are large. Wi-fi only works in the large, wood-panelled lobby. The location is very good for exploring the old part of the city.

★Magno Suites BOUTIQUE HOTEL $$$

(☎333 096 333, Whatsapp 222 755 542; www.magnosuites.com; Carretera del Aeropuerto, Paraíso; d/junior ste/exclusive ste incl breakfast CFA116,000/138,000/275,000; P❄📶🏊) Malabo's only boutique hotel, this is a superb choice in the upmarket suburb of Paraíso. It has swish modern decor, king-size beds and an excellent restaurant. An airport shuttle service is offered free of charge. Visa and MasterCard credit cards are accepted.

★Apart-Hotel Impala HOTEL $$$

(☎333 092 492, 222 287 122; www.hotelimpala.net; Calle de Enrique Nvó; s/d CFA50,000/90,000; ❄📶) Don't be put off by the tacky lobby, this place gets better upstairs, and there's a lift. The rooms are very comfortable and have tiny balconies, a fridge and good bathrooms. Staff are friendly and helpful. Be choosy about which room you take: some

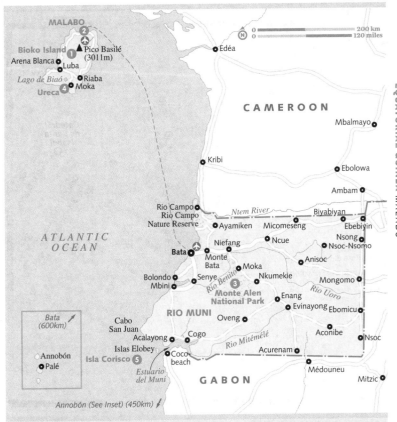

Bata
(600km)

Annobón
Palé

Annobón (See Inset) (450km)

Equatorial Guinea Highlights

❶ **Bioko Island** (p150) Going wide-eyed over the strange combination of little villages with Spanish colonial churches, dense rainforest, rare wildlife and oil platforms.

❷ **Malabo** (p150) Exploring the colonial architecture, bustling markets and buzzing nightlife of this city of contrasts.

❸ **Monte Alen National Park** (p158) Whispering during forest walks in search of gorillas, elephants, chimpanzees and a glorious array of colourful birds and insects.

❹ **Ureca** (p154) Watching marine turtles come ashore to lay their eggs from November to January in this region of forests, waterfalls and deserted beaches.

❺ **Isla Corisco** (p157) Treading softly on the squeaky-clean sand of this undiscovered paradise isle before the crowds descend.

look out directly onto the Pizza Place terrace next door, and could be noisy.

Hotel Bahia 2   HOTEL **$$$**
(☎333 096 609; bahia2caracolas@yahoo.com; Calle de los Parques de África, Caracolas; s/d CFA60,000/110,000; P❄🛜) The original version of this brand-new hotel used to be

situated at the port in central Malabo, but it has relocated to this modern building in the suburb of Caracolas off the airport road. Rooms are nicely decorated and comfortable, and staff are pleasant. It all seems eerily empty, though. The restaurant serves mains from CFA9000.

Malabo

EQUATORIAL GUINEA MALABO

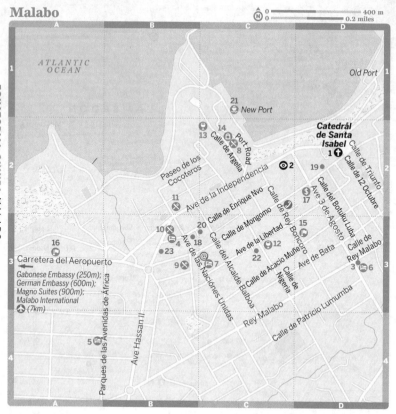

Malabo

◎ Top Sights
1 Catedrál de Santa Isabel......................D2

◎ Sights
2 Equatoguinean Cultural Centre............C2

◎ Activities, Courses & Tours
3 Ruta 47..D3

◎ Sleeping
4 Apart-Hotel Impala................................B3
5 Hotel Bahia 2...A4
6 Hotel Yoly & Hermanos.........................D3
7 Internet Hostal......................................C3

◎ Eating
8 La Luna Complex....................................C2
9 L'Atelier...B3
10 Pizza Place..B3
11 Restaurant Bidji Binia............................B2

◎ Drinking & Nightlife
12 Aviator Pub & Café.................................C3
13 Bahia Sound Lounge..............................C2
L'Atelier Cabaret Lounge ....(see 9)

◎ Shopping
14 African Crafts..C2

◎ Information
15 Cameroonian Embassy............................D3
16 French Embassy.......................................A3
17 Pecunia Express......................................D2
18 Satguru Travels & Tours Services.........B3

◎ Transport
19 CEIBA Airlines...D2
20 Cronos Airlines.......................................C3
Elobey Ferry.....................................(see 21)
21 New Port, Malabo...................................C1
22 Punto Azul..C3
23 Royal Air Maroc......................................B3

✗ Eating

There are plenty of restaurants from Senegalese to Italian, Spanish, Lebanese and French. It is worth seeking out those that serve local dishes such as *pepe* soup, giant snails and a local shellfish called *bilolá*. The upmarket hotels often serve buffet lunches on Sundays, while smaller cafes offer tortillas or croissants for breakfast.

Restaurant Bidji Binia   ITALIAN $$
(☑333 093 878; 359 Ave de la Independencia; pizzas from CFA6500; ⊙8am-noon Mon-Fri, 9am-noon Sat & Sun; ▣🔊) 'Food like mama makes' is what the name means, and she'd be proud of the pizzas. Pastas and salads are also on offer. There are two levels in the cool interior, and a pleasant terrace at the front. Staff are friendly and this is a popular place with expats. Takeaway is also available.

Pizza Place   LEBANESE $$
(☑333 093 450; Ave Hassan II; mains from CFA5000; ⊙7am-2am; ▣▣) This huge place spreads over several floors, including a lounge with sports screen and a terrace with shisha. There's a wide Lebanese menu with dishes great for sharing and an enormous lunchtime buffet every day for CFA10,000. Wi-fi is intermittent and costs CFA1000 per hour.

★ L'Atelier   AFRICAN $$$
(☑222 000 030, 555 877 436; Calle Waiso; mains from CFA7000; ⊙noon-3.30pm Mon-Wed, noon-2am Thu-Sun; ▣🔊) All wood, brick and leopard print, this modish restaurant is the place to be seen. There's a bar at the entrance and a cabaret lounge upstairs. The menu features African dishes including giant snails and chicken or fish with chocolate sauce, as well as Cameroonian dishes such as *ndolé* and *follon*. The menu changes weekly.

La Luna Complex   INTERNATIONAL $$$
(☑333 096 096; www.lalunamalabo.com; Calle de Argelia; mains from CFA7500; ⊙8am-11pm; ▣🔊♪) Superb sea views from the wide terrace complement the good food here. The menu is mostly French with a few African options. There's a huge buffet on Sundays (CFA17,000) and a daily happy hour from 5pm to 7pm. You could spend the whole day here, using the pool, too.

🍸 Drinking & Nightlife

Aviator Pub & Café   PUB
(☑222 185 534; www.facebook.com/AviatorMalabo; 322 Ave de la Libertad; ⊙9am-3am Mon-Sat; 🔊) The Aviator is a stylish new pub, all dark green walls and some outside seating.

There are sports screens, very popular karaoke on Thursdays and live music on Fridays and Saturdays. There's food to soak up the beer: the English owner offers a full English breakfast (CFA4000) and fish and chips (CFA7000). Takeaways are available, too.

L'Atelier Cabaret Lounge   LOUNGE
(Calle Waiso; ⊙10pm-2am Thu-Sun) Featuring rococo chairs, silver gilt and chandeliers, this 'cabaret lounge' is a great place to sip a cocktail and enjoy live music on weekends. There's no entry fee.

Bahia Sound Lounge   CLUB
(☑222 091 538; www.facebook.com/BahiaSound Lounge; Calle de Argelia; ⊙7pm-2am Wed-Sun) There's a great bar here and an open-air dance floor overlooking the sea. It's always popular though entrance and drinks prices are high.

🛍 Shopping

African crafts   ARTS & CRAFTS
(Luna Complex, Calle Argelia; ⊙10am-10pm) Carved wooden crafts such as figurines and masks are on sale at the entrance to the Luna Complex.

ℹ Information

INTERNET ACCESS
Many hotels, restaurants and cafes offer free wiifi.
Cibermax (Ave de la Naciones Unidas; per hour CFA500; ⊙8am-noon & 4-10pm Mon-Fri, 8am-noon Sat) is a useful internet cafe in a central location.

MEDICAL SERVICES
La Paz Hospital (☑556 666 156, 556 666 160; www.lapazmalabo.org; Sipopo; ⊙24hr) The top hospital in the country, staffed by Europeans and Israelis. There's a pharmacy and five-star hotel on-site.

MONEY
Banks and some upmarket hotels will exchange foreign currency.
Pecunia Express (Ave 3 de Agosto; ⊙8am-5.30pm Mon-Fri, 10am-2pm Sat) An exchange bureau in the centre of town.

TRAVEL AGENCIES
Satguru Travels & Tours Services (☑333 090 506, 333 096 326; marketing@satgurutravel. com; Calle de Enrique Nvó; ⊙8am-8pm Mon-Fri, 10am-8pm Sat) An efficient travel agency for booking international and internal flights. It does not offer tours in the country, though.

EQUATORIAL GUINEA URECA

DAY TRIP FROM MALABO

A day trip from Malabo around the northern two-thirds of Bioko Island is well worth taking. Contact a tour operator such as Ruta 47 (p150) to arrange transport and expect to pay around CFA131,000.

The excellent tarred road with well-tended verges will take you clockwise around the island, passing through small towns and villages. The beautiful Mt Cameroon is visible in the distance as you leave Malabo.

Look out for the pretty yellow Sagrada Familia Church (Basakoto) a pretty town with a small lighthouse, a pink church and a large house belonging to the former prime minister. Here the road turns west towards Moka and climbs into the central region. You will see huge, stately ceiba trees, the national emblem of Equatorial Guinea. At an elevation of 1000m, Moka is cooler and home to one of the president's palaces complete with two helipads. Continue on to Luba on the west coast, which is a good place to stop for lunch. Arena Blanca has a lovely yellow-sand beach, clouds of breeding butterflies and a few drinking shacks, all very popular on Sundays. Finally, you'll pass the extension of the university campus, and a striking mosque as you return to Malabo.

ℹ Getting There & Away

AIR

The easiest way to get from Malabo to Bata is to fly. The local airlines:

CEIBA Airlines (ceiba@fly-ceiba.com; Calle de Kenia; ⊙ 8.30am-5pm Mon-Fri, 9am-4pm Sat)

Cronos Airlines (✐ 333 090 471; www.cronos air.com; Calle de Enrique Nvó)

Punto Azul (✐ 222 605 949, 222 111 100; www. flypuntoazul.gq; ⊙ 8am-4pm Mon-Fri, 8am-noon Sat)

For international flights, **Royal Air Maroc** (✐ 333 099 593, 333 099 592; www.royalair maroc.com; Ave Hassan II; ⊙ 8am-noon & 4-7pm Mon-Fri) has an office in the centre of town.

BOAT

There is a ferry service called the **Elobey** (New Port, Malabo; CFA33,000) that runs weekly between Malabo and Bata, departing Friday at 6am and returning on Sunday. It is best to visit the New Port a few days before you intend to leave to try to buy tickets and confirm departure times. Expect to pay around CFA33,000 one way. The journey takes five to 10 hours, depending on the sea and the weather.

ℹ Getting Around

A shared taxi around town costs CFA1000. Expect to pay CFA2000 for longer journeys to the airport or Ministry of Tourism.

Ureca

POP 2000

This tiny village lies in a spectacular location in the southernmost region of Bioko and is one of the wettest places on earth, receiving some 10,450mm of rain per annum. During the dry season (November to January), turtles come ashore on the beaches at Ureca to lay their eggs. Four types of turtles are represented: Atlantic Green (*Chelonia mydas*), Leatherback (*Dermochelys coriacea*), Hawksbill (*Eretmochelys imbricata*) and Olive Ridley (*Lepidochelys olivacea*). When you're not sunning yourself on the beaches or watching the cycle of life unfold, there are excellent opportunities for hiking in the nearby jungle.

Part of the Bioko Biodiversity Protection Program, Ureca Nature Center (www.bioko. org/unc.html; Ureca Village; hikes per person from CFA5000, min charge CFA15,000; ⊙ 9am-4pm) has three components: an ecotourism program offering comfortable overnight trips aided by local guides, porters, cooks and camp attendants, concentrating on marine turtle ecology, Bioko's diurnal monkeys and visitor responsibility; an Ecoguard Vigilance Point to emphasise sustainable conservation; and the Bioko Artisan Collective shop selling handicrafts made by locals.

If you are taking part in a camp organised through the Moka Wildlife Center they will help you organise transport from Malabo. Otherwise, arrange transport with a tour operator in Malabo as the access road is so steep that you'll need a 4WD vehicle.

RIO MUNI

From the remote Rio Campo Nature Reserve where turtles come ashore to lay their eggs, to the pristine white sands and azure sea of the beautiful island of Corisco, the coast of mainland Equatorial Guinea is reason enough to visit. Best of all, you'll probably have it to yourself. Venture inland and discover the dense rainforest of the Monte Alen National Park, which teems with animals, including forest elephants, lowland gorillas and chimpanzees.

Bata is the major city, larger even than the capital, Malabo, though a new capital, Oyala, is being constructed in the central region.

Bata

POP 256,914

Sitting within striking distance of some of the most beautiful (and deserted) stretches of sand on the continent, the city of Bata is the capital and logistical centre of travel in Equatorial Guinea's mainland region of Rio Muni. Besides providing access to the beaches, it also acts as a jumping-off point for ventures into the wilds of Monte Alen National Park.

The city itself, with wide streets and colourful buildings, has a dilapidated colonial charm. Along the beachfront, dusty cranes hover over half-finished hotels and office blocks, acting as poignant reminders of times when oil money and expats flowed in.

🛏 Sleeping

★Hotel Finisterre San Pedro HOTEL $
(☑555 612 472, 222 612 473; fassane624@gmail. com; Calle Mbogo Nzogo; d CFA25,000-40,000; ❄️🛜) Situated behind the Chinese hotel under construction, this Senegalese-owned hotel is bright, clean and well furnished. Some rooms have a bathtub as well as a shower. The cheapest rooms share a bathroom and the largest have fridges. The friendly family also owns the Restaurant Naby next door.

Hotel Carmen HOTEL $$
(☑222 677 688; yannismalabo@hotmail.com; Paseo Marítima; d/ste CFA50,000/75,000; 🅿❄️🛜🌊) While the rooms are fairly plain here, there is a lovely pool by the sea, surrounded by thatched cabanas. There's a restaurant and bar, too. The hotel is on the airport road north of town.

★Aparthotel Plaza HOTEL, APARTMENTS $$$
(☑333 080 253; www.hotelplaza.com; Edificio 3 de Agosto; d CFA90,000; ❄️🛜) Even the standard rooms here are enormous, with a lounge area and bathroom. It's all dark wood with leather armchairs. There are larger apartments for longer stays, including the Presidential suite at CFA400,000. There are good deals to be had over weekends. The bar

MOKA WILDLIFE CENTER

The **Moka Wildlife Center** (www.bioko. org; Moka; per person CFA5000 (minimum charge of CFA15,000); ◷9am-5pm Sat & Sun) belongs to the Bioko Biodiversity Protection Program that has been in operation since 1998. It is involved in education, research and conservation. Since training people to act as guards to patrol the beaches during nesting season, the local market for both turtles and eggs has gradually decreased. They offer various guided hikes around Moka at weekends. Weekday hikes can be arranged by appointment.

Moka can easily be reached from Malabo by shared taxi (CFA2500). It is possible to visit Moka on a day trip from Malabo.

is on the ground floor, and the restaurant on the 1st floor (mains from CFA9000).

🍴 Eating

Big Bites EUROPEAN $
(Calle Jesús Bacale; burgers CFA3500, pizzas CFA5000; ◷8am-11pm) Lebanese hummus, pizzas, pastas and burgers are on the menu at this friendly place with a large terrace. KFC Big Bites are CFA4000, just don't mention copyright laws.

Restaurant Naby AFRICAN $
(☑222 612 473; Calle Mbogo Nzogo; mains CFA4000; ◷8am-10pm Mon-Sat) Part of the Hotel Finisterre San Pedro, this restaurant is set in a shady terrace and offers good pastries and omelettes for breakfast (but no coffee). There are crêpes, pizzas and salads, but the Senegalese specialities are the best options: *yassa* fish or meat is CFA4000.

Bar Central EUROPEAN $$
(☑333 274 307; El Cruce Santy; mains from CFA7000; ◷7am-11pm; ❄️) If you spend any time at all in Bata, you will gravitate to this friendly bar and restaurant. Set on a crossroads, the terrace is surrounded by plants that seem to usher in a welcome cool breeze. There's a wide menu with the usual pizzas, meat and fish. Try the calamari à la Central, dipped in beer batter (CFA10,000).

★La Ferme Beach EUROPEAN $$$
(☑222 257 333, 333 08 32 81; Bome Beach, south of Bata; mains from CFA7500; ❄️) La Ferme (pronounced Fermay for taxi drivers) is a

lovely beach resort about 20 minutes south of Bata port. It has a large terrace, gorgeous pool surrounded by palm trees and spacious restaurant. Fish is the best option here and it couldn't be fresher. The amuse-bouche of tortilla and empanadilla is a nice touch.

Utonde Beach Club
EUROPEAN $$$
(⬛555 123 893; Utonde; ⊘11am-2am; 🅿🕸📶) This is one of two beach resorts in Utonde and was about to open at the time of our visit. It's very stylish, with thatched umbrellas set around a large pool. Chef Rafi conjures up the usual staples of pizzas, fish and steaks. A great place to escape the city.

🍸 Drinking & Nightlife

Rolex Discoteca
CLUB
(Calle 3 de Agosto; admission CFA10,000; ⊘10pm-5pm Thu-Sun) The place to be seen in Bata, this place rocks over the weekend with its dark interior, loud music, mirrors and lasers. It's not cheap, though, with its high entrance price and drinks around CFA5000 each. It's next to the Aparthotel Plaza.

Cervezeria Elik Melen
BAR
(Hotel Elik Melen, Calle 3 de Agosto & Ave Patrice Lumumba; ⊘10am-2am) The 1st-floor terrace at this hotel has sea views, while the bar inside has wood panelling and blasting air-con. It's a convivial place, especially when the football is on TV.

Bar Estadio
SPORTS BAR
(Calle Mbogo Nzogo; San Miguel beer CFA1500; ⊘noon-midnight) An open-air bar with some sports screens, located next to the old stadium, this is a great place for a beer, especially on match nights.

🛍 Shopping

African crafts
ARTS & CRAFTS
(Calle Mbogo Nzogo, Bata) This small shack has a range of African souvenirs such as carved wooden figurines, masks and beads.

Information

MEDICAL SERVICES
There are plenty of pharmacies in Bata. **Farmacia Afrom** (Calle Mbogo Nzogo, Bata; ⊘9am-4pm Mon-Fri) is well stocked and in a central location.

For medical emergencies, head for the Bata branch of **La Paz Hospital** (⬛333 083 515/8, 222 633 344; www.lapazmalabo.org).

MONEY
Bata has a number of banks. The most central:

Banco Nacional (Ave Papa Juan Pablo II, Bata; ⊘8am-2pm Mon-Fri, to noon Sat)

Ecobank (Ave de la Naciones Unidas; ⊘9am-5pm Mon-Fri, to 2pm Sat)

SGBGE (Ave de la Independencia; ⊘8am-2pm Mon-Fri, to noon Sat)

Pecunia Express (⬛222 080 807; Ave Papa Juan Pablo II; ⊘8am-5.30pm Mon-Fri, 10am-2pm Sat) For exchanging foreign currency.

TOURIST INFORMATION
INDEFOR-AP (⬛222 240 159, 222 561 660; ayetebemme@yahoo.es; Calle Jesús Bacale, Bata; ⊘8am-4pm Mon-Fri) Permits to visit Monte Alen National Park and the coastal parks of Rio Campo and Tika are available here. It has excellent brochures on Monte Alen.

Getting There & Away
Bata International Airport (Paseo Marítimo) has several flights a week to Malabo.

Getting Around
➤ Taxis around town cost around CFA500 to CFA1000. Expect to pay more to reach the beach resorts south of the port.

➤ A taxi to the airport will set you back CFA2000.

➤ The **taxi rank** (Mercado 5, Colombo) for journeys to towns south of Bata is located at Mercado 5 (5km from the city centre). A private taxi to Mbini takes about an hour, and costs CFA8000 for the whole vehicle, or CFA2000 for one place in a shared taxi. Oliver Rodriguez is a good **private driver** (⬛222 581 772) with a 4WD vehicle.

Rio Campo
POP 1105
Rio Campo is the region in the far northwest of Rio Muni. The tiny village of the same name is separated from Cameroon by the Ntem River. The main reason for visiting this region is to enjoy the Reserva Natural de Rio Campo with its nesting turtles, and the beautiful deserted beaches.

⦿ Sights

Reserva Natural de Rio Campo
NATURE RESERVE
(Rio Muni; permit per day CFA10,000) This reserve, in the far northwest of Rio Muni, spans 335sq km and is a Ramsar Wetland of International Importance. Turtles, hippos and goliath frogs abound. It is managed by INDEFOR-AP (p156) in Bata, from whom you can obtain permits to visit.

Activities

TOMAGE
WILDLIFE WATCHING

(Tortugas Marinas de Guinea Ecuatorial; ☑ 222 561 660; www.facebook.com/tortugasguinea/) This is a conservation project situated between Punta Tika and Punta Cuche in the northwest of the Rio Campo reserve. It is managed by INDEFOR-AP in Bata, where permits are available (costing CFA10,000 per day). Between December and February you can see turtles come ashore to lay their eggs. There is also a small eco-museum at Punta Tika.

Sleeping

Camping on the beach here is the best option. There are some cabins in the nature reserve, but they are not always open – check with INDEFOR-AP when you apply for your permit.

Eating

Pescaderia Bar
AFRICAN $

(Rio Campo) One of the only places to eat in Rio Campo, the Pescaderia Bar has snacks and is in the southern part of the town.

Information

Register your presence at the **Comisario** (Rio Campo Village) when you arrive in the village of Rio Campo. They will want a copy of your passport, visa and tourist permit.

Getting There & Away

It is best to take your own vehicle so that you can explore more of the reserve than just the village of Rio Campo. If you prefer local transport, a taxi from Mercado 5 in Bata to the village of Rio Campo takes about two hours, and costs CFA12,000 for the whole vehicle.

It is not possible for foreigners to cross the border into Cameroon here.

Cogo
POP 4693

Cogo (or Kogo) is the jumping-off place for reaching Isla Corisco with its beautiful beaches. It's a small town with a lot of construction going on: the Club Marina & Nautica with a hotel and a marketplace is under construction along the new beachfront corniche.

The tiny Fang village of Evouat is worth visiting for its spectacular beach. Standing on the clean sweep of sand, you can see Gabon and the Elobey Islands across the sea. There are dugout canoes on the beach which local people use to catch fish that they smoke for a living. They're a friendly bunch and their wares are tasty.

Evouat lies 8km southwest of Akoga, a small town 13km north of Cogo. Turn southwest at the Somagec cement works and follow a dirt road to the coast.

Cogo is about one hour's drive south of Mbini along a good road. A taxi one way will cost around CFA5000. Alternatively, visit as part of a day trip from Bata.

It's here that locals can cross by pirogue to Gabon. Foreigners can get to Corisco on the **Somagec ferry** (⊘ no fixed time, Mon-Sat) free of charge or by pirogue for CFA10,000. A pirogue to Elobey Grande costs about CFA5000. When it's raining, there are a few bars around the jetty to wait in.

Isla Corisco
POP 3000

For the ultimate getaway with white-sand beaches, warm blue sea and swaying palm trees, look no further than Corisco. And now is the time to go, before the airport becomes operational and plans for a tourist hub take off. For now, swimming and relaxing on the beach are just about the only pastimes.

Known locally as Mandji, this idyllic island is located 44km off Cogo in the Rio Muni estuary. The largest village is Combo on the southwestern side, where you'll find the only hotel. The beach here is excellent, but for that true desert-island feeling, walk to the more remote Arena Blanca in the southeast. This is the beautiful beach that dreams are made of, the one that features on Equatorial Guinea's glossy brochures, all white sand, azure sea and palm trees. A five-star hotel is planned for this area.

There is no electricity on the island except that provided by generators, and almost no phone signal.

Sleeping

Complejo Turistico Las Islas de Corisco
RESORT $$$

(☑ 222 274 932, 222 272 737; Combo; d CFA60-70,000; ❄) Currently this is the only place to stay on Corisco and it is in a perfect spot. Rooms have air-con and a fridge though the electricity is turned off at night. Naturally enough, the restaurant specialises in fish, and there's a bar overlooking the sea.

Getting There & Away

The **Somagec ferry** docks on the northeastern side of the island, so the only way to get to Combo in the southwest is to walk or hitch a lift with one of the Moroccan truck drivers.

Monte Alen National Park

The jewel in Equatorial Guinea's crown is Monte Alen National Park (⬚ office in Bata 222 240 159; ayetebemme@yahoo.es; permits per person per day CFA10,000, guide per day CFA10,000). Covering some 2000 sq km of mountainous rainforest, it's home to forest elephants, western lowland gorillas, chimpanzees, buffalo, crocodiles, leopards and quirky creatures such as goliath frogs.

With no working tourism infrastructure, the park is an adventurer's dream. The best way to experience it is to arrange a camping trip of at least one week, giving you enough time to explore deep into the forest. You will have to organise this yourself as no tour operator in the country offers such trips. However, guides can be found around the park entrance. Permits are available from INDEFOR-AP (p156) in Bata. The Director of Monte Alen, Jesús Mba Mba Ayetebe, has to sign the permit himself, or give his authorisation by phone if he is away.

For a taster, the tour company Ruta 47 (p150) in Malabo offers day trips from Bata including a six-hour hike to the Mosumo Falls.

❶ Getting There & Away

The park lies south of Bata along an excellent road. The park centre (which is not in operation), with its hotel, eco-museum and staff accommodation, is 91km from Bata. It's best to hire your own vehicle to get to the park to transport all your equipment, food and water. If, however, you decide to take public transport, head for the taxi rank at Mercado 5 (5km from the city centre) in Colombo, Bata. Expect to pay about CFA12,000 to the park entrance.

UNDERSTAND EQUATORIAL GUINEA

Equatorial Guinea Today

Equatorial Guinea exports an annual US$12 billion worth of goods, mostly crude oil, petroleum gas and timber. The World Bank puts per-capita income at US$12,820 (2015). While this is high in comparison with most of the rest of Africa, it has dropped significantly in recent years as the price of oil diminishes (it was US$18,530 in 2013). Profits do not trickle down to most of the population, who linger in appalling poverty while the government generates an oil revenue of about US$8 billion a year. The reduction in the oil price has also meant fewer jobs in the oil industry, tourism and construction. According to the anti-corruption watchdog Transparency International, Equatorial Guinea is one of the most corrupt countries in the world. The group accuses President Obiang of using public money on fancy cars, sleek jets and luxury homes around the world. Obiang, Africa's longest-serving leader, shows no sign of releasing his grip: in 2016 he was voted in for another presidential term, in an election that banned EU monitors and some foreign media. Obiang won, as he predicted he would, gaining 93.5% of the vote.

In November 2011 the government held a referendum proposing changes to the constitution, which it claimed would facilitate democratic reform. However, critics of the changes say that the reforms, which were endorsed by voters, will in fact cement Obiang's position. Presidents are now limited to two terms of seven years in office, of which Obiang has started his second. A vice-presidency was created, the post awarded to Obiang's son, Teodoro Nguema Obiang Mangue, known as Teodorin. He is expected to take his father's place. But Teodorin's expensive tastes – ranging from Paris apartments to Bugattis, Lamborghinis and Ferraris as well as Michael Jackson's sequinned glove – have raised suspicions of money-laundering and accusations of squandering the country's assets: in 2016 the International Criminal Court instigated proceedings against him while France and Switzerland seized assets.

While the official government line is that today's regime offers a much better deal than the horrors of the Macías Nguema years, there is opposition both at home and abroad. In 2014 opposition leaders were granted amnesty and invited by the president to a 'national dialogue'. Participants, including political parties and some independent activists, agreed to several changes relating to elections and political pluralism.

As the price of oil continues to drop and reserves threaten to run dry, Equatorial Guinea will eventually have to diversify, forgo its rigid bureaucracy and allow tourism to flourish as recommended by the government's Horizon 2020 policy. A US$1 billion investment fund was established by the government in 2014 to encourage growth in sectors other than energy.

History

The Early Days

Bantu tribes, including the Bubi, came to the mainland in the 12th century from other parts of West and Central Africa. The Bubi are said to have fled to Bioko to escape the Fang, who are believed to have become the dominant ethnic group in the 1600s. Europeans made their first contact on the distant island of Annobón, which was visited by the Portuguese in 1470. In the 18th century, Bioko, Annobón and parts of the mainland were traded to Spain in exchange for regions in Latin America. Bioko subsequently became an important base for slave-trading in the early 19th century and was later a naval base for England, which by then was trying to stop the slave trade. Cocoa plantations were started on the island in the late 19th century, making Malabo Spain's most important possession in equatorial Africa.

Equatorial Guinea attained independence in October 1968 under the presidency of Macías Nguema. Months later, relations with Spain deteriorated rapidly and Nguema's 10-year dictatorship began. Thousands of people were tortured and publicly executed or beaten to death in the forced-labour camps of the mainland. Much of the violence was tribally motivated – the Bubis were particularly sought. By the time Nguema's regime was finally toppled in 1979, only a third of the 300,000 Guineans who lived there at the time of independence remained. In August 1979 Nguema was overthrown by his nephew Teodoro Obiang Nguema, who then ordered his uncle's execution.

Independence & Coup Attempts

Though it's not far from the warm waters of the Atlantic, the whitewashed prison at Playa Negra (Black Beach) is one of Africa's most notorious hellholes. It's here that South African mercenary Nick du Toit and fellow coup plotter Simon Mann were locked up for their roles in a 2004 attempted coup, an operation that aimed to overthrow President Obiang and install exiled opposition leader Severo Moro in his place. Oil rights were promised to the coup's financiers and plotters, among them Mark Thatcher, the son of former British prime minister Margaret Thatcher. But the coup attempt failed spectacularly: in March 2004 Mann, du Toit and 60 others were arrested when their Boeing jet landed in Harare, Zimbabwe, on a weapons-gathering stop. While du Toit was sent to Black Beach immediately, Mann served four years in jail in Zimbabwe before being extradited to Malabo in 2007, where he was handed a 34-year sentence. President Obiang released Mann, du Toit and other accused prisoners in early 2009, citing good behaviour.

Perhaps hoping to avoid further coup attempts, the president commissioned the building of Oyala, a new capital deep in the central jungle, in 2011. It will house 200,000 people and is expected to be finished in 2020. So far there are six-lane highways, hotels, an airport, shopping centres and the American University of Central Africa.

People of Equatorial Guinea

On the mainland 80% of the population is Fang, while on Bioko Island the Bubis are the most numerous group, making up about 15% of the total population. Smaller groups, including the Benga, inhabit the other islands.

The majority of the population is Roman Catholic, thanks to 400 years of Spanish occupation, but traditional animist beliefs are strong and are often practiced concurrently.

Traditional rituals and arts including dance are still performed and there's a strong oral tradition, with stories passed down through the generations, often involving the same cast of famous characters such as the grumpy tortoise and the wily monkey.

Arts & Crafts

Equatorial Guinea shares a similar background in the arts to its neighbours Cameroon and Gabon. Wooden mask-making and traditional sculpture are at the forefront of local crafts, particularly among the Fang ethnic group. Masks are used in celebrations, religious events and funerals. Artisanal jewellery and woven baskets can also be found.

Music and dance play an important part in cultural life. The *balélé* is a Bubi dance usually performed on holidays. The Fang national dance is the *ibanga*, where performers cover themselves in a white powder, while Ndowe *ivanga* dancers paint their faces. Musical accompaniment for these dances

SLEEPING PRICE RANGES

The following price ranges refer to a double room with bathroom.

$ less than CFA33,000

$$ CFA33,000–66,000

$$$ more than CFA66,000

comprises drums, xylophones and the *mbira* or *sanza*. The Fang are known for their singing tradition, accompanied by the *mvet*, a harp-zither made from a gourd, with up to 15 strings. Most villages have a chorus and drum group where members sing in a call-and-response style. However, there are few places to perform in public, and many artists have left the country to pursue their careers in Spain.

The modern scene is dominated by music from Cameroon, Nigeria and the Democratic Republic of Congo, which you'll hear blasting out from shared taxis. Equatorial Guinea has produced a number of well-known artists such as hip-hop and rapper Jota Mayúscula and the female duo Hijas Del Sol.

Environment

Both Bioko Island and the mainland hide a wealth of wildlife, most of which is endangered. Rio Muni is home to a hefty wedge of Central African rainforest with gorillas, chimpanzees and forest elephants. It is unknown exactly how many large mammals remain. Large sections of the interior have been set aside as protected areas, including Monte Alen National Park, which covers much of the centre of Rio Muni and offers some amazing hikes. Corrupt logging procedures, deforestation, poaching and the bushmeat trade are still big problems.

Since 1998 conservation staff at the Bioko Biodiversity Protection Program have recorded the number of animals – from monkeys and duikers to wild rats, squirrels and pythons – in meat markets. These tend to be hunted for sale to wealthy locals rather than for subsistence consumption.

PRACTICALITIES

Electricity Equatorial Guinea uses a European-style two-pin 220V AC plug.

Weights & measures The metric system is used.

SURVIVAL GUIDE

Directory A–Z

ACCOMMODATION
Malabo and Bata have a reasonable choice of medium and upmarket accommodation options, but few in the budget range. Beyond the cities, you will find pricey beach resorts and basic hotels in small towns. There are no hotels in the Monte Alen National Park or Rio Campo, so camping is the only option.

DANGERS & ANNOYANCES
➡ Travelling in Equatorial Guinea is generally safe, including for women on their own.

➡ Police requests for bribes have lessened and you probably won't be asked for a bribe if all your papers are in order. However, you might occasionally be asked for a 'fanta' (a tip to buy a drink).

EMBASSIES & CONSULATES
Cameroonian Embassy (333 093 473; 37 Calle del Rey Boncoro, Malabo; 8.30am-5pm Mon-Thu, to noon Fri)

French Embassy (333 092 005; www.ambafrance-gq.org; Carretera del Aeropuerto, Malabo; 10am-1pm & 3-5pm Mon-Fri)

Gabonese Consulate (222 528 048; Pl de Ayuntamiento, Bata; 8.30am-5pm Mon-Thu, to noon Fri)

Gabonese Embassy (333 093 180; Paraiso, Malabo; to drop off documents 10am-2pm Mon-Fri, to collect documents 11am-2pm Tue, Wed & Thu)

German Embassy (333 093 117; embajada.alemania.malabo@diplo.de; 8.30am-5pm Mon-Thu, to noon Fri)

US Embassy (333 095 741; http://malabo.usembassy.gov; Malabo II; 8am-5.30pm Mon-Thu, to noon Fri)

There is no British Embassy in Equatorial Guinea, but in an emergency, consular assistance is available from the British Honorary Consul, David Shaw, in Yaounde, Cameroon.

EMERGENCY & IMPORTANT NUMBERS

Equatorial Guinea's country code	240
Police	113
Gendarmería	114
Fire	115

There is no ambulance service.

GAY & LESBIAN TRAVELLERS
While homosexuality is not illegal in Equatorial Guinea, overt displays of affection should be avoided in this conservative Christian country.

ⓘ TOURIST PERMITS

Having a visa for Equatorial Guinea is not sufficient for travelling inside the country. As soon after arrival as possible, you must apply for an Autorización de Turismo (Tourist Permit) at the Ministerio de Turismo (p162) in Malabo II or the **Delegación de Cultura y Turismo** (3rd fl, Banco Nacional, Calle Mbogo Nzogo; ⊘8am-6pm) in Bata. You will be provided with an example of an application letter which must be typed, printed, signed and presented with the CFA15,000 fee and a copy of your passport and visa. Allow at least one day to get the permit. It has to be approved and signed by the Minister of Tourism, but what would happen if he were off sick or on holiday is not clear. In the application letter, it is essential to list everywhere you want to visit. If you are stopped somewhere not on your list, you will be turned away. The tourist permit must be produced along with a copy of your passport and visa whenever you are stopped by police. Take copies of the permit to avoid handing over the precious original. Printing and copying can be done at Cibermax (p153).

When you arrive in a small town or village and intend to stay for a few days, it is advisable to register your presence with the local authority, the Delegado or police station (Comisario). They will require a copy of your passport, visa and tourist permit.

INTERNET ACCESS

The few internet cafes in Equatorial Guinea are found in Malabo. Many hotels, restaurants and cafes offer free wi-fi, though access can be patchy. Bans on some social media such as Facebook and Twitter are imposed from time to time.

MONEY

The currency is the Central African Franc as used across the region (CFA). It is stable at CFA655 to the euro, and CFA600 to the US dollar.

ATMs At all banks in Malabo and Bata, but not elsewhere. They often don't work, only take Visa cards and only give small amounts (usually no more than CFA100,000 per day), meaning frequent trips to the bank.

Changing Money You can change euros or US dollars at banks in most towns or bureaux de change such as **Pecunia Express** (p153) that has branches in both Malabo and Bata.

Australia	A$1	CFA452
Canada	C$1	CFA440
Europe	€1	CFA656
Japan	¥100	CFA538
NZ	NZ$1	CFA415
UK	UK£1	CFA774
US	US$1	CFA600

Credit Cards Only in top-end hotels and restaurants. You can't withdraw cash over the counter in banks using your credit card.

Cash Cash is king in Equatorial Guinea. Make sure you have plenty of foreign currency to exchange for large purchases such as airline tickets.

Tipping Not expected in most restaurants and hotels. However, at those frequented by expats, staff have come to expect a tip. Guides and private drivers also appreciate a tip of around 10%.

OPENING HOURS

Shops and offices 8am to 1pm and 4pm to 7pm Monday to Friday, some are open 8am to 1pm Saturday

Banks Hours vary, but usually 8am to 2pm Monday to Friday, 8am to noon Saturday

Restaurants and cafes 7am or 9am to 11pm Monday to Saturday

Clubs 10pm to 4am Thursday to Saturday

PUBLIC HOLIDAYS

New Year's Day 1 January
Good Friday March or April
Labour Day 1 May
Corpus Christi Feast May or June
President's Day 5 June
Freedom Day 3 August
Constitution Day 15 August
Independence Day 12 October
Feast of the Immaculate Conception 8 December
Christmas Day 25 December
If a public holiday falls on a weekend, the next working day becomes a holiday.

ⓘ EATING PRICE RANGES

These price ranges refer to a main course.

$ less than CFA5000
$$ CFA5000–7500
$$$ more than CFA7500

TELEPHONE

There are no area codes.

Local SIM cards can be used in any unlocked phone. They are available only from **GETESA Central** (cnr Avenida del Rey Bonocoro & Calle de Mongomo; ⊙ 8am-1pm & 4-7pm Mon-Fri) in Malabo and cost CFA3000. You need to present a copy of your passport and visa, and two photographs. Recharge cards are available everywhere.

TOURIST INFORMATION

INDEFOR-AP (p156) Supplies permits for Monte Alen National Park and Rio Campo in Rio Muni.

Ministerio de Turismo (Ministry of Tourism; Ministerios District, Malabo II; ⊙ 8am-6pm) (Ministry of Tourism) Has a glossy flyer with photographs, but can provide no information (In Malabo).

VISAS

All nationalities need a visa for Equatorial Guinea except for US residents, who nevertheless still have to complete the form.

Visas for Equatorial Guinea can take some time to obtain. Allow at least three weeks.

❶ Getting There & Away

AIR

The only way to get to Equatorial Guinea is to fly in to Malabo. All land border crossings were closed for non-nationals at the time of writing.

Airports & Airlines

Malabo International Airport (Santa Isabel Airport; 🗐 222 091 554; adge@malabo.aero; 9km west of Malabo city centre) lies 9km west of the city centre. At the time of writing, an impressive new airport was being built adjacent. It's a chaotic place; get there at least two hours before your flight.

Check-in for CEIBA flights is in a separate building to boarding. In the main building, there is a cafe, a bank that is only open during banking hours, and an ATM that often does not accept cards. It's worth having euros or dollars in small denominations if you are unable to withdraw cash and have to pay for a taxi in foreign currency (the taxi into town should cost CFA2000).

The following international airlines fly into Malabo:

Africa's Connection from São Tomé (www.africas-connection.com)

Air France from Paris (www.airfrance.com)

CEIBA Intercontinental (Equatorial Guinea's own airline; site under construction at the time of research, but it should eventually be www.fly-ceiba.com)

❶ ARRIVING IN EQUATORIAL GUINEA

Malabo International Airport Taxis into the city (9km) cost CFA2000.

Bata International Airport (p156) Taxis wait across the car park and cost CFA2000 into the city.

Ethiopian Airways from Addis Ababa (www.ethiopianairlines.com)

Iberia from Madrid (www.iberia.com)

Lufthansa from Frankfurt (www.lufthansa.com)

Royal Air Maroc from Casablanca (www.royalairmaroc.com)

Bata International Airport (p156) is also termed 'international', but so far the only international airline flying into Bata is Niger Airlines from Niamey. The airport lies 4km north of the city.

❶ Getting Around

AIR

Flying is the best option between Malabo and the mainland. There are several national carriers with offices in Malabo and Bata.

BOAT

The Elobey Ferry (p154) between the New Port in Malabo and Bata plies the waters once a week.

BUS

In Rio Muni there is an interprovincial bus service, **Kassav Express** (🗐 222 721 516). However, shared taxis are more comfortable and easier to use.

CAR & MOTORCYCLE

Roads are excellent in Equatorial Guinea. There are tolls on all roads outside of the cities that cost CFA500 per vehicle.

Car hire is expensive: expect to pay at least CFA70,000 per day, and there's a hefty deposit of around CFA250,000. **Europcar** (🗐 333 091 902; www.europcar.com/location/equatorial-guinea; Malabo International Airport; ⊙ 8am-1pm & 4-10pm Mon-Fri, 9am-10pm Sat, 8am-10pm Sun) and **Avis** (🗐 333 090 769; www.avis.com/en/locations/eq/malabo; Malabo International Airport; ⊙ 24hr) have offices at Malabo airport. **Autos Litoral** (🗐 666 591 355, 222 043 518; www.autoslitoral.com; Ibis Hotel, Carreterra del Aeropuerto, Malabo; ⊙ 9am-8pm Mon-Fri) has a desk at the Ibis Hotel close to the airport and another office in Bata. They provide drivers if required. If you are driving yourself, you will need an International Driving Permit.

The Gambia

220 / POP 2 MILLION

Best Places to Eat

➡ Calypso (p171)

➡ Sea Shells (p172)

➡ Butcher's Shop (p171)

➡ Gida's Garden (p171)

➡ Ngala Lodge (p170)

➡ Mandina River Lodge (p174)

Best Places to Sleep

➡ Chimpanzee Rehabilitation Project Camp (p175)

➡ Mandina River Lodge (p174)

➡ Ngala Lodge (p170)

➡ Leo's (p175)

➡ Footsteps Eco Lodge (p175)

Why Go?

The Gambia may be the smallest country on the continent, but its captivating array of attractions belies its tiny size. Surrounded by Senegal, The Gambia has a mere 80km of coastline, but what a magnificent stretch it encompasses: golden beaches backed by swaying palms and sprinkled with scenic lagoons, sleepy fishing villages and biologically rich coastal reserves.

Of course there's much more to The Gambia than just sun and surf. Its namesake river is teeming with wildlife, including nearly 600 bird species, plus manatees, hippos, crocodiles and troops of wily colobus monkeys. Boat trips and overnights at forest ecolodges reveal some of the great wonders of the hinterland, from a chimpanzee island reserve to the ruins of a 17th-century British fortress. The greatest treasures, though, are the warm-hearted Gambian people, who more than live up to their homeland's moniker of the 'the smiling coast of Africa'.

When to Go
Banjul

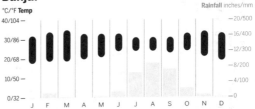

Nov–Feb The dry season and the best time to watch wildlife and birds.

Late Jun–Sep Rainy season. Many places close but you'll avoid the crowds.

Oct & Mar–May Decent weather and ideal for bagging a shoulder-season discount.

The Gambia Highlights

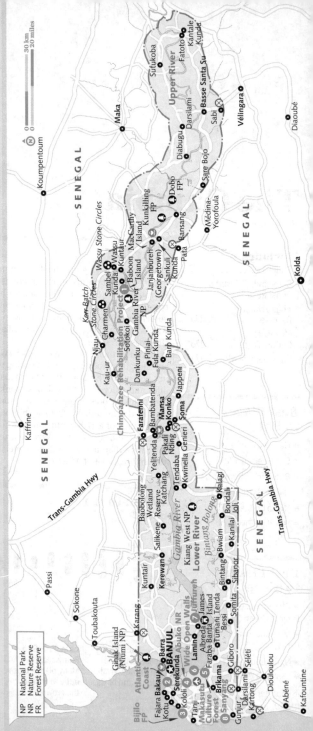

① **Chimpanzee Rehabilitation Project** (p177) Boating past river islands where great apes rule.

② **Atlantic Coast resorts** (p167) Indulging in fresh seafood while watching the sunset over the seaside.

③ **Bijilo Forest Park** (p167) Being teased by monkeys on the 4.5km nature trail.

④ **Abuko Nature Reserve** (p173) Looking out for rare birds and giant crocodiles.

⑤ **Makasutu Culture Forest** (p173) Sailing along mangrove-lined waterways.

⑥ **Wide Open Walls** (p174) Checking out the eye-popping murals covering village homes.

⑦ **National Museum of Albreda** (p176) Contemplating history at the slavery museum.

⑧ **Sanyang** (p177) Basking on powdery sands along the picturesque beaches.

NP National Park
NR Nature Reserve
FR Forest Reserve

BANJUL

POP 38,000

It's hard to imagine a more unlikely or con-sistently ignored capital city than the tiny seaport of Banjul. It sits on an island and sulks, crossed by sand-blown streets and dot-ted with fading colonial structures. It's also the least-populated capital on the African mainland. And yet, it tempts with a sense of history that the plush seaside resorts lack, and is home to a busy harbour and market that show urban Africa at its best.

⦿ Sights

★ St Joseph's Adult Education & Skills Centre SCHOOL
(⬜ 4228836; stjskills@qanet.com; Ecowas Ave; ⏱10am-2pm Mon-Thu, to noon Fri) Tucked away inside an ancient Portuguese building, this centre has provided training to disadvan-taged women for the last 20 years. Visitors can take a free tour of sewing, crafts and tie-dye classes, and purchase reasonably priced items such as patchwork products, embroi-dered purses and cute children's clothes at the on-site boutique.

Albert Market MARKET
(Russell St; ⏱8am-6pm) Since its founding in the mid-19th century, the Albert Market, an area of frenzied buying, bartering and bargaining, has been Banjul's main hub of activity. This cacophony of Banjul life is intoxicating, with its stalls stacked with shimmering fabrics, hair extensions, shoes, household and electrical wares and the myriad colours and flavours of the fruit and vegetable market.

Old Town AREA
West from the ferry terminal towards the wide Ma Cumba Jallow St (Dobson St) is a chaotic assembly of decrepit colonial buildings and Krio-style clapboard houses (steep-roofed structures with wrought-iron balconies and corrugated roofs). It's no coin-cidence they resemble the inner-city archi-tecture of Freetown in Sierra Leone, as many of them still belong to families who came to Banjul from Freetown, some as early as the 1820s.

Arch 22 MONUMENT
(Independence Dr; D50; ⏱9am-6pm) This mas-sive 36m-high gateway, built to celebrate the military coup of 22 July 1994, grants excel-lent views. There's also a cafe and a small museum that enlightens visitors about the coup d'état and houses a few ethnographic exhibitions.

🏃 Activities

Tanbi Wetland Complex BIRDWATCHING
The 6.3-sq-km site of the Tanbi Wetland Complex, with its mangroves and creeks, is a great birdwatching area, with Caspian terns, gulls, egrets and several species of wader.

🛏 Sleeping

Not many tourists stay in Banjul as the best hotels are along the coast. There are a few budget guesthouses if the need arises.

Princess Diana Hotel HOTEL $
(⬜ 4228715; 30 Independence Dr; r D1200) This is slightly better than most Banjul dosshouses, simply because it has doors that lock plus occasional live music in the bar.

🍴 Eating

Banjul's restaurant scene is a culinary desert and many eateries roll down the blinds be-fore the evening has even started. Around Albert Market you can find several cheap chop shops serving inexpensive plates of rice and sauce.

Nefertiti Bar & Restaurant SEAFOOD $
(⬜ 7776600; Marina Pde; mains D300-400; ⏱11am-11pm; 🛜) Smack on the beach with a gorgeous view, this laid-back spot serves up local seafood and is a popular location for drinks in the late afternoon and evening.

Ali Baba Snack Bar MIDDLE EASTERN $
(⬜ 4224055; Nelson Mandela St; mains D150-250; ⏱9am-7pm Mon-Sat, 10am-5pm Sun) Banjul's main snack bar has a deserved reputation for tasty shwarma (sliced, grilled meat and salad in pita bread) and felafel sandwiches.

ℹ Information

DANGERS & ANNOYANCES
Albert Market has its share of pickpockets as well as pushy sales people and bumsters, who want to be your friend/guide for the day. The Barra ferry and the ferry terminals are also places to watch out for pickpockets.

MONEY
PHB Bank (⬜ 4428144; 11 Liberation St; ⏱8am-4pm Mon-Thu, to 1.30pm Fri) Has an ATM and changes money.
Standard Chartered Bank (⬜ 4222081; Ecowas Ave; ⏱8am-4pm Mon-Thu, to 1.30pm Fri) Withdraw at ATM or change money here.

THE GAMBIA BANJUL

Banjul

Arch 22 (50m); Serekunda (15km);
Banjul International (24km)

Nefertiti Bar & Restaurant (140m)

ATLANTIC OCEAN

Marina Pde

Independence Dr

Samba Mammen
Nyang St
Tafsir Demba Ndow St
Ousman Jeng St
Antouman Faal St
Ousman Njie Keen
Dawur Gaye St

This Area Strictly Out of Bounds

Gelli-gellis & Shared Taxis to Bakau

State House

Tafsir Wally Joot St
Pierre Njie Tce

Amie Sarr St
Jack Chow St
Jallow Jallow St
Sagarr Jobe St

Mosque Rd

Alhassan Ndure St

Master Fowlis St
J R Forster
Rebecca Savage St

Freedom Lane

October 17 Roundabout

July 22 Sq

Russell St

Alpha Tapsiru St
Mam Mberry Njie St
Rev William Cole St
Hannah Forster St

Gelli-gellis & Shared Taxis to Serekunda & Brikama

Nelson Mandela St

Standard Chartered Bank

Liberation St

Abdou Wally Mbye St

Rene Blain St

Ma Cumba Jallow St

Daniel Goddard St
Davidson Carrol St

OAU Blvd

Ecowas Ave

PHB Bank

Tanbi Wetland Complex

Marma Bah St

Serign Sillah St

OLD TOWN

St Joseph's Adult Education & Skills Centre

Imam Lamin Bah St

Kankujeri Rd

Tafsir Balla Joot St

Tafsir Ebou Samba St

Ferries

POST

Main Post Office (Russell St; ⊙ 8am-4pm Mon-Sat) Near Albert Market.

ⓘ Getting There & Away

Banjul International Airport (BLJ; ☑ 4473000; www.banjulairport.com) is at Yundum, 24km from Banjul city centre and 16km from the Atlantic coast resorts.

Ferries (☑ 4228205; Liberation St; passengers D25, cars D400-500) travel between Banjul and Barra, on the northern bank of the Gambia River. They are supposed to run every two hours

from 7am to 9pm and take one hour, though delays and cancellations are frequent.

Gelli-gellis (minibuses) and shared taxis to **Bakau** (Independence Dr) (D15, 45 minutes) and **Serekunda** (D18, one hour) leave from their respective taxi ranks near the National Museum. Note that you might have to pay a bit more for luggage. A private taxi to the coastal resorts will cost around D400 to D500.

ⓘ Getting Around

A short ride across Banjul city centre (known as a 'town trip') in a private taxi costs about D40 to D80.

Banjul

◎ **Top Sights**
1 St Joseph's Adult Education &
   Skills Centre D4

◎ **Sights**
2 Albert Market D2
3 Old Town C4

🎯 **Activities, Courses & Tours**
4 Tanbi Wetland Complex......................B5

🛏 **Sleeping**
5 Princess Diana Hotel A1

🍴 **Eating**
6 Ali Baba Snack Bar D3

ℹ **Information**
7 German Embassy A1
8 Guinean Embassy C3
9 Sierra Leonean Embassy C4

SEREKUNDA & ATLANTIC COAST RESORTS

POP 390,000

Chaotic, splitting-at-the-seams Serekunda is the nation's largest urban centre, and appears to consist of one big, bustling market. The nearby Atlantic Coast resorts of Bakau, Fajara, Kotu Strand and Kololi are where the sun'n'sea tourists flock. This is a great place to spend long days on the beach and late nights on the dance floor.

◎ Sights

★ **Bijilo Forest Park**   WILDLIFE RESERVE
(📷7784902; Kololi; D150; ⊙8am-6pm) This small 51-hectare reserve makes for a lovely escape. A series of well-maintained walking trails (ranging from 900m to 1400m) takes you through lush vegetation, gallery forest, low bush and grass, towards the dunes. You'll likely see green vervet, red colobus and patas monkeys – avoid feeding them, as this only encourages them further.

★ **Kachikally**
Crocodile Pool   WILDLIFE RESERVE
(📷7782479; www.kachikally.com; off Salt Matty Rd, Bakau; D100; ⊙7am-7pm) One of The Gambia's most popular tourist attractions is a sacred site for locals. As crocodiles represent the power of fertility in Gambia, women who experience difficulties in conceiving often come here to pray and wash (any child called Kachikally tells of a successful prayer at the pool). The pool and its adjacent nature trail are home to dozens of Nile crocodiles that you can observe basking on the bank.

Sakura Arts Studio   ARTS CENTRE
(📷9928371; Latrikunda; ⊙10am-5pm) Art lovers should visit Njogu Touray's Sakura Arts Studio for a private viewing of the acclaimed painter's colourful works.

🏃 Activities

Arch Tours   TOURS
(📷7734941; http://arch-tours.com; Senegambia Strip; excursions from D2500; ⊙9am-8pm) This Gambian-owned outfit receives high marks for its wide range of professionally run excursions and competitive prices. The most popular day trips are the Alex Haley *Roots* cruise and the 4-in-1 tour, taking in markets, Kachikally Crocodile Pool, a school and a remote beach visit. Also goes to Fathala Game Reserve in Senegal.

Sportsfishing Centre   FISHING
(Denton Bridge) The Sportsfishing Centre is the best place in Serekunda to arrange fishing and pirogue excursions. Various companies are based here, including **African Angler** (📷3086500; www.african-angling.co.uk; Denton Bridge), which runs fishing excursions.

🧭 Tours

Tilly's Tours   TOURS
(📷7707356; www.tillystours.com; Senegambia Strip, Kololi; half-/full-day excursions from D1400/2400) Small company with responsible tourism products. In addition to many day excursions, Tilly's also offers multiday trips to the highly recommended Chimpanzee Rehabilitation Project in the River Gambia National Park.

Gambia Experience   TOURS
(📷4461104; www.gambia.co.uk; Senegambia Beach Hotel, Kololi; ⊙9am-5pm) Gambia's biggest tour operator. Does everything from charter flights and all-inclusive holidays to in-country tours.

Gambia Tours   TOURS
(📷4462602, 4462601; www.gambiatours.gm) Efficient, family-run enterprise.

🛏 Sleeping

★ **Luigi's**   HOTEL **$**
(📷9908218; www.luigis.gm; Palma Rima Rd, Kololi; s/d D1400/1700, apt from D2200; ❄🛜🏊) This impressive family-run complex has a mix of

Serekunda & Atlantic Coast Resorts

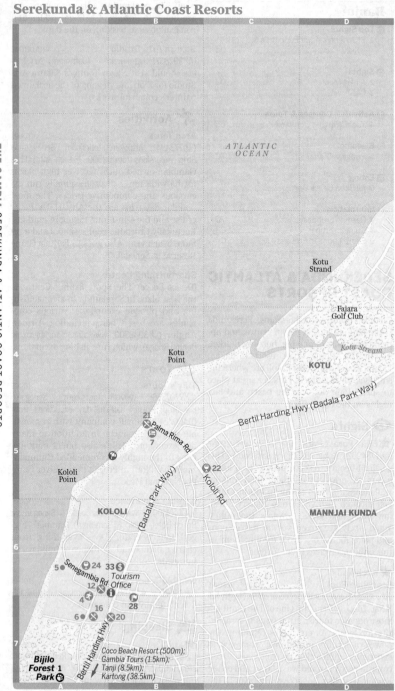

ATLANTIC OCEAN

Kotu Strand

Fajara Golf Club

Kotu Stream

KOTU

Kotu Point

Bertil Harding Hwy (Badala Park Way)

21 Palma Rima Rd

7

Kololi Point

22

Kololi Rd

KOLOLI

MANNJAI KUNDA

(Badala Park Way)

5 ● 24 33 ⑤

Senegambia Rd Tourism Office

12

4

28

6 ● 16 20

Bertil Harding Hwy

Bijilo Forest Park 1

Coco Beach Resort (500m);
Gambia Tours (1.5km);
Tanji (8.5km);
Kartong (38.5km)

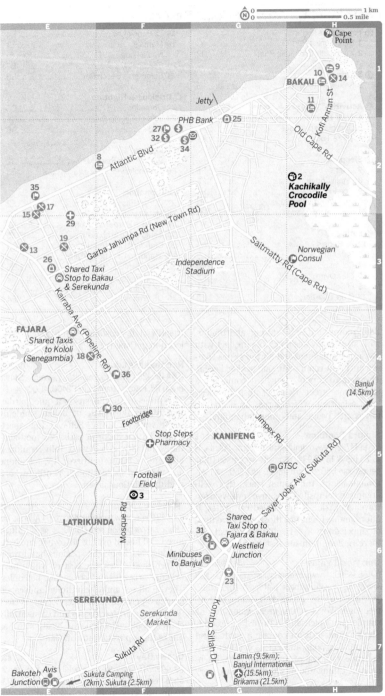

Cape
Point

1 km
0.5 mile

BAKAU

10
9
14

11

Kofi Annan St

Old Cape Rd

Jetty

25

PHB Bank
27
32
34

2
Kachikally
Crocodile
Pool

8
Atlantic Blvd

35

17
15
29

19
13
26

Garba Jahumpa Rd (New Town Rd)

Shared Taxi
Stop to Bakau
& Serekunda

Independence
Stadium

Saltmatty Rd (Cape Rd)

Norwegian
Consul

Kairaba Ave (Pipeline Rd)

FAJARA
Shared Taxis
to Kololi
(Senegambia)

18
36

30
Footbridge

Stop Steps
Pharmacy

KANIFENG

Jimpex Rd

Banjul
(14.5km)

GTSC

Sayer Jobe Ave (Sukuta Rd)

Football
Field
3

LATRIKUNDA

Mosque Rd

31

Shared
Taxi Stop to
Fajara & Bakau

Westfield
Junction

Minibuses
to Banjul

23

SEREKUNDA
Serekunda
Market

Sukuta Rd

Kombo Sillah Dr

Bakoteh
Junction

Avis

Sukuta Camping
(2km); Sukuta (2.5km)

Lamin (9.5km);
Banjul International
(15.5km);
Brikama (21.5km)

THE GAMBIA SEREKUNDA & ATLANTIC COAST RESORTS

Serekunda & Atlantic Coast Resorts

B&B rooms and self-catering apartments, with attractively designed lodgings set with modern furnishings and all the extras (flat-screen TV, in-room wi-fi, safe, fridge, kettle). There's also a pool, though it could use a touch more greenery. Don't miss the excellent restaurant, which serves up deep-dish pizzas, rich pastas and other Italian fare.

Sukuta Camping CAMPGROUND **$**
(☑9917786; www.campingsukuta.com; Sukuta, N 13°25,169 W 16°42,934; campsite per person D190, per car/van D60/85, s/d from D600/750; ☎) Although it's off the beaten track, this well-organised campsite earns rave reviews from travellers. Aside from shaded campsites, it offers simple rooms for those who have tired of zipper doorways. Facilities are great and there's a decent on-site restaurant.

One World Village GUESTHOUSE **$$**
(☑6834569; www.oneworldvillage.eu; 10 Kofi Annan St; r with/without bathroom D1220/810; ☀☎☒) Run by a Swedish-Gambian couple, One World offers great value for its simple but pleasantly furnished rooms. The grounds in front contain a garden and a swimming pool, and guests can feel right at home with use of the living room, kitchen and dining room. Other bonuses: very friendly staff, reasonable wi-fi and a great location in Cape Point.

Roc Heights Lodge LODGE **$$**
(☑4495428; www.rocheightslodge.com; Samba Breku Rd, Bakau; d/apt from D2400/4000; ☀☎) This three-storey villa sits in a quiet garden that makes the bustle of Bakau suddenly seem very far away. Self-catering apartments, with a decor of polished wood-and-tile simplicity, come with fully equipped kitchens, bathtub, hairdryer, TV, telephone and plenty of space (though 'penthouse' is a slightly ambitious label).

★**Ngala Lodge** LODGE **$$$**
(☑4494045; www.ngalalodge.com; 64 Atlantic Rd, Fajara; ste per person from D3100; ☀@☒) Much loved and fussed over by its owner, the Ngala Lodge has 24 bright, spacious handsomely furnished suites, the best of which have original artwork and sea-facing balconies. They're all set amid beautifully landscaped gardens perched over the ocean. Perfect down to the frosted glasses and thoughtfully chosen book collection, the Ngala also has one of the top restaurants in Gambia.

Ocean Bay HOTEL **$$$**
(☑4495787; www.oceanbayhotel.com; Kofi Annan St; d from D5300; ☀☎☒) This massive, 195-room property in Bakau has bright, hand-

somely furnished rooms and suites with all the mod cons – air-con, in-room safe, flat-screen TVs. Pricier rooms have balconies with sea views. The huge pool, exercise room, bar, and restaurant (with a great breakfast buffet) add to the value – though the biggest draw is having the beach right at your (back) door.

✖ Eating

La Parisienne   CAFE $
(Karaiba Ave; mains D100-400; ⊙7.30am-midnight; 🛜) Famed for its piping-hot croissants and other bakery items, La Parisienne also serves up great coffee and snacks (pizzas, salads, sandwiches). The terrace is a good spot for a bit of wi-fi.

Solomon's Beach Bar   SEAFOOD $
(☑4460716; Palma Rima Rd, Kololi; mains D200-300; ⊙9am-11pm) At the northern end of Kololi beach, this breezy roundhouse serves excellent grilled fish in a buzzing, youthful atmosphere. As light and sunny as the reggae classics on loop. Grab one of the outdoor tables for prime wave-gazing. There's live music on Thursday nights.

Ali Baba's   MIDDLE EASTERN $
(Senegambia Strip, Kololi; mains around D300-350; ⊙noon-2am) Everyone knows Ali Baba's, so it's as much a useful meeting point as a commendable restaurant. A fast-food joint during the day, it serves dinner with a show in its breezy garden. There's live music most nights, and important football matches on a big screen.

⭐Calypso   INTERNATIONAL $$
(☑9920201; off Kofi Annan St, Chez Anne & Fode, Bakau; sandwiches/mains around D350/550; ⊙9am-late daily Nov-Apr, 10am-11pm Sat & Sun May-Oct) Much-loved Calypso serves delicious grilled fish, snacks (such as prawn spring rolls), panini and an African dish of the day, plus a full English breakfast. For peaceful views over the waterfront, head to the upper-level deck or grab one of the private thatched-roof *palapas* (huts) with comfy deckchairs sprinkled around the garden.

El Sol   MEXICAN $$
(☑7149709; www.elsolgambia.com; Senegambia Strip; mains D380-500; ⊙10am-10.30pm Tue-Sun; 🛜☑) One of the best eateries in the Senegambia area, El Sol spreads a Latin feast, with enchiladas, quesadillas and fajitas, plus a first-rate grilled red snapper, all of which goes down nicely with a few rounds of margaritas or mojitos. It's an upscale spot, with a stylish interior and a few outdoor tables on the covered front deck.

Gida's Garden   INTERNATIONAL $$
(☑3709008; www.facebook.com/pg/gidasgarden; off Atlantic Blvd; mains D300-550; ⊙12.30pm-midnight) This hidden oasis tucked one block south of the Atlantic Blvd is best known for its delectably prepared grilled meats (grilled T-bone, barbecue ribs), though you'll also find a changing array of seafood and excellent desserts. It's a quite the magical and tranquil setting by night, with low-lit tables overlooking the flower-filled gardens. Book ahead.

Mama's   INTERNATIONAL $$
(☑7646452; mains D200-350; ⊙9am-midnight Tue-Sun) Mama's is a long-running institution in Fajara, with a huge menu of satisfying comfort food: brochettes, grilled fish, schnitzel, spaghetti, salads and local specialities like chicken yassa. You can dine alfresco in the garden, which draws a friendly crowd in the evening – particularly for Friday's seafood buffet (D475) and Sunday's roast pork (D450).

Clay Oven   INDIAN $$
(☑4496600; off Atlantic Blvd; mains D400-650; ⊙noon-midnight; 🛜) In a converted house surrounded by gardens, the Clay Oven serves up excellent Indian food, with classics like palak paneer, chicken tikka massala and sizzling tandoori grills. On Tuesday, you can try a variety of dishes served tableside for D795 a person.

⭐Butcher's Shop   MOROCCAN $$$
(☑4495069; www.thebutchersshop.gm; 130 Kairaba Ave, Fajara; mains lunch D230-500, dinner D385-895; ⊙9am-10pm) Driss, the Moroccan celebrity chef (and TV star), fires up some of the best cooking in The Gambia at this elegant eatery with terrace seating on busy Kairaba Ave. You'll find perfectly grilled fish and juicy steaks, along with global dishes such as rich Moroccan tagines, Italian-style duck confit and high-end comfort classics like fish pie.

Ngala Lodge   INTERNATIONAL $$$
(☑4494045; Atlantic Rd, Fajara; mains D400-900) One of Gambia's most renowned restaurants, this has always been the top address for sumptuous and lovingly presented meals; the service and sea-view setting are impeccable.

THE GAMBIA SEREKUNDA & ATLANTIC COAST RESORTS

★ **Sea Shells** INTERNATIONAL $$$
(☑ 7760070; Bertil Harding Hwy; ⊙ 11am-10pm)
Despite the unfortunate location on the highway, Sea Shells is well worth a visit for its creative and beautifully prepared dishes. Pop by at lunchtime for fresh vegetable tarts, curried chicken salad, salmon burgers with beetroot chutney and other light fare. At night, the menu shines with coconut-dusted prawns, roast ladyfish with a crab salad, and a famous beef Wellington.

Drinking & Nightlife

Reo's BAR
(www.facebook.com/reosbarandrestaurant; off Senegambia Rd; ⊙ 10am-late) Reo's is a sleek but welcoming space that ticks all the boxes, with football matches playing on the big screens, a pool table for lazy afternoons, and DJ-fuelled grooves on weekends – plus good pub grub at all hours. There's also a raised deck in front where you can take in the passing street scene.

Jokor CLUB
(☑ 4375690; 13 Kombo Sillah Dr, near Westfield Junction; ⊙ 10pm-6am Thu-Sat) This nightclub is a raucous local affair, and makes a convincing claim to be the most entertaining club of all. It draws crowds on weekends (after about 11pm), and there's occasionally a live band, usually *mbalax* (percussion-driven, Senegalese dance music) or reggae, on Friday and Saturday. Cool off in the courtyard garden.

Come Inn BEER GARDEN
(☑ 8905724; Palma Rima Junction; ⊙ 10am-2am; ⊚) For a good draught beer and a solid dose of local gossip, there's no better place than this German-style beer garden. There's also a big menu of hearty international fare (mains D200 to D450).

🛍 Shopping

Timbooktoo BOOKS
(3 Garba Jahumpa Rd; ⊙ 10am-7pm; ⊚) A delightful bookshop that stocks a good selection of West African titles, plus fiction and children's books. You'll also find a selection of African music CDs, and there's a cafe upstairs.

Bakau Cape Point Market ARTS & CRAFTS
(Atlantic Rd; ⊙ 9am-7pm) A good place to pick up sculptures, batiks and souvenirs is this shaded open-air market on the main road. You can watch the carvers and craft makers in action.

ⓘ Information

DANGERS & ANNOYANCES

Crime rates in Serekunda are low. However, tourists (and especially women) will have to deal with the constant hustling by 'bumsters' (touts). Decline unwanted offers firmly – these guys are hard to shake off. There are also a number of persistent ganja peddlers. Steer clear of the beaches after dark.

INTERNET ACCESS

Wi-fi connections are increasingly common at restaurants and hotels, where they are typically free for guests. Connections are usually slow. Internet cafes are a dying breed here.

MEDICAL SERVICES

Medical Research Council (MRC; ☑ 4495446; Fajara) If you find yourself with a potentially serious illness, head for this British-run clinic.
Stop Steps Pharmacy (☑ 4371344; Serekunda; ⊙ 9am-10pm Mon-Sat) Well stocked; has several branches.

MONEY

The main banks have ATMs, but withdrawal limits (D5000) makes relying on them impracti-

---

BEACHES

The erosion that used to eat its way right up to the hotels has largely been reversed, so that the beaches of Kotu, Kololi and Cape Point are once again wide, sandy and beautiful. Kotu is particularly attractive, with sand and palm trees, beach bars and juice sellers on one side, and an area of lagoons a bit further north, where Kotu Stream cuts into the land (that's where birdwatchers go).

Cape Point, at the northern tip of Bakau, has the calmest beaches. As this is a more residential area, you get less hassle from touts.

Most beaches in this area are relatively safe for swimming, but currents can sometimes be strong. Care should be taken along the beach in Fajara, where there's a strong undertow. Always check conditions before plunging in.

If the Atlantic Ocean and fending off 'bumsters' doesn't appeal, all the major hotels have swimming pools. Most places allow access to nonguests with a meal, a drink or for a fee.

cal. You can also change money at hotels, or at exchange booths around town.

PHB Bank (☎ 4497139; Atlantic Rd, Bakau)

Standard Chartered Bank (☎ 4396102; Kairaba Ave)

Standard Chartered Bank (☎ 4495046; Atlantic Rd)

Trust Bank (☎ 4465303; Wilmon Company Bldg, Badala Park Way)

Trust Bank (☎ 4495486; Atlantic Rd)

POST

Gampost Bakau (☎ 8900587; Atlantic Rd, Bakau; ⊗ 8.30am-4pm Mon-Thu, to noon Fri & Sat) Small, but has a convenient location near the shore.

Main post office Off Kairaba Ave, about halfway between Fajara and Serekunda.

TOURIST INFORMATION

Bijilo Forest Park Headquarters (p167) Park and trail information.

Tourism Office (www.visitthegambia.gm; ⊗ 11am-6pm Mon-Thu) Next to the Senegambia craft market, it doles out info on the region.

❶ Getting There & Away

For journeys eastward, the new **GTSC** (☎ 4380000; www.gtsc.gm; Kanifing Depot, off Banjul Serrekunda Hwy) bus is a godsend. Its new, comfy buses make regular scheduled trips between Serekunda and Bassa Santa Su, stopping at key destinations along the way.

There are also bush taxis and gelli-gellis leaving from Westfield Junction. Destinations include Brikama (D30, one hour), Soma (D130, five hours) and Janjanbureh (D230).

For transport heading to the south coast villages of Tanji, Sanyang, Gunjur (D40) and Kartong (D50), take a bush taxi or gelli-gelli from Bakoteh Junction, where Kololi Rd and Sayerrjobe Ave intersect (about 1km west of Karaiba Ave).

CAR & MOTORCYCLE

Avis (☎ 4399231; www.avis.com; Banjul International Airport) Handily located at the airport.

Tippa petrol station (Bakoteh Junction, Serekunda)

Petrol Station (Kombo Sillah Dr)

Petrol Station (Kairaba Ave (Pipeline Rd))

❶ Getting Around

Shared taxis called *six-six* (a short hop costs D15) operate on several routes around the coastal resorts. Shared taxis to Bakau and Serekunda connect Bakau to **Westfield Junction** and Serekunda, passing through **Sabina Junction** near the Timbooktoo bookshop at Fajara. You can also get *six-six* from the traffic-lights junc-

tion in Fajara to Senegambia Strip in Kololi and from there to Bakau. Simply flag a taxi down, pay your fare and get off where you want.

For Banjul, there's a minibus stop near Westfield Junction. You can also hire yellow or green taxis (they're more expensive) for trips around town. Rates are negotiable.

WESTERN GAMBIA

Abuko Nature Reserve

Abuko (Brikama Hwy; adult/child D35/15; ⊗ 8am-5.30pm) is rare among African wildlife reserves: it's tiny, it's easy to reach and you don't need a car to go in. With amazing diversity of vegetation and animals, this well-managed reserve is one of the region's best bird-watching haunts (more than 250 bird species have been recorded in its environs). Abuko is located about 11km from the Atlantic Coast and makes an easy day's excursion from most lodging near the beach.

The reserve is particularly famous for its Nile crocodiles and other slithering types such as pythons, puff adders, green mambas, spitting cobras and forest cobras.

To get to Abuko, take a private taxi (around D500 to D600) or a minibus headed for Brikama from Banjul (D25) or Serekunda (D18). Most travel agencies and hotels offer organised trips to the reserve.

Makasutu Culture Forest

Like a snapshot of The Gambia, **Makasutu Culture Forest** (☎ 9951547; www.mandina lodges.com/makasutu-forest; from D800) bundles the country's array of landscapes into a dazzling 1000-hectare package. The setting is stunning, comprising palm groves, wetlands, mangroves and savannah plains, all inhabited by plenty of animals, including baboons, monitor lizards and hundreds of bird species.

A day in the forest includes a mangrove tour by pirogue; guided walks through a range of habitats, including a palm forest where you can watch palm sap being tapped; a visit to a crafts centre; and demonstrations of traditional dancing. The tours are well organised and run by excellent staff. This is a great day out, especially for families seeking a taste of nature away from the beaches and without the hassle of braving the up-country roads.

◉ Sights

★ Wide Open Walls   PUBLIC ART
(www.instagram.com/wideopenwalls) Two huge ibex grazing amid swirling waves, a blue tattooed lion, and a lovestruck blacksmith are just a few of the striking images awaiting visitors who stumble upon the village of Kubuneh, located a few kilometres outside of Makasutu Culture Forest. The simple homes of this African settlement have been transformed into a riotous collection of thought-provoking street art, courtesy of a talented group of international artists who have brought a touch of surreal beauty to this corner of West Africa.

⊨ Sleeping

Mandina River Lodge   LODGE $$$
(☑ in Gambia and international 00 220 3026606, in UK 01489 866 939; www.mandinalodges.com; s/d incl half board from D5000/9000; ❋ ⊠) ⦿ If you feel like a treat, you can stay in the forest at this exclusive and very stunning eco-retreat, an elegant marriage of lavishness and respect for nature.

❶ Getting There & Away

To get here from the Atlantic Coast, take the GTSC bus (D20, one hour) from Serekunda to Brikama. A private taxi from Brikama costs around D300 (15 minutes).

Any tour outfit in Serekunda can arrange a day-trip, though Gambia Experience (p167) are noted Makasutu specialists.

Tanji

This petite village is home to the charming Tanji Village Museum, and provides access to the Tanji River Bird Reserve.

◉ Sights

Tanji Fish Market   MARKET
Colourful pirogues roll in the waves, women ferry fish elegantly to shore atop their heads, and crowds swarm the beachfront at this charismatic fish market. On show and on sale is everything from smelly sea creatures and colourful peppers to bright flip-flops and clothing. It's busier in the morning, but in the late afternoon it's incredibly photogenic – step inside a smoke house, which preserves masses of *bonga* (shad fish), and you'll see entrancing rays of light cutting through the thick air.

Tanji River Bird Reserve   WILDLIFE RESERVE
(☑ 9919219; entry D35, guide D400; ☺ 8am-6pm) The Tanji River Bird Reserve is an area of dunes, lagoons and woodland, and contains Bijol Island, a protected breeding ground for Caspian terns. True to name, the reserve is home to many bird species – over 300 at last count.

Tanji Village Museum   MUSEUM
(☑ 9926618; www.tanjevillagemuseum.com; adult/child D200/50; ☺ 9am-5pm) This fascinating cultural museum presents Gambian nature and life scenes by recreating a traditional Mandinka village, where you can peer into huts and learn about craftmaking, traditional music, customs and beliefs, medicinal plants and the local fauna and flora.

There's a lovely mosaic-covered restaurant here (mains around D200) and visitors can overnight in rustic bungalows (per person D500).

⊨ Sleeping

Tanji Village Museum   BUNGALOW $
(☑ 9926618; per person D500) On the grounds of the Tanji Village Museum, guests can get a taste of the simple life by overnighting in a simple bungalow. It's bare-bones but clean, with a bit of light provided by solar panels. The restaurant here (open 9am to 10pm) serves simple plates of roast fish, grilled chicken, seafood kebabs and the like.

Nyanya's Beach Lodge   LODGE $$
(☑ 6134188; Tanji; s/d D700/1200) Nyanya's Beach Lodge has ageing bungalows in a leafy garden on the bank of a Gambia River branch. Although the lodging is basic, it's hard to beat the location just steps from the beach.

❶ Getting There & Away

To get to Tanji by public transport, catch a bush taxi or gelli-gelli from Bakoteh Junction in Serekunda (D15, 35 minutes).

Brufut
POP 22,000

Located just to the south of the Atlantic Coast resorts, Brufut has rapidly changed from a tranquil fishing village to a built-up tourist centre – though it's still less hectic than its northern neighbours. The golden sands, backed by palms, are the chief draw here, but there's also some fine birdwatching in the forests to the south.

🛏 Sleeping

Leo's
BOUTIQUE HOTEL **$$$**

(☏7212830; http://leos.gm; Brufut Heights 46; s/d D5400/6600, ste for 1/2/3/4 people D6600/7500/8400/9400; ❋ 🛜 ❄) Perched on a cliff behind Brufut beach, Austrian-run Leo's has five bright, well-appointed rooms and one suite, all attractively furnished. Rooms have sliding glass doors that open onto a shared balcony overlooking the pool with the ocean in the distance. It's a kid-free place, though you might encounter a few families at the excellent on-site restaurant (mains D410 to D730).

Hibiscus House
B&B **$$$**

(☏7784552; www.hibiscushousegambia.com; r incl breakfast from D3950; ❋ 🛜 ❄) Although it's 2km from the beach, this delightful guesthouse in the village has earned many admirers for its warm welcome, great food and sparkling pool surrounded by lush grounds. Staff can help arrange trips to deserted beaches in the south and other excursions.

❶ Getting There & Away

To get here by public transport take a Tan-Western Gambiaji-bound bush taxi or gelli-gelli from Bakoteh Junction in Serekunda. Note that several hotels in the area are not convenient to public transport (being well off the main road), including Hibiscus House and Leo's.

Gunjur

POP 17,800

The tranquil fishing village of Gunjur, one of The Gambia's largest fishing centres, lies 10km south of Sanyang. This place is all about fish, guts and nets, though there are some fine opportunities to explore The Gambia's wild side at the avian-rich wetlands of the Bolong Fenyo Community Wildlife Reserve.

The **Bolong Fenyo Community Wildlife Reserve** (www.thegambiawildlife.com) is a 320-hectare reserve encompassing a mix of savanna and wetland habitats, including a freshwater lagoon, and has exceptional birdlife, with some 150 species spotted here

🛏 Sleeping

★ Footsteps Eco Lodge
LODGE **$$**

(☏7700125; www.footstepsinthegambia.com; s/d D2500/3300, cabins D4200; ⊙closed Jul–mid-Oct; ❋❄) 🍃 This beautiful ecofriendly property on the south coast has nine cheerfully decorated en-suite roundhouses which surround a freshwater swimming pool, along with several more spacious log cabins. Lush forest surrounds the buildings, and it's a pleasant 1km walk down to the beach. There's an excellent restaurant here, with locally sourced produce (including some grown on site).

Balaba Nature Camp
HUT **$$**

(☏9919012; www.balabacamp.co.uk; Medina Salaam; r incl full board D2200) 🍃 Set amid a pristine swath of Gambian forest, this locally run, ecofriendly option has rustic thatched-roof accommodation with mosquito nets and shared toilets and well water for bathing (bucket-and-jug style). With over 100 bird species around, this is a fantastic place for birdwatchers – but obviously not ideal for prima donnas.

❶ Getting There & Away

To reach this part of the coast by public transit, take a bush taxi or a gelli-gelli that departs from Bakoteh Junction in Serekunda (around D40, 70 minutes).

LOWER GAMBIA RIVER

Albreda, Juffureh & Kunta Kinteh Island

When Alex Haley, the American author of *Roots*, traced his origins to Juffureh, the tiny village quickly turned into a popular tourist destination. Together with adjoining Albreda village and Kunta Kinteh Island further offshore, this historical site preserves the memory of the dark legacy of slavery. The entire area was named a Unesco World Heritage site in 2003. Today the area can feel like a bit of a tourist circus, though it still remains a pilgrimage site for Americans with African heritage.

Fort James was an important British colonial trading post from 1661 and the departure point of vessels packed with ivory and gold, as well as slave ships. Over subsequent decades, it was the site of numerous skirmishes. Variously held by British, French and Dutch traders, as well as a couple of privateers (pirates), it was completely destroyed at least three times before being finally abandoned in 1829.

WORTH A TRIP

JANJANBUREH

Janjanbureh (Georgetown) is a sleepy former colonial administrative centre. It is situated on the northern edge of Mac-Carthy Island in the Gambia River, and is reached via ferry from either bank. The main reason to come here is to stay in a local lodge and take advantage of the superb birdwatching opportunities. However, a walk around town does reveal a few historic buildings.

There's little in terms of infrastructure – no banks and no hospital. Most visitors come on multiday excursions from the coast, such as those offered by Tilly's Tours (p167) and Arch Tours (p167), with an overnight at Janjanbureh along the way.

The small National Museum of Albreda (☑ 7710276; www.ncac.gm; Albreda; D100; ☉ 10am-5pm Mon-Sat) focuses on slavery in The Gambia, with displays detailing the gruesome treatment these human captives suffered. There's also a room dedicated to the *Roots* connection, with photos and memorabilia related to Alex Haley and the subsequent film. Also here is a replica slave ship. Admission includes entrance to Kunta Kinteh Island.

The easiest way to visit Juffureh and Kunta Kinteh Island is with an organised tour. Otherwise, take the ferry to Barra and find a shared (D40) or hire taxi (return D1500, including wait time) to Albreda. Once at Albreda, you'll have to hire a pirogue (from around D800) to get out to Kunta Kinteh Island.

Baobolong Wetland Reserve & Kiang West National Park

Together, this pair of protected areas straddles the Gambia River and provides habitats for various wildlife, including an array of bird species. A pirogue cruise through the *bolongs* (creeks) and thick mangroves of the Baobolong Wetland Reserve on the north bank is great for birdwatching. On the south bank is the less-accessible Kiang West National Park, which has even more birdlife on show, as well as bushbucks and sitatungas. An easy-to-reach viewpoint, within the boundaries of

Kiang West National Park on the south bank, is Toubab Kollon, from where an escarpment follows the river. Its view over woodlands makes a fine spot for watching birds, particularly early in the morning.

Located on the south bank of the Gambia River, Tendaba Camp (☑ 9911088; d from D1000) is well past its prime, with battered lodging and run-down facilities. However, it's one of the best places to arrange excursions in the area, with regular boat trips to the Bao Bolong Wetland Reserve and less frequent excursions to Kiang West National Park.

The easiest way of exploring these parks is by organised tour from Serekunda, usually overnighting at Tendaba Camp. By public transport it's difficult to explore these sights, though you can take a GTSC bus from Serekunda to Kwinella (D90, three hours), and walk or catch a lift for the remaining 6km north to Tendaba Camp.

BASSE SANTA SU

POP 20,400

With its dusty roads and packed trading stalls, The Gambia's easternmost town almost spills into the scenic river bend that frames it. It's a lively market and border town with a few old Victorian buildings and a feel quite different from the coast – thanks to the influence of Senegalese, Guinean and Malian traders. And while attractions are few, for those seeking an authentic side of The Gambia, well off the beaten track, Basse (as it's usually called) is an intriguing place to explore.

There are plenty of simple chop shops in town and street stalls dolling out belly-filling bowls of *fufu* (a fermented flour dish). The pick of lodging in town, Basse Guest Inn (☑ 7724822; 22 Mansajong St; s/d from D600/800; ❄) is a well-run spot that has clean, modern rooms with nice extras (including a fridge). Meals can be arranged.

Joe's Bar is a fine place for a drink with a riverside setting.

ⓘ Information

Trust Bank and Standard Chartered Bank can change money (no ATMs).

If you haven't found all the necessary immigration officials at the border, you can get your entry stamp from the immigration office in town.

ⓘ Getting There & Away

The best way to get here from the Atlantic Coast is aboard one of the GTSC (p173) buses that make the trip regularly (D220 to D260, around eight hours) in the morning (before noon).

Gelli-gellis go to the ferry ramp for Janjanbureh (D100, one hour) and Serekunda (D320, eight hours).

RIVER GAMBIA NATIONAL PARK

Established in 1978 this lush stretch of riverside covers some 500 hectares of biologically rich forest. Its centrepiece is a group of small islands that are home to the remarkable Chimpanzee Rehabilitation Project (CRP; ☑6868826; www.facebook.com/Chimpanzee RehabilitationProjectCrpInTheGambia).

This project forms the beating heart of River Gambia National Park. Comprised of so-called Baboon Island and several smaller islands, this is one of the most important wildlife sites in The Gambia. Despite the main island's moniker, it is really the kingdom of chimps – over 100 of the primates live across it and three other islands in four separate communities.

No one is allowed to set foot on Baboon Island (including staff), but visitors can see many of the simians during a boat tour around the islands. There's also other wildlife in the area, including hippos, manatees, crocodiles and abundant birdlife, not to mention other primates, such as red colobus monkeys, green vervet monkeys and – yes – even baboons. Knowledgeable guides can share the story of how this reserve came to be, and give insight into the lives and character of the island apes.

At the Chimpanzee Rehabilitation Project Camp (☑6868826; baboonislands@gmail. com; s/d incl boat tour & full board £120/220; ☺Thu-Sun) you can listen to the hoots of the chimpanzees from across the water. Accommodation is decidedly flashpacker, in comfy South African–style safari tents perched on a cliff, with private decks overlooking the river. Prices include a boat tour around the islands, and meals served at the pleasant Waterhouse, which juts over the Gambia River.

If you're travelling on public transport, best to take a GTSC bus from Barra along the north bank and disembark at Kuntaur (D140, four to five hours). By prior arrangement, a CRP boat can pick you up there.

SANYANG

POP 6300

The beautiful beaches of Sanyang, south of Tujering on the coast, are popular with tour groups. That said, the golden sands feel remarkably untouched, and if it is paradise views that you're after, this is a fine place to add to the itinerary.

🛏 Sleeping

Kajamor HOTEL $$
(☑9890035; www.kajamorhotelgambia.com; d from D1500; 🛜) This friendly place makes a great base for taking in Sanyang, with simple, reasonably priced accommodation just steps from the sun-kissed beach. There's a good seafood-slinging restaurant on hand and you can arrange excursions. Kajamor draws mostly Spanish travellers.

🍸 Drinking & Nightlife

Rainbow Beach Bar,
Restaurant & Lodge BAR
(☑9726806; www.rainbow.gm; Sanyang; d from D900, mains from D275; 🛜) This place has a perfect location for drinks, though it's often swamped with tour groups all afternoon (between noon and 5pm). Come early or around sunset to enjoy the food and drink without the circus.

ⓘ Getting There & Away

Regular gelli-gellis leave from Bakoteh Junction in Serekunda, heading down the coast to Sanyang (D25, one hour) and other stops. Public transport isn't very practical though, as it's still a 2.5km walk from the highway at Sanyang to the beach.

WORTH A TRIP

TUJERING

Quirky and wonderful, Tunbung Arts Village (☑3524875; Tujering; donations accepted) is a ragged assembly of skewed huts, wildly painted walls and random sculptures that peer out behind walls and from treetops. It's the creative universe of Etu Ndow, a renowned Gambian artist. Sadly, Etu died in 2014, but his nephew Abdoulie continues to keep the memory of his uncle alive.

If you're not coming with your own vehicle, catch a bush taxi or gelli-gellis from Bakoteh Junction in Serekunda (D20, 45 minutes).

WASSU STONE CIRCLES

This 1200-year-old arrangement of megaliths captures your attention and commands your respect. The stones, weighing several tonnes each, stand between 1m and 2.5m in height. Archaeologists believe the sites may have been used as burial grounds; locals sometimes place a small rock atop the megaliths and make a wish. You'll also find a small historical museum here. The site is about 25km northwest of Janjanbureh, near Kuntaur.

Kairoh Garden (☑ 9830134; www.kairoh garden.com; Kuntaur; r per person from D500) is a riverside spot with simple rooms and a delightful open-sided restaurant overlooking the water. Kairoh means 'peaceful' in Maninka, and it lives up to its name,

Wassu lies off the northbank road. Visit as a side trip while travelling upriver along the north bank, or on a day trip from Janjanbureh.

By public transport, take a GTSC bus from Barra to Wassu (D135). The lodges in Janjanbureh can also arrange trips.

UNDERSTAND THE GAMBIA

The Gambia Today

New hope has returned to The Gambia. In a presidential election held in December 2016, former businessman Adama Barrow won a surprise victory over long-time ruler Yahya Jammeh. The momentous event caught many by surprise, not least of all Jammeh himself, a strong-armed leader who, since overthrowing the government in a 1994 coup, had shown little desire to relinquish power. When Jammeh reneged on his promise to accept defeat, the international community intervened, strongly condemning his actions, and several West African nations sent troops into Banjul. In January 2017 Jammeh went into exile (likely in Equatorial Guinea, though his exact whereabouts remain unknown), allegedly absconding with more than US$11 million from state coffers.

President Barrow has ambitious plans, and has taken aim at The Gambia's widespread corruption, starting with his predecessor. Shortly after winning office, Barrow announced plans to establish a truth commission to investigate Jammeh's alleged human rights abuses. Barrow's other pledged goals include creating a free and independent judiciary and laying the foundation for job creation, particularly among the youth. The Gambia certainly faces grave challenges, with nearly 60% of the nation mired in poverty.

History

Ancient stone circles and burial mounds indicate that this part of West Africa has been inhabited for at least 1500 years. The Empire of Ghana (5th to 11th centuries) extended its influence over the region, and by the 13th century the area had been absorbed into the Empire of Mali. By 1456 the first Portuguese navigators had landed on James Island (now Kunta Kinteh Island), turning it into a strategic trading point.

Built in 1651 by Baltic Germans, the James Island fort was claimed by the British in 1661 but changed hands several times. It was an important collection point for slaves until the abolition of slavery in 1807. New forts were built at Barra and Bathurst (now Banjul), to enforce compliance with the Abolition Act.

The British continued to extend their influence further upstream until the 1820s, when the territory was declared a British protectorate, ruled from Sierra Leone. In 1886 Gambia became a Crown colony.

Gambia became self-governing in 1963, although it took two more years until real independence was achieved. Gambia became The Gambia, Bathurst became Banjul, and David Jawara, leader of the People's Progressive Party, became Prime Minister Dawda Jawara and converted to Islam, while the queen remained head of state.

High groundnut prices and the advent of package tourism led to something of a boom in the 1960s. Jawara consolidated his power, and became president when The Gambia became a fully fledged republic in 1970. The economic slump of the 1980s provoked social unrest. Two coups were hatched, but thwarted with Senegalese assistance. This cooperation led to the 1982 confederation of the two countries under the name of Senegambia, but the union had collapsed by 1989. Meanwhile, corruption increased, economic decline continued and popular discontent rose. In July 1994, Jawara was overthrown in a reportedly bloodless coup led by Lieutenant Yahya Jammeh. After a brief flirtation with military dictatorship, the 30-year-old Jammeh bowed to international pressure, inaugurated a second republic, turned civilian and won the 1996 election comfortably.

People

With around 115 people per square kilometre, The Gambia has one of the highest population densities in Africa. The strongest concentration of people is around the urbanised zones of the Atlantic Coast. Forty-five per cent of the population is under 14 years old.

The main ethnic groups are the Mandinka (comprising around 34%), the Fula (around 22%) and the Wolof (about 12%). Smaller groups include the Diola – also spelled Jola (11%), the Serer and Manjango. About 96% of the population is Muslim. Christianity is most widespread among the Diola.

Arts & Craft

The *kora*, Africa's iconic stringed instrument, was created in the region of Gambia and Guinea-Bissau after Malinké groups came here to settle from Mali. Famous *kora* players include Amadou Bansang Jobarteh, Jali Nyama Suso, Dembo Konte and Malamini Jobarteh.

In the 1960s The Gambia was hugely influential in the development of modern West African music. Groups like the Afro-funky Super Eagles and singer Labah Sosse had a huge impact in The Gambia, Senegal and beyond. Today, it's locally brewed reggae and hip-hop that get people moving. Even the president has been seen rubbing shoulders with the world's reggae greats, proud to hear his country nicknamed 'Little Jamaica'.

Environment

At only 11,295 sq km, The Gambia is mainland Africa's smallest country. It's also the most absurdly shaped one. Its 300km-long territory is almost entirely surrounded by Senegal and dominated by the Gambia River that runs through it. The country is flat, and vegetation consists mainly of savannah woodlands, gallery forests and saline marshes. Six national parks and reserves protect around 4% of the country's landmass. Some of the most interesting ones are Abuko, Kiang West and Gambia River. The Gambia boasts a

few large mammals, such as hippos and reintroduced chimps, but most animal lovers are drawn to the hundreds of spectacular bird species that make The Gambia one of the best countries in West Africa for birdwatching. The main environmental issues are deforestation, overfishing and coastal erosion.

SURVIVAL GUIDE

 **Directory A–Z**

ACCOMMODATION

At the Atlantic Coast resorts of Bakau, Fajara, Kotu Strand and Kololi the choice of accommodation ranges from simple hostels to five-star hotels. Upcountry, your options are normally limited to basic guesthouses and hotels.

During the low season (May to October), some places drop their prices by 25% or even 50%. Keep in mind that many places close for several weeks or even months during the low season. It's wise to book ahead.

CHILDREN

➡ Start doing your research well in advance. Vaccinations for young ones may require multiple injections spaced a month apart.

➡ Most travelling parents err on the side of extra caution when it comes to mosquitoes, bringing coils, nets and plenty of spray.

➡ A pram isn't always handy negotiating the sandy and rutted streets. You may prefer to do as locals do and simply carry your child on your back.

➡ Once you get over the logistical hurdles, you'll find The Gambia a warm and welcoming place for children. There's plenty to keep kids amused, from days on the beach or at the hotel pool to wildlife-watching on short excursions.

DANGERS & ANNOYANCES

Serious crime is fairly rare in The Gambia, though muggings and petty theft do occur, particularly around the tourist centres. Avoid walking around alone after dark. Kids will often hassle you for money or tours, but usually this is just a harmless annoyance. Beach boys are another matter.

Beach Boys

A beach boy, also referred to as a *sai sai* or bumster, is a womaniser, a smooth operator, a charming hustler, a con man or a dodgy mixture of all of these. These guys are usually young, often good-looking men, who approach women (sometimes bluntly, sometimes with astonishing verbal skills) in towns, nightclubs, bars and particularly on beaches. While some of them

> ### ℹ️ SLEEPING PRICE RANGES
>
> The following price ranges refer to a double room with bathroom.
>
> **$** less than D1000
>
> **$$** D1000-3000
>
> **$$$** more than D3000

are fairly harmless (just don't get your heart broken), others can pull some pretty sly jobs, involving sexual advances, tricking you out of money or downright stealing.

Use the same yardsticks you would at home before getting involved. It's best to ignore these guys completely. They might respond with verbal abuse, but it's all hot air.

EMBASSIES & CONSULATES

Several European countries have honorary consuls, including Belgium (at the Kairaba Hotel, Kololi), Denmark, Sweden and Norway (Saitmatty Rd, Bakau).

German Embassy (☏ 221 33 889 4884; www. auswaertiges-amt.de; Ave Pasteur, Dakar, Senegal; ⊗8am-1pm, closed Tue)

Guinean Embassy (☏4226862, 909964; 78A Daniel Goddard St, top fl, Banjul; ⊗9am-4pm Mon-Thu, 9am-1pm & 2.30-4pm Fri)

Guinea-Bissau Embassy (☏4494884; 78 Atlantic Rd, Bakau; ⊗9am-2pm Mon-Fri, to 1pm Sat)

Malian Embassy (☏4228433; 26 Rev William Cole St, Banjul)

Mauritanian Embassy (☏4491153; Badala Park Way, Kololi; ⊗8am-4pm Mon-Fri)

Norwegian Consul

Senegalese Embassy (☏4373752; www.gouv. sn; off Kairaba Ave, Fajara; ⊗8am-2pm & 2.30-5pm Mon-Thu, to 4pm Fri)

Sierra Leonean Embassy (☏4228206; 67 Daniel Goddard St, Banjul; ⊗8.30am-4.30pm Mon-Thu, to 1.30pm Fri)

UK Embassy (☏4495134, 4495133; http:// ukingambia.fco.gov.uk; 48 Atlantic Rd, Fajara; ⊗9am-noon Mon-Fri)

US Embassy (☏4392856, 4375270; http:// banjul.usembassy.gov; 92 Kairaba Ave, Fajara; ⊗2-4pm Mon, Wed, Fri)

> ### ℹ️ EATING PRICE RANGES
>
> The following price ranges are for a main meal.
>
> **$** less than D350
>
> **$$** D350–650
>
> **$$$** more than D650

EMERGENCY & IMPORTANT NUMBERS

The Gambia's country code	☏220
Ambulance	☏16
Fire	☏18
Police	☏17

GAY & LESBIAN TRAVELLERS

The Gambia is not the place to be out. Open displays of affection can in fact place you in serious danger. Travellers have been arrested in the past for 'propositioning' locals (which included something as harmless as asking where other gay men hang out).

That said, the vast majority of gay travellers who visit The Gambia have no problems. As long as you exercise the utmost caution, there is little to worry about.

INTERNET ACCESS

Wi-fi is common at most hotels and guesthouses, as well as some restaurants. There aren't many internet cafes left in the country.

MONEY

The local currency, dalasi (D), fluctuates strongly. It's best to have hard currency (British pounds, euros or US dollars) on hand and exchange it as needed. ATMs exist on the coast, but are not practical.

ATMs

There are ATMs around the coast, but relying on them is impractical with such low daily withdrawal limits (D5000). There are no ATMs up-country; it's best to chnage all the cash you think you'll need at the coast.

Changing Money

There aren't any official changing points at the border, just very persistent black-market changers. You'll be fine using CFA, though, until you get to the coast, where changing money is easier. Many hotels can recommend an informal changer, though the rates may be similar to those the banks propose. Many hotels will accept UK pounds sterling.

Exchange Rates

Australia	A$1	D34
Canada	C$	D33
Europe	€1	D50
Japan	¥100	D41
New Zealand	NZ$1	D31
Senegal	CFA100	D7
UK	£1	D59
USA	US$1	D45

Tipping

Restaurants Tipping isn't expected at smaller local restaurants; at more touristic places, a 10% tip is fairly common.

Guides At many reserves and parks, guides will be available – sometimes even included in the admission price. Regardless, it's always polite to tip the guide. While it's hard to give guidelines, D50 or more per hour is a benchmark.

Bumsters Don't tip people who hassle you or harass you for money.

OPENING HOURS

Banks From 1pm to 4pm Monday to Thursday, with lunch break from 1pm to 2.30pm Friday.

Government offices From 8am to 3pm or 4pm Monday to Thursday, and from 8am to 12.30pm Friday.

Restaurants Lunch from 11am to 2.30pm, dinner from 6pm.

Shops and businesses From 8.30am to 1pm and 2.30pm to 5.30pm Monday to Thursday; from 8am until noon Friday and Saturday.

POST

The postal service is fairly reliable for postcards and letters. For packages, you may want to use a private service such as DHL.

PUBLIC HOLIDAYS

As well as religious holidays, a few public holidays are observed.

1 January New Year's Day

18 February Independence Day

1 May Workers' Day

May or June Eid al Fitr

July or August Eid al Adha

22 July Revolution Day

15 August Assumption

25 December Christmas

TELEPHONE

If you have an unlocked phone, you can purchase inexpensive SIM cards along with talk time and data bundles at service centres around the coast. The only problem: you may have to visit a few shops, as they often run out of SIM cards.

The main mobile providers are Africell, Q Cell and Gamtel.

Coverage is generally good all around the coast, but can be spotty when you head up-country.

TOURIST INFORMATION

The Gambia Tourism (www.visitthegambia. gm) This website has a wealth of information.

Tourism Office (www.visitthegambia.gm; ⊙11am-6pm Mon-Thu) Located on the Senegambia strip in Kololi.

TRAVELLERS WITH DISABILITIES

The Gambia can be a challenging place to visit for travellers with disabilities. Badly pockmarked and unpaved roads, broken and missing footpaths, and a general lack of facilities pose the greatest obstacles.

A handful of places along the coast offer accessible rooms, including the following:

Hibiscus House (p175)

Luigi's (p167)

Ocean Bayl (p170)

VISAS

Visas are not needed for nationals of the UK, Germany, Italy, Australia, Belgium, Canada, Luxembourg, the Netherlands, New Zealand, and Scandinavian and Ecowas countries for stays of up to 90 days.

ⓘ Getting There & Away

AIR

Most people arrive on charter flights with **Gambia Experience** (in UK 01489 866939; www. gambia.co.uk) or **Thomas Cook** (www.thomas-cookairlines.com). There are a limited number of carriers flying to The Gambia, so it's wise to plan ahead.

Airports & Airlines

Banjul International Airport (p166) is in Yundum, about 15km southeast of the coast.

Charter flights aside, the only scheduled airlines flying to Gambia are the following:

Arik (www.arikair.com) Flies between Accra (Ghana) and Banjul.

Brussels Airlines (www.brusselsairlines.com) Flies to Brussels as well as Dakar (Senegal).

Royal Air Maroc (www.royalairmaroc.com) Direct flights to Casablanca, Morocco.

Vueling (www.vueling.com) Connects to Spain.

LAND

Minibuses and bush taxis run regularly between Barra and the Senegalese border at Karang (D60, one hour), where you can take care of exit/entrance formalities. From there, hire a taxi

---

ⓘ PRACTICALITIES

Electricity 220V. Most plugs have three square pins (the same as the UK); two round pins (same as continental Europe) are also in use

Newspapers *The Point i*s a daily newspaper published in Bakau.

Weights & measures The Gambia uses a mix of the UK imperial system and the metric system.

(or motorbike, which are more prevalent, D15), for 2km further to the bush-taxi garage, where you can catch onward transport to Dakar (D700, six hours) .

To get to southern Senegal (Casamance), minibuses and bush taxis leave from Bakoteh Junction (D220, five hours). Transport also goes from Brikama to Ziguinchor.

At the far-eastern tip of The Gambia, bush tax-is run from Basse Santa Su to Vélingara, Senegal (D80, 45 minutes; 27km), and from there bush taxis go to Tambacounda (D90, three hours).

ⓘ Getting Around

BUS

Gambia's new **GTSC bus service** (☑ 4380000; www.gtsc.gm; Kanifing Depot, off Banjul Ser-rekunda Hwy) provides much-improved trans-port up-country, with regular buses travelling along both the south bank and the north bank of the Gambia River.

Along the south bank, buses depart from a depot in Kanifing, about 5km southeast of the coastal resorts. Buses run hourly (from about 6am to 10pm) all the way to Basse Santa Su (D260).

To access points along the north bank, take the ferry from Banjul to Barra and catch one of the five daily buses connecting Barra with Laminkoto (D140), and points in between.

CAR & MOTORCYCLE

Driving in The Gambia presents the usual chal-lenges of West African road travel: potholes, nonexistent signage and an abundance of pe-destrians, slow-moving vehicles and free-roam-ing livestock. Always take it slow. You'll also have to contend with numerous police/immigration/customs/military checkpoints. Make sure your papers are in order, and don't be surprised if you get hit up for 'tea money' at every stop (D50 is usually a sufficient bribe to avoid lengthy delays with the authorities). Avoid driving at night, as a lack of streetlights ensures a blanket of dark-ness, and other drivers don't always use their headlights.

Driving

Gambians drive on the right-hand side.

Hire

A good 4WD is handy once you leave the main highways.

Reliable car-hire companies include **Afriq Cars** (☑ 3344443; www.afriqcars.com; Senegambia Hwy; ☉ 9am-5pm Mon-Thu, to 1pm Fri & Sat) and multinational chains such as Avis (p173).

If you don't want to self-drive, you can usually hire a car and driver for slightly more than you'd pay for a rental. Just make sure you agree on all terms beforehand – whether the cost includes fuel, driver's food and accommodation, any repairs that may arise, etc.

LOCAL TRANSPORT

To reach the south coast, head to Bakoteh Junc-tion (p173), where you'll find *sept-place* (shared seven-seater) taxis and gelli-gellis (battered, crammed minibuses) that head to the southern villages of Tanji, Sanyang, Gunjur and Kartong.

For north-bank destinations, you'll have to take the ferry from Banjul to Barra, then hop onto a *sept-place* taxi to Kerewan, from where you can change for transport heading further east.

Sept-place taxis are by no means a comfy way of travelling; however, they are infinitely better than the gelli-gellis. A few green, govern-ment-owned 'express' buses also ply the major roads.

Ghana

🎵 233 / POP 28 MILLION

Best Places to Eat

➡ Khana Khazana (p190)

➡ Baobab Vegetarian Moringa Restaurant (p198)

➡ View Bar & Grill (p205)

➡ Asanka Restaurant (p190)

➡ Santoku Restaurant & Bar (p190)

Best Places to Sleep

➡ Escape3points (p203)

➡ Lou Moon Lodge (p201)

➡ Four Villages Inn (p205)

➡ Mountain Paradise (p194)

➡ Zaina Lodge (p209)

Why Go?

Hailed as West Africa's golden child, Ghana deserves its place in the sun. One of Africa's great success stories, the country is reaping the benefits of a stable democracy in the form of fast-paced development. And it shows: Ghana is suffused with the most incredible energy.

With its welcoming beaches, gorgeous hinterland, rich culture, vibrant cities, diverse wildlife, easy transport and affable inhabitants, it's no wonder Ghana is sometimes labelled 'Africa for beginners'.

It's easy to come here for a week or a month, but no trip can be complete without a visit to Ghana's coastal forts, poignant reminders of a page of history that defined our modern world.

Travel north and you'll feel like you've arrived in a different country, with a different religion, geography and cultural practices. The beauty is that this diversity exists so harmoniously, a joy to experience and a wonder to behold in uncertain times.

When to Go
Accra

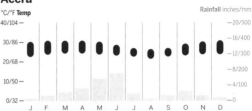

Apr–Jun The heaviest of the two rainy seasons (autumn can also be wet).

Nov–Mar The dry and easiest season to travel.

Dec–Apr Best for wildlife viewing, with good visibility and animals congregating at water holes.

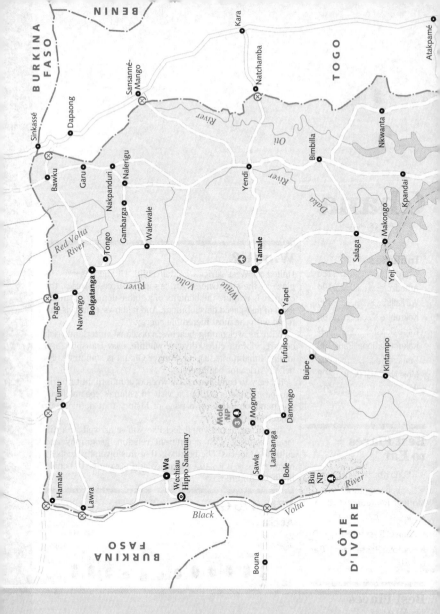

Ghana Highlights

1 Cape Coast Castle (p197) Gaining a chilling insight into the history of the slave trade.

2 Volta Region (p194) Hiking, climbing waterfalls and swimming in the former German Togoland, in Ghana's east.

3 Mole National Park (p208) Joining a safari for some close-up encounters with herds of elephants.

4 Kejetia Market (p203) Shopping till you drop (and getting very lost) in West Africa's biggest market in Kumasi.

5 Accra (p186) Spending a day or two sampling the fine restaurants, nightclubs and city beaches of Ghana's lively capital.

6 Busua (p202)
Taking a surf lesson, eating fresh lobster on the beach and chilling out in a beach bar at Ghana's favourite backpacker hangout.

2 Volta Region

LOMÉ

ACCRA

ATLANTIC OCEAN
Gulf of Guinea

NP	National Park
NR	National Reserve
WS	Wildlife Sanctuary
FR	Forest Reserve

100 km
60 miles

Map labels:
Jasikan, Wli, Hohoe, Mt Afadjato (885m), Klouto, Kpalimé, Kpetoe, Liáti Wote, Fume, Kpandu, Tafi Atome, Tafi Abuipe, Mt Gemi, Ho, Mt Adaklu, Amedzofe, Akatsi, Denu, Afiao, Keta, Keta Lagoon, Dabala, Anloga, Sogakope, Ada Kasseh, Ada, Kpong, Akosombo, Atimpoku, Somanya, Aburi, Tema, Kokrobite, Winneba, Apam, Kade, Asamankese, Oda, Saltpond, Anomabu, Cape Coast, Kakum NP, Elmina, Shama, Takoradi, Sekondi, Busua, Dixcove, Akwidaa, Cape Three Points, Axim, Agona Junction, Ankobra, Beyin, Half Assini, Ankasa NR, Elubo, Aboisso, Wiawso, Bibiani, Bia NP, Bia River, Agnibilékrou, Sunyani, Berekum, Techiman, Nkoranza, Ejura, Tarkwa, Dunkwa, Obuasi, Kumasi, Ejisu, Abono, Lake Bosumtwe, Kuntanáse, Konongo, Adanwomase, Ntonso, Bonwire, Bobiri FR, Mampong, Owabi WS, Nkawkaw, Koforidua, Digya NP, Lake Volta, Volta River, Pra River, Kokrobite

ACCRA

🎵 030 / POP 2.9 MILLION

Ghana's beating heart probably won't inspire love letters, but you might just grow to like it. The capital's hot, sticky streets are perfumed with sweat, fumes and yesterday's cooking oil. Like balloons waiting to be burst, clouds of dirty humidity linger above stalls selling mangoes, *banku* (fermented maize meal) and rice. The city's tendrils reach out towards the beach, the centre and the west, each one a different Ghanaian experience.

The city doesn't have any heavy-hitting sights like Cape Coast or Elmina but it does have good shopping, excellent nightlife and definitely the best selection of eating options in Ghana.

⊙ Sights

Jamestown   AREA

(Map p188) Jamestown originated as a community that emerged around the 17th-century British James Fort, merging with Accra as the city grew. These days, Jamestown is one of the poorer neighbourhoods of Accra – full of beautifully dishevelled colonial buildings, clapboard houses and corrugated iron shacks – but it remains vibrant. For a great view of the city and the busy and colourful fishing harbour (haze and pollution permitting), climb to the top of the whitewashed lighthouse (Map p188; C5).

Makola Market   MARKET

(Map p192; ⊙ 8am-6pm) There is no front door or welcoming sign to the Makola Market. Before you know it, you've been sucked in by the human undertow from the usual pavements clogged with vendors hawking food, secondhand clothes and shoes to the market itself. For new arrivals to Africa, it can be an intense experience, but it's a fun – if, perhaps, a little masochistic – Ghanaian initiation rite.

Bojo Beach   BEACH

(adult/child C15/5) Bojo Beach is so clean and chilled out that you'd never guess it was such a short drive west of Accra city. On arrival there's a small entrance fee to pay, and you'll then be rowed across a clear strip of water to a pristine strip of beach, where there are sun loungers and refreshments. It's a worthy alternative to hectic Labadi Beach.

Labadi Beach   BEACH

(admission C5) Come the weekend people flock to Accra's most popular beach to play ball games, frolic in the surf, go horse riding along the sand or party to loud dance music in the bars and restaurants that line the shore. Needless to say, if you're looking for a quieter experience, come on a weekday. Labadi is about 8km east of Accra; to come here, take a tro-tro (minibus) at Nkrumah Circle in Central Accra or along the Ring Rd.

Flagstaff House   NOTABLE BUILDING

(Golden Jubilee House; Map p188; Liberation Rd) This dramatic structure was completed in 2008 amid huge controversy around the tens of millions of dollars it cost to construct. Built to resemble an Asante Golden Stool, it is the office and residence of the President of Ghana.

Kwame Nkrumah Park
and Mausoleum   MEMORIAL

(Map p192; High St; park & museum adult/child C10/2; ⊙10am-5pm) This tranquil park is full of bronze statues, fountains and wandering peacocks, with the mausoleum of Kwame Nkrumah, Ghana's first leader, at its heart. It's a pleasant enough place to wander around, but the park museum is rather dishevelled. It houses a curious collection of Nkrumah's personal belongings, including the smock he wore while declaring Ghana's independence, as well as copies of personal correspondence and numerous photos of him and various world leaders.

National Museum   MUSEUM

(Map p192; 🎵 030-2221633; www.ghanamuseums.org; Barnes Rd; C40; ⊙9am-4.30pm) Set in pleasant grounds, the national museum features excellent displays on various aspects of Ghanaian culture and history. The displays on local crafts, ceremonial objects and the slave trade are particularly noteworthy. The museum was closed for renovation at the time of writing and was scheduled to reopen in 2017.

☞ Tours

★ Nima Tours   WALKING

(🎵024 6270095, 024 2561793; www.ghana-nima-tours.yolasite.com; Nima; per person per hour C25) The knowledgeable and affable Charles Sablah offers fun and informative two-hour walking tours of his neighbourhood, one of the most deprived areas of Accra. Tours vary according to the day, time, and what you'd like to do, but could include a stroll around the market, visiting local houses, or listening to a traditional drumming group.

Jamestown Walking Tours WALKING

(Map p188; www.jamestownwalkingtours.word
press.com; Jamestown Lighthouse, High St; C25;
☺2pm Sat) Jamestown is Accra's oldest
suburb, and it has sites that reveal its slavery past, colonial architecture and poor
but vibrant fishing community. Joining
Jamestown Walking Tours for a Saturday
afternoon stroll immerses you in the Ga culture. Visit a family house, taste street food
and watch fishers return with their catch.
The tours are operated by the Jamestown
Community Theatre Centre, a cultural hub
helping young people express themselves artistically. Tours start at the lighthouse.

🛏 Sleeping

Agoo Hostel HOSTEL $

(Map p188; ✆030-2222726; www.agoohostel.
com; C93/5 Keta Close, Nima Residential; dm/d
US$17.50/45; [P][✳][⌘]) A fantastic new addi-
tion to Accra's hostel scene, Agoo offers spacious private rooms, squeaky clean dorms
with bright yellow bunks and batik bedspreads, and a candy-coloured self-catering
kitchen. There's also plenty of lounging
space, including a large balcony and a garden. Breakfast is included and home-cooked
meals are available on request.

Somewhere Nice HOSTEL $

(Map p188; ✆054 3743505; www.hostelaccra.com;
9 Cotton Ave, Kokomlemle; dm/d €10/50; [P][⌘][✳])
🖋 The rooms and dorms at this hostel are
very nice indeed. They come with balconies;
en-suite bathrooms (with rainfall showers!);
and rustic, locally made furniture, much of
it recycled. There's also a pool, a garden, and
a semi-open-air lounge. The free (excellent)
breakfast and filtered drinking water is a
bonus.

Sleepy Hippo Backpacker Hotel HOSTEL $

(Map p188; ✆026 1113740; www.sleepyhippohotel.
com; 38 Duade St, Kokomlemle; dm from US$10,
d US$50, with shared bathroom US$30; [✳][⌘][✳])
One of a growing number of Accra backpackers hostels, the Sleepy Hippo has a
homely atmosphere and is a good place to
meet other travellers. The dorms and rooms
are clean and spacious, and there are plenty
of spaces to chill out in after a sweaty day on
Accra's streets, including a cafe-bar, a roof
terrace and a teeny plunge pool.

Crystal Hostel GUESTHOUSE $

(✆030-2304634; 27 Akorlu Close, Darkuman;
dm/s/d from US$10/18.50/25; [⌘]) The hosts go
out of their way to make travellers welcome
at this lovely budget set-up in the quiet
suburb of Darkuman. Rooms have private
bathrooms, TV and fridges. There's a leafy
communal lawn area and a rooftop terrace.
Campers can pitch their tents in the garden
or on the roof terrace (US$5).

Urbano Hotel HOTEL $$

(Map p188; ✆030-2788999, 030-2779688; Oxford
St, Osu; s/d/ste US$80/120/160) The rooms
may be snug at this new Osu spot, but
they're cool, spotless and pretty good val-
ue for the area. Plus there's no need to stay
in your room when there's a restaurant, a
Moroccan-style courtyard, a rooftop lounge
and a balcony overlooking the action, all
decked out in stylish mid-century replica
furniture.

Chez Delphy B&B $$

(Map p188; ✆026 2989722, 050 8979778; www.
chezdelphy.com; r from US$125; [P][✳][⌘]) A cosy
bolthole close to the bars and restaurants of
Labone, Chez Delphy offers welcome respite
from the heat and noise of Accra. The rooms
are simple but comfortable, there's a peaceful lounge and garden, and excellent dinners
are available given advance notice.

Frankie's Hotel HOTEL $$

(Map p188; ✆030-2773567; Oxford St, Osu; d/ste
from US$100/150; [✳][@][⌘]) A good deal, right
in the centre of the action. Smart modern
rooms come with all the necessary ameni-
ties, and there's Frankie's (mains C30-50;
☺7am-midnight; [✳][⌘]) restaurant downstairs
if you get hungry. It can be noisy at night,
however.

Paloma HOTEL $$

(Map p192; ✆030-2231815; www.palomahotel.
com; Ring Rd Central; s/d C520/650; [P][✳][@][⌘])
Cool rooms and bungalows with every comfort. The complex includes an excellent restaurant, a sports bar, a garden area and a
cocktail bar. The hotel also has a free airport
shuttle service.

La Villa Boutique Hotel BOUTIQUE HOTEL $$$

(Map p188; ✆030-2730333; www.lavillaghana.com;
Nii Saban Atsen Rd, Osu; s/d/apt US$225/255/315;
[P][✳][⌘]) This stylish boutique hotel is very
popular and deservedly so – it's brilliantly
located in the heart of lively Osu, yet manag-
es to feel serene. The rooms are the epitome
of understated chic, and there's a great Ital-
ian restaurant, not to mention a small pool.

GHANA ACCRA

Accra

1 km
0.5 miles

Wide St
Senchi St
Lutumba Rd

Accra Mall (200m);
La Chaumière (300m);
Josie's Cuppa Cappuccino (500m);
Santoku Restaurant & Bar (1.2km);
Wild Gecko Handicrafts (2.2km);
Lister Hospital (4km)

Accra Tourist
Information
Centre

Kotoka
International
Airport

Burma Camp Rd

Liberation Ave
Agostino Nieto Rd

Borstal Rd
Liberation Rd

Giffard Rd

37 Circle

37 Military
Hospital

CANTONMENTS

Cantonments
Circle

Jawaharlal Nehru Rd

Liberation Rd

Josef Broz Tito Ave

Sankara
Interchange

Gamel Abdul
Nasser Ave

Osu St

Kanda High Rd

Nima Hwy

Independence Ave

Ring Rd East
Nyadji Cres

NORTH
RIDGE

Mango Tree Ave

Ridge Rd

Education
Loop

Castle Rd

Hill St

Kusia St

New Town Rd

KOKOMLEME

ASYLUM
DOWN

Cathedral
Square

WEST
RIDGE

Kojo Thompson Rd

Farrar Ave

ADABRAKA

Brewery Rd

Graphic Rd

Abasi Okai Rd

Ring Road West

Larnptey
Circle

Intercity
STC Ring
Road

Kaneshie Motor Park (11km);
Swan Hotel (2.5km);
Crystal Hostel (5.5km)

Enlargement

200 m
0.1 miles

M&J Travel & Tours

Cantonments Rd

Ring Rd East

Danuah
Circle

SharpNet

Adgoate St

GY Oddol St

Oxford Link

Ring Rd East

OSU

GY Oddol St

Oxford St

6th St

Nii Noi Sekan St

Master Barnor St

Trust
Hospital

Nii Kofi Aniefi St

Naa
Amponsua St

Angola St

First St

Nells

Palm St

Kuku Hill
Cres

Dr Esther Ocloo St

Walakataka Rd

Asafoatse
Tempong St

Accra

◎ Sights
1	Flagstaff House	E3
2	Jamestown	B6
3	Jamestown Lighthouse	B6

⊕ Activities, Courses & Tours
	Jamestown Walking Tours	(see 3)

⊜ Sleeping
4	Agoo Hostel	D3
5	Chez Delphy	G6
6	Esther's Hotel	G1
7	Frankie's Hotel	A3
8	La Villa Boutique Hotel	A1
9	Sleepy Hippo Backpacker Hotel	C2
10	Somewhere Nice	D3
11	Urbano Hotel	B2
12	Villa Monticello	G1

⊗ Eating
13	Buka	A2
14	Burger & Relish	B3
15	Café Kwae	G2
16	Chez Clarisse Mama Africa	A2
17	Duncan's	A3
	Frankie's	(see 7)
18	Simret	E1
19	Vida e caffè	G2

◉ Drinking & Nightlife
20	JamesTown Cafe	B6
21	Republic Bar & Grill	A3
22	Rockstone's Office	E4

◉ Entertainment
23	+233	D3
24	Alliance Française	F2

◉ Shopping
25	Artists Alliance Gallery	G6
26	Global Mamas	B2
27	Woodin	B2

◉ Information
28	Australian High Commission	F4
29	British High Commission	D4
30	Burkinabé Embassy	D3
31	Canadian High Commission	E4
32	Dutch Embassy	E4
33	French Embassy	E3
34	German Embassy	D4
35	Immigration Office	E4
36	Ivorian Embassy	A3
37	Togolese Embassy	F4
38	US Embassy	G4

GHANA ACCRA

Villa Monticello BOUTIQUE HOTEL **$$$**
(Map p188; ☑ 030-2773477; www.villamonticello.
com; No 1A Mantaka Ave Link, Airport Residential
Area; s/d from US$385/435; P❄@⧖❄) Be-
hind the austere khaki concrete facade hides

a sleek boutique hotel. The opulent rooms were designed according to themes – Soho, Coco Chanel, Last Emperor, Out of Africa – and are furnished with exquisite taste.

Esther's Hotel
BOUTIQUE HOTEL $$$

(Map p188; ☑ 030-2765751; www.esthers-hotel. com; 4 Volta St, Airport Residential Area; s/d from US$150/180; P❄☎) Long one of Accra's more upscale addresses, Esther's is not as flashy as some of Accra's newer boutique hotels, but for many that's a bonus. It's homely and friendly, with cosy, understated rooms and lovely gardens, complete with wandering peacocks.

✗ Eating

★ Khana Khazana
SOUTH INDIAN $

(Map p192; ☑ 057 0656557, 027 5834282; www. khanakhazanagh.com; Kojo Thompson Rd; mains around C20-30; ☺9am-11pm) 🍴 Tucked behind a petrol station (Engen Filling Station), next to Avenida Hotel), this outdoor Indian restaurant is a gem – cheap, delicious and with long opening hours. One of the house specialities is the dosa (savoury parcel made of rice flour normally eaten for breakfast). Sunday is thali (set meal) day.

Café Kwae
CAFE $

(Map p188; ☑ 020 4004010; www.lovecafekwae. com; ground fl, One Airport Sq, Airport City; cakes C12; ☺8am-10pm Mon-Fri, from 10am Sat; ☎) Despite Accra's large population, you won't find many real cafes here. That's changing with the recent opening of this cafe inside the extravagant facade of One Airport Sq. Treat yourself with homemade pies, light lunches, a wide variety of teas, freshly ground coffee or cold-pressed juice as you make use of the free wi-fi.

Duncan's
AFRICAN $

(Map p188; Asafoatse Tempong St, Osu; mains from C15; ☺10am-11pm) Duncan's is an example of the low-key, outdoor chop bars that manage to get it right. Fresh, grilled fish and simple Ghanaian dishes draw a mixed, appreciative crowd.

★ Buka
AFRICAN $$

(Map p188; ☑ 030-2782953, 024 4842464; www. thebukarestaurant.com; Nii Noi Sekan St, Osu; mains C16-40; ☺noon-10pm Mon-Sat, to 7pm Sun; P🖶) Ever-popular Buka serves some of the best West African food in Accra, in stylish surroundings to boot. Hearty plates of *jollof rice*, tilapia and groundnut soup are served

on a pretty terrace, which fills up with the local office crowd every lunchtime.

Chez Clarisse Mama Africa
AFRICAN $$

(Map p188; ☑ 024 2984828; 8th Lane; mains C30; ☺8am-midnight) You have two choices: tender chicken or whole grilled tilapia topped with onions and tomatoes. The small menu doesn't make this Ivorian favourite any less popular though; this real African food experience includes plastic chairs, eating with your hands and sauces that keep fans coming back. Cutlery available upon request for the less adventurous.

Simret
ETHIOPIAN $$

(Map p188; ☑ 050 7408938; www.simret-restaurant.com; Villa Almaz, 7A Roman Rd, Roman Ridge; buffet from C70; ☺6.30-10pm Tue-Sat; P) 🍴 The welcome is warm and the authentic Ethiopian food served buffet style at this low-key place. There's a decent selection of veggie options and dinner is finished off with strong Ethiopian coffee and cake.

Asanka Restaurant
AFRICAN $$

(Map p192; Ring Rd Central; mains C20-50; ☺9am-9pm) Not to be confused with Asanka Local in Osu, this friendly and rather upmarket joint serves fantastic Ghanaian food, including groundnut soup, *red-red* (bean stew) and grilled tilapia with homemade chilli sauce.

Burger & Relish
BURGERS $$$

(Map p188; ☑ 054 0121356; www.burgerandrelish.com; cnr Adjoate & Dadebu Sts; burgers C35-55; ☺noon-11pm Mon-Wed, noon-1am Thu-Sat, 10.30am-11pm Sun; P❄☎🖶) Gourmet burgers have come to Accra in this hip, industrial restaurant, which doubles as a trendy cocktail bar in the evenings, and a family-friendly brunch spot at the weekend. If you can fit anything else in after one of the delicious burgers, there are brownies and ice-cream sundaes. Regular live-music nights here and at sister branch in East Legon.

Santoku Restaurant & Bar
JAPANESE $$$

(☑ 054 4311511; www.facebook.com/Santoku Accra; Villaggio Vista, North Airport Rd, East Dzorwu-lu; mains C60-120; ☺noon-3pm & 6.30-10.45pm; P❄) Stunning Japanese food, impeccable service and elegant decor make Santoku one of the best restaurants in the country.

La Chaumière
FRENCH $$$

(☑ 030-2772408; Liberation Rd, Airport Residential Area; mains C50-90; ☺12.30-2.30pm & 7-11pm Mon-Fri, 7-11pm Sat; ❄) There's stiff competition these days, but La Chaumière remains one of Accra's best and fanciest restaurants. It excels in old-school elegance, with soft lighting, polished wooden floors, classical music and delicious French fusion gastronomy. La Chaumière is renowned for its steaks but there is plenty of seafood on the menu too, as well as the odd North African flavour. Bookings essential.

🍸 Drinking & Nightlife

JamesTown Cafe   BAR
(Map p188; ☎ 030-2522248; www.facebook.com/Jamestowncafe; High St; 🛜) This stylish architect-owned cafe, bar and music venue sits in a beautifully restored building right in the heart of old Accra, just across from the sea. There's local and international food, great cocktails and live music daily. Once a week, the party spills outside.

Rockstone's Office   CLUB
(Map p188; Osu Ave Extension; ⊗ 6pm-late Wed-Sat) Owned by hiplife legend Reggie Rockstone. There's a lounge bar decked out with white leather sofas, an outdoor terrace and regular live music. At the weekend an energetic crowd parties till dawn to hiplife (a highlife/hip-hop hybrid) and hip-hop. It's near the police headquarters, behind the Japanese embassy.

Republic Bar & Grill   BAR
(Map p188; Asafoatse Tempong St, Osu; ⊗ noon-midnight; 🛜) With its bright red walls, black-and-white photos, vintage postcards and outdoor wooden deck, this fab bar wouldn't look out of place in Brooklyn. Here, it delights happening young Ghanaians and expats in equal measure, and is renowned for its innovative cocktails made from local booze such as palm wine. Live music is also fantastic here, with many a highlife giant having turned up to play to exuberant crowds.

☆ Entertainment

★ +233   LIVE MUSIC
(Map p188; ☎ 023 3233233; Ring Rd East, North Ridge; ⊗ 5pm-midnight) This 'Jazz Bar & Grill', as the strapline goes, is probably the best live-music venue in Accra. Bands come from all over the continent and there is a great atmosphere.

Alliance Française   LIVE MUSIC
(Map p188; ☎ 050 1287814; www.afaccra.org; Liberation Link, Airport Residential Area; concerts around C20) With several concerts a week (rock, jazz, reggae, hip-hop), exhibitions and various cultural events, the cultural arm of the French embassy is a good bet whenever you're in town.

🛍 Shopping

★ Global Mamas   FASHION & ACCESSORIES
(Map p188; www.globalmamas.org; Adjoate St, Osu; ⊗ 9am-8pm Mon-Sat, from 1pm Sun) 🏷 This shop, which stocks pretty dresses, hats, tops, accessories (including lush scented shea butter) and kids clothes in colourful fabrics, is part of a bigger Fair Trade enterprise that promotes sustainable income-generating activities for women. Everything sold here is handmade in Ghana.

Woodin   CLOTHING
(Map p188; ☎ 030-2764371; Oxford St; ⊗ 8am-7pm Mon-Sat, noon-6pm Sun) The place to come for Ghanaian wax print fabrics, Woodin so proved so popular that there are branches throughout Ghana. If you've no time to find a seamstress, there are off-the-peg clothes for men, women and children.

Artists Alliance Gallery   ART
(Map p188; ☎ 024 5251404; www.facebook.com/Artists-Alliance-Gallery; Labadi Rd; ⊗ 9am-5.30pm Mon-Sat, from noon Sun) A well-respected gallery with three neatly organised floors of painting and sculpture by established and up-and-coming Ghanaian artists. Every item has an official, non-negotiable price label, so this popular gallery might not give you the frenetic experience of the city's street markets, but it is a safe bet to find quality items while ensuring a fair amount of the money goes to the artist.

Centre for National Culture   MARKET
(Arts Centre; Map p192; 28th February Rd; ⊗ 8am-6pm) A warren of stalls selling arts and crafts, known simply as the Arts Centre, this is the place to shop in Accra. The level of aggressive hassling may make you want to keep your cedis in your pocket but if you have the patience and wherewithal, you can come away with good-quality handicrafts from all over Ghana.

ℹ Information

DANGERS & ANNOYANCES
Accra is one of Africa's safest cities, with little violent crime against tourists. Bag-snatching and pickpocketing is more common, particularly at markets or bus stations. Avoiding

Central Accra

0   500 m
0   0.25 miles

GHANA ACCRA

Ring Rd West
VIP

Neoplan
Motor
Park

Nkrumah
Circle

Kokonte St

Star Ave

Busy
Internet

Ring Rd

Paradise St

ASYLUM
DOWN

4

5

Aksanoma Rd

Kente St

Ghana Car
Rentals

Odanta St

Samora Machel Rd

Afram St

Mango Tree Ave

Farrar Ave

Eseefo Rd

Farrar Ave

Manyo Plange St

Tackie Tawiah Ave

6

ADABRAKA

Watson Ave Loop

ASYLUM
DOWN

Adama Rd

Kwame Nkrumah Ave

Kojo Thompson Rd

Castle Rd

Cathedral
Square

3

Brewery Rd

Eighth Ave

Graphic Rd

Liberia Road Nth

Liberia Road Sth

Education
Cl

Seventh Ave

Morocco Rd

WEST
RIDGE

6th Ave

Train
Station

Adjaben Rd

Barnes Rd

Independence Ave

Liberia Rd

Agbogbloshi Rd

Tudu Rd

Tudu Crescent Rd

5

Okai-Kinbu Rd

Kinbu Rd

NORTH
ACCRA

Barnes Rd

Kinbu
Gardens

Mamleshie Rd

Station Rd

Intercity
STC Tudu

2

Kinbu Rd

Tema
Station

Commercial St

Kimberly Ave

Makola
Market

Derby Ave

CITY
CENTRE

Makola
Circle

Selwyn Market St

Rawlings Park

USSHER
TOWN

Zongo La

VICTORIABORG

Oval Rd

Asafoatse
Nettey Rd

Lutterodt
Intersection

Pagan Rd

Thorpe Rd

John Evans Atta Mills High St

7

Lutterodt St

High St

Barclays Bank
Headquarters

1

Central Accra

⦿ Sights

▣ Sleeping

✘ Eating

⦿ Shopping

carrying obvious bags or valuables can miti-
gate the risk.

Negotiating the city on foot during daylight
hours is generally fine – the greatest risk you'll
face is from the traffic or open sewers. Avoid
walking around at night, however, which is
when (thankfully rare) violent incidents tend
to occur.

INTERNET ACCESS

Most midrange and top-end hotels and guesthouses offer free wi-fi, as do many cafes and
restaurants.

Busy Internet (Map p192; Ring Rd Central; per
hr C7.50; ☺7am-8pm Mon-Fri, 9am-8pm Sat;
📶) Fast browsing and printing services.

SharpNet (Map p188; Ring Rd East; per hr C3,
between midnight & 7am C1.50; ☺24hr; 📶)
Reliable 24-hour browsing.

Vida e caffè (Map p188; ☑ 054 0123222; www.
vidaecaffe.com; Icon House, Stanbic Heights,
North Liberation Link; sandwiches from C20;
☺7am-7pm) All five branches have speedy wi-fi
and good coffee.

MEDIA

Time Out Accra (www.timeoutaccra.com) A
fantastic, glossy annual magazine with the lowdown on what's hot and what's not in Accra.
Great features on Ghana's cultural scene plus
a section on day trips. Available in the capital's
bookshops and large hotels. For the most up-
to-date information, visit its website.

MEDICAL SERVICES

In addition to the following you can ask your
embassy for a list of recommended doctors and
specialists. Pharmacies are everywhere.

Lister Hospital (☑ 030-3409031, 030-
3409030; www.listerhospital.com.gh; Airport
Hills, Cantonments) Ultramodern hospital. Has
lab, pharmacy and emergency services.

Trust Hospital (Map p188; ☑ 030-2761974/5;
www.thetrusthospital.com; Oxford St, Osu) A
private hospital with decent general practitioner and lab services.

37 Military Hospital (Map p188; Liberation
Ave) Large government hospital with a trauma
centre and an ICU.

MONEY

You'll find dozens of banks and ATMs all over
town.

Barclays Bank Headquarters (Map p192; High
St; ☺8.30am-4.30pm Mon-Fri) Changes cash
and travellers cheques; ATM.

POST

Main Post Office (Map p192; Asafoate Nettey
Rd; ☺8am-5pm Mon-Fri, 9am-2pm Sat) In
Ussher Town.

TOURIST INFORMATION

Accra Tourist Information Centre (Map p188;
☑ 030-2682601; Liberation Rd) This new office
provides advice on what's happening in Accra,
as well as information about travel throughout
the country, and transport and hotel booking
services. A restaurant and a small library are
planned.

Ghana Tourism Authority (Map p188; ☑ 030-
2682601; www.ghana.travel; Haile Selassie
St) Offers advice and information about travel
throughout the country.

TRAVEL AGENCIES

Abacar Tours (☑ 024 9574691, 030-2223407;
www.abacar-tours.com; 39 Bobo St, Tesano)
Reputable operator run by a Franco-Ghanaian
team, with plenty of options in Ghana and the
possibility to extend in neighbouring Togo,
Benin and Burkina Faso.

Easy Track Ghana (☑ 027 6657036; www.
easytrackghana.com) Set up by two friends,
an American and a Ghanaian, Easy Track has a
strong focus on sustainable tourism and runs
tours all over the country as well as in the rest
of West Africa.

M&J Travel & Tours (Map p188; ☑ 024
4514824, 030-2773498; www.mandjtravel-
ghana.com; Ring Rd East, Osu) Experienced
travel agent offering car hire as well as tours
throughout Ghana and into neighbouring Togo,
Benin and Burkina Faso.

VISA EXTENSIONS

Immigration Office (Map p188; ☑ 030-
2221667, 030-2224445; off Independence Ave,
North Ridge; ☺8.30am-2pm Mon-Fri) Three-
month visa extensions cost C250 and take two
weeks to process. You will need two passport
photos and a letter of application explaining the
reasons for your extension request.

❶ Getting There & Around

AIR

Kotoka International Airport (Map p188; www.gacl.com.gh), just 5km north of the ring road, is the main international gateway to the country. There are also domestic flights to Kumasi, Takoradi and Tamale.

Allow plenty of time to get to the airport: a one-hour journey is common, two or three hours not unheard of.

A taxi from the airport to the centre should cost around C30.

BUS

After a couple of problematic years, leading many services to grind to a halt, Intercity STC is back in service, complete with a brand-new fleet of buses. For the moment, however, there are fewer departures than previously. The main **Intercity STC** (Map p188; ✆ 030-2221912, 030-2221932; http://stc.oyawego.com) bus station and the **VIP** (Map p192; ✆ 020 8402080) bus station are on Ring Rd West. STC also has another depot in **Tudu** (Map p192).

Services from Accra include:

Aflao C22, three hours, one daily, Intercity STC Tudu station

Bolgatanga C80, 18 hours, three weekly, Intercity STC Ring Rd station

Cape Coast C19, three hours, one daily, Intercity STC Ring Rd station

Ho C19, three hours, one daily, Intercity STC Tudu station

Kumasi C40, 4½ hours, leave when full, VIP station

Paga C95, 20 hours, three weekly, Intercity STC Ring Rd station

Takoradi C45, four to five hours, 1pm daily, VIP station

Takoradi C27, four hours, one daily, Intercity STC Ring Rd station

Tamale C45, 11 hours, one daily, Intercity STC Ring Rd station

Wa C85, 14 hours, 3pm daily, VIP station

LOCAL TRANSPORT

Tro-tros (minibuses or pick-ups) leave from four main motor parks:

Kaneshie Motor Park (Kaneshie) Cape Coast (C20, three hours), Takoradi (C25, four to five hours) and other destinations to the west.

Neoplan Motor Park (Map p192; Ring Rd West) Kumasi (C30, four hours), Tamale and northern destinations.

Tema station (Map p192) Tema (C10, one hour), Ho (C20, three hours), Hohoe (C25, four hours)

Tudu station Aflao (C20, three hours), Akosombo (C15, 1¼ hours), Ho (C20, three hours), Hohoe (C25, four hours)

CAR

Ghana Car Rentals (Map p192; ✆ 026 4264246; www.ghana-car-rentals.com; Odanta St, Asylum Down; saloon car/4WD per day from US$85/100 including driver's expenses) is a reliable company renting vehicles with experienced drivers.

VOLTA REGION

The Volta region has to be Ghana's most underrated gem. The area is covered in lush, fertile farmland flanked by rocks, and mountains offering beautiful vistas. It is prime hiking territory and has great ecotourism ventures.

Amedzofe

✆ 036 / POP 5500

Amedzofe's claim to fame is that, at 750m altitude, it is Ghana's highest settlement. The drive to the village, through the stunning Avatime Hills, is scenic and tortuous; it almost comes as a surprise when Amedzofe suddenly appears around a bend.

The village offers breathtaking vistas, a waterfall, forests, a cool climate and plenty of hiking opportunities. There's a fantastic community-run **visitor centre** (✆ 054 7297493; www.facebook.com/amedzofe; ◷ 8am-5pm) where you can arrange hikes. Popular choices include a 45-minute walk to Amedzofe Falls – the last section is treacherous – and a 30-minute walk to the summit of Mt Gemi (611m), one of the highest mountains in the area, where there is a 3.5m iron cross and stunning views.

🛏 Sleeping

★**Mountain Paradise**   GUESTHOUSE $
(✆ 024 4166226; www.mountainparadise-biakpa.com; Biakpa; campsite C10, d/tw/f C55/80/120, s/d without bathroom C35/45) The nicest place to stay in the area is Biakpa Mountain Paradise, a former government rest home converted into a mountain hideaway near the village of Vane. It's a peaceful place, with a good restaurant that serves home-grown highland coffee. Staff can arrange hikes along the Kulugu River and bike rental.

Abraerica HOTEL **$**

(☑054 7752361, 020 8132484; www.abraerica.com; Amedzofe; s/d with fan C80/100, d/tw with air-con C120, f C300; **P**✳) The rooms in Amedzofe's only hotel are a little uninspiring, but the views – right over Mt Gemi and the hotel's own lawns – are fabulous. There's also a decent restaurant and staff can arrange hiking and mountain-biking tours.

❶ Getting There & Away

There are tro-tros between Ho and Amedzofe (C6, one hour) daily except on Sundays. It might be quicker to get a tro-tro going from Ho to Hoehoe and be dropped off at Vane, getting a share taxi on from there. A private taxi between Ho and Amedzofe will cost C40.

Tafi Atome & Tafi Abuipe

These two small villages are worthy ecotourism destinations in the region. Tafi Atome has long been known for its monkey sanctuary, while Tafi Abuipe is famed for its kente weaving tradition.

◉ Sights

Tafi Atome
Monkey Sanctuary WILDLIFE RESERVE

(☑024 7877627; tours per person C20) Set up to protect the forest and its inhabitants, the mona monkeys, this community-run sanctuary makes for a fun excursion. The monkeys, revered by the villagers, are habituated and readily come to feed off the hand of visitors. Early in the morning and late in the afternoon, they can be seen roaming the village. Visits to the sanctuary are by tour, arranged at the visitor centre.

Tafi Abuipe Cultural Centre CULTURAL CENTRE

(☑054 2680056; C15) This kente-weaving centre is fun to visit and there's less of a hard-sell than at similar villages in the Ashanti region. You can visit the weaving room, tour the village and have kente-weaving lessons. The kente in this part of Ghana is good value and with a bit of notice, villagers will produce any textile to any measurement and deliver it to where you're staying.

⏹ Sleeping

Tafi Atome Guesthouse GUESTHOUSE **$**

(☑024 5458170, 024 7877627; r from C50) This basic guesthouse is next to the visitor centre. Simple fan-cooled rooms share a spotless if spartan shower block, and local meals can

be prepared given some notice. You will need to call in advance – walk-ins aren't possible.

❶ Information

Tafi Atome Visitor Centre (⊙7am-5pm) The first port of call at Tafi Atome for Monkey Sanctuary tours or to arrange to stay at the guesthouse.

❶ Getting There & Away

Tafi Atome and Tafi Abuipe lie west off the Ho–Hohoe road, not far from the village of Fume. If you don't have your own transport, you can charter a taxi from Fume for about C20. There is an 8km footpath between Tafi Atome and Tafi Abuipe, that you could either walk or cycle.

Wli Falls

Ghana's tallest waterfalls, the Wli (pronounced 'vlee') falls stand amid an exquisite landscape of rolling hills, forests and bubbling streams. The falls are most impressive from April to October, when you can hear – and feel – the flow of water thundering down.

It takes about 40 minutes to walk from the Wli Tourist Office to the lower waterfalls (C15) along an easy path. Much more challenging is the hike to the upper falls (C35), which takes about two hours and requires clambering in places. In both cases you'll be required to take a guide, included in the price.

🏃 Activities

Wli Tourist Office TOURS

(☑020 2572400; lower/upper falls per person C15/35; ⊙9am-5pm) Organises guides for walks up to the falls (you won't be allowed up without one).

🍴 Sleeping & Eating

Big Foot Safari Lodge LODGE **$**

(☑020 8180500, 020 4431744; www.bigfootsafarilodge.com; camping per person US$10, s/d US$40/50; **P**✳🛜) This place is in a great location, close to the start of the waterfall trail, and has large airy bungalows set in a pretty tropical garden, as well as space for campers.

Waterfall Lodge at Wli LODGE **$**

(☑054 1359872, 020 5115388; www.ghanacamping.com; camping per person C20, d C75, 2-/4-bed chalet C85/120; **P**) A serene, friendly and beautiful place, with views of Wli Falls and the surrounding hills. Huts are simple but comfortable, and there's space for campers. Food is delicious, with Ghanaian and European dishes available. Staff can organise all manner of hikes in the surrounding area. No new arrivals are accepted on Tuesdays.

Wli Water Heights Hotel GUESTHOUSE $
(☎ 020 9119152; www.wliwaterheightshotel.com; d with fan/air-con C100/180, q with fan C180; ☒) The Wli Water Heights Hotel lacks the atmosphere of some of the more rustic lodges, but it is in a beautiful spot just 500m from the falls. The garden is the perfect place to wind down after a day of trekking.

ℹ️ Getting There & Away

Wli is right on the border with Togo. Regular tro-tros and shared taxis make the scenic run between Wli and Hohoe (C5, 50 minutes). If you're heading for Togo, the Ghanaian border post is on the eastern side of Wli (turn left at the junction as you enter the village).

THE COAST

Kokrobite

☎ 031 / POP 5000

Endowed with a long stretch of white sand, and just 45 minutes from the capital city, Kokrobite has long been a favourite of backpackers, volunteers and Accra weekenders. While it's not the prettiest or cleanest beach along the coast, it has a fun vibe, an excellent surf school and some great places to stay.

🏃 Activities

Mr Bright's Surf Shop SURFING
(☎ 026 4316053; www.mrbrights.com; group/private lessons per person C60/100) British surfer Brett Davies has moved his surf school down from Busua to Big Milly's in Kokrobite.

🛏 Sleeping & Eating

Kokrobite Garden GUESTHOUSE $
(☎ 054 6392850; www.kokrobitegarden.com; d bungalows with outside/inside bathroom €18/42; ☒) A quirky collection of bungalows, rooms, and even a vintage caravan sit in tranquil tropical gardens at this relaxed and friendly guesthouse, which is a short stroll from the beach. There's a small pool, a book

exchange and a top-notch Italian restaurant (mains C40 to C65).

Big Milly's Backyard LODGE $
(☎ 024 9999330; www.bigmilly.com; camping per person C25, dm C29, r from C69; ☒☀☺) An eclectic collection of dorms, huts and rooms set in a garden next to the beach, long-standing Big Milly's is popular, fun and sociable. There's a good restaurant (mains C18 to C80), a 24-hour bar and live music at the weekends. It can get noisy, however, so if you're looking for peace and quiet, head elsewhere.

Dizzy Lizzie's INTERNATIONAL $
(☎ 020 5600990; mains from C20) This chilled beach-front restaurant a short walk down the sand from Big Milly's serves a mix of international and Ghanaian food. There's live music on Friday nights and drumming on Sundays.

ℹ️ Information

Security can be an issue here, and there have been reports of muggings on the beach. Ask advice from your guesthouse on where and where not to wander.

ℹ️ Getting There & Away

Kokrobite is only 25km west of Accra, and a 45-minute drive, though at rush hour the journey can take up to two hours. Tro-tros (C2.50) to Kokrobite go from the western end of Kaneshie Motor Park (p194) in Accra. A taxi from Accra will cost around C80.

Anomabu

☎ 033 / POP 14,500

The sands and ribbons of low-key surf are certainly the big draw here, and Anomabu's stunning beaches are among the best in the country. The village has its charms too, though, including a historic fort and a number of traditional shrines.

👁 Sights

The town has a number of *posubans* (the shrines of the city's Asafo companies, ancient fraternities meant to defend the city); Posuban No 6, in the shape of a ship, is one of the largest. To find it, walk west from Fort William for about 50m towards the yellow house. When you see Posuban No 7 on your right, turn left down some steps where you'll find Posuban No 6. Company No 3's *posuban*, which features a whale between two lions, is about 50m from the main road, opposite the Ebeneezer Hotel.

Fort William FORT
(C10; ⊙ 9am-4.30pm Mon-Sat) Now open to the public, this former slave fort hosts lively and fascinating tours, delivered by enthusiastic guides. Having served as a prison from 1962 to 2000, the building itself is in a bad state of repair.

🛏 Sleeping & Eating

Anomabo Beach Resort RESORT $$
(✐ 050 1286213, 024 4331731; www.anomabo.com; camping per person US$15, s/d hut US$80/100, s/d hut without bathroom US$60/80; P ❄) Tucked away on a quiet, clean stretch of beach, this collection of huts and cottages, set within a sandy and shady grove of coconut palms, is deservedly popular with weekenders escaping the bustle of Accra. The simple huts are slightly fraying at the edges, but they're clean and spacious, and there are camping pitches and tent rental for those on lower budgets.

The open-air restaurant has gorgeous sea views and serves a mixture of international and Ghanaian dishes, including excellent seafood.

ℹ Getting There & Away

You'll have no problem finding a tro-tro (C2, 15 minutes) to or from Cape Coast along the main road.

Cape Coast

✐ 021 / POP 170,000
Forever haunted by the ghosts of the past, Cape Coast is one of Africa's most culturally significant spots. This former European colonial capital, originally named Cabo Corso by the Portuguese, was once the largest slave-trading centre in West Africa. At the height of the slave trade it received a workforce from locations as far away as Niger and Burkina Faso, and slaves were kept locked up in the bowels of Cape Coast's imposing castle. At the shoreline, slaves were herded onto vessels like cattle, irrevocably altering the lives of generations to come.

Today, Cape Coast is an easygoing fishing town with an arty vibe, fanned by salty sea breezes and kissed by peeling waves. Crumbling colonial buildings line the streets, seabirds prowl the beaches and fishermen cast nets where slave ships once sailed. Many

travellers use Cape Coast as a base to explore Kakum National Park, Anomabu and even Elmina.

◎ Sights

As well as Cape Coast Castle, you'll notice the ruins of **Fort William** (adult/student/child C10/7/2), which dates from 1820 and now functions as a lighthouse, and **Fort Victoria** (adult/student/child C10/7/2; ⊙ 9am-4.30pm), originally built in 1702, on the town's hills but you are advised not to venture to either without a guide because of muggings.

★**Cape Coast Castle** CASTLE
(✐ 033-2132529; Victoria Rd; adult/student/child C40/30/5; ⊙ 9am-4.30pm) Cape Coast's imposing, whitewashed castle commands the heart of town, overlooking the sea. Once one of the world's most important slave-holding sites, it provides horrifying insight into the workings of the trade. Staff conduct hourlong tours, during which you'll visit the dark, damp dungeons, where slaves waited for two to 12 weeks, while contemplating rumours that only hinted at their fate. A visit to the dungeons contrasts sharply with the governor's bedroom, blessed with floor-to-ceiling windows and panoramic ocean views.

🎓 Courses

★**Global Mamas** COOKING
(✐ 054 4323833; www.globalmamas.org; Market St) Set up in 2003 to empower local women by training them to produce and sell handicrafts, this fantastic outfit also organises courses in cooking (US$14), batik (US$18) and drumming and dancing (US$13, minimum two people). Courses last three or four hours and can be organised at short notice (the day before).

🛏 Sleeping

★**Baobab Guesthouse** GUESTHOUSE $
(✐ 054 0436130; www.baobab-children-founda tion.de; Commercial St; d/tr/q without bathroom C50/60/70; ☎) All profits from this charming guesthouse go to the Baobab Children Foundation, which runs a school for disadvantaged children. The simple rooms are decked out with bamboo furniture and colourful batik cloth made by the students, and some have views of the ocean or nearby Cape Coast Castle. There is an excellent vegetarian restaurant on site.

Cape Coast

Sasakawa Guesthouse GUESTHOUSE $
(☎033-2136871; sasakawa@yahoo.com; University of Cape Coast, Newsite; s/d C80/100; P❄🛜) Originally built to accommodate Cape Coast University's visiting lecturers, this modern facility on the university's beautiful campus is now open to all. It is an absolute bargain, with wi-fi, satellite TV, air-con and breakfast all included in the price, and it's a great place to meet young Ghanaians. The campus is about 5km out of town, served by a constant stream of taxis.

Oasis Beach Resort HOSTEL $
(☎024 5128322, 024 3022594, 024 4089535; www.oasisbeach-ghana.com; seafront, Victoria Park; dm C20, hut C160, deluxe d/f with air-con C270/360, d/tr/q with shared bathroom C100/110/130; P❄🛜) Like a hip party spot, a night at Oasis is loud, hot and sweaty. Backpackers, volunteers and Cape Coast's beautiful people gravitate towards the beachfront bar and restaurant, which does a good line in sandwiches, salads and cocktails. Staff are very friendly.

Kokodo Guesthouse GUESTHOUSE $$
(☎024 4673486, 024 3529191; DeGraft Johnson Rd; r from US$60; P❄🛜) This gorgeous, modern villa – formerly the house of Barclays Bank's manager – sits atop a bluff in a pretty garden. Rooms are spacious and airy, with gigantic beds. There is a tropical garden and a wonderful restaurant lounge (mains C25). The only drawback is the location, on the outskirts of town.

🍴 Eating

★ **Baobab Vegetarian Moringa Restaurant** VEGETARIAN $
(www.baobab-children-foundation.de; 054 0436130; Commercial St; sandwiches C11-21, mains C12-24; ⊙7am-8pm; 🛜🅿) 🌱 A tiny organic food bar with a wholesome touch, Baobab serves up great veggie stews and curries, black-bread sandwiches and refreshing juices, smoothies and shakes. All this and there's a great sea view too.

Orange Beach Bar & Restaurant INTERNATIONAL $
(☎057 6605250; www.facebook.com/orange-beachbarghana; Victoria Rd; mains from C20; ⊙8am-midnight) Sitting on the beach next to Cape Coast Castle, this airy and friendly cafe serves fresh organic juices and smoothies, as well as tasty breakfasts, fish grills and Ghanaian dishes. It's a good place for a party too, with regular beach bonfires and reggae nights.

Cape Coast

◉ Top Sights
  1 Cape Coast Castle C3

◉ Sights
  2 Fort Victoria...A2
  3 Fort William...B2

✪ Activities, Courses & Tours
  4 Global Mamas B3

🛏 Sleeping
  5 Baobab Guesthouse C3
  6 Oasis Beach Resort C3

✕ Eating
  Baobab Vegetarian Moringa
    Restaurant ....(see 5)
  7 Orange Beach Bar & Restaurant C3
  8 The Castle C3

✦ Transport
  9 Kotokuraba Station B1
  10 Tantri Bus Station................................ C1

The Castle　　　　　　　　　　　AFRICAN $$
(Victoria Rd; mains C20-50; ⊙7am-11pm) Though not as impressive in size as its next-door neighbour (Cape Coast Castle), this wooden bar-restaurant is a charmer. The fare (a mix of Ghanaian and international dishes) is good, though not sensational.

ℹ Information

INTERNET ACCESS
Cornell Internet (Commercial St; per hr C5; ⊙7am-7pm)

Ocean View Internet (Commercial St; per hr C5; ⊙7.30am-11pm) Printing, scanning, CD burning.

MONEY
Barclays Bank (Commercial St; ⊙8am-5pm Mon-Fri) Can change travellers cheques and cash; has an ATM.

Coastal Foreign Exchange (Jackson St; ⊙8am-4.30pm Mon-Fri, 9am-1pm Sat) A good alternative to the perennially full Barclays for changing cash.

TOURIST INFORMATION
Tourist Office (☑033-2132062; Heritage House, King St; ⊙8.30am-5pm Mon-Fri) On the 1st floor of Heritage House, a gorgeous colonial building; staff can help with practical information such as transport and directions but little else.

ℹ Getting There & Away

BUS
The Intercity STC bus station is near the Pedu junction, about 5km northwest of the town centre. Destinations for the moment are just Accra (C25, three hours, one daily) and Takoradi (C10, one hour, one daily). There are several Metro Mass services to and from Cape Coast daily.

TRO-TRO
Shared taxis and tro-tros (minibuses) to local destinations such as Anomabu (C2, 15 minutes) and Elmina (C2.50, 15 minutes) leave from **Kotokuraba station** (Johnston Rd).

For tro-tros to Accra (C20, three hours) and Kumasi (C30, four hours) head to **Tantri station** (cnr Sarbah Rd & Residential Rd). You can also pick up tro-tros to Accra from the Total petrol station.

Ciodu station (Jukwa Rd) serves destinations west of Cape Coast, such as Kakum National Park (C5, 30 minutes) and Takoradi (C8, one hour).

Kakum National Park

An easy day trip from Cape Coast, Kakum National Park (☑033-2130265, 050 1291683; admission C2, canopy walkway adult/child C50/10; ⊙6am-4pm) is a slice of native rainforest famous for its canopy walk, a series of viewing platforms linked by a string of bouncy suspension bridges 30m above ground. The park is also home to over 300 species of bird, 600 species of butterfly and 40 mammal species, but it can be difficult to see (or hear) any of them, because tours of the walkway are conducted in large groups. It's best to come on a weekday, first thing in the morning or in the late afternoon when there are fewer visitors and you can enjoy the peace of the rainforest.

If you would like to see wildlife, you will need to venture further into the park and make special arrangements with a guide the day before.

While most people will come to Kakum on a day trip from Cape Coast, it is possible to sleep at a campsite (C45) or in a treehouse (C55) inside the forest, though you'll have to be accompanied by a park ranger. Contact the Kakum National Park Information Centre (☑033-2130265, 0501291683; ⊙6am-4pm) for further details.

Kakum is easily accessible by public transport. From Cape Coast, take a tro-tro from Ciodu Station (C5, 30 minutes).

GHANA KAKUM NATIONAL PARK

Elmina

📝 021 / POP 33,500

The enchanting town of Elmina lies on a narrow finger of land between the Atlantic Ocean and Benya Lagoon. Here, the air is salty and the architecture is a charming mix of colonial remnants, elderly *posubans* (shrines) and an imposing historical legacy in the shape of St George's Castle.

The traditional name of Elmina is Anomansa, meaning inexhaustible supply of water. Watching the colourful pirogues pull in and out of the lagoon, breathing in the salty air and listening to the cacophony of shouts at the crowded Mpoben port is like having front-row theatre seats. The vast fish market is also fascinating to wander around, particularly when the day's catch is being unloaded in the afternoon.

◉ Sights

St George's Castle CASTLE
(Elmina Castle; adult/student/child C40/30/50; ⊙9am-5pm) St George's Castle, a Unesco heritage site, was built as a trading post by the Portuguese in 1482, and captured by the Dutch in 1637. It was expanded when slaves replaced gold as the major object of commerce, with storerooms converted into dungeons. The informative tour (included in the entry fee) takes you to the grim dungeons, punishment cells, Door of No Return and the turret room where the British imprisoned the Ashanti king, Prempeh I, for four years.

👉 Tours

⭐**Ghana Ecotours** CULTURAL, WALKING
(📝024 2176357, 020 8159369; www.ghanaeco tours.com; 1st floor, St George's Castle; walking tours per person C30) This sensational outfit offers highly informative walking tours that retrace Elmina's history. Tours take in the local fish market, the town's *posuban*, colonial buildings, small alleyways and great panoramas. It also offers city tours of Cape Coast, as well as nightlife tours of both cities.

🛏 Sleeping & Eating

⭐**Stumble Inn** LODGE $
(📝054 1462733; www.stumbleinnghana.com; dm C20, d C90, d with shared bathroom C70; 🅿🌬) 🌿 This pretty, ecofriendly haven gets rave reviews from travellers, and rightly so: spotless huts are set beneath palm trees on a gorgeous stretch of beach, there's a fantastic restaurant

and bar, and plenty of strategically placed bamboo loungers for enjoying the view to the full (as well as a beach volleyball court and table tennis for the more energetic).

Coconut Grove Bridge House HOTEL $$
(📝026 3000692; www.coconutgrovehotelsghana. com; s/d US$90/125; 🅿🌬📶) Set in a charming old stone building opposite St George's Castle, this is certainly the most atmospheric place to stay in town, even if the rooms are tired and overpriced. The attached restaurant, with a breezy terrace and stunning views, is a bonus.

Coconut Grove Beach Resort RESORT $$
(📝033-2191213; www.coconutgrovehotelsghana. com; village d US$65, resort d from US$120; 🅿🌬@📶🏊) This beach resort offers a variety of upmarket rooms as well as a pool, a tennis court, a nine-hole golf course and a questionable mini animal sanctuary. Rooms in the resort's extension – called 'The Village' – are more rustic but considerably cheaper, and you still get to enjoy all the fancy facilities. The resort is 3km west of Elmina.

Almond Tree Guesthouse B&B $$
(📝024 4281098, 026 5379798; www.almond3. com; r US$55-75, r with shared bathroom US$35; 🅿🌬📶) It's the hosts' friendly welcome that makes this guesthouse so special. Originally from Jamaica, the family settled in Britain and then here. The rooms, each named after a famous Jamaican, are impeccable and homely, with warm hardwood floors. Some have shared facilities while others enjoy their own little balcony.

Bridge House AFRICAN $$
(mains C20-40; ⊙9am-9pm; 🌬) With a terrace overlooking the fort and the lagoon, Bridge House is the nicest place to eat in town, and serves huge portions of European and Ghanaian food. It's inside Coconut Grove Bridge House.

❶ Getting There & Away

From the main taxi and tro-tro station (outside the Wesley Methodist Cathedral) you can get tro-tros to Takoradi (C5, one hour) or passenger taxis to Cape Coast (C2.50, 15 minutes).

Takoradi

📝 031 / POP 445,000

Takoradi was just a fishing village until it was chosen as Ghana's first deep-water seaport; since then it has prospered. Now feeding on

Ghana's oil industry, Takoradi (or Taadi, as it's known) is growing larger by the day.

There isn't much for visitors here but the town is an important transport hub so you're bound to go through it at some stage.

⊨ Sleeping & Eating

Petit Palais Guesthouse   GUESTHOUSE **$$**
(☑ 024 4337890; www.petitpalais.com.gh; Beach Rd; d US$120-140, ste US$150-170; P ❄ 🛜 ⊠) This superchic boutique hotel, decked out in shades of white and red, is one of the best places to stay in town. There's a pool, a garden and a balcony to chill out on, a homely lounge/kitchen area and excellent food is made to order.

Planter's Lodge & Spa   BOUTIQUE HOTEL **$$$**
(☑ 031-2199271; www.planterslodge.com; d/ste from C550/790; P ❄ @ 🛜 ⊠) Originally built to accommodate British Royal Air Force flying officers, this exquisite compound is now a stylish hideaway popular with oil magnates and the Takoradi jet set. The rooms have plenty of old-school colonial elegance and there's a pool, a restaurant and a teashop set in thriving tropical gardens.

Bocadillos   CAFE **$**
(⊙ 7am-7pm Mon-Sat) Perfect for pastries, baguettes, sandwiches and ice cream. Eat on the terrace overlooking the street or in the calm, chic interior.

Captain Hook's   SEAFOOD **$$**
(☑ 031-2027084; Dixcove Hill; mains from C70; ⊙ noon-3pm & 6pm-midnight; P) The place to come for huge and delicious platters of fresh seafood. There are steaks and other grills for carnivores. The wood panelling and model ships give the place a seafaring atmosphere.

❶ Getting There & Away

Starbow (www.flystarbow.com) and **Africa World Airlines** (www.flyawa.com.gh) operate two flights a day between Accra and Takoradi (45 minutes; C165). The airport is 1.5 km west of the centre.

Intercity STC (http://stc.oyawego.com/) and **Metro Mass** (www.metromass.com) provide daily services to Accra (C25 to C45, five hours).

Tro-tro (minibus or pick-ups) stops are scattered around the main market roundabout. Everyone should be able to direct you. Destinations include Accra (C25, four to five hours), Kumasi (C25, five hours) and Agona Junction (C5, 40 minutes).

Axim

☑ 031 / POP 28.000

Axim is the site of the huge Fort San Antonio, built by the Portuguese in the 16th century. It is also home to some of the country's best beaches and most idyllic resorts. Located 70km from the border with Côte d'Ivoire, Axim is pronounced with a French accent (Akzeem or Azeem).

◎ Sights

Fort San Antonio   HISTORIC BUILDING
(adult/child C10/2; ⊙ 9am-4.30pm) Built in 1515, Fort San Antonio was the second fort constructed by the Portuguese on the Gold Coast, after St George's Castle in Elmina. The entrance fee includes a guided tour, and from the top of the fort, there are spectacular views of the stunning coastline in both directions.

⊨ Sleeping & Eating

Axim Beach Eco Resort   RESORT **$$**
(☑ 031-7090099, 031-2092397; www.axim beach.com; budget r/chalet/f bungalow from US$50/80/150; P ❄ @ 🛜 ⊠) This sprawling resort is the largest in the area – with two restaurants, a pool and a playground – yet it still manages to feel friendly and intimate. The dark red thatch huts are lovely. They're scattered around a lush green hillside that slopes down to a pretty beach, and many have floor-to-ceiling windows to take in the stunning views.

Ankobra Beach Resort   RESORT **$$**
(☑ 031-2092323; www.ankobrabeachresort.com; budget d/apt US$36/94, r from US$104, chalet from US$142; P ❄ 🛜) Gorgeous bungalows decorated with African art and textiles are hidden in vibrant tropical gardens along a suitably dreamy stretch of beach. There's also fantastic food, much of it home-grown at the resort.

★ Lou Moon Lodge   LODGE **$$$**
(☑ 020 8241549, 026 4241549; www.lou-moon-lodge.com; standard/sea-view d from €75/125, standard/sea-view ste from €100/125; P ❄ 🛜 ⊠) Perhaps the loveliest beach resort in the country, Lou Moon sits on a beautiful and private sheltered bay backed by thick forest. Rooms and chalets – all polished plaster, huge windows and crisp white linen – are an exercise in understated chic, and the daily changing menu offers a small

choice of delicious dishes, including kids and veggie options (C45 to C95).

ℹ️ Getting There & Away

Regular tro-tros (C10, one hour) go from Takoradi to Axim via a smooth, paved road. If coming from the border at Elubo, the journey should take around two hours in a tro-tro.

Busua

📞 031 / POP 5000

The small village of Busua, some 30km west of Takoradi, is a magnet for volunteers and backpackers, who love coming here to relax on the beach for a few days. There's a sociable vibe, with a number of chilled out bars and cafes in which to while away the hours; and the village has developed a reputation as a surfing hot spot. There are two excellent surf schools here, both offering lessons for absolute beginners.

The downside is the occasional rubbish on the beach, and the rather neglected air in low season.

⊙ Sights & Activities

The stunning village of **Butre** is well worth the 3km walk from Busua. In fact, the walk itself is half the attraction: head east along the beach from Busua for about 2km then veer left along a path to go up a hill. The views of Butre when you reach the summit are a sight to behold, with the ruined Fort Batenstein nestled in palm trees on a bluff, Butre sandwiched between the ocean and the lagoon, and the ocean lapping a long, curvy beach beyond the lagoon. If you want to stay the night, the Green Zion Garden – a tranquil eco-lodge with a vegetarian restaurant – is lovely.

Dixcove (or Dick's Cove, as it was once known) is a large, bustling fishing village, with a very different feel from Busua. Its natural harbour is deep enough for small ships to enter – one of the reasons why the British chose to settle here and built **Fort Metal Cross** in 1696.

Dixcove is just 20 minutes' walk over the headland to the west of Busua. Locals warn against walking the track alone, however, so heed their advice and take a local guide with you (easily arranged by your accommodation).

Run by local surf instructor Peter Ansah, **Ahanta Waves Surf School & Camp**

(📞 026 9197812; www.ahantawaves.com) offers fun and professional surf lessons starting from C40 per person. The **Black Star Surf Shop** (📞 055 6267914; www.facebook.com/blackstarsurfshop) rents longboards, shortboards (C20 per hour) and bodyboards (C10). It also runs regular surfing lessons (C40, two hours).

🛏️ SLEEPING & EATING

Green Zion Garden LODGE $
(📞 020 2949398, 026 4625900; www.greenziongarden.com; Butre; camping per person US$3, 2-/4-person huts US$10/15) Set in flourishing tropical gardens, this tranquil eco-lodge offers rustic, handmade bungalows as well as camping. The vegetarian restaurant (mains C15 to C20) specialises in Indian food, and serves freshly roasted coffee and home-grown lemongrass tea.

Busua Inn GUESTHOUSE $$
(📞 020 7373579; www.busuainn.com; d from US$40; 🅿️ ❄️ 🛜) Owners Danielle and Olivier offer four clean, spacious rooms, two of which open out onto a sea-facing balcony. The romantic restaurant has a wooden deck backing right up to the water, and serves tasty French and Senegalese dishes (mains C20 to C50) as well as cocktails and good wine. Just watch out for the light-fingered resident monkey.

★**Okorye Tree** CAFE $$
(mains C15-50; ⊙ 7am-9pm) Attached to the Black Star Surf Shop, the Okorye Tree does a roaring trade in pancakes, burgers and great big burritos. Grab a table on the wooden deck, order a frozen margarita and watch the waves break.

Coconut Dream Bar & Restaurant INTERNATIONAL $$
(mains C15-40) This rustic, bamboo restaurant is painted in the colours of the Ghanaian flag and has a breezy 1st-floor dining area. At night, benches are placed out in the sand, illuminated by torchlight. Food is the usual mix of Ghanaian and international and it does a nice line in cocktails.

ℹ️ Information

The only place in town with internet is the **Busua Beach Resort** (📞 031-2093305; gbhghana.net), which has free wi-fi.

There are no banking facilities in Busua (the nearest are in Agona or Takoradi).

ℹ️ Getting There & Away

Busua is about 12km from the main coastal road between Takoradi and Axim. To get here, get a tro-tro from Takoradi to Agona (C5, 40 minutes) and then a shared taxi to Busua (C2, 15 minutes).

To get to Akwidaa, you'll need to go back to Agona; from Akwidaa to Busua, however, you could stop at Dixcove and then walk from there.

Akwidaa & Cape Three Points

Akwidaa's unique selling point is its long, pristine, white sandy beach, by far one of the best in Ghana. The village itself isn't as interesting as other settlements on the coast but you can hike in the local forests, explore cocoa and rubber plantations, organise canoe trips through mangroves or visit the windswept Cape Three Points, Ghana's most southern point. In season, you can see turtles on the nearby beaches as well as humpback whales and sperm whales.

🛏️ Sleeping

⭐ **Escape3points**   LODGE $
(☑ 026 7218700; www.escape3points.com; dm €7, chalets €20-35; P❄️📶) 🏊 Beautiful and ecofriendly, Escape3points is one of the nicest places to stay along the coast. The stilted bungalows are rustic yet stylish. They're handmade from bamboo, raffia, thatch and wood, and are naturally cooled by the sea breezes. Meals are communal and feature food from the organic gardens.

Ezile Bay Village   LODGE $
(☑ 020 7373579, 024 3174860; www.ezilebay.com; dm/hut from US$8/23; P❄️) Simple huts sit among palm trees on this gorgeous stretch of beach. The staff are welcoming and helpful, there's a great restaurant (mains C22 to C50), and the water is clean and a good deal calmer than elsewhere on this stretch of coast, so perfect for swimming.

Akwidaa Inn   LODGE $
(☑ 054 9158469, 024 3628022; www.akwidaainn.com; Dixcove-Akwidaa Old Town Rd; dm from C25, d hut from C100; P❄️) Spacious huts and a dorm sit in plant-filled grounds on a glorious stretch of unspoilt beach. The friendly staff can arrange tours around the region including boating in the mangroves and visiting a rubber plantation.

ℹ️ Getting There & Away

Akwidaa is about 16km south of the Takoradi–Axim road, and Cape Three Points is a further 6km west. Take a tro-tro from Takoradi to Agona (C6, 40 minutes) and then a tro-tro from Agona to Cape Three Points (90 minutes) or Akwidaa (C6, one hour). The driver can drop you off at your chosen lodge. Tro-tros stop in Dixcove on the way, handy if you want to get to Busua.

If you're driving you'll need a 4WD – the roads are in poor condition.

THE CENTRE

Kumasi

🎵 032 / POP 1.98 MILLION

Once the capital of the rich and powerful Ashanti kingdom, Ghana's second city is still dripping with Ashanti traditions. Its heart, the huge Kejetia market, throbs like a traditional talking drum and its wares spill into the city so that no matter where you are in Kumasi, it sometimes feels like one enormous marketplace.

Consider staying at Lake Bosumtwe – it's a gorgeous spot just one hour from here – and visiting Kumasi as a day trip.

◎ Sights & Activities

⭐ **Kejetia Market**   MARKET
From afar, the Kejetia Market looks like an alien mothership landed in the centre of Kumasi. Closer up, the rusting tin roofs of this huge market (often cited as the largest in West Africa; there are 11,000 stalls and at least four times as many people working here) look like a circular shanty town. Inside, the throbbing Kejetia is quite disorienting but utterly captivating.

Prempeh II Jubilee Museum   MUSEUM
(National Cultural Centre; adult/student/child C20/10/5; ⏰10am-4pm Mon-Fri, 6am-6pm Sat) This museum may be small but the personalised tour included with admission is a fascinating introduction to Ashanti culture and history. Among the displays are artefacts relating to the Ashanti king Prempeh II, including the king's war attire, ceremonial clothing, jewellery, protective amulets, personal equipment for bathing and dining, furniture, royal insignia and some fine brass weights for weighing gold. Constructed to resemble an Ashanti chief's house, it has a

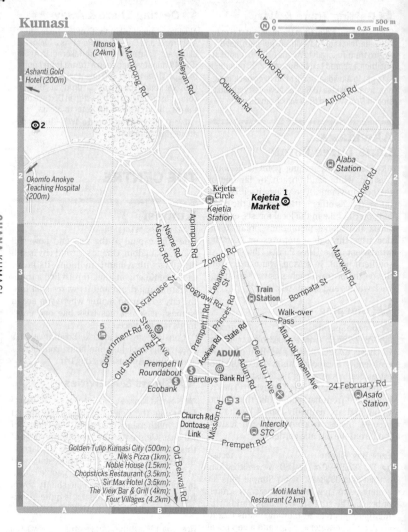

Kumasi

courtyard in front and walls adorned with traditional carved symbols.

National Cultural Centre ARTS CENTRE
(⊙9am-6pm) The National Cultural Centre is set within peaceful, shaded grounds and includes craft workshops, where you can see brassworking, woodcarving, pottery making, batik cloth dyeing and kente cloth weaving, as well as a gallery and crafts shop.

Kumasi Walking Day Tours WALKING
(☑024 9885370; kwesiannan7@gmail.com) Affable and knowledgeable Ben Kwesi Annan

offers excellent walking tours taking in the city's main sights, as well as nightlife tours of Kumasi's pubs and clubs at the weekends.

🎭 Festivals & Events

The Ashanti calendar is divided into nine cycles of 42 days called Adae, which means 'resting place'. Within each Adae, there are two special days of worship, when a celebration is held and no work is done. The most important annual festival is the **Odwira festival**, which marks the last or ninth Adae. The festival features lots of drumming, horn

Kumasi

⊙ Top Sights
1 Kejetia Market C2

⊙ Sights
2 National Cultural Centre A1
  Prempeh II Jubilee Museum........ (see 2)

🛏 Sleeping
3 Basel Mission Guesthouse C4
4 Daddy's Lodge..................................... C4
5 Kumasi Catering Rest House A4

🍴 Eating
  Kentish Kitchen............................. (see 2)
6 Vic Baboo's C4

ℹ Information
  Ghana Tourist Authority .... (see 2)

blowing, food offerings and parades of elegantly dressed chiefs. Contact the Ghana Tourist Authority (p206) for exact dates.

🛏 Sleeping

Daddy's Lodge GUESTHOUSE $
(☏ 030-22022128; www.daddyslodge.com; r from C40; 🅿❄🔊) A two-minute stroll from the STC bus station, this place can't be beat when in comes to convenience, and the simple rooms and dorm aren't too bad either.

Basel Mission Guesthouse GUESTHOUSE $
(☏ 032-2026966; Mission Rd; d/executive d C80/130, d/tw without bathroom C50; 🅿❄🔊) Set in attractive green grounds, this two-storey guesthouse is a good budget option in central Kumasi, with recently revamped rooms. The building and staff are rather austere and the bathrooms are only just clean.

★ Four Villages Inn GUESTHOUSE $$
(☏ 032-2022682; www.fourvillages.com; Melcome Rd, Poultry Junction; r incl breakfast US$106; 🅿❄@🔊) The Ghanaian-Canadian owners have pulled out all the stops at this impressive guesthouse. Each of the four enormous air-conditioned rooms is decorated in a different style, and there's a TV lounge and a tropical garden. Prices exclude the 15% VAT. The knowledgeable hosts can organise Kumasi excursions and tours, including tip-top market tours with their local guide.

Kumasi Catering Rest House GUESTHOUSE $$
(☏ 032-2026506; kcrhouse@yahoo.com; Government Rd; s/d/ste C200/260/325; 🅿❄@🔊) Massive, clean rooms with very comfortable

beds are set in pretty bungalows in spacious, shady grounds. Some of the rooms and bathrooms are looking rather outdated, however. There's a good restaurant and bar (mains C25 to C50) and a hair salon. It's a short stroll to the centre of town.

Golden Tulip Kumasi City HOTEL $$$
(☏ 032-2083777; www.goldentulipkumasicity.com; Victoria Opoku-Ware St; r from €160; 🅿❄@🔊🏊) Kumasi's plushest hotel has suitably elegant rooms and a host of upscale facilities, tennis court and pool included.

🍴 Eating

Kentish Kitchen AFRICAN $
(National Cultural Centre; mains C15-30; ⊙9am-6pm) Set in a pretty garden within the National Cultural Centre, this simple restaurant serves good Ghanaian dishes such as *red-red* (bean stew), *fufu* (fermented cassava, yams, plantain or manioc which is cooked and puréed) and *jollof rice*, as well as a few European choices.

Sir Max Restaurant GRILL $$
(Ahodwo; mains C18-50; ⊙7am-11pm; 🔊) Set within the hotel of the same name, Sir Max serves top-quality Lebanese food, including kebabs and mezze platters, on a nice terrace overlooking the hotel pool.

Vic Baboo's INTERNATIONAL $$
(Osei Tutu I Ave; mains C20-35; ⊙10am-10pm Mon-Sat, noon-9pm Sun; ❄🍴) Vic Baboo's is an institution among travellers and expats. With the biggest menu in town, this place is whatever you want it to be – Indian takeaway, decent burger joint, Lebanese deli or cocktail bar. It has a good selection of vegetarian dishes.

★ View Bar & Grill INTERNATIONAL $$$
(☏ 024 4668880; www.facebook.com/theview barandgrill; 39 Melcom Rd, Ahodwo; mains C20-125; ⊙noon-3pm & 6pm-1am; 🅿❄) Without a doubt the best restaurant in Kumasi. Delicious and beautifully presented food is served up in stylish surroundings, with expansive windows taking in views over the city. The steaks are the stars of the menu, but there are also good chicken, fish and gourmet-burger options. The cocktails are excellent and there are regular DJ parties on the roof terrace.

Moti Mahal Restaurant INDIAN $$$
(Top Martins Complex, near Asokwa Flyover; mains C30-70; ⊙noon-3pm & 7-11pm; 🅿❄) One of

CLOTH AROUND KUMASI

Ntonso, 15km north of Kumasi, is the centre of *adinkra* cloth printing. Adinkra symbols represent concepts and aphorisms; they are traditionally printed on cotton fabric by using a natural brown dye and stamps carved out of calabash. You can see the whole process explained at Ntonso's **Visitor Centre** (📞024 9547110; entry C8; ⊙9am-6pm Mon-Sat) (C8) and even create your own works; strips of fabric are sold for C40 and make a lovely keepsake.

The kente-weaving and cocoa-growing village of **Adanwomase** wins the Palme d'Or of ecotourism in Ghana. Villagers here have put a huge amount of effort into developing fun, informative tours about local culture and artistic traditions. The visitor centre offers two tours: one focusing on kente cloth, and the other on the village itself. There are direct tro-tros (minibuses; C8) from Kejetia station in Kumasi.

the fanciest and best-loved restaurants in Kumasi, Moti Mahal is a formal place serving some of the country's finest Indian cuisine in elegant, fiercely air-conditioned surroundings.

ℹ️ Information

INTERNET ACCESS

Most of the hotels offer free wi-fi.

Unic Internet (Bank Rd; per hr C5; ⊙8am-7pm) A good choice.

MEDICAL SERVICES

Pharmacies are dotted all over town.

Okomfo Anokye Teaching Hospital (📞032-2022301; www.kathhsp.org; Bantama Rd) Kumasi's main public hospital with 700-plus beds.

MONEY

There are half a dozen banks in the centre, all with ATMs and foreign-exchange facilities.

Barclays (Prempeh II Roundabout; ⊙8.30am-4.30pm Mon-Fri)

Ecobank (Harper Rd)

TOURIST INFORMATION

Ghana Tourist Authority (📞0322-035848; National Cultural Centre; ⊙8am-5pm Mon-Fri)

Staff can help arrange guided tours of the city and surrounding villages.

ℹ️ Getting There & Away

AIR

Kumasi airport is on the northeastern outskirts of town, about 2km from the centre. **Africa World Airlines** (www.flyawa.com.gh) and **Starbow** (www.flystarbow.com) both offer regular flights to Accra (one way starts around C260). A taxi from the centre to the airport costs about C20. Allow plenty of time because of the traffic.

BUS

At the time of research **Intercity STC** (📞020 4314432, 020 4314491) had just starting operating after a period of inaction, though services were subject to cancellation. VIP and VVIP offer a more frequent service, leaving from **Asafo Station** (Asafo). **Metro Mass** operates fill-up-and-go services from its station on the Western bypass.

Accra C25, four hours, leaves when full; operated by VIP.

Ouagadougou, Burkina Faso C110 + 7,000 CFA, 15 hours, three weekly; operated by STC.

Takoradi C30, six hours, once daily; operated by STC.

Tamale C45, five hours, once daily; operated by STC.

TRO-TRO

There are two main motor parks in Kumasi, each with its allocated destinations:

Alaba station (Alaba) Wa (C30, six hours), Tamale (C25, five hours)

Asafo station Cape Coast (C20, four hours), Accra (C25, four hours), Kunatase (C8, 45 minutes)

ℹ️ Getting Around

Local tro-tros around Kumasi depart from **Kejetia station** (Kejetia Circle).

Lake Bosumtwe & Abono

Formed by a huge meteorite, Lake Bosumtwe (also spelled Bosumtwi) resides in the impact crater. The 86m-deep lake is hugged by lush green hills in which you can hike, cycle and ride horses.

Located 38km southeast of Kumasi, the village of Abono is the gateway to Lake Bosumtwe; it is a popular weekend holiday spot for Kumasi residents, who come here to relax and swim. It's also a sacred site. The Ashanti people believe that their souls come here after death to bid farewell to the god Twi.

Foreign visitors will be charged C5 upon arriving in Abono.

🏃 Activities

The Green Ranch   HORSE RIDING
(☑ 020 2917058; Lake Bosumtwe; per hr C55, 10hr tour around lake C500) Enjoy the beauty of the lake and explore traditional villages on horseback, with this excellent, professional company.

🛏️ Sleeping & Eating

⭐ **Cocoa Village Guesthouse**   GUESTHOUSE **$**
(☑ 020 9891228, 020 8612675; www.cocoa-village. com; camping per person €5, dm €8, bungalow from €36; P) Bright and cosy bungalows, some handcrafted using traditional techniques, sit on a beautiful lawn with views down to the lake. A wonderful place to relax for a few days. You'll need a 4WD to negotiate the rough road to get here, or they can arrange a boat transfer from Abono (C50 one-way).

⭐ **Lake Point Guesthouse**   LODGE **$**
(☑ 024 3452922; Lake Bosumtwe; dm/d/tr C20/60/85; P ✳) Colourful huts and dorms are set on a hillside in dreamy tropical gardens at this sociable lodge. Across the small dirt road at the bottom of the property is a grassy lawn, leading down to a lakeside beach, the jumping-off point for kayaking adventures. The tin-roof bar and restaurant has a delicious daily changing menu (mains C30).

ℹ️ Getting There & Away

You can sometimes find tro-tros (minibuses) travelling directly between Kumasi and Abono, but it's more likely you'll first need to go to Kuntanase (C8, 45 minutes), a larger town to the west of Abono, and then catch a shared taxi from there (C2, 15 minutes).

THE NORTH

Tamale

☑ 037 / POP 360,000

If the northern region is Ghana's breadbasket, Tamale is its kitchen. If you can take the heat, you'll discover a town with some good food, charm and a whole lot of soul. (If

you can't, don't panic: nearby Mole National Park is generally cooler.)

Tamale's population is largely Muslim and there are several interesting mosques around town, notably on Bolgatanga Rd. The **National Culture Centre** (off Salaga Rd) is a lively place, with craft shops and regular dance and music performances.

👉 Tours

Grassroot Tours Ghana   TOURS
(☑ 054 1668682; www.grassroottours.com) Runs excellent tours around the northern region, including to Mole National Park.

🛏️ Sleeping

Clinton Lodge   GUESTHOUSE **$**
(☑ 026 2000000; www.clinton-lodge.com; d with fan/air-con & TV C40/80; P ✳ 🛜) A great-value place that's popular with volunteers and aid workers, Clinton Lodge offers simple rooms with verandas, and good food – both Western and Ghanaian. It's a little bit out of the way, but staff can order taxis for you as well as help arrange trips to Mole National Park and beyond.

Mash Lodge   HOTEL **$**
(☑ 020 6537534; s/d C150/250; P ✳ 🛜) This solid budget offering has clean and simple rooms with TV, air-con and free wi-fi. There's a decent on-site restaurant or you can pop next door to **Wooden** (☑ 037-2028943; www. wooden-gh.com; Airport St; mains from around C30; P) for a livelier atmosphere.

African Dream Hotel   GUESTHOUSE **$$**
(☑ 037-2091127, 024 3623179; www.africandream hotel.com; Bolgatanga Rd; standard/executive d C240/270; P ✳ 🛜) Set in pretty landscaped gardens complete with wandering chickens, African Dream offers charming, if slightly careworn, rooms as well as a decent restaurant and speedy wi-fi. The location, some 10km out of town, won't be for everyone, but friendly owner Abu Prince offers pick-ups and drop-offs from town and the airport. He can also arrange tours to Mole National Park and northern Ghana.

🍴 Eating

Chuck's Bar & Restaurant   INTERNATIONAL **$$**
(☑ 055 3997379, 055 4819346; Mariam Rd; mains from C35; ⏱ 5pm-1am Wed-Sat, 11am-midnight Sun) You won't see many locals in here, but as far as expat havens go, this is a good one. A wood-burning pizza oven produces excellent pizzas and the menu also includes pas-

tas, burgers and decadent desserts. There's regular live music and events, and a popular Sunday brunch. The large beer garden is perfect to sink a cold drink or two.

Luxury Catering Services   AFRICAN $$
(☑ 050 7463655; Jisonayili Rd; mains from C20; ℗) A popular choice serving tasty local and Western food as well as a decent selection of wine and real coffee. The guinea fowl is particularly good.

Swad Fast Food   INDIAN $$
(☑ 024 4712942, 037-2023588; Gumbihini Rd; mains C18-40; ⊙ 9am-10pm; ℗) The name might not be a winner, but this place remains as popular as ever. The large garden is dotted with pot plants and visited by the odd wandering goat, and there's a huge menu featuring everything from authentic curries to pizzas to Ghanaian classics.

❶ Information

Barclays (Salaga Rd; ⊙ 8.30am-5pm Mon-Fri) Changes cash and travellers cheques; ATM.
Stanbic (Salaga Rd; ⊙ 8.30am-4.30pm Mon-Fri) Changes cash; ATM.
Tamale Teaching Hospital (☑ 037-2022458, 037-2022454; Salaga Rd) The main hospital in northern Ghana, 2km southeast of town.
Vodaphone (internet per hr C5; ⊙ 9am-10pm; 📶) The fastest connection in town (still pretty slow at busy times); it's right next to the towering radio mast near the Intercity STC bus station.

❶ Getting There & Away

AIR

The airport is about 20km north of town; a private taxi here costs around C40. **Starbow** (www.flystarbow.com) and **Africa World Airlines** (www.flyawa.com.gh) fly between Tamale and Accra from C242 one way.

BUS & TRO-TRO

Buses and tro-tros congregate around the Total petrol station and the radio mast in the centre of town. There are regular tro-tros to Bolgatanga (C10, three hours) and Wa (C15, six hours).

     Intercity STC (www.stc.oyawego.com) buses go to Accra (C70, 12 hours, 6am daily), Kumasi (C40, six hours, 6am daily) and Takoradi (C58, 13 hours, 3pm Tuesday to Saturday). VVIP has a daily service to Accra (C80).

     To get to Mole National Park take a tro-tro from the **main bus station** to Wa, and change at either Damongo or Larabanga. There is also a daily **Metro Mass** (www.metromass.com) bus

to Wa, that leaves at 5am from the bus station behind the Total petrol station.

❶ Getting Around

Motorbikes, tuk-tuks, and share taxis jostle for business around Tamale's streets – a short trip should cost around C2.

Mole National Park

With its swathes of saffron-coloured savannah, **Mole National Park** (☑ 027 7564444, 024 4316777; www.molemotelgh.com; adult C40, Ghanaian/foreign car C7/35) offers what must surely be the cheapest safaris in Africa. There are at least 300 species of bird and 94 species of mammal, including African elephants, kob antelopes, buffaloes, baboons and warthogs. Sightings of elephants are common from December to April, and you're guaranteed to see other mammals year-round.

     The park headquarters offers excellent walking and driving safaris. You can arrange for an armed ranger to join you in your own 4WD, but you're not allowed to explore the park unaccompanied.

     If you tire of elephant spotting, ecotourism venture Mognori Eco Village, on the borders of the park, offers canoe safaris, village tours and the chance to learn about local culture.

☞ Tours

★ Mole National Park Headquarters Safaris   SAFARI

(☑ 024 4316777; www.molemotelgh.com/fsafari.php; walking/jeep/night safaris per person C20/40/60) Two-hour walking safaris and jeep safaris take place daily at 7am and 3.30pm. Night safaris depart at 6pm. You can also rent a safari vehicle for private tours (C80 an hour for the jeep, C10 per person, per hour for the guide). Park rangers are happy to let you pool with other travellers.

Mognori Eco Village   TOURS, SAFARI
(☑ 024 9507413, 024 6750646; canoe trip per 1-5 people C40, village tour per person C15, cultural performance per 1-4 people C70) Sitting right on the edge of Mole National Park (about 10km east of the park's visitor centre), the village of Mognori has become a flourishing ecotourism venture. Villagers here offer various activities: canoe safaris on the river, where you'll see monkeys, birds and crocodiles; village tours, on which you'll learn about shea

butter production and traditional medicine; and drumming and dancing performances.

🛏 Sleeping & Eating

Mole Motel HOTEL $$
(📞 027 7564444, 024 4316777; www.molemotelgh. com; Mole National Park; dm C60, s/d/tr with fan C80/140/210, s/d with air-con C180/220, bungalow with air-con C300; P ❄ ☒) The setting – at the top of an escarpment, with a viewing platform overlooking plains teeming with wildlife – is fantastic. Mole Motel's ugly concrete building is at odds with the natural surroundings, though, and the rooms are underwhelming. There's a small pool and a reasonable restaurant, serving a mix of Ghanaian and international fare (mains C18 to C40).

★ Zaina Lodge LODGE $$$
(📞 030-3938736, 054 0111504; www.zainalodge. com; s/d B&B US$180/240, s/d full-board incl game drives US$350/500; P ❄ 🛜 ☒) 🖉 Luxury Zaina Lodge is a game changer for Mole, and one of the nicest places to stay in all of Ghana. Entrance gates, built in traditional northern mud-and-stick style, give way to a stunning triple-height lobby/lounge with vistas over the saffron savannah – views also shared by the elegant tented rooms, the terrace and the infinity pool.

❶ Getting There & Away

A charter taxi from Tamale will cost around C400 return. Grassroot Tours Ghana (p207) can take you for the day in a 4WD with a driver for C350 excluding fuel – the advantage being that a park ranger will be able to accompany you in the car, so you won't need to hire a park vehicle.

If coming by public transport from Tamale, you could get a tro-tro headed for Wa, and ask to be dropped at Damongo or Larabanga, from where you can get a taxi or motorbike to the park.

Bolgatanga
📞 039 / POP 66,700

Bolgatanga – usually shortened to Bolga – was once the southernmost point of the ancient trans-Saharan trading route, running through Burkina Faso to Mali. Bolga is laid-back and a fine base to explore the surrounding area – and it's the last stop on the road to Burkina.

LARABANGA

The tiny Muslim village of Larabanga, just 4km from Mole National Park, is most famous for its striking Suda-nese-style mud-and-stick mosque, purported to be the oldest of its kind in Ghana. The town itself is hot, dusty and soporific; alleys wrap around traditional mud homes and bedraggled goats roam the streets.

On arrival in Larabanga you'll immediately be approached and asked to pay a visitors fee of C10 per person. Following this you'll be taken to the mosque for a quick tour and history lesson, though you are not allowed to go inside. After the tour you'll be invited to sign a guestbook and make a further donation.

From Tamale, any tro-tro (minibus or pick-up) headed to Wa can drop you at Larabanga. Or you could get the 5am Metro Mass bus from Tamale to Wa, which passes through the town.

◉ Sights

Bolgatanga Library LIBRARY
Built by award-winning American architect J Max Bond Jr, Bolga's library is a stylish piece of 1960s modernist design.

Chief's Pond CROCODILE POND
(adult/student C15/10, camera fee C5; P) The pond's reptiles, which are held sacred by the local people, are reputed to be the friendliest in Africa. Local women even do their laundry in the pond while kids frolic in the water. Legend has it that this state of blissful cohabitation goes back to a pact the town's founders made with local crocodiles not to hurt each other. While we're not totally convinced, plenty of visitors do indeed manage to pose with crocs unharmed.

🎊 Festivals & Events

Bolgatanga International Crafts & Arts Fair ART
(BICAF; 📞 038-24468; www.facebook.com/ Bolgatanga-International-Craft-and-Arts-Fair-BI-CAF-770519099638046; ☉ Dec) Showcases work by artisans from the Upper East region and across Ghana, with a handful of displays from elsewhere on the continent. The four-day event also features live bands.

🛏 Sleeping & Eating

Premier Lodge   GUESTHOUSE $
(Navrongo Rd; r from C100; P ✱ 🛜) A good-value guesthouse with spotless (if basic) rooms with air-con and free wi-fi. A decent breakfast is included and home-cooked meals are sometimes available, given advance notice. It's a little out of town, but transport is easy to find.

Nsamini Guesthouse   GUESTHOUSE $
(📞 038-2023403, 027 7316606; off Navrongo Rd; r C60, without bathroom C30; P ✱) A popular choice, this cute courtyard set-up is one of Bolga's best budget buys. Rooms are clean, and Koffi, the affable owner, will make you feel at home. It's up a lane leading off Navrongo Rd.

Swap Fast Food   INTERNATIONAL $
(📞 024 5842397; Navrongo Rd, SSNIT Bldg; mains C20; ⊙ 10am-9pm; ✱) The outdoor terrace is lovely but if the heat is too much you can always retreat to the air-con dining room. The food is good and varied – the menu includes curries, *jollof rice,* pepper steak, fried noodles – but the service is very slow.

ℹ Information

Sirius Click Internet Café (Black Star Hotel, Bazaar Rd; per hr C5; ⊙ 7.30am-9pm)
Vodafone Internet Cafe (Commercial St)

ℹ Getting There & Away

Tro-tros to Tamale (C20, three hours) and Paga (C5, 40 minutes) leave from the motor park off Zuarungu Rd, past the police station.

The Intercity STC bus station is 500m south of the centre, on the road to Tamale. There is a

---

WORTH A TRIP

WECHIAU HIPPO SANCTUARY

The much-hyped Wechiau Hippo Sanctuary (www.ghanahippos.com; C20) on the Black Volta River was initiated by local village chiefs in 1999. Hippos can usually be seen from November to March; once the rainy season (April to October) is underway, however, hippos disappear and the site becomes very hard to reach. Activities (C15 per person per hour) include river safaris, birdwatching, village tours and nature walks. Unless you have your own vehicle, you'll need to overnight at the sanctuary.

---

daily service to Kumasi (C45, eight hours) and Accra (C80, 12 hours). The VIP/VVIP station is on Zuarangu Rd, and has a daily service to Tamale, Kumasi and Accra.

THE NORTHWEST

Wa

📞 039 / POP 102,000

The sleepy capital of the Upper Northwest region is home to the Wa Na Palace, a stunning mud-and-stick mosque. There are few attractions otherwise but it has a friendly vibe and is a pleasant place to overnight before or after visiting Wechiau Hippo Sanctuary or to break the journey between Bobo-Dioulasso and Kumasi.

🛏 Sleeping & Eating

Blue Hill Hotel   GUESTHOUSE $
(📞 039-2095525; Wa-Kumasi Rd; r from C150; P ✱) The rooms in this new hotel may look as if they were designed in the 1980s, but they are clean and spacious, with plenty of mod cons. There's also a good restaurant and a small bar.

Tegbeer Catholic Guesthouse   GUESTHOUSE $
(📞 039-2022375; s/d with fan C70/90, with air-con C90/110; P ✱) The Tegbeer Catholic Guesthouse, about 3km north of Wa, is an excellent option with clean, good rooms, a pretty garden and a nice on-site bar-restaurant (mains C15 to C25).

ℹ Getting There & Away

There are regular tro-tros and buses to Wechiau (C5, 90 minutes), Larabanga (C10, 2½ hours) Tamale (C25, five hours), Hamale (C15, three hours). VIP and **Intercity STC** (www.stc.oyawego.com) both have a service to Accra (14 hours) and Kumasi (10 hours).

UNDERSTAND GHANA

Ghana Today

Once held up as an example of African growth, Ghana has faltered since 2013. A growing public deficit, high inflation and a weakening currency forced President John Dramani Mahama to turn to the International Monetary Fund (IMF) in 2015 for a bailout as world commodity prices took a nosedive.

While development continues apace in Accra, where wealthier Ghanaians and expats frequent an ever-expanding number of fancy restaurants and hotels, the picture is gloomy for most Ghanaians. Unemployment, public debt and corruption are all high.

The December 2016 presidential elections saw opposition candidate Nana Akufo-Addo beat incumbent Mahama, who conceded peacefully and immediately – a testament to Ghana's strong democratic traditions.

History

Present-day Ghana has been inhabited since 4000 BC, filled by successive waves of migrants from the north and east. By the 13th century several kingdoms had developed, growing rich from the country's massive gold deposits and gradually expanding south along the Volta River to the coast.

Power & Conflict

By the 16th century one of the kingdoms, the Ashanti, emerged as the dominant power, taking control of trade routes to the coast. Its capital, Kumasi, became a sophisticated urban centre, with facilities and services equal to those in Europe at the time. And it wasn't long until the Europeans discovered this African kingdom. First the Portuguese came prospecting around the coast; the British, French, Dutch, Swedish and Danish soon followed. They all built forts by the sea and traded slaves, gold and other goods with the Ashanti.

But the slave trade was abolished in the 19th century, and with it went the Ashanti domination. By that time the British had taken over the Gold Coast, as the area had come to be known, and began muscling in on Ashanti turf. This sparked several wars between the two powers, culminating in the British ransacking of Kumasi in 1874. The Gold Coast was soon a British colony.

Independence & the Nkrumah Years

When Ghana finally won its independence in March 1957, Kwame Nkrumah, who had been the voicve for Ghanaian independence for more than a decade, became the first president of an independent African nation. His speeches, which denounced imperialism and talked about a free, united Africa, made him the darling of the pan-African movement.

But back home Nkrumah was not popular among traditional chiefs and farmers. Factionalism and regional interests created an opposition that Nkrumah tried to contain through repressive laws, and by turning Ghana into a one-party state.

Things were starting to unravel. Nkrumah expanded his personal bodyguard into an entire regiment, while corruption and reckless spending drove the country into serious debt. Nkrumah, seemingly oblivious to his growing unpopularity, made the fatal mistake of going on a state visit to China in 1966. While he was away his regime was toppled in an army coup. Nkrumah died six years later in exile in Guinea.

The Rawlings Years

By 1979 Ghana was suffering food shortages and people were out on the streets demonstrating against the army fat cats. Enter Jerry Rawlings, a good-looking, charismatic, half-Scottish air-force pilot, who kept cigarettes behind his ear and spoke the language of the people. Nicknamed 'Junior Jesus', Rawlings captured the public's imagination with his calls for corrupt military rulers to be confronted and held accountable for Ghana's problems. The military jailed him for his insubordination, but his fellow junior officers freed him after they staged an uprising. Rawlings' Armed Forces Revolutionary Council (AFRC) then handed over power to a civilian government (after a general election).

The new president, Hilla Limann, was uneasy with Rawlings' huge popularity, and later accused him of trying to subvert constitutional rule. The AFRC toppled him in a coup in 1981, and this time Rawlings stayed in power for the next 15 years. During part of the 1980s, Ghana enjoyed Africa's highest economic growth rates.

The Democratic Era

By 1992 Rawlings was under worldwide pressure to introduce democracy, so he lifted the 10-year ban on political parties and called a general election. Rawlings won the 1992 elections freely and fairly, with 60% of the vote. In 1996 he repeated this triumph in elections that were again considered free and fair. At much the same time, the appointment of Ghanaian Kofi Annan as UN secretary-general boosted national morale.

After eight years of Rawlings and the NDC (the constitution barred Rawlings from standing for a third term in the 2000 presidential elections), his nominated successor and former vice-president, Professor John Atta Mills, lost to Dr John Kufuor, leader of the well-established New Patriotic Party (NPP). Under the Kufuor administration, primary-school enrolment increased by 25% and many of Ghana's poor were granted access to free health care.

The 2008 election was widely regarded as a test of Ghana's ability to become a modern democracy. Atta Mills won by a slim margin and despite the tensions with NPP competitor Nana Akufo-Addo, the election passed without serious violence. After Atta Mills' unexpected death in July 2012, his vice president, John Dramani Mahama, took the reins, and won the 2012 general election.

People of Ghana

Ghana's population of 28 million makes it one of the most densely populated countries in West Africa. Of this, population 44% are Akan, a grouping that includes the Ashanti (also called Asante), whose heartland is around Kumasi, and the Fanti, who fish the central coast and farm its hinterland. The Nzema, linguistically close to the Akan, fish and farm in the southwest. Distant migrants from present-day Nigeria, the Ga are the indigenous people of Accra and Tema. The southern Volta region is home to the Ewe.

In the north, the Dagomba heartland is around Tamale and Yendi. Prominent neighbours are the Gonja in the centre, Konkomba and Mamprusi in the far northeast, and, around Navrongo, the Kasena. The Sisala and Lobi inhabit the far northwest.

Religion

Ghana is a deeply religious country and respect for religion permeates pretty much every aspect of life. You'll come across churches of every imaginable Christian denomination; even the smallest village can have two or three different churches. About

70% of Ghanaians are Christian. Pentecostal and Charismatic denominations are particularly active, as are the mainline Protestant and Catholic churches.

About 15% of the population is Muslim; the majority are in the north, though there are also substantial Muslim minorities in southern cities such as Accra and Kumasi.

Many Ghanaians also have traditional beliefs, notably in spirits and forms of gods who inhabit the natural world. Ancestor veneration is an important part of this tradition. Many people retain traditional beliefs alongside Christian or Muslim beliefs.

The Arts

Music

There's no doubt about it, Ghana's got rhythm. Highlife, a mellow mix of big-band jazz, Christian hymns, brass band and sailor sonnets, hit Ghana in the 1920s, and popular recordings include those by ET Mensah, Nana Ampadu and the Sweet Talks. Accra trumpeter ET Mensah formed his first band in the 1930s and went on to be crowned the King of Highlife, later performing with Louis Armstrong in Ghana.

WWII brought American swing to Ghana's shores, prompting the first complex fusion of Western and African music. Hiplife, a hybrid of rhythmic African lyrics poured over imported American hip-hop beats, has now been ruling Ghana since the early 1990s.

Gospel music is also big, as is reggae.

Textiles

Kente cloth, with its distinctive basketwork pattern in garish colours, is Ghana's signature cloth. Originally worn only by Ashanti royalty, it is still some of the most expensive material in Africa. The cloth can be single-, double- or triple-weaved and the colour and design of the cloth worn are still important indicators of status and clan allegiance.

Kente is woven on treadle looms, by men only, in long thin strips that are sewn together. Its intricate geometric patterns are full of symbolic meaning while its orange-yellow hues indicate wealth.

SURVIVAL GUIDE

ℹ️ Directory A–Z

ACCOMMODATION

If you're looking for a bargain, Ghana probably isn't it – hotels and hostels are generally expensive for what you get, and there are few quality budget options. Budget hotels don't often provide a top sheet, so pack a sleeping liner.

CHILDREN

Aside from the daily struggle of getting them to swallow malaria tablets, travel with children in Ghana needn't be difficult. There are plenty of child-friendly restaurants in Accra, offering high chairs, kids' menus and even small play areas. Many of the larger hotels and beach resorts have a kids' pool and/or a playground and can provide cots or extra beds for children.

Narrow, uneven pavements and open drains mean that Ghana is not remotely buggy friendly, so bring a sling or infant backpack if you're travelling with a baby or toddler. Nappies are available in supermarkets and general stores throughout Ghana, though designated baby-change facilities are a rarity.

Ghanaian waters are rough, so it's best to stick to splashing in the surf, unless you are lucky enough to be at Lou Moon Lodge (p201), which has a sheltered beach with calm water, perfect for swimming.

DANGERS & ANNOYANCES

Ghana has proved to be a stable and generally peaceful country. Take care of your valuables on beaches and avoid walking alone at night. If swimming, beware of strong currents; ask locals before diving in.

Bilharzia is present in many of Ghana's freshwater lakes and rivers, so take the necessary precautions, such as applying DEET repellent before going into the water.

EMBASSIES & CONSULATES

The following are all in Accra.

Australian High Commission (Map p188; ☑ 030-2216400; www.ghana.embassy.gov. au; 2 Second Rangoon Close, Cantonments; ⊙8.30am-3pm Mon-Fri)

British High Commission (Map p188; ☑ 030-2213250; www.ukinghana.fco.gov.uk; Julius Nyerere Link, off Gamel Abdul Nasser Ave; ⊙9.30-11.30am Mon-Thu, 8.30-10.30am Fri)

Burkinabé Embassy (Map p188; ☑ 030-2221988; Nyadji Crescent, Asylum Down)

Canadian High Commission (Map p188; ☑ 030-2211521; www.canadainternational. gc.ca/ghana; 42 Independence Ave, Sankara Interchange; ⊙7.30am-4pm Mon-Thu, to 1pm Fri)

ℹ️ SLEEPING PRICE RANGES

The following prices refer to a double room with bathroom. Unless otherwise stated, breakfast is included in the price.

$ less than US$70

$$ US$70–150

$$$ more than US$150

Dutch Embassy (Map p188; ☑ 030-2214350; www.netherlandsworldwide.nl/countries/ghana; 89 Liberation Rd, Ako Adjei Interchange; ⊙9am-4.30pm Mon-Thu, 9am-3pm Fri)

French Embassy (Map p188; ☑ 030-2214550; www.ambafrance-gh.org; Presidential Dr; ⊙8am-noon Mon-Fri)

German Embassy (Map p188; ☑ 030-2211000; www.accra.diplo.de; 6 Kenneth Kaunda Rd, North Ridge)

Ivorian Embassy (Map p188; ☑ 030-774611; Naa Amponsua St, Osu)

Togolese Embassy (Map p188; ☑ 030-2777950; 4th Circular Rd)

US Embassy (Map p188; ☑ 030-2741000; http://ghana.usembassy.gov; 4th Circular Rd)

EMERGENCY & IMPORTANT NUMBERS

Ghana's country code	☑ 233
Ambulance	☑ 193
Fire	☑ 192
Police	☑ 191

FOOD

Fiery sauces and oily soups are the mainstay of Ghanaian cuisine and are usually served with a starchy staple like rice, *fufu* (cooked and mashed cassava, plantain or yam) or *banku* (fermented maize meal).

Other cuisines, particularly Indian and Chinese, are widely available throughout the country. Accra's ever-evolving dining scene offers everything from top-class sushi to gourmet burgers.

About the most common dish you'll find in Ghana is groundnut stew, a warming, spicy dish cooked with liquefied groundnut paste, ginger and either fish or meat. Palm-nut soup (fashioned from tomatoes, ginger, garlic and chilli pepper, as well as palm nut) takes its bright red colour from palm oil. *Jollof rice* is a spicy dish cooked with a blend of tomatoes and onion and usually served with meat. *Red-red* is a bean stew normally served with fried plantain.

> ### ⓘ EATING PRICE RANGES
>
> The following price ranges refer to a main course:
>
> **$** less than C20
>
> **$$** C20–50
>
> **$$$** more than C50

GAY & LESBIAN TRAVELLERS

Homosexuality is illegal in Ghana and attitudes towards gays and lesbians are for the most part conservative. In many instances same-sex couples will not be allowed to share a room.

INTERNET ACCESS

You can get online pretty much anywhere in Ghana these days. Most hotels and many restaurants offer wi-fi, all mobile phone networks have 3G and there are internet cafes in every town and city (connection costs C5 to C10 per hour).

MONEY

ATMs Virtually everywhere, with almost all accepting Visa (Stanbic's taking MasterCard and Maestro).

Changing money The best currencies to bring are US dollars, UK pounds and euros, in that order. Exchange bureaus are found in most major towns. They give lower exchange rates for small US$ denominations, so pack your $50 and $100 notes.

Credit cards Midrange and top-end hotels tend to accept credit cards, but at a surcharge.

Tipping Not common in chop houses or cheap eateries, but more expected in upscale venues (a tip of 10% to 15% should suffice). Porters or bag handlers at the airport and bus stations will often expect or ask for a tip. A cedi or two should be fine.

Travellers cheques Barclays is the only bank to exchange travellers cheques; there is a maximum of US$250 per transaction.

Exchange Rates

Australia	A$1	C3
Canada	C$1	C3.15
Euro zone	€1	C4.50
Japan	¥100	C3.70
New Zealand	NZ$1	C2.80
US	US$1	C4.10
UK	UK£1	C5.30

For current exchange rates see www.xe.com.

OPENING HOURS

Administrative buildings 8am to 2pm or so; embassies tend to keep similar hours.

Banks 8am to 5pm Monday to Friday; some additionally run until noon on Saturday.

Markets 7am to 5pm; in predominately Muslim areas, Friday is quieter; in Christian areas, it's Sunday.

Shops 9am to 5pm or 6pm every day except Sunday, when only large stores open.

POST

Accra's main **post office** (p193) is in Ussher Town, but your post will get to its destination much more quickly if you mail it from Kotoka International Airport.

PUBLIC HOLIDAYS

New Year's Day 1 January

Independence Day 6 March

Good Friday March/April

Easter Monday March/April

Labour Day 1 May

May Bank Holiday 1st Monday in May

Africa Unity Day 25 May

Republic Day 1 July

Founders Day 21 September

Christmas Day 25 December

Boxing Day 26 December

Ghana also celebrates Muslim holidays, which change dates every year.

TELEPHONE

➡ Mobile (cell) phones are ubiquitous in Ghana and the network coverage is virtually universal and excellent value.

➡ If you have an unlocked phone, SIM cards (C10) can be picked up in shopping centres and communication centres.

➡ MTN, Vodafone, Tigo and Airtel are the main networks; all have 3G.

TOURIST INFORMATION

As a rule, tourist information is pretty useless in Ghana, with staff working in tourist offices having little understanding of what travellers need. The **Ghana Tourism Authority** (p193) has an office in Accra, and the brand new **Accra Tourist Information Centre** (p193) looks like a good bet.

No Worries Ghana (www.noworriesghana.com) Published by the North American Women's Association, this guide (both paper and electronic) is more targeted at people moving to rather than travelling to Ghana; nonetheless, the dozens of eating, drinking, and entertainment listings as well as the information on shipping, transport and so on is very useful.

Touring Ghana (www.touringghana.com) Ghana's official tourism portal; worth a look for inspiration and general information.

VISAS

Visas are required by everyone except Ecowas (Economic Community of West African States) nationals. Visas upon arrival are rarely issued.

Though it's technically possible to pick up a visa upon arrival, they only get granted in rare cases so it is highly advisable you get one ahead of travelling. Single-entry three-month visas (US$60) and multiple-entry six-month visas (US$100) are standard. You can get a visa extension at the Immigration Office (p193) in Accra near the Sankara Interchange.

Burkina Faso

The embassy (p213) issues visas for three months (C146), usually in 24 hours. You need three photos and a yellow-fever certificate. Three-month tourist visas are also available at the border at Dakola, costing CFA94,000.

Côte d'Ivoire

A three-month visa costs €50 and requires a hotel confirmation. See full list of requirements at www.snedai.com.

Togo

The embassy (p213) issues visas for one month on the same day. Alternatively, you can get a visa at the border at Aflao (CFA15,000), but it's only valid for seven days and you'll need to extend it in Lomé.

Getting There & Away

AIR
Airports & Airlines
➡ Every major European airline flies to Accra; Emirates now also flies daily to Dubai, opening a host of easy connections to the Asia-Pacific.

➡ There are direct flights to the US East Coast.

➡ You'll find plenty of direct flights to other parts of Africa, including South Africa, Kenya, Ethiopia, Egypt, Morocco and most neighbouring West African countries.

A US$50 passenger service charge is included in the price of international flights.

BORDER CROSSINGS

Ghana has land borders with Côte d'Ivoire to the west, Burkina Faso to the north and west, and Togo to the east. Crossing is generally straightforward. The main border crossings:
➡ **Burkina Faso** Paga–Dakola and Hamale–Ouessa

➡ **Côte d'Ivoire** Elubo–Noe, Sunyani–Agni-bilékrou and Bole–Ferkessédougou

➡ **Togo** Aflao–Lomé, Ho–Kpalimé and Wli–Kpalimé

Border crossings are normally open 6am to 6pm. Visas are essential to enter each of these countries.

Burkina Faso
➡ Direct Intercity STC buses run to Ouagadougou from Accra (C150 + CFA1000, 24 hours) and Kumasi (C110 + CFA1000, 18 hours) three times a week.

➡ From Paga, there are frequent tro-tros (minibuses) to Bolgatanga (C4, 40 minutes); on the Burkina side, you'll find plenty of onward transport to Pô and Ouagadougou.

➡ From Wa get a tro-tro to Hamale. On the Burkina side, you'll find transport to Diebougou and then Bobo-Dioulasso.

Côte d'Ivoire
➡ Intercity STC buses run daily to Abidjan from Accra (C75 + CFA7000, 12 hours) and Kumasi (C70 + CFA7000).

➡ Otherwise you'll find tro-tros running between Takoradi and Elubo (three hours), from where you can cross into Côte d'Ivoire and find onward transport to Abidjan.

Togo
➡ The easiest way to cross into Togo is to catch a bus or a tro-tro to Aflao, pass the border on foot (visas CFA15,000) and catch a taxi on the other side to central Lomé.

➡ Overlanders may prefer to cross at the less hectic Wli border post near Hohoe.

ℹ Getting Around

AIR

Starbow Airlines (www.flystarbow.com) and **Africa World Airlines** (www.flyawa.com.gh) operate domestic flights in Ghana.

ℹ️ STREET SIGNS & NAME CHANGES

The government is part way through a street-naming project, with the aim of giving every street in Ghana a visible street sign. At the same time, many existing street names are changing. While we have endeavored to mark as many changes as possible, it is likely that more names will have changed by the time you read this.

➡ There are several daily flights from Accra to Kumasi (45 minutes), Takoradi (35 minutes) and Tamale (1¼ hours). They tend to be relatively cheap and a huge time saver when travelling north.

BUS

➡ Buses are preferable to tro-tros (minibuses) for long journeys as they tend to be more comfortable and reliable.

➡ **Intercity STC** (www.stc.oyawego.com/) is Ghana's main long-haul bus company.

➡ Other relevant bus companies for travellers include **VIP** (www.vipbusgh.com), which runs half-hourly buses between Accra and Kumasi; **VVIP**, which runs north of Accra to Kumasi and Tamale; and **Metro Mass** (www.metromass.com), which runs local services in various parts of the country.

➡ It's wise to book in advance as tickets get snapped up fast on the more popular routes.

➡ Large rucksacks or suitcases are charged a flat fee. Baggage handlers will expect a tip for loading your bags.

CAR & MOTORCYCLE

➡ Driving is on the right in Ghana.

➡ Most main roads are in pretty good condition, though most secondary roads are unsealed.

➡ You will need an international driver's licence.

➡ Fuel is inexpensive at around C4 per litre.

➡ Hiring a car with a driver is a good option if you're short on time; travel agencies can usually arrange this. Depending on the distance, car and driver experience, factor in anything from US$100 to US$150 per day, plus fuel. Ghana Car Rentals (p194) is an excellent, professional company with reasonably priced vehicles.

LOCAL TRANSPORT

Taxi

➡ Within towns and on some shorter routes between towns, shared taxis are the usual form of transport. They run on fixed routes, along which they stop to pick up and drop off passengers. Fares are generally very cheap (C1 to C2).

➡ Private taxis don't have meters and rates are negotiable. It's best to ask a local in advance for the average cost between two points.

➡ Taxis can be chartered for an agreed period of time, anything from one hour to a day, for a negotiable fee.

➡ Uber officially arrived in Accra in September 2016.

Tro-tro

Tro-tro is a catch-all category that embraces any form of public transport that's not a bus or taxi. Generally they're minibuses.

➡ Tro-tros cover all major and many minor routes.

➡ They don't work to a set timetable but leave when full.

➡ Fares are set but may vary on the same route depending on the size and comfort (air-con) of the vehicle.

➡ There is generally an additional luggage fee.

➡ The area where tro-tros and buses congregate is called, interchangeably, lorry park, motor park or station.

Guinea

Best Places to Eat

➡ Restaurant Îles des Joies (p221)

➡ Hotel SIB (p224)

➡ Le Sogue Hôtel (p222)

Best Places to Sleep

➡ Pension Les Palmiers (p218)

➡ Hotel M'lys (p218)

➡ Hotel SIB (p224)

➡ Hôtel Tata (p223)

➡ Le Sogue Hôtel (p222)

Why Go?

Imagine you're travelling on smooth highways, and then get tempted by a dusty turn-off signed Adventure. Well, that turn-off is Guinea. Little known to most of the world, this is a land of surprising beauty, from the rolling mountain plateau of Fouta Djalon to wide Sahelian lands and thick forests. Overland drivers have long been drawn here for the challenge of steering their vehicles over rocks and washed-out paths. Nature lovers lose themselves on long hikes past plunging waterfalls, proud hills and tiny villages; or by tracking chimpanzees through sticky rainforest. But the best thing about Guinea is that almost nobody else bothers to take this turn-off – meaning you'll likely have the country to yourself.

Devastatingly, the country was caught up in the West Africa Ebola outbreak in 2014. The country was officially declared Ebola-free in June 2016, and related travel restrictions were lifted, meaning now is the time to explore.

When to Go
Conakry

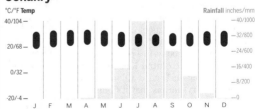

Nov & Dec Best time to visit, after the rains and before the dusty harmattan winds.

Apr Very hot everywhere and not a pleasant month to travel.

Jun–Sep Rainy season. Roads turn into mud rivers and are almost impassable. Avoid!

CONAKRY

✔ 4 / POP 1.6 MILLION

Conakry doesn't try to please its guests, and yet, slowly, many are eventually won over by its charms. There aren't many sights in this dusty (and/or muddy, depending on time of year) mess of crumbling buildings, pollution, rubbish and traffic jams, but there is plenty of buzz. From the pungent fishing port of Boulbinet and the street kitchens of Coronthie to the containers-turned-shops of Taouyah, this city goes about its business noisily and with ingenuity, proud and unruffled by the visitor's gaze.

⊙ Sights

★ Centre d'Art Acrobatique

Keita Fodeba   CULTURAL CENTRE

(✔ 624 789059; Dixinn Stadium; ⊙ 10am-2pm Mon-Fri) FREE The Centre d'Art Acrobatique Keita Fodeba is perhaps the single most amazing experience in Guinea. Every weekday morning scores of acrobats spin, twirl and flip through routines that have made them the envy of circuses the world over. As good as the acrobats are, it's the contortionists who steal the show. When they bend themselves 180 degrees the wrong way you can only wonder if they actually have backbones or if they are in fact jellyfish.

Musée National   MUSEUM

(7th Blvd, Sandervalia; GFr10,000; ⊙ 9am-6pm Tue-Fri, 10am-5.30pm Sat & Sun) The Musée National has a modest collection of masks, statues and musical instruments, many of which are used in religious or mystical ceremonies.

🛏 Sleeping

Maison d'Accueil   HOTEL $

(✔ 621 752 939; Rte du Niger, Kaloum; r with/without air-con GFr160,000/130,000; 🅿 ❄) Essentially the only real budget accommodation in the city that foreigners are likely to be able to stay at. Conakry's Catholic Mission has clean, simple rooms in a peaceful setting on the edge of the central Kaloum district. However, being such good value for money (for Conakry) means that it's often fully booked.

★ Hotel M'lys   HOTEL $$

(✔ 624 299 369; www.hotelmlys.com; Quartier Almamya, Kaloum; r from GFr705,000; ❄ 🛜) This small, central place is turning the Conakry hotel scene on its head. Gone are drowsy overpriced rooms and lacklustre service. In

are business smart rooms in soothing whites and browns, back-and-white photographic art, warm and welcoming staff, a cool delicious lipstick-red cafe-restaurant and an outdoor garden bar. All for a price that can't be knocked.

★ Pension Les Palmiers   GUESTHOUSE $$

(Chez Ghussein; ✔ 622 352 500; www.pension-lespalmiers.com; Rte de Donka, Ratoma; s/d €70/75; 🅿 ❄ 🛜 ≋) The doily-adorned couches, cute living room and caring owners make this one a five-heart guesthouse, if not a five-star hotel, and as such it seems to attract a diverse collection of business people, aid workers and the occasional tourist. The rooms are modern, and polished, with comfortable beds, reliable electricity, internet connections and plenty of hot water.

★ Noom Conakry   DESIGN HOTEL $$$

(✔ 626 333 333; www.conakry.noomhotels.com; Quartier Ignace Deen, Kaloum; s/d from GFr2,050,000/2,190,000; 🅿 ❄ 🛜 ≋) The brand-new, boat-shaped, Noom Conakry is where the city puts on its most sophisticated face. It's a face that comes with an infinity pool overlooking the ocean, several top-quality bars and restaurants, tree sculpture art and huge black-and-white photos mounted on the walls. And all that's before you've even entered one of the very swish rooms...

Riviera Royal   HOTEL $$$

(✔ 664 223 302; www.rivieraroyalhotel.com; off Corniche Nord; r from €156; 🅿 ❄ 🛜 ≋) More affordable than many of the city's top-end hotels, the Riviera Royal has a tropical-garden vibe with rooms in small blocks scattered under the palm trees. There's a huge pool, bar, restaurant, nightclub and various sporting facilities.

🍴 Eating

Conakry isn't blessed with a diverse restaurant scene. For good street food, try **Marché du Niger** (Rte du Niger, Kaloum; ⊙ 6am-5pm) or **Marché Taouyah** (⊙ 6am-4pm), where bowls of rice costs around GFr20,000.

Le Waffou   AFRICAN $

(✔ 664 337 547; off Rte de Donka, Kipé; mains GFr25,000-40,000; ⊙ noon-midnight) You can buy Ivorian *attiéké* (grated cassava) on many a Conakry street corner, but this thatch-roof eatery prepares it fresh and does it better than most. Occasional live bands at weekends.

Guinea Highlights

1 Îles de Los (p222) Stretching out on palm-fringed strands, sipping fresh coconut juice.

2 Fouta Djalon (p222) Rambling through the mountains and swimming in the waterfalls of this majestic plateau.

3 Bossou (p226) Coming face to face with cheeky, alcohol-drinking chimps during a forest walk.

4 Conakry (p218) Hopping through the capital's dubious dives, getting drunk on some of West Africa's best live music.

5 Dalaba (p223) Enjoying the endless views and soaking up the colonial ambience.

6 Parc National du Haut Niger (p226) Helping a chimp in need and watching for colourful birds in one of West Africa's last tropical dry-forest ecosystems.

7 Centre d'Art Acrobatique Keita Fodeba (p218) Bending over backwards in awe while watching some of Africa's best acrobats spin through their routines.

Le Damier　　　　　　　　BAKERY **$**
(📞655 800 000; www.damier-conakry.com; Rte du Niger, Kaloum; cakes GFr40,000, sandwiches & pizzas GFr60,000, ice cream from GFr15,000; ⏰6.30am-6pm Mon-Sat) Le Damier started over a quarter of a century ago as a simple, French-style patisserie and today still sells by far the most authentically French breads, tarts and croissants in Guinea. It's also diversified into high-class French chocolate and simple sandwiches and pizza-style meals as well as delicious ice creams.

GUINEA CONAKRY

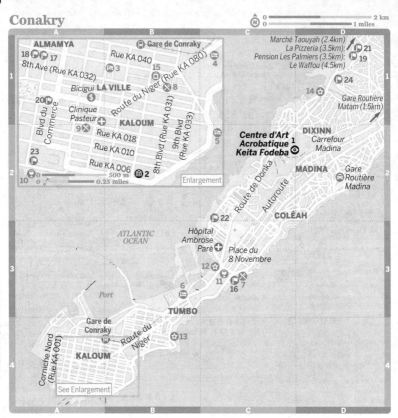

Conakry

★ **Restaurant Îles des Joies**   SEAFOOD **$$**
(☑ 664 385 652; 4th Ave, Kaloum; mains
GFr75,000-100,000; ⊘ noon-11pm Mon-Sat) Our
favourite restaurant in downtown Conakry,
this very simple, family-run place is hidden
down a dirty side-alley and, at first, looks
rather uninviting, but don't fret. The seafood
served up here – which is cooked so that it's
slightly crunchy on the outside and lush and
soft on the inside – is as fresh and delicious
as can be.

Avenue   BURGERS **$$**
(☑ 628 682 525; www.avenueconakry.com; Com-
mercial Center Residence 2000, Coléah; mains
GFr85,000-105,000; ⊘ 9am-10.30pm) Classy,
expat-popular, American-style diner serving oversized burgers stuffed with cheddar
cheese, pickles and salads. It also does fish
'n' chips and pizzas. It's currently one of the
'in' places to eat in Conakry.

🍷 Drinking & Nightlife

MLS   CLUB
(☑ 655 888 811; Pl 8 Novembre, Coléah; ⊘ 6pm-
2am Mon-Sat) This very chic place is in a
league of its own, subtly styled in polished
wood, soft fabrics, spotlighting and handmade furniture. And with a great sound system and good resident and visiting DJs to
boot it's got to be one of West Africa's class-
iest clubs. There's also a casino and lounge
bar within the same complex.

Club Obama   BAR
(Port de Boulbinet, Kaloum; ⊘ 10am-11pm)
Perched on stilts out in the water, this cute
thatch-and-wood bar covered in fish skele-
ton decorations is a great place for a sunset
drink. Whether the name will now change to
Trump Club remains to be seen...

☆ Entertainment

Conakry is one of the live-music capitals
of West Africa and there are dozens of live-
music venues, ranging from down-and-dirty
dives to big stadiums and refined cultural
centres.

★ **Faga Faga Fougou**
Espace Culturel   CONCERT VENUE
(Corniche Sud, Tumbo; entry from GFr15,000) This
is one of the most exciting live-music venues
in Conakry. The ocean-side stage hosts a diverse array of local and West African groups
performing anything from rap to world
music to Afro-funk. The atmosphere is very
chilled and welcoming and there are perfor-

mances most nights, except Sundays. Entry
fees vary depending on who is playing.

★ **Centre Culturel**
Franco-Guinéen   ARTS CENTRE
(☑ 621 904 054; www.ccfg-conakry.org; Pont du 8
Novembre, Tumbo; ⊘ 8.30am-8pm) French cultural centres in Africa usually put on diverse
and exciting events, art-house films, world
music concerts and exhibitions, and this one
is no exception. As well as a busy cultural
calender there's also a library. Closing times
vary depending on what events are taking
place that evening.

l'Echangeur   CONCERT VENUE
(☑ 622 322 390; Rte de Donka, Dixinn II; ⊘ 11am-
2am Mon-Sat) This humble bar looks completely unspectacular, yet it's where many
of Guinea's biggest stars jam at the weekend, in a space overflowing with good vibes
and cold beer. Bring a few Guinea francs
to 'spray' the musicians in thanks for the
praises they'll sing. On weekdays it's just a
chilled-out bar.

ℹ Information

DANGERS & ANNOYANCES
Incidents of military aggression and extortion
are much rarer than in years past, but they do
still happen. Always carry your passport and
vaccination certificates with you, especially if
you're out on the town after 11pm – *gendarmerie*
(police) checkpoints are set up at Pont du 8
Novembre and near the UK embassy (Résidence
2000), and you will usually have to show your
papers at night. If everything is in order, you
shouldn't have to pay any 'fines', though you
might have to discuss this a little with the often
intimidating soldiers.

Plenty of pickpockets roam Marché Madina,
Marché Niger and Ave de la République.

MEDICAL SERVICES
Most medical facilities are pretty basic. If something is seriously wrong get yourself to Dakar or
home. There are some well-stocked pharmacies
along Ave de la République.

Clinique Pasteur (5th Blvd, Kaloum;
⊘ 8.30am-6pm Mon-Sat) Fairly good for
malaria tests and minor injuries.

Hôpital Ambrose Paré (☑ 631 401 040; www.
cliniqueambroisepare.com; Dixinn) Considered
the best in Guinea, though for anything really
serious it's still best to get evacuated out of
the country.

MONEY
Bicigui (Ave de la République, Kaloum;
⊘ 8.30am-5pm Mon-Fri, 8.30am-noon Sat)

> ### ℹ ARRIVING IN CONAKRY
>
> There's no official public transport to and from Conakry International Airport (p230). Take one of the taxis waiting just beyond the gates. Expect to pay GFr100,000 to Ratoma and GFr200,000 to the city centre during daylight hours and a little more at night. There is no pre-booked taxi service.

This main bank branch claims to change travellers cheques, but doesn't always do so. The 24-hour ATM takes Visa and Mastercard.

ℹ Getting There & Away

Conakry has a number of *gares routières* for share taxis:

Gare Routière Bambeto The main station, with daily taxis to Kankan (GFr200,000, two days), Kissidougou (GFr150,000, 1½ days), N'zérékoré (GFr275,000, two days) and Labé (GFr95,000, 10 hours). Internationally, there are daily taxis to Bamako (Mali; GFr300,000, two days), Dakar (Senegal; GFr500,000, three days), Freetown (Sierra Leone; GFr130,000, nine hours) and Monrovia (Liberia; GFr480,000, three days). Taxis to Abidjan (Côte d'Ivoire; GFr650,000, four days) leave twice weekly.

Gare Routière Madina Taxis to destinations throughout Guinea. Sample fares include Kankan (GFr200,000, two days), Kissidougou (GFr150,000, 1½ days), N'zérékoré (GFr275,000, two days) and Labé (GFr95,000, 10 hours).

Gare Routière Matam (Taxis to southern destinations within Guinea as well as Bissau (Guinea-Bissau; GFr200,000, two days).

ℹ Getting Around

Taxis cost GFr2500 per 3km zone. Minibuses (*magbanas*) are a bit cheaper but much slower.

Îles de Los

A 30-minute boat ride off Conakry, the Îles de Los are a small huddle of palm-fringed islands that tempt with tropical beach dreams. There are three main islands (and a couple of rocky islets) though only two, Île de Kassa and Île Room, are kitted-out for visitors. All have beautifully forested, bird-filled interiors that reward some gentle exploration. During the dry season (October to May), the islands are a very popular weekend getaway for expats and well-to-do locals escaping Conakry. However, all's not perfect here – debris from the mountains of plastic and other rubbish that utterly blankets the Conakry shoreline drifts across to many of the island beaches in the currents. Even so, a visit here is a hugely welcome relief from the chaos of Conakry.

🛏 Sleeping

There are a couple of places to stay on both Île de Kassa and Île Room, but nothing on the other islands.

★**Le Sogue Hôtel**   HOTEL **$$**
(✆ 657 104 355; lenstonee@aol.com; d GFr700,000)
On a short stretch of private white-sand beach (entry for nonguests GFr15,000) that's swept clean every morning, this gorgeous hotel might well be the nicest place to stay in all of Guinea. The rooms are set atop granite boulders in among the trees and are subtly decorated in ocean-blue tones.

ℹ Getting There & Away

Public pirogues head to the islands from Conakry's Port de Boulbinet. It takes about 30 minutes to Île de Kassa, the nearest island. Pirogues leave when full and there's more transport at weekends. Most of the hotels on the islands also organise weekend transfers in faster, safer boats with life jackets.

FOUTA DJALON

Green rolling hills, balmy temperatures, forest-filled valleys and gushing waterfalls make the Fouta Djalon region one of West Africa's most enchanting corners. But this undulating, kilometre-high plateau isn't just pleasing to the eye, it's also superb hiking country, where experienced local guides can take you exploring along a web of walking trails snaking between interesting villages and impressive natural sites.

Mamou

Mamou, the gateway to the Fouta Djalon, is a dusty junction town and transport hub perched on a hill just above the scorching plains.

For travellers there's little in the way of attractions but there is every chance you might end up here for a night as you travel between Conakry and the Fouta Djalon or southern parts of Guinea.

🛏 Sleeping & Eating

Acacia White House   GUESTHOUSE **$**
(📞 655 295 414; road to Dabola; r GFr250,000;
🅿 ❄) It's hard to go wrong with this very
friendly and helpful family-run guesthouse
which has four spotless rooms and 24-hour
electricity thanks to a back-up generator.

Hôtel le Relais de Mamou   HOTEL **$**
(📞 660 315 944; road to Dabola, Quartier Tam-
bassa; r from GFr250,000; 🅿 ❄) This impressive and fairly new place offers good-value
rooms that are large and bright, with reliable evening electricity and hot showers. Some of the pricier rooms have sofas
and desks. Downstairs is a relaxed bar-
restaurant.

ℹ Information

There are a couple of banks with ATMs in the
town centre.

ℹ Getting There & Away

There are two *gares routières:*
Conakry Gare Routière (Conakry Rd) Taxis
to Conakry (GFr63,000, eight hours) go from
a parking area just to the west of the town
centre.
Gare Routière (Dalaba Rd) Bush taxis go from
the main station at the northern end of town
to the following destinations:
Dabola GFr45,000, 2½ hours.
Dalaba GFr20,000, 1½ hours.
Faranah GFr60,000, 2½ hours.
Kankan GFr110,000, five hours.
Kindia GFr37,000, two hours.
Labé GFr45.000, three hours.

Dalaba

POP 6500

In days past French colonialists would take
any opportunity they could get to leave
sweaty Conakry behind and decamp to the
cool, clear climes of the delightful hill town
of Dalaba (altitude 1200m). Today only a
couple of dilapidated colonial buildings and
one or two hotels redolent in yesteryear atmosphere remain, but the things that first
attracted the French to Dalaba – the eter-
nal spring-like climate, the inspiring views
down to the lowlands and the fabulous
walking – all still entice, and taken together
they make Dalaba the most pleasant town
in Guinea.

| WORTH A TRIP |

FOUTA DJALON HOTELS

The bungalows at **Hôtel Tata** (📞 657
926 150; www.hoteltata.com; r GFr250,000;
🅿 📶), with their woven, patterned roofs
and colourful bedspreads, are as pretty
as the tropical birds that fill the leafy
garden each morning. There's a relaxed
bar-restaurant with a real wood-fired
pizza oven (pizzas from GFr70,000).
Camping (GFr100,000) is also available.
  Hôtel Sister (📞 628 176 528; r
GFr200,000; 🅿), a Guinean-Welsh–run
place on the edge of town, is the exception to Pita's otherwise grotty offering
of hotels. Pretty pink rooms have a
pleasingly twee look and feel to them,
and are set around a large courtyard.
There's hot water and 24-hour electricity. Yes, you read that right! Solar panels
in the garden ensure its operation (after
a while in Guinea you'll understand how
wonderful that is!)

⊙ Sights

Jardins Auguste Chevalier   GARDENS
(GFr20,000; ⊙ 8am-6pm) Established by a
French botanist in 1908 to discover what
European and Asian plants would flourish
in Guinea, the Jardins Auguste Chevalier
offer an enjoyable place to unwind in the
shade of huge century-old oaks and forests
of bamboo. The gardens are 7km north of
Dalaba, just off the Pita road and close to the
village of Tinka.

Chutes de Ditinn   WATERFALL
One of Guinea's tallest – and certainly one
of its most beautiful – waterfalls takes a
120m drop straight down off a cliff. Ditinn
village is 35km from Dalaba and the falls are
5km further on from the village (a 20-min-
ute walk). A private taxi will charge around
GFr150,000 for the round-trip, with waiting
time.

Villa Sili   HISTORIC BUILDING
(GFr10,000) The old French governor's residence, Villa Sili (1936), which was for many
years almost on the verge of collapse, has
been recently renovated and is a fun place
to explore. Look out for the horse statues in
the garden. There are no set opening hours
but the guardian will, as if by magic, appear
and open up for you.

GUINEA DALABA

HIKING THE FOUTA DJALON

With over 16 years' experience in organising hiking adventures in the Fouta Djalon for tourists, as well as researching new routes, **Fouta Trekking** (☑622 912 024; www.foutatrekking.org; ⊘one-day trek GFr200,000, overnight trek per person per day €31) has identified the best hikes, cliffs, mountains and waterfalls in the area and developed a number of superb hiking circuits that many people find to be the highlight of their trip to Guinea.

A one man trekking, entertainment and hosting show, **Hassan Bah** (☑622 457 553; guided tour per half-/full-day GFr150,000/250,000) has been leading tours (in French or English) around Doucki for years and nobody who has the good fortune to come into contact with him regrets the encounter. He can organise hikes around the region lasting anything from a half-day to several days.

Cooperative des Cordonniers ARTS CENTRE (⊘7am-7pm) FREE This small cooperative of artisans is one of the best places in Guinea to watch high-quality leather goods such as sandals, wallets and bags being made. And yes, you can add to your baggage by buying a few items.

🥾 Activities

Pont de Dieu HIKING
There are many possible walking trails around Dalaba but the most popular half-day hike is to the Pont de Dieu, a series of small waterfalls that pass under a natural rock bridge. The route passes through pine forests, farmland and tiny villages (and even straight through a few family compounds where you'll likely be invited to stop and chat).

There are lots of variations on the route and it can be extended into a full-day hike. Hire a guide through the tourist office.

🛏 Sleeping & Eating

⭐**Hotel SIB** HISTORIC HOTEL $
(☑625 700 745; r from GFr160,000; 🅿) If this hotel were anywhere else on Earth it would have been converted into a luxury heritage hotel. As it is, this 1930s colonial building, which was originally constructed to house soldiers recuperating from WWII, is

a creaky, character-laden place, dripping in yesteryear romance.

Auberge Seidy II GUESTHOUSE $
(☑669 418 379; r GFr80,000) Koffi, the English-speaking and ever-laughing owner of the Auberge Seidy II, has created a lovely little guesthouse with clean and well-maintained rooms on the edge of the town, but even better than the rooms are the delicious meals and fun barbecues he puts on for guests. Great value.

Restaurant Moderne AFRICAN $
(☑620 306 380; mains GFr10,000-30,000; ⊘8am-10pm) Locals will rightly tell you that this friendly place, which is a proper restaurant rather than just a market stall, is the best place in town to eat. Dishes include rice and peanut sauce, chicken and chips, and spaghetti bolognese.

ℹ Information

The town has a well-established and helpful, privately run **tourist office** (☑657 604 011; ⊘8.30am-noon & 2-5pm Mon-Sat).

ℹ Getting There & Away

Bush taxis go to the following:
Labé GFr45,000, 2½ hours.
Mamou GFr20,000, one hour.
Pita GFr20,000, one hour.

Mali-Yemberem

POP 5000
The little village of Mali-Yemberem sits on the edge of the spectacular Massif du Tamgué, just before its precipitous drop towards Senegal and the plains far below. Not only is the scenery superb, but at over 1400m, this is the highest, and coolest – sometimes even cold – town in the Fouta. Mali-Yemberem is also famous for Mt Loura (1515m), known as La Dame de Mali, a mountainside resembling a woman's profile.

The incredible landscapes ensure that hiking here is top class – with a guide and time, there are near endless hiking possibilities.

La Dame de Mali (The Lady of Mali; guide from GFr70,000) is a curiously shaped mountain outcrop (its real name is Mt Loura) some 7km northeast of the village. There are a number of different walks around the edge of the sheer mountain face. The tourist office in Mali-Yemberem can organise a guide.

Campement du Mali (🖉 for tourist office 628 891 684; hut GFr50,000) consists of two huts (with a third under construction) on the edge of the escarpment close to La Dame de Mali. They are built to mimic traditional thatched village houses and are very basic, with no running water or electricity. But there are plenty of friendly folk around who might cook for you for a negotiable fee!

ℹ️ Information

Office du Tourisme (🖉 628 891 684; ⊙ 8am-6pm) Don't get too excited by the name – it's just a shop selling school books and pens – but Sadio Sauaré, the owner, has taken upon himself to promote the surrounding area and help tourists. He can organise guides (half-/full day GFr70,000/100,000) for walks ranging from a half-day to three days. He's also the person to speak to about the Campement du Mali and home stays.

ℹ️ Getting There & Away

There are reasonably frequent bush taxis between Mali-Yemberem and Labé (GFr47,000). The 'road' is horrendous and in the dry season it can easily take five to seven hours or longer to cover the 140km. In the wet season you could be counting in days.

To Kedougou (Senegal; GFr100,000) the road is equally tortuous but there are daily bush taxis and, if all goes well, you can be there in eight hours. Be aware, however, that it probably won't all go well!

FOREST REGION

Kissidougou

POP 103,000

Kissidougou, a large, bustling and colourful market town, serves as the entry to *Guinée forestière* (forest region). Even though it's hard to avoid the temptation to push on south to the forests, it's worth spending a day exploring here.

🛏️ Sleeping & Eating

Hôtel Savanah HOTEL **$**
(🖉 620 962 714; hotelsavanah2014@gmail.com; r from GFr250,000; P❄) With a wonderfully helpful management who'll go out of their way to please, and quiet, tidy rooms with floral bedsheets, this is as good as it gets in rural Guinea. Hot water comes by the bucket and there's reliable electricity all night.

Hôtel Fritz CABIN **$$**
(Hôtel de la Aeroport; 🖉 622 525 877; cabins from GFr500,000; P❄🏊) Prepare for a very big shock. Impeccable, spacious and tastefully decorated rooms set within individual cabins beside a clean, deep blue swimming pool. Yes you read that right. In fact, this resort-like place is so unexpected you'll most likely start to wonder if you're even in rural Guinea at all.

ℹ️ Getting There & Away

Bush taxis line up along the road through the centre of town. Taxis go daily to:
Conakry GFr140,000, 15 hours.
Faranah GFr35,000, 2½ hours.
Gueckedou GFr35,000, 2½ hours.
Kankan GFr75,000, six hours.
Macenta GFr75,000, five to six hours.

N'zérékoré

POP 110,000

N'zérékoré is the major city of southern Guinea and it has all the facilities you might have missed elsewhere in the country. Besides the general buzz and a few markets to keep you happily occupied for a day, it serves as a useful base for nearby forest explorations and chimpanzee encounters.

⊙ Sights

Centre d'Exposition Artisanal de N'zérékoré ARTS CENTRE
(⊙ 8am-6pm Mon-Sat) **FREE** This modern and impressive arts and handicrafts centre allows you to watch craftspeople carving, weaving, hammering and stitching dyed mudcloth, wooden carvings and raffia bags, among other things. If you're lucky you'll also get to catch some traditional dancing. There are a few statues and carvings on display as museum pieces.

🛏️ Sleeping & Eating

Grand Hôtel de Mont Nimba HOTEL **$**
(🖉 666 559 753; Quartier au Sud; r from GFr300,000; P❄🏊) This large place is where all the (many) NGO workers set up base and staff are very used to foreigners. The rooms are spacious and clean but lack much character. There's a decent restaurant (mains around GFr80,000) and a swimming pool – but don't rely on it being full of water.

Auberge Golo
GUESTHOUSE **$**

(☑ 622 601 389; Quartier Telepoulou; r GFr250,000; **P** ❋) This is a great-value place out on the edge of town. The rooms are actually suites that come with living rooms with sofas and armchairs, a large bedroom with flowery bedspreads, and bathrooms with hot showers. Meals are available with advance notice.

Mission Catholique
HOTEL **$**

(☑ 626 372 955; Quartier Dorota; r GFr100,000; **P** ❋) The Catholic Mission has simple but tidy rooms with mosquito nets and shared toilets. It's a nice, quiet location downhill behind the church at the eastern end of town. Actually finding someone with the room keys can take time!

ⓘ Information

There are several banks in town. The main branches of the Eco Bank and the Bicigui have ATMs that accept foreign cards and give out up to GFr800,000 per transaction.

ⓘ Getting There & Away

Bush taxis depart daily from the *gare routière* for:

Conakry (GFr180,000, 20 to 22 hours)
Lola (GFr10,000-12,000, one hour)
Macenta (GFr40,000, four hours)

Allow a full day to travel to Monrovia (Liberia). The road is rough and there's no shortage of checkpoints. Bush taxis go to the border at Diéké (GFr50,000; three hours) where you can walk 2km over the border to Ganta and then get another car to take you deeper into Liberia.

Bossou

The fragmented forests around the village of Bossou are home to a small troop of eight chimpanzees who can be visited on a chimp-tracking walk organised through the **Institut de Recherche Environnementalde Bossou** (☑ 622 259 829; chimpanzee tracking GFr500,000, Mt Nimba hike GFr1,000,000). The chimps are very well habituated to humans, so it's almost a given that you will see them – and at very close quarters.

Leering up into the clouds to the east of Bossou is the forest-covered hulk of **Mt Nimba** (guided tour per group GFr1,000,000). At 1752m, this is the highest mountain in Guinea and a Unesco World Heritage Site on account of its unique – and now very threatened – ecology, which includes some endemic amphibians and a sizeable population of chimpanzees. The Institute de Recherche Environnemental de Bossou can organise very long (12 hours without breaks) day hikes to the summit of Mt Nimba.

There's nowhere to stay here. The town of Lola offers the nearest rooms, but the village of N'zérékoré makes for a more enjoyable base.

Biscuits are available from a few little market stalls and shops plus some fruit but that's about the limit.

Bush taxis to/from Lola charge GFr15,000 (one hour). Once in Lola you can change for N'zérékoré (GFr10,000).

PARC NATIONAL DU HAUT NIGER

Covering some 1200 sq km, the **Parc National du Haut Niger** (per person per day admission/vehicle/camping/guide GFr50,000/100,000/50,000/150,000) is one of West Africa's last significant stands of tropical dry forest and one of the most important protected areas in Guinea. The forest, which is pockmarked with areas of tall grassland savannah and run through by the Niger River, has plenty of wildlife including significant numbers of chimpanzees, buffalo, duikers and waterbuck as well as crocodiles and hippos. You will be very lucky indeed to actually see much wildlife, however, thanks to the dense foliage, a general sense of caution from most of the animals and a near total lack of visitor facilities. Dedicated birders will likely find the forest highly rewarding.

The one place in the Parc National du Haut Niger that you are guaranteed to see large mammals is the **Centre de Conservation pour Chimpanzés** (www.projetprimates.com/chimpanzee-conservation-center; Somoria; GFr50,000). This is a French-run project in which chimpanzees rescued from the exotic animal pet trade are brought here and, over time, reintroduced to the wild. Don't get too excited about seeing wild chimps though, because visits are strictly controlled and the chimps that visitors get to see live in large enclosures.

There is no formal accommodation anywhere within the park. Bring a tent, a guide and a big dollop of adventure.

There's no public transport to the park. You'll need your own set of wheels and they'll need to be able to cope with a lot of mud, bumps and 'roads' that are nothing of the sort.

To get here take the dirt road leading east from Faranah to the village of Sanbaya (Sambonya) via Beindou. The park starts just to the north of the village.

UNDERSTAND GUINEA

Guinea Today

The Ebola epidemic that swept the region from 2014 until 2016 and killed 11,310 people began in a village not far from N'zérékoré, after a two-year-old boy became infected after coming into contact with bats.

The virus spread with lightning speed and deadly efficiency through many parts of Guinea, Sierra Leone and Liberia. Airlines cancelled all flights, cross-border road transport was dramatically reduced, international companies repatriated their foreign staff, development projects halted and investment into Guinea trickled away.

The number of people infected with the virus peaked in October 2014 and in June 2016 Guinea was finally declared Ebola free, but the epidemic cost at least 2500 Guineans their lives and had a major impact on the country's already weak economy and development.

Today, the international community is slowly returning to the country, development projects that were put on hold during the epidemic are picking up again, and there is a sense on the streets that Guinea may, finally, be about to enter a brighter future.

History

Guinea was part of the Empire of Mali, which covered a large part of western Africa between the 13th and 15th centuries; the empire's capital, Niani, is in eastern Guinea. From the mid-1400s Portuguese and other European traders settled Guinea's coastal region, and the country eventually became a French colony in 1891.

The end of French West Africa began with Guinea. In 1958, Sekou Touré was the only West African leader to reject a French offer of membership in a French commonwealth, and instead demanded total independence. French reaction was swift: financial and technical aid was cut off, and there was a massive flight of capital.

Sekou Touré called his new form of state a 'communocracy', a blend of Africanist and communist models. It didn't work; the economy went into a downward spiral, and his growing paranoia triggered a reign of terror.

Days after Touré's death in March 1984, a military coup was staged by a group of colonels, including the barely known, barely educated Lansana Conté, who became president. He introduced austerity measures, and in 1991 bowed to pressure to introduce a multiparty political system. Conté claimed victory in three highly disputed elections. Conté stayed in power until his death in December 2008.

In the Grip of the Military

Following the death in December 2008 of president Lansana Conté, an army contingent under Captain Moussa Dadis Camara took power in a coup d'état. His initial measures, such as cracking down on Guinean drug rings (Guinea is one of West Africa's hubs of the cocaine trade), and announcing anti-corruption measures and new mining deals (the country is hugely rich in natural resources, owning 30% of the world's bauxite resources), gained him many followers.

However, his announcement in 2009 that he would consider standing in the upcoming elections, and increasing violence committed by members of the army, provoked furious reactions. On 28 September 2009, army elements quashed a large demonstration with extreme violence. A UN commission denounced the events as a crime against humanity, and it is thought that over 150 people were killed. Two months later, Dadis was shot (but not killed) following a dispute with his aide-de-camp Toumba Diakite. A provisional government supervised the transition to civilian rule at the end of 2010.

After half a century in opposition, Alpha Conde, from the Malinke ethnic group, was declared winner in Guinea's first democratic election since independence from France in 1958. However, the vote kindled ethnic tensions. Conde's defeated rival, Cellou Dalein Diallo, is a member of the Fula ethnic group, to which 40% of Guineans belong. Diallo has consistently accused the president of marginalising his constituents, including many Fula.

After many false starts and disputed polls, in October 2015, presidential elections were

GUINEA GUINEA TODAY

held and again Conde won, with 58% of the vote. Despite violence and accusations of irregularities, in the post-election report the EU and AU concluded that the process overall was valid and Conde was sworn in for another term in December 2015.

SURVIVAL GUIDE

❶ Directory A–Z

ACCOMMODATION

Guinea is a country of two tales when it comes to hotels. Conakry has lots of top-end hotels (and ever more are being built), a fair few mid-range hotels and virtually nothing in the budget category. Up-country things are almost totally reversed with almost all hotels being budget or, just about, mid-range and nothing at all in the top-end. Only in Conakry's pricier places can you expect 24-hour electricity.

DANGERS & ANNOYANCES

➡ Avoid walking around Conakry and large towns at night due to the threat of muggings.

➡ Carry your passport and vaccination cards with you at all times.

➡ Electricity and running water are intermittent even in fairly large towns.

Driving & Roads

➡ Avoid road travel at night. There has been an increase in armed car-jackings.

➡ There are many police and military road blocks throughout the country and they've long had an unsavoury reputation for demanding bribes. However, in the last couple of years this problem has diminished considerably and many people now get through the country without paying a single bribe.

Photography

➡ Avoid taking photos in Conakry and large towns.

➡ Never photograph anyone without their express permission (in general people in Guinea do not like having their pictures taken).

---

❶ SLEEPING PRICE RANGES

The following price ranges refer to a double room with bathroom (when available). Unless otherwise stated, breakfast is included in the price.

$ less than GFr450,000

$$ GFr450,000-900,000

$$$ more than GFr900,000

➡ Never point a camera at police, military or anything that could be considered 'sensitive'.

EMBASSIES & CONSULATES

The following are just some of the major embassies found in Conakry:

French Embassy (☑ 621 000 010; www.amba france-gn.org; Ave du Commerce, Kaloum; ⊘8am-noon Mon-Fri)

German Embassy (☑ Mobile 621 221 706; www.conakry.diplo.de; Kaloum; ⊘8am-noon Mon-Fri)

Guinea-Bissau Embassy (☑ 664 271 533; Rte du Donka, Bellevue; ⊘8am-1pm Mon-Fri)

Ivoirian Embassy (☑ 622 363 485; www.guinee.diplomatie.gouv.ci; Blvd du la République, Kaloum; ⊘7.30am-6pm Mon-Fri)

Liberian Embassy (☑ 666 144 651; Rte de Donka, Bellevue; ⊘9am-1pm Mon-Fri)

Malian Embassy (☑ 669 399 403; Camayenne corniche, Dixinn; ⊘7.30am-1pm Mon-Fri)

Senegalese Embassy (☑ 631 900 202; Villas 41 et 42, Cite des Nations, Boulbinet; ⊘8am-1pm Mon-Fri)

Sierra Leone Embassy (☑ 631 356 566; Carrefour Bellevue; ⊘9am-1pm Mon-Fri)

UK Embassy (☑ 631 355 329; www.gov.uk/government/world/organisations/british-embassy-conakry; Villa 1, Residence 2000, Corniche Sud; ⊘8am-4.30pm Mon-Thu, 8am-1pm Fri)

US Embassy (☑ 655 104 000; https://conakry.usembassy.gov; Koloma; ⊘8.30am-noon Mon-Fri)

EMERGENCY & IMPORTANT NUMBERS

Guinea's country code	☑ 224
International access code	☑ 00
Police	☑ 122
Ambulance	☑ 442-020
Fire	☑ 1717

FOOD

Make no mistake about this. You do not come to Guinea for the food. Even in Conakry proper restaurants are a little thin on the ground and in the interior most towns have next to no proper restaurants. Your diet will normally be limited to a lacklustre hotel restaurant meal or a street stall serving *riz gras* (rice fried in oil and tomato paste and served with fried fish or meat).

GAY & LESBIAN TRAVELLERS

As in most African countries homosexuality and lesbianism is not just frowned upon but is something that is utterly incomprehensible to the huge majority of Guineans. LGBTI travellers in Guinea should be extremely discreet and careful, as situations could quickly become dangerous. Same-sex relations are prohibited by law and can attract prison terms.

INTERNET ACCESS

Most hotels in Conakry offer (slow) wi-fi nowadays and there are a few internet cafes – but far fewer than in most African capitals. By and large forget using the internet once you head inland, unless you bring your own internet dongle or use your smart phone. There are currently no hotels outside of Conakry offering internet access and very few internet cafes.

MONEY

→ The unit of currency is the Guinea franc (GFr) and it seems to be in a slow but permanent slide against major international currencies.

→ The banking system in Guinea has improved recently and some major towns now have ATMs that work with international Visa and Mastercard (the latter though is less likely to be accepted). Most ATMs, however, only allow a very small amount to be withdrawn with each transaction.

→ Most travellers continue to bring all the money they might need with them in cash (euros are best, followed by US dollars).

→ You can change money inside a bank, with moneychangers on the street in Conakry, or with hotels. There isn't a black market as such, as street moneychangers offer the same rates as banks.

→ Guinea is a cash economy. Only the major five-star hotels in Conakry and international airline offices will accept plastic.

→ Forget travellers cheques.

Exchange Rates

Australia	A$1	GFr6870
Canada	C$1	GFr6670
Euro zone	€1	GFr9954
Japan	¥100	GFr8160
New Zealand	NZ$1	GFr6310
UK	UK£1	GFr11,768
US	US$1	GFr9125
West Africa CFA	CFA1000	GFr15,000

For current exchange rates, see www.xe.com.

Tipping

Restaurants In the best restaurants in Conakry a 10% tip is normal. Elsewhere tipping is not expected.

Tourist guides and drivers A tip is expected. If you hired a guide or driver for a week expect to tip the equivalent of one extra day's work.

 EATING PRICE RANGES

The following price ranges refer to a main course.

$ less than GFr45,000

$$ GFr45,000–90,000

$$$ more than GFr90,000

OPENING HOURS

Banks 8.30am to 12.30pm & 2.30 to 4.30pm Monday to Thursday, 8.30am to 12.30pm and 2.45 to 4.30pm Friday.

Businesses and shops 8am to 6pm Monday to Saturday, except Friday when they might close for an hour to go to the mosque.

Government offices 8am to 4.30pm Monday to Thursday and 8am to 1pm Friday.

Museums 8am to 5pm Monday to Saturday.

POST

Guinea's postal service is notoriously unreliable; packages especially often get 'lost'. Postcards should get through; for anything valuable use a private shipping firm.

PUBLIC HOLIDAYS

New Years Day 1 January

Easter March/April

Declaration of the Second Republic 3 April

Labour Day 1 May

Assumption Day 15 August

Independence Day 2 October

Christmas Day 25 December

All major Islamic holidays (dates change each year) are also observed, with Eid al-Fitr being one of the country's biggest holidays.

TELEPHONE

Mobile phones are ubiquitous in Guinea and service is available in even remote villages. SIM and top-up cards are available from shops and street stalls everywhere and calls and text messages are cheap. In towns 3G service is generally available and you can purchase internet data bundles through the top-up cards.

You will likely be asked to show some form of ID when buying a SIM card, otherwise the process of buying it and getting it all set up is fast and easy.

TOURIST INFORMATION

There are no tourist information offices. Try the following website:

Fouta Decouverte (www.foutadecouverte.over-blog.com) A private tourist information website.

🛈 PRACTICALITIES

Weights & measures Guinea uses the metric system.

VISAS

Visas are required by visitors of most nationalities except those of some West African nations.

➧ Visas are generally easy to get and normally require a return air-ticket, or some other ticket in and out of the country, and a hotel booking for at least the first few days.

➧ Visas are usually valid for 30 days but can be extended to 90 days without much fuss.

➧ Visas must be obtained in advance; they are not available at the border.

VOLUNTEERING

There is very little scope for volunteering in Guinea although the Centre de Conservation pour Chimpanzés (p225) based in the Parc National du Haut Niger (p226) does accept untrained, paying volunteers on six-month stints to work with orphaned chimpanzees. Conditions are very rough.

🛈 Getting There & Away

AIR

Guinea's only international airport is **Conakry International Airport** (www.aeroport-conakry. com), 13km from the centre of Conakry. In 2016 the ageing airport was upgraded and it's now fairly fast and efficient to get through the airport.

There is no national airline, though Conakry is served by a small but slowly growing list of international and regional airlines. Regional airlines also connect Conakry with Senegal and Côte d'Ivoire.

Major carriers:

Air France (www.airfrance.com)
Aigle Azur (www.aigle-azur.com)
Brussels Airlines (www.brusselsairlines.com)
Emirates (www.emirates.com)
Royal Air Maroc (Royal Air Maroc)

BORDER CROSSINGS
Cote d'Ivoire

The land border between Guinea and Côte d'Ivoire had been closed to overland traffic for some time but it reopened in late 2016. The most frequently travelled route is between Lola and Man via Nzo and Danané. The road is in bad shape and in the rainy season can be close to impassable. There is also a route that goes from Kankan to Odienné via Mandiana, but this is an even remoter and more challenging route that few people use.

Guinea-Bissau

Most people travelling by bush taxi get to Guinea-Bissau via Labé, Koundara and Gabú. The road is now in good condition except for a dreadful stretch between Gabú and Koundara where it starts to climb up onto the Fouta Djalon plateau. At the time of research crews were busy upgrading that part as well, which means that very soon it will be an easy day by share taxi between Guinea-Bissau and Labé.

A slower alternative route is via Boké to Québo.

Liberia

There's quite a lot of traffic between Guinea and Liberia. The primary route is from N'zérékoré to Ganta via Diéke. Bush taxis go frequently to the border at Diéké where you can walk across and get a ride to Monrovia.

From Macenta, bush taxis go via Daro to the border and on to Voinjama, although the road is in a bad way.

Another route goes from Lola via Bossou to Yekepa but there's very little traffic on this route (indeed taxi drivers in Lola might instruct you to return to N'zérékore and travel to Liberia from there).

Mali

Taxis travel directly to Bamako from Kankan, Siguiri and Conakry. The road is sealed and in very good condition from Kankan to Bamako. At the time of research it was considered safe to travel between Guinea and Bamako, but make sure you check the security situation in Mali first.

Senegal

Taxis to Senegal going via Koundara, the busiest route, stop at Diaoubé, a small town with a huge market, where you can connect to almost anywhere, including Dakar. To get to Koundara most people go from Labé and the road between the two towns is now in generally good shape making it quite an easy run to Senegal. If you get stuck in Koundara there are a couple of very basic hotels. You can also get to Senegal on another route from Labé travelling via Mali-Yemberem and finishing in Kedougou in Senegal, but the route is dreadful all the way from Labé and after rain can be impassable. (When we last travelled this route we saw trucks stuck in potholes where the mud went up as high as the driver's door – and that was at the start of the dry season!)

Sierra Leone

The road from Freetown to Conakry via Kambla and Parnelap is now sealed and an easy day-long trip. There are several other routes in and out of Sierra Leone, but the roads on these routes are all generally in bad shape and transport far less frequent than the main crossing point.

CAR & MOTORCYCLE

Travelling overland in your own vehicle or by motorbike is a popular way to arrive in Guinea and, assuming you have all the car ownership, insurance and tax papers in order, presents no major hurdles although you might be asked to pay a bit of money every now and then in order to smooth out 'problems'.

Most of Guinea's border-crossing points are in remote areas with few facilities if you break down en-route to the border. Petrol stations are also unlikely to be found on most roads to the borders. Fill up in the nearest big town.

Most public transport crossing the Guinea borders, or dropping passengers at the borders, takes the form of bush taxis.

🛈 Getting Around

However you do it, getting around Guinea takes time, patience and a passion for potholes...

AIR

Despite the fact that every town of a reasonable size seems to have an airstrip (and Faranah has a runway that was designed so a Concorde could land there!) there is actually no internal flight network. Nor, indeed, is there a national airline.

CAR & MOTORCYCLE

If you're driving your own vehicle or a hired vehicle in Guinea, be sure the insurance and registration papers are in perfect order as they will be checked at the police roadblocks many times along the way. All vehicles must carry a warning triangle and police will ask to see this as well. Hiring a car for travel outside of Conakry is usually very expensive (count on US$150 to US$200 per day) and vehicles are hard to come by. One recommended private vehicle owner who rents out a jeep for very reasonable rates

is the owner of the website **Fouta Decouverte** (www.foutadecouverte.over-blog.com).

TAXI-BROUSSE

Normally a battered Peugeot 505 that looks as if a tank has driven over it, these vehicles might be smaller than buses but drivers generally attempt to cram in as many passengers as a bus would take anyway. Whereas in most of West Africa taxis carry seven passengers, here in Guinea they squeeze in nine and then, for good measure, stick a few more on top of the mountain of luggage strapped to the roof. Comfortable, safe and reliable they absolutely are not, but in the right frame of mind they could be described as an 'experience'.

Expect at least one breakdown on even the shortest journey, meaning that any travel times the driver (or we) might give are purely indications on what it should take in an ideal, breakdown and delay-free world. Guinean drivers are extreme risk takers, placing their lives and the lives of their passengers completely in the hands of God, tempting Him with racing in rusty vehicles and overtaking manoeuvres on blind corners. The saving grace is that many times the road is so rutted and torn that drivers cannot go too fast.

Taxis leave when they're full, and most people travel in the morning. You'll always have the quickest getaway around 7am to 8am.

Fares can fluctuate depending on both current fuel prices and demand along that route on any given day. It can also be more expensive if there's a lot of uphill driving to be done as that uses more fuel.

Guinea-Bissau

Best Places
to Eat

➡ Oysters on Quinhámel beach (p238)

➡ O Bistro (p234)

➡ Afrikan Ecolodge Angurman (p237)

Best Places
to Sleep

➡ Ponta Anchaca (p238)

➡ Afrikan Ecolodge Angurman (p237)

➡ Ecocantanhez (p239)

➡ Ledger Plaza Bissau (p233)

➡ Africa Princess (p234)

Why Go?

Like a microcosm of Africa, this tiny nation contains multitudes – of landscapes, peoples, cultures and plant and animal life. All of it within reach of the capital, Bissau. Faded colonial-era houses sag, from tropical decay and the weight of history. Decades of Portuguese colonisation were followed by a long painful liberation struggle and then cycles of civil war and political chaos.

Despite hardships and poverty, Bissau-Guineans persevere. The jokes, like the music, are loud but tender. The bowls of grilled oysters are served with a sauce spicy enough to give a kick, but not so strong as to mask the bitterness.

The jewel in the country's crown is the labyrinth of tropical islands that make up the Arquipélago dos Bijagós. Long white-sand beaches are lapped by waters brimming with fish. Hippos, monkeys, chimps and buffaloes thrive in protected reserves and hundreds of bird species call its vast mangroves and wetlands home.

When to Go
Bissau

Dec–Feb The coolest, driest months, when sea turtles emerge from their nests.

Mar–Jul Hot, humid and sweaty; travel with plenty of water and sunscreen.

Jul–Oct The rainy season.

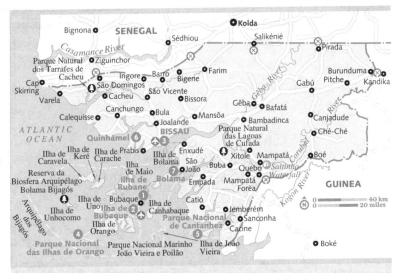

Guinea-Bissau Highlights

1 **Ilha de Rubane** (p238) Relaxing amid world-class facilities and natural splendour.

2 **Ilha de Bubaque** (p236) Experiencing village life, a short walk from your island getaway.

3 **Bissau Velho** (p233) Tangoing in cobbled streets by candlelight, after a dinner

of salty *bacalau* and red wine in the capital.

4 **Parque Nacional das Ilhas de Orango** (p237) Locking eyes with hippos as they emerge from the warm saltwater lagoons.

5 **Parque Nacional de Cantanhez** (p239) Following chimpanzee, elephant and

buffalo trails through dense forests.

6 **Quinhámel** (p238) Dipping oysters in hot lime sauce after a day in the water.

7 **Bolama** (p236) Sitting on the steps of the abandoned town hall, with its crumbling Greek-style pillars.

BISSAU

POP 492,000

Built on a low-lying estuary where the Gêba River flows into the Atlantic, apart from the hectic traffic, Bissau is a low-key, unassuming capital. In the early evening, the fading sunlight lends the crumbling colonial facades of Bissau Velho (Old Bissau) a touch of nostalgic glamour. Generators set parts of the town trembling at night, although, street lights or not, people get out of their homes and gather at ramshackle bars.

Sights

Bissau Velho, a stretch of narrow alleyways and derelict buildings, is 'guarded' by the **Fortaleza d'Amura**. The rebuilt neoclassical **presidential palace** (Praça dos Heróis Nacionais) and brushed-up **Assembleia Ministério da Justiça** (cnr Avs Francisco Mendes & do Brazil)

are architectural expressions of the country's hopes for order and democracy.

Festivals & Events

Carnaval CARNIVAL

Bissau and Bubaque's Carnaval are the country's biggest parties. It takes place every year in February or early March during the week leading up to Ash Wednesday and the beginning of Lent. Music, masks, drinking and dancing are the order of the day.

Sleeping

Ledger Plaza Bissau HOTEL **$$**

(245 955 577007; www.laicohotels.com; Av Combatentes Liberdade da Pátría; r from CFA60,000;) Bissau's most luxurious hotel, the Ledger (known to taxi drivers by its former name Lybia Hotel) is where politicians, businesspeople and the small expatriate community congregate – the latter primarily on

Bissau

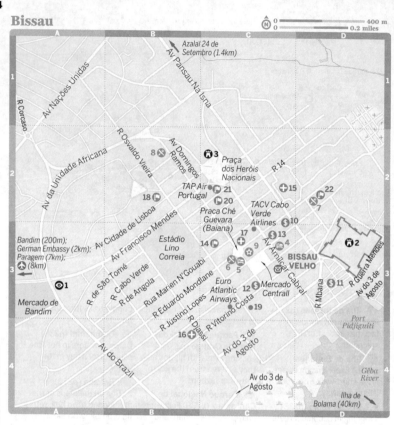

Sundays for a day by the pool and a pricey buffet lunch (CFA20,000). It's efficiently designed with contemporary furnishings and rooms – even the small economy ones are comfortable.

Coimbra Hotel & Spa   BOUTIQUE HOTEL **$$**
(☑245 3213467; www.hotel-coimbra-spa.com; Av Amílcar Cabral; r incl breakfast from CFA76,000; ❄@☎) It looks like a hardware store from the street, buit climb the steps from the side entrance to the bougainvillea-fringed terrace and you'll find a lovely oasis in the centre of town. Sparsely furnished rooms are nice enough (shower pressure can be a nuisance), and downstairs houses a spa and restaurant with a good lunch and dinner buffet.

🍴 Eating

Restaurant Samaritana   AFRICAN **$**
(Av Domingos Ramos; mains CFA2500; ☺8am-11pm) It's made from a cut-out container and buzzes with Guineans of all ranks and

incomes, all eager to sample Mamadou's reliably delicious meals.

Kalliste Restaurant   INTERNATIONAL **$$**
(Praça Ché Guevara; meals from CFA4000; ☺8am-late) Hotel Kalliste's crumbling poplant-lined courtyard buzzes at night, attracting everyone from tired UN lawyers to politicians, activists, international volunteers and mosquitoes. There's live music most evenings. The pizzas are pretty good, as is the espresso.

O Bistro   FRENCH **$$**
(☑245 3206000; Rua Eduardo Mondlane; mains CFA4000; ☺noon-3pm & 7pm-late; ❄🍴) This Belgian-owned spot has all the right ingredients: excellent, reasonably priced mains, including good pasta, fresh catches, sautéed vegetables and *crepes au chocolat;* friendly service; a well-stocked bar; and a warm ambience that transcends the air-con. Bring mosquito repellent if you want the big table on the veranda.

Bissau

🍷 Drinking & Nightlife

As far as nightlife goes, your best bet is to head to Praça Che Guevara and wander the surrounding streets. The terrace at the Kalliste Restaurant is a good spot.

ⓘ Information

INTERNET ACCESS
Most accommodation in the city offers wi-fi access.
Centre Culturel Franco-Bissao-Guinéen (CCF; ☑245 3206816; Praça Ché Guevera; ◷9am-10pm Mon-Fri; 🛜) Charges CFA2000 per day.
Hotel Kalliste (☑245 6765662; kallistebissau@hotmail.com; Praça Ché Guevara) The terrace has wi-fi.

MEDICAL SERVICES
Pharmacia Nur Din (Rua Vitorino Costa) A reasonably well-stocked pharmacy.
Policlinica (☑245 3207581; info@policlinica.bissau.com; Praça Ché Guevera) A better option for illnesses than a trip to the hospital.
Raoul Follerau Hospital (Av dos Combatentes da Liberdade da Pátria) Probably city and country's best hospital.
Simão Mendes (☑245 3212861; Av Pansau Na Isna) Bissau's main hospital in the centre; in a poor state.

MONEY
Banque Atlantique (Av Pansau Na Isna) ATM.
BAO (Banco da Africa Occidental; Rua 19 Setembro; ◷8.30am-3pm) Changes money.
Casa Cambio Nacional (Av Domingos Ramos; ◷hours vary) Changes money at good rates.

Ecobank (Av Amílcar Cabral; ◷7.30am-4.30pm Mon-Fri, 9am-noon Sat) Changes dollars and euros; ATM.

POST
Main Post Office (Av Amílcar Cabral; ◷8am-6pm Mon-Sat) Housed in a large building built c 1955.

TOURIST INFORMATION
Institute for Biodiversity and Protected Areas (IBAP; ☑245 207106; www.ibapgbissau.org; Av Dom Settimio Arturro Ferrazzetta) Established by the Bissau-Guinean government in 2005, IBAP is charged with managing, protecting and conserving the country's biodiversity and natural ecosystems. Contact for information on visiting any of the country's national parks.

TRAVEL AGENCIES
Satguru (☑245 5994211; www.satgurutravel.com; Rua Osvaldo Vieira) Travel agency that can book any airline, as well as car rentals; shares office (and desk) with ASKY Airlines.

ⓘ Getting There & Away

AIR
There are flights to Bissau's Osvaldo Vieira International Airport (OXB) with TACV Cabo Verde Airlines via Praia/Dakar, Euro Atlantic Airways and **TAP Air Portugal** (TP; ☑245 3201359; www.flytap.com; Praça dos Heróis Nacionais; ◷9am-5.30pm Mon-Fri) from Lisbon, and Royal Air Maroc from Casablanca.

BOAT
Reaching the Arquipélago dos Bijagós can be complicated, as the former ferry between the islands and Bissau no longer runs. A

GUINEA-BISSAU BISSAU

replacement ferry was said to be on its way from abroad.

LAND

Once in Bissau, you can get *sept place* taxis (Peugeot 504s with seven seats) and *transporte misto* buses to just about anywhere in the country at the *gare routière* (bus station), inconveniently located about 10km (CFA1000 by taxi) outside town.

ℹ️ Getting Around

The airport is 9km from the town centre. A taxi to town should be around CFA3000 (more at night).

Shared taxis – generally blue, well-worn Mercedes – are plentiful and ply all the main routes. Trips cost between CFA250 and CFA1000. Rates for longer routes vary and have to be negotiated.

Blue-yellow *toca-tocas* (minibuses) serve main city routes (for CFA100), including Av de 14 Novembro towards the *paragem* (bus station) and airport.

ARQUIPÉLAGO DOS BIJAGÓS

The Bijagós islands look like the perfect postcard from paradise. From the skies above, their complexity is fully revealed: islands, creeks, mangroves, islets, sandy bays and more than 20 settlements on 87 islands. Dolphins, hippos, manatees and sea turtles inhabit the waters, and the mangroves are important breeding grounds for migratory birds.

Protected by swift tides, treacherous sandbanks and the Unesco heritage fund, the Bijagós, a matriarchal people, eluded Portuguese control until the 1930s. Their rites and ceremonies remain largely hidden from visitors, conducted far away from the beaches in the heart of the forests.

Africa Princess (📞 245 969 283386, in Dakar, Senegal 351 91 722 4936; www.africa-princess.com; 7-day trip per person in double cabin €950; ☉ late Sep-late Jul) 🛥️ is the most convenient and comfortable way of seeing the most islands in the Arquipélago dos Bijagós. A large enough group of passengers can customise its own itinerary, but generally visits include Canhabaque and the two national-park areas. Sleeps up to eight in simple and tight cabins on a 15m two-hull catamaran. Solar panels provide most of the power.

Ilha de Bubaque is the gateway to the rest of the Bijagós.

Ilha de Bolama

POP 21,000

Geographically closer to Bissau than any other island in the Bijagós, eerily beautiful Bolama feels worlds away, both aesthetically and socially. The shores of Bolama town, Portuguese capital of Guinea-Bissau from 1879 to 1943, are awash with crumbling relics that were abandoned after independence. Tree-lined boulevards are mapped out by lamp posts that no longer shine, and the colonial barracks have been recast as a hospital, now – like much of the island – in a dark and desolate state.

The former town hall, flanked by Greek style pillars, was built in 1870; these days huge splinters hang like stalactites from its ceilings. The turrets of the once grandiose Hotel Turismo sit in an overgrown nest of lianas, 3m-tall weeds and snakes. It's worth walking out to Ofir Beach, around 3km from the town, to see the spooky sweeping staircase of a beach hotel that no longer exists.

🛏️ Sleeping

Formaca Pesqueria   HOSTEL $

(📞 245 5286345; Bolama town; r CFA15,000) You can rent a breezy room at the fishing training centre around 200m north of the port. There is electricity, but the rooms do not have fans. Meals can be arranged upon request.

Hotel Gã-Djau   HOTEL $

(📞 245 955 288717; Bolama town; r CFA13,000) Hotel Gã-Djau is basic, but it's the smartest option. It's a 15-minute walk from the market (ask for directions there). The rooms have fans, but the generator shuts off late at night.

ℹ️ Getting There & Away

Canoas (motor canoes; CFA350) operate three times per week between São João on the mainland and Bolama town. You can also reach Bolama by taking a *sept place* to Buba (three hours), where you can overnight before hiring motorbikes for the journey (three hours, CFA15,000) along rough forest roads to the pirogue at São João.

Ilha de Bubaque

POP 11,300

A single jetty marks the centre of Bubaque town, the archipelago's largest town and the geographic centre of the Bijagós. It's a ramshackle affair, with a small enclosed market, dirt paths and a few bars and basic shops. If you can't make it to more remote islands, Bubaque, the transport hub of the islands, makes a comfortable place to unwind and a good weekend getaway from Bissau.

🛏 Sleeping

Casa Dora   HOTEL $
(☑245 969 063585; www.hotelcasadora.yola-site.com; Bubaque town; s/d incl breakfast CFA16,000/22,000; ☎) Staffed by Dora and her very helpful and service-oriented daughters, the rooms at this budget haunt are fairly basic – little furniture, a fan and concrete walls and floors. In the garden restaurant (meals CFA5000) you get to dig into large platters of seafood in the shade of mango trees.

★ **Kasa Afrikana**   LODGE $$
(☑245 7243305; www.kasa-afrikana.com; Bubaque town; per person from CFA40,000; ❄ ☎ ☎) Gilles' fishing lodge hits the right ratio of charm to luxury, with comfortable rooms, pretty landscaped grounds, a freshwater swimming pool and excellent food. Come to escape the grind, get closer to nature, fish, visit villages or follow tracks into the Bubaque forest. The only slight downside is that it's located on the inland side of the road along the island's edge.

Dakosta Island Beach Camp   BUNGALOW $$$
(☑245 969 119999; www.dakostabc.com) Newly opened by Bissau-Guinean-American champion kickboxer Adlino Costa, this camp on Ilha de Bubaque feels worlds away from the relative bustle of town – it's situated at the far southern end of the island. Well-built bungalows are tucked just back from a beautiful white-sand beach. The pièce de résistance is an amazing communal table built from a dugout canoe.

❶ Getting There & Away

Your choice to/from Bissau is between rough and risky *canoas* (per person CFA2500, six hours) and a speedboat (per four-seater boat CFA150,000 to CFA250,000, 1½ to two hours).

Ilha de Orango

POP 2500

The heart of **Parque Nacional das Ilhas de Orango** (www.ibapgbissau.org; CFA2000) – several other islands are also part of the park's protected reserve) – Ilha de Orango is the burial site of the Bijagós kings and queens.

WORTH A TRIP

BIJAGÓS SLEEPING

Afrikan Ecolodge Angurman
(☑245 9553077; www.afrikanecolodge.com; Ilha d'Angurman; s/d with full board CFA50,000/66,000) 🌿 is a true Robinson Crusoe experience, minus the building work. That's been done by Francois, a grizzled, friendly and passionate Frenchman who runs this small out-of-the-way retreat on 50-hectare Angurman Island. Three simple bungalows with cold-water bathrooms and porches front the shoreline. An enormous baobab tree, straight out of Avatar, towers over an idyllic spot where meals are served.

Occupying one half of a tiny islet (Ilha de Keré), **Hotel Keré** (☑245 966 993827; www.bijagos-kere.com; Ilha de Keré; 7 days full board from €750) is an isolated fishing lodge made up of a collection of thatched-roof bungalows – it's ideal for those who like their escapism to come with a little luxury. Prices here are slightly cheaper than those on Ilha de Rubane for a similar experience.

Travellers know it more as the site of Anôr Lagoon, where you can spot rare saltwater hippos – considered sacred, they live in both the sea and freshwater. Local guides (around CFA10,000, plus the park entry fee) lead you on a sandy path through tall grass and swampy wetlands, more reminiscent of the prototypical African savannah than other islands. Be sure to wear shoes you don't mind muddying or sandals with straps, as well as pants you can roll up or shorts. It's a pretty walk, though shade is scarce.

There's a long, beautiful beach, basically between the point where the Orango Parque Hotel is located and where you disembark for hippo-spotting walks. No shade, however.

Orango Parque Hotel (☑245 955 352446; www.orangohotel.com; r incl full board CFA70,000) 🌿 is a collection of large and well-kept thatched-roof bungalows atop a hill a short walk up from a beautiful white-sand beach. Food and drinks are served in an outdoor patio area, and there's a small museum with traditional masks and figurines. Well managed and run, it feels remote and far removed from the hustle of Bubaque.

GUINEA-BISSAU ILHA JOÃO VIEIRA

DON'T MISS

ILHA DE RUBANE

On the uninhabited island of Ilha de Rubane, you'll find one of Guinea-Bissau's best places to stay.

Superlatives don't do **Ponta Ancha-ca** (☑ 245 966 067393, 245 966 394352; www.pontaanchaca.net; s/d with full board from €140/220; ❄ ❂ ❀) justice. Gorgeous. Idyllic. Heavenly. You won't want to leave after disembarking onto a long postcard-perfect white-sand beach. And some guests don't, choosing to buy one of the resort's charming and sophisticated beachfront bungalows. While there's much to do – fishing, kayaking, trips to other islands – it's tempting to simply do nothing for once.

Ilha João Vieira

This idyllic island is part of the **Parque Nacional Marinho João Vieira e Poilão**, a grouping of four islands (including Mëio, Cavalo and Poilão) in the southeast of the archipelago and one of the most important nesting areas for endangered sea turtles in the Eastern Atlantic. During the main egg-laying season in October and November, the shorelines, especially Mëio and Poilão, can teem with these rare creatures. João Vieira, owned and seasonally inhabited by the Canhabaque people, also houses a guardhouse for the park and its only formal accommodation.

Run by a French couple and situated on a beautiful soft, sandy beach fronting turquoise waters is **Chez Claude** (☑ 245 955 968677; per person full board CFA51,000; ⊗ Dec-May) . It's a modest collection of simple concrete and thatched-roof bungalows and an outdoor eating area. Meals can be provided.

The owner can arrange speedboat pick-up from Bubaque town (around CFA200,000 per boatload).

THE NORTHWEST

Quinhámel

POP 3100

Quinhámel, 35km west of Bissau, makes an interesting day or weekend trip. A wide,

palm-shaded promenade adds a little grandeur, fittingly as it's the regional capital of the Biombo region and the traditional home of the Papel people. About 2km away, nestled between the mangroves, is a local **beach** popular with families and young people at the weekends.

The region in general is known for its oysters, which are found in nearby mangroves. A few places by the river are picturesque spots to give them a try, as is the restaurant at **Hotel Mar Azu** (☑ 245 966 197280; r incl lunch CFA40,000; @)l.

Varela

☑ 95

Varela's charm lies in its remoteness, and the fact that this means its white-sand, windswept beaches are deserted. This is due to the 45km road from São Domingos being rough, even in a good 4WD. The prettiest beach is **Praia Niquim**, accessible only on foot.

Aparthotel Chez Hélène (Chez Fatima; ☑ 245 5301373; f.cirell.38@gmail.com; d/ste CFA15,000/20,000) consists of nine brightly coloured huts in a pretty garden setting. The thatched-roof huts are lovingly decorated and have fans, mosquito nets and bathrooms. The restaurant offers Italian food and fresh juices (it grows its own tomatoes and passion fruits). Call ahead for information on road conditions. The generator kicks in after dark. Check out the Facebook page for more information.

A *transporte misto* (minibus) leaves every afternoon from São Domingos (CFA3000, 53km), taking around four hours, and returns the following morning. If you're driving by 4WD, plan on at least two hours.

THE SOUTH

Parque Natural das Lagoas de Cufada

Sandwiched between the Buba and Corubal Rivers, the 890-sq-km **Parque Natural das Lagoas de Cufada** (www.ibapgbissau.org) is the largest wetlands reserve in Guinea-Bissau. Kayaking across placid waters on an early morning amid twittering birds (there are an estimated 250 species here) makes the effort to get here worthwhile. There's an observation post where you can sit, appreciate the view and tick-off sightings. There are also African buffaloes, gazelles, hyenas, white hippos and crocodiles in the park.

Buses to Bissau, 223km away via asphalt roads, leave early in the morning. It's easier to travel by *sept place* (CFA3500, three hours), though you might have a long wait for the vehicle to fill up. A two-hour drive through the Parque Natural das Lagoas de Cufada – you need a 4WD vehicle – brings you to São João, where you can get a *canoa* to Ilha de Bolama.

Parque Nacional de Cantanhez

The hardest-to-reach places are often the most beautiful, and so it goes with Parque Nacional de Cantanhez – over 1000 sq km of the country's last rainforest. With a dense web of giant kapok trees, lianas and palm trees (a total of more than 200 plant species), you'll need to get out on a trail to spot elephants, baboons, buffaloes, colobus monkeys, Africa's westernmost troupe of chimpanzees and hundreds of species of birds. In the mangrove and island areas that form part of the protected zone, you'll see plenty of fish, manatees, small hippos and other bird species.

🛏 Sleeping

Ecocantanhez – Jemberém   BUNGALOW $
(www.ecocantanhez.org; s/d/q CFA10,000/15,000/ 25,000) Ecotourism project designed to encourage sustainable ways of drawing visitors to the Parque Nacional de Cantanhez. Has three thatched-roof bungalows in Jemberém. You can also camp out or park your overland vehicle for the night. Has running cold water and electricity at night.

Ecocantanhez – Faro Sadjuma   BUNGALOW $
(www.ecocantanhez.org; bungalows CFA15,000) Part of the ecotourism project designed to encourage sustainable ways of drawing visitors to the Parque Nacional de Cantanhez, the camp at Faro Sadjuma consists of three bungalows with 24-hour solar-powered electricity. It's surrounded by mango, pineapple and avocado trees.

❶ Getting There & Away

You'll need time and patience to get to the access point at Jemberém. Only go in the dry season and in a 4WD; dirt tracks turn into rivers in the rainy season.

From Buba to Mampatá Forèa the road is OK. You leave the tarmac for the remaining 70km to Jemberém. No signposts mean the best option is to hire a car or guide from outside the park to direct you.

UNDERSTAND GUINEA-BISSAU

Guinea-Bissau Today

A telling fact and microcosm of the country's political instability is that there have been five prime ministers since May 2014. One resigned after 48 hours in office. In late 2016 President José Mário Vaz once again dissolved the government. A new prime minister, Sissoko Embalo, was sworn in. Once again things are in limbo.

Because of the political instability, there's little tourism to speak of, except in the Bijagós. Fishing stocks are said to be hijacked by Chinese boats, and drug-trafficking (while declining) is rampant enough for some to label the country a 'narco-state'. Outside of cashew production, the economy is largely based on international project funding.

History

In around 1200, when a group of Malinké was led to present-day Guinea-Bissau by a general of Sunjata Keita, the region became an outpost of the Empire of Mali. In 1537, it became a state in its own right – the Kaabu Empire. Gabù became the capital of this small kingdom.

European Arrival & Colonisation

Portuguese navigators first reached the area around 1450, and established lucrative routes for trading slaves and goods. With the abolition of the slave trade in the 19th century, the Portuguese extended their influence beyond the coast towards the interior in order to continue extracting wealth.

Portuguese Guinea descended into one of the most repressive and exploitative colonial regimes in Africa, particularly when dictator António Salazar came to power in Portugal in 1926.

GUINEA-BISSAU WILDLIFE

In the Bijagós archipelago you find rare saltwater hippos, aquatic turtles, dolphins, manatees and sharks. The rainforests of the southeast are the most westerly home of Africa's chimpanzee population. There is also a stunning variety of birds, especially within the coastal wetlands, including cranes and peregrine falcons.

War of Liberation

By the early 1960s African colonies were rapidly winning independence, but Salazar refused to relinquish control. The result was a long and bloody war of liberation for Guinea-Bissau and Cape Verde, fought on Guinean soil. Many Guineans were recruited to fight for the Portuguese, essentially pitting brothers against brothers and neighbours against neighbours.

The father of independence was Amílcar Cabral, who in 1956 helped found the Partido Africano da Independência da Guiné e Cabo Verde (PAIGC). In 1961 the PAIGC started arming and mobilising peasants, and within five years controlled half of the country. Cabral was assassinated in Conakry in 1973, but independence had become inevitable. When Salazar's regime fell in 1974, the new Portuguese government recognised the fledgling nation.

Independence & Instability

Once in power, the PAIGC government was confronted by staggering poverty, lack of education and economic decline. Politically, it wanted a unified Guinea-Bissau and Cape Verde; however, the idea died in 1980 when President Luis Cabral was overthrown in a coup while visiting Cape Verde to negotiate the union. João 'Nino' Vieira, an important military leader in the independence struggle, took over and initially continued the country's socialist policies. In 1986, after a coup attempt, President Vieira reversed course and privatised state enterprises.

Intractable poverty, several coup attempts and growing corruption under Vieira culminated in national strikes in 1997, which spiralled into civil war. Senegal and Guinea became involved in the conflict, sending soldiers in support of government troops loyal to the president. Vieira was killed in a 2009 coup and instability has been endemic ever since, fuelled by deep tensions between the government and the military, which includes ageing officers who fought in the war of independence. The squabble for profits from Bissau's main cash cow – not the humble cashew, but cocaine – is a symptom of these tensions.

Constant Inconstancy

In 2012, President Malam Bacai Sanha died from illness, plunging the country into another bout of instability and adding another name to the long list of presidents who have failed to complete a full term in power. A coup d'etat ousted the prime minister and election frontrunner three months later and a transitional government was installed, headed by Manuel Serifo Nhamadjo, who was chosen by West African bloc Ecowas. Nhamadjo's time in power was shaken by coup attempts and attacks, and elections in 2013 were held amid rising tensions between the Balanta and other ethnic groups.

People

Guinea-Bissau's 1.7 million inhabitants are divided among more than 27 ethnic groups. The two largest are the Balanta (30%) in the coastal and central regions and the Fula (20%) in the east and south. Other groups with significant numbers include the Mankinka, Papel and Manjaco; there are also smaller populations of Beafada, Mancanha, Felupe and Balanta Mane. The offshore islands are mostly inhabited by the Bijagós people. In the last few years, tensions have been growing between the Balanta and other ethnic groups.

About 45% of the people are Muslims and 10% Christians. Animist beliefs remain strong along the coast and in the south.

Arts & Crafts

Eastern Guinea-Bissau is a centre of kora (a harplike instrument with over 20 strings) playing, being the ancient seat of the Kaabu kingdom, where the instrument was invented. The traditional Guinean beat is gumbé, though contemporary music is mainly influenced by zouk (a style of popular music created in the Caribbean and popular across Africa, with a lilting, sensual beat) from Cape

Verde. Besides the reformed Super Mama Djombo, perhaps the country's most famous band, other contemporary artists include Manecas Costa, Justino Delgado, Dulce Nevas and Rui Sangara. However, the centre of Guinean pop is Lisbon, not Bissau.

SURVIVAL GUIDE

ℹ️ Directory A–Z

ACCOMMODATION
Bissau has a range of accommodation to suit most budgets. However, unless you're paying top dollar, you're unlikely to find anything comfortable and inviting. Conditions are generally more basic elsewhere in the country (the luxury lodges of the Bijagós are an exception). National electricity is severely limited, forcing hoteliers to rely on expensive generator power.

DANGERS & ANNOYANCES
In Guinea-Bissau periods of calm can be followed by violent flare-ups.
➡ Attacks and coup attempts rarely wound civilians or visitors.
➡ Shops, banks, businesses and, more rarely, borders may close during tense periods.
➡ Even with blackouts and scarce streetlights, you can generally walk most city streets with a modicum of care.
➡ Depending on weather and the boat, travel to and around the Arquipélago dos Bijagós can be uncomfortable or dangerous.
➡ Beware of stingrays swimming in the Bijagós.
➡ There are poisonous green mamba snakes and cobras.
➡ Land mines from past conflicts are scattered in the following regions: Bafata, Oio, Biombo, Quinara and Tombali. Most have been located and removed.

EMBASSIES & CONSULATES
All embassies and consulates are in Bissau. The UK and the Netherlands share an **honorary consul** (☎245 966 622772; mavegro@hotmail.com; Rua Eduardo Mondlane, Supermercardo Mavegro, Bissau). US interests are run out of the embassy in Dakar. The US does have a **Bissau Liaison Office** (☎245 3256382; Rua Josi Carlos Schwarz, Edificio SITEC, Barrio d'Ajuda) for basic services and hosts a 'virtual' Guinea-Bissau presence at http://guinea-bissau.usvpp.gov.
French Embassy (☎245 3201312; www.ambafrance-gw.org; Av dos Combatentes da Liberdade da Patria, Barrio da Penha)
German Embassy (☎245 443255020; escritorio-bissau@web.de; SITEC Bldg, Barrio d'Ajuda; ⏰9-11am Mon-Fri)

Guinean Embassy (☎245 3201231; amba guibissau@mae.gov.gn; Rua Marien N'Gouabi; ⏰8.30am-3pm Sat-Thu, to 1pm Fri)
Portuguese Embassy (☎245 3203379; www.consulado-pt-gb.org; Av Cidade de Lisboa; ⏰8am-noon)
Senegalese Embassy (☎245 3212944; Rua General Omar Torrijos, off Praça dos Heróis Nacionais; ⏰8am-noon)
Spanish Embassy (☎245 9667222 46; emb.bissau@maec.es; Praça dos Heróis Nacionais; ⏰8am-noon)

EMERGENCY & IMPORTANT NUMBERS

Guinea-Bissau country code	☎245
International access code	☎00
Fire	☎118
Police	☎117

GAY & LESBIAN TRAVELLERS
Bissau-Guinean society is relatively tolerant, though no doubt there are still social taboos against homosexuality that discourage public displays of affection. No laws criminalise sexual orientation, and there are no official discriminatory policies or reports of violence or rights abuses targeting the country's gay and lesbian community.

INTERNET ACCESS
Wi-fi is increasingly common in hotels and restaurants in Bissau. Roaming is possible on phones, but connections are generally slow. Outside the capital internet is more scarce. Only a small percentage of Bissau-Guineans are connected to the internet.

MONEY
ATMs ATMs that accept international MasterCard and Visa cards can be found at a handful of banks in Bissau, as well as several hotels, including the Malaika and Ledger Plaza. There is also an ATM immediately outside the arrivals hall of the airport in Bissau. Some ATMs work; others don't.
Cash The unit of currency is the West African CFA franc. This currency is also used by its neighbours in Senegal, Burkina Faso, Benin, Togo, Mali, Niger and Côte d'Ivoire. CFA stands

> ### ℹ️ EATING PRICE RANGES
>
> Prices represent the cost of a main dish.
>
> **$** less than CFA3100
>
> **$$** CFA3100–6200
>
> **$$$** more than CFA6200

for 'Communauté Financière d'Afrique' (Financial Community of Africa). It was adopted in 1997 when the country abandoned the Guinea-Bissau peso.

Changing Money It's best to change money in Bissau at Ecobank, BAO or Casa Cambio Nacional, one of the moneychangers. You can also ask your hotel, though these tend to have the worst exchange rates. It's probably best to arrive in Guinea-Bissau with a bundle of francs already on hand.

Credit Cards MasterCard and Visa are accepted at top-end hotels in Bissau. Cards are mostly useless elsewhere, including in the Arquipélago dos Bijagós.

Tipping You'll often be asked for a *cadeau* (gift), whether you've been helped or not. It's up to you to decide whether it's appropriate in return for services rendered. At top-end hotels, one gratuity for cleaning staff, completely at your discretion. For restaurants, none expected at basic places; upscale, with decent service, 10% to 15%. Loose change is appreciated by taxi drivers. Tips are always expected for guides and drivers, around 10% or more if especially good and for multiday trips.

Exchange Rates

Australia	A$1	CFA452
Canada	C$1	CFA440
Euro zone	€1	CFA656
Japan	¥100	CFA538
New Zealand	NZ$1	CFA415
Switzerland	Sfr1	CFA605
UK	UK£1	CFA774
US	US$1	CFA600

For current exchange rates, see www.xe.com.

> ### ℹ️ PRACTICALITIES
>
> **Electricity** Supply is 220V and plugs are of the European two-round-pin variety.
>
> **Weights & measures** The metric system is used.

Tipping

You'll often be asked for a *cadeau* (gift), whether you've been helped or not. It's up to you to decide whether it's appropriate in return for services rendered.

➡ **Hotels** At top-end hotels, one gratuity for cleaning staff, completely at your discretion.

➡ **Restaurants** None expected at basic places; upscale, with decent service, 10% to 15%.

➡ **Taxis** Loose change appreciated.

➡ **Guide and driver** Always expected, around 10% or more if especially good and for multiday trips.

OPENING HOURS

Banks and government offices Usually 8am to noon and 2pm to 5pm Monday to Friday, although hours vary.

Shops From 8am or 9am until 6pm Monday to Saturday. Some close for lunch.

Corner grocers In most towns you can find ones open until 10pm or later.

POST

The postal service is slow. You're better off posting mail home from Senegal or The Gambia. Post offices generally open Monday to Friday mornings only, but the main post office (p235) in Bissau is open 8am to 6pm Monday to Saturday.

PUBLIC HOLIDAYS

Islamic feasts, such as Eid al-Fitr (at the end of Ramadan) and Tabaski, are celebrated. Guinea-Bissau also celebrates a number of public holidays.

New Year's Day 1 January

Anniversary of the Death of Amílcar Cabral 20 January

Women's Day 8 March

Easter March/April

Labour Day 1 May

Pidjiguiti Day 3 August

Independence Day 24 September

Christmas Day 25 December

TELEPHONE

If you don't have your own mobile telephone, try your hotel or the call centre at the main post office. Guinea-Bissau's country code is 📞245, and its international access code is 📞00.

TOURIST INFORMATION

There are no functioning official tourism offices in Guinea-Bissau. An unofficial website that might prove useful is www.gbissau.org. But your best bet is asking for information at your accommodation.

VISAS

According to Guinea-Bissau's Permanent Mission to the UN office in New York City, visas are not issued upon arrival at the airport in Bissau. However, travellers report it's possible to get a visa upon arrival at the airstrip in Bubaque for those flying on a small plane from Cap Skirring or Dakar in Senegal.

The UN office in New York City issues 30-day single-entry visas for US$100; two passport photos are required and the process generally takes three to five days.

Guinea-Bissau's embassies and consulates elsewhere (in Europe, there are embassies in Berlin, Brussels, Madrid, Paris and Lisbon) reportedly can do the same, though the price and time varies.

There is an official government-sponsored website (www.rgb-visa.com) that purports to process visa requests electronically for US$66 (single entry) and US$77 (multiple entry) prior to arrival. Its responsiveness and effectiveness is uneven, to say the least.

❶ Getting There & Away

AIR

Osvaldo Vieira International Airport (p235) is located 9km north west of the centre of Bissau. It's small and has few facilities other than a single cafe. The small airstrip on Ilha de Bubaque services charter flights from Bissau and Cap Skirring and Dakar in Senegal.

Guinea-Bissau does not have its own national carrier. Senegal Airlines was not operating to Guinea-Bissau at the time of research; however, flights could resume in the future. Private planes can also be arranged.

The main airlines flying to Guinea-Bissau:

ASKY Airlines (p235)

Euro Atlantic Airways (☑ 245 5361081; www.flyeuroatlantic.pt; Rua Vitorino Costa; ☺ 8.30am-5.30pm Mon-Fri) Weekly flights via Lisbon.

Royal Air Maroc (☑ 245 6652000; www.royalairmaroc.com) Via Casablanca. Very early morning arrival and departure times.

TACV Cabo Verde Airlines (VR; ☑ 245 3206087; www.tacv.com; Av Amílcar Cabral; ☺ 8.30am-5.30pm Mon-Fri)

TAP Air Portugal (p235) Resuming flights in early 2017 after a four-year hiatus. Via Lisbon.

LAND
Guinea

Transport to Guinea (plan on 24 to 48 hours to reach Conakry, depending on road/taxi conditions) leaves from Gabú, crosses the border at Burunduma (Guinea-Bissau) and Kandika

(Guinea) and traverses a rough pass through the beautiful Fouta Djalon mountains.

Visas for Guinea can be acquired at its embassy in Bissau. Generally, they take several hours. Have your yellow-fever vaccination card handy for Guinea immigration at the border.

Senegal

The busiest crossing point to/from Senegal is at São Domingos, on the main route between Ingore and Ziguinchor. From Ziguinchor's *gare routière* (bus station), it's a three- to four-hour ride on a minibus (CFA3500) to Bissau (around CFA500 extra for luggage).

There are also crossing points between Tanaf and Farim; at Salikénié, just south of Kolda; and near Pirada, north of Gabú on the route to/from Vélingara and Tambacounda.

❶ Getting Around

BOAT

The regular ferry linking Bissau to Ilha de Bubaque was not operating at the time of research. A replacement was supposedly on its way. Otherwise, for a fee speedboats from various resorts in the islands are open to nonguests joining if there is a space. *Canoas* (motor canoes) also make the trip; however, these are unreliable, uncomfortable and potentially dangerous. *Canoas* also operate between individual islands.

SEPT PLACE & TRANSPORTE MISTO

Sept places are Peugeot 504 seven-seaters that link the main towns. More common and far less comfortable are large minibuses called *transportes misto* (literally 'mixed transport') or *toca-toca*; most fares are a dirt-cheap CFA100. Before 8am is the best time to get transport.

The main roads between Bissau and Bafatá, Gabú, São Domingos and Buba are all sealed and generally good. Stretches between Buba and Jemberém and São Domingos and Varela are unpaved and in bad condition.

CAR & MOTORCYCLE

While a few major roadways are paved and in relatively good condition, a 4WD is recommended for most trips. There are few signposts, and animals, chickens, cows, pigs and goats are always a hazard. Your best bet to rent a vehicle in the country is to ask at the Ledger Plaza Bissau (p233), the **Azalaï 24 de Setembro** (☑ 245 955 803000; www.azalaihotels.com; Av Pansau Na Isna) or a travel agency in Bissau.

Liberia

♫ 231 / POP 4.5 MILLION

Best Places to Eat

➡ Pak Bat (p252)

➡ Sweet Lips (p248)

➡ Evelyn's (p248)

Best Places to Sleep

➡ Mamba Point Hotel (p248)

➡ Libassa Eco-Lodge (p250)

➡ Kwepunha Retreat & Villas (p250)

Why Go?

Liberia, a lush, green, friendly and vibrant land, offers everything from excellent surf spots and shops selling wares by edgy local designers to days spent lolling in a comfy hammock on the edge of the rainforest while listening to tropical birds sing. It's home to one of West Africa's best national parks, and still hangs on to a confident American spirit mixed with West African roots. And despite the ravages of the past, it is a fantastic place to travel, full of hope and energy.

After a decade of dusting themselves off and resuming normal life following their brutal civil war, Liberians experienced another deadly conflict in 2014 – the Ebola virus. While the nation is officially Ebola-free per the WHO, it's struggling economically to recover. With travel restrictions lifted, tourism can play a huge role in this.

When to Go
Monrovia

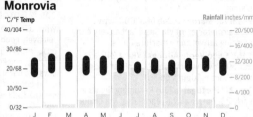

Dec–Jul Dry season and the most popular time to visit.

May–Oct Rainy season; spectacular stroms and good waves for surfers.

Oct–Jan Peak tourist season; prices are at their highest.

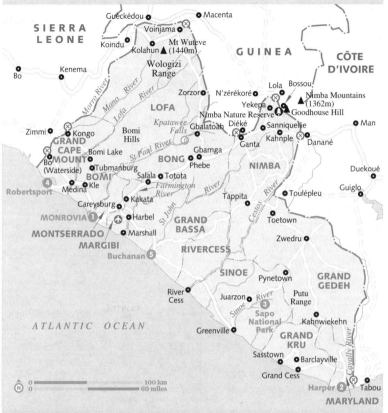

Liberia Highlights

1 Monrovia (p245)
Exploring the relics of Liberia's rich history and the American influence that still shapes the capital.

2 Harper (p252) Hitting the long, bumpy road to this pretty town that's blessed with southern American

architecture and an end-of-the-line feel.

3 Sapo National Park (p251) Venturing into the habitat of the endangered pygmy hippo, camping beneath the forest canopy and listening to the sounds of the rainforest.

4 Robertsport (p250)
Riding the waves with Liberian surfers, running your hands through the phosphorescent swell and eating fresh lobster in the shade.

5 Buchanan (p250)
Camping on the wild and beautiful beaches and relaxing at the port.

MONROVIA

🎵 0880 / POP 1.8 MILLION

Monrovia has been everything over the decades – a splendid African capital brimming with elegant stores and faces, a party city monitored by sheriffs wearing secondhand US police uniforms, a war zone marred by bullet holes, and a broken-hearted city struggling to climb to its feet after both war and a deadly Ebola outbreak.

Walk along Broad St, Monrovia's main boulevard, and you'll hear the original beat of locally brewed hip-co and the gentle rhythm of Liberian English. You'll see the architectural ghosts of Monrovia's past and the uniformed school children of its future. You'll watch entrepreneurs climb into sleek,

Monrovia

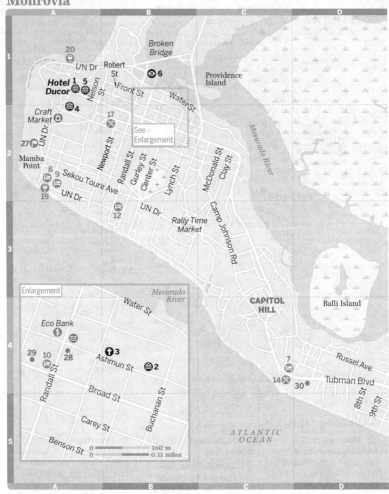

low-slung cars, market men sell coconuts from rusty wheelbarrows, and models sashay in tight jeans and heels. Monrovia has shaken off many of its old epithets and is infused with a new, exciting energy.

◉ Sights

With the weather on your side and half a day to spare, you can see most of Monrovia's major architectural landmarks on foot. Worthwhile historic buildings include the retro **Rivoli Cinema** (Broad St) and the **EJ Roye building** (Ashmun St), which dominates the skyline and was once home to a spectacular auditorium.

The imposing **Masonic Temple** (Benson St) overlooks the city at the western end of Broad St, in the shadow of the abandoned **Hotel Ducor** (Broad St) `FREE`; this was West Africa's finest hotel in the 1970s, where Idi Amin swam in the pool and Miriam Makeba sang in the bar.

Waterside Market   MARKET
(Water St, opposite Providence Island) Chaotic Waterside Market offers almost everything for sale, including colourful textiles, shoes, leather goods and pottery, all with a dose of foul smells and lots of noise. Haggle hard,

Monrovia

◉ Top Sights
1 Hotel Ducor..............................A1

◉ Sights
2 EJ Roye Building B4
3 First United Methodist Church B4
4 Masonic Temple.......................A2
5 Rivoli Cinema A1
6 Waterside Market B1

⊟ Sleeping
7 Bella Casa C4
8 Cape Hotel A2
9 Mamba Point Hotel..................A2
10 Palm Hotel A4
11 Royal Grand Hotel....................E5
12 St Theresa's Convent................B3

✕ Eating
13 Evelyn's F4
14 Golden Beach C4
15 Living Room E5
16 Sajj House F5
17 Sweet Lips B2

⊖ Drinking & Nightlife
18 Deja Vu F5
19 Lila Brown's A2
20 Tides A1

ⓘ Information
21 French Embassy E5
22 Ghanaian Embassy...................E4
23 Guinean Embassy F5
24 Ivoirian Consulate E5
25 JFK Hospital F5
26 Lucky Pharmacy F5
27 US Embassy A2

ⓘ Transport
28 Brussels Airlines A4
29 Kenya Airways.........................A4
30 Royal Air Maroc.......................D4

🛏 Sleeping

smile, and embrace raw Monrovia to its fullest.

Silver Beach BEACH
This pretty beach is fun and relatively easy to get to, plus it's home to the best beach snack joint in the area. It's located about 15km southeast of Monrovia (a US$12 charter taxi ride).

First United Methodist Church CHURCH
(cnr Gurley & Ashmun Sts) You might spot President Ellen Johnson Sirleaf attending a Sunday service here. The church is open to the public.

St Theresa's Convent HOSTEL **$**
(📞 0886 784 276; archdiocesanpastoralcenter@ yahoo.com; Randall St; r US$30, without bathroom US$20, ste US$50) Cheap and cheerful St Theresa's has rooms that back onto the convent and religious centre. There's a 10pm curfew.

Palm Hotel HOTEL **$$**
(📞 0886 585 959, 0880 425 980; www.palmhotel monrovia.com; cnr Broad & Randall Sts; s/d incl breakfast from US$115/135; ✳ @ 🛜) Located in the very heart of the city, the Palm is secure, clean and comfortable, with free in-room wi-fi and a great rooftop restaurant. Try to score a room with a balcony.

Cape Hotel HOTEL $$

(☑077 006 633; www.thecapehotelliberia.com; United Nations Dr, Mamba Pt; s/d from US$170/$250, ste or apt from US$400; P꘎🌢🏊) This reasonably priced option features an on-site terrace restaurant, parking and a pool. It's a particularly well-maintained space with a lovely terrace to while away hot afternoons; friendly, helpful staff will provide endless local tips. The smaller 'suites' are really just slightly larger rooms; the larger suites have kitchenettes, and apartments have full kitchens.

Bella Casa BOUTIQUE HOTEL $$

(☑077 692 272, 077 444 110; www.bellacasaliberia.com; cnr 3rd St & Tubman Blvd, Sinkor; d from US$115; P꘎🌢) A sound midrange boutique-style option, Bella Casa is a short walk from Capitol Hill and the UN building. They might not quite evoke dreams of Italy, but the rooms are comfortable, clean and come with air-con, desks and free wi-fi. The suites are large, with stylish bed linen and a more luxurious touch.

★Mamba Point Hotel LUXURY HOTEL $$$

(☑06 544 544, 06 440 000; www.mambapointhotel.biz; United Nations Dr; r/ste US$240/400; P꘎🌢🏊) Monrovia's finest hotel is an institution. It has 60-plus beautiful rooms, decked out with stylish furnishings and luxurious bathrooms (the suites are divine, with stunning sea views). Staff are top-notch. There's an excellent terrace restaurant, adjacent sushi bar, a casino, a pool, a gym and a cocktail bar.

Royal Grand Hotel LUXURY HOTEL $$$

(☑077-777 788; royalhotelliberia@yahoo.com; cnr 15th St & Tubman Blvd; r from US$260; P꘎🌢) The Royal is one of the classiest hotels in town. The complex holds plush rooms (including presidential suites from US$890), a coffee shop, a hair salon, an art gallery, an Asian-fusion restaurant and a rooftop cocktail bar. If you want pampering and the closest thing to five-star service in Monrovia, this is it.

✖ Eating

Sweet Lips LIBERIAN $

(Newport St; meals US$1.50-3; ⊙11am-9pm Mon-Sat) This firm favourite is said to serve up the very best Liberian food in town – try the excellent *fufu* (puréed, fermented cassava) and palm butter.

Silver Beach snack stand SEAFOOD $

(Silver Beach; mains US$5-15; ⊙11am-10pm) This snack stand with a few tables is one of the best around. It serves up platters of grilled grouper, shrimp and lobster, and on Sundays there's dancing (mainly to salsa and reggae, but anything goes and the tunes change frequently).

★Evelyn's INTERNATIONAL $$

(☑0777 001 155, 0886 710 104; www.evelyns-restaurant.com; Gibson Ave; mains US$6-18; ⊙11am-8pm Mon-Sat; ꘎🌢) This is hands-down Monrovia's favourite spot for lunch and early-evening cocktails. Evelyn's offers upmarket Liberian dishes (such as palm butter and rice), American mains including sandwiches, and an all-you-can-eat lunch buffet on Wednesdays (US$20). You can order sides of cassava fries, stuffed plantain and fried chicken, while for dessert there's papaya pie and cornbread muffins.

Golden Beach INTERNATIONAL $$

(3rd St, Sinkor; meals US$5-13; ⊙noon-late Mon-Sun; P🖐) Life in Liberia doesn't get better than this. Exhale, kick off your shoes and start your evening here, where tables sink into the sand and sunsets dip behind gin and tonics. Nobody's in a hurry here, including the chefs, who prepare Liberian/West African, European and Vietnamese food.

Sajj House LEBANESE $$

(☑06 830 888; cnr Tubman Blvd & 18th St, Sinkor; mains US$5-14; ⊙9am-10pm; P🌢🍴) Lebanese meze, cheese-and-spinach pies, sandwiches and pizzas are served beneath the awnings of a large traditional Liberian garden hut. Popular with salsa-dancing expats on Friday nights, Sajj has a fully stocked bar, blender (try the frozen fruit juices) and dessert menu, featuring chocolate crêpes. The volume dial turns with the clock.

Living Room SUSHI $$

(☑06 850 333; Royal Grand Hotel, cnr Tubman Blvd & 14th St; sushi US$5-15, mains from US$15; ⊙11am-9pm) Celebrated by expats for its transcendent tuna salad, Monrovia's top sushi bar feels very glamorous with smart leather chairs, sleek black tables and a gleaming sushi counter. Takeaway is available.

🍷 Drinking & Nightlife

Lila Brown's BAR

(UN Dr; ⊙5pm-late Mon-Sun; 🌢) Lila B's is an elegant duplex bar nestled between the

Mamba Point Hotel and the Atlantic, set in an old colonial home. Downstairs there's a food menu and a party vibe on weekend nights. Climb the wooden staircase for sea views, waiter service and relaxed tables shielded from rainy-season downpours by stylish shower curtains.

Deja Vu CLUB
(☑ 05 555 000; Airfield Short Cut, Sinkor; ☺ 10pm-4am Tue-Sat) Join the shimmering, moneyed party people at Liberia's sleekest club, which hosts DJs and regular special nights. No shorts or sandals for men.

Tides BAR
(☑ 0777 666 444; United Nations Dr; ☺ 4pm-late Wed-Sun) Wicker armchairs and loveseats line the wide veranda at the oceanfront Tides, where you get views with style. Inside, find the cocktail list scribbled on a blackboard (try the bissap margarita), a pool table and a long bar beneath a safari-lodge ceiling. The kitchen (sandwiches, cassava fries and crispy fried plantain, known as *kelewele*) opens after 4.30pm.

🛍 Shopping

★ KaSaWa CLOTHING
(☑ 0886 698 005; 1st St, Sinkor; ☺ 10am-6pm Mon-Sat) 🖉 A fair-trade initiative that brings together designers and producers from Robertsport. The assortment includes colourful bags and clothes. The group often funds local charities – ask what's currently on its radar when you visit.

Leslie Lumeh ART
(☑ 0886 430 483; www.leslielumeh.com) Leslie sells his watercolour and acrylic paintings and is *the* go-to source of info on the Liberian contemporary art scene. He does not have a gallery per se but give him a ring if you want to see his work and he will set something up.

Craft Market ARTS & CRAFTS
(☺ 10am-6pm) This cluster of craft vendors on the hilltop above the US embassy offers a mix of masks, clothing and other trinkets. It's a good place for bargains.

ℹ Information

DANGERS & ANNOYANCES
Be careful around Waterside and avoid West Point and most of the beaches in town, for both security and health reasons. Watch your back

(and head) if you choose to zip around on the back of a *pen-pen* (motorbike taxi).

MEDICAL SERVICES
Medical care is limited in Liberia.
JFK Hospital (Tubman Blvd, Sinkor) Monrovia's main hospital is fine for basic needs (it can do malaria tests), but should be avoided for more serious matters, unless the hospital's annual flying surgeons are in town.
Lucky Pharmacy (Tubman Blvd; ☺ 8.30am-late Mon-Sun) Opposite JFK Hospital, this pharmacy is trusted by international organisations and has knowledgeable staff.
SOS Clinic (☑ 0886 841 673; Tubman Blvd, Congo Town) Head here in the first instance if you fall sick; this clinic is the best-equipped in the country, trusted by expats. It's between the YWCA and Total Garage.

MONEY
Eco Bank (Asmun St; ☺ 10am-4pm Mon-Fri)

POST
Main Post Office (cnr Randall & Ashmun Sts; ☺ 8am-4pm Mon-Fri, to noon Sat)

ℹ Getting There & Away

Flights arrive at **Roberts International Airport** (ROB; Robertsfield), 60km southeast of Monrovia, from where a taxi into the city costs around US$80. There is also the little-used Spriggs Payne Airport (MLW) in Sinkor.

Bush taxis for Robertsport and the Sierra Leone border leave from Duala Motor Park, 9km northeast of the town centre. Transport for most other domestic destinations leaves from the Red Light Motor Park, Monrovia's main motor park, 15km northeast of the centre. Nearby Guinea Motor Park has buses heading to Guinea and Côte d'Ivoire.

THE COAST

Marshall

The rural area surrounding Marshall makes for an easy weekend escape from the city. You can camp on the quiet beaches here or see the chimps at Monkey Island.

⊙ Sights

Monkey Island ISLAND
(donation US$10-20) This small archipelago is home to chimpanzees that were evacuated from a hepatitis research lab during the war. Enquire in town about the most up-to-date

options for heading there by canoe (US$5 to US$10) – it can be hit or miss, but there will usually be someone around who can take you.

Firestone Rubber Plantation PLANTATION
(Harbel) This is the world's largest rubber plantation, which is leased from the government on a controversial 99-year plan. You can view how rubber is processed (not official tours, just ask at the entrance and they will normally oblige), or play a round at the 18-hole golf course. The only way to get here from Marshall is by car. The journey takes roughly an hour.

🛏 Sleeping

⭐**Libassa Eco-Lodge** LODGE $$$
(📱 0888 555 563, 05 940 930; www.libassa.com; day entry fee US$10, huts US$125, honeymoon ste US$250; P 🏊) 🏄 With pretty, solar-powered huts (named after endangered Liberian species) on the edge of the forest, Libassa makes for a gorgeous weekend retreat near Marshall. Pack your swimsuit: there's a pool, a lagoon and a beach. There's also a lunch buffet run by helpful staff. The 2km stretch of road beyond Kpan Town is rough and only accessible by 4WD (45 minutes from Monrovia, 15 minutes from Marshall).

RLJ Kendeja RESORT $$$
(📱 0886 219 939; www.rljkendejaresort.com; r from US$205; P 📶 🏊) This sleek, dreamy resort is spread across a beach in the environs of the airport. Interlinked walkways take you to the pool, the plush bar and restaurant, and the spa. Sunday brunch is a hit with expat NGO workers and there are romantic getaway deals.

❶ Getting There & Away

It's a short drive from Roberts International Airport and an hour from Monrovia.

Robertsport

📱 0880 / POP 4100
Framed by gold-spun beaches, phosphorescent waves and a thick mane of forest, this pretty capital of Grand Cape Mount, just a fishing village a few years ago, has largely retained its simple, paradise-found feel. Now, as you emerge from the rust-red roads and wind your way through the old town with its architecture in various states of undress (look out for the stunning scarlet ruins of the defunct Tubman Center of African

Culture), you're greeted by surf lodges and body-boarding tourists.

◉ Sights

Casava Point is a beach for ambitious surfers – it heaves towards the shiny granite rocks. **Cotton Trees** has beautiful surf along its shallow sand bar. **Fisherman's Point** is the closest of the surf beaches to town, and is good for beginners.

Destroyed during Liberia's war, the shambles of the **Tubman Center of African Culture**, a former museum and now a ruin, yields a few onlookers. Its draw is to see how the overgrowth keeps gaining ground. Remnants of its bright red colour can still be seen in spots and its grand pillars are still majestic, even in their dilapidated state.

🛏 Sleeping & Eating

⭐**Kwepunha Retreat & Villas** GUESTHOUSE $
(📱 0888 132 870; www.kwepunha.com; Fisherman's Beach; s/d US$55/90; P) 🏄 Run by Californian surfers in conjunction with community initiatives, this blue-and-yellow beach house offers pleasant, breezy rooms with wooden four-poster beds. You can join grassroots-style surf retreats here, or book the rooms independently. The house is situated on Fisherman's Beach, where you can tuck into fish tacos and margaritas.

Nana's Lodge LODGE $$
(📱 086 668 332; Cassava Beach; canvas/wooden bungalows for 2 from US$75/115; P) 🏄 Robertsport's original eco-lodge, Nana's has 11 bungalows overlooking the beach. The wooden huts are pricier than the canvas ones, but both styles of accommodation come with two comfortable double beds, fans and balconies. The sandy cantina down on the beach is a top sunset spot.

❶ Getting There & Away

Bush taxis cover the intermittently unpaved 120km route between Robertsport and Monrovia (L$375 to L$400, four to five hours). The same route is possible in 3½ hours via private taxi (US$150) or 4WD (US$200, plus the cost of petrol).

Buchanan

📱 0880 / POP 35,250
Liberia's second port hosts wild, beautiful beaches that are perfect for camping, plus an annual dumboy festival in January: two

good reasons to make it here. Pre-Ebola it was on the way up; these days it's still gorgeous but development has ceased. Still, its stunning coast means there is much potential for this place.

🛏 Sleeping & Eating

Teepro Lodge
LODGE $

(☑ 0880 961 568; Roberts St, next to the Buchanan Renewables site; r with net & fan US$35) You can sleep at the clean, quiet and reasonably comfortable Teepro Lodge. The staff are extremely friendly and helpful. Should the lodge be full, staff will be happy to advise on beach camping options nearby.

Sparks Hotel
HOTEL $$

(cnr Gardner & Church Sts; r US$80-110; P ❄ 🛜) Although loud and brash, this is still the best choice in town, with functional, spartan rooms. It serves decent Lebanese and African fare (US$13 to US$25), and it is home to a so-so nightclub.

ℹ Information

Be aware of the strong currents if you swim. And it's advisable to hire an overnight security guard if camping on the beach.

ℹ Getting There & Away

Bush taxis ply the route from Monrovia (L$450, three hours) or you can charter a car (US$120 one way) or a 4WD (US$180 plus petrol per day) for the 125km to Buchanan, which is mostly paved.

THE SOUTHEAST

Zwedru

☑ 0880 / POP 24,700

Flanked by thick, lush rainforest that runs along the Côte d'Ivoire border, Zwedru is the capital of Grand Gedeh, one of Liberia's greenest counties. This is the hometown of Samuel Doe, who stole power in a bloody coup in 1980. His mark is still evident in Zwedru, where he installed pavements and was in the process of constructing a house on the edge of town when he was murdered. Many in Grand Gedeh, particularly those who feel forgotten by the Monrovia administration, remain vocal supporters of Doe.

WORTH A TRIP

MOUNT NIMBA

Beautiful **Mt Nimba** (☑ 777 397 418; Zortopa; guide for 1 day US$8-15) is Liberia's tallest peak, 1362m above sea level, and you can feasibly climb it if you have a few days on your hands (it's a rewarding way to beat the heat of Monrovia). You can camp along the way if you have your own equipment, hiking along the peaks. Bring a GPS and warm clothing as it can get misty and very cool at night.

The jumping-off point is the curious town of Yekepa, a 10-hour drive from Monrovia and a Truman Show–esque mining town owned by Arcelor Mittal. The road to Mt Nimba is paved for almost three-quarters of the way to the top; you can drive to the peak using a 4WD. The **Noble House Motel** (Yekepa; ☑ 077 285 158; main road; r from US$22) is the only sleeping option of note in Yekepa.

These days, the best reason to visit is to experience the exceptional primary rainforest of Sapo National Park.

👁 Sights

Sapo National Park
NATIONAL PARK

(scnlib2001@yahoo.com) **FREE** Sapo, Liberia's only national park, is a lush 1808-sq-km tract containing some of West Africa's last remaining primary rainforest. Within it lurk forest elephants, pygmy hippos, chimpanzees, antelopes and other wildlife, although these populations suffered greatly during the war.

🛏 Sleeping

Munnah Guesthouse
GUESTHOUSE $$

(☑ 0886 485 288; r from US$40; P) The best place to stay is the Munnah Guesthouse – it's used by NGOs working in the area's Ivoirian refugee camps. The modern, airy rooms have fans.

Monjue Hotel
HOTEL $$

(☑ 0880 748 658; r US$50-70; P) A basic hotel that can be noisy at weekends.

🍴 Eating

The main road that runs through town has an assortment of snack bars and one eatery.

Florida Restaurant
AFRICAN $

(main road; mains US$10-18) This is a popular meeting spot that serves cheap Liberian dishes and European mains.

ⓘ Getting There & Away

From Monrovia, Zwedru can be reached by bush taxi for roughly L$800, a private taxi will generally cost around US$500 and a 4WD upwards of US$600 (plus petrol). It's only 200km, but you'll need to allow around nine to 10 hours to get here as the route is long, rough and bumpy.

Harper

☑ 0880 / POP 17,900

Charming, small-town Harper feels like the prize at the end of a long treasure hunt. The capital of the once-autonomous Maryland state, this gem is shingled with decaying ruins that hint at its former grandeur.

◉ Sights

Cape Palmas Lighthouse LIGHTHOUSE

FREE This lighthouse can be climbed for an outstanding panoramic view of the cape. Although no longer functional, it's on a UN base, so get permission first, and don't attempt to scale the small, slippery steps during the rainy season. Don't miss the stunning, palm-lined beach at nearby Fish Town (not to be confused with the larger town of the same name), but take care with the currents if you swim.

William Tubman mansion HOUSE

(Maryland Ave) **FREE** In the early evenings, the soft light gives an eldritch feel to the shell of the presidential mansion of former president William Tubman, who was born in Harper, and the remnants of the Morning Star Masonic Lodge, built by Tubman, himself a Grand Master Freemason.

⌂ Sleeping

Adina's Guest House GUESTHOUSE $

(☑ 0886 620 005; Maryland Ave; r US$55) Adina's has several basic rooms with fans, but it's a spotless place to rest your head and is arguably the best place to stay in town. Be sure to book as far in advance as possible: this place fills up quick. It's on the main road, next to the church.

Pastoral Center HOSTEL $

(Ivory Coast Rd; d US$30-40) The Pastoral Center offers basic dorm beds at low prices

– worth it if you are truly on a budget and need a secure place to rest your head.

✗ Eating

Pak Bat ASIAN $

(mains US$4-6) There's great South Asian food to be had at Pak Bat, the Pakistani UN peacekeepers' battalion, so long as you're prepared to hang with pretty much only NGO workers.

Sophie's LIBERIAN $

(Mechlin St; mains US$5-11) Sophie's offers good potato greens and cassava-leaf stew.

Jade's LIBERIAN $$

(cnr Walter & Mechlin Sts; mains US$5-10; ⊙ 11am-9pm) Jade's (or Sweet Baby, as some locals lovingly call it) serves fish, chicken and rice, as well as sandwiches and pizzas if the delivery truck has brought supplies.

ⓘ Getting There & Away

Reachable after two days on some of Liberia's worst road. The drive from Monrovia to Harper can be broken up in Zwedru (10 to 11 hours), from where it's around five to six hours further south. It's inadvisable to attempt this route during the rainy season, even if you're travelling by 4WD.

UNDERSTAND LIBERIA

Liberia Today

Liberia's Nobel Peace Prize–winning president, Ellen Johnson Sirleaf, won a second term in power in 2011, after rival party Congress for Democratic Change (CDC) – led by Winston Tubman and former AC Milan footballer George Weah – boycotted the second round of the violence-ridden vote, complaining of fraud. 'Ellen', as she is widely known, enjoys support from a loyal band of Liberians. Others criticise her for being a part of the old set of politicians and accuse her of failing to understand their woes.

Ellen also failed in 2010 to implement the findings of Liberia's Truth and Reconciliation Commission, a post-conflict justice organ that was modelled on South Africa's. The body's final report recommended that the president herself be barred from holding public office for 50 years, after she admitted partially bankrolling former leader Charles Taylor's rebellion that sparked the civil war.

Taylor was sentenced to 50 years behind bars by a UN-backed war crimes tribunal in The Hague in 2011. Many Liberians expressed frustration that Taylor was tried not for his role in the painful Liberian conflict, but for masterminding rebel operations during Sierra Leone's war.

Many middle-class Liberians were excited about the country's new dawn, but for others – particularly those outside Monrovia – the fresh coats of paint and eager investors in the capital did little to heal old wounds.

Today, Liberia is still recovering from the effects of the Ebola virus, which devastated the country economically and ruptured its struggling healthcare system. At time of writing, all eyes were on the 2017 presidential elections and what changes that might bring to a country that is struggling to stay on its feet.

History

Liberia was ruled along ethnic lines until American abolitionists looking for a place to resettle freed slaves stepped off the boat at Monrovia's Providence Island in 1822. They saw themselves as part of a mission to bring civilisation and Christianity to Africa, but their numbers were soon depleted by tropical diseases and hostile indigenous residents.

The surviving settlers, known as Americo-Liberians, declared an independent republic in 1847, under the mantra 'The Love of Liberty Brought Us Here'. However, citizenship excluded indigenous peoples, and every president until 1980 was of American freed-slave ancestry. For nearly a century, Liberia foundered economically and politically while the indigenous population suffered under forced labour. They were not afforded the right to vote until 1963.

During William Tubman's presidency (1944–71) the tides began to change. Foreign investment flowed into the country, and for several decades Liberia sustained sub-Saharan Africa's highest growth rate. Firestone and other American companies made major investments during this time.

Yet the influx of new money exacerbated existing social inequalities, and hostilities between Americo-Liberians and the indigenous population worsened during the era of William Tolbert, who succeeded Tubman. While the elite continued to live the high life, resentment among other Liberians quietly simmered.

In 2005 Liberia made headlines by electing economist and Nobel Peace Prize–winner Ellen Johnson Sirleaf as Africa's first female head of state. She has been credited with reducing Liberia's debt, maintaining peace and improving infrastructure in the country, but has been criticised for some of the ways she handled the 2014 Ebola outbreak. At the time of writing, she was wrapping up her last year of presidency among multiple contenders for the 2017 presidential election.

From 2014 to 2016 the Ebola virus infected around 10,700 people, killed an estimated 4900 and devastated the economy (the majority of infections occurred in 2014). Liberia was declared Ebola-free in 2015, had several small outbreaks and was then again declared free of the virus in 2016. At the time of writing it was still on the long road to economic and emotional recovery.

Culture

Liberia remains a country of exceptions. The old inequality hang-ups haven't gone away; you'll notice that Americo-Liberians and returning, educated Liberians often enjoy better treatment than those with indigenous roots. Various initiatives are under way to even things out, but the road to cultural equality is likely to be long.

Regardless of their roots, one thing all Liberians have in common is their devotion to family. Many people you meet will be supporting a dozen others. Religion is also important, with Christian families regularly attending revivals at churches.

The Liberian handshake has Masonic origins and involves a snappy pull-back of the third finger, often accompanied by a wide grin.

People

The vast majority of Liberians are of indigenous origin, belonging to more than a dozen major tribal groups, including the Kpelle in the centre, the Bassa around Buchanan and the Mandingo (Mandinka) in the north. Americo-Liberians account for barely 5% of the total. There's also an economically powerful Lebanese community in Monrovia.

Close to half of the population are Christians and about 20% are Muslim, with the remainder following traditional religions.

Arts & Crafts

Liberia has long been famed for its masks, especially those of the Gio in the northeast, including the *gunyege* mask (which shelters a power-giving spirit), and the chimpanzee-like *kagle* mask. The Bassa around Buchanan are renowned for their *gela* masks, which often have elaborately carved coiffures, always with an odd number of plaits.

Environment

Illegal logging both during and after the conflict has threatened a number of species in Liberia, including the forest elephant, hawk, pygmy hippo (nigh-on impossible to see), manatee and chimpanzee. Liberia's rainforests, which now cover about 40% of the country, comprise a critical part of the Guinean Forests of West Africa Hotspot, an exceptionally biodiverse area stretching across 11 countries in the region.

Liberia's low-lying coastal plain is intersected by marshes, creeks and tidal lagoons, and bisected by at least nine major rivers. Inland is a densely forested plateau rising to low mountains in the northeast. The highest point is Mt Nimba (1362m).

SURVIVAL GUIDE

ℹ️ Directory A–Z

ACCOMMODATION

Accommodation prices in Monrovia are on the high side due to the presence of private companies and NGOs. You can expect to pay top dollar in the capital, comparable to large European or US cities, with a few exceptions. Upcountry, both prices and standards are lower and the range of

---

ℹ️ SLEEPING PRICE RANGES

The following price ranges refer to a double room.

$ less than US$50

$$ US$50–100

$$$ more than US$100

---

accommodation options generally cover budget to midrange.

DANGERS & ANNOYANCES

➡️ Liberia has some of the strongest rip currents in the world. Check with locals before you swim, never swim alone and learn how to negotiate rip tides before you dip your toes into the ocean.

➡️ The biggest dangers are the roads.

➡️ The security situation is somewhat stable, although it's wise not to walk in Monrovia after dark and be vigilant about staying in secure lodging.

➡️ Exercise caution if using motorbike taxis and don't be afraid to ask the driver to go slow.

➡️ Electric shocks are common in badly wired buildings; wear shoes before plugging in appliances.

EMERGENCY & IMPORTANT NUMBERS

| Liberia's country code | 231 |
| Emergency (Fire, Police, Ambulance) | 911 |

EMBASSIES & CONSULATES

Canadians and Australians should contact their high commissions in Abidjan, Côte d'Ivoire and Accra, Ghana, respectively.

French Embassy (031 235 576; German Compound, Congo Town; 11am-3pm Mon-Thu)

German Embassy (0886 438 365; Tubman Blvd, UNMIL Bldg, Congo Town; 10am-4pm Mon-Fri)

Ghanaian Embassy (077 016 920; cnr 15th St & Cheesman Ave, Sinkor; 11am-3pm Mon-Fri)

Guinean Embassy (0886 573 049; Tubman Blvd btwn 23rd & 24th Sts, Sinkor; 10.30am-4pm Mon-Fri)

Ivoirian Consulate (0886 519 138; Warner Ave btwn 17th & 18th Sts, Sinkor; 10am-4pm Mon-Fri)

Nigerian Embassy (0886 261 148; Tubman Blvd, Nigeria House, Congo Town; 10am-4pm Mon-Fri)

Sierra Leonean Embassy (0886 427 404; Tubman Blvd, Congo Town; 10am-3pm Mon-Fri)

UK Embassy (06 516 973; chalkleyroy@aol.com; United Nations Dr, Clara Town, Bushrod Island; 10am-4pm Mon-Fri) Honorary consul, emergency assistance only; otherwise contact the British High Commission in Freetown, Sierra Leone.

US Embassy (077 054 826; http://monrovia.usembassy.gov/; United Nations Dr, Mamba Point; 11am-4pm Mon-Fri)

FOOD

Rice and spicy meat sauces or fish stews are popular Liberian dishes. Palm butter with fish and potato greens are two favourites. Other popular dishes include palava sauce (made with plato leaf, dried fish or meat and palm oil) and *jollof rice* (rice and vegetables with meat or fish). American food is popular in Monrovia. Restaurants in Monrovia are sophisticated and varied; outside the capital, options are more limited.

GAY & LESBIAN TRAVELLERS

Homosexual acts in Liberia are punishable by one year in jail, and the idea of making a same-sex relationship a felony crime (punishable with a 10-year prison sentence) has been floated by the government. LBGT campaigners in the country have also been targets of violence. Needless to say, gay travellers need to be extremely cautious travelling here.

INTERNET ACCESS

Internet cafes are popping up more and more, but service (always slow) is limited in rural areas. Wi-fi spaces are increasing (especially in Monrovia). Internet access costs from US$4 to US$6 per hour; wi-fi in hotel lobbies and bars is usually free with a purchase.

MONEY

The Liberian dollar is tied to the US dollar. When in the country, US dollars are used for anything over approximately US$5. You can pay for anything in US dollars and your change may be in either currency (often a mix of both).

Make sure your US dollars are new (ideally issued after 2000) and in good shape, or risk them being rejected. Counterfeit US dollars is a serious issue, so be sure to closely inspect any bills you receive as change.

Monrovia has ATMs that dispense cash in US dollars. Elsewhere, bring cash. Western Union and Moneygram operate in most towns.

Exchange Rates

Australia	A$1	US$0.77
Canada	C$	US$0.76
Euro zone	€1	US$1.05
Japan	¥100	US$0.88
New Zealand	NZ$	US$0.72
UK	£1	US$1.25

For current exchange rates, see www.xe.com.

Tipping

Restaurants Add 10% for all meals except takeaway.

Taxis You don't need to tip taxi drivers, but if you hire a guide or a driver for the day, tip roughly 5%.

OPENING HOURS

Banks 9am to 4pm Monday to Friday, 9am to noon Saturday.

Shops 9am to 6pm Monday to Friday, 9am to 4pm Saturday.

Businesses 9am to 5pm Monday to Friday.

PUBLIC HOLIDAYS

New Year's Day 1 January

Armed Forces Day 11 February

Decoration Day Second Wednesday in March

JJ Roberts' Birthday 15 March

Fast & Prayer Day 11 April

National Unification Day 14 May

Independence Day 26 July

Flag Day 24 August

Liberian Thanksgiving Day First Thursday in November

Tubman Day 29 November

Christmas Day 25 December

TELEPHONE

The country code is 231.There are no area codes or landlines.

Pick up a Cellcom or Lonestar SIM card from booths on the street for US$6 to US$8.

TOURIST INFORMATION

There are no formal tourist information offices in the country.

VISAS

Visas are required by all except nationals of Economic Community of West African States or South Korea. Costs vary depending on where they are procured.

ⓘ Getting There & Away

AIR

Monrovia Roberts International Airport (p249) is the main airport in Liberia. Drastic cuts to service were made during the Ebola crisis and, at the time of writing, few airlines served Roberts.

Airlines serving Monrovia:

Brussels Airlines (www.brusselsairlines.com; Randall St)

Kenya Airways (KQ; ☑ 06 511 522, 06 556 693; www.kenya-airways.com; Broad St, KLM Bldg)

Royal Air Maroc (AT; ☑ 06 956 956, 06 951 951; www.royalairmaroc.com; Tubman Blvd)

LAND
Côte d'Ivoire

Border crossings with Côte d'Ivoire are just beyond Sanniquellie towards Danané, and east of Harper, towards Tabou.

From Harper, you must cross the Cavally River by ferry or canoe to reach the Ivoirian border. Plan on two days if you want to reach Abidjan via San Pedro using public transport along this route.

Alternatively, daily bush taxis go from Monrovia to Ganta and Sanniquellie, from where you can continue in stages to Danané and Man (12 to 16 hours).

Guinea

For Guinea, the main crossing is just north of Ganta. From just north of Ganta's Public Market

you can take a *moto-taxi* (motorcycle taxi) the 2km to the border and walk across. Once in Guinea, there are frequent taxis to N'zérékoré. From Sanniquellie's bush-taxi rank, known as the 'meat packing', there are irregular bush taxis via Yekepa to the Guinean town of Lola (US$6.50). A place in a shared taxi is the same price. A *moto-taxi* (if you can find one!) from Yekepa to the border should cost US$1, after which there are Guinean vehicles to Lola. There is also a border crossing at Voinjama to Macenta via a bad road from Gbarnga (often impassable in the wet season).

Sierra Leone

Using a 4WD, you can reach Freetown in about 10 to 12 hours from Monrovia. The main Sierra Leone crossing is at Bo (Waterside). There are frequent daily bush taxis between Monrovia and the Bo (Waterside) border (three hours), from where it's easy to find onward transport to Kenema (six to eight hours in the dry season and 10 to 12 hours in the wet), and then on to Freetown.

ⓘ Getting Around

BUSH TAXI & BUS

Bush taxis go daily from Monrovia to most destinations, including Buchanan, Gbarnga, Ganta, Sanniquellie and the Sierra Leone border, although distant routes are severely restricted during the rainy season. Minivans (called 'buses') also ply most major routes, although they're more crowded and dangerous than bush taxis.

CAR & MOTORCYCLE

Vehicle rental can be arranged through better hotels from about US$130 per day plus petrol for a 4WD. You can travel by private taxi in Monrovia for US$5 to US$7 per short hop; contact the well-run and trusted network of Guinean taxi drivers, **Alpha** (☑ 0886-600 022), for more information, including on airport pick-ups. Motorbike taxis known as *pen-pens* ply the streets of Monrovia and other cities. In the capital they have a 10pm curfew for a reason; ride with caution.

Mali

♩ 223 / POP 14.5 MILLION

Fast Facts

➡ **Area** 1,240,140 sq km

➡ **Capital** Bamako

➡ **Currency** West African franc (CFA)

➡ **Languages** French, Bambara, Fulfulde, Tamashek, Dogon and Songhai

Introduction

Like an exquisite sandcastle formed in a harsh desert landscape, Mali is blessed by an extraordinary amount of beauty, wonders, talents and knowledge.

Yet for now, its landscapes, monuments and stories are off-limits, sealed from tourists by a conflict that is threatening the very culture of Mali.

The heart of the nation is Bamako, where Ngoni and Kora musicians play to dancing crowds from all ethnicities, while in the Dogon country villages still cling to the cliffs as they did in ancient times.

Further west, Fula women strap silver jewellery to their ears and their belongings to donkeys, forming caravans worthy of beauty pageants as they march across the *hamada* (dry, dusty scrubland).

And in the northeast, the writings of ancient African civilisations remain locked in the beautiful libraries of Timbuktu, until a new dawn comes for Mali, and they – and it – can be rediscovered by travellers.

Top Sights

➡ **Dogon Country** A fairytale of rose-coloured villages, big blue skies, sacred crocodiles and sandstone cliffs.

➡ **Djenné** The world's most captivating mudbrick mosque.

➡ **Bamako** The sounds of live music, sprawling markets and motorbikes purring along the banks of the Niger River.

➡ **Timbuktu** Ancient libraries, monuments and texts of wisdom on philosophy and astronomy.

➡ **Segou** Acacia trees, shea butter, pottery and waterside *griots* (prase singers).

➡ **Niger River** The life-blood of Mali and Africa's third-longest river, it bends and twists its way to ancient Sahelian trading kingdoms.

UNDERSTAND MALI

Mali Today

Mali's fall from grace in 2012 came as a surprise to many, although not to close watchers of former president Amadou Toumani Touré (commonly referred to as ATT), who was deposed in a coup in April 2012. A band of mutinous soldiers ousted the president and his cabinet in the run-up to elections in which ATT was not planning to stand, claiming the leader was not adequately supporting the under-equipped Malian army against a Tuareg rebellion in the northeast of the country.

Somewhat ironically, the coup only worsened the situation in the northeast, allowing Islamist groups to gain hold of the region. They in turn pushed out the Tuareg groups and went on to install sharia law in the ancient towns of Gao and Timbuktu, destroying ancient monuments, tombs and remnants of history. Seven hundred thousand civilians were forced to flee in 2012 and early 2013, winding up in refugee camps in neighbouring countries as, at the request of the Malian government, French forces and Regional West African Ecowas (Economic Community of West African States) troops launched air raids and ground attacks, successfully and quickly pushing back the Islamists from many of their strongholds. French forces began to draw down in April 2013, and in July of that year they handed over control of military operations to a UN force. At the same time presidential elections were held and won by Ibrahim Boubacar Keïta, but none of this did anything to curtail the instability in the north, and as the French departed, violence increased and Tuareg and rebel groups retook some northern towns.

By mid-2015 the government signed peace agreements with a number of rebel Tuareg groups in exchange for a degree of regional autonomy and the dropping of arrest warrants that had been issued for their leaders. Although this helped to partially improve the security situation in the north, it has done little to halt attacks by Islamic militants on government forces and public places.

The continuing instability is deeply felt by most Malians: many businesses have closed, tourism revenue has dropped dramatically and important sites in Gao and Timbuktu have been destroyed. Sadly, many people feel that it is not only Mali's future that is under threat but also its long-celebrated culture and history.

History

The Early Empires

Rock art in the Sahara suggests that northern Mali has been inhabited since 10,000 BC, when the Sahara was fertile and rich in wildlife. By 300 BC, large organised settlements had developed, most notably near Djenné, one of West Africa's oldest cities. By the 6th century AD, the lucrative trans-Saharan trade in gold, salt and slaves had begun, facilitating the rise of West Africa's great empires.

From the 8th to the 16th centuries, Mali formed the centrepiece of the great empires of West African antiquity, most notably the empires of Ghana, Mali and Songhaï. The arrival of European ships along the West African coast from the 15th century, however, broke the monopoly on power of the Sahel kingdoms.

The French arrived in Mali during the mid-19th century. During the French colonial era, Mali was the scene of a handful of major infrastructure projects, including the 1200km Dakar–Bamako train line, which was built with forced labour to enable the export of cheap cash crops, such as rice and cotton. But Mali remained the poor neighbour of Senegal and Côte d'Ivoire.

Independence & Conflict

Mali became independent in 1960 (for a few months it was federated with Senegal), under the one-party rule of Mali's first president, Modibo Keïta. In 1968, Keïta was overthrown by army officers led by Moussa Traoré. Elections were held in 1979 with Traoré declared the winner.

During the Cold War, Mali was firmly in the Soviet camp. Food shortages were constant, especially during the devastating droughts of 1968–74 and 1980–85. One bright spot came in 1987 when Mali produced its first grain surplus.

The Tuareg are the largest ethnic group in the northern regions of Mali and have long complained of a feeling of marginalisation from the political and economic mainstream. In 1990 this frustration boiled over and the Tuareg rebelion began. The follow-

Mali

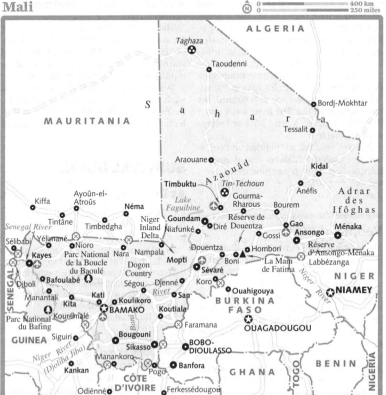

ing year a peaceful pro-democracy demonstration drew machine-gun fire from security forces. Three days of rioting followed, during which 150 people were killed. The unrest finally provoked the army, led by General Amadou Toumani Touré (General ATT as he was known), to seize control from Traoré.

Touré established an interim transitional government and gained considerable respect when he resigned a year later, keeping his promise to hold multiparty elections. But he was rewarded for his patience and elected president in April 2002.

The Tuareg rebellion gained ground in 2007 and was bolstered in 2011 and 2012 by an influx of weapons and unemployed fighters following the Libyan civil war. Islamist fighters, including those linked to Al-Qaeda, gained footing in the northeast soon after, ousting the main Mouvement pour le Liberation d'Azawad (MNLA) Tuareg group and forcing 400,000 civilians to flee the region

after harsh sharia law was imposed and ancient monuments destroyed. A transitional government, headed by Dioncounda Traoré, was installed, but deemed too weak to handle the crisis alone. French forces and later Ecowas troops launched air and ground offensives in an attempt to push back the Islamists in January 2013.

Culture

For the majority of Malians, life continues as usual, although the impact of the conflict weighs heavily on their minds. For those who eke out a living working in shops or businesses, the emphasis is on earning enough to take care of their (large) families on a day-to-day basis. But many have placed long-term plans on hold, as they simply can't predict what the future will bring.

In the northeast of the country, life has changed drastically. The imposition of sharia law has meant that many bars and restaurants have been closed. The majority of Malians are Muslim, but the strain of Islam that is traditionally followed is moderate and liberal – many enjoy dancing, drinking and being social butterflies. Now in the north women must cover their heads, couples are stoned to death for having sex outside marriage and live music is banned. For those who have not fled from areas under this strict Islamist control life has become fairly miserable.

Malians hold fast to tradition and politeness is respected. Malians find it rude to ask questions or stop someone in the street without first asking after their health and their families.

People of Mali

Mali's population is growing by almost 3% per year, which means that the number of Malians doubles every 20 years; 47% of Malians are under 15 years of age.

Concentrated in the centre and south of the country, the Bambara are Mali's largest ethnic group (34% of the population). Fulani (15%) pastoralists are found wherever there is grazing land for their livestock, particularly in the Niger inland delta. The lighter-skinned Tuareg (1%), traditionally nomadic pastoralists and traders, inhabit the fringes of the Sahara.

Almost 95% of Malians are Muslim, and 2% are Christian. Animist beliefs often overlap with Islamic and Christian practices, especially in rural areas.

Environment

Mali has four national parks, but for all intents and purposes they're merely parks on paper rather than fully functioning, well-protected conservation areas, and in general Mali's wildlife has been devastated by decades of human encroachment and a drying climate.

Mali's most urgent environmental issues are deforestation (at last count just 10.3% of Mali was covered in forest), overgrazing and desertification (an estimated 98% of the country is at risk from desertification).

Despite the urgency of the situation, while the political and security situation remains so fragile, it's unlikely that any real attention will be paid to environmental issues.

SURVIVAL GUIDE

ⓘ Directory A–Z

DANGERS & ANNOYANCES

Do not travel in Mali without good reason and careful consideration.

Almost every Western government advises against all travel to the northern two-thirds of the country, and against all but essential travel to the southern third. You should heed this advice. Not just is the risk very real, but your travel insurance will probably be invalid.

➡ Check the situation very carefully before travelling to Mali.

➡ Avoid demonstrations and areas popular with expats, diplomats and NGO workers.

➡ Do not travel anywhere after dark.

➡ Carry your passport with you at all times.

➡ Do not try to photograph police, military or sensitive sites.

VISAS

Despite the troubles within the country Malian tourist visas are being issued with minimal fuss. As long as you have a visa, getting in and out of the country via any of the main southern border crossings is fairly painless. Do not attempt to enter the country via Mauritania, Algeria or Niger.

Mauritania

222 / POP 4 MILLION

Best Places to Eat

➡ La Palmeraie Cafe & Bakery (p263)

➡ Azalaï Hôtel Marhaba (p262)

➡ La Tissayade (p265)

Best Places to Sleep

➡ Villa Maguela (p267)

➡ Auberge Diaguili (p262)

➡ Maison d'Hôtes Jeloua (p262)

➡ Parc National du Banc d'Arguin (p268)

Why Go?

Driving through the vast, sun-bleached landscape of Mauritania, you'd be forgiven for expecting to see a tricked-out post-apocalyptic hot rod from *Mad Max: Fury Road* on the horizon. Instead, a solitary, turbaned figure tending a herd of goats tells the story of survival amid millennial-old geological forces. Mauritania, with one of the world's lowest population densities, is almost equally divided between Moors of Arab-Berber descent and black Africans, a striking cultural combination that is part of its appeal.

There's no doubt that Mauritania has some of the continent's grandest scenery. The Saharan Adrar region, with its World Heritage–listed caravan towns, is currently off-limits for security reasons, but the desert is a constant presence elsewhere, pushing hard up against the Atlantic Coast. Millions of migratory birds winter along the coast at Parc National du Banc d'Arguin, and the expanding capital Nouakchott is where modernity takes root in the desert.

When to Go
Nouakchott

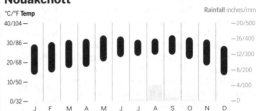

Nov–Mar Pleasantly warm for visiting the desert, although nights can be surprisingly cold.

Jul–Sep Short rainy season throughout the south; Nouakchott prone to flooding after downpours.

Mid-Jun–Aug Mauritanians from the coast head to oases towns to celebrate the date harvest.

NOUAKCHOTT

🎵 222 / POP 1 MILLION

Sixty years old, youthful by most standards, Nouakchott mushroomed quickly from a small village to the country's capital and largest city. Near, but not on the coast, building continues apace, even where roads are non-existent. Certainly, they're a strange sight: massive, gated homes plonked down in the desert. The city is unassuming and seemingly unplanned, as if on an overnight caravan stop it was left to grow by accident. Most travellers use it as a staging post before the Adrar, Banc d'Arguin or the next international border.

Nouakchott is sleepily idiosyncratic and you could do worse than spend an afternoon at the gloriously frantic fish market (one of the busiest in West Africa), treat yourself to a comfy hotel or feast in a good restaurant. Laid-back and safe – bliss after the rigours of the desert – the city is chock-a-block with international organisations and geared less to travellers, more to business people.

👁 Sights

Major landmarks in the centre include the Grande Mosquée (Mosquée Saudique; Rue Mamadou Konaté) and the large Mosquée Marocaine (Rue de la Mosquée Marocaine), which towers over a bustling market area.

Port de Pêche (Fish Market) is Nouakchott's star attraction. Lively and colourful, you'll see hundreds of teams of mostly Wolof and Fula men dragging in heavy fishing nets. Small boys hurry back and forth with trays of fish, which they sort, gut, fillet and lay out on large trestles to dry. The best time to visit is late afternoon, when the fishing boats return. Before or after, it's no less an impressive sight with the pirogues crammed like sardines on the beach.

There are two decent beaches around 5km north of the centre, Plage Pichot and Plage Sultan. Both offered covered alfresco dining areas and tents with pillows and mattresses for overnighting; Les Sultanes is recommended. These are popular with the small expat community on weekends; otherwise, you might have the place to yourself. Beware of undertows.

🛏 Sleeping

⭐ Maison d'Hôtes Jeloua   GUESTHOUSE $
(🎵 222 3636 9450; www.escales-mauritanie.com; r UM10,000-16,000; 🅿 ❄ @ 🛜) This is a lovely and deservedly popular *maison d'hôtes* (B&B), with a leafy garden, highly recom-

mended restaurant and a homey and friendly vibe. The somewhat challenging-to-find location is the only downside. The neighbourhood streets, for lack of a better term, are wide sandy lots or narrow alleys.

Les Sultanes   TENTED CAMP $
(🎵 222 4969 4140; tent UM7000) With a powdery sand beach uninterrupted as far as the eye can see, this small compound with a shady restaurant (mains UM3000) and handful of semi-permanent tent sites is as close to a beach resort as you'll get in Mauritania.

Auberge Diaguili   GUESTHOUSE $$
(🎵 222 4646 0003; www.diaguili.com; r incl breakfast UM18,000; ❄ 🛜) Owners Nadia and Pascal have created a friendly and warm environment, especially good for long-term stays. Rooms are simply furnished; there's a shared kitchen and tastefully designed lounge area.

Al Khaima City Center   HOTEL $$
(🎵 222 4524 2222; www.akcc.mr; 10 Rue Mamadou Konaté; r from UM25,000; ❄ @ 🛜) A downtown high-rise of solid value, the Al Khaima has small rooms that are surprisingly stylish, with boutique design elements and comfortable bedding. It's surprising because of the utilitarian lower lobby and lower floors, which include a bank, travel agency, electronics store and other offices. The 10th-floor cafe has unbeatable views of the city from the outdoor terrace.

Hôtel Monotel Dar el Barka   HOTEL $$$
(🎵 222 4524 2333; www.monotel-mr.com; Zone des Ambassades; r from UM51,000; ❄ @ 🛜 🏊) A large, low-slung complex with tight security near the French embassy, Dar el Barka is one of the more popular business-class hotels in the city. Sundays are especially crowded with expats enjoying the leafy central patio and pool area, and the all-you-can-eat buffet. Conferences, meetings and weddings are common, however room furnishings are a little old-fashioned.

Azalaï Hôtel Marhaba   HOTEL $$$
(🎵 222 4529 5051; www.azlaihotels.com; Ave Abdal Nasser; r/ste UM42,000/50,000; ❄ @ 🛜 🏊) The newest luxury business-class hotel to open in downtown Nouakchott, the Azlaï is part of a chain of hotels throughout West Africa. More than US$8 million was invested in upgrading what was once a Mercure hotel into a sparkling oasis with a top-flight restaurant and boutique-style rooms.

Mauritania Highlights

1 **Réserve Satellite du Cap Blanc** (p267) Tracking down a rare colony of charismatic Mediterranean monk seals in the country's remote north.

2 **La Tissayade** (p265) Tasting Mauritanian cooking in Nouakchott's best and most atmospheric restaurant.

3 **Parc National du Banc d'Arguin** (p268) Observing vast flocks of birds from a traditional pirogue.

4 **Port de Pêche** (p260) Witnessing the amazing tableau of hundreds of fishing boats returning to the beach just outside Nouakchott.

5 **Iron-Ore Train** (p266) Hopping on one of the world's longest trains – be ready for the most epic journey of your life!

✕ Eating

Perhaps the most inviting cluster of restaurants is along Rte des Ambassades, just south of the intersection with Rue de l'Ambassade du Senegal. Another few are grouped around a little further north off Ave Moktar Ould Daddah, just east of the Stade Olympique. Most high-end hotel restaurants are fairly stuffy and unremarkable; the Azalaï Hôtel Marhaba is the exception.

La Palmeraie Cafe & Bakery CAFE **$**
(☎222 4525 7344; Rue Ahmed Ould Mohamed; sandwiches UM1200; ☺7am-8pm Sun-Thu, to 11pm Fri; ☀☎) Widely considered the best breakfast spot in the city. Enjoy a sit-down meal of crêpes or a set continental breakfast in a contemporary-style dining room, or pick up a croissant and other freshly baked pastries and deserts (gelato as well) to go in bakery

Nouakchott

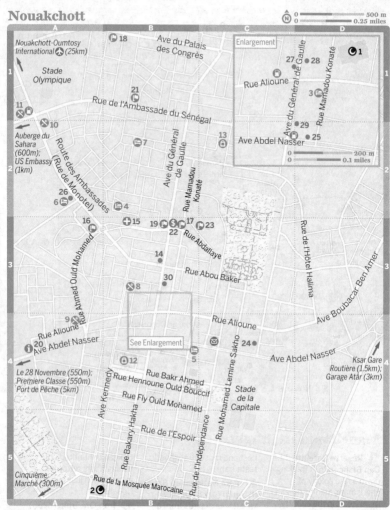

MAURITANIA NOUAKCHOTT

at the front. Other times of day pizzas and sandwiches available.

Café Tunisie
TUNISIAN $

(Ave Kennedy; set breakfast UM1000; ☺6.30am-8pm) This cafe is fine for coffee and smoking a water pipe, plus good-value breakfasts – freshly squeezed orange juice, bread, jam, pastries, yoghurt, coffee and a bottle of mineral water. Mains, like *merguez* (spiced sausage) or chicken brochette, come with fries, rice, bread and a salad. Street-front office furniture and couches under tattered awnings make it a good people-watching spot.

Tafarit
SEAFOOD $$

(mains UM3000; ☺noon-11pm; 🛜) Known for its seafood, which you can hand-pick from a tank (lobster runs around UM6000) in a sunny, slightly tattered dining room. Live music Friday nights adds a lovely, and rare for Nouakchott, soundtrack to your meal.

Le Manara
LEBANESE $$

(formerly Pizza Lina; Rte des Ambassades; mains from UM2000; ☺12.30-3.30pm & 7-11pm Tue-Sun; 🛜) Known around town, at least within the expat community, as one of the best places for steak in Nouakchott. Also serves some Asian dishes.

Nouakchott

⭐ **La Tissayade**   MAURITANIAN $$$
(📞 222 3636 9450; Maison d'Hôtes Jeloua; mains UM3000-5000; 🍴) Easily the restaurant with the best atmosphere in the city, La Tissayade is located in the shady front courtyard of Maison d'Hôtes Jeloua. Daily specials like vegetable quiche and a menu of beef, chicken, shrimp and lobster (order 24 hours in advance).

☆ Entertainment

CIMAN   LIVE MUSIC
(Conservatoire International de Musique et des Arts de Nouakchott; 📞 222 4685 5161; ciman.nkc@gmail.com) Hosts regular classical and traditional music concerts.

🛍 Shopping

⭐ **Zein Art**   ARTS & CRAFTS
(📞 222 4651 7465; www.zeinart.com; ⊘3.30-7.30pm Tue-Fri, 10am-7.30pm Sat) A gallery curating the very best work from Mauritanian artists and craftspeople. Periodically hosts exhibitions themed around art and artists in the region.

Marché Capitale   GIFTS & SOUVENIRS
(Grand Marché; Ave Kennedy) You'll find a bit of everything at Marché Capitale, including brass teapots, silver jewellery, traditional wooden boxes and colourful fabrics.

ℹ Information

MEDICAL SERVICES

Bureaux de Change There are bureaux de change on Ave du Général de Gaulle and on Ave du Gamal Nasser, as well as in the Marché Capitale. Euros, US dollars, CFA and Moroccan dirhams are most easily changed.

Cabinet Médical Fabienne Sharif (📞 222 4525 1571) English-speaking doctor, recommended by expats.

Doctor Melhem Hanna (📞 222 4525 2398) Lebanese cardiologist able to handle other general medical issues.

Le Phare du Désert (📞 222 4644 2421; www. desertmauritanie.com) A reliable tour operator that organises trips throughout the country.

Main Post Office (Ave Abdel Nasser; ⊘8am-3pm Mon-Thu, to noon Fri)

Societe Generale (Ave du Général de Gaulle) Two branches 100m apart; both have ATMs.

ℹ Getting There & Away

AIR

The major airlines have offices in Nouakchott. Mauritania Airlines has flights to Nouâdhibou (UM31,000, 45 minutes) daily, except Wednesday.

You can purchase domestic or international air tickets at one of the many travel agencies around town, including **Asfaar** (📞 222 4529 0406; asfaar@asfaar.mr; Ave Charles de Gaulle) and **PSV Voyages** (☑ 222 3630 1342; khattary@ amadeus.mr; 2nd fl, Al Khaima City Center).

Air Algérie (☑ 222 529 0922; www.airalgerie. dz; cnr Ave du Général de Gaulle & Ave Abdel Nasser)

Air France (☑ 222 4525 1808; www.airfrance. com; Rte des Ambassades, connected to Monotel Dar El Barka; ⊘ 8.30am-5pm Mon-Thu, to 1pm Fri)

Mauritania Airlines (☑ 222 4525 4767; www. mauritaniaairlines.mr; Ave du Général du Gaulle)

Royal Air Maroc (☑ 222 4525 3564; www. royalairmaroc.com; Ave du Général de Gaulle)

Tunis Air (☑ 222 525 8762; www.tunisair.com; Ave Kennedy)

Turkish Airlines (www.turkishairlines.com; Ave du Général de Gaulle)

BUSH TAXIS

For Nouâdhibou (about UM5000, six hours), several companies including **Premiere Classe** (Autoroute Nouadhibou), Le 28 Novembre, Gulf Transport and Prince Voyage, are all clustered together on the N2 (Autoroute Nouâdhibou), just north of the intersection with Ave Gamal Abdel Nasser.

For Rosso (about UM2500, 3½ hours), Garage Rosso is at Carrefour Madrid, a roundabout southeast of the centre.

❶ Getting Around

A taxi ride within the centre costs around UM200. It's possible to cover some ground in the centre on foot, however the heat, damaged or non-existent sidewalks and unruly traffic are challenges.

For the Nouakchott-Oumtosy International Airport, 25km north of the city, a convenient shuttle leaves from the Air France office in town to

the airport at 6.30pm on Mondays, Wednesdays, Fridays and Sundays (UM2000). Otherwise, a taxi or hotel van should run around UM5000.

Europcar (☑ 222 4430 3241; www.europcar. com; Ave du Général de Gaulle; ⊘ 8am-6pm Mon-Thu & Sun, 9.30am-12.30pm Fri & Sat) is the only rental vehicle outlet in the city.

ATLANTIC COAST

Nouâdhibou

☑ 222 / POP 118,000

Stretching along the Baie du Lévrier in the middle of a narrow 35km-long peninsula, the fishing port of Nouâdhibou marks the end of the road in many respects. The rail line from the interior ends. The country's northern border is a few kilometres away. Shipwrecks are marooned in the waters south of the city. From the air, the divide with Morocco, mostly empty desert bordering the Atlantic, is stark.

The city itself sprawls north to south; mostly low-slung buildings, paved roads petering out into sandy pathways a few blocks from the main artery. Often bypassed by travellers making a dash to the capital or to the Adrar, its sleepiness is its selling point. North of the centre, the Baie de l'Étoile resembles a mini Banc d'Arugin and a destination for intrepid kitesurfers. Daily life – the call of the muezzin, afternoon football, joggers hugging the coastal road – feels close.

AN EPIC JOURNEY ON THE IRON-ORE TRAIN

Africa offers some pretty wild train trips, but the train ferrying iron ore from the mines at Zouérat to Nouâdhibou might just be the wildest. One of the longest trains in the world (typically a staggering 2.3km long), when it arrives at the 'station' in Nouâdhibou, a decrepit building in the open desert, a seemingly endless number of ore wagons pass before the passenger carriage at the rear finally appears. The lucky ones – ie most aggressive in a scrum – find a place on one of the two long benches (UM2500); the rest stand or sit on the floor. There are also a dozen 'berths' (UM3000) that are so worn out you can see the springs. It's brutally basic. It's also possible to clamber into the ore cars and travel for free. Impossibly dusty, this is only for the hardcore. Plastic sheets are essential to wrap your bags (and person), plus plenty of warm clothes, as the desert can get fearsomely cold at night, as well as food and drink.

The train leaves Nouâdhibou at around 2pm to 3pm daily. Most travellers get off at Choûm, 12 hours later, where bush taxis wait to take passengers to Atâr, three hours away. In the other direction, the train leaves Zouérat around midday and passes through Atâr at about 5.30pm.

⊙ Sights

Réserve Satellite du
Cap Blanc   WILDLIFE RESERVE
(UM2000; ⊙10am-5pm Tue-Sat) A small nature
reserve with an excellent information centre, dedicated to the colony of endangered
Mediterranean monk seals *(phoque moin)*
that live here. Resembling elephant seals,
these grey-skinned animals have been hunted since the 15th century for their valuable
skins and oil. The protected colony here of
roughly 150 seals is one of the last on earth
(less than 500 worldwide). The colony is at
the foot of the cliffs; you have a reasonable
chance of seeing them swimming offshore.

🏃 Activities

With your own equipment you can enjoy
some outdoor activities around Nouâdhibou, including surf fishing on the remote
peninsula around Cap Blanc – but security
checkpoints can be a hassle. Shallow waters
and brisk winds make the bay an excellent
spot for kitesurfers. And you can swim near
the Centre de Pêche, around 12km north
of the airport.

🛏 Sleeping

Bungalow Dauphins   BUNGALOW $
(www.auberge-des-nomades-du-sahara.com; r
with full board from UM12,000) Located on an
otherwise lonely stretch of road north of
the city, this collection of well-designed
solar-powered bungalows overlooks the Baie
de l'Etoile. Be sure to make a reservation in
advance since it's geared towards groups of
kitesurfers coming from its sister resort in
Dakhla in the Western Sahara and not necessarily independent travellers.

Camping Baie du Lévrier   HOSTEL $
(☑222 4574 6536; Blvd Médian; s/d
UM3000/5000; ▣) Also known as Chez Ali,
this *auberge*-style place has a good location.
Rooms are a bit cell-like, and bathroom facilities are shared, but there is a tent to relax
in and cooking facilities.

★ Villa Maguela   VILLA $$
(☑222 2295 0820; www.facebook.com/villamague
la; r UM17,000) Easily the nicest place around
Nouâdhibou, nay, the nicest place on the
entire Mauritanian coast. This simple mud-
walled compound is set directly on a magnificent piece of rocky coastline around
8km north of the city. The room design and
furnishings are comfortable, if basic, but the

WORTH A TRIP

PARC NATIONAL DIAWLING

The little-known Parc National Diawling (www.pnd.mr; adult UM1200) is a sister to the adjacent Djoudj National Bird
Sanctuary in Senegal. It has important
mangroves and acacia forest (any bit of
greenery comes as a relief), as well as
large coastal dunes. Incredibly rich in
birdlife – you're also likely to spot monkeys, warthogs and monitor lizards – it's
well worth a detour if you have a 4WD.
Most people breeze through on their
way to Senegal via the border crossing
at Diamma. Facilities are almost completely undeveloped.

wind and lapping waves lulling you to sleep
is magnificent.

🍴 Eating

In the centre, you'll find a slew of cheap restaurants along Rue de la Galérie Mahfoud.
They're nothing fancy, serving fish and *mafé*
(groundnut-based stew) for around UM300
a plate.

Restaurant Oasis Tunisien   MOROCCAN $
(Blvd Maritime; mains UM1200; 🛜) Moroccan
owned (despite the name), this is a good-
value spot for chicken and shwarma served
up with fries and a small salad. If you can
stand the sun, a few street-front tables are
a pleasant spot for people-, and more commonly, vehicle-watching.

Restaurant La Paillotte   MEDITERRANEAN $$
(☑222 4574 3218; Blvd Maritime; mains UM1500-
4000; ⊙noon-3pm & 7-11.30pm, closed Sat)
Above-average seafood and more-standard
meat and chicken dishes; located inside the
Italian-owned Hotel Mauritalia.

ⓘ Information

Most of the hotels offer wi-fi, as do some restaurants. A few internet outlets along Blvd Médian
double as telephone offices.

There are several bureaux de change along the
city's main drag, Blvd Médian, as well as a couple
of banks with ATMs.

Société Générale Mauritanie (Blvd Médian;
⊙8am-4pm Sun-Thu) ATM open 24 hours.

ⓘ Getting There & Away

Mauritania Airlines (☑222 4574 4291; www.
mauritaniaairlines.mr; Blvd Médian) flies daily

(except Wednesday) to Nouakchott (UM31,000, 45 minutes; departure times vary), and three times a week to Casablanca in Morocco and Las Palmas in the Canary Islands (round trip UM161,500). Tickets can be purchased at the airline office or at any one of the handful of travel agencies around town.

There are plenty of minibuses and bush taxis to Nouakchott (UM5000, six hours); the former, of course, are more comfortable and leave from various company offices around the city. Premiere Classe is recommended – best to book a day in advance.

There is a train (p266) that runs from Nouâdhibou to Choûm and Zouérat (UM3000). The train 'station' is about 5km south of town.

Parc National du Banc d'Arguin

This World Heritage–listed park (www.pnba. mr; permit per person per day UM1200) is an important stopover and breeding ground for birds migrating between Europe and southern Africa, and as a result is one of the best birdwatching sites on the entire continent. It extends 200km north from Cape Timiris and 235km south of Nouâdhibou. The ideal way to approach the birds is by traditional fishing boat (UM20,000, plus UM5000 for the guide), best organised from the fishing village of Iwik. Cape Tagarit, 40km north of Tidra, offers beautiful views and the water is crystal clear.

Permits are issued in the park, or at the headquarters (☑222 425 8541; Ave Abdel Nasser; permits per day UM1200) in Nouakchott; the park office (☑222 574 6744; www.pnba. mr/pnba; Blvd Médian; ◷8am-4pm Mon-Thu, to noon Fri) in Nouâdhibou is of less help. The Nouakchott office sells a map and guide (English available) with GPS waypoints. There's also a useful map available at the University of Texas website (www.lib.utexas. edu/maps/africa/arguin_map.jpg).

To visit the offshore islands you need to request a special permit from the park office.

🛏 Sleeping & Eating

Inside the park there are official campsites (UM4000/800/12,000 per small/medium/large tent) equipped with traditional tents. Some, located directly on sandy beaches where you can swim, are also wonderful for bonfires and stargazing.

Meals can be ordered at the official campsites.

🛈 Getting There & Away

There's no public transport, so you'll need to hire a 4WD with a knowledgeable driver in Nouakchott (you're less likely to find one in Nouâdhibou), allowing a couple of days for the trip.

THE ADRAR

The Adrar is the undoubted jewel in Mauritania's crown, but sadly it remains firmly off-limits for security reasons – all Western governments currently advise their nationals against travelling to the Adrar. When it again becomes safe to visit, it's epic Saharan country, and shows the great desert in all its variety: the ancient Saharan towns of Chinguetti and Ouadâne, mighty sand dunes that look sculpted by an artist, vast rocky plateaus and mellow oases fringed with date palms.

UNDERSTAND MAURITANIA

Mauritania Today

President Mohamed Ould Abdel Aziz, considered strong in terms of security, has made less progress battling corruption and ensuring Mauritania's rich natural resources accrue to the benefit of all. Despite speculation to the contrary, Aziz, who won re-election to another five-year term in 2014, announced in October 2016 that he would not seek constitutional changes to allow him to run for a third term. Opposition voices – whether in politics or the media – are given little room to breathe in Mauritania.

A prominent blogger, Mohamed Ould Cheikh, was accused of blasphemy and sentenced to death in 2014; and an anti-slavery activist, Biram Ould Dah Ould Abeid, was jailed for 18 months after publicly burning Islamic legal texts purporting to advocate slavery. Abeid turned to politics and was Aziz's primary opposition in the 2014 presidential election. He was jailed again and released in May 2016. The country now looks to 2019, which could mark Mauritania's first transfer of power from one elected president to another.

History

From the 3rd century AD, the Berbers established trading routes all over the Western Sahara, including in Mauritania. In the 11th century, the Marrakesh-based Islamic Almoravids pushed south and, with the assistance of Mauritanian Berber leaders, destroyed the Empire of Ghana, which covered much of present-day Mauritania. That victory led to the spread of Islam throughout Mauritania and the Western Sahara. The descendants of the Almoravids were finally subjugated by Arabs in 1674.

As colonialism spread throughout Africa in the 19th century, France stationed troops in Mauritania, but it was not until 1904 that, having played one Moorish faction off against another, the French finally managed to make Mauritania a colonial territory. Independence was fairly easily achieved in 1960 because the French wanted to prevent the country from being absorbed by newly independent Morocco. Mokhtar Ould Daddah became Mauritania's first president.

Ould Daddah took a hard line, especially against the (mainly black African) southerners, who were treated like second-class citizens and compelled to fit the Moors' mould. Any opposition was brutally suppressed.

The issue of Western Sahara (Spanish Sahara) finally toppled the government. In 1975 the very sandy Spanish Sahara (a Spanish colony) was divided between Morocco and Mauritania. But the Polisario Front launched a guerrilla war to oust both beneficiaries from the area. Mauritania was incapable, militarily and economically, especially in the midst of terrible droughts, of fighting such a war. A bloodless coup took place in Mauritania in 1978, bringing in a new military government that renounced all territorial claims to the Western Sahara.

Ethnic tensions culminated in bloody riots between the Moors and black Africans in 1989. Around 100,000 Mauritanians were expelled from Senegal and more than 70,000 black Africans were expelled to Senegal, a country most had never known.

Riots over the price of bread in 1995 worsened the political situation. Cosmetic elections were held in 2001; opposing political parties and Islamists were deemed threats to the regime and both were repressed.

The 2000s were marked by more instability until elections in March 2007 saw Sidi Ould Cheikh Abdallahi returned as Mauritania's first democratically elected president. He openly condemned the 'dark years' of the late 1980s, and sought rapprochement with the expelled black Moors – a move that angered the traditional elites and which led, in part, to his overthrow by General Mohamed Ould Abdel Aziz in a coup in August 2008. Despite international condemnation, Aziz's position was consolidated the following year in elections that saw him narrowly returned as president.

Culture

The extended family, clan or tribe still remains the cornerstone of Mauritanian society, especially with the Moors.

As in many Muslim countries, religion continues to mark the important events of life. Although slavery was declared illegal in 1980, it is reported to still exist and the caste system permeates society's mentality.

Only a third as many women as men are literate and few are involved in commercial activities. Female genital mutilation and forced feeding of young brides are still practised in rural communities. However, Mauritanian women do have the right to divorce and exert it routinely.

People

Of Mauritania's estimated three million inhabitants, about 60% are Moors of Arab and Berber descent. The Moors of purely Arab descent, called 'Bidan', account for 40% of the population, and hold the levers of political power. The other major group is black Africans, ethnically split into two groups. The Haratin (black Moors), the descendants of people enslaved by the Moors, have assimilated the Moorish culture and speak Hassaniyya, an Arabic dialect. Black Mauritanians living in the south along the Senegal River constitute 40% of the total population and are mostly Fulani or the closely related Tukulor. These groups speak Pulaar (Fula). There are also Soninke and Wolof minorities.

Islam links the country's disparate peoples – more than 99% of the population are Sunni Muslims.

Arts & Crafts

The traditional music of Mauritania is mostly Arabic in origin, although along its southern border there are influences from

MAURITANIA HISTORY

the Wolof, Tukulor and Bambara. One of the most popular Mauritanian musicians is Malouma. She has created what is called the 'Saharan blues' and is to Mauritania what Cesária Évora is to Cabo Verde. One of the country's few other internationally known artists was Dimi Mint Abba, who passed away in 2011. Her 1990 album *Khalifa Ould Eide & Dimi Mint Abba: Moorish Music from Mauritania* (Eide was her husband) can be found online. Weddings, raucous and lively affairs, are the best venues to experience Mauritanian music in all its microtonal and often very loud glory. Otherwise, most taxi drivers are happy to pop in a cassette of their favourite tracks.

Environment

Mauritania is about twice the size of France. About 75%, including Nouakchott, is desert, with huge expanses of flat plains broken by occasional ridges, sand dunes and rocky plateaus, including the Adrar (about 500m high).

The highest peak is Kediet Ijill (915m) near Zouérat. Mauritania has some 700km of shoreline, including the Parc National du Banc d'Arguin, one of the world's major bird-breeding grounds and a Unesco World Heritage Site. The south is mostly flat scrubland.

Major environmental issues are the usual suspects of desertification, overgrazing and pollution. As drought, depleted soil fertility and dusty sandstorms diminish harvests, such as for dates in the Adrar, the rural exodus continues. Overfishing is another concern, with hundreds of tonnes of fish caught every day off the Mauritanian coastline.

SURVIVAL GUIDE

❶ Directory A–Z

ACCOMMODATION
There's an expanding number of high-end hotels catering to international business travellers in Nouakchott and, to a much lesser extent, Nouâdhibou and Atâr. In the desert, you'll find numerous basic *auberges* or *campements*. They consist of a series of *tikits* (stone huts) or *khaimas* (tents) that come equipped with mattresses on the floor.

DANGERS & ANNOYANCES
Mauritania is generally one of the safest countries in Africa, particularly the coastal region from Senegal to Morocco, but the previously popular tourist region of the Adrar was off-limits at time of writing for security reasons.

Other than petty theft, easily preventable through common-sense precautions, and somewhat chaotic driving patterns in Nouakchott, there's little to worry most travellers. In fact, and remarkably so compared to many other countries in the region, you're unlikely to attract any unwanted attention or be hassled when out and about. If anything, one's status as a foreigner and especially as a tourist will only elicit hospitality, warmth and kindness.

Travel Warnings
➡ US and European embassies caution against travel to large swaths of Mauritania, especially areas in the east. These will likely seem hyperbolic and unfair to Mauritanians and expats who know the country well. Of course, warnings should be taken very seriously, but these should be supplemented by up-to-date advice from locals in the area you intend to visit.

➡ Between late 2007 and 2011, there were a handful of incidents, mostly involving Al-Qaeda in the Islamic Maghreb. The popular Paris–Dakar rally was cancelled in 2008 because of threats against Mauritania by Islamist groups.

➡ Regional security threats, especially instability in neighbouring Mali, are concerns. Be sure to check the current security situation before travelling to border areas.

EMBASSIES & CONSULATES
The majority of embassies and consulates have locations in Nouakchott.

Canadian Consulate (☏ 222 4529 2697; www.canadainternational.gc.ca/morocco-maroc; Al Khayma city center, 3rd fl, Rue Mamadou Konaté)

French Embassy (☏ 222 4529 9699; www.ambafrance-mr.org; Rue Ahmed Ould Mohamed)

German Embassy (☏ 222 4529 4075; www.nouakchott.diplo.de; Rue Mamadou Konaté)

Malian Embassy (☏ 222 4525 4081; Ave du Palais des Congress)

Moroccan Embassy (☏ 222 2525 1411; Ave du Général de Gaulle)

Senegalese Embassy (☏ 222 4525 7290; Rue de l'Ambassade du Sénégal)

Spanish Embassy (☏ 222 4529 8650; www.exteriores.gob.es/embajadas/nouakchott; Rue Mamadou Konate)

US Embassy (☏ 222 4525 2660; cnr Autoroute Nouadhibou & Rue Ambassade du Sénégal)

EMERGENCY & IMPORTANT NUMBERS

Mauritania's country code	222
Police	17
Fire	18

FOOD

The desert cuisine of the Moors is rather unmemorable and lacks variety. Dishes are generally bland and limited to rice, mutton, goat, camel or dried fish. With negligible agriculture, fruit and vegetables are imported, and hard to find outside Nouakchott. Mauritanian couscous, similar to the Moroccan variety, is delicious. The cuisine of southern Mauritania, essentially Senegalese, has more variety, spices and even a few vegetables.

GAY & LESBIAN TRAVELLERS

Homosexuality is explicitly illegal in Mauritania. According to religious law, the maximum penalty is death if witnessed by four individuals. For what it's worth, however, there is little evidence of government-sponsored violence or discrimination. Regardless of the legality, Mauritanians are conservative in their attitudes towards gay and lesbian people. In most places, discretion is key and public displays of affection should be avoided, advice that applies to homosexual and heterosexual couples alike.

INTERNET ACCESS

You can get online in any reasonably sized town, although outside Nouakchott connection speeds can often be wanting. Expect to pay around UM200 an hour. Top-end and midrange hotels and many restaurants in Nouakchott and Nouâdhibou generally offer free wi-fi.

MONEY

The unit of currency is the ouguiya (UM). There are plenty of ATMs in Nouakchott and a handful in Nouâdhibou. It's best to take euros or US dollars as back-up.

Changing money Only crisp recently issued bills are accepted at bureax de change. Exchange rates at the Nouakchott airport aren't much different than those offered in town. Either way, it's quick and hassle-free with no commissions. Rates at top-end hotels are generally worse.

Credit cards Visa and MasterCard, but not Amex, are accepted at top-end hotels and larger businesses.

Tipping Leave a gratuity for hotel cleaning staff at your discretion. No tip is expected at basic restaurants; leave between 10% and 15% in more upmarket places. Loose change is appreciated by taxi drivers on short trips. For guides and drivres, tips are always expected;

ℹ️ SLEEPING PRICE RANGES

The following price ranges refer to a double room with bathroom.

$ less than UM18,000

$$ UM18,000–36,000

$$$ more than UM36,000

begin around 10%, more for multiday trips or if service has been particularly good.

Exchange Rates

Australia	A$1	UM271
Canada	C$1	UM263
Euro zone	€1	UM392
Japan	¥100	UM322
Morocco	MAD 1	UM36
New Zealand	NZ$1	UM285
Senegal	CFA100	UM60
UK	UK£1	UM464
US	US$1	UM359

For current exchange rates, see www.xe.com.

OPENING HOURS

Mauritania is a Muslim country, and for business purposes adheres to the Monday to Friday working week. Friday is the main prayer day, so many businesses have an extended lunch break on Friday afternoon. Many shops are open every day.

Government offices, post offices and banks are usually open 8am to 4pm Monday to Thursday and 8am to 1pm on Friday.

POST

The headquarters for Mauripost, the company that runs the country's postal service is in Nouakchott. Post is generally slow and unreliable.

PUBLIC HOLIDAYS

New Year's Day 1 January
National Reunification Day 26 February
Workers' Day 1 May

⚠️ WARNING

At the time of writing, travel to the Adrar region of Mauritania and Mauritania's border regions with Mali were considered dangerous. Check the local security situation before considering a trip here.

MAURITANIA DIRECTORY A–Z

ⓘ EATING PRICE RANGES

The following price ranges refer to a main course.

$ less than UM1800

$$ UM1800–3500

$$$ more than UM3500

African Liberation Day 25 May
Eid al-Fitr (end of Ramadan) 7 July
Armed Forces Day 10 July
Aid el-Adha (Feast of Sacrifice) 13 September
Islamic New Year 3 October
Independence Day 28 November

Mauritania also celebrates other Islamic holidays.

TELEPHONE

You can make international calls at post offices. The innumerable privately run phone shops in the major cities and towns cost about the same and are open late.

There are no telephone area codes.

A GSM SIM card for the Mauritel, Chinguitell or Mattel networks costs around UM2000 (a SIM with 3G runs around UM3000); a new phone with a pre-installed SIM card should run around UM20,000. Coverage is generally good and the best way of staying connected while travelling.

TOURIST INFORMATION

The official Ministry of Tourism has two offices, one at the airport in Nouakchott and another in Nouakchott proper, however neither is of much use. Even if open, they're unlikely to have good maps on hand.

ⓘ PRACTICALITIES

Electricity Current is 220V AC, 50Hz and most electrical plugs are of the European two-pin type.

Newspapers For the news (in French), pick up Le Calame or Horizons.

TV Mauritania has two state-owned TV stations (TVM and TVM2) with programs in Hassaniyya and French; the five privately owned stations are Elwatania, Chinguitty TV, Sahel TV, El-mourabitoune and Dava. Top-end hotels have satellite TV.

Weights & measures Mauritania uses the metric system.

VISAS

Visas are required for everyone, except nationals of Arab League countries and some African nations.

In countries where Mauritania has no diplomatic representation, including Australia, French embassies often issue visas.

However, visas (US$130) are also issued upon arrival at the airport in Nouakchott, as well as at border crossings from Senegal and Morocco. The process itself, which involves biometric fingerprinting and a photograph, is quick, however the wait can be long, both at the airport and land borders. For the former, de plane as quickly as possible, grab the form and fill it out while you're standing in line.

There's a rumour the visa fee will be reduced substantially in coming years.

One-month visa extensions can be obtained for UM46,000 at the **Sûreté** (222 4525 0017; off Ave Abdel Nasser; ⊘ 8am-3pm Mon-Thu) in Nouakchott.

Mali

One-month visas (UM6500) are issued within 24 hours at the embassy in Nouakchott. You need two photos and a passport photocopy.

Morocco

Most nationalities do not require visas, and simply get an entry stamp valid for 90 days on arrival. Nationalities that do (mostly Africans, including Mauritanians) must pay around UM9000 and provide two photos and passport photocopies and (according to whim) an air ticket.

Senegal

Americans, Australians, Canadians and Europeans do not need a visa to enter Senegal. Its helpful to have a photocopy of your Mauritanian visa page for officials on the Mauritanian side of the border.

WOMEN TRAVELLERS

Mauritania is a conservative Muslim country, but it is by no means the most extreme in this regard. Women might receive the odd bit of sexual harassment, but it's nothing in comparison with some North African countries. It's wise to dress modestly, covering the upper legs and arms and avoiding shorts or skimpy T-shirts.

ⓘ Getting There & Away

AIR

With its own national carrier and several international airlines flying to Nouakchott, Mauritania is relatively easily accessible by air. Gateways are Paris, Istanbul and Casablanca.

Opened in June 2016, the Nouakchott-Oumtosy International Airport handles most air traffic. It's 25km north of the city, essentially plopped in the middle of the desert. It's polished to a shine, if also mostly empty of facilities. There is a bureau de change and a tourist office with brochures and country maps. Nouâdhibou and Atâr also have small international airports.

LAND
Mali

At the time of writing, the border crossings between Mauritania and Mali were considered off-limits due to the dangerous security situation in the area.

Morocco

The trans-Sahara route via Mauritania was once, now less so, a very popular route from North Africa into sub-Saharan Africa. This crosses the internationally disputed territory of Western Sahara, although the border itself is administered by Morocco.

The only border crossing between Morocco/Western Sahara and Mauritania is north of Nouâdhibou. Crossing this border is straightforward, though the process can be painfully slow, and the road is entirely tarred to Nouakchott, except for the 3km no-man's land that separates the two border posts. Note, generally motorcycles are allowed to skip to the head of the car line.

There are direct bush taxis heading north from Nouâdhibou to Dakhla (Western Sahara), but travelling in the opposite direction you'll need to change vehicles at the border. The 425km trip can easily be accomplished in a long day.

Senegal

The main border crossing for Senegal is at Rosso (by ferry), but it's also possible to cross by the bridge over a dam at Diamma (Keur Masséne), west of Rosso. The latter is a much calmer and overall prefererable experience, but is only for the dry season.

From Dakar to Nouakchott by public transport usually takes from 11 to 13 hours. At Rosso, most travellers without vehicles cross by pirogue (UM200/CFA500, five minutes) as the ferry crosses only four times daily (free for foot traffic). The border is open from 8.30am to noon and 3pm to 6pm.

Vehicles cost CFA5000. Customs fees are around UM1500 if you're entering Mauritania, CFA2000 for Senegal; keep your paperwork (and vehicle) in good order.

 ARRIVING IN MAURITANIA

Nouakchott-Oumtosy International Airport Best to arrange pick-up in advance; via your accommodation is easiest. By the time you're through the potentially long line for visas, taxis are often gone and the parking lot mostly vacant. Otherwise, a few taxis are available for arriving passengers.

Nouâdhibou International Airport Few taxis await arriving flights. You can flag one down on the street.

Getting Around

AIR

Mauritania Airlines flies daily (except Wednesday) between Nouakchott and Nouâdhibou (UM31,000, 45 minutes), and twice a week via Zouérat (UM39,000, three hours). Tickets can be purchased at the airline's office (p266) in Nouakchott or most travel agencies.

CAR & MOTORCYCLE

Mauritania's primary road network is mostly good, with tarred roads leading from the border with Western Sahara to Nouakchott, and on to the Senegalese and Malian borders at Rosso and Nioro respectively. Police checkpoints abound.

MINIBUS & BUSH TAXI

Minibus routes stitch together the main towns and cities linked by tarmac roads. Where tarmac is replaced by *piste,* the bush taxi *(taxi brousse)* – often Mercedes 190s and Peugeot 504s – take over, along with pick-up trucks for the rougher routes.

With long stretches of nothingness, including the route between Nouakchott and Nouâdhibou, basic, gritty rest stops feel like revelations of civilisation. Some, including the petrol station between the two major cities, offer food, including camel sandwiches (UM600).

TRAIN

The Nouâdhibou–Zouérat train is certainly an epic adventure when the security situation permits, and it is a masochists' dream. It's an iron-ore train with no passenger terminals, but it's become a passenger train for lack of better alternatives. The trip takes 16 to 18 hours, but most travellers get off at Choûm (close to Atâr), 12 hours from Nouâdhibou.

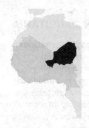

Niger

227 / POP 17.8 MILLION

Includes ➡

Fast Facts

➡ **Area** 1,267,000 sq km

➡ **Capital** Niamey

➡ **Currency** West African franc (CFA)

➡ **Languages Spoken** French, Hausa, Djerma, Fulfulde, Tamashek

Introduction

Niger rarely makes waves in the international consciousness, and when it does it's invariably for all the wrong reasons: coups, rebellions and famines. But those who have been lucky enough to visit this desert republic normally return with stories of a warm and generous population living in ancient caravan cities at the edge of the Sahara.

In the north, the stark splendour of the Aïr Mountains hides Neolithic rock art and stunning oasis towns. Within the expansive dunes of the Ténéré Desert are dinosaur graveyards and deserted medieval settlements, while to the south is the ancient trans-Saharan trade-route town of Agadez and the sultanate of Zinder.

As good as it all could be, though, the current security situation means that Niger is still largely off limits to travellers. Attacks against foreigners have occurred across the Sahel, and the threat of kidnapping remains high.

Top Sights

➡ **Agadez** A spiky summit of a majestic mud mosque overlooking town and the Sahara

➡ **Kouré** West Africa's last wild herd of giraffes.

➡ **Zinder** The sultan's palace within the fascinating Birni Quartier of this Hausa city tells of a brutal history.

➡ **Parc Regional du W** Home to lions, crocodiles, monkeys and elephants.

➡ **Ténéré Desert** A sublime section of the mighty Sahara.

➡ **Aïr Mountains** Where camel caravans plod through red sands and past mystical blue rocks.

Niger

UNDERSTAND NIGER

Niger Today

A series of unpleasant events have defined Niger to the outside world in recent years. In 2007 the Tuareg in the north of the country began a rebellion against Niger's government, whom it accused of hoarding proceeds from the region's enormous mineral wealth and failing to meet conditions of previous ceasefires, in a conflict that has reignited at regular intervals since the early 20th century.

A year later Niger again made headlines around the world for less-than-positive reasons when in a landmark case an Economic Community of West African States (Ecowas) court found Niger guilty of failing to protect a young woman from the continued practice of slavery in the country. According to anti-slavery organisations, thousands of people still live in subjugation. In 2014 a man was sentenced to four years in jail on a conviction of slavery. The first such prosecution of its kind.

There have been several high-profile terrorist attacks and kidnappings of tourists and foreign workers over the past few years by groups linked to Al-Qaeda factions operating in the Sahel and Sahara zone. The largest such attack was a coordinated assault by Islamic militants on military and mining sites in the north of the country in 2013. The Islamist takeover of northern Mali in 2012 created a security vacuum and opened up a safe haven for extremists and organised crime groups in the Sahara Desert. But even though terrorist attacks were on the rise in Niger, tens of thousands of refugees flooded into the country from neighbouring conflict zones.

Niger's economy continues to putter and struggle along. The country's main export, uranium, is prone to price fluctuations, and the industry has been hurt by the threat of terrorism and kidnapping. Niger began producing and refining oil in 2011 following a US$5 billion joint-venture deal with China.

In March 2016 Mahamadou Issoufou was re-elected president in a run-off election that was boycotted by opponents.

History

Before the Sahara started swallowing Niger around 2500 BC, it supported verdant grasslands, abundant wildlife and populations thriving on hunting and herding. Long after the desert pushed those populations southward, Niger became a fixture on the trans-Saharan trade route. Between the 10th and 18th centuries, West African empires, such as the Kanem-Borno, Mali and Songhaï, flourished in Niger, trafficking gold, salt and slaves.

Colonial Period

The French strolled in late in the 1800s and met stronger-than-expected resistance. Decidedly unamused, they dispatched the punitive Voulet-Chanoîne expedition, destroying much of southern Niger in 1898–99. Although Tuareg revolts continued, culminating in Agadez's siege in 1916–17, the French had control.

French rule wasn't kind. They cultivated the power of traditional chiefs, whose abuses were encouraged as a means of control, and the enforced shift from subsistence farming to high-density cash crops compounded the Sahara's ongoing migration.

In 1958 France offered its West African colonies self-government in a French union or immediate independence. Countless votes disappeared in the ensuing referendum, enabling France to claim that Niger wished to remain within its sphere of influence.

Independence & Uranium

Maintaining close French ties, Niger's first president, Hamani Diori, ran a repressive one-party state. After surviving several coups, he was overthrown by Lieutenant Colonel Seyni Kountché after food stocks were discovered in ministerial homes during the Sahel drought of 1968–74. Kountché established a military ruling council.

Kountché hit the jackpot in 1968 when uranium was discovered near the town of Arlit. Mining incomes soon ballooned, leading to ambitious projects, including the 'uranium highway' between Agadez and Arlit. Yet not everyone was smiling: inflation skyrocketed and the poorest suffered more than ever.

The 1980s were unkind to all: uranium prices collapsed, the great 1983 drought killed thousands, and one-party politics hindered democracy. By the 1990s, Nigeriens were aware of political changes sweeping West Africa. Mass demonstrations erupted, eventually forcing the government into multiparty elections in 1993. However, a military junta overthrew the elected president, Mahamane Ousmane, in 1996.

Democracy?

In 1999, during widespread strikes and economic stagnation, president Mainassara (a 1996 coup leader) was assassinated and democracy re-established. Peaceful elections in 1999 and 2004 witnessed victory for Mamadou Tandja.

In 2009 Mamadou Tandja won a referendum allowing him to change the constitution to allow him to run for a third term. In the presidential elections that year Tandja won by a large margin, though the Economic Community of West African States (Ecowas) did not accept the result and suspended Niger's membership. The tables were turned on Tandja in February 2010 when a military coup in Niamey led to his arrest. A year-long military junta ended when veteran opposition leader Mahamadou Issoufou was declared winner of a presidential poll in March 2011.

Culture

Niger boasts the highest birth rate in the world: in 2015 it was estimated that women have a staggering average of just under seven children each. The population is predicted to reach 21.4 million by 2025.

More than 90% of Nigeriens live in the south, which is dominated by Hausa and Songhaï-Djerma, making up 53% and 21% of Niger's populace respectively. The next largest groups are nomadic Tuareg (11%) and Fulani (6.5%), both in Niger's north, and Kanuri (5.9%), who are located between Zinder and Chad.

Nigeriens are predominantly Muslim (over 80%), with small percentages of Christian urban dwellers. Several rural populations still practise traditional animist religions. Due to the strong influence of Nigeria's Islamic community, some Muslims around the border town of Maradi call for sharia law.

Despite most Nigeriens being devoutly Muslim, the government is steadfastly secular and Islam adopts a more relaxed aura than in nations with similar demographics. Women don't cover their faces, alcohol is quietly consumed and some Tuareg, recognising the harshness of desert life, ignore Ramadan's fast.

While Islam plays an important role in daily life, shaping beliefs and thoughts, little is visible to visitors. The biggest exceptions are *salat* (prayer), when Niger grinds to a halt – buses even break journeys to partake.

Religion aside, survival occupies most people's days. Around 90% make their tenuous living from agriculture and livestock, many surviving on US$1 or less per day. Producing numerous children to help with gruelling workloads is a necessity for many, a fact contributing to population growth. The need for children to work has led to staggering adult illiteracy rates.

Niger's best-known artisans are Tuareg silversmiths, who produce necklaces, striking amulets, ornamental silver daggers and stylised silver crosses, each with intricate filigree designs representing areas boasting Tuareg populations. The most famous cross is the *croix d'Agadez*. To Tuareg, crosses are powerful talismans protecting against ill fortune.

Leatherwork by *artisans du cuir* is well regarded, particularly in Zinder, where traditional items – such as saddlebags, cushions and tasselled pouches – rank alongside attractive modernities like sandals and briefcases.

Beautifully unique to Niger are vibrant *kountas* (Djerma blankets), produced from bright cotton strips.

Environment

Three quarters of Niger is desert, with the Sahara advancing south 10km a year. The remaining quarter is Sahel, the semi-desert zone south of the Sahara. Notable features include the Niger River (Africa's third-longest), which flows 300km through Niger's southwest; the Aïr Mountains, the dark volcanic formations of which rise over 2000m; and the Ténéré Desert's spectacularly sweeping sand dunes.

Desertification, Niger's greatest environmental problem, is primarily caused by overgrazing and deforestation. Quartz-rich soil also prevents topsoil anchoring, causing erosion.

The southwest's dry savannah woodland hosts one of West Africa's better wildlife parks, Parc Regional du W (although many governments have marked the Niger section of this trans-frontier park as unsafe to visit).

SURVIVAL GUIDE

ℹ Directory A–Z

DANGERS & ANNOYANCES
Niger has never had a reputation as a safe and easy place to travel, but today the situation is worse than normal.

Almost every Western government advises against all travel to virtually the entire country. The only exception is for travel to Niamey and a narrow band across the south, and even then most governments advise against all but essential travel.

➡ Check the situation carefully before travelling to Niger.

➡ Avoid demonstrations and areas popular with foreign residents.

➡ Do not travel anywhere after dark.

➡ Carry your passport with you at all times.

➡ Do not photograph police, military or sensitive sites.

VISAS
Should you decide to ignore the advice of most governments and go to Niger anyway, the good news is that tourist visas are not overly hard to come by.

➡ Visas are available in most neighbouring countries.

➡ Allow up to two weeks for a visa to be issued.

➡ Outside West Africa, Niger embassies are few and far between.

Nigeria

🔊 234 / POP 186 MILLION

Best Places to Eat

➡ Terra Kulture (p279)

➡ Bogobiri House (p279)

➡ Indigo (p283)

➡ Purple at the Blowfish (p282)

Best Places to Sleep

➡ Bogobiri House (p279)

➡ Nike Ambassador Guest House (p290)

➡ Wheatbaker (p282)

➡ Nordic Villa (p292)

Why Go?

Nigeria is a pulsating powerhouse: as the most populous nation on the continent – nearly every fifth African is Nigerian – it dominates the region. Recently, though, the boom has shown a few signs of bust: the economy has been hit by the drop in crude oil prices. But Lagos, the main city, is resurgent: with burgeoning tech industries, posh restaurants and clubs, and an exploding arts scene, this megacity is the face of modern Africa.

Outside Gidi (as Lagosians call their city), you may feel as if you're a lone explorer getting a glimpse of the raw edges of the world, immersing yourself in deep and layered cultures. From Yoruba shrines to the slave ports, from the ancient Muslim cities of the north (currently out of bounds for security reasons) to the river deltas, and among stunning natural environments – there are plenty of wonderful antidotes to a sometimes exhausting journey.

When to Go
Lagos

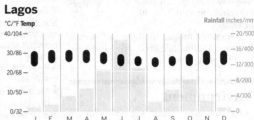

Nov–Feb Dry season; many events, such as carnival in Calaba and Felebration in Lagos.

Apr–Sep Rainy season; heavy rainfall particlary in the south

Mar & Oct Shoulder season; some rain in the south but dry in the north.

LAGOS

📄 01 / POP 21 MILLION

The economic and cultural powerhouse of the country thanks to an influx of oil money, Lagos has an exploding arts and music scene that will keep your *yansh* engaged far past dawn. If you're headed to Nigeria, you'll have no choice but to jump right in.

As well as brilliantly buoyant culture, Lagos has bumper-to-bumper cars, noise and pollution beyond belief, a high crime rate, and maxed-out public utilities. Elevated motorways ringing the island city are jammed with speed freaks and absurd traffic jams ('go-slows') on top, and tin-and-cardboard shacks underneath. It's a divided city, but an undeniably exciting one.

Named after the Portuguese word for lagoon, Lagos has been a Yoruba port, a British political centre and, until 1991, Nigeria's capital.

⊙ Sights

On Lagos Island look out for examples of old Brazilian architecture in the distinctive houses built by former slaves and their descendants who returned from Brazil.

★ **Terra Kulture**   GALLERY
(Map p286; www.terrakulture.com; Plot 1376 Tiamiyu Savage St, VI) FREE Close to Bar Beach, this welcoming arts centre with a high bamboo roof has a traditional restaurant which is one of the best and most attractive places to eat in town: try the catfish with pounded yam and spicy soup. There's an art gallery, a bookshop with funky crafts, literary readings and events, and a theatre.

★ **Nike Art Gallery**   GALLERY
(📞 0803 4096 656; www.nikeart.com; 3rd Roundabout, Epe Expressway, Lekki; ⊙ 10am-6pm) FREE One of Nigeria's most important artists, Nike Okundaye, runs this enormous gallery full of contemporary and traditional Nigerian arts. Nike herself is like an incarnation of love and beauty, which is reflected in this astonishing four-storey space. If you're lucky she'll be there and may grace you with a new Yoruba name. There's a small cafe in the grounds.

★ **Lekki**
Conservation Centre   WILDLIFE RESERVE
(📞 01 264 2498; www.ncfnigeria.org; Km 19, Lagos-Epe Expressway; N1000; ⊙ 8.30am-5pm Mon-Sat, 8.30am-noon Sun; 🚌 flag down a bus on VI along Maroko Rd) FREE Run by the Nigerian Conservation Foundation, this centre has a huge tract of wetlands set aside for wildlife

viewing. Canopy walkways enable you to see monkeys, crocodiles and various birds; early morning is the best time to visit. There is a conservation centre and a library.

★ **Kalakuta Republic Museum**   MUSEUM
(Map p282; 7 Gbemisola St, Ikeja; N500; ⊙ 10am-5pm) Legendary musician Fela Kuti's former house and revolutionary headquarters is now a fascinating museum with everything intact from Fela's bedroom to his (very small) underwear. Breath deep and you may even catch a high. And hang around on the rooftop terrace and you might catch a band rehearsal or performance.

★ **Lekki Market**   MARKET
(Elegushi Market; off Epe Expressway, Lekki) A rich variety of crafts from all around Nigeria and West Africa: this is a brilliant place to wander and look for affordable gifts. You can also buy fabrics and get clothes run up on the spot here.

African Artists' Foundation   GALLERY
(Map p286; www.africanartists.org; 3b Isiola Oyekan Close, VI; ⊙ 10am-5pm Mon-Fri, noon-4pm Sat) FREE An organisation supporting young African and international artists with a great gallery of contemporary Nigerian art.

🛏 Sleeping

Peerage Retreat   HOTEL $
(Map p286; 📞 805 633 2902; peerageretreat@yahoo.com; 1 Olabode George St, VI; r N10,000; ❄) The best option for the money on the island, this family-run hotel is clean, friendly and well run. Given the deal, it fills up fast. Just make sure the electricity is working.

Ritz Hotel   HOTEL $
(Map p284; 📞 01 263 0481; King George V Rd; r with fan & without bathroom N2000, with air-con N2900-4000; ❄) The name's a bit of a misnomer, but this hotel is a reasonably decent budget option. Rooms are fine in a grubby 'by the hour' sort of way, but they're secure and management is friendly.

Hotel Victoria Palace   HOTEL $$
(Map p286; 📞 01 262 5901; victoriapalace@gmail.com; 1623 Sake Jojo St; r N14,000; 🅿❄) Basic rooms and friendly staff; a good budget-ish choice on Victoria Island.

★ **Bogobiri House**   BOUTIQUE HOTEL $$$
(Map p286; 📞 706 817 6454; www.bogobiri.com; 9 Maitama Sule St, Ikoyi; r from N50,000; ❄@📶) This charming boutique hotel, beautifully decorated with paintings and sculptures by local artists, serves as the hub of the vibrant

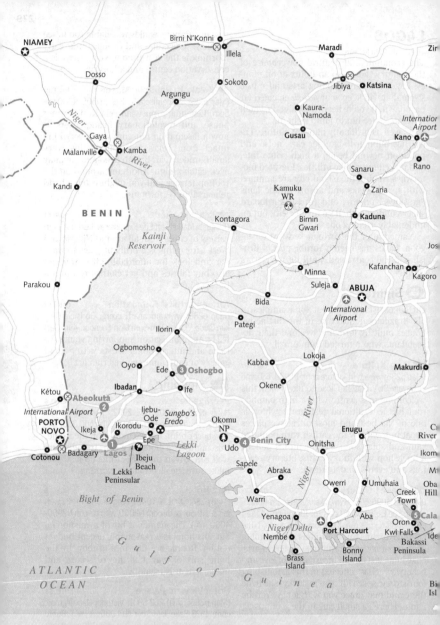

Nigeria Highlights

1 Lagos (p279) Joining the gold rush of the country's super-confident boom city, and exploring its insatiably lively art and music scene.

2 Abeokuta (p288) Climbing the sacred rock via historic hideouts and shrines, and looking out on the picturesque rooftops from a high vantage point.

3 Oshogbo (p289) Learning about traditional crafts, browsing the impressive galleries and losing yourself on the river bank in the sacred grove.

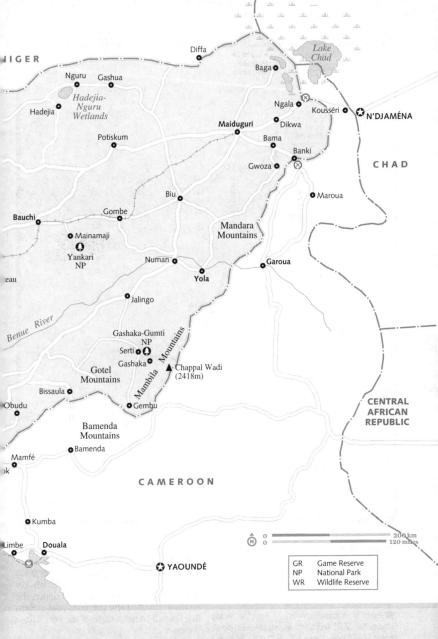

NIGER

Diffa

Lake Chad

Baga

Nguru   Gashua

Hadejia-Nguru Wetlands

Hadejia

Ngala   Kousséri

N'DJAMÉNA

Potiskum

Maiduguri   Dikwa

Bama

Banki

CHAD

Gwoza

Biu

Maroua

Bauchi   Gombe

Mainamaji

Mandara Mountains

Yankari NP

Numan   Garoua

Yola

Jalingo

...eau

Benue River

Gashaka-Gumti NP

Serti   Gotel Mountains

Gashaka

Chappal Wadi (2418m)

CENTRAL AFRICAN REPUBLIC

Bissaula

Obudu   Gembu

Bamenda Mountains

Mamfé   Bamenda

...ok

CAMEROON

Kumba

0   200 km
0   120 miles

Limbe   **Douala**

YAOUNDÉ

GR	Game Reserve
NP	National Park
WR	Wildlife Reserve

④ **Benin City** (p290) Wandering the Brass Casters St, governed by a secret ancient guild, and catching a flavour of the former glory of the marvellous Benin empire.

⑤ **Calabar** (p291) Taking in colonial history and cutting-edge conservation in the easygoing old river port.

Lagos

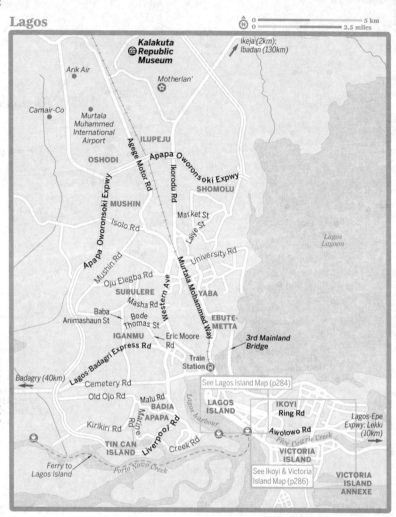

See Lagos Island Map (p284)

See Ikoyi & Victoria Island Map (p286)

NIGERIA LAGOS

art and cultural scene. The rooms are decorated by different local artists. The restaurant has some of the best Nigerian favourites in the city, and there is often excellent live music.

★ **Purple at the Blowfish**   HOTEL **$$$**
(Map p286; ☎ 01 463 1298; www.theblowfishhotel.com; 17 Oju Olobun Close, VI; r N30,000; ❄🛜🏊)
Not only a great boutique hotel with classy and comfortable rooms, the Blowfish's restaurant Purple offers nice dining by the pool with Indian, Italian Thai, Lebanese and continental menus.

Wheatbaker   BOUTIQUE HOTEL **$$$**
(Map p286; ☎ 01 277 3560; www.legacyhotels.com; 4 Onitolo Rd, Ikoyi; r from N90,000; 🅿❄@🛜🏊)
A luxury boutique hotel, the Wheatbaker ranks at the absolute top. Experience the secluded grounds and gorgeous pool at Sunday brunch to get a taste of the elite Lagos lifestyle.

✗ Eating

Broad St and Campbell St in Lagos Island are good for chop houses and *suya* (Nigerian kebab); the better restaurants are in Ikoyi and Victoria Island. Some of the best places to eat are attached to hotels and cultural centres, such as Bogobiri House, Terra Kulture and Purple at the Blowfish. There are cheap eats at the Bar Beach market.

Sherlaton INDIAN $
(Map p286; 01 269 1275; 108 Awolowo Rd; mains less than N1500; noon-3pm & 7-10pm;) Vegetarians suffer a lot in Nigeria, but this Indian restaurant really comes to the rescue. The Sherlaton is generally considered to be the city's best curry option.

Ikoyi Hotel Suya AFRICAN $
(Map p286; Kingsway Rd, Ikoyi Hotel, Ikoyi; suya from N100; 10am-10pm) Lagosians claim the best *suya* in town can be found at the stall outside the Ikoyi Hotel. Not just beef and goat, but chicken, liver and kidney, plus some great fiery *pepe* (pepper) to spice it all up.

★**Indigo** INDIAN $$
(Map p286; 0805 235 9793; www.indigolagos.com; 242b Muri Okunola St; mains N1800; noon-midnight;) Subtly flavoured Indian food served in a refined atmosphere. There's a picture window onto the traditional clay oven, where fresh bread is baked at high speed. Lots of choice for vegetarians.

Pizze-Riah PIZZA $$
(Map p286; 13 Musa Yardua St, VI; pizzas N1500; noon-11pm) Brick-oven pizza in a lovely outdoor setting, with a play area for kids.

Cactus BAKERY $$
(Map p286; Maroko Rd; mains from N1200; 8am-10pm) This place labels itself primarily as a patisserie, but it also serves up proper meals throughout the day. Breakfasts of pancakes or bacon are good, as are the pizzas, and the club sandwiches with salad and chips are simply huge – excellent value at N1800. Giant fresh juices cost N1200.

Art Cafe CAFE $$
(Map p286; www.thehomestoresng.com/artcafe; 282 Akin Olugbede St, VI; suya/mains N700/4000; 7.30am-11pm;) A lovely little cafe-pub which also sells arts and crafts. It does good coffee and snacks, and the laid-back arty vibe is a nice contrast to the bland feel of parts of Victoria Island.

Yellow Chilli AFRICAN $$
(Map p286; 01 280 6876; www.yellowchilling. com; 27 Oju Olubun Close, VI; mains N1500-2500; noon-midnight;) Well-presented Nigerian dishes in swish surroundings. It's carried off well, with tasty dishes in reasonable portions and good service – a great way to eat your way around the country without leaving your table.

Drinking & Nightlife

As they say in Lagos, what happens in Gidi stays in Gidi. In other words, Lagos' nightlife is legendary. Be prepared to stay up past dawn. Note that what's hot is constantly changing, and that you have to dig beneath the bling to find the city's earthier venues.

Ask around for the best nights out or check out www.nothingtodoinlagos.com. Bars are best up until midnight, when the clubs and music venues heat up.

★**Bogobiri II/Nimbus** BAR
(Map p286; 706 817 6454; www.bogobiri.com; Maitama Sule St, Ikoyi; 8am-11pm) Part of Bogobiri House, this is a lovely place for a drink (and eat) – mellow in the day and happening at night. There's an attached art gallery with works from local artists, and at weekends

---

FELA KUTI: MUSIC IS THE WEAPON

The impact of Fela Anikulapo Kuti's music in Nigeria, and worldwide, cannot be overstated. Fela Kuti (1938–97) is Africa's musical genius, the creator of Afrobeat – a genre combining traditional African highlife, jazz, James Brown funk grooves and Latin rhythms into a unique mix that is wholly his own – and a revolutionary. Fela's politically inflammatory songs laid bare the corruption, violence and greed of the ruling regimes in his country and beyond. He was arrested over a hundred times by the Nigerian government, and ultimately 1000 soldiers invaded and destroyed the Kalakuta Republic – Fela's living and performing compound that he shared with his 27 wives – sending nearly all of the inhabitants to the hospital, or worse. Despite the death of his own mother due to the siege, Fela never stopped fighting the powers of imperialism, colonialism, conformity and racism with – as the legend himself put it – music as his weapon. Due to the re-release of his music worldwide and, interestingly, a Broadway musical based on his life, Fela's legacy is enjoying renewed attention and a reinvigorated profile in Nigeria. The Lagos government even donated money to launch the Kalakuta Republic Museum (p279), and Felabration is celebrated for a week each year around his birthday on 15 October.

Lagos Island

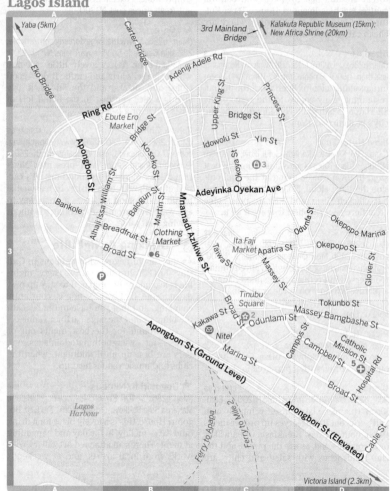

there's live music. At the open mic night on a Thursday you'll hear some astonishing young musicians.

Elegushi Beach BAR
Dancing bumper-to-bumper, bottles of the hard stuff – the party does not get better than Elegushi Beach on a Sunday night. Go with a local; there have been robberies. Not for the faint of heart. During the day, pay a fee (N1000) to enjoy the semi-private beach.

Vapours BAR
(Map p286; 879 Samuel Manuwa St, VI; ⊙10pm-6am) Starts late, gets good even later. Nigeria's elites, socialites and pop stars come here for the post-party partying. If you get the munchies, head across the street, outside the gate of 1004 Housing Estates, to Chopbox; it's always open.

☆ Entertainment

★ **New Afrika Shrine** LIVE MUSIC
(Adeleye St, Ikeja; cover charge N500; ⊙6pm-1am Thu-Sun) Just by showing up you'll get a political education, a lesson in shakin' it and a contact high. Though Fela's original Shrine was burnt down, this replacement run by his children is the best show in town. Femi

Motherlan'   LIVE MUSIC
(Map p282; ☑ 802 067 8899; 64b Opebi Rd, Ike-ja; N1000; ⊙ Thu-Sun) Owned by renowned mask-wearing musician Lagbaja, this is a big outdoor venue with lots of live music and a robust local following.

🛍 Shopping

★ **Jazz Hole**   BOOKS
(Map p286; www.glendorabooks.net; 168 Awolowo Road, Ikoyi; ⊙ 10am-8pm Mon-Sat, 4-8pm Sun) An offspring of the great Glendora Books, Jazz Hole is primarily a book and record store. In this oasis of calm in the mile-a-minute city, sip tea in the lovely cafe and get cultural lessons from the proprietor – ask to see his own book about Abeokuta. Special events and performances in the evenings.

★ **Quintessence**   ARTS & CRAFTS
(Map p286; ☑ 803 327 5401; www.quintessenceltd. com; Plot 13, Block 44, Parkview Estate, off Gerrard Rd; ⊙ 8am-5pm Mon-Fri, 9am-4pm Sat & Sun) Out in the gated Parkview estate, Quintessence sells artworks and crafts, with an especially good selection of clothes and some antique carvings and artefacts. Some of the colourful and original garments are made here, and there are lovely embroidered Senegalese dresses.

Jankara Market   MARKET
(Map p284; off Adeyinka Oyekan Ave; ⊙ 8am-6pm) Jankara Market is the largest market in Lagos and sells everything from tie-dyed cloth, trade beads and jewellery to pirate cassettes, pottery and clothing. There is also a fetishes market where you can buy herbs, traditional medicines and *juju* potions and powders.

Kuti plays on Thursdays (free) and Sundays. Fela's most approximate reincarnation Seun Kuti plays the last Saturday of the month.

Freedom Park   LIVE MUSIC
(Map p284; www.freedomparklagos.com; Old Prison Ground, Broad St, Lagos Island) Formerly the Old Broad Street Prison, a colonial-era instrument of oppression, it has recently been turned into a cultural centere, venue for events and concerts, a museum, a food court and a market. Some of the old prison structures are still standing.

NIGERIA LAGOS

Ikoyi & Victoria Island

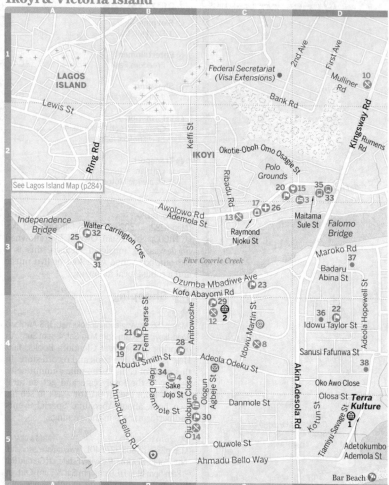

ℹ️ Information

DANGERS & ANNOYANCES

Contrary to popular perception, violent crime has decreased in recent years. Most crime against foreigners targets expats in expensive cars, and travellers are unlikely to encounter any serious problems. Still, never carry more money than is necessary and avoid flaunting valuables and walking outside at night – particularly around hotels and restaurants frequented by foreigners.

INTERNET ACCESS

Internet cafes are everywhere and cost upwards from N200 per hour. Most upscale restaurants and cafes also have wi-fi.

Bogobiri House Have lunch here for a fast connection.

Cafe Royale (Map p286; http://royalteas.com.ng/cafe-royal; No 267A, Etim Inyang Cres, VI; ⏱7am-10pm; 📶) Satisfy your sweet tooth and wireless needs at this bakery-restaurant.

Mega Plaza Internet (Map p286; Idowu Martin St, Mega Plaza; ⏱10am-6pm)

Ikoyi & Victoria Island

◎ Top Sights

◎ Sights

🛏 Sleeping

✕ Eating

🍷 Drinking & Nightlife

🛍 Shopping

ⓘ Information

ⓘ Transport

MEDICAL SERVICES

Healthplus Integrative Pharmacy (Map p286; ☏ 0802 802 5810; Unit 54, The Palms Shopping Centre, Lekki; ⊗ 8am-9pm Mon-Sat, 10am-9pm Sun) With branches in Ikeja, Yabo and the airport.

St Nicholas Hospital (Map p284; ☏ 0802 290 8484; www.saintnicholashospital.com; 57 Campbell St) Has a 24-hour emergency clinic.

MONEY

Find exchange bureaus at Alade Market on the mainland, or outside Federal Palace and Eko Meridien hotels on Victoria Island.

POST

Main Post Office (Map p284; Marina St; ⊗ 8am-4pm Mon-Sat)

Post Office (Map p286; Adeola Odeku St, VI; ⊗ 8am-4pm Mon-Sat)

> ℹ️ **ARRIVING IN LAGOS**
>
> **Murtala Muhammed International Airport** Take a licensed taxi to your accommodation; these will be waiting to meet incoming flights. Ask the fee before getting in (30 minutes to one hour depending on traffic; around N6000).

ℹ️ Getting There & Away

Murtala Muhammed International Airport (MMA1; p297) is the main gateway to Nigeria and is roughly 10km north of Lagos Island. The domestic terminal (MMA2) is 4km away; tickets can be bought on departure or from an agent. Though there are airline offices at the airport and in Lagos, it's best to use a travel agency that can sort your flights all-in-one.

Ojota Motor Park (with Ojota New Motor Park next door), 13km north of Lagos, is the city's main transport hub. Minibuses and bush taxis leaving to all destinations depart from here. Sample fares are Benin City (N3000, four hours), Ibadan (N1000, two hours), Oshogbo (N2500, three hours) and Abuja (N5000, 10 hours).

Mile-2 Motor Park serves destinations east of Lagos, including the Benin border at Seme (N800, 90 minutes). You'll also find a few minibuses going as far north as Ibadan from here.

ABC Transport (Map p286; ☑ 01 740 1010; www.abctransport.com) is a good intercity 'luxury' bus company, serving many major cities, as well as destinations in Benin, Ghana and Togo. The depot is at Jibowu motor park, but there's a useful **booking office** (Map p286; ☑ 01 740 1010; Awolowo Rd, Block D, Falomo Shopping Centre) inside a shoe shop at Falomo Shopping Centre.

The following airlines fly in and out of Lagos:
Air France (Map p286; ☑ 01 461 0777; www.airfrance.com; Idejo Danmole St)

Arik Air (Map p282; ☑ 01 279 9999; www.arikair.com; Lagos Murtala Muhammed International Airport)

Camair-Co (Map p282; ☑ 01 291 2025; www.camair-co.cm; Murtala Muhammed International Airport)

Ethiopian Airlines (Map p286; ☑ 01 461 1869; www.ethiopianairlines.com; 3 Idowu Tayor St, Victoria Island)

Kenya Airways (Map p286; ☑ 01 271 9433; www.kenya-airways.com; Badaru Abina St, Churchgate Tower)

KLM (Map p286; ☑ 0703 415 3801; www.klm.com; 1 Adeola Odeku St, Sapetro, VI)

Lufthansa (Map p284; ☑ 01 461 2222; www.lufthansa.com; Churchgate Tower, VI)

South African Airlines (Map p286; ☑ 01 270 0712; www.flysaa.com; 28c Adetukonbo Ademola St, VI)

ℹ️ Getting Around

Traffic in Lagos is legendary, and it's not getting any better – especially with occasional governmental edicts outlawing *okada*, small (and sometimes unsafe) motorcycles that are your best best for skirting the 'go-slow'.

A taxi costs from N4000 to reach Lagos Island. Always allow way more time than you think to get to the airport when catching a flight. There are no airport buses.

Arriving in Lagos can be complicated and you may be dropped at one of several motor parks – Oshodi, Yaba and Oju Elegba Junction are the likeliest candidates. Minibuses run from these to more central points, such as **Obalende Motor Park** (Map p284) on Lagos Island.

Yellow minibuses (*danfos*; fares N70 to N250 according to distance) serve points all over Lagos – prices increase when you cross a bridge from one part of Lagos to another. Yellow private taxis start at N500.

Keke napep (motorised tricycles that can carry three passengers) are useful for short-distance travel and have replaced the services previously provided by *okada*. Fares from N100.

A decent, cheap option to avoid traffic, the official city Bus Rapid Transit (BRT) buses have routes that stretch from Lagos Island to the mainland. Buy tickets (N70 to N150) at terminals scattered around Lagos. Boarding may require waiting in long queues.

SOUTHERN NIGERIA

Abeokuta

POP 494,700 / ☑ 35

Abeokuta is a remarkable place, backed by the huge Olumo Rock. Grand but dishevelled Brazilian and Cuban mansions built by returned slaves sit alongside basic shacks with hand-painted signs, historic mosques and churches and the rounded mass of the rocks, creating an unforgettable streetscape.

Abeokuta has its own very strong cultural identity, well known as the birthplace of many famous Nigerians, notably Afrobeat legend Fela Kuti and writer Wole Soyinka, whose autobiography, *Aké*, is a vivid depiction of a childhood spent here.

It's a poor town, unused to visitors except those visiting the rock, and while wandering around is fascinating, you'll feel conspicuous.

☉ Sights

Olumo Rock   SHRINE

(off Ijemo Rd; N2500, guide from N1000) The founding site of Abeokuta, famed Olumo Rock has a rich history and great spiritual significance. Hire a guide and climb the rock – at one point it is smooth and quite steep, so go via the steps if you're not confident. You'll see shrines, sacred trees, tribal wartime hideouts, and ultimately, at the top, an astonishing view of the city.

🛏 Sleeping

Most people visit Abeokuta on a day trip from Lagos: accommodation is limited, but the Quarry Imperial Hotel is friendly and comfortable enough, as long as the electricity is functioning.

Quarry Imperial Hotel   HOTEL $

(☑811 358 6172; www.quarryimperialhotels. com; 52 Quarry Rd; r N10,100-57,100; ❀🛜🌊) A grandly named place, built on a weirdly large scale. It's often almost empty, and staff will be delighted to see you. Rooms are large and fairly comfortable, the restaurant is decent and there's even a pool. The electricity and water supplies come and go. Take a motorbike or taxi to the rock.

🍴 Eating

You'll find cheap eating joints throughout the town, and vendors sell snacks around the rock. There's a basic cafe at the foot of the shrine through the entrance gate.

❶ Getting There & Away

To make the two-hour trip from Lagos take a bush taxi (N300) from Ojota Motor Park. You'll arrive at Kuto Motor Park, where you can hop on an *okada* (N100) or catch a taxi.

Ibadan

POP 3.3 MILLION / ☑02

The word sprawling could have been invented to describe Ibadan, now the biggest city in West Africa. You're likely to pass through this major transport junction, but you'll find few formal sites. There's an acclaimed university, and the Gbagi market has an enormous selection of fabric, but otherwise just keep on driving.

University of Ibadan Guest House

(☑012 273 9865; Benue Rd, University of Ibadan Campus; r N8000; P❀@) is a bit grimy but on the campus at Nigeria's premier university, with many amenities.

Kakanfo Inn (☑812 094 6333; www.kakan-foinn.com; 1 Nihinlola St, Ring Rd, Ibadan; r N15,000; P❀@🛜🌊) is decent choice, with a pool, a good Indian restaurant and friendly staff. The wi-fi may be theoretical though.

Ibadan's favourite Asian restaurant, **Kabachi Chinese Fusion Bistro** (☑705 555 0000; Sango Rd, Ventura Mall; mains N2500; ⊘11am-10pm; ❀) has teppanyaki chefs whipping up meat, fish and veg dishes such as chow mein and Sichuan beef. Great service and attractive decor, with lanterns and oriental screens.

❶ Getting There & Away

Iwo Rd is Ibadan's major motor park; minibuses run to all points from here, including Lagos (N500, 90 minutes), Abuja (N2000, eight hours) and points north. For Oshogbo (N300, 90 minutes), go to Gate Motor Park in the east of the city.

Oshogbo

POP 681,600

This very special city has been a traditional centre for Yoruba spirituality and, since the 1950s, the birthplace for much contemporary Nigerian art. The best sight is the Osun Sacred Grove, believed to be the dwelling of Osun, the Yoruba fertility goddess.

☉ Sights

★Osun Sacred Grove   FOREST

(Osun Shrine Rd; N200; ⊘10am-6pm) The Sacred Grove is a large area of rainforest on the outskirts of Oshogbo. Within the forest is the beautiful Shrine of Oshuno, the River Goddess. In addition to natural beauty, there are many stunning sculptures by Suzanne Wenger (known locally as Aduni Olosa, the 'Adored One'), an Austrian painter and sculptor who came here in the 1950s.

Suzanne Wenger's House   CULTURAL CENTRE

(41A Ibokun Rd; by donation) Susanne Wenger's remarkable house sits in the heart of Oshogbo: a tall Gothic place decorated outside with terracotta swirling sculptures, and inside with a mass of wooden votive figures. Sit on one of the fantastical carved chairs at the household shrine (first take your shoes off) and you may hear about Susanne's incredible life from one of her adopted children.

Nike Centre
for Art & Culture   CULTURAL CENTRE

(www.nikeart.com; Old Ede Rd; ⊘9am-5pm) FREE Get your shopping groove on at this fabulous gallery, where you can browse Nike's own paintings, and buy a terrific range of fabrics, batik garments and jewellery.

**Jimoh Buraimoh's
African Heritage Gallery**   GALLERY
(📞 806 797 9333; www.buraimoh.com; 1 Buraimoh St; ⊙ 9am-5pm) FREE Jimoh pioneered a technique of bead painting – you can see his colourful and dynamic works in the gallery, where he also runs workshops.

✨ Festivals & Events

Osun Festival   CULTURAL
(⊙ Aug) Thousands descend on Oshogbo in late August for this festival held in honour of the river goddess. Music, dancing and sacrifices form one of the centrepieces of the Yoruba cultural and spiritual year.

🛏 Sleeping & Eating

⭐ **Nike Ambassador
Guest House**   GUESTHOUSE $
(📞 080 340 96656; www.nikeart.com; Ofatedo Rd; r N8000) It's essential to book ahead to stay in this wonderfully tasteful home, decorated with artworks inside and out. It's centred around an internal courtyard, where you can read at low sofas beneath the paintings. Vivid sculptures made from recycled metal dot the garden. You eat breakfast out here with the peacock, and the in-house team can arrange trips and meals.

❶ Getting There & Away

Okefia Rd is the main motor park. Minibuses leave regularly for Ibadan (N500, 90 minutes) and Lagos (N700, three hours).

WORTH A TRIP

IE-IFE

Ie-Ife is considered the birthplace of Yoruba civilisation, where people still worship traditional deities at revered spiritual sites. At the 18th-century **Oòni's Palace** (Ile-Ife; around N2000), one of the king's servants will, for a fee, show you the shrine within the palace walls, take you to see Oduduwa's staff, and teach you fantastic Yoruba creation stories including the tale of Moremi the warrior-princess.

To get here, take a bush taxi from Oshogbo (N400, 45 minutes).

Benin City

POP 1.5 MILLION / 📞 052

Benin City, which served as the capital of the Benin kingdom, starting in the 15th century, gave rise to one of the first African art forms to be accepted internationally – the Benin brasses (often given the misnomer bronzes). Today the city is the centre of Nigeria's rubber trade, and a sprawling metropolis.

Virtually nothing of the historic city survives: it was destroyed by the British in an epic act of vandalism in 1897. But the culture and the royal family is still deeply venerated here, with the *oba* (king) held in higher esteem than any mere politician.

◎ Sights

Brass Casters Street   AREA
(Igun St) On the Unesco-protected Brass Casters St, sculptors reviving the 'lost-wax' sculpture technique can show you their works in progress and sell you one to take home: there are small ornaments as well as hugely impressive figurative statues. The street is governed by an ancient and secretive guild.

National Museum   MUSEUM
(King's Sq; N100; ⊙ 9am-6pm) The National Museum has displays of beautiful brasses. There are photographs of pieces which were stolen by the British during the sacking and destruction of the city and are now displayed in the British Museum.

✨ Festivals & Events

Igue Festival   CULTURAL
(⊙ Dec) Held in Benin City, usually in the first half of December, this festival has traditional dances, a mock battle and a procession to the palace to reaffirm loyalty to the *oba*. It marks the harvest of the first new yams of the season.

🛏 Sleeping & Eating

Lixborr Hotel   HOTEL $
(📞 802 459 1750; Sakowpba Rd; r N12,000; ✳) A popular, well-run place with comfortable rooms though a slightly subterranean murky feel. It's opposite Brass Casters St: look for the giant statue of the Benin woman. The in-house gallery is impressive.

Hexagon   HOTEL $$
(📞 052 941185; www.thehexagonnetwork.com; 2 Golf Course Rd, GRA; r N18,000; ℗ @ 🛜) Owned by a prince of the Benin royal family, Hexagon has a gallery which displays ancient artworks as well as contemporary pieces; the

outdoor Coconut Bar, which serves grilled grub and beer; a nightclub; and 19 rooms. These are spacious, with extremely comfortable beds and good bathrooms. The highlight of a stay here, though, is the excellent live bands at the Coconut Bar.

ℹ Getting There & Away

Arik Air (p288) has daily flights from Lagos (N45,000, 40 minutes). Iyaro Motor Park is the main place for minibuses to Lagos (N1600, six hours) and Calabar (N1900, up to 10 hours, depending on the state of the road). Also try the depot next to the Edo-Delta Hotel on Akpakpava Rd, which serves most destinations.

Calabar

POP 500,000 / ☎ 087

Tucked into Nigeria's southeastern corner, the capital of Cross River state has a rich history and is well worth a trip. Originally a cluster of Efik settlements, Calabar was once one of Africa's biggest slave ports, and later a major exporter of palm oil. A popular stopover for travellers heading to Cameroon, this tourist-friendly city has a fantastic museum and an excellent primate-conservation centre.

◉ Sights

★ **Afi Mountain Drill Ranch**   WILDLIFE RESERVE
(www.pandrillus.org; green grant N250, guides N1000, car/motorbike N500/250, campsites N2000, huts N6000) The excellent Afi Mountain Drill Ranch near Cross River National Park is one of Nigeria's highlights, with a rainforest canopy walk, close primate encounters and superb accommodation. Its **headquarters** (Pandrillus; ☎ 0803 5921262; Nsefik Eyo Layout, off Atekong Rd; donations appreciated; ☺ 9am-5pm) is in Calabar.

Slave History Museum   MUSEUM
(☎ 080 3441 1080; Calabar Marina Resort; ☺ 8am-6pm Mon-Fri, noon-6pm Sat & Sun) FREE The museum sits on the site of a 15th-century slave-trading warehouse. Exhibits explore local slave markets, the grim paraphernalia of the trade including shackles and chains, and the variety of currencies used to buy people, such as copper bars, brass bells and flutes.

Calabar Museum   MUSEUM
(Court Rd; N100; ☺ 9am-6pm) Housed in the beautiful 1884 British governor's building overlooking the river, the museum has a fascinating collection covering Calabar's days as the Efik kingdom, the slave and palm-oil trade, and the colonial period.

✵ Festivals & Events

Calabar Festival   CULTURAL
(☺ Dec) Calabar hosts a festival throughout December with concerts from national and international stars scheduled closer to Christmas. The highlight of the festival is the cultural masquerade carnival when tens of thousands of costumed revellers descend on the city.

⊨ Sleeping

Nelbee Executive Guesthouse   GUESTHOUSE $
(☎ 08 723 2684; Dan Achibong St; r from N3500; ℙ ❄) Close to Watt Market is this handy budget option. Rooms are comfortable, the management is friendly, and there's a terrifically formal dining room.

Jacaranda Suites   HOTEL $$
(☎ 08 723 9666; off Atimbo Rd; r from N12,000; ℙ ❄ ☆) Lovely suites, a lively outdoor thatch-roof bar with secluded cabanas, and a restaurant serving Cross River specialities and grilled fish, Jacaranda is an easy choice for high-end sleeping and eating. It was being restored at the time of writing.

Marian Hotel   HOTEL $$
(☎ 703 445 2736; www.marianhotels.com; Old Ikang Rd; r N7000-8000; ℙ ❄) The Marian features spacious, tidy and comfortable rooms. It's a little on the dingy side, but the welcome is great and the location ideal.

✗ Eating & Drinking

Calabar has the usual selection of hotel eating places and chop houses. But you'll find some great street food down at the Marina near the Slave History Museum, and at the Municipal Park.

Municipal Park   BEER GARDEN
(☺ noon-11pm) Grassy area with a stage for nighttime concerts (free) and thatched cabanas where you can buy beers, smoothies and street food, including fiery baked fish.

ℹ Getting There & Away

Arik Air (p288) flies daily to Lagos and Abuja (for around N55,000).

In theory **Fakoships** (☎ 0806 9230753) sails every Wednesday and Friday around 7am to Limbe in Cameroon (N6000, seven hours), but at the time of writing the service wasn't running.

The main motor park is tucked between Mary Slessor Ave and Goldie St. Sample minibus fares include Lagos (N3200, 10 hours) and Ikom (for Afi Mountain Drill Ranch; N700, three hours).

WORTH A TRIP

CREEK TOWN

A day trip to Creek Town is an immersion in the surrounding watery landscape, and the rich history of the area.

Once there, get in touch with **Itaeyo** (☑ 0803 741 2894), who will show you the prefab colonial buildings and artifacts, traditional architecture and the king's palace (bring booze as a gift for the king). Also learn about the legacy of Scottish missionary Mary Slessor, who ended the traditional practice of killing twins.

You can reach Creek Town by boat (N400) from the wharf on Marina road, leaving around 7am and noon, coming back at 4pm.

NORTHERN NIGERIA

Abuja

☑ 9 / POP 2.7 MILLION

Nigeria's made-to-measure capital, Abuja was founded during the boom years of the 1970s. After the divisive Biafran War, the decision was made to move the capital from Lagos to the ethnically neutral centre of the country. Clean, quiet and with a good electricity supply, sometimes Abuja hardly feels like Nigeria at all. There's not much to do, but it's a good place to catch your breath and do some visa shopping.

Nike Centre for Art & Culture (☑ 080 2313 1067; www.nikeart.com; Km 7.5 Abuja International Airport Rd, Piwoyi Village) **FREE** is the wondrous Nike gallery's Abuja outpost on the airport road; there are also branches in Lagos, Oshobgo and Ogidi. You can buy artworks and take part in craft workshops, creating tie-dye fabric for example. It's worth asking if they can accommodate you here too.

Abuja has a range of hotels, with mainly upmarket options geared to business people. The city tends to empty at weekends, with people leaving for more exciting destinations, so many hotels offer discounts for Friday and Saturday nights. Hotel restaurants in Abuja are generally reliable if unexciting. It's a good place to seek out Chinese and Indian restaurants if you need some culinary variety.

The **Nordic Villa** (☑ 809 994 4480; www.thenordicvilla.com; 52 Mike Akhigbe Way; r from N37,000; P ✱ ☎ ☒) is a modern Scandinavian-style guesthouse that feels more like a home, with helpful staff, a calm atmosphere and good internet access. A lovely breakfast is included. It's located near Jabi Lake.

Wakkis (☑ 09 291 1002; www.wakkis.com; 171 Aminu Kano Cres; ⊙ noon-midnight; ☑) is an excellent Indian restaurant in a pointy-roofed brick building: there's a charcoal pit in the open kitchen for cooking up tandoori classics. Good for vegetarians.

❶ Getting There & Around

The airport is 40km west of Abuja (N3500 by taxi). Flights depart hourly for Lagos with several airlines (N54,000, one hour). There are also daily flights to Kano and Port Harcourt, as well as flights several times a week to Ibadan, Calabar and Maiduguri.

Jabi Motor Park (also called Utoka) is the main terminus for Abuja. Transport goes to all points from here; sample minibus fares include Kano (N1000, four hours), Jos (N800, three hours), Ibadan (N1500, eight hours) and Lagos (N2600, 10 hours).

Okadas have been banned in Abuja but there are plentiful green taxis (around N200 a trip).

UNDERSTAND NIGERIA

Nigeria Today

After years of coups and military rule, in 2011 Nigeria elected a democratic leader: President Goodluck Jonathan. In another democracy first for Nigeria, Jonathan conceded defeat to reformed military leader Muhammadu Buhari in 2015 (Buhari was in power in the 1980s, having staged a coup). Buhari has pledged to suppress the jihadist-fuelled violence of northern separatist group Boko Haram, and to combat corruption.

Nigeria's economic growth – due almost entirely to the influx of oil money – has ushered in a time of modernisation and development. But these advances run alongside government mismanagement and corruption. Images of barefoot children hawking fruit alongside slick SUVs are a reminder that new wealth doesn't often trickle down.

History

Early Nigeria

Northern and southern Nigeria are essentially two different countries, and their histories reflect this disparity. The first recorded empire to flourish in this part of West Africa was Kanem-Borno around Lake Chad, which grew rich from the trans-Saharan trade routes. Islamic states based in the Hausa cities of Kano, Zaria and Nupe also flourished at this time.

Meanwhile, the southwest developed into a patchwork of small states, often dominated by the Yoruba. The Ijebu kingdom rose in the 10th century and constructed the mysterious earthworks at Sungbo's Eredo. Most famously the Benin kingdom became an important centre of trade and produced some of the finest metal artwork in Africa. In the southeast, the Igbo and other agrarian peoples never developed any centralised empires, instead forming loose confederations.

Colonial Era

The first contact between Yoruba empires and Europeans was made in the 15th century, when the Portuguese began trading in pepper and, later, slaves. In contrast, the northern Islamic states remained untouched by European influence until well into the 19th century.

In the early 19th century the British took a lead in suppressing slavery along the Niger delta, leading to the annexation of Lagos port – a first colonial toehold. This led to further annexation to thwart the French, who were advancing their territory along the Niger River. By the beginning of the 20th century, British soldiers had advanced as far north as the cities of Kano and Sokoto, where Islamic revivalism had created a rapidly expanding caliphate.

Nigeria was divided in two – the southern, mainly Christian, colony and the northern Islamic protectorate. The British chose to rule indirectly through local kings and chiefs, exacerbating ethnic divisions for political expediency.

Military Misrule

The ethnic divisions came back to haunt Nigeria when independence came in October 1960. Politics split along ethnic lines, and in 1966 a group of Igbo army officers staged a coup. General Johnson Ironsi took over as head of state. Another coup quickly followed on its heels, along with massacres of Igbos, which in 1967 provoked civil war by secessionist Igbos. The war dragged on for three years. Biafra was blockaded, and by the time its forces capitulated in 1970, up to a million Igbos had died, mainly from starvation.

An oil boom smoothed Nigeria's path to national reconciliation, but as the army jockeyed for political control, the next two decades were marked by a series of military coups, with only a brief democratic interlude in the early 1980s. When General Ibrahim Babangida offered elections in 1993, he annulled them when the result appeared to go against him, only to be toppled in a coup soon after by General Sani Abacha.

Abacha was ruthless, purging the army and locking up intellectuals, unionists and pro-democracy activists. His rule reached a nadir in 1995 with the judicial murder of the Ogoni activist Ken Saro-Wiwa, an act that led to Nigeria's expulsion from the Commonwealth.

Salvation finally came in June 1998, in what Nigerians called the 'coup from heaven'. Aged 54, and worth somewhere between US$2 billion and US$5 billion in stolen government money, Abacha died of a heart attack while in the company of two prostitutes. His successor immediately announced elections and in February 1999 Olusegun Obasanjo, a former military leader and ex-president, was returned as president.

Culture

With 186 million people, Nigeria has a huge and expanding population. The main ethnic groups are the Yoruba (in the southwest), the Hausa (north) and the Igbo (southeast), each making up around a fifth of the population, followed by the northern Fulani (around 10%). It's thought that up to 500 languages are spoken in Nigeria.

In many towns and villages traditional belief systems remain strong, despite the presence of American-style evangelical mega-churches. The north is predominantly Muslim, but elsewhere you'll find the boundaries between Islam, Christianity and animist beliefs refreshingly fluid.

Chinua Achebe documented the early collision of African religion and Christianity in his ground-breaking novel *Things Fall Apart* (1958). Achebe was Nigeria's most famous author and is still revered for his genius and wisdom; he died in March 2013. Other acclaimed writers from Nigeria include the Nobel Laureate Wole Soyinka, Booker Prize winner Ben Okri (*The Famished Road*) and Chimamanda Ngozi Adichie, who documented the tragedy of the Biafran War in *Half a Yellow Sun*.

Some of Africa's best-known musicians are Nigerian. Two styles have traditionally been dominant – Afrobeat and *juju* – with their respective masters being the late great Fela Kuti and King Sunny Ade.

Environment

The north touches on the Sahel and is mostly savannah with low hills. Mountains are found only along the Cameroon border in the east, although there is a 1500m-high plateau around Jos in the centre of the country. The coast is an almost unbroken line of sandy beaches and lagoons running back to creeks and mangrove swamps and is very humid most of the year.

An underfunded national parks service does exist, but in practice very little land in Nigeria is effectively protected. The expanding population has contributed to widespread deforestation – 95% of the original forests have been logged. However, the oil industry has caused the greatest number of environmental problems: oil spills and gas flaring have damaged the fishing industry, with little of the industry's wealth trickling down to the local level.

SURVIVAL GUIDE

 Directory A–Z

ACCOMMODATION

Hotels in Nigeria are generally reasonable if uninspired. The holy grail is functioning air-con, running water, loo roll and a towel; count yourself lucky if you find all four.

The exception is some expensive and extravagant options in Lagos, and the odd soulful guesthouse.

CHILDREN

While children will be treated kindly in Nigeria, you may find the practicalities difficult. The broken pavements are very difficult for prams, and public toilets tend to be dire, with no baby-change facilities. Bus journeys are hot and crowded, with few loo breaks.

 SLEEPING PRICE RANGES

The following price ranges refer to a double room with bathroom. Unless stated, breakfast is not included in the price.

$ less than N15,000

$$ N15,000–30,000

$$$ more than N30,000

Child-friendly sights:

Lekki Conservation Centre (p279) Climb the canopy walkways to get close to the monkeys in this wetland reserve.

Afi Mountain Drill Ranch (p291) Watch drill monkeys and a very lively chimpanzee up close in Calabar.

Osun Sacred Grove (p289) Vervet monkeys scamper through the trees of the grove, but thankfully the snakes and alligators stay well hidden.

DANGERS & ANNOYANCES

→ The most dangerous region is northern Nigeria, where Boko Haram has been waging a low-grade war against the federal government.

→ Lagos has a reputation for petty, violent crime, not always undeserved, although it's been on the decline in the past few years.

→ You're unlikely to have trouble with large-scale corruption and bribery. Police roadblocks are common, but fines and bribes are paid by the driver. Take care on the major highways into Lagos, where armed robbery is a problem at night.

→ Enugu has a reputation for kidnapping schemes, but they're more likely to be after wealthy oil execs than travellers.

EMERGENCY & IMPORTANT NUMBERS

Nigeria's country code	234
Ambulance	112 or 199
Fire	112 or 199
Police	112 or 199

EMBASSIES & CONSULATES

Some embassies have yet to relocate from Lagos to Abuja.

Australian Embassy (☑ 09 461 2780; www.nigeria.embassy.gov.au; 48 Aguyi Ironsi St, 5th fl, Oakland Centre, Maitama, Abuja; ⊙8am-4.30pm Mon-Thu, 8am-1pm Fri)

Beninese Embassy Abuja (☑ 09 413 8424; Yedseram St; ⊙9am-4.30pm Mon-Fri); Lagos (Map p286; ☑01 261 4411; 4 Abudu Smith St, VI; ⊙9am-11am Mon-Fri)

Burkinabé Embassy (Map p286; ☑01 268 1001; 15 Norman Williams St, Lagos, Ikoyi)

Cameroonian Embassy Calabar (☑087 222782; 21 Ndidan Usang Iso Rd; ⊙9am-3.30pm Mon-Fri); Lagos (Map p286; ☑01 261 2226; 5 Femi Pearse St, VI; ⊙8am-11am Mon-Fri)

Canadian Embassy Abuja (☑09 461 2900; 13010G, Palm Close, Diplomatic Dr; ⊙8am-4.30pm Mon-Thu, 8am-1.30pm Fri); Lagos (Map p286; ☑01 271 5650; 4 Anifowoshe St, VI; ⊙8am-6pm)

Dutch Embassy (Map p286; ☑ 01 261 3005; 24 Ozumba Mbadiwe Ave, Lagos, VI; ⊙9am-6pm)

French Embassy (Map p286; ☑ 01 269 3430; 1 Oyinkan Abayomi Rd, Ikoyi; ⊙8am-2pm Mon-Fri)

German Embassy (Map p286; ☑ 909 724 9554; 15 Walter Carrington Cres, VI; ⊙8am-6pm)

Ghanaian Embassy (Map p284; ☑ 01 263 0015; 23 King George V Rd, Lagos Island; ⊙9am-3pm)

Irish Embassy (☑ 09 462 0611; 11 Negro Cres, off Aminu Kano, Maitama, Abuja; ⊙8am-4.30pm Mon-Thu, 8am-1pm Fri)

Ivoirian Embassy (Map p286; ☑ 01 261 0963; 5 Abudu Smith St, VI; ⊙9am-2pm)

Nigerien Embassy Abuja (☑ 09 523 6205; 7 Sangha St, off Mississippi St; ⊙9am-3pm Mon-Fri); Kano (☑ 064 64 38 06; 1A Katsina Road; ⊙9am-3pm Mon-Fri); Lagos (Map p286; ☑ 01 261 2300; 15 Adeola Odeku St, VI; ⊙9am-2.30pm Mon-Fri)

Spanish Embassy (Map p286; ☑ 01 261 5215; 21c Kofo Abayomi St, VI; ⊙8am-6pm)

Togolese Embassy (Map p286; ☑ 01 261 7478; Plot 976, Oju Olobun Cl, VI; ⊙8am-3pm Mon-Fri)

UK Embassy Abuja (☑ 09 462 2200; www.ukinnigeria.fco.gov.uk; 19 Torrens Close, Mississippi; ⊙8.30am-noon Mon-Thu, 8.30-11am Fri); Lagos (Map p286; ☑ 01 261 9531; 11 Walter Carrington Cres, VI; ⊙8.30am-noon Mon-Thu, 8.30-11am Fri)

US Embassy Abuja (☑ 09 461 4000; http://nigeria.usembassy.gov; Plot 1075, Diplomatic Dr, Central Business District; ⊙8.30am-2pm Mon-Thu, 8.30am-noon Fri); Lagos (Map p286; ☑ 01 261 0150; 2 Walter Carrington Cres, VI; ⊙8am-6pm)

FOOD

Nigerians like their food ('chop') hot and starchy. The classic dish is a fiery pepper stew ('soup') with a little meat or fish and starch – usually pounded yam or cassava (*garri, eba,* or slightly sour *fufu*). Another popular dish is *jollof* – peppery rice cooked with palm oil and tomato. Cutlery isn't generally used – yam or cassava soaks up the juices of the stew. Eat only with your right hand.

GAY & LESBIAN TRAVELLERS

Homosexual sex is illegal in Nigeria. The draconian 'Same Sex Marriage Prohibition Bill' permits 14-year prison sentences for those entering into a same-sex marriage, or those witnessing or supporting a same-sex marriage. There are 10-year sentences for those who operate gay clubs and organisations.

ℹ PRACTICALITIES

Electricity Supply is 220V. Plugs are square British three pin, but most hotels have European two-pin adaptors.

Newspapers Privately owned English-language daily newspapers include the *Guardian, This Day,* the *Punch* and *Vanguard.*

TV There are over 30 national and state TV stations, broadcasting in English and all major local languages. South African satellite DSTV is hugely popular.

Weights & measures Nigeria uses the metric system.

INTERNET ACCESS

Decent connections are widespread in major towns, for around N200 per hour. Never use internet banking in a Nigerian cybercafe.

MONEY

ATMs are increasingly widespread and many are connected to international systems such as MasterCard or Visa. GTB is the most reliable.

Cash The unit of currency is the naira (N).

Credit cards Accepted at only a few places; use them with caution. Notify your bank before you use your cards in Nigeria as fraud scams have made it a red-flag country for transactions. For online purchases such as buying internal flights your card may be refused. You may have to ask a trusted local to make the transaction for you, then reimburse them.

Changing money Bring higher denomination dollars or pounds for the best exchange rate. There are moneychangers in each town and they are almost always Hausa. Western Union branches are useless unless you have a Nigerian bank account.

Tipping For hotels, tip N1000 or so for help with bags. For decent service in restaurants, 10% is customary. Taxi tips are not expected, but add one for good service.

Exchange Rates

Australia	A$1	N230
Canada	C$1	N223
Europe	€1	N333
Japan	¥100	N273
New Zealand	NZ$	N211
UK	UK£1	N394
US	US$1	N305

For current exchange rates, see www.xe.com.

NIGERIA DIRECTORY A–Z

ⓘ WARNING: BOKO HARAM

Between 2009 and 2016, Boko Haram, a jihadist organisation based in the northeast of Nigeria, has been fighting a low-level war against Christian communities and the central government, killing thousands. Known for bombing churches and markets, assassinating police, and motorcycle drive-bys, the group, whose name means 'Western education is sinful' in Hausa, has made travel to northern Nigeria impossible.

Attacks were sporadic and took place in Adawama, Gombe, Yobe, Jigawa and Plateau States, occasionally in an outskirt of Abuja or Jos, with many incidents centred on Maiduguri, the capital of Borno State.

The situation has begun to stabilise after a military campaign directed by President Buhari. But there are now many displaced people and severe food shortages in the north.

At the time of writing the guidance was to avoid northern Nigeria altogether. Read your government's travel advisory and ask locals before attempting to head north.

OPENING HOURS

General business hours are from 8.30am to 5pm Monday to Friday. Sanitation days are held on the last Saturday of the month – traffic isn't allowed before 10am for street cleaning.

Banks 8am to 4pm Monday to Friday.

Government offices 7.30am to 3.30pm Monday to Friday

Shops and supermarkets 7.30am to 3.30pm Monday to Friday, 7.30 to 1pm Saturday

POST

Mail sent to or from Nigeria is notoriously slow. Worldwide postcards cost about N80. For parcels, use an international courier like DHL or FedEx, which have offices in most towns.

PUBLIC HOLIDAYS

New Year's Day 1 January

Easter March or April

May Day 1 May

National Day 1 October

Christmas 25 December

Boxing Day 26 December

Islamic holidays are observed in northern Nigeria.

TELEPHONE

Nigeria is in love with the mobile phone, and cellular networks are more reliable than landlines.

Calls at roadside phone stands are quick and easy to make, costing around N20 per minute inside Nigeria, and around N60 for an international call. Most mobile numbers start with 080.

Having a local SIM card to use in a smart phone is extremely useful. The best service is Etisalat (SIMs cost N300) though MTN has the widest coverage. Street vendors everywhere sell top-up scratch cards.

VISAS

Everyone needs a visa to visit Nigeria, and applications can be quite a process. Three-month visas cost up to US$300, according to nationality.

Obtaining Visas

Many Nigerian embassies issue visas only to residents and nationals of the country in which the embassy is located, so it's essential to put things in motion well before your trip. Exact requirements vary, but as a rule of thumb, forms are required in triplicate, along with proof of funds to cover your stay, a round-trip air ticket, and possibly confirmed hotel reservations. You also need a letter of invitation from a resident of Nigeria or a business in the country.

If you're travelling overland to Nigeria, the embassy in Accra (Ghana) is consistently rated as the best place in West Africa to apply for a visa, as no letter of introduction is required. The embassy in Niamey (Niger) also claims to issue visas the same way.

Visa Extensions

Visas can reportedly be extended at the **Federal Secretariat** (Map p286; Forest St; ⊙8am-5pm Mon-Fri) in Lagos, but it's a byzantine process of endless forms, frustration and dash, with no clear sense of success.

Visas for Onward Travel

Benin One-month visas cost around CFA15,000 (CFA, not naira), with two photos, and take 24 hours to issue. The embassy in Lagos carries an uninviting reputation, and unexpected extra fees are not unknown.

ⓘ EATING PRICE RANGES

The following price ranges refer to a main course.

$ less than N1500

$$ N1500–N3000

$$$ more than N3000

Cameroon A one-month single-entry visa costs CFA50,000 (CFA, not naira), with two photos, and is issued in a day. As well as Lagos and Abuja, there's a useful consulate in Calabar.

ⓘ Getting There & Away

AIR

The vast majority of flights to Nigeria arrive in Lagos, although there are also international airports in Abuja, Port Harcourt and Kano. Airports are well organised and have official porters, but plenty of touts outside.

Lagos' airport is **Murtala Muhammed International** (Map p282; www.lagosairport.net). Arik Air (p288) operates domestic and some international flights, for example to Douala in Cameroon.

LAND
Benin

The main border crossing is on the Lagos–Cotonou (Benin) highway. Expect requests for bribes. There's a good direct Cotonou–Lagos bus service run by Nigerian bus company **ABC Transport** (☑ 81 4255 2436, 0805 300 1000; www.abctransport.com). An alternative border crossing is further north at Kétou on the Benin side.

Cameroon

The southern border crossing is at Mfum (Nigeria), near Ikom. The road infrastructure collapses pretty much as soon as you cross to Ekok (Cameroon), making this border problematic during the rainy season, so consider taking the Calabar–Limbe ferry instead during the wettest months. However, at the time of writing the ferry was not functioning.

Northern border posts between the two countries were not safe at the time of writing.

SEA

A ferry sails from Calabar to Limbe every Tuesday and Friday evening (N6000, five hours), returning on Monday and Thursday. It's an overnight trip in each direction. Your passport is collected on boarding and returned at immigration. Try to keep hold of your luggage – if it gets stowed in the hold, you'll be waiting hours to get it back. Note that there are safety issues with the ferry, and at the time of writing it wasn't functioning. Take local advice.

ⓘ Getting Around

AIR

Internal flights are a quick way of getting around Nigeria. Flights start at around N20,000. Most cities are linked by air to Lagos.

The most reliable domestic airline with the best connections is **Arik Air** (p288).

BUS

Each town has at least one motor park serving as the main transport depot full of minibuses and bush taxis.

Vehicles have signs on their roofs showing their destination, while touts shout out destinations. Minibuses don't run on any schedule but depart when full.

CAR & MOTORCYCLE

Nigeria's road system veers unpredictably between good and appalling. Accident rates are high, the only real road rule is survival of the fittest and road signage is minimal.

Foreigners driving in Nigeria shouldn't get too much hassle at roadblocks, particularly if your vehicle has foreign plates. If you get asked for dash, a smile and some patience will often defuse the request. It's a legal requirement to wear a seatbelt; not doing so leaves you open to both official and 'unofficial' fines. Petrol stations are everywhere, but fuel shortages are common, causing huge queues and worsening the already terrible traffic. Diesel can sometimes be hard to come by, so keep your tank topped up.

Hiring a good local driver takes a lot of the stress out of car transport: it will cost around N80,000 per day. Ask at your hotel for suggestions.

LOCAL TRANSPORT

The quickest way to get around town is on the back of a motorcycle-taxi called an *okada* (*achaba* in the north). Because of their general lawlessness, the government has banned *okada* in a few of the major cities, badly affecting traffic and driving up the prices with drivers who are willing to flout the law.

São Tomé & Príncipe

📞 239 / POP 195,000

Best Places to Eat

➡ Bom Bom Resort (p308)
➡ Papa Figo (p302)
➡ 5 Sentidos (p302)
➡ Celvas (p303)
➡ Roça São João (p305)

Best Places to Sleep

➡ Roça Belo Monte (p308)
➡ Mucumbli (p303)
➡ Makaira Lodge (p308)
➡ Sweet Guest House (p300)
➡ Praia Inhame Ecolodge (p305)
➡ Bom Bom Resort (p308)

Why Go?

Floating in the Gulf of Guinea, this two-island nation, Africa's second-smallest, blends natural wonders with a gripping history. Once a vast network of plantations and a centre of global cocoa production, São Tomé & Príncipe (STP) has suffered an economic collapse since independence from Portugal in 1975. In the countryside, squatters inhabit once great mansions; in the capital, historic colonial buildings slowly decay on broken streets. Nevertheless, the country remains amazingly safe and welcoming to visitors, particularly ecotourists, for whom the advancing jungle is a delight. This is particularly true on tidy and unspoiled Príncipe, an island of just 7000 people. A canopy of green broken by spires of primordial rock, Príncipe is a magnificent Lost World, offering fantastic beaches, jungle exploration, snorkelling, fishing, birdwatching and a handful of interesting (if expensive) accommodation options, with minimal tourist pressure. While both islands have their natural rewards, Príncipe should not be missed.

When to Go
São Tomé

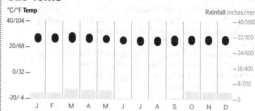

| Jun–Sep Dry season; ideal for climbing Pico de São Tomé or trekking the Volta a Ilha. | Oct–May Rainy season; particularly wet in the southwest. | Year-round Temperatures in the high 20s (°C); areas of cloud, rain and sun can be found any time. |

São Tomé & Príncipe Highlights

❶ Baía das Agulhas (p307) Boating past Príncipe's extraordinary volcanic skyline, a spectacular trip back in time.

❷ Plantation History Visiting *roças* (plantations) like Roça Agua Izé (p304) for an eye-opening look at a national calamity.

❸ World-Class Seafood (p302) Eating thick slabs of deep-sea fish at restaurants such as Papa Figo in São Tomé.

❹ Pico de São Tomé (p306) Climbing the highest peak in the country for an unforgettable jungle adventure.

❺ Praia Banana (p307) Admiring the golden curves, swaying palms and turquoise waters of a paradise beach – all by yourself.

SÃO TOMÉ

Ecotourists, listen up: this is an island where nature offers the best rewards. By combining the island's two major ecolodges, Mucumbli in the north and Praia Inhame in the south, you can enjoy the best the island has to offer, including jungle hikes, exploring remote beaches, seeing local wildlife, visiting a *roça* (plantation) or two, and climbing the Pico de São Tomé, all for a very reasonable price. You may also want to splurge on Ilhéu das Rolas, a satellite resort island with exotic twists of its own, including classic tropical beaches.

São Tomé (City)

POP 53,300

São Tomé city ought to be one of the world's great port towns. It contains an extraordinary collection of colonial buildings, located on a broad curving bay, and is the economic and political hub of the country. Unfortunately STP's long economic decline has devastated its infrastructure. The historic architecture is decaying on every street, the roads are choked with potholes, and the central market is filthy. Even so, stay long enough for a plate of world-class seafood, the city's finest attribute.

◉ Sights

★ **Claudio Corallo**
Chocolate Factory   FACTORY
(📞 222 2236; www.claudiocorallo.com; Ave Marginal 12 de Julho; €4; ⊙ tours 4.40pm Mon, Wed & Fri, tickets on sale from 8am) Claudio Corallo is both an extraordinary person and a local institution. For over 40 years this native Italian has pursued an overriding passion for coffee and cocoa in Africa, first in Zaire and later in STP, where he has two plantations and a factory in the capital. The results are on display in this fascinating little tour, which takes you not only through the chocolate production process, but through all the thought and experimentation that went into developing the bean.

CACAU   CULTURAL CENTRE
(📞 994 3810, 222 2625; www.facebook.com/pg/cacau.cultural; Ave Marginal 12 de Julho; ⊙ 7.30am-11.30pm) The Casa das Artes, Criação, Ambiente e Utopias (House of the Arts, Creativity, Environment and Utopias) is an ambitious attempt to create a true cultural centre in the capital. Located in a huge warehouse, it has various elements: a restaurant/cafe/bar, an exhibition space, a crafts shop, and

a stage/movie theater. It can be very quiet, however, without a special event going on. See 'Events' on its Facebook page.

Mercado Grande   MARKET
(Great Market; Ave Geovany & Rua do Municipio; ⊙ 6am-5.30pm Mon-Sat) Alternately fascinating and repellent, the Mercado Grande is divided into two cavernous and adjacent halls, the Mercado Municipal and the newer, and cleaner, Mercado Novo. They both contain the same goods, mostly food and clothing, which also spill into the street outside, creating a few blocks of densely packed commerce. The spectacle is the point. Photography is not appreciated, so be discreet.

🏃 Activities

Marapa   WILDLIFE WATCHING
(📞 993 3240, 222 2792; www.marapa.org; Largo Bom Despacho; small donation requested) On Monday, Wednesday and Friday in turtle-nesting season (November to February) this marine conservation organisation provides a 5pm briefing, followed by a late night measuring, tagging and collecting eggs on nearby beaches. These are then protected from poachers in a guarded enclosure until they hatch, after which they are released into the sea, a process you can also witness.

TropicVenture   DIVING
(📞 993 4199; www.facebook.com/Divingcenter saotome; ES-1/Airport Rd, Praia Lagarto; 1-tank dive €40; ⊙ 8am-6pm) Experienced dive master João Santos is an expert on local waters, and books up quickly by word of mouth. Offering various PADI courses, free equipment and two 6m boats, he can craft any diving itinerary for the north of the island. The typical outing is a two-tank dive (three if a night dive is added).

🛏 Sleeping

★ **Sweet Guest House**   HOTEL $
(📞 903 1313, 999 0763; www.sweetguesthouse. com; Vila Dolores; ⊙ s/d €45/52, with shared bath €35/42; 🅿 ❋ 🛜) The budget traveller's salvation, this hotel performs its role perfectly. It feels like a cabin, with a large wooden balcony on the 2nd floor, and panelled rooms. While not in the cheeriest neighborhood, its walled compound has 24-hour security (with parking). One of the few backpacker havens in STP, with an interesting array of global travellers to match.

Kayla   B&B $
(📞 989 8240; kayla.guesthouse@yahoo.com; Rua Palma Carlos, 113B, top floor; s/d incl breakfast

São Tomé Town

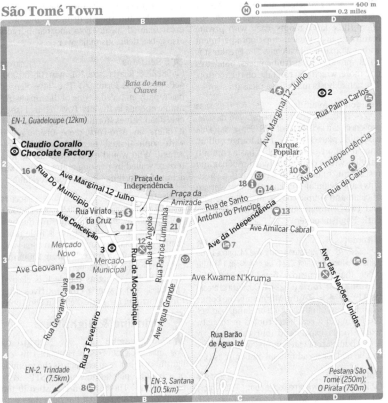

São Tomé Town

◎ Top Sights
1 Claudio Corallo Chocolate
Factory A2

◎ Sights
2 CACAU D1
3 Mercado Grande B3

✛ Activities, Courses & Tours
4 Marapa C1

🛏 Sleeping
5 Kayla D1
6 Miramar D3
7 Residencial Avenida C3
8 Sweet Guest House A4

✗ Eating
9 5 Sentidos D2
10 B-24 .... D2
11 Papa Figo D3

12 Pastelaria Central B3

🍷 Drinking & Nightlife
13 Pico Mocambo C3

🛍 Shopping
14 Pica Pau C2

ℹ Information
15 Banco International de Sao
Tomé & Príncipe B3
16 Mistral Voyages A2
17 Navetur B3
18 Tourism Bureau C2

ℹ Transport
19 Hanna & Silva Rent-a-Car A3
STP Airways ....(see 18)
20 TAAG A3
21 TAP B3

€35/50; 🌐 🛜) A super option, this family B&B on a quiet residential street near the sea offers three large rooms, each with private bathroom, in a spacious top-floor apartment with a wraparound balcony. The breakfast is a full spread of local fruits, juices, omelettes and more, which you can take on the rooftop. The genial hosts make for a pleasant stay.

Residential Avenida HOTEL **$$**

(🖉 224 1700; ravenida@cstome.net; Ave da Independência; s/d incl breakfast €79/95; 🌐 🛜) This easygoing place is the best midrange option. Spread out on ground level, it has a communal vibe, with a central thatched-roof bar and restaurant (mains €9 to €15; fish is a speciality) and popular TV. There's a nice spread of clean and simple rooms, including triples and two-bedroom suites, but they're a bit dark. English spoken.

Miramar HOTEL **$$$**

(🖉 222 2778; www.pestana.com; Ave Marginal 12 de Julho; s/d incl breakfast €124/130; 🌐 🛜 🏊) While older than its nearby flagship sister, the **Pestana São Tomé** (🖉 224 4500; s/d incl breakfast €195; 🅿 🌐 🛜 🏊), the Miramar is the better deal. Instead of entering resort-land, you get the feeling of a real hotel rooted in the city, where locals, expats and tourists all mix. A secret bonus: renovated rooms with seaviews can be had for no additional cost (just ask).

Omali Lodge RESORT **$$$**

(🖉 222 2479; www.omalilodge.com; ES1/Airport Rd, Praia Lagarto; s/d incl breakfast €150/200; 🅿 🌐 🛜 🏊) Striking the right balance between European standards and local ambience, the laid-back Omali is where locals, expats and foreign visitors all meet. Located between the city and the airport, it provides convenient access to either one. Rooms are mildly worn but spacious, and arranged around a large pool set in palms.

🍴 Eating

B-24 SEAFOOD **$**

(Parque Popular; mains Db100,000-150,000; ⊙ 7.30am-11pm) The best of the many restaurant shacks lining Parque Popular, this simple thatched hut packs an enormous punch with its fish of the day, as its many patrons reveal.

⭐ **Papa Figo** SEAFOOD, PUB FOOD **$$**

(Ave Kwame Nkrumah; mains Db60,000-250,000; ⊙ 7am-11.30pm) This charming, well-kept and ever-popular tin-roofed patio restaurant is laid-back in style, but no slouch in the kitchen. Everything on the menu has an interesting new twist. The thick fish steaks

are world class: don't miss the barracuda. Tasty sides and special drinks round out a great seafood meal. Pizza and hamburgers also gets a delicious makeover.

⭐ **5 Sentidos** FUSION **$$**

(🖉 981 8798; Rua da Caixa, 201; mains Db200,000-400,000; ⊙ 6-11.30pm; 🖉) The 'Five Senses' has rapidly emerged as one of the top gastronomic options in the city. Powered by Lisbon chef João Nunes (formerly of Omali Lodge), it offers an Afro-Portuguese fusion menu with sophisticated meals beautifully presented. Who would expect this cuisine in a terrace walled by packing crates, with a parachute for a ceiling? Reserve on weekends.

O Pirata SEAFOOD **$$**

(Estrada de Pantufo; mains Db200,000-250,000; ⊙ 9am-midnight, to later Fri) Enjoying the best location in the city, the Pirate is little more than a deck perched on a crashing sea wall, facing a rusting shipwreck barely 100m distant. The seafood is excellent, with huge portions. On Friday nights the deck is cleared of tables, and a young crowd arrives after 10pm, forming the hottest club in São Tomé.

🍷 Drinking & Nightlife

⭐ **Pico Mocambo** COCKTAIL BAR

(Ave Amilcar Cabral; ⊙ 8am-midnight) This delightful rum bar is spread across the grounds of a historic plantation house – STP needs more of this! The bar itself is nestled in the top floor, and strikes just the right note with its plantation shutters and bamboo furniture, not to mention cocktails. Picks up after 9pm.

🛍 Shopping

⭐ **Pica Pau** ARTS & CRAFTS

(Rua de Santo Antonío do Príncipe; ⊙ 8am-7pm) Looking for a souvenir? This artisans cooperative contains a fantastic collection of wood carvings, by far the best in the city, and more limited jewellery. Various vendors are on hand, and freely interrupt one another for your attention. Be prepared to haggle! Some fine gifts can be had for under €20.

ℹ Information

Moneychangers operate around Praça da Amizade. The Miramar and Pestana São Tomé offer cashback service on credit cards for up to €100 to guests for a 5% fee. **BISTP** (BISTP; 🖉 224 3105; www.bistp.st; Praça de Independência; ⊙ 8am-3pm Mon-Fri, to noon Sat) will also offer cashback for a steep €10 fee PLUS 11% on the transaction, no matter how small it may be. In an emergency, **Navetur** (p301) may be able to help.

CST (Ave da Independência; ⊙7am-7pm) Purchase SIM cards and top up your phone here.

Internet Access Free wifi is available in the lobby of the Miramar and Pestana São Tomé hotels; you'll need to ask for the code at the restaurant-bar at the Omali, and downtown at **Pastelaria Central** (Rua de Angola; ⊙7am-8pm; ✳ 🛜).

Mistral Voyages (☑ 222 3344; www.mistral-voyages.com; Ave Marginal 12 de Julho; ⊙8am-6pm Mon-Fri) Travel agency with ticketing services.

Navetur (☑ 222 2122; www.navetur-equatour. st; Rua Viriato da Cruz; ⊙8am-12.30pm & 3-5.30pm Mon-Fri, to noon Sat) Travel agency with ticketing services. The best stop for English speakers, particularly if you are also booking tours through them.

Post Office (Ave Marginal 12 de Julho; ⊙7am-noon & 2-5pm Mon-Fri)

Tourism Bureau (☑ 222 1542; www.turismo. gov.st; Ave Marginal 12 de Julho; ⊙8am-noon & 2-5pm Mon-Fri, to noon Sat) Has an attractive tourist map for €3, but that's about it. No English spoken.

ⓘ Getting There & Around

The taxis that depart from the Mercado Grande (p300) head all over the island. Sample shared fares include Santana (Db15,000, 30 minutes), Neves (Db25,000, one hour), São João dos Angolares (Db25,000, one hour) and Porto Alegre (Db30,000, two hours).

Hanna & Silva Rent-a-Car (☑ 222 6282; www. facebook.com/hannaesilvarentacar; Rua Geovane Caixa; 4-person Suzuki Jimny with full insurance per day €42; ⊙8am-12.30pm & 3-5.30pm Mon-Fri, to 1pm Sat) is a cheerful small company with about 10 vehicles including some inexpensive 4WDs. If Hanna & Silva is out of cars, try **Tortuga Car Rental** (☑ 991 1913; tortuga.stp@gmail. com) – the cars are insured, but service is slow, and be very clear about the price.

You can reach anywhere in the city by motorbike taxi, hailed on any street, for Db10,000.

Northern Coast

The northern coast of São Tomé offers some fine beaches, historic *roças* and one long road, the EN-1. This gets increasingly remote the further you travel upon it, until it disappears completely into the jungle. Here you can pursue numerous activities, including boating the coastline, hiking the Pico de São Tomé, and mountain biking to the road's end, a dramatic journey where the

ⓘ **ARRIVING IN SÃO TOMÉ**
....
São Tomé International Airport Taxis wait for arrivals. A shared ride into the city takes 15 minutes and costs €2 to €3. A private taxi costs €10. Agree on the fee ahead of time. This is the only form of transport available (apart from a motorcycle, if you have no luggage).

waves crash on one side while the Pico rises on the other.

One of the island's best beaches, **Praia dos Tamarindos** is a beautiful white crescent facing an emerald sea, with excellent swimming. An easy drive from the capital, it's empty during the week but crowded on weekends. Reaching Guadelupe from the capital, turn right at the monument in the middle of the road, then a further right at the primary school.

Museo do Mar e da Pesca Artesanal (Morro Peixe; €2; ⊙8am-6pm Mon-Fri, to 3pm Sat) is a charming marine and fishing museum located in a whitewashed fisherman's shack up on stilts by the water's edge. Created by local marine conservation organisation Marapa (p300), it has some intelligent displays with English signage and is definitely worth a stop. You can also arrange night trips to see nesting turtles here. Located at end of road to Morro Peixe.

🍴 Sleeping & Eating

★**Mucumbli**   ECOLODGE $$
(☑990 8736; www.mucumbli.wordpress.com; EN-1, Neves; s/d bungalows incl breakfast €58/68; 🅿🛜) 🗲 STP's finest ecolodge is situated in a cliffside forest overlooking the sea. Nicely designed wooden bungalows offer plenty of space, light and dreamy views for two to four people. But it's hard to leave the dining area, with its coastal vista, convivial atmosphere and superb food (mains €6 to €12; visitors welcome). This is your launch pad for multiple itineraries, and great value.

★**Celvas**   FUSION $$$
(☑223 1093, 993 5849; www.restaurante-cel vas.com; EN-1, Guadeloupe; mains Db180,000-400,000; ⊙8.30am-4pm, dinner on reservation only, reserve before 3pm same day) Hidden behind a wall on the main street of Guadeloupe, this restaurant comes as a shockingly good surprise. You'll find two gazebos set in a garden, with tables draped in white tablecloths. A generous wine selection

complements sophisticated meat and fish dishes blending Portuguese and São Toméan flavours. Three garden rooms (singles/doubles €35/47) were also being renovated during research.

ⓘ Getting There & Around

A shared taxi from the capital to Mucumbli (one hour) is Db25,000 per seat. You may need to double that for luggage.

If you wish to explore the area on your own you will need to rent a mountain bike (€10 per day) from Mucumbli or bring a rental car from the capital.

Southern Coast

The southern coast offers diverse attractions, including beach resorts, jungle hikes, diving, and some fine accommodation. These are concentrated in two main areas, near Santana (and hence within range of the capital) and near Porto Alegre, at the southern tip of the island. The entire coast is linked by the EN-2, a 2½-hour drive from end to end. The southern half of this road is particularly pleasant, a jungle drive with little traffic and the awesome sight of Cão Grande, the symbol of São Tomé, rising in the distance. From Porto Alegre a potholed dirt road continues along the coast to a trio of bungalow beach resorts, offering various outdoor activities. As elsewhere, the villages are not the focus of your trip.

Cão Grande (Great Canine) is the poster image of São Tomé, and an awesome sight. An enormous tooth of rock 663m high, it is a hardened column of magma, the remains of an ancient volcano whose softer outer shell has long since eroded away. Its diminutive

---

TREKKING VOLTA A ILHA

This two-day trek along the roadless southwestern coast of São Tomé connects the end of the EN-1 to the end of the EN-2. It also includes the island's two best ecolodges, Mucumbli (p303) and Praia Inhame (p305). Those who want to begin in the north should arrange their trek through the former, while those who want to start in the south should organise it through the latter. It is best done in the dry season (June to September), as the wet season makes crossing several ravines difficult.

---

sibling, **Cão Pequeno**, is a phonolite tower best seen from Ilhéu das Rolas.

Ilhéu de Santana is an interesting island facing Santana Resort, unique in that a natural tunnel runs straight through the centre of it. Boat trips operated by the Atlantic Diving Center (€8) can get most of the way through before the ceiling lowers too far. You can also snorkel off the island's cliffs, revealing some interesting underwater formations.

Roça Agua Izé   PLANTATION

One of the original 'Big Five' *roças* of São Tomé, this was the plantation that kicked off the cocoa industry in STP, and it still farms the bean, albeit at a much lower production level. If you've seen other *roças* a lap around the buildings will suffice. Otherwise this is a good introduction to the plantation chapter of São Tomé history, assuming you can find a guide on site that speaks your language – a hit-or-miss proposition.

🏃 Activities & Tours

Atlantic Diving Center   DIVING

(☑ 224 2400; www.atlanticdivingcenter.com; Club Santana resort; 1-tank dive €45; ⊘ 8am-1.30pm) STP's best dive center is a very ship-shape operation, offering all PADI courses up to divemaster, with nitrox forthcoming. It reaches about six good dive sites from here on a regular basis. Expect warm clear water, interesting geological formations, and tropical life, although overfishing means that big fish are scarce. Inexpensive boat trips to Ilhéu de Santana are also offered.

Marapa   ECOTOUR

(☑ 991 7602; www.marapa.org; EN-2 (Malanza); per person €10) If you have never been in a mangrove swamp, you might find this hourlong trip into one interesting, but pass otherwise. It is fun to canoe up a tropical river, but there is no life to be seen apart from a few mudskippers. Departs from the bridge just south of Malanza. Portuguese only.

🛏 Sleeping

⭐ **Pousada Roça São João**   POUSADA $

(☑ 226 1140; www.facebook.com/rocasaojoao; EN-2, São João dos Angolares; d incl breakfast €35) This budget charmer is the best *roça* to stay in on the island. It's a classic administrator's house, with two stories of wraparound veranda and endless interior rooms (including its famous restaurant) full of books and art. There's lot of places to hang out, including a hammock in the restaurant (grab it!). A herd of ducks guards the entrance.

★ **Praia Inhame Ecolodge** ECOLODGE $$
(📞 991 6552; www.hotelpraiainhame.com; Praia Inhame; bungalows incl breakfast from €80; 📶) 🏖
At the remote southern end of the island, this ecolodge has been a great success due to its excellent management, which pays attention to details. Nicely situated on its own private beach, with a view toward Ilhéu das Rolas, it offers clean wooden bungalows on stilts. The bungalows are of various sizes, with comfy beds and wide decks nestled in the trees.

Jalé Ecolodge ECOLODGE $$
(📞 222 2792; www.ecolodgejale.com; Praia Jalé; bungalows incl breakfast €45-60) 🏖 You have reached the end of the road. And that is why you are here. Compared to São Tomé's other ecolodges, Jalé is primitive, with three bungalows, a small restaurant, minimal staff and few activities. What it does have is a long, empty, roaring palm-fringed beach. This is where you come to escape the Feds. Or to see nesting turtles (September to April).

Praia N'Guembu BUNGALOW $$
(📞 991 3630; Praia N'Guembu; s/d bungalow €40/60) This bungalow resort was about to open during research. It's similar to neighbouring Praia Inhame ecolodge, but with a few disadvantages: the beach is not as protected, the restaurant (menu €15) is a hike up a hill, and the bungalows have tiny decks. It's brand new, however, and nicely furnished.

★ **Ondas Divinas** COTTAGE $$$
(📞 990 4382; www.facebook.com/casaondas divinas; Santana; 2-/8-person cottage €130/200; 📶) STP needs more of this! Trailblazing entrepreneur Yves has built five fantastic beach cottages on a cliff overlooking the sea, with spectacular views from all rooms. A precipitous walkway takes you to the castaway beach below. Arrive with all your groceries, or sign up for the delicious half board (€20), as Yves was a professional chef.

★ **Club Santana** RESORT $$$
(📞 224 2400; www.clubsantana.com; Praia Messias Alves; s/d bungalows with half board €160/180; 🅿 ❄ 📶 ⛱) This resort has a welcome lack of pretension. While its tar-paper roofs resemble a tropical research station, it's so dated it's retro cool, and fits the island perfectly. The 1980s air-conditioned bungalows are spread over a hillside above a beautiful crescent beach, within sight of a fishing village on an attractive cove.

Eating

★ **Roça São João** FUSION $$
(📞 226 1140; EN-2, São João dos Angolares; menu €12; ⏰ 7am-10pm; 🅿) This well-known restaurant, an ever-popular weekend drive from the capital, occupies a sprawling deck at a classic *roça* administrator's house, with valley views towards the sea. The food is a mélange of European, African and São Toméan tastes, but best when it sticks to creative takes on local fare, be it chicken or fish. The prix fixe menu makes choosing easy.

Mionga SEAFOOD $$
(📞 226 1140; EN-2, São João dos Angolares; menus €10; ⏰ 7am-11pm) Located in two colourful waterfront shacks on a swampy peninsula, this is an excellent stop for creative seafood, above and beyond the normal plates of fried fish and banana chips found elsewhere. The only drawback is the flies. Reserve ahead weekends.

❶ Getting There & Away

Transport is all by shared taxi. A seat from the capital to São João dos Angolares (one hour) costs Db25,000, and to Porto Alegre (two hours) costs Db30,000.

Ilhéu das Rolas

Ilhéu das Rolas is a small island straddling the equator off the southern tip of São Tomé. It is essentially a resort island, the home of the Pestana Ecuador resort, although there is also a small village in which most of the resort workers live. The island takes about an hour to walk from top to bottom, and two to three hours to circumnavigate, but packs in quite a few attractions, more than enough for a day's adventure. Ideally you should spend a night to get the full experience.

TREKKING ROÇA CIRCUIT

Beginning at Roça São João, this easy 2½-hour circuit takes in the neighbouring *dependencias* (satellite plantations) of Roça Soledade and Roça Fraternidade (both in ruins), and follows the beachfront at São João dos Angolares before returning by wading a stream. Along the way you'll catch great views of Pico Maria Fernandez and Cão Grande (p302). Hire a guide (€30 per couple) through Pousada Roça São João (p304).

◉ Sights & Activities

★ Praia Bateria
BEACH

So perfect it stops you in your tracks, this cute little beach is a scallop of sand wedged between long walls of rock. Swimming here is like being in your own private bath. Definitely the couple's first choice, you'll either have it to yourself or you won't want to intrude on someone else.

★ Praia Café
BEACH

In the running for island's best beach, Praia Café is a short walk from the pier, and should not be missed. A beautiful arc of sand, it also offers excellent snorkeling when the waves are calm.

Costa Norte
DIVING, FISHING

(📞 999 3715; www.costanorte.pt; Pestana Ecuador Resort; 1-/2-tank dive €55/100; ⊙ 8am-5pm) Although 80% of its business is diving, Costa Norte also offers sport fishing (four/eight hours €375/550), whale and dolphin watching (€40 per hour), and an inexpensive boat trip around Rolas (€25, two-person minimum). It also has an office in the Pestana São Tomé (p302).

🛏 Sleeping

Pestana Ecuador
RESORT $$$

(📞 226 1195; www.pestana.com; d with full board €255; ❀ 🛜 🏊) Occupying the northern end of the island, this resort offers spacious duplex cabins of varnished wood with decks in a garden setting, overlooking a massive saltwater pool. There's a nice beach facing São Tomé, and others (like Praia Café) within walking range.

❶ Getting There & Away

Access to the island is via a ferry run by the Pestana Ecuador resort twice a day. The crossing takes 30 minutes. The ferry departs Ponta Baleia, the peninsula opposite Porto Alegre, at 10.10am and 5.30pm. It departs the resort pier at 9.30am and 4.30pm. The cost is €14 per person round trip. There is also a €6 per person island fee paid upon landing.

Travellers are advised not to try to hire a boat in Porto Alegre to reach Ilhéu das Rolas, as these boats are prone to accidents in the channel.

Interior

The interior of São Tomé offers the chance to head deep into mountainous jungle along old plantation roads, with some stretches still paved in stone. Cool air, huge trees, roadside waterfalls, alluring vistas and a reflective peacefulness await. The key routes are the EN-3 to Bom Sucesso, and the even better ride to more remote Roça Bombaim.

Pico de São Tomé is an impressive peak soaring 2024m above the sea like a great green tooth bleeding mist. You can see it best from the EN-1 as you drive from Neves to Santa Catalina. Or you can reach the summit by making the country's signature climb. **Cascata São Nicolau** is a nice roadside waterfall (*cascata*), with a bridge across the pool below.

Roça Monte Café (museum & tour €4; ⊙ 8am-4pm Mon-Fri, to 1pm Sat & Sun) is the most pleasant *roça* to visit. A hillside village of plantation houses, it offers a small museum and formal tour of the coffee production process (the arabica variety grows well at this 600m altitude). The tour nicely ties the entire plantation together, including a school with 150 children. Tastings at the small gift shop. English-speaking guide available. The obvious entrance is located on the right about 6km inland from Trindade on the EN-3.

Trekking routes from the interior extend out to the east and west coasts of the island, offering some fine long-distance journeys. Heading east from Roça Bombaim, you can reach Roça Agua-Izé in six hours. Heading west from Bom Sucesso, you can reach Roça Ponta Figo via Lagoa Amelia and Pico de São Tomé (p304), a two-day event. Bombaim and Bom Sucesso are further joined by a six-hour trek, with basic accommodations at either end. Guides are generally available at the office at the **Jardim Botânico** (Bom Sucesso; tour €2; ⊙ 8am-5pm), or book through Navetur (p301). Don't forget your rain gear.

One of the island's better hikes is the-hour-long trek from the Jardim Botânico in Bom Sucesso, where you pick up a guide (€20 to €30), to **Lagoa Amelia**. The name notwithstanding, this is no lagoon, but a unique crater filled with water and covered with a thick layer of earth, so that you can walk on it.

🛏 Sleeping

Pousada Bombaim
POUSADA $

(📞 987 5978; Roça Bombaim; s/d €30/40, full board €54/64) Set in spectacular jungle surroundings in the remote heart of the island, Pousada Bombaim occupies the central plantation house on the otherwise eerily abandoned Roça Bombaim. Unfortunately this classic home with its two-storey verandas has seen better days. What should be a five star inn is now a hostel with basic rooms, plain food and a widespread lack of maintenance.

Albergue Bom Sucesso AGRITURISMO $
(Bom Sucesso; d/tr €30/35) The botanical garden in Bom Sucesso offers a few clean and simple en suite rooms with a basic communal kitchen. This is a transit point for several long distance treks, with meals available for €10. Book through Navetur (p301).

ℹ️ Getting There & Away

While you can reach Bom Sucesso, and possibly Bombaim, by taxi, renting a 4WD for the day is the best option, so you can move around at your own pace. You will also need a guide to not only understand what you are seeing, but to explore a region with no road signs. Guides can be hired through Navetur (p301), or at the Jardim Botânico in Bom Sucesso.

PRÍNCIPE

POP 7000

Príncipe is in many ways a smaller version of São Tomé, with a port capital in the north, a vast uninhabited forest in the south, and a few *roças* (plantations) sprinkled around. However, due to its much smaller population this island is more unspoiled, feels more remote and is ultimately more attractive. Nature rules here, and beautifully so: an intact canopy covers everything with the exception of the airport and the tiny capital, Santo António, creating an emerald isle accented by fantastic beaches. Raw phonolite towers of various shapes punch through the forest, forming a crazy skyline, and making the entire island feel like Jurassic Park – without the dinosaurs, although there are some interesting endemic species that won't eat you. Recognising this natural patrimony, Unesco made Príncipe a World Biosphere Reserve in 2013. Given recent infrastructure upgrades, including a new international airport, perhaps you should visit sooner rather than later.

Once the subject of a world-famous Bacardi advertisement (you'll remember it when you see it), the picture-perfect tropical beach of **Praia Banana** is located on the grounds of Roça Belo Monte, a 15-minute walk from the front gate. It is first seen from above, at a clifftop *mirador* (overlook; where the ad was shot), before descending to sea level, where you'll find its golden sands.

The spectacular **Baía das Agulhas** (Bay of Spires) is not just Príncipe's top attrac-

tion, but STP's as well. It's best seen from the water, where the postcard view of the island's world-class skyline slowly unfolds, including phonolite towers named (for obvious reasons) the Father, the Son and the Grandson, along with Table Mountain. You expect to hear the primordial roar of T-Rex at any moment. If you've flown all this way, you do not want to miss this.

Praia Macaco is an excellent swimming beach. It's wonderfully private and isolated, so bring everything you'll need. The best way to find it is to ask the guard at the front gate to Roça Belo Monte; you may also hire a guide here if necessary.

Praia Boi is a postcard tropical beach, with turquoise water, swaying palms and no people. You will need to bring your own food, but it is perfect for a picnic. Located around the headland from Praia Macaco, it is accessed by car via a signless complex of rough dirt roads best navigated with local assistance. The guard at the entrance to Roça Belo Monte is a good source of information, and may be able to find you a local guide.

🏃 Activities

Activities including hiking, diving, boat tours, stand-up paddleboarding and quad biking are offered to all comers by the resorts, particularly Bom Bom and Roça Belo Monte. Makaira Lodge is the source for deep-sea fishing. All have guides who speak English.

Quad Biking

Quad bikes are the perfect way to explore Príncipe, as you can access many of the old plantation roads that interlace the island. Roça Belo Monte offers three-hour quad tours with guide for €40 per person – a bargain.

Baía das Agulhas Boat Tour

Fully taking in the country's top sight really requires a boat journey, and several resorts offer trips. The best is led by Bom Bom Resort – its three-hour tour costs €150 for the boat (maximum six people). While in the calm bay you can take in the views on a stand-up paddleboard. Or you can dip beneath the waters for some interesting snorkelling among the great variety of fish that inhabit the shoreline.

🛏️ Sleeping

Hotel Rural Abade POUSADA $$
(📞 991 6024; www.abadeprincipe.com; Roça Abade; d incl breakfast €70) These basic rooms, some with shared bathroom, in the former administrator's house of Roça Abade are

TREKKING PORTO REAL TRAIL

In the town of Porto Real, Príncipe's only official self-guided trail has been constructed, a 6km three-hour hike into the forest that ends with a beautiful view. The trailhead is indicated by a big wooden sign, and located to the right of the old hospital ruins, now overrun by jungle. Anyone in the village can direct you.

only a good option if you really want to get away from it all, as they require a significant drive to a remote part of the island. The chief attractions are the low price and the beautiful view of Ilhéu Caroço (Jockey Cap island).

★ **Bom Bom Resort**   RESORT $$$
(☑225 1114; www.bombomprincipe.com; bungalows with pool or garden view and half board s/d €260/320; ❄️🛜🏊) 🍴 It's hard to find fault with this slice of tropical paradise, for while that term is highly overused, it does apply here. The resort has an extraordinary location encompassing both a coastal peninsula, where the bungalows are, and tiny Bom Bom island, where the bar-restaurant is. The two are connected by a 140m-long wooden bridge flanked by two gorgeous beaches.

★ **Roça Belo Monte**   POUSADA $$$
(☑225 1152; www.belomontehotel.com; s/d incl breakfast €152/235; ❄️🛜🏊) This beautifully renovated and fast-expanding *roça* is the best of its kind in STP. High up on a hill, it affords marvellous views of the coastline from various points, most notably its lovely veranda. There is a great variety of spacious rooms in a quadrangle of outbuildings, the most luxurious being in the main house, as well as several well-appointed cottages.

Makaira Lodge   TENTED CAMP $$$
(☑906 5935; www.makaira-adventure.com; Praia Campanha; s/d/tr with half board €135/165/215) Here lies the great secret of Príncipe lodging. During research Makaira Lodge had just opened, and was putting the finishing touches on its dipping pool. The lodge is brilliantly simple: six high-end safari tents on a beautiful secluded beach. The canvas tents are spacious and furnished with all electrics, private bathrooms and thoughtful design flourishes, beginning with the canopy beds.

❶ Getting There & Away

The only scheduled transport to or from Príncipe is the twice-daily STP Airways shuttle between Príncipe Airport (PCP) and São Tomé International Airport (TMS). The plane leaves TMS around 9am and returns around 11am. In the afternoon it departs TMS around 4pm and returns around 6pm. The flight lasts around 45 minutes and costs around €150 return.

Santo António

POP 1500

While it's the island capital, Santo António is just a small grid of unkempt streets scattered with concrete-block buildings. It has an otherwise pretty location astride a river that empties into a narrow bay. The best views of the area are from the yellow hospital at the entrance to the bay. Looking inland affords a dramatic view of Pico Papagaio (Parrot Peak), the island's tallest mountain at 680m. Come here for the island's least expensive accommodation, to top up your phone, change money or mail that postcard.

Your best in-town option, **Complexo Mira Rio** (☑986 9003, 990 6454; gruposalvador51@gmail.com; Rua Martires da Liberdade; s/d €50/70; ⏱6am-10pm; ❄️🛜) is a spick-and-span hotel nicely located opposite the Papagaio River bridge, with a small grocery store downstairs. The rooms are well lit, with comfy mattresses. Best of all there is a nice terrace restaurant overlooking the river, with food cooked to order, including some very generous sandwiches. This is the best place in town to hang out.

If Complexo Mira Rio is full, default to **Residential Palhota** (☑225 1060, 993 8153; hotelpalhota@gmail.com; Ave Martires da Liberdade; s/d €50/70; ❄️). Beaten up but serviceable, it includes the adjacent thatched hut restaurant (menu €10) which is open all day. Book ahead as rooms fill up.

Run by the former chef at Bom Bom resort, the humble **Pastelaria** (☑991 9539; António Segundo II; dinner menu Db100,000; ⏱6-10pm, lunch on request) punches well above its weight. The very clean kitchen turns out a dinner menu each night. Also has a small bar.

Top up your phone at CST, and change money at **BISTP** (Ave Carneiro; ⏱8am-3pm Mon-Fri, to noon Sat). The post office is on Marcelo da Veiga Sq.

There's no public transport in Santo António. Travellers typically arrange transport through their hotel, which can contact informal taxi services. For short trips, flag down a passing motorcycle.

UNDERSTAND SÃO TOMÉ & PRÍNCIPE

São Tomé & Príncipe Today

São Toméans face a harsh historical reality: independence has impoverished the country. The elderly will tell you that colonial times may not have been ideal, but at least there was electricity, sanitation, running water and a public bus service.

Deep in the jungle, one comes upon forgotten roads and bridges carefully made of stone, amid cocoa plants gone wild. In the capital, shipwrecks dot the harbour, potholes scar the streets, and scores of once-beautiful colonial homes lie rotting; only one has been restored, with EU funding. Outside the capital, people eke out a living in ramshackle fishing villages, with rudimentary sanitation.

The current prime minister is Patrice Trovoada (son of Miguel Trovoada, the country's first prime minister), who was elected in 2014. With the once-promising search for offshore oil having ground to a halt, the silent question hanging over the people is when the slow, unending decline in their living conditions will finally prompt a revolution. Today 85% of the annual budget consists of foreign aid.

History

There are essentially two chapters in the history of São Tomé and Príncipe: before 1975, and after 1975. Both are on view everywhere.

Before 1975, STP was one of Portugal's four African colonies. The Portuguese discovered the uninhabited islands in the late 15th century, and transformed them into breadbaskets of tropical agriculture, in two historic waves. The first was based on sugar, powered by slave labour (with freed slaves also part of the social fabric) and lasted for much of the 16th century. Following two centuries of decline, during which the islands became an outpost of the transatlantic slave trade, the 19th century brought two new crops, coffee and cocoa, and extraordinary growth: by the early 20th century São Tomé was one of the world's largest cocoa producers.

The 19th-century agricultural boom transformed STP into an enormous network of plantations, known as *roças* ('clearings'). On São Tomé five major *roças* evolved and over 100 major *dependencias* (satellites), all linked by stone roads and a narrow-gauge rail network that eventually brought crops to the pier for transportation to Europe. The *roças* were towns unto themselves, with a grand administrator's mansion, huge hospitals, warehouses, bean drying sheds, and housing for hundreds of workers and their families. Collectively, they turned STP into one enormously productive farm.

In 1975, all of this changed, and rapidly so, with the independence of STP from Portugal. In 1974, a bloodless coup had restored democracy to Portugal. Tired of fighting costly insurrections in all of its other African colonies, Portugal decided to liberate them all at once. In STP, the effect was immediate. Facing the nationalisation of their property, and fearing for their personal safety, the Portuguese quickly abandoned the entire country, leaving behind a mostly unskilled, illiterate population.

The country first turned to Communism, which lasted 15 years until the fall of the Soviet Union. It remained closely aligned with Angola, Cuba and communist eastern Europe until the demise of the Soviet Union, when São Toméans began to demand multiparty democracy. The first elections were held in 1991. Since then, the islands have experienced a long period of political instability, with several coups and major corruption scandals upending and reinstalling various presidents and prime ministers in a complex soup of events. Neither form of government was able to prevent an economic apocalypse. Without the ability to run the *roças* as profitable businesses, the economic foundation of the entire country collapsed.

The People

São Toméans consist of *mestiços,* mixed-blood descendants of Portuguese colonists and African slaves; Angolares, reputedly descendants of Angolan slaves who survived a 1540 shipwreck and now earn their livelihood fishing; Forros, descendants of freed slaves; Tongas, the children of *serviçais* (contract labourers from Angola, Mozambique and Cape Verde); and Europeans, primarily Portuguese repatriates, who have started many island businesses.

Environment

Every country is the product of its environment, but with its far-flung locale, unique topographical features and endemic wildlife,

STP is more so than most. When you step foot here, you'll feel a long way from anywhere. Many of the species that inhabit the islands perilously arrived on natural rafts flushed into the sea from the rivers of West Africa.

SURVIVAL GUIDE

ⓘ Directory A–Z

ACCOMMODATION

STP is top-heavy: budget accommodation of acceptable quality is relatively scarce. Be very careful of accommodation at *roças* (plantations): only a handful – Roça Sao João (p304), Roça Belo Monte (p308), Roça Bombaim (p306) and soon Roça Sundy – offer acceptable accommodation. Most are either abandoned or squatter settlements with squalid conditions.

DANGERS & ANNOYANCES

São Tomé and Príncipe is an extremely safe destination. However, thefts of personal belongings are common on beaches, particularly those next to villages, where a smartphone is worth an annual salary. The beaches near Morro Peixe, north of São Tomé city, are known for such thefts.

EMERGENCY & IMPORTANT NUMBERS

Country Code	📞 239
International Access Code	📞 00
Emergency	📞 112

GAY & LESBIAN TRAVELLERS

Homosexuality was decriminalised in 2012. However, there are no lesbian or gay organisations and some social stigma remains. Otherwise the *leve leve* ('easy easy') attitude prevails.

INTERNET ACCESS

All major hotels have wi-fi, as do some cafes. When purchasing a SIM, an additional €12 buys you 4GB of web-surfing, and there is coverage virtually everywhere.

ⓘ **SLEEPING PRICE RANGES**

The following price ranges refer to a double room with bathroom:

$ less than €50

$$ €50–100

$$$ more than €100

MONEY

There are no international ATMs, and only certain high-end hotels accept credit cards, with two offering limited cash back (p303), ie they run your credit card for a certain amount and hand it to you in cash. Bringing cash in euros is the best option.

Cash Bring cash denominated in euros, as the dollar is increasingly less common. The dobra can only be used in-country, so you must exchange euros for dobras after you arrive, and dobras for euros before you leave.

Changing money Foreign exchange is normally done through informal brokers (cheapest) or through a bank or a hotel. Don't be put off when approached by moneychangers on the street in São Tomé city, as this is the normal way of doing business, and entirely legal. Just agree on the rate, use your calculator, and count your money. In Príncipe you must use the bank.

The euro can be used almost anywhere, although you will often receive change in dobras, and only dobras. It is also generally more expensive to spend euros, as one way or another an exchange fee gets added in.

Tipping Tipping is not customary, and at the customer's discretion. However, 5% goes a long way locally.

Exchange Rates

Australia	A$1	Db16,930
Canada	C$1	Db16,440
Euro zone	€1	Db24,530
Japan	¥100	Db20,110
New Zealand	NZ$1	Db15,550
UK	£1	Db28,990
US	$1	Db22,480

For current exchange rates, see www.xe.com.

OPENING HOURS

Banks 8am to 3pm Monday to Friday.

Bars & Clubs 10pm to 2am weekends, some during week as well.

Restaurants 11am to 3pm and 6 to11pm (generally closed Mondays).

Shops 8am to 12.30pm and 2 to 5pm Monday to Friday, 8am to 1pm Saturday (although not all shops observe the siesta).

POST

The main post offices are in the island capitals, São Tomé city (p301) and **Santo António** (Marcelo da Veiga Sq; ⊙7am-noon & 2-3.30pm Mon-Fri). STP stamps are particularly valued by collectors!

PUBLIC HOLIDAYS

New Year's Day 1 January

Rei Amador Day 4 January
Heroes Day 3 February
Labour Day 1 May
Independence Day 12 July
Agricultural Reform Day 30 September
São Tomé Day 21 December
Christmas Day 25 December

TELEPHONE

Mobile phone coverage is excellent, reaching all developed areas. SIM cards are available from CST (p301) in São Tomé city and **CST** (225 1100; Ave Martíres da Liberdade; ⊘7am-noon & 2-7pm Mon-Fri, 7am-7pm Sat) in Santo António (Príncipe) for €3, and work with unlocked phones. Add a few euros of credit for local use, and use wi-fi for international calls. Skype users should check the cost of international pay calls to/from STP, as the fees can be exorbitant.

TOURIST INFORMATION

There is limited tourist information available on STP. Web surfers will quickly discover that many official websites do not even function, including that of the government's national tourism office. However, a new website, www.turismo.gov.st, is reportedly coming online soon...

The only tourism bureau (p301) in STP is in São Tomé city.

VISAS

Visas are necessary and a significant headache to obtain. There is an online system (www.smf. st/virtualvisa), but it's known to malfunction for long periods of time.

A 15-day visa is free for citizens from the EU, USA, Canada, and lusophone (Portuguese-speaking) countries, €20 otherwise. A 30-day visa costs €80. Given the problems that may arise in this process, it is best to apply early.

If you book a car rental or hotel booking through the travel agent Navetur (p301), it will sort your visa for you – by far the easiest route. Otherwise you must deal with the closest embassy, of which there are only a few (some offer a mail-in service):

Africa Gabon, Angola, Equatorial Guinea, Nigeria
Asia Taiwan
Europe Lisbon (covers Spain) and Belgium
USA New York

ℹ Getting There & Away

AIR

There are two commercial airports in the country, São Tomé International Airport (TMS) and Príncipe Airport (PCP). At time of research Príncipe's runway had been extended in antic-

---

ℹ EATING PRICE RANGES

The following price ranges represent the cost of a main dish:

$ less than €5
$$ €5–10
$$$ more than €10

---

ipation of direct international flights but none had yet been scheduled.

From Europe, all flights to TMS originate in Lisbon, with one of two carriers: **TAP** (222 2307; www.flytap.com; Rua de Santo António do Príncipe; ⊘24/7), the Portuguese national airline, or **STP Airways** (222 1160; www.stpairways. st; Ave Marginal 12 de Julho; ⊘7.30am-4.30pm Mon-Fri, 9am-noon Sat). STP Airways tickets are significantly cheaper than TAP, but do not show up on conventional booking engines. All online ticketing is done via their website.

From Africa, flights to TMS originate from Luanda, Angola (**TAAG** (122 2593; www.taag. com; Rua Geovane Caixa; ⊘8am-3pm Mon-Fri)); Douala, Cameroon (CEIBA, www.ceibaintercontinental.com); Libreville and Port-Gentil, Gabon (CEIBA and Afrijet, www.flyafrijet.online); Accra, Ghana (TAP); and Malabó, Equatorial Guinea (Punto Azul, www.flypuntoazul.gq). TAAG, CEIBA, Afrijet and Punto Azul are all on the European blacklist.

There is a €20 departure tax.

ℹ Getting Around

AIR

STP Airways (p311) flies back and forth between São Tomé and Príncipe Monday to Saturday (€165, 45 minutes). Seats fill up so book early.

BOAT

Travellers are advised not to use the intermittent ferry service between the islands. The six-hour, open-ocean voyage is both uncomfortable and dangerous, with two ships having sunk in recent years, one of which capsized in São Tomé harbour due to overloading.

CAR & MOTORCYCLE

Shared taxis are the most common form of transport, but to ensure a modicum of comfort sit in front and buy two seats. Motorcycle taxis are also used, but for safety reasons you should limit to in-town use, rather than long distance. Otherwise you will need to rent a car. The only established rental agencies are on São Tomé.

Senegal

♪ 221 / POP 14.5 MILLION

Best Places to Eat

➡ Le Lagon I (p321)

➡ La Kora (p330)

➡ La Guingette (p325)

➡ Casa-Resto (p335)

Best Places to Sleep

➡ Au Fil du Fleuve (p329)

➡ Espace Sobo Badè (p327)

➡ Keur Saloum (p327)

➡ Lodge des Collines de Niassam (p326)

➡ Cisko Centre Culturel (p335)

➡ Hôtel du Phare (p317)

Why Go?

Though it's one of West Africa's most stable countries, Senegal is far from dull. Perched on the tip of a peninsula, Dakar, the capital, is a dizzying, street-hustler-rich introduction to the country: elegance meets chaos, snarling traffic, vibrant markets and glittering nightlife, while nearby Île de Gorée and the beaches of Yoff and N'Gor tap to slow, lazy beats.

In northern Senegal, the enigmatic capital of Saint-Louis, a Unesco World Heritage Site, tempts with colonial architecture and proximity to scenic national parks. Along the Petite Côte and Cap Skirring, wide strips of beaches beckon and the wide deltas of the Casamance invite mesmerising boat journeys amid astounding biodiversity, including hundreds of bird species.

Whether you want to mingle with the trendsetters of urban Africa or be alone with your thoughts and the sounds of nature, you'll find your place in Senegal.

When to Go
Dakar

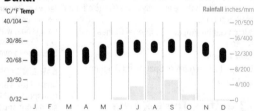

Nov–Feb Senegal's main tourist season is dry and cool.

Dec & Mar–Jun When most music festivals take place, including the Saint-Louis Jazz Festival.

Jul–late Sep Rainy, humid season; some hotels close, others reduce prices by up to 40%.

DAKAR

POP 1.2 MILLION

Dakar is a city of extremes, where horse-cart drivers chug over swish highways and gleaming SUVs squeeze through tiny sand roads; where elegant ladies dig skinny heels into dusty walkways and suit-clad business-men kneel down for prayer in the middle of the street. Once a tiny settlement in the south of the Cap Vert peninsula, Dakar now spreads almost across its entire triangle, and keeps growing.

For the traveller, there's much to discover, from peaceful islands just off-shore to ver-tiginous nightlife dancing to mbalax beats. You can spend your days browsing frenetic markets and taking in the sights of bustling downtown, followed by sunset drinks over-looking the crashing waves. At once both intimidating and deeply alluring, Dakar is a fascinating introduction to Senegal.

◎ Sights

★ Île de N'Gor   ISLAND

(Map p320) For a quick escape from the fre-netic streets of Dakar, head to peaceful Île de N'Gor, a tiny island just off Dakar's north shore. It has a few calm beaches on the bay side, and some legendary surf on the north-ern coastline. Most visitors just come for the day, to relax on the beaches, stroll the sandy lanes of the village and have lunch in one of the waterside eateries, but there are several appealing guesthouses here as well.

★ Musée Théodore Monod   MUSEUM

(Musée IFAN; Map p318; ☑ 33 823 9268; Pl de Soweto, Plateau; adult/child CFA5000/1000; ⊙ 9am-5pm Tue-Sun) The is one of Senegal's best museums. Exhibitions delve into Afri-can art and culture with over 9000 objects on display. Lively displays of masks and traditional dress from across the region (including Mali, Guinea-Bissau, Benin and Nigeria) give an excellent overview of styles without bombarding you with more than you can take in.

Village des Arts   ARTS CENTRE

(Map p320; ☑ 33 835 7160; Rte de Yoff; ⊙ 9.30am-7pm) FREE An arts tour around Dakar is simply not complete without a visit to this famous art complex, where some of Sene-gal's most promising and established paint-ers, sculptors and multimedia artists create, shape and display their works in individu-al studios scattered around a large garden space. There's also an on-site gallery, which exhibits works by artists both home-grown and from abroad.

Médina   AREA

(Map p316) A bustling popular *quartier* with tiny tailor's shops, a busy **Marché Tilène** (Map p316; Ave Blaise Diagne; ⊙ 8am-4pm) and streets brimming with life, the Médina was built as a township for the local pop-ulace by the French during colonial days. It's the birthplace of Senegalese superstar and current minister of culture Youssou N'Dour. Besides being a very real neighbour-hood, where creative ideas and new trends grow between crammed, makeshift homes, it's also home to Dakar's 1664 **Grande Mosquée**, impressive for its sheer size and landmark minaret.

☆ Activities

Dakar's best beaches are found in the north of the peninsula. **Plage de N'Gor** (Map p320) is often crowded; if so, you're better off catching the frequent pirogues (CFA500) to Île de N'Gor, which has two small beaches.

Dakar has decent waves and a growing surf scene. In Yoff, **Plage de Virage** (Map p320; Yoff) is good; **Plage de Yoff** (Map p320) is rubbish-strewn in parts but waves are strong enough for surfing. Malika Surf Camp (p317), **École Surf Attitude** (Map p320; ☑ 77 034 3434; www.senegalsurf.com; Plage des Viviers, Corniche des Almadies; 2hr surf class CFA15,000, 10-class package CFA120,000) and **N'Gor Island Surf Camp** (Map p320; ☑ 77 336 9150; www.gosurf.dk; dm/s/d with half-board CFA25,000/50,000/80,000; ⚛ ⚛) can point out additional surf spots; they also run courses and hire out boards.

Nautilus Diving   DIVING

(Map p320; ☑ 77 637 1422; www.nautilus-diving. com; N'Gor; discovery dives CFA28,000, two dives CFA53,000; ⊙ 9am-7pm Tue-Sun) Operating out of the Maison Abaka (p318), this pro-fessional, French-run outfit offers diving to suit all levels (and courses for those who want to learn). The friendly owners, Hilda and Philippe, also speak English (and some Spanish).

☞ Tours

Andaando (☑ 77 793 9432; www.andaando. com; Sicap Mbao 199, Thiaroye) A recom-mended agency with trips to Saint-Louis, the desert of Lampou, the Casamance

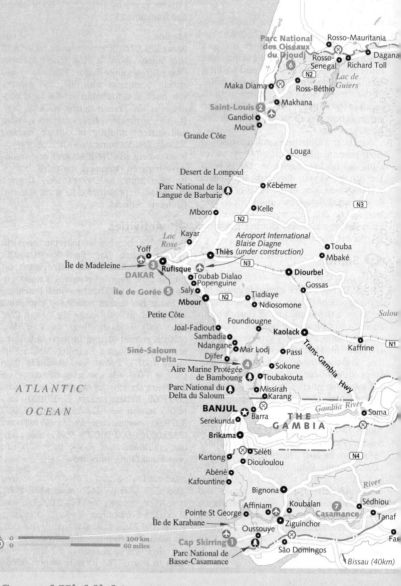

Senegal Highlights

1 **Cap Skirring** (p333)
Weaving your way via tiny villages to Senegal's best beaches and kicking back for a day of doing absolutely nothing.

2 **Saint-Louis** (p327)
Wandering the cobblestone streets past colourful French colonial buildings in a Unesco World Heritage Site.

3 **Dakar** (p313) Spending sleepless nights touring the vibrant nightclubs and bars of the capital.

4 **Siné-Saloum Delta** (p325) Gliding through

Senegal *River*
Podor
Île à Morphil
Bogué
Taredji
Saldé

MAURITANIA

Kifa

Mbout

Réserve Slvo-Pastorale s Six Forages

Kankossa

N2

Réserve de Faune du Ferlo-Nord
Ouro Sogui
Matam

nguère

N3

N2

Senegal

Réserve de Faune du Ferlo-Sud

Bakel

River

Réserve Sylvo-Pastorale Siné-Saloum

Kayes

River

Kidira ⊗ Diboli

Koumpentoum

Koussanar
Tambacounda

N1

Sadiola

MALI

Maka

Dialafar

Janjanbureh (Georgetown)
⊗
Pata

Gambia

Saïnsoutou

Basse Santa Su

Sabi
Vélingara

Dar Salam

N7

Niokolo-Koba

Kolda
N6

Diaoubé

Simenti

River

Geba River

Parc National de Niokolo-Koba
▲ Mt Assirik (311m)

Saraya

Salikénié
⊗
⊗

Ethiowar

Salémata
Iwol
Bassari Country
Kédougou ⊗

GUINEA-BISSAU

Ethiolo
Ibel
Bandafassi

Koundara
Dindéfelo
Ségou
Niagalankome

Gabú

Dande

Fongolimbi

GUINEA

mangroves in a pirogue (traditional motorised canoe).

5 **Île de Gorée** (p324) Contemplating history at Maison des Esclaves and browsing the handiwork of

local artists on this peaceful island.

6 **Parc National des Oiseaux du Djoudj** (p330) Spotting flamingos, black-

crowned night herons and dozens of other bird species.

7 **Casamance** (p331) Exploring a lush, tropical island or sandy shore.

Dakar

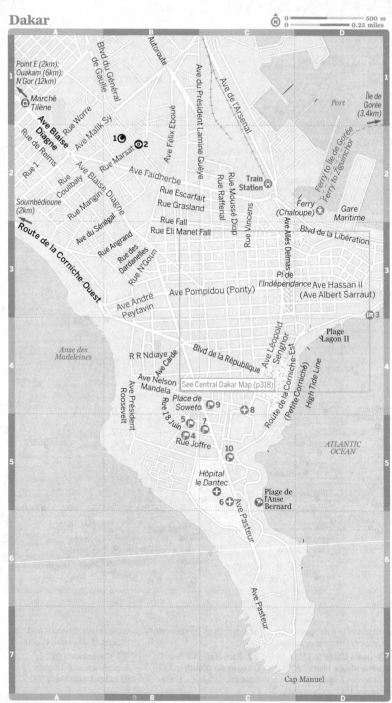

N

0 ————————————— 500 m
0 ————————————— 0.25 miles

Point E (2km);
Ouakam (6km);
N'Gor (12km)

Marché
Tilène

Île de
Gorée
(3.4km)

Port

Blvd du Général
de Gaulle

Autoroute

Ave du Président Lamine Guèye

Ave de l'Arsenal

Rue Worre

Ave Malik Sy

Rue Marsat

Ave Félix Eboué

Rue de Reims

Rue 1

Ave Blaise Diagne

Ave Faidherbe

Rue Escarfait

Rue Grasland

Train
Station

Rue Moussé Diop

Rue Raffenal

Ferry
(Chaloupe)

Gare
Maritime

Ferry to île de Gorée
Ferry to Ziguinchor

Rue Coulibaly

Rue Mangin Diagne

Ave Blaise Diagne

Rue du Sénégal

Rue Fall

Rue Eli Manel Fall

Rue Vincens

Ave Alliés Delmas

Blvd de la Libération

Soumbédioune
(2km)

Route de la Corniche-Ouest

Ave André
Peytavin

Rue Angrand

Rue des
Dardanelles

Rue N'Goun

Ave Pompidou (Ponty)

Pl de
l'Indépendance

Ave Hassan II
(Ave Albert Sarraut)

Plage
Lagon II

Anse des
Madeleines

R R Ndiaye

Ave Carde

Blvd de la République

Ave Nelson
Mandela

Ave Léopold
Senghor

See Central Dakar Map (p318)

Ave Président
Roosevelt

Rue 18 Juin

Place de
Soweto

Route de la Corniche-Est
(Petite Corniche)

High Tide Line

ATLANTIC
OCEAN

Rue Joffre

Hôpital
le Dantec

Plage de
l'Anse
Bernard

Ave Pasteur

Ave Pasteur

Cap Manuel

SENEGAL DAKAR

Dakar

◉ Sights
1 Grande Mosquée B2
2 Médina..B2

🛏 Sleeping
3 Le Lagon II...D3

ℹ Information
4 Cabo Verdean Embassy B5
5 Canadian Embassy...............................B5
6 Clinique du Cap C5
7 German Embassy C5
8 Hôpital Principal...................................C4
9 Spanish Embassy C4
10 UK Embassy C5

and the big national parks, plus day trips around Dakar.

Boumak NDofféene Diouf (✎ 77 339 7712) English-speaking guide; ask for him at Via Via.

Nouvelles Frontières (Map p320; ✎ 33 859 4447; www.nfsenegal.com; Lot 1 Mamelles Aviation, Rte des Almadies; ⊙ 8.30am-6pm Mon-Fri, 9am-12.30pm Sat) Offers a wide range of tours: Lac Rose, Saint-Louis, Parc National de Niokolo-Koba, the Petite Côte and other destinations.

SenegalStyle (✎ 77 791 5469; SenegalStyle@ gmail.com; Cité Africa, Unit 13, Ouest Foire) Offers customised tours (by car or motorbike), plus activities like drumming lessons.

✪ Festivals & Events

Dak'Art Biennale   ART
(✎ 33 823 0918; www.facebook.com/dakartbien nale; ⊙ May) Held on even-numbered years, this festival of painting and sculpture is the queen of Dakar's festivals. It drowns the town in colour for the whole of May, with exhibitions all across Dakar. Unmissable.

🛏 Sleeping

Quicksilver
Boardriders Dakar   GUESTHOUSE, HOSTEL $
(Map p320; ✎ 78 196 9349; www.quiksilver-board riders-dakar.com; Rond-point N'Gor, Les Almadies; dm/s/d from CFA10,000/15,000/20,000; 🖁🗷) Tucked behind the Quicksilver shop is this appealing guesthouse, with the hip-but-laid-back vibe you'd expect from the well-known clothing brand. Rooms are clean and well-kept, if minimally furnished, and overlook a lovely patio with a pool and outdoor bar that's great to meet other travellers.

Malika Surf Camp   GUESTHOUSE $
(Map p320; ✎ 77 113 2791; www.surfinsenegal. com; Yoff Plage; r per person with half board from CFA17,000; 🖁) This small, Italian-run place on Yoff beach has a bohemian vibe that draws a mix of surfers, aspiring surfers and those just wanting to enjoy the beach. Rooms are basic, but there's a small court-yard strung with hammocks, and a roof deck where you can sit on a bamboo chair, cold drink in hand, and watch the waves roll in.

Via Via   GUESTHOUSE $
(Map p320; ✎ 33 820 5475; www.viavia.world/ en/africa/dakar; Rte des Cimetières, Yoff; s/d CFA17,000/28,000, dm/s/d with shared bathroom CFA9500/12,000/22,000; 🖁🗷) Offers clean, simple rooms with fan and mosquito nets set around a courtyard. The welcoming staff is great here, and in season (November to March) they whip up tasty traditional meals, serve cocktails (a rarity in Yoff) and host monthly events, such as live music and film screenings.

Keur Diame   HOTEL, HOSTEL $
(Map p320; ✎ 33 820 9676; www.aubergekeur diame.wordpress.com; Cité Djily Mbaye 265, Yoff; s/d CFA21,000/29,000, s/d with shared bathroom CFA15,000/23,000; 🖁🗷) On a peaceful street by the beach, this friendly, Swiss-owned guesthouse offers attractively furnished rooms decorated with touches of African textiles. Three of the seven rooms have ocean views. There's ample space to relax with a roof deck, a courtyard and an indoor dining area with a small lending library.

★ Hôtel du Phare   HOTEL $$
(Map p320; ✎ 33 860 3000; www.hotelduphare-dakar.com; 36 Cité des Magistrats, Les Mamelles; r CFA23,000-42,000; 🖁🗷) This attractive and welcoming guesthouse has 10 cheerfully painted rooms, a book-filled lounge, and a restaurant with seats in a small courtyard. The rooftop deck, though, is the best fea-ture, and a fine spot for tapas and sunset cocktails – plus occasional events like film screenings and music jams.

La Maison d'Italie   GUESTHOUSE $$
(Map p320; ✎ 77 572 4306; www.chezcarla hotel.com; Deuxieme Plage, Île de N'Gor; s/d from CFA29,000/40,000; 🖁🗷) A charming guest-house with five bright, cheerfully painted rooms and a terrace with sea views. The res-taurant is also a draw, with a deck perched out over the water and good seafood and Italian plates (mains CFA6000 to CFA9500).

Central Dakar

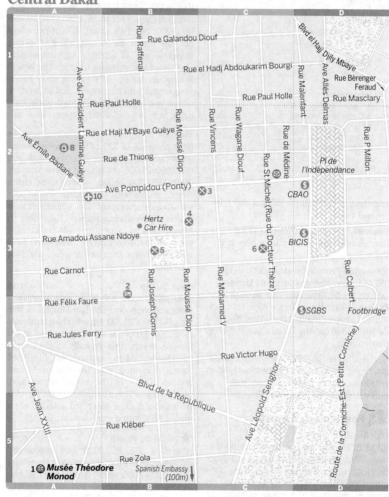

Fleur de Lys HOTEL **$$**
(Map p318; ☑ 33 849 4600; www.hotelfleur
delysdakar.com; 64 Rue Félix Faure; s/d/ste
CFA56,000/87,000/120,000; ❈ 🛜 🌊) This
12-storey hotel offers well-designed rooms
and suites with all the essentials, plus extras
like rain showers and balconies with views
in the pricier chambers. There's a gym, an
11th-floor restaurant with views and a roof-
top pool overlooking the city centre.

La Demeure GUESTHOUSE **$$**
(Map p320; ☑ 33 820 7679; www.lademeure-guest
house.com; off Rte de N'Gor; s CFA50,000-69,000,

d CFA59,000-79,000; ❈ 🛜 🌊) Oozing laid-back
elegance, this little guesthouse offers pleasant rooms (all with balconies) in a rambling,
well-maintained house filled with a clutch of
tasteful art collected by its engaging owner.
It boasts a fantastic terrace with views over
the greenery and out to the ocean – the perfect spot for a sunset drink from the bar.

Maison Abaka HOTEL **$$**
(Map p320; ☑ 33 820 6486; www.maison-aba
ka.com; Plage de N'Gor; d CFA40,000-70,000;
❈ 🛜 🌊) This handsomely designed guest-
house has airy and lovingly decorated rooms

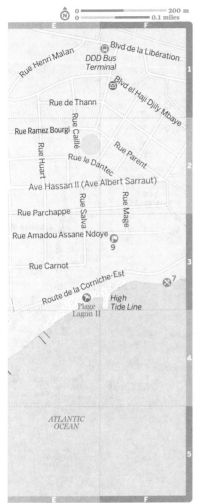

0   200 m
0   0.1 miles

SENEGAL DAKAR

I, you can drift off to sleep to the sound of waves lapping at the shore.

✖ Eating

Le Bideew   INTERNATIONAL $$
(Map p318; ☑ 33 823 1909; 89 Rue Joseph Gomis; mains CFA3500-6000; ☺ 10am-11pm Mon-Sat; ☑) In the cool shade of the garden of the Institut Français Léopold Sédar Senghor, this colourful arts cafe is perfect for a break from the city. The varied menu features vegetable curry, octopus salad, chargrilled pork and creative dishes such as grilled prawns with *bissap* chutney. Sunday brunch is a hit (10am to 2pm).

Le Djembé   AFRICAN $$
(Map p318; ☑ 33 821 0666; 56 Rue St Michel; dishes CFA2500-5000; ☺ noon-7pm Mon-Sat) A block west of Pl de l'Indépendance, this inviting, colourful eatery is the whispered insider-tip for anyone in search of a filling platter of *thiéboudienne* (rice baked in a thick sauce of fish and vegetables). There's also *poulet yassa* (grilled chicken in onion and lemon sauce), *bissap* juice (a purple drink made from water and hibiscus leaves), lively music and a good mix of locals and expats.

Ali Baba Snack Bar   FAST FOOD $$
(Map p318; ☑ 33 822 5297; Ave Pompidou; sandwiches around CFA 1700, mains CFA3500-5000; ☺ 8am-2am) Dakar's classic fast-food haunt keeps on turning thanks to the undying love

located right behind the beach. The patio is the highlight, with a tiny bar on hand (also good food in the evenings) and small tables that give breezy views over the shore.

Le Lagon II   HOTEL $$$
(Map p316; ☑ 33 889 2525; www.lelagondakar.com; Rte de la Corniche Est; s/d/ste CFA101,000/112,000/193,000; ❋ ☎) Tucked along waterfront Corniche Est, this place feels like a nautical hideway, with modern, nicely set rooms, all with balconies perched right over the ocean. After dining next door at the good seafood restaurant Le Lagon

Greater Dakar

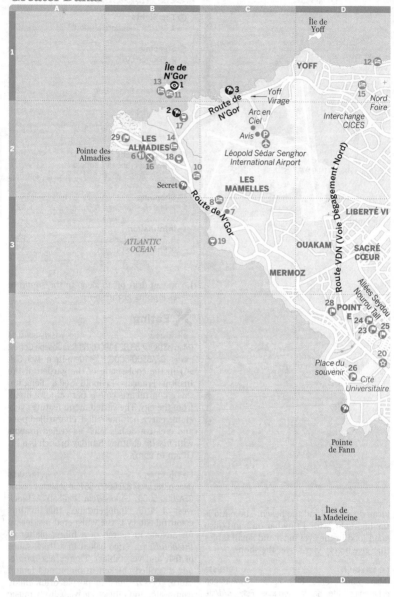

Île de
Yoff

YOFF

12

15   Nord
Foire

Île de
N'Gor

13   1

11

2   3   Yoff
Virage

Route de
N'Gor

Arc en
Ciel

Avis

Interchange
CICES

17

29   14   LES
ALMADIES

Pointe des
Almadies

6   18

16   10

Léopold Sédar Senghor
International Airport

Secret

LES
MAMELLES

Route de N'Gor

8   7

19

LIBERTÉ VI

OUAKAM   SACRÉ
CŒUR

MERMOZ

ATLANTIC
OCEAN

Route VDN (Voie Dégagement Nord)

28   POINT
E   24   25

23   20

Place du
souvenir   26   Cité
Universitaire

Pointe
de Fann

Îles de
la Madeleine

SENEGAL DAKAR

of the Senegalese. Serves the whole fast-food range: kebabs, shwarmas and other quick snacks.

Chez Loutcha   AFRICAN $$

(Map p318; ☑ 33 821 0302; 101 Rue Moussé Diop; mains CFA4300-7600; ☉ noon-3pm & 7-10pm Mon-Sat) This friendly, always overflowing place serves up huge Senegalese and Cabo Ver-

the bay, Le Lagon is one of Dakar's top seafood spots, with a spread of culinary treasures – oysters, sea urchins, chargrilled fish, pastas with mixed seafood. You can dine outside on the breezy waterside deck, or in the classy dining room, amid hanging swordfish, brass sailing instruments and a vintage diving suit.

Estendera Vivier Beach   INTERNATIONAL **$$$**
(Map p320; ☑78 459 8181; www.facebook.com/estendera.vivierbeach; mains CFA6000-7500; ☺10am-11pm Tue-Sun; ⛵) A charming little eatery with tables overlooking the crashing waves, Estendera has a small, well-executed menu of seafood, grilled meats and Italian plates. Start off with barracuda carpaccio, then move on to seafood tagliatelle, chicken with porcini mushrooms or oven-baked lasagne.

🍷 Drinking & Nightlife

⭐**Phare des Mamelles**   BAR
(Map p320; ☑77 343 4242; www.pharedesmamelles.com; ☺7pm-3am Thu-Sat, 10am-3pm Sun) On the hilltop in front of Dakar's iconic lighthouse, this open-air bar draws a dance-loving crowd on Friday nights, when it hosts live music jams. On Saturday nights DJs rule the roost (the cover for either night is CFA5000). At the moment, the Phare is one of the best places to be on a weekend night.

Bayékou   COCKTAIL BAR
(Map p320; ☑77 631 3888; www.facebook.com/bayekou; Plage de N'Gor; ☺6pm-1am Tue-Sun) Head upstairs to this stylish, open-sided drinking den near the beach for well-made cocktails, delicious sharing plates (including a tangy red tuna ceviche) and breezy views over the shore. There's also a blackboard menu of well-executed dishes like grilled octopus. It draws a mostly expat crowd. Occasional nights of DJs and live jazz.

Duplex   CLUB
(Map p320; ☑33 820 9646; Rte de N'Gor; ☺11pm-5am) One of the anchors of the Dakar club scene, Duplex draws a well-dressed crowd who come to show off their moves on the dance floor. Although it's mostly DJs on rotation here, the occasional live band here takes the stage on Friday or Saturday night.

☆ Entertainment

⭐**Institut Français**
Léopold Sédar Senghor   ARTS CENTRE
(Map p318; ☑33 823 0320; www.institutfrancais-senegal.com; 89 Rue Joseph Gomis) This

dean plates to its loyal followers – note that it gets packed at lunch.

⭐**Le Lagon I**   SEAFOOD **$$$**
(Map p318; ☑33 821 5322; Rte de la Corniche-Est; mains CFA9000-15,000) Perched on stilts over

spacious arts centre occupying a whole city block is one of the main hubs of cultural activity in Dakar. It features an open-air stage (a fantastic place to catch a live-music gig), a good cafe, and exhibition and cinema rooms, and also houses a couple of artists' workshops and shops in its vast garden.

Just 4 U LIVE MUSIC
(Map p320; ☎77 248 9799; Ave Cheikh Anta Diop; ⊘7pm-3.30am) If you only have time for one live-music venue, don't miss Just 4 U. The small stage of this outdoor restaurant has been graced by the greatest Senegalese and international stars, from jazz to rap to folk and reggae. There's a concert on most nights (best on Thursdays through Saturdays), and you often get to catch the big names.

Closed during Ramadan.

Thiossane LIVE MUSIC
(Map p320; ☎33 824 7078; Rue 10) Owned by Youssou N'Dour, one of Africa's most notable musicians and Senegal's tourism and culture minister, this legendary club is always packed and jamming to anything from mbalax to international beats. Unfortunately, the schedule can be erratic – phone ahead before heading over.

🛍 Shopping

Marché Sandaga MARKET
(Map p318; cnr Ave Pompidou & Ave du Président Lamine Guèye; ⊘9am-5pm) In the endless sprawl of street stalls here you can buy just about anything (as long as no one steals your purse): you'll find tapestries, wood carvings, wildly patterned clothing, beaded jewellery and original paintings, among many other things.

ⓘ Information

DANGERS & ANNOYANCES
➡ Dakar's notorious street hustlers and hard-to-shake-off traders do a pretty good job of turning any walk around town into mild punishment, particularly for women. Stride purposefully on and throw in a brief *bakhna* ('it's OK') and they'll eventually leave you alone.

➡ Many of them also double as pickpockets – be particularly vigilant at markets and in town.

➡ Muggings – often at knifepoint or from passing scooters – are not uncommon. Avoid walking around after dark. Trouble spots include the Petite Corniche (behind the presidential palace), the Rte de la Corniche-Ouest and the beaches.

MEDICAL SERVICES
Hospitals are understaffed and underequipped; for faster service try a private clinic. Pharmacies are plentiful in Dakar; most are open 8am to

8pm Monday to Saturday and rotate with 24-hour shifts.

Clinique de Cap (Map p316; ☑ 33 889 0202; www.cliniqueducap.com; Ave Pasteur) One of the biggest private medical clinics in Dakar.

Hôpital le Dantec (Map p316; ☑ 33 889 3800; www.hopitaldantec.gouv.sn; 30 Ave Pasteur) A modern, full-service hospital in the Plateau.

Hôpital Principal (Map p316; ☑ 33 839 5050; www.hopitalprincipal.sn; 1 Ave Nelson Mandéla) Main hospital and emergency department.

Pharmacie Guigon (Map p318; ☑ 33 823 0333; 1 Ave du Président Lamine Guèye; ⊙ 8am-11pm Mon-Sat) One of the best-stocked options.

MONEY

ATM-equipped banks are never too far away in Dakar. Main branches are at Pl de l'Indépendance.

BICIS (Map p318; ☑ 33 839 0390; Pl de l'Indépendance; ⊙ 9am-4pm Mon-Thu, to noon Fri)

CBAO (Map p318; ☑ 33 849 9300; Pl de l'Indépendance; ⊙ 9am-4pm Mon-Thu, to noon Fri)

SGBS (Map p320; ☑ 33 842 5039; Rue de Kaolack; ⊙ 10am-4pm Mon-Thu, to 1pm Fri)

SGBS (Map p318; ☑ 33 839 5500; 19 Ave Léopold Senghor; ⊙ 9.30am-4pm Mon-Thu, to noon Fri)

POST

Main Post Office (Map p318; ☑ 33 839 3400; Blvd el Haji Djily Mbaye; ⊙ 7am-7pm Mon-Fri, 8am-5pm Sat)

Post Office (Map p318; ☑ 33 839 3400; Ave Pompidou)

ⓘ Getting There & Away

AIR

Léopold Sédar Senghor International Airport (DKR; Map p320; ☑ 24hr info line 33 869 5050; www.aeroport-dakar.com) is in Yoff. This is likely to be out of service when the new airport, **Aéroport International Blaise Diagne** (www.aibd.sn), opens in Ndiass, 50km southeast of Dakar. The airport is scheduled to open by 2018.

Arc en Ciel (Map p320; ☑ 33 820 2467; www.arcenciel-aviation.com) offers charter fights from Dakar to Bissau and Bubaque in the Arquipélago dos Bijagós.

BOAT

Three ferries travel between Dakar and Ziguinchor (in the Casamance), with a total of four weekly departures in each direction (Tuesday, Thursday, Friday and Sunday). Buy your ticket in advance from the **office** (COSAMA; Map

ⓘ ARRIVING IN DAKAR

Léopold Sédar Senghor International Airport, Dakar Book transport through your hotel or guesthouse (which will charge CFA5000 and up to collect you from the airport). Otherwise, taxi touts line up along a fence just outside the airport exit. Pay no more than CFA5000 if going all the way across town to the Plateau, and less if going to Yoff, N'Gor or Les Almadies (in the ballpark of CFA3500).

p320; ☑ 33 821 2900, 33 821 3434; 1 Blvd de la Libération, Gare Maritime; one-way CFA16,000-31,000) in Dakar's *gare maritime*.

BUS & BUSH TAXI

Road transport for long-distance destinations leaves from the **Gare Routière Baux Maraîchers** (☑ 30 118 4644; Pikine) – a taxi from Place de l'Indépendance should cost around CFA3500. Main destinations include Mbour (CFA2000), Saint-Louis (CFA5000), Karang (at the Gambian border; CFA6000), Tambacounda (CFA10,000) and Ziguinchor (CFA10,000).

While ticket prices are fixed, you'll have to pay extra (and negotiate) over luggage charges, which could be CFA1000 to CFA5000.

CAR & MOTORCYCLE

Avis (Map p320; ☑ 33 849 7755; www.avis.com; ⊙ 8am-midnight) Car rental at the airport.

Hertz (Map p318; ☑ 33 889 8181; www.hertz.sn; 64 Rue Joseph Gomis) This rental agency is in the city centre; also has a branch at the airport, and at the hotel **Fleur de Lys** (p318).

ⓘ Getting Around

BUS

Dakar Dem Dikk (www.demdikk.com) buses are a pretty good way of travelling cheaply; fares cost beween CFA150 and CFA300. In downtown, northeast of Place de l'Indépendance is a useful **DDD Bus Terminal** (Map p318; Ave de la Libération).

More frequent but less user-friendly are the white Ndiaga Ndiaye minivans and the iconic blue-yellow *cars rapides*, Dakar's battered, crammed and dangerously driven symbols of identity.

CAR & MOTORCYCLE

Though he doesn't speak much English, **Adama Ba** (☑ 77 461 7108) is highly recommended for trips in and around Dakar and around the country; count on about CFA35,000 per day, plus fuel.

TAXI

Taxis are the easiest way of getting around town. Rates are entirely negotiable. A short hop costs from CFA1000 upwards. Dakar centre to Point E is around CFA1500; it's up to CFA2500 from the centre to N'Gor and Yoff.

AROUND DAKAR

Île de Gorée

POP 1300

Ruled in succession by the Portuguese, Dutch, English and French, the historical, Unesco-designated Île de Gorée is enveloped by an almost eerie calm. There are no sealed roads and no cars on this island, just narrow alleyways with trailing bougainvilleas and colonial brick buildings with wrought-iron balconies – it's a living, visual masterpiece.

But Gorée's calm is not so much romantic as meditative, as the ancient, elegant buildings bear witness to the island's role in the Atlantic slave trade. The island is also home to an active artist community with small studios sprinkled around the island.

◉ Sights

IFAN Historical Museum MUSEUM
(Institut Fondamental d'Afrique Noire; ☑33 822 2003; adult/child CFA500/100; ☉10am-5pm Tue-Sun) Gives a glimpse of island (and regional) history dating back to the 5th century.

Exhibitions cover cultural lore, megalithic sites, key figures in the resistance against European colonisers – and in room 9, the heartbreaking slave trade. Head upstairs for fabulous views of Dakar from the old fortress walls.

🛏 Sleeping & Eating

Hostellerie du Chevalier de Boufflers GUESTHOUSE $
(☑33 822 5364; boufflers@live.fr; r CFA19,000-25,000; 🖲) Set in one of Gorée's classic, elegant old homes, this places is mainly famous for its garden restaurant (mains CFA4500 to CFA8000) serving seafood-focused fare, but also offers five tastefully decorated rooms.

Chez Valerie et Amy GUESTHOUSE $$
(ASAO; ☑33 821 8195; www.csao.fr; 7 Rue St Joseph; r CFA15,000-45,000; 🖲) Set in a picturesque Goréen home, this low-key guesthouse has four lovely rooms painted in rich colours and decorated with folk art. There's a craft shop below.

Villa Castel B&B $$
(☑77 263 6075; www.villacogelsgoree.com; Rue Castel; s/d/tr CFA35,000/40,000/45,000; 🖩🖲) Guests feel right at home in this charming, Belgian-run guesthouse with attractive rooms opening on to a courtyard garden. The roof deck makes a fine vantage point for sunsets and stargazing.

L'Amiraute SEAFOOD $$
(Rue St-Germain; mains CFA4000-6500; ☉11am-8pm) Escape the crowds filling the beachside eateries at this peaceful spot just past the Maison des Esclaves. You can sit on the

---

THE SLAVE HOUSE

Île de Gorée was an important trading station during the 18th and 19th centuries, and many merchants built houses in which they would live or work in the upper storey and store their human cargo on the lower floor.

La Maison des Esclaves (Slave House; Rue St-Germain; CFA600; ☉10.30am-noon & 2.30-6.30pm Tue-Sun) is one of the last remaining 18th-century buildings of this type on Gorée. It was built in 1786 and renovated in 1990 with French assistance, with its famous 'doorway to nowhere' opening directly from the storeroom on to the sea.

Walking around the dimly lit dungeons, you can begin to imagine the suffering of the people held here. It is this emotive illustration that really describes La Maison des Esclaves as a whole.

The island's precise status as a slave-trading station is hotly debated. But the number of slaves transported from here isn't what matters in the debate around Gorée. The island and museum stand as a melancholy reminder of the suffering the Atlantic slave trade inflicted on African people.

outside terrace overlooking the sea and enjoy decent plates of fresh seafood.

❶ Getting There & Away

A **ferry** (Liaison Maritime Dakar-Gorée; Map p316; ☑ 33 849 7961, mobile 78 120 9090; https://lmdg.wordpress.com; Gare Maritime, 21 Blvd de la Libération; adult/child return CFA5200/2700) runs every one or two hours from the *gare maritime* (passenger port) in Dakar to Gorée (20 minutes). Departures are roughly every hour or two from 6.15am (7am Sundays) to after midnight.

PETITE CÔTE & SINÉ-SALOUM DELTA

The 150km Petite Côte stretches south from Dakar and is one of Senegal's best beach areas. Where the Siné and Saloum Rivers meet the tidal waters of the Atlantic Ocean, the coast is broken into a stunning area of mangrove swamps, lagoons, forests and sand islands, forming part of the magnificent 180-sq-km Siné-Saloum Delta.

Mbour & Saly

POP 280,000 (COMBINED)

Eighty kilometres south of Dakar, Mbour is the main town on the Petite Côte and the region's most vibrant and important fishing centre. Nearby Saly, with its strip of big ocean-front hotels, is the perfect corner for a beach holiday of soaking up the sun and sipping cocktails.

Mbour's busy, slightly nauseating fish market on the beach, where the catch is immediately gutted and dispatched, is a sight to behold.

◉ Sights

Réserve Naturelle Somone NATURE RESERVE
(Rte Ngaparou-Somone, Somone; CFA1500) This serene 700-hectare reserve is a great spot for seeing some of the avian wildlife along the coast. Pelicans, egrets, herons and flamingos are among the commonly observed species. The best way to see it all is on a short boat trip; from the beach beside the Royal Decameron Baobab, guides ask for about CFA6500 per person (for a roughly one-hour trip), including the CFA1500 admission fee to the reserve.

🛏 Sleeping & Eating

★**Ferme de Saly & Les Amazones** GUESTHOUSE, APARTMENT $$
(☑ 77 638 4790; www.farmsaly.com; Saly; s/d with half board CFA16,500/33,000, apt per person with half board CFA27,000; ❇ ☀) At this iconic place on the beach you'll find appealing rooms and cottages, great food and a hearty welcome from host Jean-Paul. The lush grounds and sizeable swimming pool make for some leisurely days, though you can also arrange excursions.

Au Petit Jura GUESTHOUSE $$
(☑ 33 957 3767; www.aupetitjura.ch; Saly; d CFA38,000; ❇ 🛜 ☀) Au Petit Jura is a small, charming, Swiss-run guesthouse located just a short stroll to the beach. Days can be spent lounging poolside, strolling the beach or exploring nearby villages on an excursion offered by the guesthouse. Good meals are available, too.

Tama Lodge LODGE $$$
(☑ 33 957 0040; www.tamalodge.com; Mbour; s/d from CFA80,000/105,000, with half board from CFA95,000/137,000; ❇ 🛜) Scattered across a peaceful beachfront property, these nine exquisitely designed bungalows are made of local materials and set with carvings and textiles from across Africa. The open-air thatched-roof restaurant serves up some of the best meals along the coast.

Le Soleil de Saly AFRICAN $$
(☑ 33 958 2865; www.lesoleildesaly.com; Rte de la Somone; mains CFA4000-6000; ☻ noon-11pm) The buzzing new favourite in town has a central location on the main drag and serves up tasty grilled meat and fish dishes, with live music three nights a week (Thursday through Saturday). Owner Mamadou Basse is easy to spot: look for the kind-hearted man in the fedora.

★**La Guinguette** FRENCH $$$
(☑ 77 158 0808; http://laguinguettedesaly.simple site.com; Saly; mains from CFA6000; ☻ 7.30-10pm Thu-Tue & noon-2.30pm Sun) Tucked down a small lane near the entrance to Saly, La Guinguette earns rave reviews for its delectable, market-fresh cuisine and its colourful garden setting. Reserve ahead.

❶ Getting There & Away

There are plenty of transport options heading down the coast, including *sept-place* taxis and minibuses. Things get a little more complicated

SENEGAL MBOUR & SALY

JOAL-FADIOUT

Joal is a sleepy fishing town at the pro-verbial end of the road south of Mbour. Nearby mangroves and placid waters lend an air of peace to the settlement. It's also the gateway to Fadiout, a small island made of clam and oyster shells (even the houses, streets and cemeteries!), reached by an impressive wooden bridge. It's dreamy to wander around the island's narrow alleys, admire the shell-world and pop into artisan workshops dotted around.

A guide is required to visit Fadiout; you can find them at the foot of the bridge leading to the island. The going rate is around CFA5000 for a small group.

Minibuses go to/from Mbour (CFA800, one hour) and Palmarin (around CFA1200, 1½ hours). In the morning you can catch an early bus direct to Dakar leaving at 5am or 6am (CFA1500, three hours).

reaching Ndangane and Palmarin, requiring a transfer and waiting time at key transport hubs on the main highway. To get to Toubakouta and Missirah, you'll have to go Kaolack first and transfer from there.

Palmarin

POP 7200

Palmarin, with its soft lagoons, tall palm groves and labyrinthine creeks, is one of Senegal's most underrated destinations. It's not one community, but rather a string of tiny villages scattered for more than 12km along the coast. The big draw is enjoying a peaceful, relatively empty stretch of beachfront.

🛏 Sleeping

Sangomar BUNGALOW $
(☑77 536 4425; moussengomar59@gmail.com; Palmarin Djifer; s/d CFA12,600/21,200, with half-board CFA19,600/31,200, camping per person CFA2500) In the village of Djifer, Sangomar has pleasant bungalows made of native materials that are set amid eucalyptus and palms and front on to a calm beach (which is clean for Djifer, though there are better options further north along the peninsula). The friendly host offers walking or pirogue excursions.

Djidjack LODGE $$
(☑33 949 9619; www.djidjack.com; Palmarin Nguedj; bungalow s CFA21,500, d 23,000-33,000, camping per person CFA3500; ☎🏊) Run by a Swiss couple, welcoming Djidjack has round bungalows with conical thatch ceilings, African artwork and a small terrace. Budget travellers can also camp (mattress and mosquito net provided).

⭐**Lodge des Collines de Niassam** LODGE $$$
(☑77 639 0639; www.niassam.com; Palmarin Ngallou; with half board s CFA85,000-98,000, d CFA118,000-140,000; ❄☎🏊) 🌿 One of Senegal's most original *campements* lies in a pristine setting on the edge of a lagoon. You can sleep in atmospheric tree houses that cling to the mighty branches of baobabs, in elegant bungalows perched on stilts over the water or in colourful savannah rooms with flower-trimmed terraces.

There's an excellent restaurant, and all manner of tours (and transfers) are available.

ℹ Getting There & Away

Palmarin is most easily reached by minibus from Mbour, via Joal-Fadiout and Sambadia (where you may have to change). The fare from Joal-Fadiout to Sambadia is CFA700 (45 minutes), and from Sambadia to Palmarin it's about CFA500 (30 minutes).

Toubakouta & Missirah

POP 9000

Toubakouta is a fantastically calm and pretty spot in the south of the Siné-Saloum Delta, and is one of the country's best places for birdwatching. Most guesthouses offer excursions exploring wildlife-filled wetlands, visiting sacred baobabs, and getting a taste of Mandinka village life.

South of Toubakouta, Missirah is the point of entry to the **Parc National du Delta du Saloum** (www.deltadusaloum.com; CFA2000).

For those not heading to wildlife parks in other parts of Africa, the 60-sq-km **Fathala Wildlife Reserve & Lodge** (☑70 986 1993; www.fathala.com; self-drive tour CFA21,000) might be worth adding to your itinerary. This reserve was created in 2006 as a habitat for the western giant eland, and today includes troops of this critically endangered antelope, as well as giraffes, rhinos, warthogs, buffaloes and several monkey species. While it's pricey to visit, it can nevertheless be thrilling to see these animals in the (semi-)wild.

🛌 Sleeping

Keur Bamboung   GUESTHOUSE $
(📞 77 510 8013; www.oceanium.org; r per person with full board CFA22,000) 🥢 Managed by local villagers on the island of Sipo, Keur Bamboung sits in a stunning location in the heart of a 68-sq-km protected marine reserve. Things are simple and green, with lodging in wooden bungalows near the water's edge. Phone to arrange pirogue pick-up from Toubakouta; it's a 30-minute boat ride to Keur Bamboung, followed by transfer in a donkey cart.

Keur Thierry   GUESTHOUSE $
(📞 77 439 8605; www.keurthierry.com; Toubakouta; ⏰ s/d/tr with fan CFA13,500/17,000/26,000; ❄️📶) Offers simple, good-value rooms set around a small, shell-strewn courtyard (rooms with air-con cost an extra CFA2500). Thierry has loads of info about the area, and can happily arrange fishing trips and other excursions. The meals here are decent.

★Keur Saloum   HOTEL $$
(📞33 948 7715; www.keursaloum.com; Toubakouta; s/d/tr incl breakfast from CFA26,000/38,000/45,000; P❄️📶🏊) This Belgian-run lodge offers quality accommodation in attractive bungalows, nicely outfitted and set amid lush grounds. But it's all the extras that have earned Keur Saloum such a solid reputation over the years, with a spacious restaurant and deck overlooking the mangroves, an enticing pool and an impressive array of tours.

ℹ️ Getting There & Around

You can catch sept-place taxis heading north or south between Kaolack and Karang. Bank on about CFA2500 one-way to either Kaolack (1½ hours) or Karang (45 minutes).

Taxis-brousses (bush taxis) make infrequent runs between Toubakouta and Missirah (from around CFA500, one hour). A private taxi from Toubakouta to Missirah costs around CFA5000 (45 minutes).

Toubab Dialao

POP 2500

Located around 55km south of the capital, Toubab Dialao (also spelt Toubab Dialaw) makes for a convenient getaway when *dakarois* need a break from the big city. The

beach is the star, a pretty stretch of golden sands backed by low cliffs strung with homes and a few guesthouses. The low-key village has an arty bohemian vibe, with colourfully decorated houses and nights of drumming, dancing and theatre. With classes and activities on offer at one of the coast's most imaginatively designed guesthouses and cultural spaces, it's easy to spend more time here than anticipated enjoying the creative life.

🛌 Sleeping

★Espace Sobo Badè   GUESTHOUSE $
(📞33 836 0356; sobobade1@hotmail.com; dm/s/d CFA5000/13,000/22,000; ❄️📶) Perched over a wave-battered stretch of coastline, Sobo Badè has the wondrous look of a Gaudì creation, with its imaginative brickwork, shell-lined archways, steeply pitched thatched roofs, and mosaic-covered fountains and railings. Haitian-born artist Gerard Chenet (b 1927) is the visionary behind this imaginative space, which has become a magnet for artists, musicians and other creative types.

ℹ️ Getting There & Away

Collective sept-place taxis run from Dakar's gare routière (around CFA600 per person, 1½ hours). From the same station, you can also find buses to Toubab Dialaw, though you will likely have to change at Diamniado.

Once the new airport opens, you'll be less than 20km away from the terminal – meaning it'll be faster to come straight here rather than going to Dakar.

NORTHERN SENEGAL

Saint-Louis

POP 178,000

With its crumbling colonial architecture, horse-drawn carts and peaceful ambience, West Africa's first French settlement has a unique historical charm – so much so that it's been a Unesco World Heritage Site since 2000. The old town centre sits on an island in the Senegal River, but the city sprawls into Sor on the mainland, and on to the Langue de Barbarie, where you'll find the lively fishing community of Guet N'Dar.

The island is reached via the 500m-long Pont Faidherbe, a feat of 19th-century engineering.

Saint-Louis

◎ Top Sights

◎ Sights

◆ Activities, Courses & Tours

⊜ Sleeping

⊗ Eating

◎ Drinking & Nightlife

◎ Entertainment

ⓘ Information

◎ Sights & Activities

★ Pont Faidherbe
BRIDGE

Transferred to Saint-Louis in 1897, the Pont Faidherbe is the city's most significant landmark. The metal arches of this bridge linking Saint-Louis to the mainland were designed by Gustav Eiffel and originally built to cross the Danube. You'll cross its steel planks when driving into town.

Parc National de la Langue de Barbarie
NATIONAL PARK

(CFA5000, guide CFA3000; ⊙8am-sunset) This park includes the far southern tip of the Langue de Barbarie peninsula, the estuary of the Senegal River (which contains two small islands) and a section of the mainland on the other side of the estuary. The park covers a total area of 20 sq km, and is home to numerous water birds, swelled from November to April by migrant birds from Europe.

Place Faidherbe   SQUARE

With its statue of the French governor who led the colonial expansion eastwards and initiated many ambitious infrastructural projects, this square sits adjacent to several intact 19th-century houses, including the **Governor's Palace** (Place Faidherbe), and on its north and south side, former barracks known as the **Rogniat Casernes** (Place Faidherbe). Next to the Governor's Palace, you'll find a lovely 1828 **cathedral** (Rue de l'Eglise; ⊙ irregular hours) with a neoclassical facade worth admiring.

Bou El Mogdad   CRUISE

(☎ 33 961 5689; www.bouelmogdad.com; Rue Blaise Diagne; 6-day cruise per person from €730) The 52m tourist boat *Bou El Mogdad* sails from Saint-Louis, travelling along the scenic Senegal River en route to Podor with stops and excursions along the way. Departures happen four times a month (twice a month from each direction) from late October to early May. Book through Sahel Découverte (p330).

⭐ Festivals & Events

Saint-Louis Jazz Festival   MUSIC

(www.saintlouisjazz.org; ⊙ May) The most internationally renowned festival in West Africa is held annually in early or mid May and attracts jazz greats from around the world. The main event usually happens at the **Quai des Arts** (☎ 33 961 5656; Ave Jean Mermoz; ⊙ 7pm-late) or on an open-air stage in Place Faidherbe, though there are fringe events all over town.

Les Fanals   CULTURAL

(⊙ Dec) Celebrated on one night during the last week of December between Christmas and New Year's Eve, this historic lantern procession has its roots in the lantern-lit marches to midnight Mass once made by the *signares*. Today it evokes Saint-Louisian history and reaffirms the town's unique identity.

🛏 Sleeping

Zebrabar   BUNGALOW $

(☎ 77 638 1862, 33 962 0019; www.zebrabar.net; Mouit; campsites per person CFA5000, s CFA7000-22,000, d CFA13,000-32,000; 🕸) Around 22km south of Saint-Louis, this peaceful spot makes a great base for excursions into the Parc National de la Langue de Barbarie. Accommodation is available in simple huts and spacious bungalows spread across a large terrain. The restaurant with open-air tables is a fine spot for meeting other travellers.

Cafe des Arts   GUESTHOUSE $

(☎ 77 613 8914; Quai Giraud; dm CFA5000, r CFA10,000-15,000) This tiny guesthouse in the north of the island has a handful of simple but brightly painted rooms; the best has a balcony that opens on to the waterfront. There's also a roof deck, but not much shade up top. It's a good value if you're on a budget.

Hotel de la Poste   HOTEL $$

(☎ 33 961 1118; www.hoteldelaposte saintlouis.com; s/d/tr/ste from CFA37,000/44,000/56,000/75,000; 🕸🛜) Step back in time at this elegant 36-room hotel, which first opened its doors back in 1850 and was a favourite with aviator Jean Mermoz and other Aéropostale pilots. Old photos adorn the walls of the dapper guest rooms, and the vintage bar is a great place for a drink.

Au Fil du Fleuve   GUESTHOUSE $$

(☎ 77 379 9534; www.fildufleuve.com; 15 Rue El Hadj Malick Sy; r CFA56,000-62,000; 🛜) In the southern half of Saint-Louis, this grand 19th-century merchant's house has been transformed into a lovely boutique B&B, with three unique rooms, each displaying works by a different African artist, and a lovely courtyard. The friendly host Marie-Caroline has a wealth of information about the island, and serves up fabulous breakfasts (and dinners on request).

Siki Hotel   BOUTIQUE HOTEL $$

(☎ 33 961 6069; www.hotelsenegal.net; Rue Abdoulaye Seck; s/d from CFA35,000/44,000; 🕸🛜) A stylish Spanish-owned option in the centre, Siki Hotel has attractive rooms with wide plank floors and attractive wood furnishings. It's set in the former childhood home of Senegalese boxing champ Battling Siki. There's a first-rate tapas restaurant on the ground floor.

Jamm   GUESTHOUSE $$

(Chez Yves Lamour; ☎ 77 443 4765; www.jamm-saintlouis.com; Rue Paul Holle; s/d incl breakfast CFA56,000/66,000; 🕸🛜) One of Saint-Louis' most beautifully restored houses offers four tiled and brick-walled rooms with ceilings high enough to impress even regular churchgoers. Every tiny decorative detail has been restored with care.

La Maison Rose   HOTEL $$

(☎ 33 938 2222; www.lamaisonrose.net; Rue Blaise Diagne; s/d/ste from CFA54,000/67,000/93,000; 🅿🕸🛜) Old-time elegance meets contemporary luxuries in one of Saint-Louis' most famous old buildings: every room and suite here is unique, though they all exude a spirit of old-time comfort. The classic furniture and wonderful artworks on display add to the romance.

🍴 Eating

La Linguère AFRICAN **$**
(☑ 33 961 3949; Rue Blaise Diagne; mains CFA1500-4000; ⊘ noon-3.30pm & 7-11pm) A reliable local eatery that serves up tasty *poulet yassa*, *thiéboudienne* and other Senegalese classics. Friendly service and attention to details (and cleanliness) makes all the difference.

★ La Kora AFRICAN **$$**
(Chez Peggy; ☑ 77 637 1244; www.facebook.com/lakorachezpeggy; 402 Rue Blaise Diagne; mains CFA4000-8500; ⊘ 11.30am-3pm & 6-11.30pm Mon-Sat, 6-11.30pm Sun) La Kora has earned a stellar reputation for its fabulous cooking, the warm welcome from Peggy (the proprietor) and staff, and the lovely setting – complete with a baobab tree in the vine-trimmed courtyard and a stylish dining room slung with old photos of Saint-Louis. La Kora also hosts occasional concerts.

Le Reveil SEAFOOD, AFRICAN **$$**
(☑ 77 701 9682; Rue Abdoulaye Seck; mains CFA3000-4000; ⊘ 10am-6pm & 7-10pm) A friendly, very welcoming restaurant tucked away in the back of the bar Ambuscade, Le Reveil serves up tasty fresh seafood. The *fricassé de la mer* (a kind of mixed seafood plate) and coconut shrimp curry are both first-rate.

🍸 Drinking & Entertainment

Flamingo BAR
(☑ 33 961 1118; Quai Bacre Waly Guèye; ⊘ 11am-2am) Any night out in this town starts at the pool-adorned riverside bar and restaurant Flamingo. Always packed, it's Saint-Louis' best place for live music – and not a bad place for a meal (mains from CFA5500) around sunset.

Meyazz Club LIVE MUSIC
(☑ 33 916 6451; Route de Khor, Sor; from CFA1000; ⊘ 8pm-late Wed, 10pm-late Thu-Sat) The best new venue for live music is in Sor – well worth the taxi trip over if a concert is happening. Music is wide-ranging, from African rhythms and mbalax to reggae and global beats, and it draws a well-dressed, dance-

loving crowd. In late 2016 the open-air club even hosted its first annual world-music festival, featuring flamenco, Cuban jazz and Afrobeat.

ℹ Information

BICIS (☑ 33 961 1053; Rue de France; ⊘ 7.45am-12.15pm & 1.40-3.45pm Mon-Thu, 7.45am-1pm & 2.40-3.45pm Fri) Bank.

CBAO (☑ 33 938 2552; Rue Khalifa Ababacar Sy; ⊘ 8.15am-5.15pm Mon-Fri) Also has a Western Union office.

Post Office (Rue du Général de Gaulle; ⊘ 9am-4pm Mon-Fri) The art-deco building opposite the Hôtel de la Poste.

Sahel Découverte (☑ 33 961 5689; www.saheldecouverte.com; Rue Blaise Diagne; ⊘ 8.30am-1pm & 3-6pm Mon-Fri, 9am-1pm Sat) Travel agency. Quite simply the best company for exploring the northern region.

Saint-Louis Hospital (☑ 33 938 2400; Blvd Abdoulaye Mar Diop) Has an accident and emergency department.

Syndicat d'Initiative (☑ 33 961 2455; www.saintlouisdusenegal-tourisme.com; Gouvernance; ⊘ 9am-noon & 2.30-5pm) A haven of regional information with excellent tours.

Parc National des Oiseaux du Djoudj

With almost 300 species of bird, this 160-sq-km **park** (☑ 33 961 8621; admission CFA5000, pirogue/car/guide CFA4000/5000/6000; ⊘ 7am-dusk Nov-Apr) is one of the most important bird sanctuaries in the world. Flamingos, pelicans and waders are most plentiful, and large numbers of migrating birds travel here in November. The lush setting is no less impressive: these vast wetlands comprise lakes, streams, ponds, fords and sandbanks.

The park is best explored by pirogue. Boats trips can be arranged at the park entrance or at the hotels.

The large **Hôtel du Djoudj** (☑ 33 963 8702; www.hotel-djoudj.com; r CFA31,000; ⊘ Nov-May; ❄🛜🏊), near the park headquarters, has comfy rooms and a very inviting swimming pool. It offers regular boat trips, and you can also arrange walking excursions and 4WD trips.

The park is 25km off the main road; there's no public transport. You can either negotiate a private taxi from Saint-Louis (from CFA25,000, 90 minutes) or join an organised tour, such as one offered by Sahel Découverte.

CENTRAL SENEGAL

Tambacounda

POP 86,000

The junction town Tambacounda is all about dust, sizzling temperatures and lines of traffic heading in all directions. It's a jumping-off point for Mali, Guinea and The Gambia and is a fine place to base yourself to visit the Parc National de Niokolo-Koba. There's not much to the city, and few foreign visitors linger here.

🛏 Sleeping & Eating

Brasari GUESTHOUSE **$**

(☑ 33 981 1102; s/d/tr CFA16,000/22,000/27,000; ❋ 🛜) A welcome addition to Tomba, Brasari is a compact property on the main highway through town, with rooms set in freestanding round buildings. Each has clean African art on the walls and a neat appearance, though there's no hot water. A new restaurant was also in the works when we passed through.

Oasis Oriental Club HOTEL **$$**

(☑ 33 981 1824; Rte de Kaolack; s/d incl breakfast from CFA24,000/29,000, ste CFA45,000-82,000; P ❋ 🛜 ⊠) Try Oasis Oriental Club for some comfort and service. It has attractive rooms set in bungalows surrounding a pool and restaurant. It's outside of town, a few kilometres west of the centre (on the left when arriving from Dakar).

ℹ Getting There & Away

If you're travelling on to Mali, you get your *sept-place* taxi to Kidira (CFA4000, three hours) at Garage Kothiary, on the eastern side of town. Vehicles to other destinations go from the larger *gare routière* four blocks west of the market.

Parc National de Niokolo-Koba

This biologically rich national park is home to a spectacular array of flora and fauna, with some 350 bird species and 80 mammal species spread across a vast reserve in southeastern Senegal. Lions, leopards, baboons, hippos and antelope are all found (though not always easily spotted) here. Its terrain encompasses dry savannah, riparian forest and various waterways, including the Gambia River. Sadly, a lack of resources have left the park poorly maintained, so you'll have to anticipate bad access roads and rustic facilities.

The park is inaccessible in the wet months (June to October). The entrance fee gives you access for 24 hours. You get your obligatory guide (CFA10,000) at the entrance gate.

If you want to stay in the national park, **Hotel Sementi** (☑ 33 984 1136; r from CFA30,000) is your best bet, with lodging in simple rooms and decent thatched-roof bungalows. There's a pleasant terrace with views of the Gambia River, and meals can be arranged.

You will need a vehicle to enter the park. It's best to hire a 4WD (per day around CFA90,000) in Tambacounda. Enquire at the gare routière or at the hotels in the city.

CASAMANCE

With its lush tropical landscapes watered by the graceful, winding Casamance River, this area seems far from Dakar and its surroundings in every sense. Between the sleepy capital, Ziguinchor, and the wide, sandy beaches of Cap Skirring, the banks of the Casamance River are dotted with tiny, community *campements* that nestle between mangroves and lagoons. You'll find plenty of reason to linger here, whether basking on sandy shorelines, overnighting on forest-covered islands or taking in the beat of traditional villages – all of which are the proud homeland of the fascinating and fiercely independent Diola people.

Ziguinchor

POP 174,000

With its old houses, tree-lined streets and busy markets, this former colonial centre exudes real atmosphere. It's worth spending a night or two here to feel the pulse of this tropical, mangrove-fringed city before rushing off to the coast.

Ziguinchor is the largest town in southern Senegal, and the main access point for travel in the Casamance region.

◉ Sights

Alliance Franco-Sénégalaise CULTURAL CENTRE

(☑ 33 991 2823; www.afziguinchor.org; Ave Djignabo; suggested donation CFA1000; ⊙ 9am-7pm Mon-Sat) This is easily Ziguinchor's most stunning building, a giant *case à impluvium* (a large, round traditional house) decorated with blindingly busy South African Ndebele and Casamance patterns. Inside are exhibitions, a large concert hall (shows take place at least once a week) and a welcoming restaurant and bar (with a weekday lunch special for CFA1000).

🎓 Courses

Africa Batik   ART
(🖉 77 653 4936) Offers batik-making courses of varying duration; inquire for rates. You can also browse Mamadou Cherif Diallo's colourful creations for sale – which make brilliant souvenirs to bring home from the Casamance.

🛏️ Sleeping

Le Flamboyant   HOTEL $
(🖉 33 991 2223; www.casamance.info; Rue de France; r CFA18,000-20,000; ❋ 🛜 🏊) In a central location, Le Flamboyant offers comfort well above the price you pay. The clean, well-equipped rooms open on to a small flower- and palm-filled courtyard and swimming pool. The decent on-site restaurant and kindly staff add to the value.

Le Perroquet   GUESTHOUSE $
(🖉 33 991 2329; www.hotel-le-perroquet.com; Rue du Commerce; s/d CFA11,000/13,000, with view 13,000/15,000) Dozens of yellow-billed storks attract you with their noisy chatter to Zig's favourite budget place. Invest in an upstairs room for the small balconies with river views. The friendly restaurant is a fine spot for early evening drinks.

Hotel Kadiandoumagne   HOTEL $$
(🖉 33 938 8000; www.hotel-kadiandoumagne.com; Rue du Commerce; s/d from CFA30,000/38,000; ❋ 🛜 🏊) Never mind the tongue-twister of a name – this place ticks all the boxes, with attractive, handsomely furnished rooms overlooking the river, an appealing pool and ample outdoor space for lounging, dining and drinking. Good place to book excursions as well.

🍴 Eating

Le Erobon   AFRICAN $$
(🖉 33 991 2788; Rue du Commerce; mains CFA2000-4000; ⊘ 8am-1am) This humble outdoor eatery is highly recommended. You can come here any time of day for grilled fish, carefully spiced and served with a sea view. The ambience is wonderfully relaxed and sometimes includes live music.

Le Kassa   AFRICAN $$
(🖉 33 991 1311; Rond-Point Jean-Paul II; mains CFA3000-7500; ⊘ 8am-1am) Ziguinchor's best-known dining spot has a plant-filled courtyard and classic cooking – the Senegalese dishes are best. The kitchen stays open late and there's live music some nights.

ℹ️ Information

CBAO (Rue de France; ⊘ 9am-3pm Mon-Fri) Advances on credit cards and ATM.

French Honorary Consul (🖉 33 991 2223; www.ambafrance-sn.org; Rue de France) Across from the hotel Le Flamboyant.

Guinea-Bissau Consulate (🖉 77 512 6497; ⊘ 8.30am-2pm Mon-Fri) It's hard to find the consulate on your own: take a taxi here (around CFA200).

Hôpital de la Paix (🖉 33 991 9800; Ave Djiniabo Bassene) A new facility that opened in 2015. It's a few kilometres south of the centre.

Office de Tourisme (🖉 77 544 0332; www.casamance-tourisme.sn; Rue du Général de Gaulle; ⊘ 8am-1pm & 3-6.30pm Mon-Sat Nov-Apr; 🛜) In the town centre, this is one of the best-informed tourism offices in the country. Staff can help arrange village and birdwatching tours and other excursions (even one- or two-week guided trips). You can purchase Casamance maps, and staff have lists of artisans who make and sell handicrafts. Free wi-fi.

SGBS (Rue du Général de Gaulle; ⊘ 9am-4pm Mon-Thu, to 1pm Fri) Change or withdraw money here; there's an ATM.

ℹ️ Getting There & Around

AIR

Groupe Transair (🖉 33 865 2565; www.groupetransair.sn) flies twice daily between Dakar and Ziguinchor (one-way/return about CFA65,000/115,000).

Ziguinchor Airport (🖉 33 991 1334) is in the south of the city, about 4.5km south of the waterfront.

BOAT

There are four weekly departures each way on long, overnight journey between Dakar and Ziguinchor. The voyage takes 14 to 18 hours.

Buy your ticket (CFA16,000 to CFA31,000 one-way) in advance and in person from the *gare maritime* (passenger port). You can also buy tickets through Diambone Voyages based in Ziguinchor – a good option if you're overseas, as ferries can book up.

SHARED TAXIS & MINIBUS

The *gare routière* is to the east of the city centre. There are frequent *sept-place* taxis to Dakar

Ziguinchor

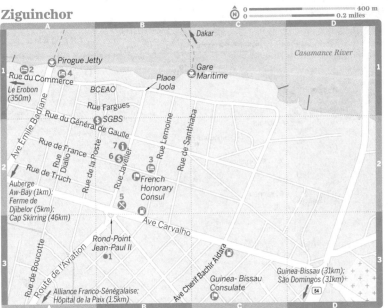

Ziguinchor

(CFA10,000 plus luggage, minimum 10 hours, 454km) and Cap Skirring (CFA2000, 1¾ hours).

You can also catch a minibus here to Oussouye (CFA1000, one hour).

To get anywhere around town by private taxi costs CFA500 (CFA700 after midnight).

Cap Skirring

POP 2300

The beaches at Cap Skirring are some of the finest in West Africa – and better still, they're usually empty. While there isn't a lot happening here culturally (aside from weekend nights of live music), Cap Skirring makes a fine base for a few days of unwinding. You can also alternate days on the beach with exploring traditional Diola villages to the east, or opt for some of the many activities on offer, including kayaking and mountain biking.

🛏 Sleeping

La Tortue Bleue GUESTHOUSE **$**
(📱77 635 1399; www.latortuebleue.org; s/d/tr CFA15,000/18,000/24,000; 🛜) Guests feel right at home in this delightful, three-room spot run by a Belgian-Senegalese couple. Brightly painted and well-equipped rooms overlook a flower-filled garden, and meals and excursions are available. It's about a 10-minute walk from the beach.

Le Paradise HOTEL **$**
(📱33 993 5129; capskirringparadise@hotmail.fr; r with fan/air-con from CFA15,000/20,000, r with shared bathroom CFA7000; ❄🛜) On the coastal road about 2km south of the village, welcoming Le Paradise has clean, well-maintained rooms – both rustic (in a traditional *case à impluvium)* and comfy (tiled with air-con and sea views). Plus you can organise tours, eat well (mains CFA3500 to CFA5000) and enjoy perfect beach access.

Casamance

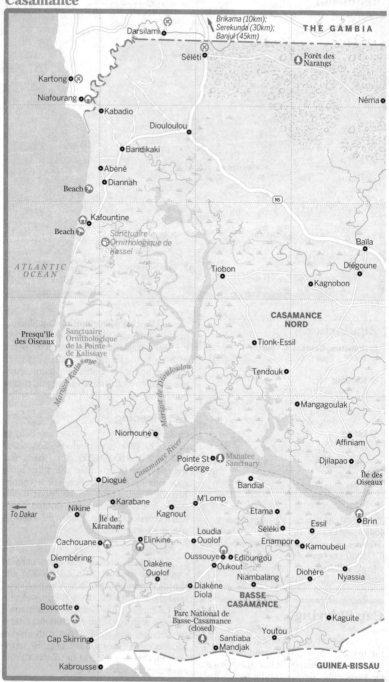

Darsilami

⊗

Brikama (10km);
Serekunda (30km);
Banjul (45km)

THE GAMBIA

Séléti ⊗

Forêt des
Narangs

Kartong ⊗

Niafourang

Kabadio

Néma

Diouloulou

Bandikaki

Abéné

Diannah

Beach

Kafountine

Beach

Sanctuaire
Ornithologique de
Kassel

ATLANTIC
OCEAN

Baïla

Diégoune

Tiobon

Kagnobon

CASAMANCE
NORD

Presqu'île
des Oiseaux

Sanctuaire
Ornithologique
de la Pointe
de Kalissaye

Marigot Kalissaye

Tionk-Essil

Tendouk

Mangagoulak

Niomoune

Marigot de Diouloulou

Casamance River

Pointe St
George

Manatee
Sanctuary

Affiniam

Djilapao

Île des
Oiseaux

Diogué

Bandial

To Dakar

Nikine

Karabane

Île de
Karabane

Kagnout

M'Lomp

Etama

Séléki

Essil

Brin

Cachouane

Elinkine

Loudia
Ouolof

Enampor

Kamoubeul

Diembéring

Diakène
Ouolof

Oussouye

Oukout

Edioungou

Niambalang

Diohère

Nyassia

Diakène
Diola

BASSE
CASAMANCE

Boucotte

Parc National de
Basse-Casamance
(closed)

Kaguite

Youtou

Cap Skirring

Santiaba
Mandjak

Kabrousse

GUINEA-BISSAU

SENEGAL CAP SKIRRING

Auberge Le Palmier   GUESTHOUSE **$**

(✆33 993 5109; r CFA11,000-17,000; ❄️🛜) In Cap Skirring village (near the roundabout), the small Auberge Le Palmier is a decent budget bet with clean rooms (but noisy fans), and a good front-terrace restaurant. It's about a 10-minute walk from the beach.

⭐**Cisko Centre Culturel**   HOTEL **$$**

(✆33 990 3921; www.ciskocentre.com; s/d CFA46,000/62,000, ste CFA114,000-181,000; ❄️🛜🏊) Created by the Senegalese musician Youssouph Cissoko, this sprawling, high-end property is the go-to destination for music lovers, with weekend concerts held on the open-air stage throughout the year. Rooms here are beautifully designed, with African art and textiles, and there are fine places to unwind with a palm-fringed pool (and pool bar) and a good restaurant.

Kaloa les Palétuviers   HOTEL **$$**

(✆33 993 0666; www.hotel-kaloa.com; s/d incl breakfast from CFA16,000/30,000; ❄️🏊) This riverside hotel is one of the more upmarket options and sits among lovely mangroves. Decent facilities, with a pool flanked by palms, a pleasant restaurant and a bar that hosts DJ-fuelled dance parties on weekends.

Villa des Pêcheurs   HOTEL **$$**

(✆33 993 5253; www.villadespecheurs.com; s/d with full board CFA40,000/62,000; ❄️🛜🏊) An excellent option on the beach. It also has a brilliant restaurant and offers the best fishing expeditions in town.

🍴 Eating

⭐**Casa-Resto**   INTERNATIONAL **$$**

(✆77 796 2071; mains CFA3500-5000; ⏲noon-3pm & 7-11pm) Set on the main road about 400m south of the village roundabout, Casa-Resto may lack the sea views and flashy setting, but it serves up some of the best meals in Cap Skirring. The menu has a bit of everything: good pizzas (made by William at the pizza station out front), seafood spaghetti, juicy steaks and grilled fish.

Le Biarritz   INTERNATIONAL **$$**

(mains CFA1500-4000; ⏲10am-late) This much-loved classic serves up reliable plates of pasta with shrimp, grilled fish, sandwiches and ever-flowing drinks. On weekend nights, Le Biarritz embraces its wild side, with DJs (or bands) and dancing – and sometimes stays open till 6am.

Diaspora   INTERNATIONAL **$$**

(✆33 993 0304; CFA3500-6000; ⊙11am-10pm)
Just off the road leading to the beach, Diaspora is an elegant but welcoming setting for nicely prepared crab ravioli, pork cutlets and pizza, as well as grilled seafood. There's live music some nights, too.

Casa Bambou   FRENCH **$$**

(mains CFA2500-4000; ⊙10am-11pm) Offers tasty grilled seafood and roast chicken in a cheery, open-sided setting on the main road. The *plat du jour* (daily special) is a steal at CFA1000. Next door the restaurant has a bar-disco that draws a dance-minded crowd on Friday and Saturday nights.

❶ Getting There & Away

Aéroport de Cap Skirring (✆33 993 5194) is served by **Groupe Transair** (p332), which flies twice a week (Fridays and Sundays) between Dakar and Cap Skirring (one-way from around CFA75,000, 45 minutes). There are also charter flights from Paris Orly airport.

Otherwise you can take a *sept-place* taxi (around CFA2000, 1¾ hours) from Ziguinchor.

UNDERSTAND SENEGAL

Senegal Today

One of West Africa's most successful democracies, Senegal continues to be a role model for its political stability and steady economic growth. Hoping to further strengthen Senegal against future strongmen, President Macky Sall even championed a referendum in 2016 that curtailed presidential powers, shortening a president's time in office to a maximum of two consecutive terms, and shortening each term from seven to five years. Sall's ambitious economic plan 'Emerging Senegal' has helped spur growth (reaching over 6% annually in both 2015 and 2016), with major investments in infrastructure, tourism and agriculture. Enormous challenges remain, not least creating opportunities for Senegal's least fortunate – over 40% of the population still lives below the poverty line.

History

Senegal was part of several West African empires, including the Empire of Ghana (8th century), and the Djolof kingdom, in the area between the Senegal River and Dakar (13th and 14th centuries). In the early 16th century Portuguese traders made contact with coastal kingdoms, and became the first in a long line of 'interested' foreigners: soon the British, French and Dutch jostled for control of strategic points for the trade in slaves and goods. In 1659 the French built a trading station at Saint-Louis; the town later became the capital of French West Africa.

Dakar, home to tiny fishing villages, was chosen as capital of the Senegalese territory, and as early as 1848 Senegal had a deputy in the French parliament.

Independence

In the run-up to independence in 1960, Senegal joined French Sudan (present-day Mali) to form the Mali Federation. It lasted all of two months, and in August 1960, Senegal became a republic. Its first president, Léopold Sédar Senghor, a socialist and poet of international stature, commanded respect in Senegal and abroad. His economic management, however, didn't match his way with words. At the end of 1980, he voluntarily stepped down and was replaced by Abdou Diouf, who soon faced a string of mounting crises.

The 1980s saw the start of an ongoing separatist rebellion in the southern region of Casamance, a three-year diplomatic squabble with Mauritania and rising tensions over the government's economic austerity measures.

In March 2000 the hugely popular opposition leader Abdoulaye Wade won in a free and fair presidential election, thanks to his hope-giving *sopi* (change) campaign. The following year a new constitution was approved, allowing the formation of opposition parties and consolidating the prime minister's role.

Though initially popular, Wade's government wasn't able to lead the country out of economic crisis. The Constitutional Council allowed Wade to run for a highly controversial third term (when already in his mid-80s, no less), but voters rejected him in favor of Macky Sall, who had previously served as prime minister under Wade (from 2004 to 2007).

Macky Sall became president in early 2012, and quickly set about tackling corruption. He also made ambitious plans for new investment in infrastructure, healthcare, agriculture and tourism.

People & Culture

More than 95% of the population is Muslim, and many of them belong to one of the Sufi brotherhoods that dominate religious life in Senegal. The most important brotherhood is that of the Mourides, founded by Cheikh Amadou Bamba. The marabouts who lead these brotherhoods play a central role in social life and wield enormous political and economic power (possibly the power to make or break the country's leaders).

The dominant ethnic group is the Wolof (39% of the population), whose language is the country's lingua franca. Smaller groups include the Pular (around 27%), the Serer (15%), the Mandinka (4%) and the Diola (4%). Senegal's population is young: just over 40% are under 14 years old.

Senegal has a vast music scene; names such as Youssou N'Dour and Baaba Maal are famous worldwide. The beat that moves the nation is mbalax. Created from a mixture of Cuban music (hugely popular in Senegal in the 1960s) and traditional, fiery *sabar* drumming, mbalax was made famous by Youssou N'Dour in the 1980s.

SURVIVAL GUIDE

ⓘ Directory A-Z

ACCOMMODATION

Senegal has a very wide range of places to stay, from top-class hotels to bare-bones budget guesthouses. Dakar has the biggest choice, with surfer camps and art-filled boutique guesthouses. If you're after beach getaways, check out Saly and Cap Skirring. Many rural areas, particularly the Casamance, have pleasant *campements* (guesthouses).

DANGERS & ANNOYANCES

The main concern for visitors is street crime and annoying hustlers in Dakar. Civil unrest in the Casamance is no longer a threat, though it's best to seek out the latest advice before venturing to this southern region.

EMBASSIES & CONSULATES

The embassies listed are located in Dakar. Most close late morning or early afternoon Monday to Friday, so set off early.

Bissau-Guinean Embassy (Map p320; ☎ 33 850 2574, 33 825 9089; Rue 6, Point E; ⊙ 8am-12.30pm Mon-Fri) There's a consulate in Ziguinchor (p332).

Cabo Verdean Embassy (Map p316; ☎ 33 860 8408; 3 Rue Mermoz, Plateau)

Canadian Embassy (Map p316; ☎ 33 889 4700; www.canadainternational.gc.ca; Rue Gallieni, Plateau; ⊙ 8am-12.30pm & 1.15-5pm Mon-Thu, 8am-12.30pm Fri)

French Embassy (Map p318; ☎ 33 839 5100; www.ambafrance-sn.org; 1 Rue Amadou Assane Ndoye, Plateau; ⊙ 8am-noon Mon-Fri)

Gambian Embassy (Map p320; ☎ 33 820 1198; Villa 128, Cité des Jeunes Cadres, Yoff Toundoup Rya)

German Embassy (Map p316; ☎ 33 889 4884; www.dakar.diplo.de; 20 Ave Pasteur, Plateau; ⊙ 9am-noon Mon-Fri)

Ghanaian Embassy (Map p320; ☎ 33 869 1990; Rue 6, Point E)

Guinean Embassy (Map p320; ☎ 33 824 8606; Rue de Diourbel, Point E)

Ivoirian Embassy (Map p320; ☎ 33 869 0270; www.ambaci-dakar.org; Allées Seydou Nourou Tall, Point E)

Malian Embassy (Map p320; ☎ 33 824 6250; 23 Rte de la Corniche-Ouest, Point E; ⊙ 9am-1pm Mon-Fri)

Mauritanian Embassy (Map p320; ☎ 33 823 5344; Mermoz; ⊙ 8am-2pm Mon-Fri)

Moroccan Embassy (Map p320; ☎ 33 824 3836; Ave Cheikh Anta Diop, Mermoz)

Spanish Embassy (Map p316; ☎ 33 849 2999; www.exteriores.gob.es; 30 Ave Nelson Mandela, Plateau; ⊙ 9am-2.30pm Mon-Fri)

UK Embassy (Map p316; ☎ 33 823 7392; www.gov.uk/government/world/senegal; 20 Rue du Dr Guillet, Plateau; ⊙ 8am-4.30pm Mon-Thu, to 12.30pm Fri) One block north of Hôpital le Dantec.

US Embassy (Map p320; ☎ 33 879 4000; www.dakar.usembassy.gov; Rte des Almadies, Les Almadies; ⊙ 8am-5.30pm Mon-Thu, to 1pm Fri)

EMERGENCY & IMPORTANT NUMBERS

Senegal's country code	☎ 221
International access code	☎ 00
Ambulance (SOS Médecins)	☎ 33 889 1515
Fire	☎ 18
Police	☎ 17

SENEGAL DIRECTORY A-Z

ℹ️ PRACTICALITIES

Electricity 220V. Plugs have two round pins (same as continental Europe

Newspapers *Le Soleil* (www.lesoleil.sn) is the main daily paper.

Post Service is fairly inexpensive, though not entirely reliable. The main post office is in Dakar.

Television RTS (www.rts.sn) is Senegal's public broadcasting channel, featuring independent programming (sometimes delving into culture and history).

Weights & measures Senegal uses the metric system.

FOOD

Dakar has a great many restaurants, catering to a wide range of budgets (though prices tend to be higher here than in other parts). Saint-Louis, Saly and Cap Skirring all have a small but vibrant dining scene, but elsewhere, options are sparse, and you'll likely be taking your meals wherever you lodge for the night.

Senegal's national dish is *thiéboudienne* (rice cooked in a thick tomato sauce and served with fried fish and vegetables). Also typical are *poulet yassa* or *poisson yassa* (marinated and grilled chicken or fish) and *mafé* (peanut-based stew).

GAY & LESBIAN TRAVELLERS

In Senegal things feel a little less severe than in neighbouring The Gambia (where gay travellers have been arrested, and the former president promised violence against gays). However, homosexual acts are still illegal in Senegal and can carry a prison sentence of one to five years. Violence and discrimination against gays is a very real threat. Gay travellers need to be extremely cautious travelling here. Being out is simply not an option in Senegal.

INTERNET ACCESS

Internet cafes are a dying breed in Senegal. Free wi-fi is available in many places (particularly in Dakar), and common in most accommodation catering to foreign tourists.

ℹ️ EATING PRICE RANGES

The following price ranges refers to a main course.

$ less than CFA3000

$$ CFA3000–6000

$$$ more than CFA6000

MONEY

Senegal uses the West African CFA (*SAY-fuh*) franc. All larger towns have banks with ATMs. US dollars and euros are the most easily exchanged currencies.

Tipping Not expected at budget eateries; 10% customary at pricier restaurants, though sometimes included in the bill. If you hire a guide or a driver for the day, however, you should plan on tipping (assuming the service wasn't abysmal).

Exchange Rates

Australia	A$1	CFA452
Canada	C$	CFA440
Euro zone	€1	CFA656
The Gambia (Dalasi)	D10	CFA133
Guinea (Guinean franc)	GF1000	CFA66
Japan	¥100	CFA538
New Zealand	NZ$1	CFA415
UK	£1	CFA774
US	US$1	CFA600

OPENING HOURS

Banks 9am to 4pm; a few open Saturday morning.

Bars 5pm to 2am.

Business and government offices 8.30am to 1pm and 2.30pm to 5pm Monday to Friday.

Cafes 8am to 7pm.

Clubs 10pm to 5am, mostly Thursday to Saturday.

Restaurants Lunch from noon to 2.30pm and dinner from 7pm; many closed on Sunday.

Shops 9am to 6pm Monday to Thursday and Saturday, to 1pm Friday; most close on Sunday.

PUBLIC HOLIDAYS

As well as Islamic religious holidays, Senegal celebrates a few principal public holidays.

New Year's Day 1 January

Independence Day 4 April

Workers Day 1 May

Assumption 15 August

TELEPHONE

➡ Good mobile phone coverage means that most of the public *télécentres* have now closed.

➡ The country code is 221. For directory assistance dial 1212.

TOURIST INFORMATION

There isn't much official tourist information available for travellers. One exception is the **Office de Tourisme** (p332) in Ziguinchor, which is an excellent source of info on the Casamance.

Given the lack of tourism posts (and online info), your best bet is to get local information from your guesthouse or hotel.

Visitors from the EU, USA, Canada, Australia, New Zealand and 80-plus other countries can enter Senegal without a visa for stays of up to 90 days.

Getting There & Away

AIR
Dakar is one of Africa's transport hubs, with links across Africa, Europe and America. Dakar's current airport, Léopold Sédar Senghor International Airport (p323), is slated to close once the new airport opens – which might be as early as 2018.

LAND
The Gambia

From Dakar there are *sept-place* taxis south to Karang (CFA7000, six hours, 250km) at the Gambian border, where you connect to Barra and then via ferry to Banjul.

From southern Senegal, *sept-place* taxis run regularly between Ziguinchor and Serekunda (CFA5000, five hours, 145km), and between Kafountine and Brikama (CFA3600, two hours, 60km).

In Eastern Senegal, *sept-place* taxis go from Tambacounda to Vélingara (CFA2500, three hours, 98km), and from there to Basse Santa Su (CFA1500, 50 minutes, 27km).

Guinea

Coming from the north, head to Tambacounda, where you can usually find Guinea-bound transport, down through Kalifourou and on to Koundara (Guinea).

If coming from the Casamance, your best bet is by *sept-place* from Diaoubé (Senegal). The enormous market on Wednesday makes it the ideal day to find transport out.

The road is generally in fair shape in Senegal, but deteriorates rapidly when you cross the border.

Guinea-Bissau

Sept-place taxis leave every morning from Ziguinchor for Bissau (CFA6000, four hours, 147km), via the main border post at São Domingos, and Ingore. The road is sealed and in good condition.

Mali

The security situation in Mali remains difficult – check the latest information before visiting. *Sept-place* taxis leave regularly from Tambacounda to Kidira (CFA4000, four hours, 190km), where you cross the border to Diboli in Mali; from Diboli long-distance buses run to Kayes and Bamako.

Mauritania
Sept-place taxis run regularly from Dakar to the main border point at Rosso (CFA7500, seven hours, 384km), a crowded, hasslesome place, where four daily ferries (free for passengers, CFA5000 for a vehicle) cross to Rosso-Mauritania.

If you have your own wheels, it's less hassle to cross at the Maka Diama dam, 97km southwest of Rosso and just north of Saint-Louis, where the border crossing is swift and largely free of hustlers.

Getting Around

AIR
Groupe Transair (p332) flies between Dakar, Ziguinchor and Cap Skirring.

BOAT
A regular ferry service travels between Dakar and Ziguinchor. There are currently four departures heading in each direction per week (see the latest times and prices on www.cap-skirring.voyage). All are operated by **COSAMA** (☑ 33 821 3434; info@cosamasn.com).

A regular ferry service travels between Dakar and Île de Gorée. Senegal's other islands can be visited by pirogue, including Île de N'Gor, Mar Lodj and Île de Karabane.

The luxury Bou El Mogdad (p329) travels in the north of the country on six-day voyages between Saint-Louis and Podor along the Senegal River.

BUS & SEPT-PLACE TAXIS
The quickest (though still uncomfortable) way of getting around the country is by *sept-place* taxi – battered Peugeots that negotiate even the most ragged routes. Slightly cheaper, but infinitely less reliable are the minibuses (Ndiaga Ndiaye or grand car), carrying around 40 people. Vehicles leave from the *gare routière* (transport station) when they're full, and they fill up quickest in the morning, before 8am.

Prices are theoretically fixed, though there's an extra, negotiable charge for luggage (10% to 20% of the bill).

In Dakar, long-distance transports arrive and depart from the Gare Routière Baux Maraîchers (p323) in Pikine.

CAR & MOTORCYCLE
You can hire vehicles in Senegal (Dakar's airport is the best place for this). To rent a vehicle, you'll need your home licence and, technically, an international drivers licence (though this isn't always asked for).

For less of a headache, you can often hire a car with driver for about the same price as a self-drive (starting from around CFA30,000 per day). Most guesthouses can help arrange this.

Sierra Leone

🔊 232 / POP 6 MILLION

Best Places to Eat

➜ Franco's (p348)

➜ Oasis (p345)

➜ Tokeh Beach (p348)

➜ Mamba Point Lagoonda (p346)

➜ Tessa's (p345)

Best Places to Sleep

➜ Freetown Oasis (p344)

➜ Tacugama Sanctuary Lodge (p347)

➜ Rogbonko Village (p349)

➜ Ategbeh Garden (p347)

➜ Cockle Point (p348)

Why Go?

For the traveller, Sierra Leone is still West Africa's secret beach destination. Sweet sands rise from the soft waters of the Atlantic, with the backdrop dressed in sun-stained hues, rainforest green and the red, red roads of the north.

In Freetown, colourful stilted houses remember the days when freed slaves from the Caribbean were resettled upon these shores. In the north, the Loma Mountains form the highest point west of Cameroon. Further east national parks and rainforest shelter endangered species like the black-and-white colobus monkey and the elusive pygmy hippo.

The scars of Sierra Leone's civil wars had just healed when the 2014–15 Ebola outbreak knocked the country off its feet once again. Tourism can play an important role in helping its recovery, so join the island-hoppers and adventurers, camp in little-visited rainforests and crack open fresh lobster in the shade of skinny palms and rope-strung hammocks.

When to Go
Freetown

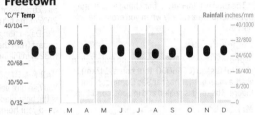

Nov–Jun The dry season is marked by mild, dusty harmattan winds in December, January and February.

April The average daytime temperature is 32°C.

Jun–Nov In the rainy season, spectacular coastal storms mean up to 3200mm of precipitation.

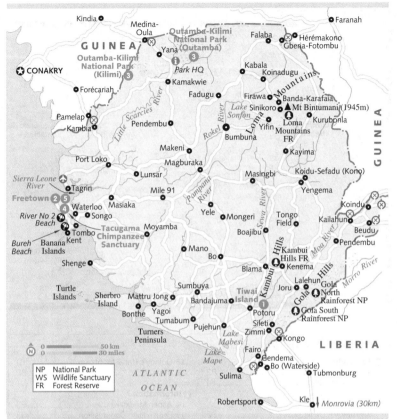

Sierra Leone Highlights

1 Tiwai Island (p351) Joining a nighttime hike through the forest in search of the elusive pygmy hippo.

2 Freetown Peninsula (p347) Eating barbecued lobster pulled fresh from the sea at one of the peninsula's stunning beaches.

3 Outamba-Kilimi National Park (p350) Gliding down the river by dugout canoe while monkeys and birds chatter in the surrounding forest.

4 Tacugama Chimpanzee Sanctuary (p347) Learning about conservation efforts

and viewing chimps playing in their sanctuary home.

5 Freetown (p341) Soaking up the atmosphere: spotting colourful Krio houses, strolling the beach and dancing till dawn at one of the city's energetic clubs.

FREETOWN

022 / POP 1.1 MILLION

Strung between the mountains and the sea, Sierra Leone's capital is a cheeky, quicksilver city bubbling with energy, colour and charm. One minute it's calm, offering up quiet beaches, friendly Krio chat and warm plates of soup and rice. The next it's frenzied and playing dirty, throwing you into the

back of a shared taxi and hurtling you up and down its pretty little hills.

And it might just be the only capital in the world where when you emerge from the airport, blinking after an overnight flight, you find yourself standing on the wooden deck of a port flanked by a backdrop of mountains, beaches and palm trees so idyllic you wonder if it's real. Well it's real, all of it – the chatter and the chaos and the colour and

Greater Freetown

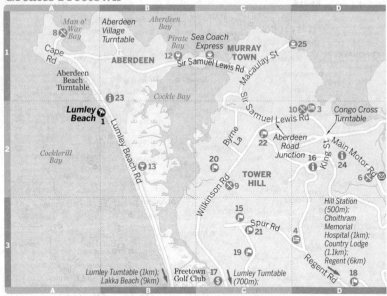

Greater Freetown

the dirt and the lush lobster dinners and the devastating history of war and Ebola – and those lovely white sands too.

◉ Sights

★ **National Railway Museum** MUSEUM
(Map p342; ☎ 077 423575; www.sierraleonerailwaymuseum.com; Cline St; ⊙ 9.30am-4.30pm Mon-Fri; 🚼) FREE You don't have to be a rail fan to

enjoy this Clinetown museum, where enthusiastic staff guide you around a surprising collection of restored locomotives, including one commissioned for the Queen of England in 1961. Other attractions include a display of model trains, and fascinating photos of the glory days of the Sierra Leone railway. There's also a small gift shop. Admission is free but donations are encouraged.

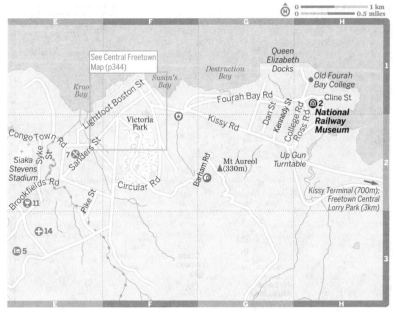

★**Lumley Beach**　　　　　　　BEACH
(Map p342) This wide sweep of beach has lost some of its atmosphere since the 2015 demolition of dozens of bamboo and thatch food shacks, and the numerous, ugly construction projects lining the beach road don't add to its appeal. During the week it feels deserted, save for a few joggers pounding the paved beach walkway, but it comes into its own on weekends and public holidays, when Freetown's residents come out to relax and party on the golden sands.

★**Sierra Leone National Museum** MUSEUM
(Map p344; ☑022 223555; Siaka Stevens St; ◷10.30am-4pm Mon-Fri) FREE There are two galleries inside the Sierra Leone National Museum – one housing a collection of cultural and historical artefacts, including Temne Guerrilla leader Bai Bureh's drum, clothes and sword; and another devoted to temporary exhibitions (at the time of research a fascinating collection of photographs and documents detailing the city's colonial past).

★**State House**　　　　HISTORIC BUILDING
(Map p344; Independence Ave) The State House, up on Tower Hill and overlooking the downtown area, is an example of Freetown's old Krio architecture, which features brightly washed buildings and higgledy-piggledy window frames. This building incorporates the bastions and lion gate from Fort Thornton (built at the turn of the 19th century).

★**Old Fourah Bay College**　　UNIVERSITY
(Map p342; College Rd) Gutted by fire in 1999, only the stone shell of the Old Fourah Bay College remains, but this 1848 building is graceful even in its decay. The World Monuments Fund lists it as one of the world's 100 most-endangered historic sites.

Cotton Tree　　　　　　　GARDENS
(Map p344) Freetown's most famous landmark is the fat Cotton Tree, which looms large over the buildings of central Freetown. Rumoured to be hundreds of years old, it is said to have played a key role in the city's history, when poor black settlers rested in its shadows after landing in Freetown in 1787.

🛏 Sleeping

There's no getting around it – accommodation in Freetown is expensive, and while there are plenty of chic options for those with deep pockets, good-value budget and midrange digs are hard to find. For those looking to make their leones stretch further, home-sharing websites such as Airbnb offer an excellent value alternative.

Central Freetown

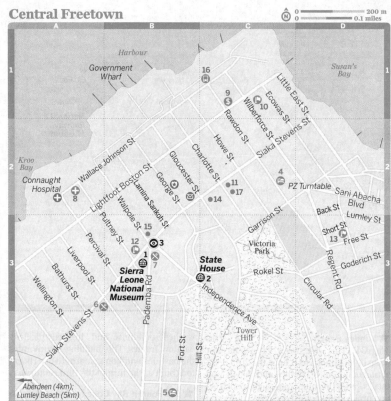

YMCA HOSTEL **$**

(Map p344; ☐ 078 952818; www.sierraleoneymca. org; 32 Fort St; s/d incl breakfast from Le220,000, with shared bathroom Le100,000/150,000; ⓟ❋🛜) The simple rooms here are the best deal in the city centre. Balconies on each floor provide sweeping views over the city, and there's a restaurant serving hearty local food (Le12,000).

Hedjazi Hotel HOTEL **$**

(Map p344; ☐ 076 601094, 076 790750; 32/24 Rawdon St; s/d Le100,000/150,000; ❋🛜) Cheap and cheerful is this centrally located budget hotel. Basic rooms have air-con and running water, and there's a guest lounge and wi-fi. As with the neighbouring Sierra International Hotel, this place can get pretty noisy, so ask for a room that faces away from the street.

★Freetown Oasis GUESTHOUSE **$$**

(Map p342; ☐ 076 605222; 33 Murray Town Rd; ⓟ❋🛜) Wander down the lane off busy Mur-

ray Town Rd to find nine homely, airy rooms in a surprisingly tranquil garden setting, with sea views. There's a wonderful cafe serving healthy meals and fresh fruit smoothies.

Lacs Villa Guesthouse GUESTHOUSE **$$**

(Map p342; 9 Cantonment Rd; s/d incl breakfast US$115/138; ⓟ❋🛜) The location is special – an old colonial house set in pretty green gardens, that seems miles away from the bustle of the city. The rooms in the old building come with high ceilings and polished wood furniture, and are a little more atmospheric than those in the newer annexe.

Hub BOUTIQUE HOTEL **$$$**

(Map p342; ☐ 088 112120; www.thehub-hotel.com; 6 Regent Rd; ⓟ❋🛜🏊) This fancy new spot offers plush rooms that wouldn't look out of place in London or New York, as well a pub, a restaurant and an excellent sushi bar. Oh, and not forgetting the rooftop pool, complete with city and beach views.

Central Freetown

Country Lodge HOTEL **$$$**
(☏076 691000; www.countrylodgesl.com; Hill Station; r US$200-320, ste US$350-500; P❄@🛜🛗) Perched on top of a hill, with stunning views out over the city and the ocean, Country Lodge is one of Freetown's fanciest addresses, popular with everyone from businessmen to VIPs. Rooms are suitably plush, and there's also a pool, gym and tennis court. If you can't afford to stay here, you're welcome to hole up in the excellent restaurant and use the free wi-fi.

✕ Eating

Senegalese Restaurant AFRICAN **$**
(Map p342; mains Le40,000-50,000; ⊙11am-10pm) Ignore the no-frills interior – this tiny gem serves up delicious West African meals and cold beers. The *yassa* chicken (or fish) is excellent and it even does a nice line in Senegalese deserts.

Salgus Restaurant AFRICAN **$**
(Map p344; ☏078 664404; cnr Pademba Rd & Independence Ave; ⊙8.30am-7.30pm Mon-Sat; P) A good place for a filling breakfast or to mingle with the lunchtime office crowd. Grills, sandwiches and *jollof rice* (rice and vegetables with meat or fish) are on the menu here, and there's a terrace overlooking the Cotton Tree.

Balmaya Restaurant AFRICAN **$**
(Map p342; 32 Main Motor Rd; mains Le40,000-50,000; ⊙8am-6pm) This is a friendly spot with a lovely terrace overlooking the street. Simple dishes of chicken, fish and rice are served with charm, if not speed.

Caribbean Fusion Restaurant CARIBBEAN **$**
(Map p342; ☏022 220226; Sanders St; mains Le40,000-60,000; ⊙7am-7.30pm Mon-Sat; ✎)

Krio goes back to its roots at this no-frills Caribbean joint. Written up on the chalkboard outside you'll find a choice of two or three mains a day (perhaps fish curry, jerk chicken or *jollof rice*), as well as a selection of fresh juices and other homemade drinks – it does a mean ginger beer!

D's Bazaar AFRICAN **$**
(Map p344; ☏077 248759, 076 999993; cnr Liverpool & Siaka Stevens Sts; mains Le15,000-30,000) Both the name and the food beat the decor at this local *plasas* spot. The menu changes daily, according to what's on hand, but you can expect to fill up with sour-sour, cassava leaves or simple rice and fish for less than Le15,000. There's a second branch on Wilkinson Rd.

★Oasis RESTAURANT **$$**
(Map p342; ☏076 605222; 33 Murray Town Rd, near Boyle Lane; P❄🛜✎) ✿ This charming little cafe is an oasis indeed. Set in a garden off Murray Town Rd, it feels hundreds of miles away from the chaos of Freetown. Though it's famous for its smoothies, the food here is also excellent and wholesome – think black bean soup, Thai chicken curry and indulgent brownies.

Tessa's AFRICAN **$$**
(Map p342; ☏076-800085; 13 Wilkinson Rd; mains Le40,000-60,000; ⊙11.30am-10pm; P) Authentic Sierra Leonean dishes such as black-eyed beans with plantain, palm-oil stew, *fufu* (fermented cassava, cooked and puréed) and sour-sour are on the menu here, served by super-friendly staff in either the simple dining room or the garden. There are a few European and Asian menu options too.

Mamba Point Lagoonda
SEAFOOD $$$

(Map p342; ☑ 099 100100; 53 Cape Rd, off Aberdeen Rd; P✷☎) Mamba Point is one of Freetown's most popular (and expensive) restaurants. Come for dinner in the chic dining room, or just to sink a few cocktails and smoke on a shisha pipe on the expansive terrace, which has gorgeous views over Man o' War Bay. On the menu are grilled fish and meats, pastas, and excellent sushi. There's a casino upstairs.

🍷 Drinking & Nightlife

★Quincy's Bar & Nightclub
CLUB

(Map p342; 63 Sir Samuel Lewis Rd; ⊙2pm-9am) A Freetown institution, Quincy's claims that it shuts 'when the last person leaves', and in their case, it's true. Come the weekend, an exuberant crowd of local posers, government ministers and expats parties well past dawn.

Roy's
BAR

(Map p342; ☑079 655677; ⊙11am-late) Watch the sun go down and the party people wake up on the expansive split-level terrace at Roy's, a perfect sundowner spot on Lumley Beach. It's hard to find a beef with this place – everyone from backpackers to ministerial employees seems to come here.

China House
BAR

(Map p342; Youyi Building, cnr Main Motor & Brookfield Rds) Mingle with ministers at China House, strangely located in the compound of the ministerial building. There's regular live music, although you might want to watch who you elbow on your way to the bar.

ℹ Information

DANGERS & ANNOYANCES

Freetown has less crime than you'd imagine, but it still makes sense to be cautious and avoid having valuables on display, or walking alone at night. Petty crime is an issue in markets and other crowded areas, and there have been many reports of muggings around Lumley Beach. Don't walk on the beach after dark, and exercise caution on weekdays, when it is almost deserted.

By far the most dangerous creatures in Freetown are not the mosquitoes but the (admittedly cheap) motorbike taxis – take one at your peril and wear a helmet (most drivers carry a spare).

MEDICAL SERVICES

Aspen Medical (Map p342; ☑ 099 500800, emergencies 099 888000; www.aspenmedicalintl.com)

Central Pharmacy (Map p344; ☑ 076 615503; 30 Wallace Johnson St) Reasonably well-stocked pharmacy.

Choitram Memorial Hospital (☑ 076 980000, emergency 076 888880; www.cmhfreetown.com; Hill Station) Freetown's best hospital.

Connaught Hospital (Map p344; ☑ 076 490595)

MONEY

There's an exchange bureau at **Lungi International Airport** with reasonable rates. There's also an ATM just outside the terminal building, which may or may not be working. Forex bureaus are found throughout the city.

Ecobank is located on **Wilkinson Rd** (Map p342; 157 Wilkinson Rd) and **Lightfoot Boston St** (Map p344; Lightfoot Boston St). Other major banks, including UBA and Rokel Commercial

---

ℹ ARRIVING IN FREETOWN

All international flights land at **Lungi International Airport** (☑ 099 714421), which is across the water from Freetown. While you can get to the city road, it's a four-hour journey, so it makes much more sense to get a speedboat or ferry.

Speedboats arranged through **Sea Coach Express** (Map p342; ☑ 033 111118; one-way US$42) take around 30 minutes. They run in coordination with the airport's flight schedule, and drop passengers off at Aberdeen Bridge. Rival company **Sea Bird Express** (Map p342; ☑ 077 606084; 36 High Broad St, Murray Town; one-way US$42) provides a similar service at a similar price, dropping passengers off at High Broad St in Murray Town.

The ferry service (1st/2nd class Le11,000/5000) leaves from Tagrin Ferry Terminal, a 15-minute taxi or *okada* (motorcycle taxi) ride from the airport. It takes around an hour and drops passengers off at the Kissy Ferry Terminal, in eastern Freetown.

If your flight arrives late at night, you could stay at **Lungi Airport Hotel** (☑ 076 660055; budget r US$80, standard s/d US$120/140; P✷☎☒) and cross over the water in the morning.

Bank, have Visa-card-linked ATMs. There are several ATMs in central Freetown.

POST

DHL (Map p342; ☑ 099 547672; 30 Main Motor Rd; ⊙ 8am-6pm Mon-Fri, 9am-5pm Sat)

Post Office (Map p344; 27 Siaka Stevens St; ⊙ 8.30am-4.30pm Mon-Fri) You can send international mail and set up a PO Box.

TOURIST INFORMATION

Conservation Society of Sierra Leone (Map p342; ☑ 030 522579, 076 633824; www. facebook.com/conservationsl; 14a King St; ⊙ 9am-5pm Mon-Fri) Helpful for travellers to Sierra Leone's natural reserves, including the Turtle Islands.

National Tourist Board (Map p342; ☑ 025 216362; www.welcometosierraleone.sl; Lumley Beach Rd; ⊙ 8am-5pm) Government-run, it can provide useful information about travel throughout the country.

TRAVEL AGENCIES

IPC Travel (Map p344; ☑ 077 444453; info@ ipctravel.com; 22 Siaka Stevens St; ⊙ 8.30am-5.30pm Mon-Fri) Can arrange tours, car hire, flight bookings and airport transfers.

Visit Sierra Leone (Map p342; ☑ 076 877618; www.visitsierraleone.org; 28 Main Motor Rd) A brilliant one-stop shop for tours, information, transport, guides and historical knowledge.

ⓘ Getting There & Away

From the **main bus station** (Map p344) at Wallace Johnson St, reasonably well maintained government buses leave for cities including Bo (6am daily, Le20,000), Kenema (6am daily, Le25,000), Makeni (6am daily, Le15,000) and Conakry, in Guinea (6am Monday to Thursday, Le50,000). Shared bush taxis head to the same destinations, stopping at villages and communities along the way. They leave from **Freetown Central Lorry Park** (Bai Bureh Rd) on the far east side of town. Taxis to Conakry park along Free St near Victoria Park Market.

ⓘ Getting Around

Shared taxis and *poda-podas* (minibuses) cost Le2000 per short hop and run on fixed routes around town. You can also bargain for a charter taxi (expect to pay around Le20,000 for a short journey, such as Lumley to town).

FREETOWN PENINSULA

The Freetown Peninsula is the star attraction of Sierra Leone's tourist industry – a deep green interior of mountains and for-est, kissed by a dazzling stretch of beaches, each one with its own special appeal. From powdery white sands nudged by a shallow turquoise lagoon, to a saffron bay shaded by palms and studded with boulders, to a wide sweep of thundering waves, perfect for surfing. And just off the tip of the peninsula lie the Banana Islands; an untrammelled hideaway, perfect for snorkelling, fishing and lazy days – or for jumping off an adventure to the storybook Turtle Islands.

◉ Sights & Activities

★**Tacugama**
Chimpanzee Sanctuary   WILDLIFE RESERVE
(☑ 076 611211, 044 625107; www.tacugama.com; adult/child Le100,000/35,000; ⊙ tours 10.30am & 4pm, bookings required) In the dense rainforest of Western Area National Park, Sri Lankan founder Bala created Tacugama Chimpanzee Sanctuary, a leafy, waterfall-framed hideaway set up with the purpose of rescuing and rehabilitating endangered primates, and in the process educating humans about one of our closest relatives. The passionate and committed staff offer twice-daily tours of the sanctuary, during which you'll watch rescued chimps frolic in enclosures and spot those who have been released to a larger area in the mountains beyond.

Bureh Beach Surf Club   SURFING
(☑ 078 044242, 077 934956; burehbeachsc@gmail. com) Run by a group of locals, with all profits going back into their community, Bureh Beach Surf Club offers board rental (Le60,000 per hour) and beginners surf lessons (Le80,000 for a two-hour lesson) on a beautiful golden beach 90 minutes south of Freetown.

🛌 Sleeping & Eating

★**Ategbeh Garden**   GUESTHOUSE $
(☑ 078 870119; www.ategbehgarden.co.uk; Cambeltown Rd, Waterloo; 🅿 ❄) Run by a British–Sierra Leonean couple, this little guesthouse, surrounded by flourishing tropical gardens and local farms, is the perfect antidote to busy Freetown life. The little cabins are calm and cool, with high ceilings, hardwood floors and verandas overlooking the birds and the trees. The food, cooked by your hosts or a local village cook, is wholesome and delicious.

★**Tacugama Sanctuary Lodge**   LODGE $$$
(☑ 044 625107; www.tacugama.com; incl breakfast d US$90-140, 4-person lodges US$180; 🅿) 🖋

SIERRA LEONE FREETOWN PENINSULA

Near enough to Freetown for an overnight visit, yet deep enough in the mountains to feel as if you're lost in the wilderness, Tacugama is a wonderfully romantic experience. The four cabins, two of which have bedrooms level with the treetops, overlook mist-shrouded forest, so you can fall asleep to the sound of chattering chimps. Rates include a sanctuary tour.

★**Franco's**   ITALIAN **$$**
(Florence's Resort; ☑ 076 744406, 077 366366; www.florencesresort.com; 20 Michael St, Sussex Village; mains Le50,000-100,000; ⊙ 9am-11pm; P 🛜 🐹) Half an hour from Freetown is Sierra Leone foodie institution Franco's, sprawled on Sussex Beach (beside the lagoon). Run by an Italian–Sierra Leonean couple, this place specialises in seafood and pasta, and is a favourite spot for a long, wine-fuelled Sunday lunch.

Banana Islands

Dublin (*doo-blin*), Ricketts and Mes-Meheux are the three bananas in this pretty archipelago, hanging from the southern tip of the Freetown Peninsula like a ripe bunch of fruit. The islands were first settled by the Portuguese in the 17th century and were later inhabited by freed slaves from the Caribbean – the descendents of those who live here now.

A private taxi from Freetown to Kent will cost around Le100,000 or you could get a poda poda to Waterloo (Le20,000) and find a shared taxi from there. After paying a Le5000 community 'entry fee', head straight for the port. There you'll receive plenty of offers from young men keen to take you across in a wooden boat (Le100,000). Alternatively, the owners of **Dalton's Banana Guest House** (☑ 076 278120; www.daltonsbananaguesthouse.com; budget/standard/deluxe Le100,000/250,000/300,000) can organise sea transport (the 30-minute crossing costs Le120,000 per boat one-way).

River No 2

This beach shot to fame after a Bounty bar ad was filmed here, and the sugary white sands don't disappoint. The popular Sankofa Complex, managed by the local community, organises activities and is home to a popular restaurant and guesthouse. You'll have to pay for the privilege though – there's an entrance fee of Le5000 per person.

🛏 Sleeping

★**Cockle Point**   GUESTHOUSE **$**
(☑ 077 073998, 076 687823, 078 717871; www.cocklepoint.com; s/d from US$50/80, tent US$15) A tranquil place with gorgeous views over River No 2, this guesthouse has four lovely thatch-roof bungalows. Two are traditional round huts, and two are split-level with balconies and 1st-floor bedrooms perfectly poised to receive the ocean breezes. The owners also have a couple of tents that they'll happily put up under thatch shelter for those on lower budgets.

River No 2 Guesthouse   GUESTHOUSE **$**
(☑ 078 349941, 088 330597; r incl breakfast Le250,000; P ❄) A community-run spot within the Sankofa Complex that has simple, clean rooms, with beautiful water views.

🍴 Eating

Africa Point   CAFE **$**
Just across the river from the Sankofa Complex, Africa Point's wooden tables and sunloungers make a worthwhile alternative for lunch – with fresh fish and cold beer on the menu.

Sankofa Complex   INTERNATIONAL **$$**
(☑ 088 33059; mains around Le50,000; P) At the relaxed restaurant in the Sankofa Complex you can eat under thatch or on bright-red tables set out on the sand. Food includes lobster, shrimp, barracuda. It's Le20,000 to hire a table and chairs, regardless of how much food you order.

ℹ Getting There & Away

Until the stretch of road between River No 2 and Tokeh Beach is completed, there is limited public transport, and you'll be better off hiring a taxi in Freetown (Le80,000).

Tokeh Beach

Tokeh Beach is one of the most spectacular beaches on the peninsula, a wide stretch of soft white sand, cradled by palm trees and forested hills. It is the most upmarket destination on the peninsula, and was purportedly popular with European celebs before the war.

☐ Sleeping & Eating

Tokeh Beach Resort   HOTEL **$$**

(☑078 911111; r US$60-180; P☀🛜) Tokeh Sands, which has sleek, white rooms with 24-hour power and air-con, opened here in 2013. You can swim out to the old helipad nearby, or kick off your sandals and nap in one of the hammocks strung between the palms while you contemplate your dinner options. There are some basic wooden huts for budget travellers here, but at US$60/80 for a single/double they seem expensive, especially considering that you share a bathroom.

The Place   HOTEL **$$$**

(☑099 604002; www.stayattheplace.com; P☀🛜⌨) The most luxurious hotel on the peninsula, The Place offers airy bungalows with soaring ceilings, large bathrooms, flat-screen TVs, iPod docks and coffee makers, where you can seal yourself up in an air-conditioned stupor and forget that you're even at the beach. There's also a pricey (and excellent) restaurant and bar, with ground- and 1st-floor terraces overlooking the water.

ⓘ Getting There & Away

Get a *poda poda* to Waterloo and from there you can find a share taxi to Tokeh. Tokeh Beach is just around the bend from River No 2 and it's possible to walk between the two at low tide.

Bunce Island

Once a major trading post for the transatlantic slave trade, Bunce Island lies some 30km up the Sierra Leone River from the ocean. Men, women and children who were kidnapped in the interior were brought to the fort to be traded. Until the British outlawed the industry in 1808, some 30,000 passed through the island and onto slave ships bound for the Americas, many to Georgia and South Carolina. Among those who have been traced back to here are the Gullah families of South Carolina.

Bunce Island is on a tentative list for inclusion as a Unesco World Heritage site, but unlike similar sites in Ghana and Senegal, it sees few visitors, mostly because it's costly and difficult to get to. Its isolation, coupled with the fact that it has never been used for any other purpose – essentially abandoned since the 1800s – makes a visit here feel even more haunting.

Visit Sierra Leone (p347) in Freetown can arrange a trip with a boat and guide for US$260 per group, as can the Sierra Leone National Museum (p343), at a similar price. You could also try hiring a boat yourself from Kissy Ferry Terminal (count on spending around US$200 for a return journey).

Those on lower budgets could try going via Pepel, the nearest village. You could get the public ferry from Kissy Terminal to Tagrin (1st/2nd class Le11,000/5,000), from where Pepel is a 90-minute ride by taxi or *okada*.

THE NORTH

Makeni

POP 126,000

Makeni is a good base for exploring the northern highlands, and all of the city's hotels will be able to advise you on getting out into the countryside, including rock-climbing and hiking.

The annual **Sierra Leone Marathon** (www.sierraleonemarathon.com) was set up in 2012. Runners follow a route through the villages and communities surrounding Makeni, raising funds for the charity Street Child (www.streetchild.co.uk). Over 100 international runners travelled to the town for the most recent event in 2016.

☐ Sleeping

★**St Josephs School for the Hearing Impaired**   GUESTHOUSE **$**

(☑088 509755; Teko Rd; s/d Le150,000/200,000, with shared bathroom Le100,000/200,000; P☀🛜) You'll get a warm welcome at St Josephs, by far the nicest place to stay in town. It's set in a beautiful old colonial building, which has a wraparound veranda, and the airy rooms come with high ceilings and splashes of colour from local fabrics. There's also a small dining room where meals are served (lunch/dinner Le30,000/50,000, order in advance). Be sure to tour the well-run school while you're here.

★**Rogbonko Village**   GUESTHOUSE **$**

(☑076 877018; www.rogbonkovillage.com; per person US$20) Experience life in a rural Sierra Leonean village at this excellent, community-run initiative, where guests are invited to take part in daily village life and

YORK

A little Krio village steeped in history, York was settled in the early 1800s by freed slaves starting a new life, including many Royal African Corps (liberated slaves who served Britain in the Napoleonic wars). It's a wonderful place to wander around for an hour or so. The streets are laid out in a grid fashion, and are full of colourful Krio board houses, reminiscent of those found in the southern states of the USA.

SIERRA LEONE MT BINTUMANI

sample (or even learn to cook) local country food. The village is beautifully set in native forest, and surrounded by rivers, ripe for exploring.

✖ Eating

Club House   INTERNATIONAL $$
(mains Le45,000-60,000; ⊙11am-11pm Mon-Fri, 10am-midnight Sat & Sun) Popular with the expat crowd, the place to come for burgers, grills, pizzas and breakfast, or just to drink a cool beer in the courtyard. It's all for a good cause too – profits go towards Street Child Sierra Leone.

De Rock's   INTERNATIONAL $$
(☑076 558150; Lunsar Makeni Hwy; ⊙9am-10pm; ❄) An air-conditioned space above Adnams Supermarket, this restaurant serves grilled meat, burgers, pizza and pasta.

❶ Getting There & Away

Bush taxis and *poda-podas* run to many destinations, including Freetown (Le25,000, four hours).

Mt Bintumani

Also known as Loma Mansa, the breathy King of the Mountains, 1945m-high Mt Bintumani is the second-highest peak in West Africa, after Mt Cameroon. The mountain range is rich in highland birds and mammal species, including duikers, colobus monkeys, buffalo, leopards and snakes. And it's well worth the two- to five-day adventure; the spectacular summit looks out over most of West Africa, veiled by soft, cool mist.

Any climbing attempt should be taken seriously, not just because of the difficulty of the climb, but because of the poor condition of the access roads (you might want to

stay away during the slippery rainy season!). You'll also need to come prepared with GPS and hiking and camping equipment, as well as adequate provisions for the climb, including plenty of water, and snacks for energy. Hiring a guide/porter who knows the mountain is essential.

Simple accommodation is often available in the villages surrounding Mt Bintumani, or they'll at least find you somewhere in the village to camp. Ask the chief of the village on arrival. On the mountain, camping is the only option, and you'll have to bring all equipment with you.

For Sokurala, you'll have to come via Makeni. Take the road east towards Koidu, then north to Sangbania via Kurubonla. You'll have to leave your car there and walk the final stretch (about an hour) to Sokurala. If coming on public transport, you'll need to get a shared taxi from Makeni to Koidu and from there arrange an *okada* to Sangbania.

To get to Sinekoro, first get to Kabala and then either drive (you'll need a 4WD) or arrange an *okada*. You can reach Yfin from either Kabala or Makeni. If coming from Makeni, head north on the Kabala road, turning right at Binkolo, and following the road past Bumbuna and Alikalia.

Outamba-Kilimi National Park

About 300km north of Freetown, **Outamba-Kilimi** (Le7500) 🍃 is a magical place, a mixture of jungle and savannah embedded between two hippo-filled rivers, and home to nine species of primate, pygmy hippo and, reputedly, leopard. While it doesn't match the grandeur of East Africa's parks and reserves, there are more gentle pleasures to be had here, such as searching for elusive forest elephants or gliding down the river listening to the chatter of monkeys and birds in the overhanging trees.

Safari Village (☑079 189718; next to the Kabba ferry; huts US$15; ℗) is a guesthouse with simple thatch huts and mosquito nets set right next to the river. There's a kitchen for self-catering or meals available on request.

The incongruous **White House** (☑079 189718; r from US$45; ℗❄), built to resemble that well-known building in Washington, DC, has pleasant air-conditioned rooms and a 24-hour bar.

About 15km south of the park's main entrance is the town of Kamakwie, an eight-hour journey from Freetown. Take a bus (Le25,000) or *poda poda* (Le30,000) to Makeni and pick up onward transport there. The cheapest way from Kamakwie to the park is by *okada*.

THE SOUTH

Bo

POP 306,000

Sierra Leone's second city is a pleasant place to spend a day or two, dodging the *okadas* that zip about at breakneck speed, or chatting to one of the many students that call this university town their home. There are no must-see attractions here, but it serves as a useful stop-off for travellers heading east to Tiwai Island, or south to Bonthe.

Rooms at the **Sir Milton Hotel** (Kissy Town Rd; s/d Le100,000/120,000; ※ 🛜) are simple but clean and come equipped with air-conditioning and hot water. The restaurant on the ground floor serves decent plates of grills and rice (mains around Le20,000) and shows football matches on the flat-screen TV.

The fanciest place to stay in Bo is **Doha's Hotel** (📞 079 944444; www.dohashotel.net; 103 Towama Rd; s/d Le375,000/525,000; 🅿 ※ 🛜 🏊), where spacious rooms with cool tile floors and wi-fi are set across a series of stupefyingly ugly two-storey villas. There's also a pool (though if the hotel isn't busy, it may not be filled), a bar and a restaurant specialising in Lebanese food.

It's smooth tarmac all the way from Freetown, a journey of three to four hours by either government bus (Le20,000) or *poda poda* (Le25,000). Bush taxis to Freetown (Le25,000) and the Liberian border (Le45,000) depart from Maxwell Khobe Park near the centre. You can also pick up bush taxis to Freetown from the lorry park on the Bo–Freetown highway. The quickest way to Kenema is usually to go out to Shell-Mingo on the highway and jump in a shared taxi there (Le10,000).

Turtle Islands

This beautiful, remote eight-island archipelago in Sierra Leone's southwest peninsula is made from soft golden sand, thick shavings of palm fronds, the purest turquoise water, and, quite frankly, dreams. Tethered to a traditional way of life, the islands swing to their own rhythms. You can explore most of them with the exception of Hoong, which is a male-only island reserved for rites of passage.

Arrange a fully catered trip through one of the guesthouses on the peninsula. Dalton's Banana Guest House (p348) offers excellent three-day camping trips from Banana Island to the Turtle Islands (a journey of around five hours, depending on the weather) for US$750 per group, including all camping equipment and food (maximum four people).

Tiwai Island

One of the few remaining tracts of ancient rainforest in West Africa, Tiwai Island, meaning 'Big Island' in the Mende language, is Sierra Leone's most popular and accessible nature reserve. Set on the Moa River, the entire island is run as a conservation research project – known as the Tiwai Island Wildlife Sanctuary. Tiwai covers a mere 12 sq km, but teems with an astonishing range of flora and fauna, and is most famous for its primate population. Although not part of the island, Gola Rainforest National Park shares the same tract of rainforest as Tiwai Island.

◉ Sights

Tiwai Island
Wildlife Sanctuary   WILDLIFE RESERVE
(📞 076-755146; www.tiwaiisland.org) Sierra Leone's most visited natural reserve is home to over 700 different plant species, 135 bird species (including eight species of hornbill), plus otters and sea turtles. Tiwai is most famous for its primate population – the forests are home to the striking black-and-white Diana monkey as well as chimpanzees. The endangered, elusive pygmy hippopotamus is also a resident here – of the estimated 2000 left in the wild, they are only found in Sierra Leone, Liberia, Guinea and Côte D'Ivoire.

🏃 Activities

For a proper introduction to life on Tiwai Island, take one of the excellent tours, such as guided forest walks (day/night from Le25,000/50,000 per person). If you're keen to do it yourself, there are a few self-guided forest trails.

If you want to spend more time in the area, and experience life in the communities that surround the nature reserve, there's a community-managed initiative called the **Tiwai Heritage Trail** (www.tiwaiheritagetrails. weebly.com). As well as including time on Tiwai Island and/or the Gola Rainforest National Park, multi-day trips follow bush trails and include stays in Mende villages, eating local food and learning about daily village life, culture and history.

🛏 Sleeping

Accommodation is provided either in tents (complete with foam mattresses and bedding) under a thatch canopy (US$30 to US$35), or in a bed at the simple research lodge (US$35). Either way, you'll get clean indoor shared bathrooms and a solid breakfast included in the rate. Drifting to sleep to the sounds of the rainforest makes for an atmospheric stay.

❶ Getting There & Away

From Bo, take a bus or *poda-poda* to Potoru (Le30,000, about three hours), but be warned that the last section of road is rough and unpaved and can be impassable in the wet season. From Potoru, you'll have to get an *okada* to Kambama, a 30-minute ride via a narrow stretch of road rising up through the forest. Once in Kambama, which sits on the banks of the Moa River, you can cross the river by canoe or speedboat (the journey is included in the Le100,000 entry fee).

If you'd rather have the comfort of an organised excursion, the Environmental Foundation for Africa started running regular weekend trips to Tiwai in November 2016. The trips leave Freetown on Friday mornings (two-/three-night packages US$110/142 per person; see www. tiwaiisland.org for more information).

Gola Rainforest National Park

Part of the same tract of rainforest as Tiwai Island, the **Gola Rainforest National Park** (☑ 076 420218; www.golarainforest.org) is home to an abundance of creatures great and small, from rare, intricately patterned butterflies to lost, lumbering forest elephants having a hard time locating the rest of their species (as in most parts of West Africa, their numbers are critically low). The park runs from Tiwai Island in the south up to the rocky Malema hills in the north. In September 2016, the Liberian side of the rainforest became the Liberian Gola Forest National Park, and together with the Sierra Leonean side becomes a trans-boundary peace park protecting some 1600 sq km.

Almost all visitors tour the park on a pre-arranged package through the **park headquarters** (☑ 076 420218; 164 Dama Rd) in Kenema, which include all food, park entry fees, guides and accommodation. Among the 10 packages on offer are camping and canoeing trips (from Le208,000 per person for two days), multiday forest hikes in search of primates and elephants (from Le600,000 per person for a four-day trip), and two-day community stays (from Le147,000 per person). As part of efforts to minimise impact on the park, tours are accompanied by a national park staff member and a community guide.

You can either bed down in a forest campsite (Le30,000 per person; Le15,000 if you bring your own equipment), or in one of three community lodges (Le30,000 per person), each of which has simple rooms with mosquito nets, a clean shared bathroom with running water, and a small lounge. All accommodation must be booked in advance.

Simple local meals, which must be arranged in advance, cost Le10,000 per person per meal.

❶ Getting There & Away

There are three main entry points to the park: Belebu, Lalehun and Sileti, all accessed via Joru, some 30 km south of Kenema. All roads leading to the park are unpaved and require a 4WD vehicle (the journey should take between two and three hours, depending on which part of the park you are heading to). If you don't have your own wheels, the guys at the office in Kenema can arrange transport for you, or you can make the journey by *okada* (around Le90,000).

UNDERSTAND SIERRA LEONE

Sierra Leone Today

In 2013, things were on the up in Sierra Leone. Ernest Bai Koroma had just won a second term in power in an election hailed as a marker of the peaceful postwar era, and the country was poised for an iron ore boom, as well as increased interest in tourism. Then in 2014 the devastating Ebola epidemic hit, freezing much of the country's economy. This was swiftly followed by a crash in the world price of metals and the collapse of two of the country's biggest mining companies, resulting in the loss of tens of thousands of jobs. The country had gone from one of Africa's fastest-growing economies in 2013 to the world's fastest-shrinking economy in 2015.

With Sierra Leone finally declared Ebola-free by the World Health Organization in March 2016, and the government implementing plans to expand agricultural growth, the country is slowly starting to rebuild itself – a revival that will hopefully be bolstered by much needed growth in the tourist industry now that the country is safe to visit once more.

History

The North American slave trade was effectively launched from Freetown in 1560, and by the 18th century Portuguese and British trading settlements lined the coast. In the late 1700s, freed slaves from places such as Jamaica and Nova Scotia were brought to the new settlement of Freetown. Soon after, Britain abolished slavery and Sierra Leone became a British colony. Many subsequent settlers were liberated from slaving ships intercepted by the British navy and brought here. These people became known as Krios and assumed an English lifestyle, together with an air of superiority.

But things didn't run smoothly in this brave new world. Black and white settlers dabbling in the slave trade, disease, rebellion and attacks by the French were all characteristics of 19th-century Sierra Leone. Most importantly, indigenous people were discriminated against by the British and Krios, and in 1898 a ferocious uprising by the Mende began, ostensibly in opposition to a hut tax.

Diamonds Are Forever

Independence came in 1961, but the 1960s and 1970s were characterised by coups (once there were three in one year, an all-African record), a shift of power to the indigenous Mende and Temne peoples, and the establishment of a one-party state (which lasted into the 1980s). By the early 1990s, the country was saddled with a shambolic economy and rampant corruption. Then the civil war began.

Foday Sankoh's Revolutionary United Front (RUF) seized large swathes of the country, including Sierra Leone's diamond and gold fields, with looting, robbery, rape, mutilation and summary execution, all tools of the RUF's trade. While their troops plundered to make ends meet, Charles Taylor in Liberia and the RUF's leaders enriched themselves from diamonds smuggled south.

The Sierra Leone government was pretty ineffective and tried using South African mercenaries against the RUF. In 1996, elections were held and Ahmad Tejan Kabbah was declared president, but a year later, after peace talks had brought some hope, the country descended into bloodshed.

Hopes & Fears

In March 1998, the Economic Community of West African States Monitoring Group (ECOMOG), a Nigerian-led peacekeeping force, retook Freetown and reinstated Kabbah. In January 1999, the RUF and AFRC launched 'Operation No Living Thing'. The ensuing carnage in and around Freetown killed 6000 people and mutilated many more (cutting a limb off was an RUF calling card). A massive UN peacekeeping mission (Unamsil) was deployed. Three hundred UN troops were abducted, but as the RUF closed in on Freetown in mid-2000 the British government deployed 1000 paratroopers and an aircraft carrier to prevent a massacre and shift the balance of power back to Kabbah's government and UN forces. Kabbah was re-elected and the RUF's political wing was soundly defeated.

Unamsil became the largest and most expensive peacekeeping mission in UN history up until that time, and also one of its most effective. The last of the 17,500 soldiers departed in 2005. Peace had won.

The Special Court for Sierra Leone, a UN-backed judicial body charged with investigating war crimes during the conflict, was set up in 2002 and took 10 years for proceedings against more than 15 people to be completed. The court's most famous convictee is Charles Taylor, the former president of next-door Liberia, who received a jail sentence of 50 years in 2012.

Culture

The two largest of the 18 tribal groups, the Temnes of the north and Mendes of the south, each make up about one-third of the population. Krios, mostly living in Freetown, constitute about 1.5% of the population but a large percentage of the professional class.

About 70% of Sierra Leoneans are Muslim; around 20% Christian; and a further 10% or so are followers of traditional or animist faiths. The majority of Christians live in the south. Sierra Leoneans are very tolerant, and mixed marriages are common.

SURVIVAL GUIDE

ⓘ Directory A–Z

ACCOMMODATION

Freetown has a growing number of accommodation choices, although you may have to pay through the roof for 24-hour power, water and internet. Elsewhere in the country, choices are more limited, but you can still find some gems.

DANGERS & ANNOYANCES

Sierra Leone is generally safe, although the biggest dangers are the roads and the tides, both of which can claim travellers who aren't vigilant about safety. Read up on rip tides before you travel, and be sure to wear a seatbelt whenever possible: driving safety standards aren't always of the highest. Avoid walking on Freetown's beaches alone – you should be fine on the peninsula – and it's best to walk in a group at night. Motorbike taxis are not the safest way to travel, especially in Freetown and other places with smooth roads. Make sure that your driver has a spare helmet.

EMBASSIES & CONSULATES

Most embassies are located in Freetown.

British High Commission (Map p342; ☑ 076 780713; www.ukinsierraleone.fco.gov.uk; 6 Spur Rd; ⊗ 8am-4.30pm Mon-Thu, 8am-1pm Fri) Assists French nationals.

Gambian High Commission (Map p344; ☑ 022 225191; 6 Wilberforce St)

German Embassy (Map p342; ☑ 078 732120; 3 Middle Hill Station; ⊗ 9am-noon Mon-Fri)

Ghanaian High Commission (Map p342; ☑ 076 100502; www.ghanahighcommission-freetown.sl; 43 Spur Rd)

Guinean Embassy (Map p342; ☑ 022 232584, 022 232469; 6 Carlton Carew Rd)

Liberian Embassy (Map p342; ☑ 022 230991; 2 Spur Rd)

Malian Consulate (Map p342; ☑ 022 231781; 40 Wilkinson Rd)

Nigerian Embassy (Map p344; ☑ 022 224229; 37 Siaka Stevens St)

Senegalese Consulate (Map p344; ☑ 022 222948; 9 Upper East St)

US Embassy (☑ 099 105500; http://freetown. usembassy.gov; Southridge, Hill Station; ⊗ 8am-5pm Mon-Thu, 8am-12.30pm Fri)

EMERGENCY & IMPORTANT NUMBERS

Sierra Leone's country code	☑ 232
Police	☑ 999
Ambulance	☑ 999
Fire	☑ 019

FOOD

Sierra Leone is known for its cuisine, and every town has at least one *cookery* (basic eating house) serving *chop* (meals). Rice is the staple and *plasas* (pounded potato or cassava leaves, cooked with palm oil and often fish or beef) is the most common sauce. Other typical dishes include okra sauce, groundnut stew and pepper soup. Street food, such as fried chicken, roasted corn, chicken kebabs and *fry fry* (simple sandwiches), is easy to find.

GAY & LESBIAN TRAVELLERS

Homosexuality is illegal in Sierra Leone and most gay relationships are carried out in secrecy. Many hotels and guesthouses will refuse to let same-sex couples share a room.

INTERNET ACCESS

Most of the good hotels, and some of the restaurants, offer free wi-fi. Most expats get by with USB pay-as-you-go internet sticks. You can also pick up internet-ready SIM cards for smartphones and tablets.

MONEY

ATMs Ecobank and UBA ATMs in Freetown spit out up to Le400,000 per day for those with Visa credit and debit cards. Don't rely on them too heavily, however, as they sometimes don't work. If leaving Freetown (to head down to the peninsula, for example), it pays to take all the cash you think you'll need with you, and then some.

SIERRA LEONE CULTURE

Changing money The most easily exchangeable currencies in Sierra Leone are US dollars, UK pounds and euros, in that order. Large denominations get the best rates. Forex bureaus (and street traders, though avoid them unless somebody you trust makes the introduction) invariably offer better rates than banks.

Credit cards Not widely accepted in Sierra Leone – you can generally only use them at top end hotels – but some Rokel Commercial Bank branches give cash advances on Visa cards.

Tipping At your discretion for hotels; staff at top-end hotels are more like to expect it. Not expected at restaurants, but always welcome. It is common practice to tip guides and drivers at the end of a trip or tour. When visiting a village it's polite to make a cash offering to the local chief.

Exchange Rates

Australia	A$1	Le5670
Canada	C$1	Le5500
Euro zone	€1	Le8200
Japan	¥100	Le6800
New Zealand	NZ$1	Le5200
UK	UK£1	Le9700
USA	US$1	Le7525
West African franc	CFA 1US$1	Le9000

OPENING HOURS

Banks Usually 8.30am to 4pm Monday to Friday, with a select few also open 9am to 1pm Saturday.

General shops and offices 9am to 5.30pm Monday to Saturday, though some places close at 1pm on Saturday.

PUBLIC HOLIDAYS

Besides the Islamic and Christian holidays, Sierra Leone celebrates New Year's Day (1 January) and Independence Day (27 April).

TELEPHONE

SIM and micro-SIM cards are widely available. Airtel and Africell offer 3G coverage and mobile broadband.

TOURIST INFORMATION

National Tourist Board (p347) Might be helpful.
Visit Sierra Leone (p347) A great source of pre-departure information.

❶ Getting There & Away

AIR

Brussels Airlines (Map p344; ☑ 076 333777; www.brusselsairlines.com; 30 Siaka Stevens St; ☺9am-5pm Mon-Fri, 10am-noon Sat) serves its hub in Brussels, **Kenya Airways** (Map p344; ☑ 077 001001; www.kenya-airways.com; 19 Walpole St) flies from Nairobi and Accra; **Royal Air Maroc** (AT; Map p344; ☑ 022 221015; www.royalairmaroc.com; 19 Charlotte St) flies from London via Casablanca, and Air France flies from Paris via Abidjan. KLM is launching direct fights from Amsterdam to Freetown in 2017.

LAND
Guinea

The main route to Guinea is via Pamelap. Bush taxis from Freetown to Conakry run regularly (Le60,000), and government buses leave central Freetown at 6am Monday to Thursday (Le50,000). The journey usually takes eight to 10 hours.

From Kamakwie to Kindia (Guinea) there's little transport on the Sierra Leone side, where the road is quite bad. Four-wheel drives usually leave Kamakwie every two or three days (Le80,000, eight to 10 hours). Alternatively, hire an *okada* (motorcycle taxi) to the border (they'll ask for around Le150,000), where it's about a 1.5km walk to Madina-Oula in Guinea. Here you might be able to find a bush taxi; if not, an *okada* can take you all the way to Kindia.

Liberia

Taxis (Le90,000) and sometimes *poda-podas* (minibuses; Le80,000) depart from Bo and Kenema to the border post at Gendema (taking six to eight hours in the dry season and 10 to 12 hours in the wet), where you walk over to Liberia and continue in one of the frequent taxis to Monrovia.

❶ Getting Around

CAR & MOTORCYCLE

Car hire is expensive (starting at around US$100 a day for a car with a driver in Freetown, and at least US$150 to head upcountry, not including the driver's expenses), but don't choose a company only on the price; ask about the terms too. Visit Sierra Leone (p347) and IPC Travel (p347) both hire reliable vehicles with drivers. Another good company is **Sierra Leone Car Hire** (☑ 076 345687, 077 461316; www.sierraleonecarhire.com).

You could also just charter ('*chatah*') a taxi. In Freetown, you can usually negotiate an hourly rate of Le30,000 per hour.

LOCAL TRANSPORT

Bush taxis and *poda-podas* (minibuses) link most towns; however, except for departures to and from Freetown and between Bo and Kenema, you'll find that traffic is usually pretty sparse, especially on Sunday. Buses will usually cost a little less, but they are slower.

Togo

📖 228 / POP 7.7 MILLION

Best Places to Eat

→ Côté Jardin (p359)

→ La Belle Époque (p361)

→ Le Fermier (p364)

→ Centre Grill (p366)

Best Places to Sleep

→ Chez Alice (p359)

→ Côté Sud (p358)

→ Hôtel Napoléon Lagune (p359)

→ Hôtel Coco Beach (p359)

→ La Douceur (p366)

Why Go?

For those fond of travelling off the beaten track, Togo is a rewarding destination. Its great diversity of landscapes ranges from lakes and palm-fringed beaches along the Atlantic coastline to the rolling forested hills in the centre; heading further north, the mantle of lush forest is replaced by the light-green and yellowy tinges of savannah. It's an excellent playground for hikers – there's no better ecofriendly way to experience the country's savage beauty than on foot.

Another highlight is Togo's melting-pot culture. The fortified compounds of Koutammakou are a reminder that the country's ethnically diverse population didn't always get along, but nowadays voodoo, Muslim, Christian and traditional festivals crowd the calendar and are often colourful celebrations for all. The cherry on top is Lomé, the low-key yet elegant capital, with its large avenues, tasty restaurants and throbbing nightlife – not to mention the splendid beaches on its doorstep.

When to Go
Lomé

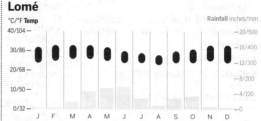

Mar & Apr The hottest period throughout the country is best avoided.

May–Oct Rainy season; there's a dry spell in the south mid-July to mid-September.

Nov–Feb Best time to visit, with pleasant temperatures. Perfect for outdoor activities.

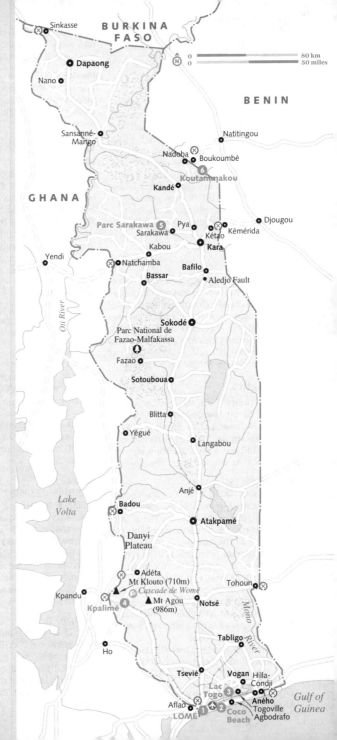

Togo Highlights

1 **Lomé** (p358)
Soaking up the the mellow vibes, jazz clubs and vibrant markets of the coastal capital.

2 **Coco Beach** (p358) Unwinding on this blissful stretch of sand in a hammock while sipping a sundowner.

3 **Lac Togo** (p363) Relaxing on the shores of this serene lake and taking a spin on a pirogue, a traditional local canoe.

4 **Kpalimé** (p363) Hiking in lush forested hills and cooling down with a dip beneath waterfalls.

5 **Parc Sarakawa** (p366) Tracking buffaloes, ostriches and antelope at Togo's most underrated wildlife reserve.

6 **Koutammakou** (p366) Seeking out northern Togo's remote clay-and-straw fortresses, the *tata* compounds.

COCO BEACH

Past the port and customs east of Lomé is another world – a mellow land of beachfront auberges where you can recharge your batteries. The best option on this part of the coast is Hôtel Coco Beach, with boardwalks leading to a great restaurant (meals CFA5700 to CFA7100), a seafront bar, a pool and a private beach with deckchairs and *paillotes* (shaded seats) for hire. It's also the safest beach to swim from, thanks to a reef that blocks the strong under-tow. Rooms are bright and comfortable but devoid of character.

LOMÉ

POP 754,000

Togo's capital – once dubbed 'the pearl of West Africa' – may be a shadow of its former self, but it retains a charm and nonchalance that is unique among West African capitals. You'll probably appreciate its human scale and unexpected treats and gems: from tasty *maquis* (street-side eatery) food to colourful markets and palm-fringed boulevards.

⊙ Sights

Centre Culturel Français   CULTURAL CENTRE
(☑ 22 53 58 00; www.institutfrancais-togo.com; 19 Ave du 24 Janvier; ⊙ 10am-8pm Tue-Sat, 5-8pm Sun) Offers regular films, concerts and exhibitions, and has a good selection of books and up-to-date newspapers.

Marché des Féticheurs   MARKET
(Fetish Market; ☑ 227 20 96; Quartier Akodesse-wa; admission & guide CFA4000, camera/video CFA7000/11,000; ⊙ 8.30am-6pm) The Marché des Féticheurs, 4km northeast of the centre, stocks all the ingredients for traditional fetishes, from porcupine skin to serpent head. It's all a bit grisly but it's important to remember that a vast majority of Togo-lese retain animist beliefs and fetishes are an integral part of local culture. Guides are not required, but it's helpful to hire one as they'll explain what is on offer and how the items are used in voodoo.

To get there charter a taxi (CFA1500) or a *taxi-moto* (motorcycle taxi; CFA700).

Grand Marché   MARKET
(Rue du Grand Marché; ⊙ 8am-4pm Mon-Sat) The labyrinthine Grand Marché is Togo at its most colourful and entrepreneurial. You'll find everything at this market, from Togo-lese football tops to cheap cosmetics.

Presidential Palace   NOTABLE BUILDING
The home of the president is an imposing modern structure, worth a few pics and the chance to see the guards dressed in their finest.

⛬ Tours

1001 Pistes   TOURS
(☑ 90 27 52 03; www.1001pistes.com) Run by a French couple, 1001 Pistes offers excellent excursions across the country. These range from easy day walks from Lomé to several-day hikes and 4WD adventures with biv-ouacs to whale-watching outings along the Atlantic coast. They also offer guided mountain bike tours in Lomé and elsewhere in the country. Pick-up from your hotel is included.

⛭ Sleeping

All budgets are catered for in Lomé. As in the rest of the country, security is always an issue, so even at the top establishments, be aware.

★ Marie-Antionette   HOTEL $
(☑ 90 05 73 13; www.kara-tg.com; Blvd 30 Août; r without/with AC CFA9000/12,500; P❄🖧) A fantastic choice, with bright clean rooms. Extra touches like colourful wall murals in the rooms put a smile on your face each morning, as does the over-the-top service. Exceptional value and worth being a bit outside town for.

★ Côté Sud   GUESTHOUSE $
(☑ 91 93 45 50, 23 36 12 70; Rue Nima; r CFA24,000-32,000; ❄🖧) Seeking a relaxing cocoon in Lomé with homely qualities? This champ of a guesthouse, run by a Frenchman who fell in love with Togo, has all the key ingredients, with five spacious, light and spick-and-span rooms, prim bathrooms and a small garden. The on-site restaurant (mains CFA3600 to CFA6100) is a winner for tasty French dishes with an African twist.

My Diana Guesthouse   GUESTHOUSE $
(☑ 91 25 08 80; Rue des Jonquilles; r CFA6350-9000, with air-con CFA10,000-16,000; ❄) A fam-ily affair, this lovely guesthouse is a simple but proudly maintained establishment. The room includes use of the kitchen, a spacious garden terrace and TV lounge. It's a great bargain.

★ **Chez Alice** GUESTHOUSE **$$**

(☑ 22 27 91 72; chezalice@hartmann-design.com; Blvd du Mono; campsites per person CFA1600, r CFA24,000-33,000; P ❄ 🛜) This perennial favourite is run by a friendly and efficient Swiss woman. Rooms in the massive wood structure are spotless and bright; camping is available on the grounds and the owner and the staff know everything about the area and will happily help out travellers. Meals are CFA3500 to CFA5000.

★ **Hôtel Napoléon Lagune** HOTEL **$$**

(☑ 22 27 07 32; www.napotogo.com; Route 20 Bé; d CFA42,000-62,000; P ❄ 🛜 ☀) The Napoléon Lagune is not in the centre but its perch on a lively stretch of the Bé lagoon is outstanding. It offers a range of well-equipped (if unspectacular) rooms at reasonable prices. Good service, satellite TV, a plant-filled garden, a small pool and an excellent restaurant (mains CFA3500 to CFA6200) are among the other highlights.

Hôtel Coco Beach RESORT **$$**

(☑ 22 71 49 37; www.hotel-togo-cocobeach.com; Coco Beach; s CFA31,000-39,000, d CFA33,000-60,000; P ❄ 🛜 ☀) This breezy, open hotel and grounds is a sweet place to spend a few days. Staff are attentive, the restaurant serves excellent seafood (meals CFA5700 to CFA7100) and a backup generator for the air-con keeps things cool.

Veronica Guest House GUESTHOUSE **$$**

(☑ 22 22 69 07; Blvd du Mono; d CFA36,000-55,000; 🛜 ☀) This charming 10-room hotel with professional staff, beautiful mahogany fittings and a pint-sized pool is a more Togolese alternative to the chain hotels. Both rooms and common areas are particularly spotless. Although it's on the busy highway, the rooms have thick double-glazing and views across the road to the beach. Meals are available (CFA13,000).

Hôtel Mercure-Sarakawa RESORT **$$$**

(☑ 22 27 65 90; www.accorhotels.com; Blvd du Mono; r with city view CFA112,000-119,000, with sea view CFA123,500-135,000; P ❄ ☀) Despite its concrete bunker exterior, this is one of West Africa's most exclusive hotels, 3km east of the centre on the coastal road to Benin. Rooms are comfortable, but the Sarakawa's main drawcard is its stunning Olympic-sized swimming pool set in acres of coconut grove. Rates include breakfast.

 Eating

Nopégali Plage AFRICAN **$**

(☑ 22 28 06 20; Blvd du 13 Janvier (Blvd Circulaire); mains CFA1500-2000; ⊘ 8am-10pm) You'll find no cheaper place for a sit-down meal in the centre. It's very much a canteen, but a good one, with friendly service and copious African dishes prepared like your Togolese grandma would make them.

China Town CHINESE **$**

(☑ 22 23 00 60; 67 Blvd du 13 Janvier (Blvd Circulaire); meals around CFA7500; ⊘ noon-10pm Wed-Mon) Welcoming, reliable and in a good location at the Kodjoviakopé end of the Blvd Circulaire, this place offers a great selection of steamed dumplings and meat dishes.

Brochettes de la Capitale ARABIC **$**

(Blvd du 13 Janvier (Blvd Circulaire); kebabs CFA200; ⊘ 5pm-1am) This Lomé institution is somewhat suffering from its popularity and location on the increasingly polluted Blvd Circulaire, but it's still a cool place to devour lip-smacking kebabs with a beer.

★ **Côté Jardin** INTERNATIONAL **$$**

(Rue d'Assoli; mains CFA3500-7000; ⊘ 11.30am-10.30pm Tue-Sun) Hands-down the most atmospheric eatery in Lomé, Côté Jardin has an exotic pleasure garden replete with tropical plants and woodcarvings. The supremely relaxing surrounds and eclectic menu make this a winner. Dim lighting contributes to the romantic ambience.

Big Metro AFRICAN **$$**

(Blvd du 13 Janvier (Blvd Circulaire); mains CFA1100-4700; ⊘ 11.30am-10pm) This little eatery with a pavement terrace is a great spot to catch local vibes and nosh on unpretentious yet tasty African staples. The braised fish of the day is superb.

Greenfield PIZZA, INTERNATIONAL **$$**

(☑ 22 21 21 55; Rue Akati; mains CFA4500-6000; ⊘ 11am-11pm) It's a bit out of the centre of the action, but this great garden bar-restaurant with a French owner has an original decor, with colourful lanterns and funky colonial seats with retro faux-leather cushions. The menu features wood-fired pizzas (evenings only), meat grills, salads and pastas.

Bena Grill STEAK **$$**

(☑ 22 21 50 87; Rue du Lac Togo; mains CFA2000-7500; ⊘ 8am-11pm) A nirvana for carnivores, this cheery restaurant in the market area is lauded for its top-quality meat dishes,

Lomé

N

0   400 m
0   0.2 miles

Marché des Féticheurs

Raketa (5km)

Ave Joseph Strauss

Ave Nicolas Grunitzky

Rue Moussons

Le Circus

Rue Abovey

Rue Aného

Ave F Mitterand

Ave de Nîmes

Place de l'Indépendance

Place des Martyrs

Train Station

Ave de la Nouvelle Marché

Rue Kponvenne

Ave de la Libération

Ave du 24 Janvier

Rue du Chemin de Fer

Rue Aniko Palako

Rue Kokéti

Place du Petit Marché

Ave Pompidou

Ave du Golfe

Ave Sarakawa

Eyadéma Omnisports Stadium

Ave de Duisberg

Ave Général de Gaulle

Ave de la Présidence

Presidential Palace

Route d'Aflao

Blvd du 13 Janvier (Blvd Circulaire)

Rue des Camomilles

Ghanaian border (550m)

Blvd de la Marina (République)

Beach

Disused Jetty

Atlantic Ocean (Gulf of Guinea)

Rue des Jonquilles

KODJOVIAKOPÉ

Rue Kouenou

Rue Notre Dame des Apôtres

Blvd Houphouët Boigny

Blvd du 13 Janvier (Blvd Circulaire)

Rue d'Amoutiévé

Rue Litimé

Blvd du Mono

Rue de l'Entente

Veronica Guest House (1.5km); Alt München (2.3km); Hôtel Mercure Sarakawa (2.5km)

Rue du Lac Togo

Blvd de la Marina (République)

Beach

Rue Sylvanus Olympio

Rue des Artisans

Rue de la Gare

Rue du Grand Marché

Rue Tokmaké

Rue de Kouromé

US Embassy; Service Immigration Togolaise; Gare d'Agbalépédo

Lomé

◎ Sights
1 Centre Culturel Français........................ D2
2 Grand Marché E3

⬛ Sleeping
3 Côté Sud F1
4 Hôtel Ibis-le Bénin................................ C3
5 My Diana Guesthouse A4

⬛ Eating
6 Bena Grill...F2
7 Big Metro A3
8 Brochettes de la Capitale E1
9 China Town..B4
10 Côté Jardin G2
11 La Belle Époque A4
12 Le Pêcheur... G2
13 Nopégali Plage G2

⬤ Drinking & Nightlife
14 Byblos.. F1
15 Le 54 ....B2

⬤ Entertainment
16 Cotton Club E2

17 Le Rézo C1

⬤ Shopping
18 Village Artisanal................................... C1

ⓘ Information
19 Banque Atlantique D2
20 Direction de la Promotion
      Touristique.......................................F2
21 Ecobank...E1
22 French Embassy....................................C3
23 German Embassy..................................A4
24 Pharmacie Bel Air.................................D3

ⓘ Transport
25 ABC E3
26 Air Côte d'Ivoire D3
27 Air France A3
28 Asky...D3
29 CTS..F1
30 Ethiopian Airlines D3
31 Gare de Cotonou E3
32 NTI...F1
    Royal Air Maroc ....(see 26)
33 STIF F3

including a sensational *côte porc grillée* (grilled pork rib). Also serves sandwiches, burgers and salads. It's next to the Marox supermarket.

★ La Belle Époque   FRENCH $$$
(☑ 22 20 22 40; Hôtel Belle-Vue, Kodjoviakopé; mains CFA9500-18,000; ⊙ 11am-11:30pm) One of Lomé's finest tables, La Belle Époque – all crisp white tablecloths and dimmed lighting – serves a refined, French-inspired cuisine. You can enjoy your meal in a verdant courtyard or the classy dining room inside.

Alt München   FRENCH, GERMAN $$$
(☑ 22 27 63 21; Blvd du Mono; mains CFA6200-11,300; ⊙ 11am-10pm Thu-Tue) A well-regarded restaurant just east of Hôtel Mercure-Sarakawa, offering a good selection of French and Bavarian specialities, including *jarret de porc* (pork knuckle) and *fondue bourguignonne* (meat fondue). Fish dishes are also available.

Le Pêcheur   SEAFOOD $$$
(☑ 91 59 63 50; Blvd du Mono; mains CFA8500-10,500; ⊙ 11am-3pm Mon-Fri, to 9pm Sat) The name gives it away: this is a fantastic seafood place where you'll enjoy fish fillet *a la plancha* (cooked on a griddle) and skewered *gambas* (prawns). Well worth the splurge – if only it had an outdoor terrace!

🍷 Drinking & Nightlife

Bars and clubs often fuse into one in the capital. Locals dress up when hitting the dance floor and going out for cocktails, so leave your sneakers and casual clothes at home for most dance clubs.

Le 54   BAR
(☑ 22 20 62 20; Blvd du 13 Janvier (Blvd Circulaire); ⊙ 10am-midnight Thu-Sun) A nice blend of exhibition space, affordable craft and jewellery, and a vibrant restaurant-bar. There's great live music Thursday to Sunday, catering for all musical tastes from electronic and house to rap and pop.

Byblos   CLUB
(Blvd du 13 Janvier (Blvd Circulaire); around CFA7000; ⊙ from 10pm Wed-Sun) This trendy nightclub is a favourite haunt of rich young Togolese, with music ranging from electronic to hip hop.

☆ Entertainment

Le Rézo   JAZZ
(☑ 22 20 15 13; 21 Ave de la Nouvelle Marché; ⊙ 10pm-1am) Inside, it's like a 1980s disco with its blacked-out windows, but Le Rézo is more contemporary than it looks, with giant screens showing Champions League football games, as well as karaoke nights and live jazz on Thursday.

TOGO LOMÉ

Cotton Club
JAZZ

(☑ 90 04 45 70; Ave Augino de Souza; ⊙ 6pm-late Tue-Sun) This jazz and blues lounge bar is polished, homely and welcoming. Snacks are available.

 ## Shopping

Head to the stalls of **Rue des Artisans** (⊙ 7.30am-6pm Mon-Sat) to buy woodcarvings, leather bags and sandals, as well as jewellery from across West Africa – but come with your haggling cap firmly on. It's just off Blvd de la Marina (République), one street west of Rue de la Gare.

Village Artisanal
GIFTS & SOUVENIRS

(☑ 22 16 80 70; Ave de la Nouvelle Marché; ⊙ 9am-5.30pm Mon-Sat) At this easy-going centre you'll see Togolese artisans weaving cloth, carving statues, making baskets and lampshades, sewing leather shoes and constructing cane chairs and tables – all for sale at reasonable, fixed prices.

ⓘ Information

DANGERS & ANNOYANCES
➜ There are pickpockets around the Rue de Grand Marché and along Rue du Commerce.

➜ Avoid walking on the beach alone, especially at night – muggings are common.

➜ There is a very strong undertow along coastal waters, so if you'd like a swim, head for a pool, such as the one available to nonguests at Hôtel Mercure-Sarakawa or **Hôtel Ibis-le Bénin** (☑ 22 21 24 85; www.ibishotel.com; Blvd de la Marina).

INTERNET ACCESS
There are numerous internet cafes in Lomé. Expect to pay CFA400 per hour.

MEDICAL SERVICES
Centre Hospitalier Universitaire de Tokoin
(☑ 22 12 50 10; Rte de Kpalimé) The main hospital, 1.5km northwest of the city.
Pharmacie Bel Air (☑ 22 10 32 10; Rue du Commerce; ⊙ 8am-7pm Mon-Fri, to 1pm Sat) Next to Hôtel du Golfe.

MONEY
All banks change cash. Banks with ATMs are easy to find in the centre; they accept Visa cards.
Banque Atlantique (☑ 22 20 88 92; Place du Petit Marché; ⊙ 8am-4pm Mon-Fri, 9am-2pm Sat) is the only place that accepts MasterCard in Togo; it also accepts Visa and has an ATM.
Ecobank (☑ 22 17 11 40; 20 Rue du Commerce) This branch is equipped with Visa cash machines.

POST
Post Office (☑ 22 13 19 50; Ave de la Libération; ⊙ 7.30am-5pm Mon-Fri, to 12.30pm Sat) Has an efficient poste-restante service.

TELEPHONE
Local and international calls can be made from any of the multitude of private telephone agencies around the city.

TOURIST INFORMATION
Direction de la Promotion Touristique
(☑ 22 14 31 30; www.togo-tourisme.com; Rue du Lac Togo) Located in a run-down building near Marox Supermarché. Staff are helpful (if surprised to see tourists), and can give you a reasonable road map of Togo as well as information on traditional festivals, which they are keen to promote.

ⓘ Getting There & Away

Rakieta (☑ 90 29 88 04) runs a daily bus service between Lomé and Kara (CFA5900, 6½ hours). It leaves between 7am and 7.30am (or so) from its depot in Atikoumé. Book ahead or arrive early (6am) on the day. This service is a better option than bush taxis.

Bush taxis and minibuses travelling east to Aného (CFA1400, one hour), Lac Togo/Agbodrafo (CFA950, 45 minutes) and to Cotonou (Benin; CFA7400, three hours) leave from **Gare de Cotonou** (Blvd de la Marina), just west of the STIF bus station.

Gare d'Agbalépédo (Quartier Agbalépédo), 10km north of central Lomé, serves all northern destinations. Services include Atakpamé (CFA3800, two hours), Dapaong (CFA8900, 10 to 11 hours) and Kara (CFA7900, five hours).

Minibuses to Kpalimé (CFA2000, two hours) leave from **Gare de Kpalimé** (Rue Moyama), 1.5km north of the centre on Rte de Kpalimé.

There are also international services, including to/from Ghana (p372).

ⓘ Getting Around

To the airport (5km from central Lomé) the taxi fare is about CFA1900 (but count on CFA2500 from the airport into the city).

Taxis are abundant and have no meters. Fares are from CFA480 for a shared taxi (more after 6pm) and CFA1500 for a private ride. A taxi by the hour should cost CFA3000 if you bargain well.

Zippy little *moto-taxis* (motorcycle taxis) are also popular, if rather dangerous. You should be able to go anywhere in the centre for CFA500 to CFA800.

SOUTHERN TOGO

The area between Aného, Kpalimé and Atak-pamé is one of the most alluring in West Africa, with a combination of superb beaches, a vast lake, forested hills and numerous waterfalls. If you can only visit one area in Togo, this should surely be it.

Lac Togo

On the southern shores of Lac Togo, part of the inland lagoon that stretches all the way from Lomé to Aného, **Agbodrafo** is a popular weekend getaway for frazzled Lomé residents. Swimming in the lake – which is croc- and bug-free – is blissful. It's also a good place to find a pirogue to **Togoville**, which was the former seat of the Mlapa dynasty and Togo's historical centre of voodoo.

There aren't many places to eat here. Bring your own food or eat at your hotel. East of Agbodrafo, the breezy, resort-like **Hôtel Le Lac**, (☑ 90 36 28 58; www.hotellelactogo.com; Agbodrafo; r CFA45,000-48,000, bungalows CFA68,000; [P][❄][☎][≋]) on the shores of Lac Togo, is a reliable choice. The renovated rooms are spacious, with private patios and sweeping lake views. There's a good restaurant (mains CFA2800 to CFA6000) overlooking the lake, a swimming pool and a small beach from where you can swim in the lake. Pirogue trips to Togoville (CFA3600) can easily be arranged.

The best route here is from Lomé; from its Gare de Cotonou bush taxis frequently travel along the coastal road to Aného (CFA1200) via Agbodrafo.

Aného

POP 48,000

All that remains of Aného's days as colonial capital in the late 19th century are its crumbling pastel buildings – a stroll past may have you pondering the echoes of their past residents. Local voodoo practice is also strong, but the real reason to stay here is to use it as a base for visiting Vogan's Friday market, about a half-hour from town.

◎ Sights

Vogan Friday Market   MARKET
(⊙8am-5 or 6pm Fri) This is one of the biggest and most colourful markets in Togo, with produce and bric-a-brac and a fun atmosphere. It's great for embracing local culture as well as picking up some fruit and veg.

It's located about 20km northwest of Aného. Taxis (CFA800, 30 minutes) leave from the junction of the coastal road and the highway to Lomé, on the eastern side of town.

★ Festivals & Events

Aného plays host to the **Festival des Divinités Noires** (Festival of Black Divinities), which has been held in December each year since 2006. A celebration of voodoo, it features singing, dancing, the beating of drums and parades.

⌶ Sleeping & Eating

There are some simple snack bars around town, but you'll find the quality and service better at hotel restaurants.

Hôtel Oasis   GUESTHOUSE $
(☑ 23 31 01 25; Rte de Lomé-Cotonou; d with fan/air-con CFA11,000/17,000; [P][❄]) An unbeatable location east of the bridge, looking across the lagoon and the beach to the sea. The terrace is a prime place for a sunset drink. Rooms are basic, though – you're paying for the location.

La Becca Hôtel   HOTEL $
(☑ 23 31 05 13; Rte de Lomé-Cotonou; r with fan CFA11,000-12,000, with air-con CFA16,500-21,000; [P][❄][☎]) The cheap and cheerful La Becca is a good budget option, with smallish yet well-scrubbed rooms. The air-con rooms are significantly better than the fan-cooled units.

❶ Getting There & Away

From the *gare routière* (bus station), bush taxis and minibuses head to Lomé (CFA1200, one hour), as well as to the Beninese border and Cotonou (CFA2700, 2½ hours).

Kpalimé

POP 101,500

Kpalimé is only 120km from Lomé, but it feels like another world. Hidden among the forested hills of the cocoa and coffee region, it offers some of Togo's best scenery and hiking and a lovely waterfall. It's also a busy place thanks to its proximity to the Ghanaian border and an important and lively market.

◎ Sights

Cascade de Womé   WATERFALL
(Womé Falls; ☑ 99 01 01 12; Womé; CFA1100; ⊙8am-5pm) One great attraction in the Kpalimé area is these falls, 12km from Kpalimé.

You pay the admission fee to the Association Akatamanso at the entrance of the village of Womé (ask for a receipt); then it's a further 4km to the picnic area near the falls. From there it's a short but steep descent to the waterfalls through lush vegetation. You can swim beneath the falls – bliss!

From Kpalimé, a *moto-taxi* ride to the falls should cost around CFA3600 return, including waiting time.

Market
MARKET

(⊙8am-6pm Tue & Sat) **FREE** Local farmers sell their produce here; there's also the usual bric-a-brac of plasticware and clothes. Since it's one of the biggest markets around this area, it's also the place where people meet and chat – offering some great people-watching and a chance to absorb the local culture.

As the location is close to the Ghanaian border, this market has a mix of both Togolese and Ghanaian vendors.

Tours

Adetop
TOURS

(📱90 08 88 54, 24 41 08 17; www.adetop-togo. com; Rte de Klouto) A small NGO promoting sustainable tourism, Adetop is based in Kpalimé but runs activities throughout the country. Its main activities are guided tours exploring the culture and heritage of Togo, as well as hiking. It is sensitive to local village culture and does a particularly good job visiting families and arranging meals and homestays with locals.

🛏 Sleeping

Hôtel Chez Felicia
HOTEL $

(📱22 46 33 49, 90 10 97 77; Rte de Missahoé; r with fan/air-con CFA8000/13,000; P❄) Off the road to Klouto, the discreet Hôtel Chez Felicia is an excellent bargain. This low-slung building set in verdant surrounds shelters immaculate, bright rooms with back-friendly mattresses, crisply dressed beds and impeccable bathrooms. Meals are CFA2500 to CFA4000.

Hotel Agbeviade
HOTEL $

(📱24 41 05 11; agbeviade2003@yahoo.fr; Rte de Missahoé, cnr of Rue de Bakula; r with fan CFA10,000, with air-con CFA19,500-22,500; ❄) Off the road to Klouto, the Agbeviade is a safe choice, although the smallish air-con rooms are a bit disappointing for the price. The restaurant's short menu concentrates on European dishes.

Hôtel Le Geyser
HOTEL $

(📱24 41 04 67; www.hotellegeyser.com; Rte de Missahoé; r CFA15,000-22,000; P❄🛜🏊) This tranquil place is 2km from the centre on the road to Klouto, in a balmy garden setting. Rooms are well tended, functional and airy, and the restaurant (mains CFA3500 to CFA5000) serves good African and European dishes. A real hit is the pool, larger than most others and kept impeccably clean.

Auberge Vakpo Guest House
GUESTHOUSE $

(📱24 42 56 64, 91 53 17 00; www.vakpoguesthouse. com; Kpodzi; r with fan CFA10,000, with air-con CFA12,500; P❄🛜) A well-run little number with a quiet location near the Catholic church, Auberge Vakpo offers neat rooms with good bedding, meticulous bathrooms and a lovely pleasure garden complete with flower bushes, mural frescoes and sculptures. Meals are available for CFA3700. They also organise local excursions.

Chez Fanny
INN $

(📱24 41 00 99; hotelchezfanny@yahoo.fr; Rte de Lomé; Kpodzi; r CFA18,000; P❄🛜) This jolly good villa 2km south of town is a homey retreat. The eight rooms are huge and the patio is a lovely spot for relaxing, despite the fact it overlooks the busy Rte de Lomé. The restaurant (mains CFA3000 to CFA6000) is the best in town.

🍴 Eating

⭐Le Fermier
AFRICAN, FRENCH $$

(📱90 02 98 30; mains CFA3000-4000; ⊙11.30am-9pm) For excellent European and African food, try this low-roofed, intimate spot on the northwestern outskirts of town. You can't really go wrong – everything is pretty good – but if you want a recommendation, go for the *fufu* (pounded yam), served in a clay pot.

Chez Lazare
FRENCH $$

(Rte de Missahoé/Rte de Kusuntu; mains CFA1200-5600; ⊙11am-10pm) Don't be put off by the unappealing concrete walls: Lazare cooks up excellent French specialities – how does a *côte de porc à la dijonnaise* (pork rib in mustard sauce) sound? There's pasta as well. The rooftop terrace is pleasant in the evening.

🍷 Drinking & Nightlife

Chez Fomen
BAR

(Rue de Bakula; ⊙9am-late) This cheerful, easy-going bar is a fun place for a drink.

HIKING IN THE KPALIMÉ AREA

The heartiest walk is up Togo's highest peak, **Mt Agou** (986m). The path climbs between backyards, through cocoa and coffee plantations and luxuriant forests bristling with life. Small terraced mountain villages pepper the slopes and provide fabulous views of the area – on a clear day, you can see Lake Volta in Ghana. The walk takes four hours' return from the village of Nyogbo. There's also a road to the top, so you can also walk one way and arrange a taxi for a ride back.

It's best to go with a local guide who will show you cool plants and unusual fruit and vegetables, and fill you up on local culture and history. Ask staff at your hotel to recommend the best guides.

Guides can also arrange anything from guided butterfly walks and even overnight village stays, as well as multi-day treks in the area. The area around **Mt Klouto** (710m), 12km northwest of Kpalimé, is another walking heaven, with forested hills, waterfalls and myriad butterflies; early morning is the best time to search for them.

It also shows regular football games and serves food.

Bar Alokpa BAR
(Rte de Missahoé; ⊙ 11am-late) A popular bar on the main road, north of the centre.

❶ Information

Banks with ATMs can be found in the centre.

❶ Getting There & Away

The *gare routière* is in the heart of town, two blocks east of the Shell petrol station. The road between Kpalimé and Atakpamé is the worst in the country, which means few taxis from Kpalimé travel further north than Atakpamé (CFA2500, four hours) – you'll have to change there for services to Sokodé or Kara.

You can get minibuses direct to Lomé (CFA2300, two hours), to the Ghanaian border (CFA1000, 40 minutes) and to Ho (Ghana; CFA1650, 1½ hours).

Atakpamé

POP 85,000

Once the favourite residence of the German colonial administrators, Atakpamé today is a commercial centre. There are no sights here as such, but it makes a pleasant enough stopover on long journeys.

⏍ Sleeping & Eating

Hôtel California HOTEL $
(⏍ 23 35 85 44; Rte Internationale; r with fan & shared bathroom CFA3000, with air-con CFA9500-14,000; ❄) Despite being at the back of the Total petrol station, this hotel-restaurant is a good surprise, with uncomplicated yet spotless rooms, salubrious bathrooms, ex-

cellent food (mains CFA1700 to CFA5000) and a friendly welcome. Opt for the air-con rooms, which have en-suite bathrooms and are noticeably better maintained than the fan-cooled units.

Le Sahélien AFRICAN $$
(⏍ 24 40 12 44; Rte Internationale; mains CFA1900-6200; ⊙ 11.30am-9pm) The downstairs *maquis* (an informal, street-side eatery) with its enormous grill and informal atmosphere does a brisk trade with the town's *moto-taxis*. Upstairs is more upmarket, and the roof terrace is a nice spot to catch the evening breeze. It also doubles as a hotel, but the rooms need a freshen up – we recommend staying elsewhere.

❶ Getting There & Away

Taxis and minibuses leave from the main *gare routière*, south of the centre, to Dapaong (CFA7600, eight hours), Kara (CFA4200, five hours), Kpalimé (CFA2500, four hours) and Lomé (CFA2900, two hours).

There's a secondary *gare routière* next to the market in the centre of town, from where taxis regularly go to Kpalimé (CFA2000).

NORTHERN TOGO

In the north, Islam takes over from Christianity as the dominant religion and its presence increases the further north you are. Most towns are short on sights, but for those with their own vehicle, or the determination to have a showdown with local bush taxis, fabulous highlights await in the castellated shapes of the Tamberma compounds in Koutammakou.

Kara

POP 110,000

Laid out by the Germans on a spacious scale, Kara is the relaxed capital of northern Togo and a good base for trips to Koutammakou. Because Gnassingbé Eyadéma, the president of Togo from 1967 to 2005, was from Pya, a Kabye village about 20km to the north, he pumped a lot of money into Kara and the region has remained a political stronghold of the Eyadéma clan. Kara is also the base from which to explore wildlife at Parc Sarakawa.

◉ Sights

Parc Sarakawa WILDLIFE RESERVE
(☑ 90 55 49 21; hel228@hotmail.fr; adult/child CFA5000/2500; ⊙ 8am-5pm) Unpretentious and relaxing, Parc Sarakawa is easily accessed from Kara as a day trip. While its wildlife-watching can't compare with that of the better-known parks in West Africa, this park spreads out over 607 hectares and is home to various species of antelope, buffaloes, ostriches and zebras. Game drives (CFA5000) can be arranged at the gate. There are plans to build a lodge within the park in the future.

✯ Festivals & Events

The area is famous for Evala, a coming-of-age festival held in July. The main event is *la lutte* (wrestling), in which greased-up young men try to topple each other in a series of bouts.

🛏 Sleeping & Eating

★ La Douceur INN $
(☑ 26 60 11 64; douceurkara@yahoo.fr; off Rue de Chaminade; r with fan CFA6000, with air-con CFA9000-12,000; ❄ 🛜) Down a dirt track in the stadium's neighbourhood you'll find this cosy bird's nest in a proudly maintained and flowered little compound; rooms are spotless, with simple decor. The well-stocked bar serves the coldest beer in town and the *paillote* (straw awning) restaurant serves fresh, well-prepared food (mains CFA1600 to CFA4000).

Marie-Antoinette HOTEL, CAMPGROUND $
(☑ 26 60 16 07; http://ma.kara-tg.com; Rte Internationale; camping per person CFA1600, s/d with fan CFA7500/12,500, with air-con CFA15,500/16,500; 🅿 ❄ 🛜) In a pretty house, 3km south of Kara on Rte Internationale, Marie-Antoinette has rooms of varying size and shape. The dear-er rooms are spacious, well-organised and come with hot-water bathrooms in good working order; you can also camp in the annexe across the street. One downside is the highway noise. The restaurant cooks up decent meals (CFA2800).

★ Centre Grill AFRICAN, EUROPEAN $$
(Marox; ☑ 90 70 22 33; cnr Rte de Prison & Ave Eyadéma; mains CFA3200-4900; ⊙ 8am-10pm) An attractive place with a straw roof, wicker light shades and blackboard menus, Centre Grill serves divine Togolese food and good Western dishes. Try its *fufu sauce arachide* with grilled fish or *pâte sorgho* (mashed sorghum), wash the lot down with a cold beer and polish it off with plantain fritters. Great value.

ℹ Getting There & Away

From the main *gare routière*, about 2km south of the town centre, minibuses regularly head north to Kandé (CFA1400) and south to Atakpamé (CFA4700, four hours) and Lomé (CFA4800, seven hours). Taxis heading north to Dapaong (CFA3900, four hours) are scarce – and it's common to have to wait for a half or even a full day for one to fill up.

For buses heading to Lomé, **Rakiéta** (Rue du 23 Septembre) has a daily departure at 7.45am (CFA5800, six hours) from its depot.

To get to the border with Benin via Kétao (CFA700, 45 minutes), get a minibus or bush taxi from **Station du Grand Marché** (Ave Eyadéma), next to the market.

Koutammakou

Also known as Tamberma Valley after the people who live here, Koutammakou has a unique collection of fortress-like mud houses, founded in the 17th century by people fleeing the slave-grabbing forays of Benin's Dahomeyan kings. Listed as a World Heritage Site by Unesco in 2004, the area is one of the most scenic in the country, with stunning mountain landscapes and intense light.

◉ Sights

Tamberma Compound NOTABLE BUILDING
(Nadoba; CFA1500; ⊙ roughly 9am-5pm) This is an excellent example of a typical Tamberma compound, called a *tata*. There's a variety of traditional, inhabited *tatas* here, so typically a visit includes a greeting by the head of the compound and then the opportunity to enter a select few homes. Look for the fetish statues out front – they're meant to keep

evil spirits away. The compound is about 2km from Nadoba, the area's main village. Purchase tickets at the Accueil et Billetterie office.

ℹ️ Getting There & Away

To get here turn eastward off the Kara–Dapaong highway in Kandé and follow the track in the direction of Nadoba. The track is in good condition and crosses the valley all the way to Boukoumbé and Natitingou in Benin.

If you don't have your own transport, chartering a *moto-taxi*/taxi for the day (from the centre of town) will cost around CFA7000/26,000.

Dapaong

POP 32,900

This lively little town is a West African melting pot, with the Burkinabé and Ghanaian borders both within 30km. It sits in the middle of Togo's most arid landscape and gets the full force of the dusty harmattan winds between November and February.

🍴 Sleeping & Eating

Hôtel Le Campement HOTEL $

(☎ 90 01 81 06; Rte de la Station de Lomé; r with fan/air-con CFA9800/17,600; P ❄️) This is Dapaong's only midrange hotel, but it's a tad overpriced. However, rooms are pleasant and spacious, and the overgrown garden filled with oversized sculptures is a cool place to laze around. The French bar-restaurant is expensive (mains from CFA4200), but the food is very tasty – and the desserts amazing.

Auberge Idriss GUESTHOUSE $

(☎ 27 70 83 49; off Rte Internationale; r with fan & shared bathroom CFA5000, with air-con CFA14,500-18,000; P ❄️) A tidy little guesthouse in a quiet neighbourhood 2km north of town. Rooms in the main building are spacious; those in the annexe have shared facilities but are cosier. Rooms with air-con have en-suite bathrooms.

ℹ️ Getting There & Away

Taxis leave the station on Route de Nasablé for Sinkasse on the Burkinabé border (CFA1400, 40 minutes), from where transport heads to Ouagadougou.

From Station de Lomé on Route Internationale, 2km south of the centre, bush taxis head to Kara (CFA4200, four hours) and Lomé (CFA9000, 12 hours).

TAMBERMA COMPOUNDS

A typical Tamberma compound, called a *tata*, consists of a series of towers connected by a thick wall with a single entrance chamber, used to trap an enemy and shower them with arrows. The castle-like nature of these extraordinary structures helped ward off invasions by neighbouring tribes – and, in the late 19th century, the Germans.

As in the *tata somba* in nearby Benin, life in a *tata* revolves around an elevated terrace of clay-covered logs, where the inhabitants cook, dry their millet and corn, and spend most of their leisure time.

The Tamberma (the word means 'skilled builders') use only clay, wood and straw for their houses – there are no nails or metal parts. There may be a fetish shrine in front of the compound.

Sokodé

POP 119,000

Sokodé is Togo's second-biggest city – but it certainly doesn't feel like it, with no major sites beyond the odd colonial building. It's the best base for trips to the Parc National de Fazao-Malfakassa, however; head to Fondation Franz Weber's office for more information.

◉ Sights

Parc National de Fazao-Malfakassa NATIONAL PARK

(www.ffw.ch; CFA4000; ⊙10am-5pm Dec-May) This 1920-sq-km national park is one of the most diverse West African parks in terms of landscape, with forest, savannah, rocky cliffs and waterfalls. The park boasts 203 species of bird and many species of mammal, including monkeys, antelope and around 40 somewhat elusive elephants.

The park was run by the Swiss organisation Fondation Franz Weber until 2015 and handed over to the Togolese government, but at the time of writing the park's future was undetermined, as protection from poachers dwindled in 2016 and the delicate fauna of the park was under threat. Visit the website for the most up-to-date information.

🛏 Sleeping & Eating

Hôtel Essofa   HOTEL $
(☑25 50 09 89; r without/with air-con CFA8500/15,000; ❄) This is one of the better options in Sokodé, with a nice garden and relatively clean rooms. Main meals cost CFA1800.

Hôtel Ave Kedia   HOTEL $$
(☑25 50 05 34; r without/with air-con CFA9000/16,000; ❄) As it's the only hotel in town with a generator (power cuts are all too frequent here), this is an excellent choice if you want to be assured of a cool escape and restful sleep. Rooms are simple but clean. Meals are CFA2200 to CFA4500.

Cafeteria 2000   AFRICAN $$
(mains CFA1500-5000; ⊙11am-7pm) If you're not eating at your hotel, try this basic snack bar, where the menu spells out every possible combination of meat and side dish. It's BYO beer.

🍷 Drinking & Nightlife

Bar Temps en Temps   BAR
(⊙approx 4-11pm) With its massive BBQ and candle-lit tables, this joint doubles as a beer hang-out and a great spot to grab a bite.

ℹ Information

UTB Has an ATM (but it often is out of order). They will also exchange euros or US dollars.

ℹ Getting There & Away

You can catch taxis from the *gare routière* (which is one block west of the market, behind the Shell petrol station on Route de Bassar), or on the main square between the market and the mosque.

Minibuses go regularly to Kara (CFA1800, two hours), Atakpamé (CFA3200, four hours) and Lomé (CFA5500, six hours).

UNDERSTAND TOGO

Togo Today

Togolese are generally pessimistic about the political outlook for the country. Many believe that the results of the 2010 and 2015 presidential elections, which re-elected Faure Gnassingbé, were corrupted, resulting in protests.

History

The country was once on the fringes of several great empires and, when the Europeans arrived in the 16th century, this power vacuum allowed the slave-traders to use Togo as a conduit.

Following the abolition of slavery, Germany signed a treaty in Togoville with local king Mlapa. Togoland, as the Germans called their colony, underwent considerable economic development, but the Togolese didn't appreciate the Germans' brutal 'pacification' campaigns. When the Germans surrendered at Kamina – the Allies' first victory in WWI – the Togolese welcomed the British forces.

However, the League of Nations split Togoland between France and Britain – a controversial move that divided the populous Ewe people. Following a 1956 plebiscite, British Togoland was incorporated into the Gold Coast (now Ghana). French Togoland gained full independence in 1960 under the country's first president, Sylvanus Olympio. But his presidency was short-lived. Olympio, an Ewe from the south who appeared to disregard the interests of northerners, was killed by Kabye soldiers in 1963. His replacement was then deposed by Kabye sergeant Gnassingbé Eyadéma. The new leader established a personality cult and became increasingly irrational following a 1974 assassination attempt.

In 1990, France began pressuring Eyadéma to adopt a multiparty system, but he resisted. The following year, after riots, strikes and the deaths of pro-democracy protestors, 28 bodies were dragged from a lagoon and dumped in front of the US embassy, drawing attention to the repression in Togo.

Eyadéma agreed to a conference in 1991, where delegates stripped him of his powers and installed an interim government. However, troops supporting Eyadéma later reinstalled him. Back in power, the general retaliated by postponing planned elections, which prompted strikes in 1992. The strikes paralysed the economy and led to violence, during which 250,000 southerners fled the country.

Eyadéma triumphed his way through ensuing elections throughout the 1990s – elections typically marred by international criticism, opposition boycotts and the killing of rival politicians. Amnesty International made allegations of human rights violations, such as executions and torture, and pressure on the president increased at the same rate that aid from international donors decreased.

Following Eyadéma's death in February 2005, his son, Faure Gnassingbé, seized power in a military coup, then relented and held presidential elections, which he won. Some 500 people were killed in riots in Lomé, amid allegations the elections were fixed.

Faure's Rally of the Togolese People (RPT) party won legislative elections in 2007, the first to be deemed reasonably free and fair by international observers. Opposition parties also won seats in parliament, a political first. Following this milestone, the EU resumed relations with Togo, which had been suspended for 14 years, and dealings with international agencies such as the IMF and the World Bank were restarted.

People

With about 40 ethnic groups in a population of over six million people, Togo has one of Africa's more heterogeneous populations. The three largest groups are the southern Ewe and Mina, and the northern Kabye; the latter counts President Gnassingbé among its population and is concentrated around Kara.

Religion

Christianity and Islam are the main religions in Togo (in the south and north, respectively). However, a majority of the population have voodoo beliefs, which are strongest in the southeast.

Arts & Culture

Batik and wax printing is popular throughout Togo, but the most well-known textile is the Ewe kente cloth, which is less brilliantly coloured than the Ashanti version.

Music and dance play an important part in Togolese daily life. Today, traditional music has fused with contemporary West African, Caribbean and South American sounds, creating a hybrid that includes highlife, reggae and *soukous*. Togo's most famous singing export was Bella Bellow, who, before her death in 1973, ruled the local music scene, toured internationally and released a re-cording, *Album Souvenir*. Nowadays, King Mensah is Togo's best-known artist, at home and abroad.

The fortified Tamberma compounds in Koutammakou are some of the most striking structures in West Africa.

Environment

Togo's coastline measures only 56km, but the country stretches inland for over 600km. The coast is tropical; further inland are rolling hills covered with forest, yielding to savannah plains in the north.

There's less wildlife than in neighbouring countries because larger mammals have largely been killed or scared off. Togo's remaining mammals (monkeys, buffaloes and antelope) are limited to the north; crocodiles and hippos are found in some rivers.

The coastline faces serious erosion and pollution problems.

SURVIVAL GUIDE

ℹ Directory A-Z

ACCOMMODATION

Togo has a fairly good range of accommodation options, from basic cubicle hotels to upmarket establishments with all mod cons. Unsurprisingly, Lomé has the widest range of hotels. In areas beyond the capital, lodging choices tend to be guesthouses or basic hotels with on-site restaurants; more expensive options usually offer generators and reliable air-con.

CHILDREN

➡ Togolese love children. Visitors with tots will find people extra friendly and helpful.

➡ Nappy-changing tables are available only in high-end restaurants.

➡ Finding child safety seats, nappies and formula are hit or miss – it's best to bring your own.

TOGO PEOPLE

ℹ **SLEEPING PRICE RANGES**

The following price ranges refer to a double room.

$ less than CFA30,000

$$ CFA30,000–50,000

$$$ more than CFA50,000

ℹ️ EATING PRICE RANGES

The following price ranges refer to a main course.

$ less than CFA3000

$$ CFA3000–6000

$$$ more than CFA6000

DANGERS & ANNOYANCES

➡ Petty theft and muggings are common in Lomé, especially on the beach and near the Grand Marché.

➡ *Taxi-motos* in the city may be convenient, but they are dangerous.

➡ Driving in Togo is, to say the least, hair-raising. Take care on the roads, particularly at night.

➡ The beaches along the coast are not safe for swimming because of strong currents.

EMBASSIES & CONSULATES

The following embassies are in Lomé:

French Embassy (☑ 22 23 46 00; www.amba-france-tg.org; Ave du Golfe; ⊙ 9am-2pm)

German Embassy (☑ 22 23 32 32; www.lome.diplo.de; Blvd de la Marina; ⊙ 9am-noon)

Ghanaian Embassy (☑ 22 21 31 94; ghmfa01@cafe.tg; Rue Moyama, Tokoin; ⊙ 8am-2pm Mon-Fri)

US Embassy (☑ 22 61 54 70; http://togo.usembassy.gov; Blvd Eyadéma)

British nationals should contact the **British High Commission** (☑ 030-2213250; www.ukinghana.fco.gov.uk; Julius Nyerere Link, off Gamel Abdul Nasser Ave; ⊙ 9.30-11.30am Mon-Thu, 8.30-10.30am Fri) in Accra (Ghana); the **Australian High Commission** (☑ 030-2216400; www.ghana.embassy.gov.au; 2 Second Rangoon Close, Cantonments; ⊙ 8.30am-3pm Mon-Fri) and **Canadian High Commission** (☑ 030-2211521; www.canadainternational.gc.ca/ghana; 42 Independence Ave, Sankara Interchange; ⊙ 7.30am-4pm Mon-Thu, to 1pm Fri) are also located there. New Zealand citizens should contact the **New Zealand High Commission** (☑ 012-435 9000; www.nzembassy.com/south-africa; 125 Middle St, New Muckleneuk, Pretoria) in Pretoria, South Africa.

EMERGENCY & IMPORTANT NUMBERS

Togo's country code	☑ 228
International access code	☑ 00
Ambulance	☑ 8200
Police	☑ 117
Fire	☑ 118

GAY & LESBIAN TRAVELLERS

Togolese society is quite conservative and gay and lesbian travellers should avoid making their sexual orientation known. Homosexual acts are punishable by law.

INTERNET ACCESS

In towns and cities, wi-fi is available at almost all midrange and top-end establishments. Internet cafes are easy to find in towns and cities but nonexistent in more remote areas.

MONEY

Togo uses the West African CFA franc. Major towns have Visa ATMs. A few upmarket hotels take credit cards but otherwise cash is king.

ATMs You'll find Visa ATMs in major towns. Only Banque Atlantique (p362) in Lomé accepts MasterCard.

Changing money The best foreign currency to carry is euros, which are easily exchanged at any bank or hotel.

Tipping Not the norm at local restaurants. In upmarket spots, 10% is the usual. Giving 5% to 10% to guides is reasonable.

Exchange Rates

Australia	A$1	CFA452
Canada	C$1	CFA440
Euro zone	€1	CFA656
Japan	¥100	CFA538
New Zealand	NZ$1	CFA415
UK	UK£1	CFA774
US	US$1	CFA600

For current exchange rates, see www.xe.com.

OPENING HOURS

Administrative offices 7am to noon and 2.30pm to 5.30pm Monday to Friday.

Banks 7.45am to 4pm or 5pm Monday to Friday (Many banks are open on Saturdays, too).

Bars and clubs around 6pm to late Monday to Saturday.

Restaurants 11am to 10pm daily, unless otherwise specified.

Shops 7.30am to 12.30pm and 2.30pm to 6pm Monday to Saturday.

POST

Togo's national postal service is La Poste. Expect long queues.

PUBLIC HOLIDAYS

Togo also celebrates Islamic holidays, which change dates every year according to the lunar calendar.

New Year's Day 1 January

Meditation Day 13 January

Easter March/April
National Day 27 April
Labour Day 1 May
Ascension Day May
Pentecost May/June
Day of the Martyrs 21 June
Assumption Day 15 August
All Saints' Day 1 November
Christmas Day 25 December

TELEPHONE

Landline numbers start with 2, mobile numbers with 9. You can make international calls at the private telephone agencies found in every town.

TOURIST INFORMATION

Togo's official tourist website (only in French) is at www.togo-tourisme.com.

TRAVELLERS WITH DISABILITIES

Togo has limited facilities for travellers with disabilities. The capital, Lomé, is slightly better equipped than rural areas. The best bet is to speak to your hotel and ask if you can hire a staff member after-hours for help (eg with lifting), or if they can suggest another trustworthy person.

VISAS

One-week extendable visas (CFA10,000) are issued at major border crossings with Ghana (Aflao/Lomé), Benin (Hillacondji) and Burkina Faso (Sinkasse), and upon arrival at the airport.

The **Service Immigration Togolaise** (☑ 25 07 85 60; Ave de la Chance; ⊙ 8am-4pm Mon-Fri), near the GTA building 8km north of central Lomé, issues 30-day visa extensions in one or two days. They're free when you extend the seven-day visa. Four photos are required.

The Visa des Pays de l'Entente, valid in Côte d'Ivoire, Niger, Benin and Burkina Faso, is available at the Service Immigration Togolaise (p371). Bring two photos, your passport and CFA17,800. It takes 24 to 48 hours to process, but note that the office is closed on weekends.

If you're visiting only a single country, the following embassies deliver visas:

Benin A two-week/one-month single-entry visa costs CFA12,000/17,000. You need two photos and photocopies of your passport. It takes one day to process.

Burkina Faso Contact the French Embassy (p370) in Lomé.

Ghana One-month single-entry visas are issued within three days for CFA20,000 and require four photos and a photocopy of your yellow-fever vaccination certificate.

WOMEN TRAVELLERS

The Togolese are rather conservative when it comes to marriage, so it's incomprehensible to them that women past their 20s might not be married. This will lead to many questions, but it is generally harmless. To avoid attracting any more attention, dress conservatively; if single, wear a fake wedding ring.

❶ Getting There & Away

AIR

Lomé–Tokoin International Airport (Gnassingbe Eyadema Airport; www.aeroportdelome.com; Ave de la Paix) is 5km northeast of the centre of Lomé. A few major airlines operate in Togo and have offices in Lomé.

The main international carriers are **Air France** (☑ 22 23 23 23; www.airfrance.com; Immeuble UAT, Blvd du 13 Janvier [Blvd Circulaire]), **Brussels Airlines** (☑ 22 21 25 25; www.brusselsairlines.com; Ave Joseph Strauss), **Royal Air Maroc** (☑ 22 23 48 48; www.royalairmaroc.com; Immeuble Taba, Ave Pompidou) and **Ethiopian Airlines** (☑ 22 21 87 38; www.ethiopianairlines.com; Immeuble Taba, Ave Pompidou), which offer direct flights to France, Belgium, Morocco and Ethiopia respectively, and connecting flights to the rest of the world.

Other major airlines include **Asky** (☑ 22 23 05 05; www.flyasky.com; Immeuble Taba, Ave Pompidou), which flies to major capitals in West and Central Africa; **Air Burkina** (www.air-burkina.com), with flights to Ouagadougou (Burkina Faso); and **Air Côte d'Ivoire** (☑ 22 61 18 44; www.aircotedivoire.com; Ave Jean-Paul II), which flies to Abidjan (Côte d'Ivoire).

LAND
Benin

Bush taxis regularly ply the road between Gare de Cotonou in Lomé and Cotonou (Benin; CFA7000, three hours) via Hillacondji (CFA950, one hour), while **ABC** (☑ 90 07 69 56; Rue Sylvanus Olympio) in Lomé has daily buses to Cotonou (CFA7000, three hours).

The main northern crossing is at Kétao (northeast of Kara). You can also cross at Tohoun (east of Notsé) or Nadoba (in Koutammakou country), arriving in Boukoumbé, but public transport is infrequent.

Note that Beninese visas can be issued at the border.

TOGO GETTING THERE & AWAY

Burkina Faso

The best way to get to Ouagadougou from Lomé is by bus (roughly 17 to 20 hours), via Dapaong. **NTI** (☑ 90 19 80 92; Blvd du 13 Janvier [Blvd Circulaire]), **CTS** (☑ 99 27 83 32; Blvd du 13 Janvier [Blvd Circulaire]) and **TCV** (☑ 92 29 48 93; Ave Agustino de Souza) are reliable companies. NTI and CTS have three services weekly (CFA12,800) and TCV has two weekly (CFA16,200); the ride from Lomé to Dapaong takes roughly one to two hours.

From Dapaong, you'll easily find a taxi to Sinkasse (CFA1700, 45 minutes), which straddles the border. From there it's CFA6000 to Ouagadougou by bus. The border is open from 6am to 6pm.

Ghana

From central Lomé it is only 2km by shared/chartered taxi (CFA600/1750) or taxi-moto (CFA500) to the chaotic border crossing (open 6am to 10pm) with Aflao in Ghana. From there, you can cross on foot to pick up minibuses to Accra.

STIF (☑ 99 42 72 72; off Blvd de la Marina) runs daily buses between Lomé and Abidjan via Accra (CFA7600, four hours).

There are other crossings from Kpalimé to Ho and Mt Klouto to Kpandu.

ⓘ Getting Around

BUS

Buses are the most reliable way to get around, especially for long-distance trips. **Rakiéta** (p362) buses are more reliable than those of other companies.

Buses almost always operate with guaranteed seating and fixed departure times.

CAR & MOTORCYCLE

If you're driving, you will need an International Driving Permit (IDP). Police checkpoints are common throughout the country but rarely nasty or obstructive.

Petrol stations are plentiful in major towns. At time of research, a litre of petrol cost from CFA750 to CFA900.

Cars may be hired at Lomé–Tokoin International Airport.

LOCAL TRANSPORT
Bush Taxis

Togo has an extensive network of dilapidated bush taxis, which can be anything from an old pick-up truck to a normal sedan car or nine- or 15-seat people carriers. Travel is often agonisingly slow, but unfortunately these bush taxis are generally the only way to go from town to town. Fares are fixed-ish.

Motorcycle Taxis

You'll find taxis in most cities. Taxi-motos (motorcycle taxis) – also called zemi-johns – are everywhere. A journey across town costs about CFA200, and more in Lomé. They are also a handy way to get to remote locations in the bush.

Chartering a taxi-moto will generally cost CFA2500 to CFA4000 per hour.

Understand
West Africa

West Africa Today

Life in West Africa ain't easy. Much of the Sahara and parts of the Sahel are off-limits due to ongoing violence and civil conflict sparked by an Islamist insurgency in Mali and elsewhere. Abundant natural resources have more often than not cursed countries with their side effects. And environmental degradation threatens to swallow entire countries. But with great resilience the region goes about its business, trying to build prosperity, democracy and, despite the odds stacked against its people, a peaceful future.

Best on Film

Half of a Yellow Sun (2013) Stirring love story and evocation of Nigeria's Biafran civil war in the 1960s.

Moolaadé (2005) An important film by one of West Africa's finest directors.

Blood Diamond (2006) Heart-rending Hollywood blockbuster set in Sierra Leone's diamond-fuelled civil war in the 1990s.

Ezra (2007) A searing look at the abduction of child soldiers as seen from an African perspective.

Best in Print

The Shadow of the Sun (Ryszard Kapuściński; 2002) A masterpiece by one of Africa's most insightful observers.

Journey Without Maps (Graham Greene; 1936) One of the 20th century's best writers travels through the forests of Liberia and Sierra Leone.

Things Fall Apart (Chinua Achebe; 1958) Timeless dramatisation of the collision between traditional culture and Europeans in 19th-century Nigeria.

African Silences (Peter Matthiessen; 1992) A memorable foray into West Africa by one of the 20th century's premier nature writers.

Terrorism in the Sahel

Not that long ago, travellers explored the Sahara and Sahel with ease and the world's largest desert was an undoubted regional highlight. Now the Sahara is one of the most dangerous places on earth. With Libya's 2011 disintegration, arms and rebel groups flowed down into Niger and Mali. In 2012 fundamentalist Islamist groups, with Al-Qaeda in the Islamic Maghreb (AQIM) to the fore, swept across Mali until a French force pushed them back into their desert strongholds. Bomb attacks on Bamako in 2015 and Ouagadougou in 2016 served as reminders that Mali's peace is fragile at best. At the same time, the withering conflict between Al-Qaeda-affiliated Boko Haram and government forces in Nigeria has wrought devastation in the country's north. Mali, Niger, western Mauritania and northern Nigeria are no-go zones. One consolation appears to be that the fundamentalist Islamist roots behind much of the conflicts bear little resemblance to the tolerant and moderate form of Islam practised by most in a region where the majority of the population is Muslim.

The Resource Curse

West Africa could be one of the richest places on earth. Oil in Nigeria and Equatorial Guinea and diamonds in Sierra Leone have done little to improve the lives of ordinary West Africans. Nigeria seems perennially at war with itself and living standards are too often appalling. In Equatorial Guinea, oil riches have propped up a brutal dictatorship whose members enjoy fabulous wealth while too many Equatorial Guineans live in abject poverty. Sierra Leone became a byword for Africa's resource curse in the 1990s with a vicious war and it remains an economic basket case. It's not all bad news. Sierra Leone is again at peace. Equatorial Guinea has a per-capita income higher than its former colonial ruler, Spain. And

Equatorial Guinea has some of Africa's highest adult female literacy rates. Still, West Africa has been blessed far more by natural riches than by governments capable of distributing the benefits fairly.

Rulers for Life?

The days of the dictator-for-life may be on the wane across the globe, but the tradition dies hard in West Africa. With Teodoro Obiang Nguema (who has ruled Equatorial Guinea since 1979) and Paul Biya (in power in Cameroon since 1982), the region 'boasts' the two longest-serving (non-royal) leaders on earth. And some leaders just won't go quietly – The Gambia's Yahya Jammeh, who tried to cling to power after his unexpected election loss, only departed the country after Senegalese troops organised by the Economic Community of West African States (Ecowas) moved in. The region's reaction to Jammeh's intransigence signposts how much the world has indeed changed. Elsewhere democracy holds firm in many countries of the region, including powerhouses Nigeria, Senegal and Ghana, suggesting that the region's democratic balance sheet is generally in the positive.

A Difficult Future

When it comes to living standards, most West Africans still live lives of quiet desperation: according to the UNDP's 2015 Human Development Index, a ranking of living standards based on a range of quality-of-life indicators, Niger came last and West African countries occupied 10 of the 20 lowest positions. West Africa's countries are on the frontline of environmental issues and climate-change consequences, its government and peoples grappling with some of the most pressing issues of our time. And yet, some countries offer proof that a brighter future is possible – Cabo Verde, Equatorial Guinea, Ghana and São Tomé & Príncipe have all risen to the ranks of countries determined by the UN to be of 'Medium Human Development' in the index. Given that some of these have troubled recent histories, imagine what might be possible with a little more luck and good governance.

POPULATION: **370 MILLION**

AREA: **7,257,567 SQ KM**

UNESCO WORLD HERITAGE-LISTED SITES: **34**

HIGHEST POINT: **MT CAMEROON (4095M)**

if West Africa were 100 people

51 would be Nigerian
8 would be Ghanaian
6 would be Cameroonian
5 would be Ivoirian
30 would be other

belief systems
(% of population)

Muslim

Christian

Animist

population per sq km

WEST AFRICA   AUS   USA

† ≈ 3 people

History

West Africa's story is one of history's grand epics. This is a place where the great issues and contradictions of Africa's past resonate through the present: from ancient empires to the ravages of slavery, from fabulous natural resources to the destruction wreaked by climate change, from proud independence and the colonial yoke to the more complicated sovereignty of the present. Above all, West Africa's history is about an astonishing patchwork of peoples trying to write their own history against often considerable odds.

First Footprints

West Africa's earliest history is shrouded in mystery, its archaeological evidence either residing in the belly of a termite or consumed by tropical climates and the shifting sands of the Sahara.

The first meaningful signposts to West Africa's past appeared around 10,000 years ago in the Sahara, especially the Aïr Mountains of northern Niger and the Adrar des Ifôghas in Mali, where nomads roamed across a very different West Africa from what you see today. Rivers, forests, vast lakes and savannah occupied much of what is now the Sahara, the human population was small and widely dispersed, and animals such as elephants, giraffes and the great cats were plentiful.

Around 5000 BC, domesticated cattle replaced elephants and giraffes in the carvings and finely rendered rock paintings left by hunter-gatherer peoples. This rock art, which serves as the Sahara's history books of the time, marks the moment when West Africans began to build sedentary settlements as water became scarce.

The earliest signs of organised society in West Africa date from around 1500 BC, in present-day Mauritania and northern Nigeria, where the remains of stone villages and domestic animals have been found. As settlements spread, two dominant groups emerged, the first along the Niger River and the second around Lake Chad – both areas where soils were fertile and well suited to agriculture. These groups built large stone villages and even towns. The first urban settlement of note was Jenné-Jeno, in present-day Mali, which was established around 300 BC and is often

Opinion among historians is divided as to whether knowledge of iron-working was introduced to the region from Egypt or actually originated in West Africa.

TIMELINE	200,000 BC	From 5000 BC	450 BC
	Homo erectus, the predecessor of *Homo sapiens*, occupies much of West Africa, as suggested by the tools and other artefacts found in Senegal, Guinea, Mali, Mauritania and elsewhere.	The Sahara begins to become a desert. Most of West Africa's peoples forsake transient life and settle around waterholes, begin to rely on agriculture and start to move south.	The appearance of iron-working in central Nigeria enables the clearing of forests, which expands agricultural land and commences the process of denuding West Africa's landscape.

considered the father of West African cities. By AD 500, towns and villages were dotted across the region.

The earliest inhabitants of West Africa's southern coast and its hinterland were most likely the Pygmies, who arrived in the region of what is now the Republic of Congo, Gabon and Equatorial Guinea from the east. Over the centuries they were gradually displaced or pushed deeper into the forest by peoples of Bantu origins who established kingdoms such as Kongo, Loango and Teke across the Congo River basin.

West Africa's Golden Empires

Two thirds of the world's gold once came from West Africa and the indigenous empires that controlled the West African interior, and hence the lucrative trans-Saharan trade routes were among the richest in the world.

Empire of Ghana

The Empire of Ghana was the first major state of its kind established in West Africa. It was founded in AD 300 with its capital at Koumbi Saleh, in present-day Mauritania, about 200km north of modern Bamako (Mali). By Ghana's 8th-century heyday, the empire covered much of present-day Mali and parts of eastern Senegal. Although smaller than the empires that followed it, Ghana was extremely wealthy and powerful, controlling not just trans-Saharan trade, but also massive gold deposits; rumour had it that the streets were paved with gold and that the emperor of Ghana routinely tied his horse to a nugget of pure gold.

Islam was introduced by traders from the north, but it couldn't save Ghana – the empire was destroyed in the late 11th century by the better-armed Muslim Berbers of the Almoravid Empire from Mauritania and Morocco. The Almoravids justified their invasion by pointing to Ghana's half-hearted adoption of Islam, but many historians believe that it had more to do with the Almoravid desire for Ghana's gold and control of trade routes.

Empire of Mali

The Empire of Mali, founded in the middle of the 13th century by Sundiata Keita, leader of the Malinké people, was perhaps the most legendary of West African empires. Such was its wealth and prestige that it, more than any other African empire, was to spark the outside world's interest in the continent.

Mali's heyday was the 14th century. Mali's kings controlled not only Saharan trade and the gold mines that had fuelled the prosperity of the Empire of Ghana, but also a swath of territory that stretched from

African Rock Art (2001) by David Coulson and Alec Campbell is definitive and beautifully illustrated. It's one to keep on your coffee table, not carry in your backpack.

In the 8th century AD, Jenné-Jeno (in what is now Mali) was a fortified town with 3.7m-thick walls and 15,000 inhabitants, and covering 33 hectares (just under half the size of modern Djenné), but by around 1300 it was abandoned.

300 BC	AD 300	900	Around 1000
Jenné-Jeno is founded in what is now Mali and is recognised as West Africa's first-known urban settlement. By AD 800, Jenné-Jeno is home to an estimated 27,000 people.	The Empire of Ghana is founded in what is now the western Sahel. The first of the great West African empires, it holds sway over the region for 800 years.	Islam first reaches the Sahel, almost 250 years after it crossed the Sahara. It arrives as part of the trans-Saharan caravan trade and later becomes West Africa's predominant religion.	Timbuktu is founded, near where the Niger River enters the Sahara, as a seasonal encampment for Tuareg nomads. It later becomes a great centre of scholarship and wealth, home to 100,000 people.

modern-day Senegal in the west to Niger in the east. Their ambition was matched only by the extravagance of their rule.

One such monarch, King Abubakari II, sent an expedition across the Atlantic in an attempt to discover the Americas, almost two centuries before Christopher Columbus. Only one ship returned, with stories of a great river running through the ocean's heart. Abubakari II himself led a second expedition of 200 ships. Not a single ship returned.

King Abubakari's anointed successor, King Kankan Musa (the grand-nephew of Sundiata Keita), would prove to be one of the most extraordinary of all African kings. Like all of Mali's rulers, Musa was a devout Muslim and in 1324 he made his pilgrimage to Mecca, accompanied by an entourage of more than 60,000 people and needing 500 slaves to carry all the gold. Along the way he gave away so much of his gold that the world gold price did not recover for 12 years – some say for a generation. His actions attracted the attention of European merchants in Cairo and news spread quickly about a fabulously wealthy land in the desert's heart.

Under Malian sovereignty, trans-Saharan trade reached its peak, and the wealth created meant that Mali's main cities became major centres of finance and culture. The most notable was Timbuktu, where two Islamic universities were founded, and Arab architects from Granada (in modern-day Spain) were employed to design new mosques, such as Timbuktu's Dyingerey Ber mosque.

Empire of Songhaï

While Mali was at the height of its powers, the Songhaï people had established their own city-state to the east, around Gao in present-day Mali. As Mali descended into decadence and royal squabbles, Gao became powerful and well organised. At its height, the Songhaï Empire stretched from close to Lake Chad in the east to the hinterland of the Atlantic Coast in the west. Its emperors were reported to have travelled to Mecca with 300,000 gold pieces.

A hallmark of the Empire of Songhaï was the creation of a professional army and a civil service with provincial governors. The state even subsidised Muslim scholars, judges and doctors. By the mid-15th century, the Empire of Songhaï was at its most powerful and presided over most of West Africa, and by the 16th century Timbuktu was an important commercial city with about 100,000 inhabitants and a great seat of learning with its Sankore University home to 25,000 scholars.

But the Songhaï Empire would prove to be the last of West Africa's great empires. The golden period ended with an audacious invasion by Berber armies crossing the Sahara from Morocco in 1591.

Empires of Medieval West Africa: Ghana, Mali, and Songhay (2009), by David Conrad, covers the sweep of West Africa's three greatest historical empires in one accessible tome.

Into Africa: A Journey through the Ancient Empires (1997), by Marq de Villiers and Sheila Hirtle, looks at Africa's past through the prism of modern journeys through the region.

Late 11th century	1240	1351	1375
One of West Africa's Sahelian kingdoms is overthrown by armies crossing the Sahara, as the Empire of Ghana is destroyed by Berber armies.	Sundiata Keita founds the Empire of Mali with its capital at Niani. The empire rules the Sahel for two centuries and presides over West Africa's golden age.	Ibn Battuta leaves Fez to cross the Sahara, whereafter he travels extensively throughout the Empire of Mali. His later book is one of the earliest accounts of life in the region.	Mali's King Kankan Musa is depicted on a 1375 European map of Africa holding a gold nugget. The caption reads: 'So abundant is the gold found in his country that he is the richest and most noble king in all the land'.

Other States & Empires

As the Empire of Mali declined, the Wolof people established the Empire of Jolof (also spelt Yollof) in 1360 near the site of present-day Dakar in Senegal. Meanwhile, on the southeastern fringe of the Songhaï realm, the Hausa created several powerful city-states, such as Katsina, Kano and Zinder (still important trading towns today), but they never amalgamated into a single empire.

Further east again, on the shores of Lake Chad, the Kanem-Borno Empire was founded in the early 14th century. At its height it covered a vast area including parts of present-day Niger, Nigeria, Chad and Cameroon, before being loosely incorporated into the Songhaï sphere of influence; it nonetheless remained a powerful force until the 19th century.

To the south, between the 13th and 16th centuries, several smaller but locally powerful states arose in gold-producing areas: the kingdoms of Benin (in present-day Nigeria), Dahomey (Benin), Mossi (Burkina Faso) and Akan-Ashanti (Ghana).

The Almoravids

In the 11th century the Sanhaja, the pious Saharan Berber tribe that founded the Almoravid dynasty, swept into southern Morocco from what is today Senegal and Mauritania. As they pushed north under Yahya ibn Umar and his brother Abu Bakr, they demolished brothels and musical instruments as well as their opponents. After Yahya was killed and Abu Bakr was recalled to the Sahara to settle Sanhaja disputes in 1061, their cousin Yusuf bin Tachfin was left to run military operations from a campsite that would become Marrakesh the magnificent. Almoravid power would range far beyond the city they founded, reaching deep into northern Iberia and south across the Sahara to destroy the Empire of

Sundiata: An Epic of Old Mali (2006), by DT Niane, is the most accessible English-language version of Mali's founding epic; it's like listening to the *griots* (praise singers attached to the royal court) during West Africa's glory days.

Timbuktu: The Sahara's Fabled City of Gold (2007), by Marq de Villiers and Sheila Hirtle, provides a detailed look at Timbuktu, and the Songhaï capital Gao, during the Mali and Songhaï empires.

THE EPIC OF SUNDIATA

In the annals of West African history, few tales have endured quite like the story of Sundiata Keita. In the 13th century, a sacred hunter prophesied to a minor Malinké king, known as 'Maghan the Handsome', that if he married an ugly woman she would one day bear him a son who would become a great and powerful king, known to all the world. Maghan followed the seer's advice, but his son Sundiata was born with a disability and could not walk. When Maghan's successors battled for the throne, Sundiata was bypassed and forced into exile, only to return one day as king. When he defeated his more powerful Sosso rivals in 1240, he was crowned 'Mansa', or 'King of Kings', whereafter he founded the Empire of Mali, with its capital at his village of Niani, close to the Guinea–Mali border. He drowned in 1255 but his legend lives on in the tales of *griots* (praise singers) and in songs that draw heavily on his story.

1390	1434	1482	Late 15th century
The Kingdom of Kongo, one of West and Central Africa's most successful kingdoms, is founded, with its sphere of influence extending across the Congo River basin.	Portuguese ships become the first to round Cape Bojador in almost two millennia, beginning the era of European trade along West Africa's coast. Nine years later, they reach the Senegal River.	Portugal constructs the first European structure on West African soil, the warehouse-fortress of Sao Jorge de la Mina in what is now Ghana, symbolising increasing trade between Portugal and West Africa.	The Kingdom of Benin helps Portugal to capture and export slaves, transforming the slave trade from a small-scale African concern to a much larger global trade.

Some historians believe that the Gambia River's name (and indeed the name of the country) derives from the Portuguese word *cambio*, meaning 'exchange' or 'trade'.

Ghana, thereby making them one of ancient West Africa's most successful empires.

Colonial West Africa

The appearance of Europeans on the Atlantic Coast of West Africa in the 15th century marked the beginning of the end for West African independence, and would forever change the region in ways that have rippled down through history to the present day.

RECLAIMING WEST AFRICA'S HISTORY

West African history was, for centuries, assumed to be a solely oral tradition. Later, non-African historians interpreted the absence of written records as indicating an absence of civilisation; H Trevor Roper wrote in 1963, 'Perhaps in the future there will be some African history to teach. But at present there is none. There is only the history of Europeans in Africa. The rest is darkness.'

That changed in the 1990s when an astonishing storehouse of manuscripts – up to five million across the Sahara by some estimates – was 'discovered' in Timbuktu and surrounding regions. The manuscripts, some of which dated to the 13th century, contained scholarly works of poetry, philosophy, astronomy, mathematics, geography, physics, optics and medicine.

The manuscripts also included detailed histories of the region written by Africans, as well as the first-known examples of local languages in their written form, thereby suggesting that Africans could read and write centuries before Europeans arrived. Timbuktu also had a book-making tradition far more advanced than anything that Europe could muster until the invention of movable type in the 15th century, and many books were printed on European-manufactured paper that had reached Timbuktu long before any explorers completed the journey.

According to Dr John Hunwick, a leading expert on Africa's written history, 'Africa has for too long been stereotyped as the continent of song and dance, where knowledge is only transmitted orally. We want to demonstrate that Africans think and write and have done so for centuries.' In short, the manuscripts could change forever the way we see West African history.

Sadly, when Timbuktu was overrun by Islamic militants in 2012, many of these manuscripts were deliberately destroyed. In August 2016 one of the militants was found guilty of war crimes by the International Criminal Court in The Hague for his part in destroying mosques, mausoleums and other cultural sites in Timbuktu, the court's first such conviction for cultural destruction.

The oases of the Adrar region of Mauritania also have rich manuscript collections, especially Chinguetti and Ouadâne.

1512	1591	1659	1796
Leo Africanus visits West Africa and writes, 'The rich king of Tombuto keeps a splendid and well-furnished court...a great store of doctors, judges, priests and other learned men....'	The Empire of Songhaï, the last and most extensive of the Sahel's empires, falls to al-Mansur, ruler of Marrakesh, who seizes the Songhaï political capital Gao, and its commercial and cultural capital Timbuktu.	The French establish their first permanent trading post at Saint-Louis in Senegal in 1638. Twenty-two years later, the British found a base at the mouth of the Gambia River.	The Scottish explorer Mungo Park arrives at the Niger River near Ségou and solves one of the great unanswered questions of African geography: the Niger flows east, not west.

European Footholds

By the 13th century the financial stability of several major European powers depended largely on the supply of West African gold. With gold and intriguing tales of limitless wealth making their way across the Sahara and Mediterranean, European royalty became obsessed with West Africa. Thus it was that, at the precise moment when West Africa's empires went into decline and began to fragment, Europe began to turn its attention to the region.

Prince Henry of Portugal (Henry the Navigator, 1394–1460) was the first to act, encouraging explorers to sail down the coast of West Africa, which soon became known as Guinea. In 1434 a Portuguese ship rounded the infamous Cape Bojador (in present-day Morocco), the first seagoing vessel to do so since the Phoenicians in 613 BC.

In 1443 Portuguese ships reached the mouth of the Senegal River. Later voyages reached Sierra Leone (1462) and Fernando Po (now Bioko in

The legendary Sundiata Keita, founder of the Empire of Mali in the 13th century, included a clause prohibiting slavery in his Charter of Kurukanfuga.

HISTORY COLONIAL WEST AFRICA

SLAVERY IN WEST AFRICA

Slavery had existed in West Africa for centuries, but it gained momentum with the arrival of Islam, which opened the region to more far-reaching trade networks and to distant empires where slave-trading was widespread. The Moors, Tuareg and Soninke, in particular, were known as slave traders. Later, the Portuguese took the trade to a whole new level, transporting slaves en masse to work on the large sugar plantations in Portuguese colonies across the Atlantic (including present-day Brazil) between 1575 and 1600.

By the 17th and 18th centuries, other European nations (particularly England, Spain, France and Holland) had established colonies in the Americas, and were growing sugar, tobacco, cotton and other crops. Huge profits depended on slave labour and the demand for African slaves was insatiable, not least because conditions on the plantations were so bad that life expectancy after arriving in the Americas was often no more than a few years.

In most cases, European traders encouraged Africans on the coast to attack neighbouring tribes and take captives. These were brought to coastal slaving stations and exchanged for European goods such as cloth and guns. A triangular trans-Atlantic trade route developed – the slaves were loaded onto ships and transported to the Americas, the raw materials they produced were transported to Europe, and the finished goods were transported from Europe to Africa once again, to be exchanged for slaves and to keep the whole system moving. Exact figures are impossible to come by, but it is estimated that from the end of the 15th century until around 1870, when the slave trade was abolished, as many as 20 million Africans were captured. Up to half of these died, mostly while being transported in horribly overcrowded and unhealthy conditions. There were few places not affected by slavery.

1828	1870	1884–85	1957
Frenchman René Caillié becomes the first European to reach the fabled city of Timbuktu and return home alive. Two years earlier, Scotsman Alexander Gordon Laing was murdered on the return journey.	The slave trade is officially abolished, but not before up to 20 million Africans were transported to the Americas, never to return. Around half died en route.	The Berlin Conference divides Africa. France is awarded one third of the continent and 10 West African countries in what becomes known as Afrique Occidentale Française (French West Africa).	Ghana gains independence after a long campaign entitled 'Self Government Now'. The campaign's leader Kwame Nkrumah becomes Ghana's post-independence leader and hero to millions of West Africans.

Equatorial Guinea, off the coast of Nigeria; 1472), while the first Portuguese settlers arrived on Cabo Verde in 1462. As the Portuguese made contact with local chiefs and began to trade for gold and ivory, West Africa turned on its axis and the focus of its trade (and power) began shifting from the Sahara to the coast.

In 1482 the Portuguese built a fortified trading post at Elmina, on today's Ghanaian coast. It was the earliest European structure in sub-Saharan Africa. At around the same time, Portuguese traders and emissaries made their first contact with the Kingdom of Benin (in modern-day Nigeria), an advanced, stable state whose artisans had mastered highly skilled bronze- and brass-casting as early as the 13th century. The cordial relations and resulting trade between Portugal and Benin proved highly profitable. In 1483 Portuguese explorer Diogo Cão reached a new 'further south', sailing into the interior along the hitherto uncharted Congo River and discovering the Kingdom of Kongo.

By the early 16th century, with the Songhaï Empire still ruling much of the West African interior, French, British and Dutch ships had joined the Portuguese in making regular visits along the coast, building forts as they went. But with few large rivers that allowed access to the interior, the European presence in West Africa was still largely confined to the coast and its immediate hinterland. The prolific gold mines that had first captured the attention of Europe remained in African hands.

Europe Ventures Inland

The inability to penetrate the West African interior haunted the great powers of Europe. In 1788 a group of influential Englishmen, led by Sir Joseph Banks, founded the Africa Association to promote African exploration. The French soon followed suit. Although questions of commerce and national prestige played an important role, the august men of the Africa Association and their French counterparts were driven by a burning desire to solve the great geographical questions of the age. In 1796, more than 300 years after Europeans had first begun scouting the West African coast, Mungo Park finally determined that the Niger River flowed east, while it was not until 1828 that the Frenchman Réné Caillié became the first European to reach Timbuktu and return safely.

West Africans were by no means passive bystanders, and local resistance was fierce. The most notable leader of the time was Omar Tall (also spelt Umar Taal), who led a major campaign against the French in the interior of Senegal from around 1850. After his death, the jihads known as the 'Marabout Wars' persisted in Senegal until the 1880s.

For all their progress, the European powers were largely confined to pockets of territory on the coast, among them the French enclave of Dakar (Senegal), and the British ports of Freetown (Sierra Leone) and La-

Until the Portuguese dispelled the myths, Cape Bojador was considered among sailors as the point of no return, beyond which lay monstrous sea creatures, whirlpools, boiling waters and waterless coastlines.

After the Berlin Conference, Britain's Lord Salisbury told the London *Times* in 1890: 'We have been giving away mountains and rivers and lakes to each other, only hindered by the small impediment that we never knew exactly where the mountains and rivers and lakes were.'

1958	1973	1979	1982
Guinea opts to go it alone, rejecting ongoing French rule in favour of immediate independence. France takes revenge by withdrawing all assistance to the country.	Guinea-Bissau becomes the last West African country to achieve independence. Unlike former French and British colonies, Guinea-Bissau has to fight for its freedom in a bloody war that devastates the country.	Teodoro Obiang Nguema overthrows his uncle to seize power in Equatorial Guinea.	Paul Biya takes power in Cameroon. He and Teodoro Obiang Nguema are at the time of research the two longest-serving (non-royal) leaders on earth.

gos (Nigeria). Portugal, no longer a major force, retained some territory, notably Bissau, capital of today's Guinea-Bissau. The relentless European pursuit of territory nonetheless continued, with brutal military expeditions into the interior increasingly the norm. Minor treaties were made with local chiefs, but the lives of ordinary West Africans were more often determined by unspoken understandings between European powers.

The Scramble for Africa

Europe's wholesale colonisation of Africa was triggered in 1879 by King Leopold of Belgium's claim to the Congo. The feeding frenzy that followed saw Africa parcelled out among the European powers. Africans had no say in the matter.

Togo and parts of Cameroon fell under German rule, Portugal held fast to Guinea-Bissau, Cabo Verde and São Tomé & Príncipe, Britain staked its claim to The Gambia, Sierra Leone, the Gold Coast (Ghana) and Nigeria, while the Sahel and what would become Gabon, the Republic of Congo and much of Cameroon was the preserve of the French. Spain took over what is now Equatorial Guinea. These claims, at once military realities and colonial fantasies, as many Africans had never seen a European from the country to whom his or her land now supposedly belonged, were confirmed at the Berlin Conference of 1884–85. The final adjustments to the colonial map were made after Germany's defeat in WWI: Togo went to the French and Cameroon was divided between France and Britain.

Although among the least-known European explorers, the English brothers Richard and John Lander outdid their better-known counterparts by establishing in the 1830s that the Niger River flowed into the Atlantic.

The echoes of slavery live on in a number of names still in use today, among them Liberia, Freetown and Libreville.

HISTORY COLONIAL WEST AFRICA

EUROPEAN EXPLORERS IN WEST AFRICA

➡ *Travels in the Interior of Africa,* by Mungo Park, is an epic tale of exploration on the Niger River in the late 18th and early 19th centuries.

➡ *Difficult & Dangerous Roads,* by Hugh Clapperton, is a vivid portrait of the Sahara, Niger and Nigeria in the 1820s by this haughty but ever-observant traveller.

➡ *Travels Through Central Africa to Timbuktu,* by Réné Caillié, is the account of Europe's first encounter with Timbuktu in 1828.

➡ *Travels & Discoveries in North and Central Africa 1849–1855,* by Heinrich Barth, is a fascinating insight into what is now Niger, Nigeria and Mali, from arguably West Africa's greatest explorer.

➡ *The Gates of Africa – Death, Discovery and the Search for Timbuktu,* by Anthony Sattin, is a stirring account of Europe's fascination with Timbuktu and West Africa.

➡ *The Race for Timbuktu – In Search of Africa's City of Gold,* by Frank T Kryza, covers similar terrain and is another great read.

1996	1997	2000	2004
International oil companies find large oil reserves in Equatorial Guinea's territorial waters. Oil revenues transform the country from one of West Africa's poorest to one of its richest, at least on paper.	Sierra Leone erupts in a civil war in which hundreds of thousands are killed or maimed. Conflict in neighbouring Liberia and massive refugee camps in Guinea contribute to a regional humanitarian catastrophe.	Côte d'Ivoire begins its descent into anarchy. Within years, the country is divided in two and immigrants who helped build the country's economic miracle become scapegoats.	In a tale that seemed to spring from a Frederick Forsyth novel, mercenaries, including Briton Simon Mann, launch a failed coup attempt in Equatorial Guinea.

MODERN SLAVERY

More than a century after the slave trade was abolished, slavery has yet to be consigned to history in West Africa, where people continue to be born into, and live their whole lives in, slavery. **Anti-Slavery International** (www.antislavery.org) estimates that as many as 18% of Mauritanians (or around 600,000 people) may be living in slavery. Mauritania finally criminalised slavery in August 2007, but actual change on the ground is slow in coming – in 2015 the International Labour Organization (ILO) officially expressed its concern about ongoing slavery in the country.

Mauritania is not alone in perpetuating this form of descent-based slavery where the conditions of forced labour pass from one generation to the next. In 2003, Anti-Slavery International, in partnership with local anti-slavery NGO Timidria, estimated in 2003 that 7% of Niger's population was living in conditions of forced labour, while a significant number of Malians are also believed to be living in slavery.

In October 2008 Hadijatou Mani, an escaped slave, took Niger's government to the Court of Justice of the West African regional body Ecowas (Economic Community of West African States). The court upheld her argument that Niger's government had failed to protect her by not implementing Niger's own anti-slavery legislation and awarded her substantial compensation. The decision set a legal precedent that applies in all West African countries. In 2014 a man was sentenced to four years in jail, also in Niger, for having a fifth wife, a practice known as *wahiya*, in a case brought by Timidria.

Introducing 'civilisation' to the 'natives' officially replaced trade as the raison d'être of the colonial mission, but the primary aim of European governments was to exploit the colonies for raw materials. In West Africa, gem and gold mining was developed, but the once gold-rich region disappointed the occupiers. Consequently, labour-intensive plantations were established, and cash crops such as coffee, cocoa, rubber, cotton and groundnuts (peanuts) came to dominate the economies of the fledgling colonies. Such infrastructure as was built in West Africa (the Dakar–Bamako rail line, for example) was designed primarily to benefit the colonial economy. Little or no attempt was made to improve living standards or expand education for West Africans, let alone build the institutions on which their future depended.

Walter Rodney's *How Europe Underdeveloped Africa* (1972) may be half a century old but it's still a classic text on African history and as relevant for its insights as it ever was.

During the first half of the 20th century France controlled its West African colonies with a firm hand, and through a policy of 'assimilation' allowed Africans to become French citizens if they virtually abandoned their African identity. Britain made no pretence of assimilation and was slightly more liberal in its approach towards its colonies. Portugal and Spain ruled their empires in Africa with a rod of iron.

2005	2007	2008	2009
Ellen Johnson-Sirleaf is elected president in Liberia, ending decades of civil war and in the process becoming Africa's first elected female president.	Tuareg rebels launch a rebellion in northern Niger and the conflict soon spills over into Mali. Much of the Sahara becomes the domain of rebels and government soldiers.	Ghana wins plaudits for its peaceful democratic transition. With the discovery of offshore oil and a proven track record of democracy, Ghana is widely seen as West Africa's shining light.	Boko Haram launches a campaign of violence in an attempt to have Sharia law imposed in Nigeria. Tens of thousands of people are killed in the ensuing conflict, which continues at the time of research.

Modern West Africa

The Road to Independence

Although nationalism and calls for independence grew in West Africa throughout the first half of the 20th century, it was not until after WWII that the winds of real change began to sweep the region.

In 1957 Ghana became the first country in West Africa to gain independence, with the reluctant blessing of Britain. In September 1958 the French government of Charles de Gaulle held a referendum in its African colonies in which Africans were asked to choose between immediate independence and remaining under French control. All chose the latter, except Guinea, which was to pay dearly for its independence. Affronted by Guinea's perceived lack of gratitude, the French, whose bureaucrats effectively ran Guinea and who had trained very few locals to the required level to take their place, took revenge by removing their administrative staff and all financial assistance from Guinea, leaving their former colony to fend for itself. In 1960 Benin, Côte d'Ivoire, Nigeria, Togo, Senegal and several other countries won their independence. Most other countries in the region became independent in the following few years. Only recidivist Portugal held firm, not granting independence to Guinea-Bissau until 1973 and only then with great reluctance.

France encouraged its former colonies to remain closely tied in a trade-based 'community', and most did; Guinea was a notable exception, while Senegal and Côte d'Ivoire were the darlings of Franco–West African relations. In contrast, Britain reduced its power and influence in the region. The French maintained battalions of its own army in several former colonies, while the British preferred more discreet military assistance.

Independent West Africa

The period immediately following independence was a time of unbridled optimism in West Africa. For the first time in centuries, political power was in the hands of Africans themselves. Inspirational figures such as Kwame Nkrumah in Ghana and Léopold Senghor in Senegal spoke of a new African dawn, while Guinea's Sekou Touré was lauded for having thumbed his nose at the French.

Then reality set in. Without exception, the newly minted countries of West Africa were ill-equipped for independence. Colonialism had created fragile economies based on cash crops that were prone to huge price fluctuations, while artificial boundaries and divide-and-rule policies that had favoured some ethnic groups over others quickly created tensions. Education for Africans had never been a priority for the colonial overlords and few members of the new ruling class and bureaucrats had the necessary training or experience to tackle the massive challenges faced

Wonders of the African World (1999), by Henry Louis Gates Jr, is a scholarly and enthusiastic re-evaluation of African history before colonialism; the section on Timbuktu is fascinating.

In 2016 Equatorial Guinea had a per-capita GDP of US$38,700, which was higher than the EU average (including for Italy, Portugal and its former colonial ruler, Spain).

2011	2012	2012	2013
President Laurent Gbagbo of Côte d'Ivoire refuses to accept the election victory of Alassane Ouattara; Gbagbo is later captured and sent for trial in The Hague.	The Malian army seizes power, ending the country's democratic transition; Tuareg and Islamist rebels soon capture the north, including Timbuktu and Gao; the international community approves a regional military force.	Soon after being chosen as the NDC's candidate in upcoming elections, Ghanaian president Atta Mills dies; President John Mahama, his NDC successor, narrowly wins elections in December.	With Al-Qaeda in the Islamic Maghreb (AQIM) threatening Bamako, France sends in soldiers to restore government control over much of Mali, including Gao and Timbuktu, although insecurity continues.

Bury the Chains: The First International Human Rights Movement (2006), by Adam Hochschild, is masterful in its treatment of the British campaign to abolish slavery in the 18th century.

by the new states. The catchcry of Sekou Touré – who would prove to be a particularly nasty dictator – of preferring 'freedom in poverty to prosperity in chains' soon became horribly true. Poor governance, coups d'état and massive economic problems increasingly became the norm, with civil wars, border disputes and dictatorship often thrown in for good measure. When Côte d'Ivoire – for so long an exception and a byword for West Africa's post-independence progress and optimism – descended into civil war after 2000, it was a massive blow to the region's self image.

The end of the Cold War led to dramatic changes throughout West Africa, as the popular demand for democracy gathered strength and multiparty elections were held in several countries. But even as democracy spread, West Africa's hopes of a new dawn were tempered by the scale of the challenges it faced, not least among them environmental degradation on a massive scale, widespread and worsening poverty across the region and the ailing economic health of the two regional powerhouses, Nigeria and Côte d'Ivoire. And the fact remains that many West Africans have as little control over their own destinies and economic wellbeing as they did at independence.

2013	2014	2015	2016
An outbreak of Ebola in Guinea spreads to Sierra Leone and Liberia; it's not until 2016 that all countries are declared Ebola-free. There are more than 11,300 deaths according to the World Health Organization (WHO).	Militants from Boko Haram kidnap more than 200 girls from a boarding school in Chibok, a town in northern Nigeria. Although some were later freed, many remain in captivity at the time of research.	Muhammadu Buhari becomes the first opposition leader to win elections in Nigeria.	In Cameroon's Anglophone regions, protests against President Paul Biya's rule and his government policies favouring Francophone areas become more frequent.

Culture & Daily Life

West Africa is one of the most intriguing gatherings of cultures on the planet. As a traveller, understanding even a little about the complicated issues that West Africans deal with on a daily basis – the role of traditional culture in modern life, the position of women in society and the complicated mosaic of multicultural relationships, for example – can go a long way towards gaining a foothold in the region. The region's cuisine, too, offers fascinating insights into one of Africa's least-known corners.

Lifestyle

Family life is the bedrock for most West Africans. In traditional society, especially in villages, homes are arranged around a family compound and life is a communal affair – family members eat, take important decisions, celebrate and mourn together in a space that is identifiably theirs and in a family group that spans generations. Such family structures remain strongly evident in many villages and rural areas, and family remains a critical source of support for many West Africans, not least because government welfare is largely nonexistent.

But things are changing. Vast numbers of Africans have migrated to cities, where ethnic identity takes on added significance, as recent arrivals gravitate towards those with whom they share an ethnic tradition. Most (but by no means all) form friendships with people from their own ethnic groups. This is particularly true of minorities.

If family and ethnic identity are the fundamental foundations of a West African's existence, the nation to which they belong serves to announce who they are to the rest of the world. Most West Africans proudly identify themselves as being, for example, Ghanaian, Senegalese or Nigerian, suggesting that one success of postcolonial West Africa has been the building of national identity in countries where borders often cut across longer-standing ethnic boundaries.

Traditional Culture

Before the arrival of colonialism, West African society was, in most cultures, organised along hierarchical lines: each person's place in society was determined by birth and the family's social status. At the top were traditional noble and warrior families, followed by farmers, traders and persons of lower caste, such as blacksmiths, leather workers, woodcarvers, weavers and musicians. Slaves were at the bottom of the social hierarchy. Difficult economic circumstances and urbanisation have reduced the relevance of these traditional roles to some degree, but they remain important for many West Africans. For example, although slavery no longer officially exists, many descendants of former slaves still work as tenant farmers for the descendants of their former masters. Another surviving practice in traditional societies is that older people (especially men) are treated with deference, and teachers, doctors and other professionals (usually men) often receive similar treatment.

But traditional culture is not just about immutable social roles and, as it most often manifests itself in public these days, it can often be a

In every West African country, more than half of the population is aged 24 years and below. The lowest proportion is in Cabo Verde (50.12%), and the highest is Niger (68.18%). This compares with the UK (29.59%), Australia (30.8%) and the US (35.3%).

TIPS ON MEETING LOCALS

Greetings

There are few more important elements in person-to-person encounters in West Africa than greetings. In villages, highly ritualised greetings can seem to last an eternity. In cities, the traditional greetings may give way to shorter ones in French or English, but they're never forgotten. Muslims usually start with the traditional Islamic greetings, *Salaam aleikum* and *Aleikum asalaam* ('Peace be unto you', 'And peace be unto you'). This is followed by questions, such as 'How are you?', 'How is the family?' and 'How are the people of your village?' The reply is usually *Al humdul'allah* (meaning 'Thanks be to God'). While language constraints may mean that your ability to greet West African–style is limited, launching straight into business is considered rude. Learning some greetings in the local language will smooth the way considerably in just about every circumstance.

Hand-shaking is also an important part of greetings. Use a soft – rather than overly firm – handshake. Some Muslim men prefer not to shake hands with women, and West African women don't usually shake hands with their male counterparts.

Deference

An important consideration when meeting locals is eye contact, which is usually avoided, especially between men and women in the Sahel. If a West African doesn't look you in the eye during a conversation, remember that they're being polite, not cold.

When visiting rural settlements it's a good idea to request to see the chief, to announce your arrival and request permission before wandering through a village. You'll rarely be refused.

---

celebration of what binds communities together. Village festivals (*fêtes* in French), which are fundamental to traditional life, are held to honour dead ancestors and local traditional deities, and to celebrate the end of the harvest.

Multiculturalism

West Africans know a thing or two about living side by side with people from different cultures. For a start, West Africa as you see it today is the result of centuries of population shifts and mass migrations that have created a patchwork of diverse but largely cohabiting cultures. After the colonial period and independence, most groups found themselves being asked to share a new national identity with other cultures that were, in some cases, wholly different from their own. Later, widespread urbanisation produced polyglot West African cities that are among the most multicultural on earth. And then there are the twin issues of immigration and emigration – millions of West Africans live in Europe and elsewhere, creating new levels of multiculturalism in the Western countries they now inhabit.

The movement of people in search of opportunity within West Africa is less widely reported in the international media, but operates on a much larger scale than emigration to Europe. Côte d'Ivoire's one-time economic miracle drew immigrants from across the region, providing much-needed labour for a booming economy and a livelihood for millions of citizens of neighbouring countries. However, after political instability began in 2000, the economy slumped and the country descended into a conflict that exposed the thin veneer of tolerance with which many Ivoirians viewed the immigrants.

Monique and the Mango Rains: Two Years with a Midwife in Mali (2007), by Kris Holloway, gives a human face to statistics about difficulties faced by women in traditional, rural West Africa. It's a sobering but great read.

Women in West Africa

West African women face a formidable array of barriers to their participation in public life on an equal footing with men. In much of the region, social mores demand that a women is responsible for domestic work (cooking, pounding millet, child-rearing, gathering firewood), while many women also work (often as market or street vendors) to supplement meagre family incomes. Indeed, it's depressingly common to see women pounding millet or otherwise working hard while men lounge in the shade 'working' on their social relationships. Education of girls also lags significantly behind that of boys, as evidenced by often appalling female literacy rates. Little wonder, therefore, that West African women are greatly under-represented in most professions, let alone in government or at the upper levels of industry.

Marriage & Polygamy

In traditional societies, marriages often took place between teenagers, but financial constraints and the growing demands for lavish weddings mean that many men cannot afford to get married until their late 20s or 30s.

Polygamy is quite widespread in West Africa. The practice, which predates the arrival of Islam (the Quran allows up to four wives, as long as the husband can provide for them all), is particularly strong in rural and predominantly Islamic areas; according to one study, half of all marriages in Senegal are polygamous. You will be told (by men) that women are not averse to polygamy, and that the wives become like sisters, helping each other with domestic and child-rearing duties. In reality, however, fighting and mistrust between wives is more common than marital bliss. However, as few if any countries in the region have outlawed polygamy, there's not much women can do. Leaving a marriage simply because a husband takes another wife can bring shame to the woman and her family. She might be cast out of the family home or even physically beaten as punishment by her own father or brothers.

Taking a fifth wife, a practice known as *wahiya*, is considered a form of slavery, and in 2014 a Nigerien man was sentenced to four years in prison for doing so.

Female Genital Mutilation

Female genital mutilation (FGM), often euphemistically termed 'female circumcision' or 'genital alteration' but more accurately called female genital cutting (FGC), is widespread throughout West Africa. The term covers a wide range of procedures, but in West Africa the procedure usually involves removal of the entire clitoris (called infibulation).

Although outsiders often believe that FGM is associated with Islam, it actually pre-dates the religion (historical records of infibulation date back 6000 years) and has far more to do with longstanding cultural traditions than religious doctrine; in predominantly Muslim northern Mali, FGM prevalence rates are less than 10%. The procedure is usually performed by midwives on girls and young women. They sometimes use modern surgical instruments, but more often it's done with a razor blade or even a piece of glass. If the procedure is done in a traditional setting the girl will not be anaesthetised, although nowadays many families take their daughters to clinics to have the procedure performed by a trained doctor. Complications, especially in the traditional setting, include infection of the wound, leading to death, or scarring, which makes childbirth and urination difficult.

In West Africa, FGM is seen among traditionalists as important for maintaining traditional society. An unaltered woman would dishonour her family and lower its position in society, as well as ruining her own chances for marriage – a circumcised woman is thought to be a moral woman, and more likely a virgin. Many believe that, if left, the clitoris can make a woman infertile, or damage and even kill her unborn children.

In eight West African countries the female adult literacy rate exceeds 50%: Equatorial Guinea (93%), Cabo Verde (83.1%), Ghana (71.4%), Cameroon (68.9%), São Tomé & Príncipe (68.4%) and Togo (55.3%). Women fare worst in Niger (11%), Benin (27.3%), Mali (29.2%), Burkina Faso (29.3%), Côte d'Ivoire (32.5%) and Liberia (32.8%).

Cameroon alone has around 280 ethnic groups, tiny Togo counts 40 ethnic groups among its five million people, and Guinea-Bissau, a country of less than one million people, has 23.

CULTURE & DAILY LIFE WOMEN IN WEST AFRICA

EATING ETIQUETTE

If you're invited to share a meal with locals, there are a few customs to observe. You'll probably sit with your hosts on the floor and it's usually polite to take off your shoes. It may be impolite, however, to show the soles of your feet, so observe closely what your hosts do.

The food, normally eaten by hand (remember to use only the right hand and don't be embarrassed to ask for a spoon), is served in one or two large dishes. Beginners will just pick out manageable portions with their fingers, but experts dig deep, forming a ball of rice and sauce with the fingers. Everybody washes their hands before and after eating. As an honoured guest you might be passed choice morsels by your hosts, and it's usually polite to finish eating while there's still food in the bowl, to show you've had enough.

Gogo Mama: A Journey Into the Lives of Twelve African Women (2007), by Sally Sara, includes illuminating chapters on a Liberian former child soldier, a Ghanaian ex-slave and a Malian midwife.

Some West African countries have enacted laws outlawing FGM, but poor enforcement means that, even where FGM is illegal, the practice continues as before. FGM is illegal in Guinea, for example, and punishable in some cases by life imprisonment with hard labour, yet an estimated 96% of women still undergo the procedure, according to the World Health Organization (WHO). Laws against FGM are also on the books in Burkina Faso, which nonetheless has a 76% prevalence rate, in Côte d'Ivoire (38%) and in Senegal (26%). The practice is also extremely common in Mali (89%), Sierra Leone (88%), The Gambia (76%), Mauritania (69%), Liberia (66%), Guinea-Bissau (50%) and Nigeria (27%), none of which have laws outlawing it. FGM is a particularly common practice among the Fulani.

NGO Tostan (www.tostan.org) operates throughout West Africa at the village level with a number of long-term projects to promote the ending of the practice, as well as maternal health, education and more.

Food & Drink

West Africa's combination of unfamiliar tastes and the range of influences – including local, French and even Lebanese – can result in some fine cuisine. The key is knowing where to find it (there's not much variety outside larger cities), trying not to let the rather generous amounts of oil used in cooking bother you, and learning to appreciate the atmosphere – an essential ingredient in the region's cooking – as much as the food.

The Female Genital Cutting Education and Networking Project (www.fgmnetwork.org/index.php) is an excellent resource on female genital mutilation (FGM), including statistics for many West African countries. Check also the World Health Organization (WHO; www.who.int/reproductive-health/topics/fgm/en).

The Basics

West Africa has some fine cuisine. As a general rule, West Africans don't eat out much. Cheap roadside places are popular and usually target local travellers on their way through town.

→ **Restaurants** Most restaurants worthy of the name cater to a wealthy local and expat clientele, with cheaper places available in those areas with a large backpacker scene.

→ **Cafes** Cool cafes serving food are sprinkled across the region, but are usually restricted to cities.

→ **Bars** Some bars serve food, but more often roadside stalls set up right outside to cater for those with the munchies.

→ **Supermarkets** Well-stocked but pricey supermarkets can be found in larger cities; they can be basic and extremely limited elsewhere.

Staples & Specialities

Rice, rice and more rice is the West African staple that you'll eat again and again on your travels. Millet is also common, although this grain is usually pounded into flour before it's cooked. The millet flour is steamed then moistened with water until it thickens into a stiff porridge that can be eaten with the fingers. In the Sahel, couscous (semolina or millet grains) is always on the menu.

In coastal countries, staples may be root crops such as yam or cassava (also called manioc), which are pounded or grated before being cooked. They're served as a near-solid glob called *fufu* or *foufou* (which morphs into *foutou* further north) – kind of like mashed potatoes mixed with gelatin, and very sticky. You grab a portion (with your right hand), form a ball, dip it in the sauce and enjoy. In the coastal countries, plantain (green banana) is also common.

If all that sounds a little uninspiring, remember that the secret's often in the sauce, which usually goes by the name of *riz sauce*. In some Sahel countries, groundnuts (peanuts) are common, and a thick, brown groundnut sauce (usually called *arachide*) is often served, either on its own or with meat or vegetables mixed in with the nuts. When groundnut sauce is used in a stew, it's called *domodah* or *mafé*. Sometimes deep-orange palm oil is also added. Sauces are also made with vegetables or the leaves of staple food plants such as cassava. Stock cubes or sachets of flavouring are ubiquitous across the region (Maggi is the most common brand) and are often thrown into the pot as well. When it can be afforded, or on special occasions, meat or fish is added to the sauce; sometimes succulent slices, sometimes grimly unattractive heads, tails and bones.

Some of the most memorable regional specialties include the ubiquitous *jollof rice* (rice and vegetables with meat or fish and called *riz yollof* in Francophone countries) and *kedjenou* (Côte d'Ivoire's national dish of slowly simmered chicken or fish with peppers and tomatoes). *Poulet yassa* is a Senegalese dish consisting of grilled chicken in an onion-and-lemon sauce; the sauce is also used to make *poisson yassa* (fish), *viande yassa* (meat) and just plain old *yassa*. *Tiéboudienne* is Senegal's national dish of rice baked in a thick sauce of fish and vegetables.

Street Food
Street food tends to be absurdly cheap and is often delicious, especially the grilled fish.

On street corners and around bus stations, particularly in the morning, you'll see small booths selling pieces of bread with fillings or toppings of butter, chocolate spread, yoghurt, mayonnaise or sardines. In Francophone countries the bread is cut from fresh French-style baguettes, but in Anglophone countries it is often a less enticing soft, white loaf.

In the Sahel, usually around markets, women with large bowls covered with a wicker lid sell yoghurt, often mixed with pounded millet and sugar. You can eat it on the spot or take it away in a plastic bag.

In the evenings you can buy brochettes (small pieces of beef, sheep or goat meat skewered and grilled over a fire) or lumps of roast meat sold by guys who walk around pushing a tin oven on wheels. Around markets and bus stations, women serve deep-fried chips of cassava or some other root crop.

In Francophone countries, grilled and roast meat, usually mixed with onions and spices, is sold in shacks. These food stalls are called *dibieteries* in some places, and you can eat on the spot or take away.

Another popular stand-by in the larger cities are Lebanese-style shwarmas, thin slices of lamb grilled on a spit, served with salad (optional) in Lebanese-style bread (pita) with a sauce made from chickpeas.

CULTURE & DAILY LIFE FOOD & DRINK

In Sierra Leone the maternal mortality rate is a staggering 1360 women per 100,000 live births. Other countries with extremely high rates include Nigeria (814), Liberia (725), The Gambia (706), Guinea (679) and Côte d'Ivoire (645). The lowest rates are in Cabo Verde (42) and São Tomé & Príncipe (156). In Australia the figure is six.

More than half of the population in the following countries lives in urban areas: Cabo Verde (65.5%), São Tomé & Príncipe (65.1%), Mauritania (59.9%), Cameroon (54.4%), Côte d'Ivoire (54.2%) and Ghana (54%). West Africa's least urbanised countries are Niger (18.7%), Burkina Faso (29.9%) and Guinea (37.2%).

Literature & Cinema

West Africa punches above its weight when it comes to the arts. Nigeria's writers have been celebrated as some of Africa's finest throughout the English-speaking world, while names like Côte d'Ivoire's Ahmadou Kourouma have found an appreciative audience in Francophone circles. West Africa's world-renowned film festival has provided a vehicle for some of the most impressive cinematic output on the continent.

Literature

Stories, usually in oral or musical form, have always played an important role in West African life. This is how cultural traditions and the great events of the day were chronicled and, in the frequent absence of written histories, such tales catalogued the collective memory of the region's peoples. The greatest and most famous historical tale is the *Epic of Sundiata*, the story of the founder of the Empire of Mali, which is still recounted by modern *griots* (praise singers), musicians and writers.

Modern-day West African writers have adapted this tradition, weaving compelling tales around the great issues facing modern West Africa, most notably the arrival and legacy of colonial powers, and the role of women within traditional society.

Nigeria dominates West Africa's Anglophone literary scene, while some of the best novels in Francophone West African literature have also been translated into English. A number of major West African authors have achieved international renown.

Anglophone West Africa

Although the Anglophone literary scene is dominated by Nigerians, there are some other fine writers to watch out for. Acclaimed writer William Boyd (www.williamboyd.co.uk) was born in Ghana but is generally described as Scottish. Other significant names:

TOP 10 WEST AFRICAN NOVELS

➡ Chinua Achebe, *Things Fall Apart* (1958)

➡ Ben Okri, *The Famished Road* (1991)

➡ Chimamanda Ngozi Adichie, *Half of a Yellow Sun* (2006)

➡ Helon Habila, *Measuring Time* (2007)

➡ Aminatta Forna, *The Memory of Love* (2010)

➡ Ahmadou Kourouma, *Waiting for the Wild Beasts to Vote* (1998)

➡ Ousmane Sembène, *God's Bits of Wood* (1995)

➡ Amadou Hampaté Bâ, *The Fortunes of Wangrin* (1973)

➡ Mongo Beti, *The Poor Christ of Bomba* (1956)

➡ Emmanuel Dongala, *Little Boys Come From the Stars* (2000)

➜ Aminatta Forna, from Sierra Leone, whose books include *Ancestor Stones* (2006), *The Memory of Love* (2010), *The Hired Man* (2013) and the memoir *The Devil that Danced on the Water* (2003)

➜ Ayi Kwei Armah, Ghana's foremost writer (*The Beautiful Ones Are Not Yet Born*; 1968)

➜ Ama Ata Aidoo from Ghana, with *Changes: A Love Story* (1993) and *Our Sister Killjoy* (1977)

➜ Kojo Laing, also from Ghana: *Woman of the Aeroplanes* (1988), *Search Sweet Country* (1986) and *Major Gentl and the Achimota Wars* (1992)

➜ Ayesha Harruna Attah, one of Ghana's most exciting young writers, with *Harmattan Rain* (2009) and *Saturday's Shadows* (2015)

➜ William Conton (The Gambia), whose 1960 classic *The African* is a semi-autobiographical tale of an African student in Britain who later returns to his homeland and becomes president

➜ Yaa Gyasi, a Ghanaian-American, whose *Homegoing* (2016) charts the impact of the slave trade in Ghana and the US, with much of the action taking place in and around Cape Coast

The annual Caine Prize for African Writing (www. caineprize.com), which is awarded for the best published short story by an African writer, is one of the continent's most prestigious literary awards. Recent West African winners include Helon Habila (2001), SA Afolabi (2005), EC Osundu (2009), Rotimi Babatunde (2012) and Tope Folarin (2013).

LITERATURE & CINEMA LITERATURE

Nigeria

Nigeria is credited with producing the first African novels of international quality. With *The Palm-Wine Drunkard* (1952), about an insatiable drunkard who seeks his palm-wine tapster in the world of the dead, Amos Tutuola was the first African writer to catch the world's attention by providing a link between traditional storytelling and the modern novel.

If Tutuola made the world sit up and take notice, Chinua Achebe, who died in 2013, earned for African literature the international acclaim it still enjoys to this day. His classic novel, *Things Fall Apart* (1958), has sold over eight million copies in 30 languages, more than any other African work. Set in the mid-19th century, it charts the collision between pre-colonial Ibo society and European missionaries. Achebe's *Anthills of the Savannah* (1987) is a satirical study of political disorder and corruption. It was a finalist for the 1987 Booker Prize. His memoir of the Biafra War, *There Was a Country: A Personal History of Biafra* (2012) caused waves in Nigeria but has been critically acclaimed.

Building on the work of these early pioneers, Wole Soyinka has built up an extraordinary body of work, which includes plays, poetry and novels (such as *The Interpreters*; 1964), political essays and the fantastical childhood memoir *Ake*. Praised for his complex writing style, Soyinka won the Nobel Prize for Literature in 1986; he was the first author from Africa to receive this accolade.

The exceptionally talented Ben Okri is a thoughtful essayist (*A Way of Being Free*; 1997) and an accomplished poet (*An African Elegy*; 1992), but his magical realist novels have seen him labelled the Nigerian Gabriel García Márquez. His novel *The Famished Road* (1991), which follows Azaro, a spirit-child, won the Booker Prize in 1991. When critics grumbled that to appreciate the book's style and symbolism the reader had to understand Africa, Okri recalled reading Victorian novelists such as Dickens as a schoolboy in Nigeria. His *Songs of Enchantment* (1993) and *Infinite Riches* (1998) completed his Azaro trilogy. He continues to fuse modern style with traditional mythological themes in his later novels *Dangerous Love* (1996), *Astonishing the Gods* (1995), *Starbook* (2007) and *The Age of Magic* (2014).

Buchi Emecheta is one of Africa's most successful female authors. Her novels include *Slave Girl* (1997), *The Joys of Motherhood* (1979), *Rape of Shavi* (1984) and *Kehinde* (1994), and they focus with humour and

The international availability of works by African novelists owes much to the Heinemann African Writers Series (now called the African Writers Series and published by Pearson publishing house; www. africanwriters. com), which publishes 273 novels that would otherwise be out of print or hard to find.

irrepressible irony on the struggles of African women to overcome their second-class treatment by society.

Two young Nigerian writers – Chimamanda Ngozi Adichie and Helon Habila – have successfully made the leap from promising talents to skilled novelists with a growing international following. Adichie in particular followed up her impressive first novel *Purple Hibiscus* (2004) with the exceptional *Half of a Yellow Sun* (2006), which is set in Nigeria during the Biafra War, as well as short-story collections and a number of essays. Helon Habila, too, managed to build on the success of his first novel *Waiting for an Angel* (2004) with an acclaimed follow-up, *Measuring Time* (2007), the stirring story of twins in a Nigerian village. His most recent offering is *Oil on Water* (2010).

Other young Nigerian novelists to watch out for include Helen Oyeyemi (*The Icarus Girl*, 2005; *White is for Witching*, 2009; *Boy, Snow, Bird*, 2014); Uzodinma Iweala (*Beasts of No Nation*, 2005); and Adaobi Tricia Nwaubani (*I Do Not Come to You by Chance*, 2010).

Francophone West Africa

Until recently, Francophone West African writers were little known beyond France, but a flurry of translations into English has brought them the international readership they richly deserve.

Until his death in 1991, Amadou Hampaté Bâ, Mali's most prolific novelist, was one of the most significant figures in West African literature, as well as a leading linguist, ethnographer and religious scholar. Three of his books – *The Fortunes of Wangrin* (1973; which won the 1976 'Grand Prix litéraire de l'Afrique noire'), *Kaidara* (1969) and *Radiance of the Great Star* (1974) – are available in English.

The late Ousmane Sembène, from Senegal, better known as an acclaimed movie director, has also published short-story collections and *God's Bits of Wood* (1995), an accomplished novel set in colonial Mali and Senegal. Two female Senegalese writers worth tracking down are Mariama Bâ, whose novel *So Long a Letter* (1981) won the Noma Award for publishing in Africa, and Fatou Diome, whose 2003 novel *The Belly of the Atlantic* was a bestseller in France. Nafissatou Dia Diouf is also attracting attention, although her *Retour d'Un Long Exil et Autres Nouvelles* (2001) and *Sables Mouvants* (2000) are still available only in French. The late Leopold Senghor, former Senegalese president and a literary figure of international note, is the author of several collections of poetry and writings.

Côte d'Ivoire's finest novelist, Ahmadou Kourouma, is widely available in English. His *Waiting for the Wild Beasts to Vote* (1998) is a masterpiece that evocatively captures both the transition to colonial rule and the subsequent corruption of power by Africa's leaders. *The Suns of Independence* (1968), *Monnew* (1990) and *Allah Is Not Obliged* (2002) are also great reads.

A particularly incisive account of the clash between modern and traditional views on polygamy is given in *So Long a Letter* (1981), an especially fine novel written in the voice of a widow by Senegalese author Miriama Bâ.

Cameroon's best-known literary figure is the late Mongo Beti. *The Poor Christ of Bomba* (1956) is Beti's cynical recounting of the failure of a missionary to convert the people of a small village.

Camara Laye (Guinea) wrote *The African Child* (also called *The Dark Child*), which was first published in 1954 and is one of the most widely printed works by an African.

Cinema

West Africa rarely makes an appearance in cinemas beyond the region – *Blood Diamond*, set (but not filmed) in 1990s Sierra Leone, is a rare exception – and most West African films can be difficult for travellers to track down. But, despite limited resources, West African film is high quality, a regular presence at the world's best film festivals and has, for

FESPACO

Burkina Faso may, as one of the world's poorest countries, be an unlikely venue for a world-renowned festival of film, but the biennial nine-day Pan-African Film Festival, Fespaco (Festival Pan-Africain du Cinema; www.fespaco.bf), goes from strength to strength.

Fespaco began in 1969, when it was little more than a few African film-makers getting together to show their short films to interested audiences. Hundreds of films from Africa and the diaspora in the Americas and the Caribbean are now viewed every year, with 20 selected to compete for the prestigious Étalon D'Or de Yennenga – Fespaco's equivalent of the Oscar – as well as prizes in other categories (including TV).

Fespaco is held in Ouagadougou every odd year, in the second half of February or early March, and has become an essential pillar of Burkina Faso's cultural life. Since its early days, it has also helped stimulate film production throughout Africa and has become such a major African cultural event that it attracts celebrities from around the world.

Recent West African award-winners include Nigeria's Newton Aduaka, who received the Étalon d'Or de Yennenga for *Ezra* (which also appeared at the Sundance Film Festival) in 2007, while the runner-up award the same year went to *Les Saignantes* by Cameroonian director Jean Pierre Bekolo. In 2013, the top prize was won by Senegalese director Alain Gomis for *Tey*, while third place went to another Senegalese film, *La Pirogue* by Moussa Touré. Two years later, third prize (behind films from Morocco and Algeria) was awarded to Burkinabé director Sekou Traoré for *The Eye of the Cyclone*.

decades, been quietly gathering plaudits from critics. The region also has a respected film festival of its own, Fespaco, which takes place biennially in Ouagadougou in Burkina Faso and has placed quality film-making at the centre of modern West African cultural life.

History

The 1970s was the zenith of African film-making, and many films from this era still inspire the new generation of directors working today. From the 1980s onwards, however, directors have found it increasingly difficult to find the necessary finance, production facilities and – most crucially – distribution that would give West African directors the wider recognition they deserve.

A handful of themes resonate through postcolonial West African cinema: the exploitation of the masses by colonialists; corrupt and inefficient independent governments; the clash between tradition and modernity; and traditional African values (usually in a rural setting) portrayed as suffering from Western cultural influence. As such, the region's films act as a mirror to West African society and history.

Films to watch out for include *Dakan* (1997), by Mohamed Camara of Guinea, which uses homosexuality to challenge prevailing social and religious taboos; *Clando* (1996), by Cameroonian director Jean-Marie Teno, which depicts Africans choosing between fighting corrupt regimes at home and seeking a better life in Europe; and *The Blue Eyes of Yonta* (1992), by Flora Gomes, one of the few feature films ever made in Guinea-Bissau – it captures the disillusionment of young Africans who've grown up in the post-independence era.

Senegal, Mali & Burkina Faso

West African film is dominated by Senegal, Mali and Burkina Faso.

Ousmane Sembène (1923–2007) from Senegal was arguably West Africa's best-known director. His body of work includes *Borom Sarret* (1963), the first commercial film to be made in post-independence Africa, *Xala* (1975), *Camp Thiaroye* (1988) and the critically acclaimed *Moolade* (2004).

California Newsreel (www.newsreel.org) is a terrific resource on African film with extensive reviews and a Library of African Cinema, where you can order many of the best West African films, especially Fespaco prize-winners.

Moolade, the powerful 2004 film by the Senegalese director Ousmane Sembène, is one of the few mass-release artistic endeavours to tackle head-on the taboo issue of female genital mutilation.

Mali's leading director is Souleymane Cissé, whose 1970s films include *Cinq Jours d'Une Vie* (1971) and *Baara* (1978). Later films include the wonderful *Yeelen* (1987), a lavish generational tale set in 13th-century Mali and a Cannes Festival prize winner, and *Waati* (1995). Cheick Oumar Sissoko has won prizes at Cannes and his *Guimba, un Tyran, une Epoque Guimba* won the Étalon d'Or de Yennega, Africa's 'Oscar', at the 1995 Fespaco.

Idrissa Ouédraogo, from Burkina Faso, won the Grand Prix at Cannes for *Tilä* (1990), an exceptional cinematic portrayal of life in a traditional African village. He is one of very few West African film-makers to find genuine commercial success in the West. His other movies include *Yaaba* (1989), *Samba Traoré* (1993), and *Kini and Adams* (1997). Gaston Kaboré is another fine director whose film *Buud Yam* (1997), a tale of childhood identity, superstition and a 19th-century African world about to change forever, was the 1997 winner of the Étalon d'Or de Yennenga.

Nigeria

Nigeria is home to the world's second-largest film industry (behind India, but ahead of the USA, and worth around US$250 million a year). Going by the name of 'Nollywood', it turns out massive numbers of low-budget, high-energy films (up to 200 a month) that are wildly popular on DVD, but which won't win any critics' awards.

Most industry watchers trace the birth of Nollywood to *Living in Bondage* (1992) by NEK Video Links, owned by Kenneth Nnebue in the eastern city of Onitsha. The wide reach of Igbo networks, aggressive marketing campaigns and the use of English as a primary language quickly broadened the industry's appeal. The staple of Nollywood films (and another secret of success) is their focus on the daily issues and dilemmas faced by ordinary Africans.

Thousands of films later, the industry is well established and in recognition of the growing importance of the industry to Nigeria's economy, in 2010 then-president Goodluck Jonathon announced the creation of a $200-million loan fund to help finance local movie-making.

Half of a Yellow Sun (2013), an adaptation of Chimamanda Ngozi Adichie's novel of the same name, was directed by Nigeria's Biyi Bandele and filmed in Nigeria. His follow-up, *Fifty* (2015), was well regarded by critics.

Nigerian director Chico Ejiro (widely known as 'Mr Prolific') is famous for having directed more than 80 films in just five years. He's been quoted as saying he can complete a film in just three days. For a fascinating insight into the industry, see the 2007 documentary *Welcome to Nollywood* by director Jamie Meltzer.

Religion

Close to half of all West Africans are Muslim and it's very much a north–south divide: the countries of the Sahel and Sahara are predominantly Muslim, while Christianity is more widespread in the southern coastal countries. That said, in almost every country of the region, traditional or animist beliefs are strong.

Traditional Religions

Before the arrival of Islam and Christianity, every race, tribe or clan in West Africa practised its own traditional religion. While many in the Sahel converted to Islam, and those in the south converted to Christianity, traditional religions remained strong and still retain a powerful hold over the consciousness of West Africans, even coexisting with established aspects of Islam or Christianity. When discussing traditional beliefs, terms such as 'juju', 'voodoo' and 'witchcraft' are frequently employed. In certain specific contexts these may be correct, but they are much misunderstood terms.

There are hundreds of traditional religions in West Africa, with considerable areas of overlap. What you won't find are any great temples (more modest local shrines often served the same purpose) or written scriptures (in keeping with West Africa's largely oral tradition). Beliefs and traditions can be complex and difficult to understand, but several common factors are found again and again.

The Role of the Natural World

Almost all traditional religions are animist, meaning that they are based on the attribution of life or consciousness to natural objects or phenomena. Thus a certain tree, mountain, river or stone may be sacred (such as among the Lobi of southwestern Burkina Faso) because it represents, is home to, or simply is, a spirit or deity. The number of deities of each religion varies, as do the phenomena that represents them. The Ewe of Togo and Ghana, for example, have more than 600 deities, including one that represents the disease smallpox.

Totems, fetishes (talismans) and charms are also important features of traditional religions. Among the Senoufo, for example, the dead take on the form of the clan's animal totem. Masks also play a significant role, and often serve as mediums of intercession between the human and natural worlds.

The Role of Ancestors

In many African religions, ancestors play a particularly strong role; two powerful examples of this are found among the Igbo and Yoruba of Nigeria. The principal function of ancestors is usually to protect the tribe or family, and they may on occasion show their ancestral pleasure or displeasure (eg in the form of bad weather, a bad harvest, or when a living member of the family becomes sick). There are almost as many variations on the theme as there are distinct cultural groups in West Africa. The Baoulé people of Côte d'Ivoire, for example, believe in a parallel

The Way of the Elders: West African Spirituality & Tradition (2004), by Adama and Naomi Doumbia, is one of surprisingly few books to provide an overview of the foundations of traditional West African religions.

world to our own where parallel relatives can have an important influence over the 'real' world. Many traditional religions also hold that the ancestors are the real owners of the land and, while it can be enjoyed and used during the lifetime of their descendants, it cannot be sold and must be cared for.

Communication with ancestors or deities may take the form of prayer, offerings (possibly with the assistance of a holy man, or occasionally a holy woman) or sacrifice. Requests may include good health, bountiful harvests and numerous children. Many village celebrations are held to ask for help from, or in honour of, ancestors and deities. The Dogon people in Mali, for instance, have celebrations before planting (to ensure good crops) and after harvest (to give thanks).

Religion and the Making of Nigeria (2016), by Olufemi Vaughan, is a fascinating study of the role played by Christianity, Islam and traditional religions in shaping modern Nigeria.

A Central Deity?

Several traditional religions accept the existence of a supreme being or creator, alongside spirits and deities. This being usually figures in creation myths and is considered too exalted to be concerned with humans – the belief system of the Bobo people of Burkina Faso and Mali is an example of this. In many cultures, communication with the creator is possible only through lesser deities or through the intercession of ancestors.

Islam & West Africa

Islam's Origins

Abdul Qasim Mohammed ibn Abdullah ibn Abdal-Muttalib ibn Hashim (the Prophet Mohammed) was born in 570. Mohammed's family belonged to the Quraysh tribe, a trading family with links to Syria and Yemen. By the age of six, Mohammed's parents had both died and he came into the care of his grandfather, the custodian of the Kaaba in Mecca in Saudi Arabia.

At the age of 40, in 610, the Prophet Mohammed retreated into the desert and began to receive divine revelations from Allah via the voice of the archangel Gabriel; the revelations would continue throughout Mohammed's life. Three years later, he began imparting Allah's message to Meccans. He called on them to turn away from pagan worship and submit to Allah, the one true god.

Islam provided a simpler alternative to the established faiths, which had become complicated by hierarchical orders, sects and complex rituals, offering instead a direct relationship with one deity based only on the believer's submission to Allah (Islam means 'submission'). Not surprisingly, the Prophet's message and movement appealed especially to the poorer, disenfranchised sections of society.

Islam: A Short History (2000), by Karen Armstrong, is a first-rate primer on the world's fastest-growing religion; it's distinguished by a fair-minded approach and clear language.

The Spread of Islam

When Mohammed died in 632 the Arab tribes spread quickly across the Middle East, in very little time conquering what now constitutes Jordan, Syria, Iraq, Lebanon and Israel and the Palestinian Territories. To the west, the unrelenting conquest swept across North Africa. By the end of the 7th century the Muslims had reached and conquered what is now Morocco. In 710 they marched on Spain.

The natural barrier formed by the Sahara meant that Islam took longer to trickle down into West Africa than elsewhere. It first reached the Sahel around 900, via trans-Saharan traders from present-day Morocco and Algeria. Islam cemented its position as the dominant religion in the Sahel in the 17th and 18th centuries, filling the vacuum left by the then-defunct Sahelian empires. Spiritual power was fused with political and economic hegemony, and Islamic jihads (holy wars) were declared on nonbelievers and backed by the powers of the state. In time, several Muslim states were established, including Futa Toro (in northern Senegal), Futa Djalon (Guinea), Masina (Mali) and the Sokoto state of Hausaland (Niger and Nigeria).

Although ordinary people in many regions preferred to retain their traditional beliefs, Islam quickly became the state religion in many West African kingdoms and empires, where rulers skilfully combined aspects of Islam with traditional religions in the administration of the state. The result was a fusion of beliefs that remains a feature of West African life today.

The Quran

For Muslims the Quran is the word of God, directly communicated to Mohammed. It comprises 114 suras (chapters), which govern all aspects of a Muslim's life.

It's not known whether the revelations were written down during Mohammed's lifetime, although Muslims believe the Quran to be the direct word of Allah as told to Mohammed. The third caliph, Uthman (644–56), gathered together everything written by the scribes (parchments, stone tablets, the memories of Mohammed's followers) and gave them to a panel of editors under the caliph's aegis. A Quran printed today is identical to that agreed upon by Uthman's compilers 14 centuries ago.

The Five Pillars of Islam

The five pillars of Islam (the basic tenets that guide Muslims in their daily lives) are as follows:

Shahada (the profession of faith) 'There is no god but Allah, and Mohammed is his Prophet' is the fundamental tenet of Islam.

Salat (prayer) Muslims must face Mecca and pray at dawn, noon, mid-afternoon, sunset and nightfall. Prayer times are marked by the call to prayer, which rings out across the towns and villages of the Sahel.

Zakat (alms) Muslims must give a portion of their income to the poor and needy.

Sawm (fasting) Ramadan commemorates Mohammed's first revelation, and is the month when all Muslims fast from dawn to dusk.

Haj (pilgrimage, usually written *hadj* in West Africa) All Muslims who can afford it should perform the *haj*, or pilgrimage, to the holiest of cities, Mecca, at least once in their lifetime. The reward is considerable: the forgiving of all past sins. It's not unusual for families to save up for a lifetime to be able to send only one member. Before the advent of air travel, the pilgrimage often involved an overland journey of a year or more. In West Africa, those who complete the pilgrimage receive the honorific title of Hadj for men, and Hadjia for women.

The schism between Sunnis and Shiites dates back to the 1st Islamic century and to a dispute over who should rule over the Muslim world as caliph. Beyond this early dynastic rivalry, there is little doctrinal difference between Shiite Islam and Sunni Islam. Sunnis comprise some 90% of the world's Muslims.

Some Muslims believe that the Quran must be studied in its original classical Arabic form ('an Arabic Quran, wherein there is no crookedness'; sura 39:25) and that translations dilute the holiness of its sacred texts. For Muslims, the language of the Quran is known as *sihr halal* (lawful magic).

TIPS FOR TRAVELLERS IN ISLAMIC AREAS

When you visit a mosque, take off your shoes; women should cover their heads and shoulders with scarves. In some mosques, women are not allowed to enter if prayers are in progress or if the imam (prayer leader) is present; in others, there may be separate entrances for men and women. Non-Muslims are not allowed to enter some mosques at all.

If you've hired a guide or taxi driver for the day, remember that he'll want to say his prayers at the right times, so look out for signs that he wants a few moments off, particularly around noon, late afternoon and sunset. Travellers on buses and bush taxis should also be prepared for prayer stops at these times.

Despite the Islamic proscription against alcohol, some Muslims do enjoy a quiet drink. Even so, it's impolite to drink alcohol in their presence unless they show approval.

During Islamic holidays, shops and offices may close. Even if the offices are officially open, during the Ramadan period of fasting people become soporific (especially when Ramadan falls in the hot season) and very little gets done.

Islamic Customs

In everyday life, Muslims are prohibited from drinking alcohol, eating carrion, blood products or pork (which are considered unclean), eating the meat of animals not killed in the prescribed manner, and eating food over which the name of Allah has not been said. Adultery, theft and gambling are also prohibited.

Islam is not just about prohibitions but also marks the important events of a Muslim's life. When a baby is born, the first words uttered to it are, in many places, the call to prayer. A week later there is a ceremony in which the baby's head is shaved and an animal sacrificed in remembrance of Abraham's willingness to sacrifice his son to Allah. A major event of a boy's childhood is circumcision, which normally takes place between the ages of seven and 12. When a person dies, a burial service is held at the mosque and the body is buried with the feet facing Mecca.

Islam South of the Sahara

Islamic practice in sub-Saharan West Africa is extremely varied and, perhaps more than anywhere else in the Islamic world, traditional animist beliefs are often fused with more orthodox doctrinal tenets.

In some countries, especially Senegal, *marabouts* wield considerable political power. Sufism, which emphasises mystical and spiritual attributes, was one of the more popular Islamic forms in West Africa; some scholars speculate that the importance that Sufis ascribe to religious teachers may have found favour in West Africa as it mirrored existing hierarchical social structures.

Quranic schools play an important role both socially and educationally in many Sahelian countries. In recent years, Islamic clerics (sometimes with the support of clerics and funds from Saudi Arabia) have begun to preach a stricter doctrinal line. This has particularly been the case in predominantly Muslim northern Nigeria where Sharia law has been imposed. In its most extreme form, the shift has seen the rise of fundamentalist groups such as Boko Haram (with its roots in northeastern Nigeria) and Al-Qaeda in the Islamic Maghreb (AQIM); AQIM was a powerful force in the rebel occupation of northern Mali in 2012 and its footsoldiers were responsible for destroying numerous *marabout* (saint) tombs, including some in Timbuktu.

The Lost Kingdoms of Africa (2005), by Jeffrey Tayler, is an engagingly told journey through the stories and terrain of the ancient Islamic kingdoms of West Africa's Sahel and southern Sahara.

Muslims form a majority in Burkina Faso, The Gambia, Guinea, Mali, Mauritania, Niger, Senegal and Sierra Leone, and comprise 50% of the inhabitants of Nigeria.

SONY & THE QURAN

West African Islam is generally regarded as more liberal than the Islam espoused by purists in Cairo or Mecca. In October 2008 that diversity of opinion was thrust into the international spotlight. A Sony video game, 'LittleBigPlanet', was withdrawn from sale after a Muslim playing a trial version of the game alerted Sony that a piece of background music included two phrases from the Quran. It could, he said, be considered blasphemous by Muslims for its combination of music and sacred words from Islam's holy book. Fearful of alienating Muslim gamers, Sony recalled the game and removed the song in question before releasing it back onto the market.

But the decision was viewed somewhat differently in West Africa. The offending song was 'Tapha Niang', recorded by Mali's master *kora* (harp-like instrument) player Toumani Diabaté, which had appeared on his acclaimed 2006 album *Boulevard de l'Independence*. Diabaté, a devout Muslim, denied that the song was in any way blasphemous. Expressing his disappointment, he said that it was entirely acceptable in Mali for Islamic tenets to be put to music as a way of glorifying Islam.

Christianity

Christianity arrived in West Africa later than Islam, during the age of colonial exploration; after the first wave of explorers, missionaries were among the first colonial settlers in West Africa. In general their success was limited in Sahelian countries where Islam had been established centuries before, but found more fertile ground further south where traditional religions held sway. This story is reflected in the current distribution of Christian strongholds: Christianity is the majority religion in Cameroon, Cabo Verde, Equatorial Guinea, Gabon, Ghana, Liberia, Republic of Congo and São Tomé & Príncipe, and the largest religion in Benin and Togo. There are also significant Christian minorities in Nigeria and Côte d'Ivoire.

As with Islam, many West African Christians have held on to their traditional beliefs, and these are often practised side by side with Christianity. More often, stories from traditional religions were inserted into Bible stories so as to make them more relevant to a West African audience, meaning that some liturgical and even some belief systems appear different to the practice of Christianity in the West. There has, however, been something of a backlash against such doctrinal fusions, resulting in the rise of sometimes quite conservative evangelical churches that are becoming increasingly influential in some areas, particularly in Nigeria.

Beyond Jihad: The Pacifist Tradition in West African Islam (2016), by Lamin Sanneh, is an important counter-voice to the increasing stridency of some Islamic groups in the region.

Music

Music put West Africa in the international spotlight. Years ago, even if Western music-lovers weren't sure where Senegal was, they knew that Youssou N'Dour lived there. They could tell you that Salif Keita or Ali Farka Touré came from Mali. That Nigeria was home to Fela Kuti. Reggae star Alpha Blondy defined Côte d'Ivoire. Saxophonist Manu Dibango was Cameroon, just as Angélique Kidjo was Benin. These greats lent 'world music' much needed individuality, commercial success and cred.

Music of West Africa

The international success of West Africa's pioneering musicians paved the way for an apparently bottomless pool of talent: desert rebels Tinariwen; dreadlocked Senegalese mystic Cheikh Lo and his hotly tipped compatriot, Carlou D; the fresh prince of Côte d'Ivoire, Tiken Jah Fakoly, and its fresh princess, Dobet Gnahoré; golden-voiced Mauritanian Daby Touré, and afrobeating politicos such as Nigeria's Femi and Sean Kuti (in looks, sound and sentiment, very much their fathers' sons); Mayra Andrade from Cabo Verde, with her multicultural jazz, and Malians including ethereal songbird Rokia Traore, *kora* (21-stringed lute) maestro Toumani Diabaté and husband-and-wife team Amadou and Mariam, whose eighth album, 2012's *Folila*, features such special guests as Santigold and Jake Shears from Scissor Sisters.

Mentioning these names is only scratching the surface. Music is everywhere in West Africa, coming at you in thunderous, drum-fuelled polyrhythms, through the swooping, soaring voices of *griots* (traditional musicians or minstrels; praise singers) and via socially-aware reggae, rap and hip-hop. From Afrobeat to Pygmy fusion, highlife to *makossa*, *gumbe* to Nigerian gospel, genres are as entrenched as they are evolving, fusing and reforming. Little wonder that here – in this vast, diverse region, with its deserts, jungles, skyscrapers, and urban sprawl – myriad ethnic groups play out their lives to music. Here are traditional songs that celebrate weddings, offer solace at funerals, keep work rhythms steady in the fields. Here are songs and rhythms that travelled out on slave ships to Cuba and Brazil, songs that retell history and, in doing so, foster inter-clan and inter-religious respect.

In West Africa, too, are the roots of Western music (along with guitars, keyboards, Latin influences and other legacies of colonialism).

Not for nothing did Senegalese rap crew Daara J title their 2003 international debut *Boomerang* – it illustrates how these rap artists, born in Africa and raised in America, have come full circle. But it goes both ways too, with a host of American blues musicians – Ry Cooder, Corey Harris, Taj Mahal, Bonnie Raitt – finding inspiration in West Africa, in Mali in particular.

Martin Scorsese's documentary *The Blues: Feels Like Going Home* (2003) follows musician Corey Harris' travels through Mississippi and West Africa, exploring the roots of blues music, and includes performances by Salif Keita, Habib Kolté, Taj Mahal and Ali Farka Touré.

A Potted History of West African Music

The musical history of West Africa is closely linked to its diverse and long-established empires, such as Ghana's (6th to 11th centuries), where court music was played for chiefs, music accompanied ceremonies and chores, and was played for pleasure at the end of the day. In the vast Mali Empire (13th to 15th centuries), music was the province of one social caste, the *jelis,* who still perform their folk styles today. Correspondingly in Senegal, *griots* – Wolof culture's *kora*-strumming, praise-singing caste – trace genealogies, recount epics and span generations. There are myriad musical styles in West Africa, courtesy of its hundreds of ethnic groups and various Islamic and European influences, but the *jeli/griot* tradition is arguably the best known.

Senegal, The Gambia, Guinea, Mali, Mauritania, Burkina Faso and Côte d'Ivoire all share the same *jeli* tradition, though each linguistic group calls it something different and each has its own subtly different sound. They are acknowledged as oral historians – nearly all children know the epic of Sundiata Keita, the warrior who founded the Mali Empire – and often as soothsayers but, although they top the bill at weddings and naming ceremonies, *griots* occupy a lowly rank in their hierarchical societies. Many big West African stars faced parental objections to their choice of career. Others, such as Salif Keita – a direct descendent of Sundiata and, as such, not a *jeli* – made their reputations in exile.

Oral tradition is equally strong in Nigeria, where stories of ancient Yoruba, Ashanti, Hausa and other kingdoms flourish. Like many a West African style, Yoruba music has its roots in percussion. Indeed, if there is any element common to the huge, diverse region that is West Africa, it is drumming. From the Ewe ensembles of Ghana – similar in style to those of Benin and Togo – to Senegal's *sabar* drummers, beating their giant instruments with sticks, drumming kick-started West Africa's musical heart. Often accompanied by ululation, vocal repetition, call-and-response vocals and polyrhythms, drums beat out a sound that immediately says 'Africa'.

As West African music travelled out on the slave ships (and brought other influences back with it later), so the music of the colonisers travelled in. The Portuguese presence in Cabo Verde created *morna,* music of separation, and *saudade* and creole-style *gumbe* in Guinea-Bissau. Western-style dance orchestras had the colonial elite fox-trotting on the Gold Coast. Francophone Africa fell in love with Cuban dance music, a genre, in rhythm and structure, remarkably close to Mande music. Cuban music introduced modern instruments to the region, creating a swath

CLASSIC WEST AFRICAN ALBUMS

➡ *Dimanche á Bamako* (2004) by Amadou and Mariam, and co-produced by Manu Chao

➡ *M'Bemba* (2005) by Salif Keita

➡ *In the Heart of the Moon* (2005) by Ali Farke Touré and Toumani Diabaté

➡ *Worotan* (1996) by Oumou Sangare

➡ *Zombie* (1976) by Fela Kuti

➡ *Specialist in All Styles* (2002) by Orchestra Baobab

➡ *The Rough Guide to West African Music* (1995)

➡ *Talking Timbuktu* (1994) by Ali Farke Touré and Ry Cooder

➡ *Highlife Roots Revival* (2012) by Koo Nimo

➡ *Radio Salone* (2012) by Sierra Leone Refugee All Stars

➡ *Orchestre Poly-Rythmo: The Kings of Benin Urban Groove 1972–80* (2004) by Orchestre Poly-Rythmo de Cotonou

➡ *Segu Blue* (2006) by Bassekou Kouyaté and Ngoni Ba

➡ *Aman Iman: Water is Life* (2007) by Tinariwen

MUSIC MUSIC OF WEST AFRICA

of dance bands such as Guinea's legendary Bembeya Jazz (a signifier of modern music, 'jazz' was commonly tagged onto a band's name), who played local styles with Latin arrangements.

Post-independence, the philosophy of 'negritude' – or cultural rediscovery – arose among some 1960s-era West African governments. Popular Latin sounds were discouraged in favour of folkloric material. Electric Afropop began to incorporate traditional rhythms and instruments, such as the *kora* (a harp-like musical instrument with 21 strings), *balafon* (xylophone) and *ngoni* (a stringed instrument). State-sponsored dance bands won big audiences and spawned even bigger stars. The first president of Senegal (poet Leopold Senghor) fostered the young Orchestra Baobab band, which made a phenomenal 21st-century comeback. Mali's Le Rail Band du Bamako (sponsored by the Malian Railway Company) became an African institution that launched the careers of two of Africa's greatest singers: Salif Keita and Mory Kanté.

When the young Salif Keita defected to their foreign-style rivals, Les Ambassedeurs du Motel, there was uproar. Fierce competition ensued throughout the 1970s, making Bamako the dance music capital of West Africa. Meanwhile, in Nigeria, the poppy highlife sound of the 1940s, '50s and '60s gave way to genres with a strong percussive element, such as *juju* and *fuji*. The West's popular music genres – rock, soul, jazz, funk, pop – made their mark, each spawning its own 'Afro' equivalent. Today the likes of 1960s Sierra-Leonean Afro-soul king Geraldo Pino and Beninoise voodoo heroes Orchestre Poly Rythmo de Cotonou are being rediscovered by a new generation of Western hipsters.

The recording studios of Lagos offered commercial opportunities for Nigerian performers, as did those of 1980s Abidjan in Cotê d'Ivoire – a musical mecca for artists from across the continent. But by the mid-1980s all eyes were on Paris, the city where Mory Kanté recorded his seminal club floor anthem 'Yeke Yeke' (check out Kanté's excellent 2012 album *La Guinnéenne*) and where innumerable West African musicians lived.

Big names moved back and forth between Paris, London and West Africa, recording cassettes for the local market and albums for the international one, as remains the case today. With the 1990s world-music boom, many stars – Youssou N'Dour, Salif Keita, Cesária Evora, King Sunny Ade – established their own record companies and signed up local talent.

Some savvy Western record labels pre-empted mainstream interest in West African music. London-based World Circuit signed the likes of Oumou Sangaré, Orchestra Baobab and the late Ali Farka Touré – and more recently, Malian songbird Fatoumata Diawara – arguably doing for West Africa what it did for Cuba with the Buena Vista Social Club. West African artists are now staples of international festivals including Womad and Glastonbury. Club producers have remixed Femi Kuti and Rokia Traoré. West African albums make it into mainstream charts, West African musicians sell out Western venues and Western musicians look to West Africa for inspiration.

In West Africa, big-name artists attract hordes of followers wherever they go. The politicians who try to hijack such popularity are usually shrugged off. Mory Kanté and Baaba Maal are respectively United Nations and Oxfam Goodwill Ambassadors, using their stardom to campaign against poverty, disease and illiteracy. The great Youssou N'Dour – described in *Rolling Stone* as possibly the most famous living singer in much of Africa – has been Senegal's Minister of Tourism and Culture since April 2012.

Sierra Leone's Refugee All Stars is a band formed by a group of refugees displaced to Guinea by the Sierra Leone Civil War, and who tour extensively to raise awareness of humanitarian causes. Fatoumata Diawara and Oumou Sangaré sing, however obliquely, about women's rights. The rap movement in Senegal promotes peace and love. But freedom of expression is still curtailed; both Sean and Femi Kuti's pro-democracy narratives are censored in Nigeria, just as their father's were.

Guitar-based highlife is still a staple of Ghana, where hip-life – the country's very own hip-hop – is also huge. Nigerian music isn't as popular in the West as it was; Mali and Senegal are ahead in the popularity stakes, but the demand for the back catalogue of the late great Nigerian Fela Anikulapo Kuti continues apace. After revisiting their roots with traditional acoustic albums both Salif Keita and Baaba Maal have gone on to re-embrace electronica; Keita's 2013 album Talé was produced by Phillipe Cohen Solal of Paris-based experimentalist Gotan Project.

Everywhere, musicians are creating, collaborating, experimenting. New, exciting performers are constantly emerging. Traditional styles are proudly upheld and passed down. West Africa's musical heritage is rich and ever present. It's in the DNA of its people.

Life is Hard, Music is Good (2012) is a feature-length documentary on the music of Mali, the result of over five years' worth of research by Kanaga System Krush. It mixes interviews with the likes of Toumani Diabate, Djelimady Tounkara and honorary Malian Damon Albarn with footage of life across this increasingly strife-torn country.

West African Instruments

West Africa's traditional instruments tend to be found in its rural areas and are generally fashioned from local materials – everything from gourds, stalks and shells to goat skin, cow horns and horse hair. Discarded and natural objects also have multiple musical uses: in Sierra Leone, empty Milo tins filled with stones were the core instrument for the genre called Milo-jazz. Hausa children in Nigeria beat rhythms on the inflated belly of a live pufferfish. The Pygmies of Cameroon beat rhythms on river water.

There are bells made of bronze in the Islamic orchestras of northern Nigeria, and scrapers made of iron in the south. In Cabo Verde women place a rolled-up cloth between their legs and beat it as part of their *batuco* music (the singer Lura does this live, with silver lamé). Everywhere, there is men's music and women's music, men's instruments and women's instruments: in Mauritania, men play the *tidinit,* a four-stringed lute, and women the *ardin,* a sort of back-to-front *kora.* Accordingly, there are men's dances and women's dances. And most of these, like most instrumental ensembles, are fuelled by drums.

There are wind instruments (Fula shepherds play melodies on reed flutes) and brass instruments (the Niger Tuareg favour the *alghaita,* or shawm trumpet) and voices used as instruments – such as the timeless vocals of the *griots,* the polyphonic singing of the Pygmies and the sung poetry of the Tuareg.

Across the region, percussion vies and blends with brass, wood and wind instruments. In urban areas, traditional instruments complement and ground modern ones. West Africa is, indeed, a hive of musical activity, thrumming to its own collective orchestra.

Drums & Xylophones

West Africa has a phenomenal variety of drums: kettle, slit and talking drums; water, frame and hourglass-shaped drums; log, goblet and double-headed barrel drums; drums used for ritual purposes, like the *dùndún* drums of the Yoruba, which communicate with the Orishas (minor gods); drums made from tree trunks and used for long-distance messages; drums that mark the major events of one's life – baptism, marriage, death – and drums for entertainment. There are 'talking' drums, such as the Wolof *tama,* a small, high-pitched instrument clamped under the armpit and beaten fast with a hooked stick, or the *djembe,* the chalice-shaped drum ubiquitous from Ghana to Senegal, and in the West's endorphin-inducing African drum circles.

AND THE BAND PLAYS ON

The breadth and depth of Mali's musical soundtrack is attributable not just to centuries of tradition but also to the policies of Mali's post-independence government. As elsewhere in West Africa, Mali's musicians were promoted as the cultural standard-bearers of the newly independent country and numerous state-sponsored 'orchestras' were founded. The legendary Rail Band de Bamako (actual employees of the Mali Railway Corporation) was one of the greatest, and one of its ex-members, the charismatic Salif Keita, has become a superstar in his own right.

But the 2012 coup and subsequent collapse in law and order in much of the country shook artists and musicians as well as politicians, interrupting album recordings and forcing Tuareg musicians to leave the country. The famous *ngoni* player Bassekou Kouyaté, who also served as a *griot* (traditional caste of musicians or praise singers) to ousted president ATT was in the middle of recording an album when the coup hit. He finished the record, but the mark of the coup on it – and perhaps his future sales – is indelible.

Tinariwen, an intoxicating Tuareg group of former rebels from Kidal, were caught up in the crisis multiple times in 2012, with some of their members going missing and turning up in refugee camps in neighbouring countries. Sadly, the Festival in the Desert, usually held in January and organised by Tuareg musicians, became another victim of the crisis.

Fortunately, music is harder to destroy than the ancient monuments and libraries of Timbuktu, but the crisis has certainly thwarted some musicians, restricting funding, electricity and inspiration. In the northeast, sharia law has meant that live bands and dancing venues have been silenced.

Outside Mali, the music plays on, including bluesy stuff such as that from the late Ali Farka Touré. Other much-loved blues performers include many from Ali Farka's stable, among them Afel Bocoum, Ali Farka's son Vieux Farka Touré, Baba Salah and Lobi Traoré. Some scholars believe that the roots of American blues lie with the Malian slaves who worked on US plantations.

Another well-known *griot* instrument is the *balafon*, a wooden xylophone with between 18 and 21 keys, suspended over a row of gourds to amplify the sound. The *balafon* is often played in pairs, with each musician – one improvising, one not – striking the keys with wooden mallets. The Susu people of Guinea are renowned *balafon* experts. There are other xylophones with different names in West Africa, some fashioned from huge logs or amplified by boxes and pits.

Kora & Other String Instruments

Afropop (www.afropop.org) aims to be the premier destination for web denizens interested in the contemporary music of Africa and the African diaspora; highlights include streaming audio and a searchable database.

West Africa boasts a diverse array of string instruments, from the one-stringed *viol* of the Niger Tuareg and the 13-string *obo zither* of the Igbo people in Nigeria, to the 21-string *kora* – the harp/lute of the *griots* and one of the most sophisticated instruments in sub-Saharan Africa. *Kora* players are usually virtuosos, having studied their craft from childhood. Mory Kanté's amplified rock-style *kora* helped establish its reputation as a formidable solo instrument, while *kora* master Toumani Diabaté, son of the virtuoso Sidiki Diabaté, displayed its crossover potential by collaborating with everyone from flamenco musicians to African American bluesman Taj Mahal.

Regarded by some as the precursor to the banjo, the *ngoni* (*xalam* in Wolof, *hoddu* in Fula, *konting* in Mandinka) is also popular with *griots*. A feature in the 14th-century courts of Mali, it has between three and five strings that are plucked, and is tricky to play.

West African Musical Styles

While many of West Africa's mega-successful artists might be classified as 'Afro-pop', thanks to commercial sales at home and/or in the West, the region boasts a gamut of distinctive musical styles. The following are just a few of them.

Afrobeat

Co-created by the late, great Fela Kuti, Afrobeat is a hybrid of Nigerian highlife, Yoruba percussion, jazz, funk and soul. Fela, a singer, saxophonist and band leader, and one of the most influential 20th-century African figures, used Afrobeat to give voice to the oppressed. His onstage rants, tree-trunk-sized spliff in hand, were legendary. A succession of governments tried to shut him up. When he died of AIDS in 1997, a million people joined his funeral procession through Lagos. His eldest son, Femi, has picked up the baton, releasing fine albums such as *Africa For Africa* (2011) and *No Place for My Dream* (2013), and reopening his father's Lagos nightclub, the Shrine. A host of Nigerian creatives – percussionist and singer Tony Allen, rapper Weird MC, Fela's youngest son, Seun (who in 2015 made his first appearance on stage with his brother Femi) – keep the flame alight. Afrobeat continues to cross over into dance mixes and hip-hop and reggae projects.

Cabo Verdean Music

Cabo Verdean music came late to the West. The undisputed star of the bluesy, melancholy songs (known as *morna*) was the 'barefoot diva' Cesária Evora, a cigarette-puffing grandmother who passed away in December 2011. European influences are obvious in *morna,* the equivalent to Portugal's *fado,* while Africa is at the fore in other genres such as the dance-oriented *coladeira,* accordion-led *funana* and percussive women's music, *batuco.* Look out for the 2013 international debut album by 60-year-old *morna* balladeer Zé Luis, the Lisbon-based Lura and Tcheka, a singer-songwriter and guitarist who plays beats that are normally played on percussion. Tete Alhinho – *Voz* (2004) and *Mornas ao Piano* (2015) – is another haunting *morna* voice.

Gumbe

Closely associated with Guinea-Bissau, *gumbe* is an up-tempo, polyrhythmic genre that fuses about 10 of the country's folk music traditions. Lyrics, sung in Portuguese creole, are topical and witty; instruments include guitars and the water drum, an upturned calabash floating in a bucket. *Gumbe* is sometimes used as an umbrella term for any folk music in Guinea-Bissau but should not be confused with *kizomba*, the popular dance and music originating from Angola. In Sierra Leone, *gumbe* evolved from the breezy, calypso-style guitar music called palm-wine or *maringa*. The late SE Rogie and the Ghana-based elder statesman Koo Nimo, who also play highlife, are probably the best-known exponents. From Guinea-Bissau, Manecas Costa's *Paraiso di Gumbe* (2003) is one of the more accessible examples of the genre.

MUSIC WEST AFRICAN MUSICAL STYLES

West Africa is one of the few places on earth where the cassette is king. Cassette piracy is a huge problem and many high-profile names have devoted themselves to the task of its eradication. Dakar-based singer-songwriter Carlou D only sells his CD *Audio Visa* at his live gigs for this reason.

Penned by Cuban ethnologist Carlos Moore, *Fela: This Bitch of A Life: The Authorised Biography of Africa's Musical Genius* (2010) is as it says. It's based on many hours of conversation with Kuti himself, and reissued to coincide with *FELA: The Musical*, which took London and Broadway by storm.

BEST 'NEW' WEST AFRICAN ALBUMS

➡ *Emmar* (2014) by Tinariwen
➡ *Music in Exile* (2015) by Songhoy Blues
➡ *Tzenni* (2014) by Noura Mint Seymali
➡ *New Era* (2016) by Kiss Daniel
➡ *God Over Everything* (2016) by Patoranking
➡ *Taksera* (2015) by Tamikrest

Highlife

Ghana's urban, upbeat highlife, which started off in the dancehalls of the colonial Gold Coast, has had a ripple effect throughout West Africa. Trumpeter and band leader ET Mensah was the postwar, pan-African king of this sound, a blend of everything from Trinidadian calypso, brass band music and Cuban *son*, to swing, jazz and older African song forms. Osibisa were *the* 'Afro-rock' pop/highlife group of the 1970s. Today's hybrids include gospel, hip-hop (hip-life) and the ever-popular guitar highlife. Amekye Dede and Jewel Ackah are popular highlife artists; Tic Tac, Sarkodie and FOKN Bois are living it large in hip-life. Highlife is also a staple of Sierra Leone, Liberia and Nigeria. Check out early recordings by Dr Victor Olaiya, Nigerian highlife's 'evil genius' and his band, Cool Cats.

> Just 4 U (p322), in Dakar (Senegal), is a cosy outdoor bar-restaurant that holds nightly live music shows, including gigs by some of the capital's best musicians, which, if you're lucky, might include Cheikh Lo, Carlou D or Orchestra Baobab.

Juju

Juju music evolved from a mix of traditional Yoruba talking drums and folklore, and popular palm-wine guitar music. It*s* best known ambassador, King Sunny Ade, has been deploying his relentless blend of ringing guitar lines, multilayered percussion, tight harmonies and booty shaking for four decades now. In Nigeria he's known as KSA, the Minister for Enjoyment. Competition with his rival Sir Shina Peters continues. *Juju* is not to be confused with the Arabesque percussion frenzy that is *fuji:* main players include King Wasiu Ayinde Marshal (KWAM1) and King Saheed Osupa, who uses his songs to advise and educate his fans.

Makossa

A fusion of highlife and soul, influenced by Congolese rumba and characterised by electric guitars, Cameroon's distinctive pop-*makossa* music remains one of West Africa's most vibrant dance genres. Its biggest star is still the jazz-minded octogenarian sax player and singer Manu Dibango (track down his 1973 release, *Soul Makossa*), who has worked in related genres such as *mangambe, assiko* and *bikutsi*, and still sells out London venues such as Ronnie Scott's. The 1980s saw Sam Fan Thomas popularise *makassi*, a sort of *makossa*-lite. Other *makossa* names to look out for include Petit Pays, Sam Fan Thomas, Guy Lobe and the guitarist Vincent Nguini.

> Stephen Feld's *Jazz Cosmopolitanism in Accra: Five Musical Years in Ghana* (2012) combines memoir, biography, ethnography and history in a compelling and accessible look at Ghana's coolest cats.

Mbalax

Taken from the Wolof word for rhythm, mbalax is Senegal's primary musical genre, an intensely polyrhythmic sound that evolved in the 1970s from Afro-Cuban dance bands such as the Star Band and Orchestra Baobab, and then fiercely reclaimed its African roots. Youssou N'Dour was the first to introduce more traditional elements, including *tassou* (a form of rap), *bakou* (a kind of trilling) and instruments such as the *tama* and *sabar* drums. Popular mbalax artists include Alloune Mbaye Nder and female artists Fatou Gewel, Coumba Gawlo Seck and N'Dour's sister-in-law, Vivianne.

> Akwaaba Music (www.akwaabamusic.com) is a Ghana-generated site dedicated to African music and pop culture, and finding new sounds and trends.

Reggae, Rap & Hip-Hop

Afro-reggae, rap and hip-hop are huge throughout West Africa. Elder Ivorian statesman Alpha Blondy has enjoyed a 20-year career, spawning hits like the classic 'Jerusalem', recorded in Jamaica with the Wailers. His younger, equally political, compatriots include Serge Kassy and Tiken Jah Fakoly. Ivorian hip-hop (think outfits such as 2431 and All Mighty) includes the gangsta-style *rap dogba*, which contrasts with the socially aware, anti-bling Wolof rap of Senegalese outfits such as Daara J and Positive Black Soul.

In strife-torn Mali, rap music is now at the vanguard of messaging the population through music, including clarifying the political situation in the North and in Bamako. Rappers Amkoullel, Mylmoand Les Sofas de la Republique have much to say. Daddy Showkey is a well-known Nigerian reggae artist, and Nigerian hip-hop musicians include the duo P-Square along with Ice Prince and JJC aka Skillz. Rap Nigerien is a melange of different languages spoken in Niger – as deployed by groups such as Kamikaz and Metaphor – and covers such topics as forced marriages, child labour and corruption. The Gambia is the self-styled reggae capital of Africa; well-known artists include Horicane, Stalwart and Rebellion the Recaller.

Wassoulou

Wassoulou music is named after the region of the same name, south of Bamako in Mali, and the Fula people who inhabit it. Wassoulou is not *jeli* music – they have no castes – but is based on hunting songs. The women usually sing and the men dance. The music is based on the *kamalengoni* (youth's harp) – a sort of funky, jittery bass guitar invented in the 1950s – and is augmented by the thwack and slap of the *fle,* a calabash strung with cowrie shells and thrown and spun in the air. Prominent artists include Oumou Sangare, Fatoumata Diawara and Coumbia Sidibe. Having shot to fame with her 1989 release, *Moussoulou*, Oumou Sangare is still the biggest Wassoulou star, singing in her native Bambara about injustices of life in West Africa – polygamy, the price of a bride – and is actively involved in Mali's burgeoning peace movement.

Africanhiphop.com (www.africanhiphop.com) has been mapping the development of African hip-hop culture since the '90s; it features links, new productions and contributions from the artists themselves.

Directed by Cheikhj Sene, better known as the rapper Keyti, *100% Galsen* is a 2012, 25-minute documentary about hip-hop in Senegal and a sort of grassroots version of the multi-award-winning *Democracy in Dakar*, a 2007 film that presents a model for hip-hop as a force for social change.

MUSIC WEST AFRICAN MUSICAL STYLES

Arts & Craftwork

West Africa's artistic heritage, which encompasses traditional sculptures, masks, striking textiles and jewellery, is tied very much to the land and its people. Most such works were, in their original form, representations of the natural and spirit worlds. The creation of these arts and crafts is often the preserve of distinct castes of blacksmiths and weavers, who rely on locally found or produced materials, and many pieces still carry powerful meaning for West Africa's diverse peoples.

Masks

Traditionally in West Africa masks were rarely produced for purely decorative purposes. Rather, they were highly active signifiers of the spirit world and played a central role in ceremonies that served both to accompany important rites of passage and to entertain. There is a staggering range of shapes and styles of mask, all of which are invariably rich in meaning, from the tiny 'passport' mask of the Dan (Côte d'Ivoire) to the Dogon *imina-tiou* mask (Mali), which can tower up to 10m in height.

Masks, which are usually created by professional artisans, can be made of wood, brass, tin, leather, cloth, glass beads, natural fibres and even (in the case of the Ashanti) gold. They come in numerous forms, including face masks, helmet masks (which cover the whole head), headdresses (which are secured to the top of the head), the massive *nimba* masks of the Baga people in Guinea (which are carried on the dancer's shoulders) and the famous ivory hip masks from the Kingdom of Benin (present-day Nigeria), which are worn around the waist.

West African masks are usually classified as anthropomorphic (resembling the human form) and zoomorphic (the representation of deities in the form of animals). Anthropomorphic masks are often carefully carved and very realistic. Many groups use masks representing beautiful maidens, whose features reflect the aesthetic ideal of the people. The zoomorphic masks mostly represent dangerous and powerful nature spirits, and can be an abstract and terrifying combination of gaping jaws, popping eyes and massive horns. Some masks combine human and animal features. These convey the links between humans and animals, in particular the ability to gain and control the powers of animals and the spirits they represent.

The mask is only part of a complex costume that often covers the dancer's entire body. Made of plant fibre or cloth, often with elaborate appliqué, the costume is usually completed with a mane of raffia surrounding the mask. Most masks are associated with dance, although some are used as prestige symbols and are worn as amulets.

The use of crosses in Tuareg culture (in jewellery and the shape of pommels on camel saddles) led early European explorers to speculate that the Tuareg were once Christians.

Totems & Talismans

An important feature of traditional religions is the totem, an object (usually representing an animal) that serves as an emblem for a particular ethnic group, and is usually connected with the original ancestor of that group. It is taboo for a member of the clan whose totem is, for example, a snake, to harm any snake, as this would be harming the ancestor. Other

THE MASK COMES ALIVE

Behind almost every West African mask lies a story, often known only to members of a particular ethnic group. When masks and costumes are worn for a dance, which is accompanied by percussive music and song, they come alive and convey their meaning to the audience. Masked dances are used in initiation and coming-of-age ceremonies; in burial rituals, when dancing and celebrations assist the spirit of the dead to forsake the earth and reside with ancestors; in fertility rituals, which are associated with agriculture and the appeasement of spirits to ensure a successful harvest; and in the rituals surrounding childbirth. Masks are also used for entertainment, in community-based dances and theatrical plays.

The role of the mask is, however, changing. Christianity, Islam and the 20th century have all had a major impact on the animist masked dances of West Africa. Many dances are no longer performed, and others have transformed from sacred rituals to forms of entertainment. Since the arrival in Africa of tourists and collectors, artisans have begun to produce masks for widespread sale. Although this is a departure from the mask's role in traditional society, tourism can serve to keep artisans employed in their traditional art – evidence, perhaps, that masking traditions are never static and continue to transmute over time.

It's still possible to see masked dances in West Africa, although they may be specially arranged 'tourist performances'. Getting to see the real thing is often a matter of being in the right place at the right time.

common totems include lions, crocodiles and birds, although many of the animals themselves have disappeared from the West African wild.

Talismans (sometimes called fetishes) are another important feature in animism. These objects (or charms) are believed to embody a spirit, and can take many forms. For example, bird skulls and other animal parts may be used as charms by a learned elder for helping people communicate with their ancestors. The elders (usually men) responsible for these sacred objects are sometimes called *féticheurs* (fetish priests).

The most common charms found throughout West Africa are the small leather or metal amulets *(grigri)*, often containing a sacred object, worn by people around the neck, arm or waist to ward off evil or bring good luck. Many West African Muslims (including the Tuareg) also wear *grigri,* which are called *t'awiz* in other Islamic countries; they often contain a small verse from the Quran and are only considered effective if made by a *marabout* (saint).

Figurative Sculpture

African sculpture is now considered one of the most dynamic and influential art forms around. Once relegated to curio cabinets and dusty museum storerooms, and labelled as crude, barbaric and primitive, African carving finally gained credibility in the early 20th century when Picasso, Matisse and others found inspiration in its approach to the human form.

Most West African sculpture is carved in wood, but superb bronze and iron figures are also produced, while some funerary figures are created in terracotta and mud. The strange and uncompromising forms found in West African sculpture are rarely the unique creations of an inspired artist – the sculptures have always been made to fulfil specific functions, using centuries-old designs redolent with meaning.

In West Africa, sculpture is mostly used in connection with ancestor or spirit worship. Many groups believe that the spirits of the dead can have a major impact, both positive and negative, on a person's life. Ancestral figures are carved and placed in shrines and altars where they receive libations and sacrificial blood. Some groups carve figures that are

Butabu: Adobe Architecture of West Africa (2003), by James Morris, is a stunning photographic study of West Africa's traditional architecture with informative text; a great reminder of your visit. *Banco: Adobe Mosques of the Inner Niger Delta* (2003), by Jean Dethier, Dorothee Gruner and Sebastian Schutyser is also excellent.

WEST AFRICAN ARCHITECTURE: TOP PICKS

Mudbrick Mosques
➡ Djenné Mosque (Mali)
➡ Dyingerey Ber Mosque and Sankoré Mosque, Timbuktu (Mali)
➡ Grande Mosquée, Bobo-Dioulasso (Burkina Faso)
➡ The seven mosques of Bani (Burkina Faso)
➡ Grande Mosquée, Agadez (Niger)

Fortified Villages
➡ Dogon Country (Mali)
➡ Tamberma Valley (Togo)
➡ Lobi family compounds (Burkina Faso)

Painted Facades
➡ Gourounsi homes, Tiébélé (Burkina Faso)
➡ Tichit (Mauritania)
➡ Oualâta (Mauritania)

Traditional Palaces & Forts
➡ Foumban (Cameroon)
➡ Bafut (Cameroon)
➡ Bafoussam (Cameroon)
➡ Abomey (Benin)
➡ Ashanti buildings, Kumasi (Ghana)
➡ Colonial-era forts (Ghana)

Stilt Villages
➡ Ganvié (Benin)
➡ Nzulezu (Ghana)

Colonial Architecture
➡ Saint-Louis (Senegal)
➡ Malabo (Equatorial Guinea)

cared for by women to ensure fertility and in the hope that the resulting child will inherit the fine looks represented in the sculpture. The famous *akuaba* 'doll' of the Ashanti is the best-known example of this. Prestige objects are also carved, such as figurative staffs of office, commemorative statues and other regalia used by kings, chiefs, traditional healers and diviners as emblems of power.

West African sculpture is usually created by a professional artist, who is almost always male and who has learned his craft through an apprenticeship. It's mostly a family- or caste-specific occupation, and the forms and skills are passed down from generation to generation, resulting in highly refined styles.

Across the many styles produced in West Africa, some common characteristics exist. The figure is usually symmetrical and faces forward, the features are impassive and the arms are held to the side with the legs slightly bent at the knees. Certain features may be exaggerated, and the head is almost always large in proportion to the body.

Among the British Museum's fine collection of Benin statues are 16th-century plaques depicting the Portuguese in knee breeches, boots and feathered hats, with matchlocks and cross-hilt daggers, accompanied by dogs.

The surface of the carving will often have tribal marks carved or burnt into the blackened face and torso. Sometimes the carving is highly polished, or painted with ochre or imported enamel paint.

Bronze & Brass Casting

West Africa's best-known castings were created for the Kingdom of Benin in present-day Nigeria. Plaques, statues and masks were produced to decorate the palaces and compounds of the kings and chiefs, and their discovery (and plundering) by Western governments and collectors did at least serve to challenge the prevailing view that African cultures were primitive.

West African brass and bronze is often cast using the *cire perdue* (lost wax) technique. The casting process involves creating a sculpture out of wax, which is then dipped in a silt-and-mud solution. When the sculpture is dry, clay is built around the form to create a strong mould. The mould is then heated and the wax is melted out. Molten bronze is then poured into the empty mould. When cool, the mould is broken away to reveal the bronze sculpture. Each cast is therefore unique. This process is thought to have produced the 1000-year-old beautifully intricate statues of the Ibo-Ikwu, which can be seen today in the National Museum in Lagos. Today, latex is often used instead of wax, which creates even finer detail.

The Yoruba cast ritual staffs called *edan*. These comprise male and female figures in bronze, surmounting an iron tip and joined together by a chain. Figurative weights for weighing gold were cast by the Ashanti, and often symbolised the colourful proverbs for which they are known.

Iron is no longer smelted in the Dogon Country; many Dogon blacksmiths now use iron taken from abandoned motor vehicles, which withstands heating and shaping better than new iron.

ARTS & CRAFTWORK BRONZE & BRASS CASTING

Textiles

Few places in the world can match West Africa for the beauty, vitality, colour and range of its textiles. Contrary to what many travellers expect,

THE BLACKSMITH: MASTER OF THE DARK ARTS

In many West African societies, an almost mystical aura surrounds the blacksmith who, perhaps more than any other artisan caste, occupies a special place in community life. Feared due to their strange communion with fire and iron, which is believed to render them immune to evil spirits and give them special powers, and respected for the pivotal role they play in ritual and daily life, blacksmiths provide an unbroken connection to West Africa's past. They are the makers of all manner of tools, weapons and household implements, but they also serve as intermediaries (between social groups and between the human and spirit worlds) and operate at the heart of many traditional ceremonies.

Despite their pivotal role in traditional life, blacksmiths often live on the margins of the community with whom they work. Among the Dogon people of Mali, for example, blacksmiths may not marry outside the blacksmith caste, but the blacksmith's anvil is considered the foundation of the village; if the anvil is moved, it is believed that the village may drift. Within Tuareg society, blacksmiths (known as *inaden*) are customarily viewed with suspicion by other Tuareg, and the blacksmiths traditionally lived on the periphery of towns and villages, even though Tuareg life would be impossible without them. Blacksmiths produce weapons and jewellery, and they're also healers, herbalists, poets, singers, skilled sacrificers of animals, advisers in matters of tradition and the custodians of oral traditions. Noble Tuareg women even confide in the *inaden,* using them as go-betweens in marriage negotiations and as mediators in love affairs. So important are they that no Tuareg festival could be complete without *inaden* participation, and anyone who tries to prevent them from attending is shunned by the whole community.

Other communities in which blacksmiths play a special role include the Bambara, Senoufo and Wolof.

men are the main producers of textiles (the *bogolan* cloth of Mali is an exception), weaving wool, cotton, nylon, rayon and silk on a variety of looms. Most of West Africa's textiles follow the strip-cloth technique, whereby cloth is woven in narrow strips that are then sewn together. As many West Africans now wear Western clothes and traditional textiles are largely reserved for ceremonial occasions, the skills required to produce the finer textiles are disappearing, a trend that is only partially ameliorated by sales to collectors and tourists.

African Textiles: Colour and Creativity Across a Continent (2016), by John Gillow, is at once visually eye-catching and a reasonably comprehensive study, including sections on Côte d'Ivoire, Mali, Sierra Leone, Cabo Verde and the Niger Delta.

Kente Cloth

Clothing is one of the most important marks of distinction in Ashanti society, and the colourful kente cloth is the most famous expression of Ashanti exuberance. The basic traditional garment for men is a long rectangular piece of *ntoma* (cloth) passed over the left shoulder and brought around the body like a toga. The earliest kente cloth was cotton, but from the 18th century Ashanti weavers began incorporating designs using unravelled, imported Dutch silk. Silk has since gone on to be the fabric of prestige and the most expensive kente cloths contain silk (or imported rayon).

The weaving is done exclusively by men (usually working outdoors), who weave narrow, brightly coloured strips with complex patterns and rich hues. Kente cloth is worn only in the southern half of Ghana and is reserved for prestigious events. Although you'll find kente cloth on sale across Ghana, your best bet is to head to the Ashanti heartland, especially at Kumasi's Kejetia Market or the surrounding craft villages.

Bogolan: Shaping Culture through Cloth in Contemporary Mali (2009), by Victoria L Rovine, is splendidly photographed and is a fine study of Mali's most recognisable textile art.

The Ewe also weave kente cloth, but their designs are somewhat different and include motifs of geometric figures. Every design has a meaning and some designs are reserved exclusively for royal families.

Adinkra Cloth

Just as impressive as the better-known kente cloth, *adinkra* cloth (a colourful cotton material with black geometric designs or stylised figures stamped on it) is also from Ghana. The word *adinkra* means 'farewell', and Ghanaians consider this fabric most appropriate for funerals.

Originally the printing was done on cotton pieces laid on the ground. Today, the cotton fabric is cut into long pieces, spread on a raised padded board and held in place by nails. The symbolic designs are cut on calabash stamps, and the dye is made from the bark of a local tree called *badie*. The printer dips the calabash into the hot dye and presses it onto the fabric. The rich colours are about far more than aesthetics: each colour has a special significance: vermilion (red) symbolises the earth, blue signifies love and yellow represents success and wealth.

The village of Ntonso, close to Kumasi in central Ghana, is famous for its *adinkra* cloth.

Bogolan Cloth

From the Sahel region of Mali comes *bogolan* cloth (called *bokolanfini* in Bambara, and often simply referred to as 'mud cloth'). This textile can be found in markets throughout West Africa, but its true home is in Djenné and Ségou, both in Mali.

Some art historians believe that one of Picasso's most famous paintings, *Les Demoiselles d'Avignion*, depicts women wearing ceremonial Dogon masks.

The cloth is woven in plain cotton strips, sewn together and dyed yellow using a solution made from the leaves of a local tree. If you thought mud was mud, think again – after weaving, the cloth is covered in designs using various types of mud from different sources: from sandstone outcrops for reds and oranges; from riverbeds for blacks and greys. The cloth is left to dry in the sun, and the mud designs are then removed, leaving their imprint – the effect is very striking.

Designs are traditionally geometric and abstract, but *bogolan* cloth made specifically for tourists is more representational, showing animals, markets or village scenes. Some designs are very complex and involve many hours of work by the artists, who are all women.

Indigo Cloth

Another classic West African fabric is the indigo-dyed cotton worn primarily by the Tuareg as robes and headdresses. The indigo colour comes from the indigofera plant and the indigo vine; the plant is crushed and fermented, then mixed with an alkaline solution to produce the dye. The dyed cloth is often beaten with a mallet to produce a sheen. Among the Tuareg, cheaper dyed cotton from Nigeria or even China has begun to replace true indigo cloth, which can be outrageously expensive. Other West African peoples noted for their use of indigo include the Hausa, Dogon, Baoulé, Yoruba and Soninké, and it is also characteristic of Guinea's Fouta Djalon region.

The Yoruba produce an indigo-dyed cloth, *aderi*, which has designs that are applied using the tie-dye technique, or by painting motifs with a dye-resistant starch. The Dogon also produce an indigo cloth, which has geometric patterns.

Other Textiles

The Fula have a caste of weavers, called Maboub, who produce blankets known as *khasa*. These are usually made from camel hair, although the term is sometimes used to describe cotton blankets as well. The Maboub also make rare and expensive wedding blankets. These large and elaborately detailed textiles are traditionally displayed around the marriage bed.

The Fon and the Fanti are known for their appliqué banners and flags. Shapes of people and animals are cut from colourful material and are carefully sewn onto a cloth panel.

The Hausa are famous for their embroidery, which was once hand-stitched onto their robes and caps. Although they are now machine-stitched, the designs remain unchanged. In keeping with Islam, Hausa designs are non-figurative.

Northern Côte d'Ivoire is famous for its Korhogo cloth, a coarse, cream-coloured cotton adorned with geometrical designs or fantastical animals.

Jewellery

Jewellery is an African tradition of extraordinary variety and, like all West African art forms, traditionally serves a purpose beyond the purely decorative.

Few jewellery items carry a wealth of associations quite like the humble bead, which is elevated to high art in this part of the world. Beads often represent spiritual values and can play a major role in community rituals such as birth, circumcision, marriage and death. The availability of European products, which arrived via trans-Saharan trade caravans long before Europeans themselves, accelerated during the colonial period, altering the bead-making tradition significantly. Beads are now more likely to be made of glass, after local jewellers started copying the highly decorative *millefiori* trading beads from Venice, which featured flowers, stripes and mosaic designs. Discarded bottles and medicine jars were pulverised into a fine powder to be remade into glass beads, and the Krobo in Ghana still melt powdered glass in terracotta moulds. In a slight variation, the Nupe in central Nigeria wind molten glass on long iron rods to make beads and bracelets. Referred to as *bakim-mutum* by bead traders (most of whom sell glass beads by weight, hence their other

Kente Cloth: Introduction to History (1993), by Ernest Asamoah-Yaw, is a fascinating journey through the history of Ghana's most famous textile with good coverage of pattern and name origins.

Starbook (2008), by Ben Okri, is a stirring fictional fable that takes place among a mystical group of artists and artisans in West Africa in the lead-up to the colonial era.

African Elegance (1999), by Ettagale Blauer, is a magnificently photographed chronicle of African art forms and their role in modern Africa. The sections on masks and jewellery are of particular interest.

name, 'pound beads'), beads are commonly worn by village chiefs and elders as a sign of power and wealth.

Various other materials are used in Africa for making beads, including coral, shell, copal, amazonite, silver, gold and brass. In Mali you'll see large amber beads and ornate gold earrings worn by Fula women. The Dogon also treasure amber, and use it in their necklaces, bracelets and pendants. They also use beads made of stone and terracotta incised with geometric patterns.

Rings in West Africa can be stunning. In Burkina Faso, look for Bobo bronze rings, which often have intricate designs, including a tick bird, a warrior on horseback or a chameleon. In Mali, older Dogon men wear large bronze rings as a sign of status. Cowrie shells are often used to decorate jewellery; for a long time these shells were used as money in many areas of Africa.

In most areas of the region, the preferred metal for jewellery is gold; the Ashanti are famous for their goldwork in jewellery, ornaments and staffs. In and near the Sahara, however, the Tuareg and Moors prefer silver. The Tuareg are renowned for their intricate filigree silverwork in jewellery and in the decoration on the handles of their daggers. Tuareg men and women often wear silver crosses as pendants; in Niger, Mali and neighbouring Algeria these crosses differ from place to place, the most famous being the *croix d'Agadez,* while most are characterised by protective symbolism. Some incorporate circle and phallus designs, or fertility symbols; those representing a camel's eye or jackal tracks are symbolic of power and cunning.

West Africa: African Art and the Colonial Encounter (2007), by Sidney Littlefield Kasfir, can be a little academic, but the influence of colonialism on African art forms is a fascinating subject.

Africa Adorned (1987), by Angela Fisher, is an extravagantly beautiful coffee-table book that could just be the finest of its kind, with some exceptional and detailed sections on African jewellery.

Peoples of West Africa

Perhaps more than anything else, it's West Africa's people and the richness of their cultural traditions that lure travellers to the region. Beyond the French-speaking world this is Africa's least-known corner, and the diversity of distinct languages, histories and customs you'll encounter in West Africa is astounding.

Ashanti

Inhabiting the now-thinning forest of south-central Ghana, the Ashanti, an Akan-speaking people, are among West Africa's best-known peoples. Their fame derives in part from their artefacts and symbols (among them kente and *adinkra* cloth), which have become prized among collectors in the West. But it's the Ashanti affinity with gold, with its echoes of West Africa's great empires of antiquity, which gives them their greatest resonance.

In the 18th century, the Ashanti king, the Asantehene, united the fractured feudal states of what is now Ghana and, ruling from his capital at Kumasi, brought peace and prosperity to the country; Ashanti political administration was among the most sophisticated in West Africa prior to the colonial period. Everything about the Ashanti kingdom glittered with gold: the Asantehene controlled the region's most prolific gold mines, the goldsmiths of the royal court were among West Africa's most practised artisans and the kingdom's trading reach extended across the world. The Asantehene's sacred golden stool, which may only be shown in public four times each century, became the ongoing symbol of Ashanti extravagance.

Ashanti power waned with the arrival of British colonial forces and, later, was subsumed into the multi-ethnic modern state of Ghana. But Ashanti culture maintains a strong hold over Ghana, and modern Ghanaian leaders ignore the traditional Ashanti rulers at their peril.

The 1995 silver jubilee of the then-Asantehene Otumfuo Opoku Ware II became one of the most lavish traditional ceremonies in West Africa in modern times, attended by 75,000 people and showcasing an incredible collection of golden royal regalia.

TRADITIONAL CULTURE

Chances to experience and access traditional culture include the following:

➡ The Moro-Naba ceremony is held every Friday at the Moro-Naba Palace (p57) in Ouagadougou, Burkina Faso.

➡ The Musée de Poni (p67) in Gaoua, Burkina Faso, is an excellent introduction to Lobi culture.

➡ Kumasi (p203), Ghana, is littered with monuments and museums dedicated to Ashanti traditions.

➡ Ikeji is the annual new yam festival; the most important Ikeji festival takes place in September at Arochukwu, southeastern Nigeria.

Bambara

The Bambara (also known as Bamana) are the largest ethnic group in Mali. Concentrated in the south and centre of the country, they comprise around one-third of the population.

Although the Bambara are a predominantly Muslim people, their belief systems are laced with traditional beliefs and customs. Bambara men, for example, must pass through six secret societies during a seven-year coming-of-age initiation rite, a process that culminates in a symbolic death and rebirth. Masks play a spiritually charged role in traditional Bambara culture.

Bambara tradition decrees a highly regulated occupational caste system, among whose ranks are farmers, leather-workers, poets and blacksmiths. Each occupational group or caste has its own initiation rituals, for which particular masks are required, and only blacksmiths inherit the capacity to tap into the spiritual power, or *nyama,* that enables them to transform wood and iron into masks and other religious objects. Because *nyama* is inherited, blacksmiths must marry within their own occupational group. Blacksmiths also make hoes, door locks and guns, all of which are furnished with spiritual power as well as utility. Door locks often have a water-lizard symbol to protect the house from thieves, or a long-eared creature similar to a bat that is said to hear every sound, thus protecting the household.

Genii of the River Niger (1993), by Jean-Marie Gibbal, is a fascinating study of the river peoples of eastern Mali, in particular their struggles to hold fast to traditional mythology in the face of Islam's march.

Baoulé

The Baoulé of eastern and central Côte d'Ivoire, like the Ashanti of Ghana, are an Akan-speaking farming people. Their origins lie in Ghana, which they fled in the 16th century as Ashanti power grew. As they fled west, so the story goes, they came up against a river which they were unable to cross. With their pursuers close behind, they threw their most prized possessions into the river, among them the son of their ruler, Queen Pokou, whereupon hippopotamuses rose up to provide a bridge, allowing them to cross the river. The queen's lament of *baouli* (which means 'the child is dead') became the sorrowful name of a people.

The Baoulé claim to have resisted French colonial power longer than any other West African group. They are distinguished by their belief in the *blolo* (meaning 'elsewhere' or 'the beyond'), another world, parallel to our own. A man may even have a *blolo bla,* a wife from beyond, and a woman a *blolo bian,* or other husband. Both can influence a partner's wellbeing, marital stability and sex life, usually negatively. Soothsayers play an important role in Baoulé culture; they're often used to 'call in' or 'bring down' the *blolo* partner to prevent further havoc. This can be done either by moulding a cone of fine kaolin clay mixed with secret herbs, or by fashioning a clay or wooden statue of the *blolo* partners, to control them.

Baoulé society is considered to be one of West Africa's most egalitarian: everyone, from village elders to slaves, traditionally had a voice in the important decisions of Baoulé life.

Bobo

The ancestors of the 100,000 Bobo people arrived in West Africa almost 1200 years ago and the Bobo now occupy western Burkina Faso, around Bobo-Dioulasso, and southern Mali. The Bobo traditionally showed little interest in conquest. As a result, they made few enemies and thereby managed to escape subjugation by the powerful Mossi who ruled from Ouagadougou.

The Bobo cosmology revolves around the creator god Wuro, who creates balance in the world by dividing everything into pairs. In the Bobo world view, human disruption to this natural order can only be rectified by this deity, but as Wuro may neither be addressed nor spoken of nor depicted in any form, the Bobo communicate with Wuro through a mediating deity, Do. That effort to commune with Do gives the Bobo their most recognisable cultural forms, the renowned Bobo masks, especially the famous butterfly and helmet masks. They are worn during funeral rites, and when invoking Do in planting-time ceremonies asking for rain and a good harvest. Other animals represented in Bobo masks include owls, buffaloes, antelope, crocodiles and scorpions.

Bubi

The Bubi are a Bantu-speaking people who live in Cameroon and Equatorial Guinea; they form a majority on the last's Bioko Island, which is considered their ancestral homeland. Once one of the most numerous peoples in this part of the region, their numbers fell dramatically as a result of colonial-era epidemics, slavery and targeted violence at the time of Equatorial Guinea's independence from Spain. By some accounts, 75% of Bubis were wiped out during the country's pre-independence civil war – where there were once three million Bubis, just 100,000 remain.

The form of a butterfly is used in Bobo masks because butterflies appear in great swarms immediately after the first rains and are thus associated with the planting season.

Dan

The animist Dan (also known as the Yacouba) inhabit the mountainous area around Man in Côte d'Ivoire, spilling over the border into Liberia. Although part of the wider Mande tradition, they are set apart by their Dan language, of which there are more than 320,000 speakers. Until recently Dan society lacked any overarching social organisation, with each village looking after its own affairs, although the secret leopard society (known as *go*) has become an important unifying vehicle for peacemaking between Dan communities. In Dan tradition, lavish gift-giving is considered an essential means of advancing socially.

Masks are an important element of Dan culture and the Dan mask tradition is one of Africa's most highly developed. Each village has several great masks that represent its collective memory and which are glorified during times of happiness and abundance. Masks are regarded both as divinities and repositories of knowledge. They dictate the community's values that give the clan cohesiveness and help preserve its customs. For example, harvest-time yields, or whether a woman will give birth to a son or a daughter, are believed to depend on masks, and no important action is undertaken without first addressing a mask to request its assistance.

Dogon

The Dogon, who live along Mali's Falaise de Bandiagara (Bandiagara Escarpment), are among the region's most intriguing people, having unusual belief systems, masks and ceremonies.

The Dogon are traditionally farmers, and work for both men and women is a central feature of their society. Crops such as millet and onions are planted in the fields below and atop the escarpment and on terraces created on the lower slopes. Unsurprisingly, many Dogon now choose to farm down on the plains where water is more plentiful.

Although Islam and Christianity have taken hold, traditional belief systems remain at the centre of Dogon life. Rituals surrounding masks, ceremonies, sacred spaces and relationships with the natural world are among the most intricate in Africa.

Dogon: People of the Cliffs (2001), by Agnes Pateaux, combines beautiful photography with text that gets to the heart of Dogon society, from the aura of blacksmiths to the changes assailing Dogon ways.

Ewe

The Ewe people live in Ghana and are the most important ethnic group in southern Togo. Inhabiting forests and fertile riverine soils, they are accomplished agriculturalists and their cultivation of yams (a staple of the Ewe diet) has taken on a near-mythical status. The annual Ewe Yam Festival, called Hogbetsotso, is the highlight of their year and involves farmers presenting their crops to the ancestors and purifying ceremonial stools where, the Ewe believe, ancestral spirits reside. Funeral rites are another intricate Ewe ceremony.

Ewe chiefs, who are elected by consensus, must keep their heads covered in public and must never be seen to be drinking. More generally, the Ewe are known for their hard work, tidy villages, love of education, spirituality, and the power of their traditional shrines and priests.

The arts play an important role in Ewe life, with their subtly coloured kente cloth (techniques learned from Ashanti weavers taken as prisoners by the Ewe) and for their *vu gbe* (talking drums) taking centre stage. The tonality of the Ewe spoken language and the rhythm of particular phrases and proverbs are combined in drumming to produce messages that range from the commonplace, which everyone understands, to a specialised repertoire known only to the master drummers. Drum language is used for communication, especially in times of crisis, and is an integral part of religious song and dance.

Fang

The Fang, a Bantu people, are the dominant ethnic group in Equatorial Guinea, where they make up 80% of the mainland population and wield a political power they have had since independence. They are also found in southern Cameroon.

The Fang are widely believed to have inhabited the Sahel and possibly North Africa but moved down into central Cameroon in the 7th or 8th centuries, possibly to escape invading Muslim armies and Hausa slave traders. Once wrongly thought to be cannibals – the Fang display the bones of their dead as a way of remembering their ancestors – these people suffered greatly at the hands of European slave traders from the 16th to 19th centuries. Despite their current dominance, the Fang only arrived in Equatorial Guinea in the 19th century.

They are renowned for their mix of Christian and traditional beliefs, and for the high quality of their wood and iron artworks.

Fula

One of the most widespread of West African peoples, the Fula (also called Fulani, Peul or Foulbé in French-speaking countries) are tall, lightly built people who have been settling across the West African savannah and Sahel for centuries. They number more than 12 million, and are found from Senegal to Cameroon, and sometimes beyond. The Tukulor (Toucouleur) and the Wolof of Senegal, as well as the Fulbe Jeeri of Mauritania, are all of Fula origin.

Cattle occupy a central position in their society; the Fula are traditionally nomadic cattle herders, following their herds in search of pasture and living in seasonal grass huts resembling large beehives; they're famous for putting the welfare of their animals above their own. Islam also plays a central role: town-dwelling Fula (referred to as Fulani Gida in some areas) adopted Islam as early as the 12th century and were major catalysts in its spread. Fula resistance to colonial rule was fierce, usually coalescing around an inspirational Islamic leader.

The nomadic Fula, or Wodaabé, are known for their public initiation ceremony in which young boys are lashed with long rods to the accelerating rhythm of drums, as part of their passage into manhood. There are many onlookers, including potential brides, and the boys must show no fear, though their ordeal leaves them scarred. At the annual Gerewol festival, where the young Wodaabé meet prospective marriage partners, men pay great attention to their appearance, adorning themselves with shining jewellery, feathers, sunglasses and elaborate make-up – anything to create an impression and to look their best for the women.

Half of a Yellow Sun (2006), by Nigerian novelist Chimamanda Ngozi Adichie, is a stirring tale of the Biafra War with a nuanced look at the often fraught relations between Nigeria's main ethnic groups.

Hausa

The dominant cultural group in northern Nigeria (Hausaland), the Hausa (with 27 million in Nigeria and almost six million in Niger) have played an important role in West African history. From their bases in Kano, Katsina, Sokoto and Zaria, they developed a reputation as a fiercely independent mercantile people, with Islam the dominant force. This mix of spiritual devotion and worldliness means that you'll likely see Quranic script alongside symbols of modern technology, such as bicycles and aeroplanes, in the mud-relief patterns on house walls in the old quarters of Nigerian towns such as Kano and Zaria.

The emirs of the Hausa states are known for the pomp with which they live and travel. Their bodyguards traditionally wear chain mail, carry spears and ride strikingly caparisoned horses, while attendants on foot wear red turbans and brilliant red-and-green robes. Except on ceremonial occasions, especially during the Islamic festivals of Eid al-Kebir (Tabaski) and Eid al-Fitr, these days you'll more likely see an emir riding through town in a large American car, with the horn sounding – very Nigeria.

Although the city states, caliphates and trappings of power of Hausaland are what brought the group its renown, rural communities are the bedrock of Hausa society. Many rural Hausa farm grains, cotton and groundnuts; sacks of groundnuts stacked in pyramids are one of the distinctive sights of many Hausa markets.

More than half of the almost 370 million West Africans are Nigerians. The number of Yoruba, Hausa or Igbo alone each exceeds the national population of every other country.

PEOPLES OF WEST AFRICA HAUSA

Igbo

The Igbo (also known as Ibo) occupy densely settled farming areas in southeastern Nigeria. They form Nigeria's third-largest ethnic group with around 25 million Igbos in Nigeria alone. Their proximity to the Gulf of Guinea saw them devastated by slavery, while more than one million Igbo died during the Biafran War (1967–70). The Igbo have a reputation for hard work, ambition and a love of education.

Although predominantly Christian, many Igbo still practise the traditional religion of Odinani. An Igbo receives his destiny or *chi* directly from Chukwu, the benign god or 'great spirit' of creation. At death, a person returns his *chi* and joins the world of ancestors and spirits. From this spirit world, the deceased watches over living descendants, perhaps returning one day with a different *chi*. A traditionalist's daily preoccupation is to please and appease the *alusa*, the lesser spirits, who can blight a person's life if offended and bestow rewards if pleased.

Lobi

Tucked away in southwestern Burkina Faso, northern Côte d'Ivoire and northern Ghana, the Lobi have held fast to their traditions and ancestor-based belief systems, more than most groups in the region. The Lobi are also distinguished by their architecture (they live in distinctive mud-brick compounds resembling small fortresses) and by the fact that they don't use masks. Their name means 'Children of the Forest'.

Most Lobi woodcarvings are of human figures, typically 35cm to 65cm high, which represent deities and ancestors. The woodcarvings are used for ancestral shrines, and traditionally occupied every home. The Lobi also carve staffs and three-legged stools with human or animal heads, as well as combs with human figures or geometric decorations. The carvings are distinguished by their rigid appearance and their realistic and detailed renderings of certain body parts, particularly the navel, eyes and hair.

Many Lobi ceremonies take place on or near the banks of the Mouhoun (or Black Volta) River, which divides Ghana and Burkina Faso and, in Lobi tradition, separates this world from the afterlife. Fish and animals in the river are believed to be sacred. Fetishes, the spirit world and village priests still play an important role in daily Lobi life.

Malinké

The Malinké (in some areas synonymous with, or closely related to, the Mandinka or Mandingo) are part of the larger Mande group, which also includes the Bambara and Soninké and is believed to have originated as early as 4000 years ago, when agricultural peoples of the southern Sahara merged with the indigenous hunter-gatherers of the Niger River basin. Today the Malinké are known as prolific traders and live in southern Mali as well as northern Guinea, Côte d'Ivoire, Senegal and Gambia. Historically, they were famed hunters and warriors, and were prominent converts to Islam from the 11th century. In the mid-13th century the Malinké founded the powerful Empire of Mali.

Originally the Malinké were divided into 12 clans, each with its own king and highly stratified castes. The heads of these 12 clans formed a royal council, which elected a single leader, known as a *mansa*. The traditional hunter societies of the Malinké, with their secret initiation rites, still thrive today.

Music also accompanies almost all of the important events in Malinké life and its tradition of *jelis* or *griots* (praise singers) dates back to the days of the Empire of Mali. *Griots* were traditionally the custodians of West Africa's oral traditions and many born into the *griot* caste now rank among Mali's most famous musicians.

Lobi tradition, backed by the accounts of some Christian missionaries, holds that a Lobi man once converted to Christianity and threw his fetishes in a nearby lake, whereupon the fetishes leapt from the water to reclaim him.

Mossi

When the empires of Mali and Songhaï reigned over West Africa from the 13th to 16th centuries, one group remained outside their orbit: the Mossi, now the largest ethnic group in Burkina Faso. In the 14th century they established powerful kingdoms in this area after leaving their original homeland around the Niger River, and they held off the larger empires of the time through a fierce army of feared warriors. The Mossi are known for their rigid social hierarchies and elaborate rituals, and many continue to follow traditional beliefs. They also exert considerable political influence in Burkina Faso today and the Mossi ruler, the 37th Moro-Naba, is regularly consulted on important issues by the government.

Artistically, the Mossi are best known for their tall wooden antelope masks, often more than 2m high and painted red and white. The masks were worn primarily at funerals.

African Ceremonies (1999), by Carol Beckwith and Angela Fisher, is a masterpiece – a stunning two-volume coffee-table book of photos of different rites and festivals from across Africa.

Pygmy

The Pygmy people (sometimes called Baka) inhabit the forests of Cameroon and Equatorial Guinea, and are considered the original forest-dwelling people of the region. Numbering less than one million, and generally short in stature, they have traditionally followed a hunter-gatherer lifestyle. Their history is preserved in oral form and they are renowned for their polyphonic vocal music, which plays a central role in daily life and important ceremonies.

They have also suffered widespread discrimination in the countries they inhabit and some live in conditions of semi-slavery.

Senoufo

The Senoufo, a farming people who live in Côte d'Ivoire, western Burkina Faso and southern Mali, are, like the Lobi, renowned for having maintained their traditions in the face of assaults by colonialism, Islam and Christianity. The northern Côte d'Ivoire town of Korhogo is considered the Senoufo capital.

Animals are held in high regard in Senoufo culture, and when someone dies it is believed that they are transformed into the clan's animal totem. As a result, many Senoufo dances are associated with animals. One of these is the dance of the leopard men, which is performed in Natiokabadara, near Korhogo, as well as in other Senoufo areas when young boys return from their Poro (part of the secret Lô society) initiation-training sessions. In this and other dances, spirit masks (often of animal heads) are instrumental in making contact with the gods and driving away bad spirits.

When someone dies in traditional Senoufo society, the corpse is carried through the village in a procession, while men in grotesque masks chase away the soul of the deceased to ensure it leaves the village in peace and departs for the afterlife.

Songhaï

The Songhaï, heirs to the Empire of Songhaï, live predominantly in Niger and in northern Mali, between Timbuktu and Gao. They trace their roots back to a 7th- or 8th-century exodus from Mandinke lands, while other theories claim that the Tuareg founded the original Songhaï state; yet another hypothesis states that the ancestors of the Songhaï were the original inhabitants of the Upper Niger.

Songhaï villages are divided into neighbourhoods, each of which elects a head. These heads then come together to elect a village chief, who typically is of noble descent. Most Songhaï consider themselves Muslim, although their religious practices are often mixed with strong traditional elements, including ancestor worship and witchcraft. Large communities often have both a mosque and a troupe that specialises in mediums for spirit intervention.

Tuareg

The Tuareg are a nomadic people who traditionally roamed the Sahara from Mauritania to western Sudan; they now live in Niger, Mali, Libya and Algeria, with smaller communities in Burkina Faso and Nigeria. Tuareg origins lie with the Berbers of North Africa (their language, Tamashek, has Berber roots). Droughts and political conflict have ensured that few Tuareg remain purely nomadic.

The Tuareg traditionally follow a rigid status system, with nobles, blacksmiths and slaves all occupying strictly delineated hierarchical positions. The *taguelmoust* (veils) that are the symbols of a Tuareg's identity serve as protection against the desert sand and wind-borne spirits, and as a social requirement; it is considered improper for a Tuareg man to show his face to a man of higher status.

Tuareg women – who are not veiled and who enjoy an unusual degree of independence – weave artificial strands into their plaits and attach cowrie shells. They also can be recognised by their large pieces of silver jewellery.

Wolof

The Wolof heartland is in Senegal, where they comprise about 39% of the population. They also live in Gambia (13%) and Mauritania (7%).

Although Islam has been an influence in Wolof areas since the 11th century, and Sufi Muslim Brotherhoods form the backbone of Wolof society, traditional beliefs persist. For example, there is a belief in a snake monster so terrible that to look upon it causes death. In order to guard against witches and other forms of evil, many Wolof wear leather-bound amulets containing written verses of the Quran.

Wolof society is hierarchical, with hereditary castes determining status and traditional occupations such as blacksmiths and *griots*. The

The Pastoral Tuareg: Ecology, Culture, and Society (1997), by Johannes and Ida Nicolaisen, is a comprehensive two-volume study of the Tuareg, with good photographs.

Wolof, who are of Fula origin, tend to be tall and striking in their traditional flowing robes of white, dark blue or black.

Yoruba

The Yoruba, almost 30-million strong, are perhaps the largest ethnic group in West Africa, with their homeland extending from southwestern Nigeria into neighbouring Benin. It was here that the powerful Yoruba Kingdom of Ife (12th to 16th centuries) and Oyo Empire (17th to early 20th centuries) held sway over one of the region's most populous corners.

Yoruba traditionally live in towns, migrating seasonally to their more distant farmlands; the Nigerian cities of Lagos and Ibadan are considered important centres of Yoruban life. This urban culture has facilitated the development of trade and elaborate arts, including the famous Benin bronzes. Every Yoruba town has an *oba* (crowned chief). The traditional head of all Yorubas is the *alafin,* who lives at Oyo, in Nigeria, while the *oni* (chief priest) lives at Ife. Formality, ceremony and hierarchy govern social relations, and ostentation in dress and jewellery is a social requirement for women at traditional functions.

Many Yoruba are now Christian, although traditional practices persist, among them the belief that ancestor spirits, which reside in an afterworld known as Kutome, hold powers of protection over the living. During the annual Egungun Festival, these ancestors are summoned by members of the secret Egungun masking society to return, so as to restore the cosmic balance upset by human failings, and to advise their descendants.

Famous members of the Senegalese Wolof community include musician Youssou N'Dour, the late film-maker Ousmane Sembène, and the former president of Senegal, Abdoulaye Wade.

The Yoruba have the highest ratio of twin births of any group in the world and twins occupy an important role in their mythology.

Environment

West Africa's numerous environmental woes – and the precarious subsistence conditions in which many West Africans live – exist alongside some stunning success stories such as the greening of central Niger and the survival of Mali's desert elephants. It is also, according to one UN official, the world's 'ground zero' for vulnerable communities when it comes to climate change. It's as simple and as complicated as that: West Africa faces some of the most pressing environmental issues of our time.

The Land

West Africa spans some of the great landscapes of the African continent. Its geography is the story of three horizontal lines: a northern band of desert, a southern band of woodland and forest, and a semidesert zone in between known as the Sahel. Through it all snakes the region's lifeblood, the Niger River. In the region's tropical south, the vast rainforests of the Congo River Basin cover the land.

African Silences, by Peter Matthiessen, is a classic on African wildlife; the passages on Senegal, The Gambia and Côte d'Ivoire are so beautifully written that you'll return to them again and again.

Mountains

Although West Africa largely consists of a gently undulating plateau, there are some important highland areas: the borderlands between Nigeria and Cameroon rising to Chappal Wadi (2418m); the Jos Plateau (1781m) and Shebsi Mountains (2418m) in Nigeria; Mt Bintumani (1945m) in Sierra Leone; the rocky Aïr Mountains in Niger, rising to Mt Bagzane (2022m); Mt Nimba (1752m) in the border area between Guinea, Côte d'Ivoire and Liberia; and the Fouta Djalon in western Guinea (1538m). The peaks of the volcanic Cabo Verde islands are also notable with the highest being Mt Fogo (2829m). Mt Cameroon (4095m) is the highest point in West Africa.

Rivers

West Africa's highlands create headwaters for several rivers, including the Niger. Other major rivers include the Senegal River, which forms the border with Mauritania; the Gambia River, again giving its name to the country it flows through; the Casamance River in southern Senegal; the Volta River in Ghana and Burkina Faso; and the Benue River (a major tributary of the Niger) in Nigeria and Cameroon.

Until the intrepid Mungo Park reached the Niger River close to Ségou on 21 July 1796, European map-makers were convinced that the river flowed east–west and originated in the Nile or Lake Chad.

Forests

Most of West Africa's coastal forests lie between the equator and 10 degrees north of the equator, where rainfall is heavy. Dense rain-fed lowland forest (or just 'rainforest') contains trees that can reach heights of 45m. The upper branches form a continuous canopy, blocking light from the forest floor.

Rainforests are most commonly found in the Congo Basin, a vast area that includes Equatorial Guinea and southern and eastern Cameroon. Forests and dense woodland can also be found in parts of Liberia, Sierra Leone and southwestern Côte d'Ivoire. Smaller areas of woodland exist in Benin, Ghana, Guinea, Nigeria and Togo. An especially rich bounty of

THE NIGER RIVER

Africa's third-longest river (4100km), the Niger owes its name to the Tuareg phrase *gher-n-gheren,* which means 'river among rivers', and its curious course has fascinated travellers for centuries.

The Niger begins its journey just over 200km from the Atlantic, at a spring in the Fouta Djalon highlands, on the Guinea–Sierra Leone border. Gathering strength and volume from countless mountain streams, the Niger flows deep into West Africa's heart, through the vast Niger Inland Delta of central Mali. From there, the Niger narrows and comes within touching distance of Timbuktu before it comes up against the impenetrable barrier of the Sahara and performs a long, laborious curve (known as the Niger Bend or Boucle du Niger). Thereafter, it courses down into Niger and crosses a slice of Benin before emptying into the Atlantic via a maze of swamps and channels (in Nigeria, west of Port Harcourt) called the Niger Delta.

Apart from its initial descent from the western highlands, the Niger flows on an extremely low gradient and is fed by highly variable rainfall. As such, its high and low points can vary by an extraordinary 10.7m and the river is highly susceptible to drought: in 1972 and again in 1984, the river almost dried up completely. Even more serious than the vagaries of seasonal fluctuations are the threats posed by human activity: by one estimate, the Niger's volume has fallen by 55% since the 1980s due to climate change, drought, pollution and population growth. Fish stocks have fallen, water hyacinth is a recurring problem, and the formation of sand bars has made navigation increasingly difficult. Given that an estimated 125 million people live in the Niger's basin, problems for the Niger could cause a catastrophic ripple well beyond the river's shoreline.

It may be over 25 years old, but *The Strong Brown God,* by Sanche de Gramont, remains the most comprehensive geographical and human history of the Niger.

rainforests, set amid volcanic mountains, straddles the border between Nigeria and Cameroon.

The Coast

If West Africa is overshadowed by the looming Sahara desert to the north, it is barricaded by the equally formidable Atlantic Ocean to the south. Many major cities (including 14 out of 21 West African capitals, if you include the island-based Malabo in Equatorial Guinea) are strung out along the coast like beads in a chain, in some areas forming an almost constant linear urban sprawl, cut only by national frontiers.

The Sahara

The Sahara is a notoriously unwieldy beast to quantify, but most estimates put its size at over nine million sq km, comparable in size to the continental United States. It occupies more than half of Mali, 75% of Mauritania and 80% of Niger.

The Sahara may be the world's largest dry desert, but it is also the youngest. Thousands of years ago the area was a fertile land, alternating between savannah grasslands, forests and lakes watered by relatively frequent rainfall. It was home to abundant wildlife – elephants, giraffes, hippos, lions and other African mega-fauna – as depicted in the rock art found across the Sahara, especially in Niger's Aïr Mountains and Mali's Adrar des Ifôghas. The change began around 7000 years ago, when rains became less frequent and the land more arid. It was a gradual process that took 4000 years. As the Sahara became a desert, its people and wildlife retreated south. By 400 BC, the Sahara was the desert we know today, albeit on a smaller scale.

Contrary to popular misconceptions, sand covers just 20% of the Sahara's surface and just one-ninth of its area rises as sand dunes. More

Sahara Conservation Fund (www.saharaconservation.org or www.facebook.com/SaharaCF/) is one of few sources of information on the wildlife of the Sahara, and the efforts being undertaken to protect it. Its work was instrumental in convincing Niger's government to create Africa's largest protected area, the Termit & Tin Toumma National Nature and Cultural Reserve (97,000 sq km).

typical are the vast gravel plains and plateaus such as the Tanezrouft of northwestern Mali. The Sahara's other signature landform is the desert massif, barren mountain ranges of sandstone, basalt and granite such as the Aïr Mountains (Niger) and Adrar des Ifôghas (Mali).

By one estimate, the Sahara is home to 1400 plant species and 50 species of mammals.

The Sahel

The Sahel – a horizontal band stretching from the Atlantic Coast to the Nile – is the transition zone between the forested lands of the south and the Sahara to the north. The Sahel is one of the harshest stretches of inhabited geography on earth, beset by drought, erosion, creeping desertification, periodic locust invasions and increasingly infertile land.

That said, within its boundaries are many different subregions. Among these are zones that are variously described as semidesert savannah, Guinea savannah, Sudanese savannah, dry savannah or dry woodland savannah. In the north, near the true desert, the Sahel is dry, dusty, sparsely vegetated and barely distinguishable from the Sahara, but in the south, nearer the forests, it is greener and contains areas of light woodland fed by more plentiful rains.

Although the Sahel's boundaries are not fixed, the countries of West Africa that are considered to be all or partly in the Sahel are Senegal, The Gambia, Guinea, Mali, Burkina Faso, Niger and Nigeria. The northern parts of the coastal countries of Côte d'Ivoire, Ghana, Togo, Benin and Cameroon are relatively dry and sometimes described as having a Sahelian climate or vegetation.

Wildlife

West Africa's tropical south is one of Africa's least-known yet most prolific wildlife areas, from the marine mammals of the coast to the forest species of the forested interior. Equatorial Guinea in particular is rich in mammal species. Wildlife-watching here often involves expensive and serious expeditions out into remote areas, but it's almost always worth it.

Further north, human beings rule in West Africa's northern heartland, and it's possible that, no matter how long you spend here, you may never see more than the occasional reptile or hear more than a troop of monkeys, caterwauling through the trees but out of view. The once-plentiful wildlife of the region has been reduced by deforestation, encroaching deserts, ever-expanding human populations and drought, to small, isolated pockets. As a result, West African animals are wild, wary and unaccustomed to large-scale safari tourism.

But, for all the doom and gloom, this northern section of West Africa does have some excellent national parks that are home to many of Africa's classic mammal species. Yes, you have to travel further to see the animals than elsewhere on the continent, and these animals may retreat into the canopy at the first sign of human beings, but for wildlife-watching purists, this is how wildlife safaris used to be: a place where the sense of a real quest survives without carloads of camera-toting tourists outnumbering the animals.

West Africa is also a world-class birdwatching destination.

Mammals

Across its 21 countries, West Africa has an extraordinary diversity of mammal species and, while the situation for much of the region is mostly grim, there are pockets of good news. Two of West Africa's most emblematic and endangered herds – the giraffes at Kouré in Niger and Mali's desert elephants – are holding their own in the most difficult of

---

ENVIRONMENT WILDLIFE

Forty million metric tonnes of Saharan sand reaches the Amazon annually, replenishing mineral nutrients depleted by tropical rains. Half of this dust comes from the Bodele Depression on the Niger–Chad border, although the depression covers just 0.2% of the Sahara.

SOS Sahel International (www.sossahel.org or www.sossahel.ngo) is an NGO dedicated to the Sahel environment. It can be a good source of information on grassroots projects in the region.

circumstances. And primate species are thriving down in the dense rain-forests of West Africa's tropical south.

Elephants

In the 2016 Great Elephant Census (www.greatelephantcensus.com) found just 148 elephants in northern Cameroon. For every 10 live elephants found, there were 8.3 carcasses of elephants killed by poachers, almost triple the figure for any other country. Not surprisingly, the census report concluded that 'without intervention, it is possible that the small, rapidly declining population here could go locally extinct'. Greater numbers of forest elephants likely survive in the forests of the southeast, as well as in neighbouring Gabon, Equatorial Guinea and Republic of Congo, but there are no reliable figures for these areas.

The census found that there were around 250 desert elephants remaining in Mali – Africa's northernmost herd and one that is considered at particular risk due to the ongoing conflict and instability in northern Mali. More hopefully, the area known as the W-Arli-Pendjari Complex, a network of parks that straddles the Niger, Burkina Faso and Benin borders and includes Benin's Parc National de la Pendjari, was found to have 8911 elephants. This was more than double the figure estimated 13 years earlier.

Elsewhere, in most cases, West Africa's elephants exist in small, isolated herds and are considered endangered. In Côte d'Ivoire, for example, the vast herds that gave the country its name have been reduced to around 300.

Giraffes

In 2016 the International Union for the Conservation of Nature (IUCN) downgraded the giraffe from a species of Least Concern in 2010 to Vulnerable. The world's tallest land mammal has all but disappeared from West Africa, with the last population surviving outside Kouré, east of Niamey in Niger.

Over the second half of the 20th century this herd shrunk in size from more than 3000 giraffes down to barely 50 in 1996. The threats to their existence came from the destruction of their habitat through desertification and deforestation, as well as disease, poaching, road accidents and farmers killing them to protect crops. It also didn't help that, from April to August 1996, soldiers shot around a dozen of them while trying to carry out a presidential order to capture giraffes for presentation as gifts to friendly foreign leaders.

In the late 1990s the government of Niger and international conservation groups finally launched a campaign to save the last wild giraffes left in West Africa. Intensive conservation efforts have caused a gradual increase in the population – the African Wildlife Foundation (AWF; www.awf.org) estimated in 2014 that there were 403 giraffes in the herd.

Lions

Scientists have for a long time known that lions in West Africa were in decline and that their populations were small. In 2014 they discovered that things were a lot worse than they thought.

Instead of the 21 lion populations across West Africa, just four remained, and three of these contained fewer than 50 lions. In total they found just 400 lions, including only 250 breeding adults. Lions now occupy barely 1% of their former territory range and three of the four remaining populations – in Senegal's Parc National de Niokolo-Koba (just 16 lions) and in two Nigerian Parks, Yankari and Kainji Lake – are considered to be too small to be sustainable in the long term.

The only lion population in West Africa that appears to be viable in the short to medium term consists of more than 350 lions (nearly 90% of West Africa's total) and inhabits the W-Arli-Pendjari Complex. But even there, the lion's future looks precarious without a serious injection of funds over the coming years and decades.

Primate Species

West Africa is particularly rich in primate species and this is one of the best places in the world to see gorillas, the world's largest living primates. Unlike the critically endangered eastern mountain gorilla (which inhabits the mountains of Democratic Republic of Congo, Uganda and Rwanda and numbers fewer than 800), the western lowland gorilla is doing rather well. In 2008, the Wildlife Conservation Society (www.wcs.org) 'discovered' a staggering 125,000 western lowland gorillas in the swamps of northern Republic of Congo, almost doubling previous projections. Today western lowland gorillas inhabit the rainforests of the Republic of Congo, Gabon, Equatorial Guinea and Cameroon.

Chimpanzees are the animal world's closest living relative to humans: we share 99% of their genetic make-up. There aren't many populations in West Africa, but you'll find them in Guinea in the northwest, and the chimps of Côte d'Ivoire's Parc National de Taï are famous for using tools in their daily activities.

Other primate species found in West Africa include colobus, green or vervet monkeys, mangabeys, baboons and galagos (bushbabies), as well as the rare and endangered drill.

All of West Africa's primates are at great risk from the widespread trade in and consumption of bushmeat.

Marine & River Mammals

In rivers, including the upper reaches of the Niger and Gambia Rivers, hippos can sometimes be seen, but numbers are low. Some hippos have adapted to live in salt water and exist in coastal areas such as the Orango Islands National Park in the Arquipélago dos Bijagós in Guinea-Bissau.

ENVIRONMENT WILDLIFE

WHERE TO SEE PRIMATES

Gorillas
➡ Monte Alen National Park, Equatorial Guinea
➡ Parc National de Campo-Ma'an, Cameroon

Chimpanzees
➡ Monte Alen National Park, Equatorial Guinea
➡ Bossou, Guinea
➡ Parc National du Haut Niger, Guinea
➡ River Gambia National Park, The Gambia
➡ Parc National de Taï, Côte d'Ivoire
➡ Tiwai Island Wildlife Sanctuary, Sierra Leone

Other Primates
➡ Ureca, Equatorial Guinea (red colobus)
➡ Afi Mountain Drill Ranch, Nigeria (drills)
➡ Limbe Wildlife Centre, Cameroon
➡ Tiwai Island Wildlife Sanctuary, Sierra Leone (Diana monkey)

BEST BIRDWATCHING

- ➡ Parc National du Banc D'Arguin, Mauritania
- ➡ Parc National des Oiseaux du Djoudj, Senegal
- ➡ Parc National du Delta du Saloum, Senegal
- ➡ Abuko Nature Reserve, The Gambia
- ➡ Gola Rainforest National Park, Sierra Leone
- ➡ Tiwai Island Wildlife Sanctuary, Sierra Leone

A few forest areas, including Liberia's Sapo National Park and Sierra Leone's Tiwai Island Wildlife Sanctuary, are home to very small populations of elusive pygmy hippos, which are less aquatic than their larger cousins.

Sightings of humpback whales are also possible. They can be seen off Freetown Peninsula in Sierra Leone, especially in September and January.

Dolphins, too, can be seen anywhere along the West African coast but especially where the region's rivers meet the ocean; watch especially for the rare and elusive humpback dolphin.

Highly endangered species that have somehow survived the human and climatic onslaught include the following:

Birds of West Africa, by W Serle, is a must for birders who want to know which species are present and where you're most likely to see them.

➡ manatees (sea cows, a giant seal-like relative of the elephant) in Mali's Réserve d'Ansongo-Ménaka, in Senegal's Parc National de Niokolo-Koba, or in mangrove and delta areas along the coast, including the Parque Nacional de Cantanhez in Guinea-Bissau

➡ one of the world's last colonies of monk seals along Mauritania's remote Atlantic coast, especially at the Réserve Satellite du Cap Blanc, near Nouadhibou.

Antelopes & Other Ungulates

The most easily seen mammal species include several beautiful antelope species, such as bushbuck, reedbuck, waterbuck, kob, roan, eland, oribi and several varieties of gazelle and duiker; the sitatunga is more shy. The Sahel-dwelling dama gazelle is the largest gazelle species in Africa, but it is now close to extinction as its grazing lands have been taken over by cattle and reduced by desertification. The red-fronted gazelle may still survive in Mali's remote far east. Wild pig species include giant hogs and bush pigs (the West African species is often called the red river hog), which inhabit forest areas, and warthogs, frequently seen in drier savannah areas. Buffaloes in West Africa inhabit forest regions; they are smaller and redder than the East African version.

It is estimated that 5000 million birds from Europe and Asia migrate to tropical Africa every year, a journey of up to 11,000km – less than half make it home, either dying en route or preferring to remain in Africa.

Birds

West Africa lies along one of the busiest bird migratory routes between Europe and Africa, and more than 1000 species have been recorded. Many are endemic, while others are passing migrants, flying down the Atlantic coast to and from their wintering grounds, and some are African nomads moving within the continent in pursuit of seasons of plenty. Among those you're likely to see are flamingos, storks and pelicans (around waterways), gannets and fish-eating cormorants (in coastal areas), turacos – including the striking violet turaco – and African grey and red-billed hornbills.

One of West Africa's best birdwatching destinations is tiny Gambia, with more than 560 species recorded and several easily accessed birdwatching sites, among them Abuko Nature Reserve, Tanji River Bird Reserve, Kiang West National Park and Baobolong Wetland Reserve.

Senegal also offers excellent birding, particularly in Parc National de la Langue de Barbarie and Parc National des Oiseaux du Djoudj. Both are famous for vast pelican and flamingo flocks. Parc National de Niokolo-Koba and the Parc National du Delta du Saloum are some other terrific sites, and there are several other good sites in northern Casamance near Kafountine.

Sierra Leone's Tiwai Island Wildlife Sanctuary hosts hornbills, kingfishers and the rare white-breasted guinea fowl. Around Mt Bintumani, the endangered rufous fishing-owl has been sighted, while Outamba-Kilimi National Park supports kingfishers, waders, raptors and the spectacular great blue turaco. The rainforest-rich Gola Rainforest National Park is another fine birding destination, home at last count to 333 bird species, including the Gola malimbe, while the Kambui Hills Forest Reserve is home to the white-necked rockfowl. Liberia's Sapo National Park and Côte d'Ivoire's Comoé National Park each host in excess of 500 species.

Further afield, other destinations that draw birders include Ghana's Mole National Park, Cameroon's Park National de Korup, Mauritania's Parc National du Banc d'Arguin and Equatorial Guinea's Bioko Island.

Reptiles

Crocodiles & Snakes

West Africa's most notable reptile is the Nile crocodile, which was once abundant all over the region; few remain, due to hunting and habitat destruction. Your best chance to see them is along the larger rivers such as the Gambia, Senegal and Niger, although an unlikely population also survives in Mauritania's Saharan oasis of Matmata. Two lesser-known species, the dwarf crocodile and slender-nosed crocodile, also occur.

West Africa has a full complement of both venomous and harmless snakes, but most fear humans and you'd be 'lucky' to even see one. The largest snake is the non-venomous python, which grows to more than 5m in length. It kills by coiling around and suffocating its prey – not the nicest way to go, but fortunately it doesn't usually fancy humans. The venomous puff adder, which reaches about 1m in length and enjoys sunning itself, isn't aggressive but, being very slow, it's sometimes stepped on by unwary people before it has had time to wake up. When stepped on, it bites. Take special care when hiking in bush areas, especially in the early morning when this snake is at its most lethargic. The Sahara is home to the venomous horned viper.

Turtles & Tortoises

Turtles survive along the coast of West Africa and on some of the offshore islands. The females come to the beaches to lay eggs in the sand, sometimes several hundred at a time. The threats faced by turtles are

According to the UNEP, Mt Nlonako in southwestern Cameroon is the richest single locality in the world for snake species – 63 different species.

ENVIRONMENT WILDLIFE

WILD WILDLIFE

If you set out in search of wildlife, remember that West Africa's wildlife is just that – wild. *Always* keep a healthy distance between you and any elephant, lion, rhino or other wild animal that you may be lucky enough to encounter. *Never* get between a mother and her calves or cubs, and invest in a telephoto lens instead of approaching an animal at close range. On safaris, heed the advice of your guide and respect park regulations, especially those that require you to stay in a vehicle. Exercise care when boating or swimming, and be particularly aware of the dangers posed by crocodiles and hippos.

considerable, and include damage to nesting areas by humans, hunting, and the effects of water pollution – turtles often mistake floating plastic bags for food.

These are the best places to see sea turtles:

⇒ **Ebodje, Cameroon** Turtles begin arriving from November.

⇒ **Ureca, Equatorial Guinea** Four main species (Atlantic green, leatherback, hawksbill and Olive Ridley) can be seen from November to January.

Other places where sea-turtle sightings are possible:

⇒ **Arquipélago dos Bijagós**, Guinea-Bissau

⇒ **Boa Vista**, Cabo Verde (July and August)

⇒ **Akwidaa Beach**, Ghana

The Sahara is home to an unlikely inhabitant: the spurred tortoise somehow survives in the Aïr Mountains of northern Niger.

Plants

Forest & Woodlands

The Congo Basin is one of the most important repositories of forest flora on the planet – the area of lowland rainforest along West Africa's coast from the Niger Delta to the Congo River mouth is considered the mother lode of endemic forest plant species. According to the World Wildlife Fund for Nature (wwf.panda.org), the Democratic Republic of Congo (DRC), for example, has more than 11,000 recorded forest species, around 10% of which are endemic. Much smaller Cameroon has around 8000 plant species and a staggering 227 plant species were found in a forest plot of just 100 sq metres, one of the highest counts ever recorded anywhere.

Savannah & Semidesert

In the northern parts of the coastal countries the climate is drier, and forest and woodland yield to savannah and semidesert. Here, the landscape consists primarily of well-dispersed trees, especially acacia and low scrub

ENVIRONMENT PLANTS

THE BAOBAB: KING OF THE AFRICAN BUSH

There's nothing quite like the baobab *(Adansonia digitata);* its thick, sturdy trunk and stunted root-like branches are an instantly recognisable symbol of Africa. Thanks to its unusual form, many traditional cultures believe that the tree displeased a deity who promptly plucked it in anger and thrust it back into the ground upside down. Ryszard Kapuściński declared it the elephant of the plant world.

Despite the apparent misdemeanours of its ancestor, today's baobab is revered by local people. Its wizened appearance, combined with an ability to survive great droughts and live for many hundreds of years, ensures that the baobab is believed to possess magical powers. Old trees often develop cavities, which are sometimes used to inter a revered *griot* (praise singer).

The baobab is found in most parts of West Africa and serves a variety of practical, often essential, purposes. The hollow trunk sometimes holds rainwater, making it a useful reservoir in times of drought. The tree's large pods (which resemble pendulous Christmas decorations and are sometimes called 'monkey bread') contain seeds encased in a sherbet-like substance that can be eaten or made into a juice-like drink. The pods themselves are used to make cups or bowls (often for drinking palm wine) and as fuel; they burn slowly and are especially good for smoking fish. The leaves of the baobab can be eaten when chopped, boiled and made into a sauce; they can also be dried and ground into a paste to use as a poultice for skin infections and joint complaints. Even the flowers are used as decoration at ceremonies.

bush, although ribbons of dense gallery forest occur along river courses. Gallery forest is similar to rainforest but is fed by groundwater rather than rain, so the vines characteristic of rainforest are absent.

Desert
In true desert, rainfall and vegetation growth are minimal. Apart from desert grasses and small flowers, which can carpet the desert in colour after rains (even after lying dormant for years), the most striking plant is the *Calotropis procera,* otherwise known as the apple of Sodom. Its prolific (but poisonous) green leaves should be no invitation to taste. Wild colocynth melons (think watermelons in the sand) produce brittle, gourd-like fruits that burst open in the sun and scatter their seeds on the wind, but should not be eaten.

National Parks & Wildlife Reserves
West Africa has some outstanding national parks and reserves that provide the last refuge for the region's wildlife, protected areas amid a growing sea of humanity. Others exist in name only.

Whatever their status, few West African parks are set up for tourism – national-park offices are rare and trails are often poorly maintained. Visiting these parks usually requires arranging a visit through a private agency – preferably one from the park's hinterland and with a local guide, to ensure that the proceeds of your visit benefit the local community.

Environmental Issues
There are many environmental issues confronting West Africa, all of them serious. Deforestation and desertification are perhaps the most widespread and urgent of the challenges, but soil erosion, air and water pollution, wildlife destruction, water scarcity, threats to coastal and marine ecosystems, overfishing, drought and the impact of cash crops such as cashews and rubber all pose significant threats to the West African environment.

Deforestation
West Africa was once covered in forests, but only a tiny fraction of the original forest cover remains and even that is under threat. In 1990, for example, forests covered 42.1% of Liberian territory; 15 years later, the figure had dropped to just 32.7%. Other alarming falls were recorded during the same period in Benin (30% to 21.3%) and Togo (12.6% to 7.1%). Deforestation is similarly acute in Côte d'Ivoire.

The extent of the problem is evident from the causes – increased population growth, commercial logging, the clearing of trees for farming and slash-and-burn farming techniques, loss of wildlife habitat – the effects of most of which are either irreversible or require massive investment from often-impoverished governments. Potential earnings in global timber markets, for example, are infinitely more attractive (and lucrative) than preserving wildlife for the trickle of tourists who come to see it.

Conflict and refugee movement can also have important flow-on effects for local forest coverage. During the conflicts in Sierra Leone and Liberia, neighbouring Guinea played host to one of the world's largest refugee populations, especially in the Parrot's Beak region, wedged between its two neighbours. Satellite images from 1974 show that forests completely covered the Parrot's Beak area; by 2002, satellite images showed that none of it had survived the massive human influx.

Desertification
As forest cover diminishes, all too often the desert moves in. Desertification is one of the most serious forms of land degradation, and it's one

Benin has the highest ratio (23%) of protected areas to total territory, followed by Côte d'Ivoire (16.4%), Burkina Faso (15.4%), Ghana (14.7%), and Equatorial Guinea (14.3%). Lagging behind are Cabo Verde (0.56%), Mauritania (1.7%), Mali (2.1%) and Nigeria (2.1%).

In 2016, Nigeria's government launched a $1 billion clean-up of the Niger Delta region which has been plagued by oil spills for decades. Work on the clean-up, however was not due to start until 2018 and could take 25 years to complete.

to which the countries of the Sahel are particularly vulnerable. Some areas of the Sahel are losing over 50 metric tonnes of soil per hectare per year, and the desertification that results has reached critical levels in Niger, Mali and Mauritania, each of which could be entirely consumed by the Sahara within a generation. But desertification is also a problem for countries beyond the Sahelian danger zone: a high-to-moderate risk of desertification exists in Sierra Leone, Liberia, Guinea, Ghana, Nigeria and Senegal, which all suffer from serious erosion.

The major causes of desertification are easy to identify – drought, deforestation and the over-exploitation of fragile soils on the desert margin – and are the result of both human activity and climatic variation. But one of the most significant causes in West Africa is the use of deliberately started fires. Such fires are sometimes necessary for maintaining

MAJOR NATIONAL PARKS & WILDLIFE RESERVES

NATIONAL PARK	COUNTRY	WILDLIFE	BEST TIME TO VISIT
Parc National de la Pendjari (p50)	Benin	elephants, leopards, buffaloes, hippos, lions	Mar-May
Parc Regional du W	Benin/Niger/ Burkina Faso	leopards, lions, cheetahs, elephants, baboons, Nile crocodiles, hyenas, over 300 bird species, 500 plant species	Mar-May; open mid-Dec–mid-Jun
Réserve de Nazinga (p68)	Burkina Faso	elephants, monkeys, crocodiles	Jan-Mar
Parc National de Campo-Ma'an (p125)	Cameroon	rainforest, buffaloes, elephants, mandrills	Dec-Apr
Park National de Korup	Cameroon	oldest rainforest in Africa, 50 large mammal species, over 300 bird species	Nov-May
Réserve de Biosphere du Dja	Cameroon	rainforest, buffaloes, grey-necked rockfowl	Dec-Apr
Parc National de Takamanda	Cameroon	Cross River gorillas	Dec-Apr
Parc National de Taï (p144)	Côte d'Ivoire	rainforest, chimpanzees	Dec-Feb
Monte Alen National Park (p158)	Equatorial Guinea	forest elephants, western lowland gorillas, chimpanzees, buffaloes, crocodiles, leopards, goliath frogs	Jun-Aug
Kiang West National Park (p176)	The Gambia	baboons, colobus monkeys, hyenas, dolphins, crocodiles, over 300 bird species	Nov-May
Tanji River Bird Reserve (p174)	The Gambia	over 300 bird species	Nov-May
Kakum National Park (p199)	Ghana	rainforest, elephants, colobus monkeys, antelopes, 300 bird species, 600 butterfly species	Jan-Mar
Mole National Park (p208)	Ghana	94 mammal species (including elephants), over 300 bird species	Jan-Mar
Wechiau Hippo Sanctuary (p210)	Ghana	hippos	Nov-Jun

soil quality, regenerating savannah grasslands and ecosystems, enabling livestock production and as a form of pest control. But all too often the interval between fires is insufficient to allow the land to recover, thereby exposing the soil to wind and heavy rains, and degrading it beyond the point of recovery.

West Africans are often blamed for the destruction of their own environment, but the reality is far more complex and there are other causes that date back a long way. Many of the problems began in colonial times, when farmers were encouraged to plant thirsty cash crops (such as the peanut) that require intensive farming – traditional methods involved fallow periods, which allowed the soil to regenerate. Thus deprived of essential nutrients, the soil required fertilisers to recover, but these were often too expensive for poor farmers to afford. The soil began to unravel.

NATIONAL PARK	COUNTRY	WILDLIFE	BEST TIME TO VISIT
Parc National du Haut Niger (p226)	Guinea	dry rainforest, hippos, chimpanzees	Nov-Apr
Parque Nacional Marinho João Vieira e Poilão (p238)	Guinea-Bissau	sea turtles	Oct-Nov
Parque Nacional das Ilhas de Orango (p237)	Guinea-Bissau	saltwater hippos, crocodiles	Nov-Apr
Parque Nacional de Cantanhez (p239)	Guinea-Bissau	chimpanzees, elephants, colobus monkeys, baboons, manatees	Nov-Apr
Sapo National Park (p251)	Liberia	forest elephants, pygmy hippos, chimpanzees, over 500 bird species	Nov-Apr
Parc National du Banc d'Arguin (p268)	Mauritania	migratory birds	Dec-Jan
Afi Mountain Drill Ranch (p291)	Nigeria	rescued drills, chimpanzees	Oct-Feb
Parc National de la Langue de Barbarie (p328)	Senegal	hundreds of bird species	Nov-Apr
Parc National des Oiseaux du Djoudj (p330)	Senegal	pelicans, flamingos, over 350 bird species	Nov-Apr
Parc National de Niokolo-Koba (p331)	Senegal	lions, 80 mammal species, 350 bird species	Dec-May
Parc National du Delta du Saloum (p326)	Senegal	red colobus & patas monkeys, hyenas, sea turtles, dolphins	Nov-May
Gola Rainforest National Park (p352g)	Sierra Leone	rainforest, 333 bird species, elephants, leopards, zebras, duikers	Nov-Apr
Tiwai Island Wildlife Sanctuary (p351)	Sierra Leone	pygmy hippos, chimpanzees, 120 bird species	Nov-Apr
Outamba-Kilimi National Park (p350)	Sierra Leone	elephants, primates, hippos,	Nov-Apr
Parc National de Fazao-Malfakassa (p367)	Togo	elephants, monkeys, antelopes, over 200 bird species	Dec-May

ENVIRONMENT ENVIRONMENTAL ISSUES

BIODIVERSITY HOT SPOT: GUINEAN FORESTS OF WEST AFRICA

Of 34 internationally recognised 'biodiversity hotspots', eight are in Africa. In order to qualify as a biodiversity hot spot, a region must contain at least 1500 species of vascular plants (ie more than 0.5% of world's total) and have lost at least 70% of its original habitat. Although only one of these – the Guinean forests of West Africa – is in West Africa, it is so vast that it passes through nine of the 19 West African countries. This hot spot covers the heavily populated coastal belt and its hinterland, and includes Guinea, Sierra Leone, Liberia, Côte d'Ivoire, Ghana, Benin, Togo, Nigeria and southwestern Cameroon, as well as Equatorial Guinea and São Tomé & Príncipe. As such, it's a hugely significant indicator of the state of West Africa's environment.

The original extent of West Africa's Guinean forests was 620,314 sq km, of which only 93,047 sq km remain. It is also home to 31 endemic threatened birds, 35 endemic threatened mammals and 45 endemic threatened amphibians. The most prominent of the threatened mammals are pygmy hippos, Liberian mongoose, 12 primate species (including chimpanzees and gorillas), the African golden cat and the elephant. It also has what is easily the highest population density of any of the world's hot spots – 137 people per sq km.

The Guinean forests are home to 320 mammal species (more than 25% of Africa's mammals and including more than 20 primate species), 785 bird species, 210 reptile species, 221 amphibian species and over 9000 plant species, of which 1800 are endemic. Despite being such an important storehouse for Africa's biodiversity, less than 20% of the territory is adequately protected. The hot spot's landmark conservation parks – Sapo National Park (Liberia), Kakum National Park (Ghana), Korup National Park (Cameroon) and Takamanda National Park (Cameroon) – provide an example of what can be done, but many more protected areas are needed, as is the development of conservation corridors, agro-forestry projects and a greater emphasis on ecotourism. Major threats include unregulated logging, mining, hunting (especially the trade in bushmeat) and human encroachment.

This process was exacerbated by well-intentioned animal husbandry and well-building schemes funded by the EU in the 1960s and '70s. Herd sizes increased without any accompanying growth in pasturelands. In the absence of fodder, the additional cattle and goats ate the grasses and thorns that bound the soil together. Patches of desert began to appear around villages that once lay many kilometres south of the desert's southern boundary. As populations increased and enticements by Western seed companies prompted more farmers to increase the land under cultivation, the few remaining trees and forests were cut down, thereby accelerating a process that began centuries ago.

Sahara: A Natural History (2002), by Marq de Villiers and Sheila Hirtle, covers the natural and human history of the Sahara like no other recent book, and the lively text makes it a pleasure to read.

Community-Based Conservation

Sustainable environmental protection usually only works if it involves local communities and provides them with the material benefits (tourism, sustainability of resources for future generations) that derive from preserving pristine environments.

The Gambia is the star performer among West African countries when it comes to ecotourism, with a host of community projects, eco-lodges and wildlife parks. In addition to these, several forestry projects in The Gambia recognise this delicate balance, fusing environmental protection with traditional sources of livelihood. Natural woodland areas are not simply fenced off, but rather used in a sustainable way for the benefit of local communities, with the emphasis on sustainable resource management. In The Gambia's Kiang West National Park, limited cattle grazing and (more controversially) rice cultivation is permitted. Dead wood can be used for timber, fruits and edible leaves can be collected, and grasses

ENVIRONMENT ENVIRONMENTAL ISSUES

PURIFY YOUR WATER & SAVE THE ENVIRONMENT

When confronted by West Africa's often overwhelming environmental issues, it's easy to feel helpless. But there is one small but very significant thing you can do to minimise your impact on the environment: don't buy bottled water. Instead, purify tap water for your drinking needs. Plastic water bottles and plastic bags are one of the most visible blights on the West African landscape; you'll find plastic water bottles (and half-litre bags of mineral water) everywhere for sale when they're full, and then again littering the streets, fields and roadsides once empty. Water purification has come a long way since the days of unappealing iodine treatments, and one purification system we've trialled on the road in West Africa are Micropur tablets, although there are plenty of other brands on offer. The impact of travelling this way is easily calculated: if you drink 150L of purified water, you'll keep around 100 plastic water bottles off the streets, not to mention saving a considerable amount of money (in the UK Micropur costs UK£15 per 100 tablets, enough to purify 100L).

can be harvested for thatch. These products can be used or sold, but all activities take place without destroying the growing trees. In this way, local people view the forest as a source of produce, income or employment, and have a real incentive to protect it in the long term. Local inhabitants also take a leading role in environmental planning – at Niumi National Park, also in The Gambia, community groups have been established to give local people a formal voice in the park's management structure.

In Burkina Faso, small-scale NGO projects encourage farmers to return to traditional methods of cultivation, in particular the laying of *diguettes*, stone lines along field contours, which slow water run-off, maximise water penetration and reduce erosion. And in Niger, putting land conservation in the hands of local farmers has proved to be a stunning success.

Wildlife conservation is another area where involving local communities is beginning to reap rewards. Apart from several locally run sanctuaries in Ghana – such as the Tafi Atome Monkey Sanctuary and Wechiau Hippo Sanctuary – some of the best results are to be seen in protecting Mali's desert elephants, and protecting primates and sea turtles in the region's southwest.

Local community projects around Toubab Dialao and the Réserve de Popenguine in Senegal are fine examples of community-driven conservation. In Côte d'Ivoire, a village tourism project reduced forest clearing and poaching in one of West Africa's largest stands of rainforest in Parc National de Taï prior to the conflict; however, many such projects are yet to restart now that peace has returned to the country.

The UNEP's *Africa: Atlas of Our Changing Environment* (2008) is the dated, but still-definitive study of Africa's environment, with a detailed continental overview, country-by-country statistics and before-and-after satellite photos. It's available from www.earthprint.com.

Bushmeat & Poaching

West Africa has not been spared the poaching holocaust that has decimated elephant and rhino populations in Southern and East Africa. According to the African Wildlife Foundation (AWF; www.awf.org), in February 2012 heavily armed poaching gangs swept down from Sudan and massacred 50% of the elephant population in northern Cameroon's Bouba N'djida National Park. In 2012 and 2013 an estimated 2000 elephants were killed by poachers in Cameroon, and reports of elephant killings continue to emerge from the country with disturbing regularity. In 2016 Cameroon's government publicly burned six tonnes of ivory and ivory products. Even so, the slaughter continues.

Bushmeat – the killing of wildlife for food – is a grave problem across the region and it follows a familiar pattern. As logging and the commercial exploitation of the region's forests increases, roads and human

Nearly half of Togo's land is considered arable, making it one of only two countries in Africa with more than 40% of its land suitable for farming. Just 0.2% of Mauritania can support agriculture.

settlements penetrate ever deeper into the forests, and bushmeat becomes a subsistence food for people living and working in these often-remote areas.

An example of the scale of the problem comes from Equatorial Guinea where the Bioko Biodiversity Protection Program (www.bioko.org) conducts extensive research into local bushmeat practices. Their results found that more than 197,000 wild animals (including more than 35,000 monkeys) passed through Malabo's bushmeat market from 1997 to 2010.

Elsewhere, a 2014 report by the Center for International Forestry Research (CIFOR) found that locals in West and Central Africa consume up to five million tonnes of bushmeat every year.

The dangers posed to wildlife populations are obvious, but there are also serious risks for those who eat bushmeat. Highly contagious viruses, including the Ebola virus and HIV, are thought to have been spread, in some cases, through the human consumption of primate meat.

Survival Guide

Safe Travel

It's difficult to make generalisations about the personal-safety situation in West Africa. While there may be considerable risk in some areas, most places are completely safe. It's always important to be aware of potential problems and to keep your wits about you, but don't be paranoid, and do remember that most travellers experience no problems.

Common Dangers

Beaches

Although you should be careful of thieves and hustlers on West Africa's beaches, a potentially greater risk awaits you in the water. In many places along the West African coast, the beaches can slope steeply and the waves can create a vicious undertow. Never plunge into the ocean without first seeking reliable local advice.

Cities

The danger of robbery with violence is much more prevalent in cities and towns than in rural or wilderness areas, where it's relatively rare. Most cities have their dangerous streets and beaches, but towns can differ; there's more of a danger in places frequented by wealthy foreigners than in those off the usual tourist track. Major cities with questionable reputations include Abidjan, Dakar, Douala, Lagos and Yaoundé. Muggings do occur, although pickpocketing and bag-snatching are more frequent.

Road Safety

Perhaps the greatest danger faced by travellers to West Africa is road accidents. Road conditions outside capitals are bad and, apart from potholes and the inevitable chickens, dangers include people as well as wandering camels, cows and other animals moving into your path. Keep in mind that many locals do not drive, and are thus not aware of braking distances and similar concepts. One of the biggest hazards is overtaking blind or on curves. Throughout the region, travelling by road at night is unsafe; avoid doing so wherever possible.

Scams

The main annoyances you'll come across in West Africa are the hustlers, touts and con artists who prey on tourists. Scams are only likely to be tried in tourist areas; on most occasions, especially in remote or rural areas, you're more likely to come across genuine hospitality. Some examples of scams:

SAFETY TIPS

⇒ Carry as little as possible and lock up what you don't carry.

⇒ Avoid conspicuous displays of wealth, including expensive watches, mobile phones and bulging wallets.

⇒ Keep a small amount of cash separate from your other money, so you don't need to pull out large wads of bills for small expenses.

⇒ Walk purposefully and confidently and be discreet about consulting maps and guidebooks.

⇒ Always take a taxi at night in city areas.

⇒ Avoid getting in taxis with two or more men inside – especially at night and especially if you're female.

⇒ Consider hiring somebody locally to accompany you when walking around a risky area – ask at your hotel for a reliable recommendation.

⇒ Keep your backpack or suitcase locked whenever you leave it anywhere, whether it's on the roof of a bush taxi or in your hotel room.

➤ You may be invited to stay in someone's house in exchange for a meal and drinks, but your new friend's appetite for food and beer may make this an expensive deal. More seriously, someone else might be back at the house going through your bag.

➤ Street sellers offering boxes of cassettes by local musicians frequently sell duds – try to listen to tapes before buying them.

➤ If you're unwise enough to sample local narcotics, or spend time with those who are taking drugs, don't be surprised if the dealers are in cahoots with the local police.

➤ Local lads may approach you in the street pretending to be a hotel employee or 'son of the owner'. Can you lend him some money? Don't be fooled, no matter how much he seems to know about you.

➤ Sock sellers bend down to show you how well the socks would go with your outfit while a friend relieves you of your wallet.

➤ Don't accept drinks from newly found acquaintants on buses or trains, or you may soon find yourself asleep while your new friend runs off with your wallet.

Region by Region
The Sahel & Sahara

The major concern for travelling in the region at the time of research is the Sahara, most of which is off-limits. Much of Mali and Niger remain dangerous, with kidnapping and attacks by Al-Qaeda in the Islamic Maghreb (AQIM) an ever-present possibility in both countries. Northern Burkina Faso is also considered unsafe, although

GOVERNMENT TRAVEL ADVICE

The following government websites offer travel advisories and information for travellers.

➤ **Australian Department of Foreign Affairs & Trade** (www.smartraveller.gov.au)

➤ **Canadian Department of Foreign Affairs & International Trade** (www.voyage.gc.ca)

➤ **French Ministère des Affaires Étrangères et Européennes** (www.diplomatie.gouv.fr/fr/conseils-aux-voyageurs)

➤ **Italian Ministero degli Affari Esteri** (www.viaggiaresicuri.mae.aci.it)

➤ **New Zealand Ministry of Foreign Affairs & Trade** (www.safetravel.govt.nz)

➤ **UK Foreign & Commonwealth Office** (www.gov.uk/foreign-travel-advice)

➤ **US Department of State** (www.travel.state.gov)

the rest of the country is generally fine. Attacks on hotels in Bamako (2015), Grand Bassam (2016) and Ouagadougou (2016) serve as a reminder that the Sahara's problems occasionally impact beyond its remote confines.

The Coast

Most coastal countries in West Africa are considered safe for travel, including Cameroon, Benin, Togo, The Gambia, Ghana, Liberia, Sierra Leone, and Equatorial Guinea; this includes inland regions of these countries. Offshore, Cabo Verde and São Tomé & Príncipe could just be the region's safest destinations.

Senegal, too, is considered safe, but check the prevailing security situation if you're travelling to the Casamance region.

The security situation in Côte d'Ivoire improves with each passing year, but the fragile nature of the peace means that you should exercise great caution, especially in the north and west of the country. Safe travel was possible in Guinea and Guinea-Bissau at the time of research but the ongoing potential for instability in both countries means you should check the situation before travelling.

Nigeria

As with most things in West Africa, Nigeria deserves special mention. This perennially complicated country has one of the highest road accident rates in the world, the extremist group Boko Haram poses a serious risk in the north of the country, crime rates are high in Lagos and outbreaks of violence from the north to the Niger Delta are always possible. And yet, for all its challenges and potential pitfalls, we certainly don't recommend against travelling to Nigeria. Just be careful...

Directory A–Z

Accommodation

Most midsized and larger towns in West Africa offer some sort of accommodation, although quality and price vary widely. In smaller towns, accommodation possibilities are often severely limited.

➡ **B&Bs** Some excellent choices in Burkina Faso.

➡ **Campements** The stalwarts of West Africa's accommodation scene, a cross between a campsite and a basic guesthouse.

➡ **Hotels** Everything from fleapits to local business hotels and up to five-star palaces; such choice is rarely possible beyond cities.

➡ **Missions** Basic rooms offered by Catholic missions are spread across the region.

➡ **Resorts** Senegal, The Gambia and Cabo Verde have dozens of beach resorts catering to fly-in-fly-out visitors.

B&Bs

Burkina Faso is leading the way in smaller, more intimate alternatives to hotels with a range of excellent B&Bs. Pric-es are usually cheaper than hotels, and the warmth and personality of the owners (often a French-Burkinabé couple) is a big drawcard. They're also known as *chambres d'hôtes* or *maisons d'hôtes*. Similar places are appearing in Mali, Mauritania and elsewhere in Francophone West Africa.

Campements

Many towns and many villages in Francophone countries have a *campement* whose primary purpose is not as a campsite in the traditional sense, although some do provide areas where you can pitch a tent and have access to shower facilities. *Campements* offer cheap and simple accommodation, containing the bare necessities, shared facilities and little else, but some are very good quality, with prices on a par with midrange hotels. Either way, they're often the best (and sometimes only) option in small towns. Here, 4WDs fill the compound, and overlanders mingle with backpackers who've just arrived on the latest bush taxi.

In some trekking areas, it is established practice for visitors to sleep on the roof of the *campements* in each village, as this is usually preferable to the stifling rooms.

Camping

There are few dedicated campsites in West Africa, and those that do exist cater mainly for overlanders in their own vehicle. Some hotels and *campements* allow camping or provide an area where tents can be pitched. Grassy knolls on which to pitch your tent are rare – you often have to force pegs through hard-packed gravel. Camping in the wild is risky in most countries as theft can be a problem; if you do decide to camp, always seek permission from the local village chief before setting up.

Hotels

Most hotels (often called *auberges*) charge for a bed only, with all meals costing extra. If breakfast is included it's usually on a par with the standard of accommodation: a full buffet in more expensive places, instant coffee and bread further down the scale.

Independent travellers on tight budgets are fairly well catered for, but there are almost no backpacker lodges. Although you will come across some gems, most of what's on offer is basic, devoid of any discernible character, and ranges from the recently swept to downright grubby. The showers and toilets are usually shared and often of the squat variety. Some hotels in this price range double as brothels.

Midrange hotels tend to be at their best in the capitals or major towns where you're likely to find at least one place with lovingly maintained rooms, private bathrooms, splashes of local colour, satellite TV and even a swimming pool. Most midrange places, though fine, fall somewhat short of this ideal. Most offer a choice between a fan and air-con.

West Africa has very few top-end hotels outside the capitals and offers little in the way of exclusive wildlife lodges or tented camps as found in East or Southern Africa.

Missions

If you're travelling on a tight budget, mission accommodation can be a good alternative to budget hotels, although rooms are usually reserved for mission or aid workers and are open to others only on a space-available basis. Usually called *missions catholique,* they're invariably clean, safe and good value, although these are not places to stagger home drunk at 4am – at many missions travellers are only allowed to stay if they respect the rules.

Outdoor Sleeping

In many parts of West Africa, particularly in the Sahel during the hot season, people often sleep outside their hut or on the flat roof of their house as it's much cooler. In some cheap hotels this is also possible, and carrying a mattress onto the roof – where you'll have some breeze and views of the stars – is usually allowed if you ask. Remember, however, to take all necessary precautions when it comes to mosquitoes.

Resorts

You'll find European-style resorts all along the West African coast, but the best

facilities are at those that cater to Europeans looking for a comfortable, two-week beach holiday. These are especially popular in Senegal, The Gambia and Cabo Verde, where you'll find all-inclusive packages of meals, accommodation and airport transfers. Although it's occasionally possible to get a room by simply walking in off the street, most rooms (and the best deals) are reserved for those who book the whole package through a travel agency in Europe.

Activities

West Africa has some world-class activities to get involved in, with diving and snorkelling, deep-sea fishing, hiking, rock climbing, surfing and windsurfing all possible. Unlike elsewhere in the world, you may be the only traveller taking part, but the flipside is that infrastructure can be rudimentary.

Cycling

In several parts of West Africa, bicycles can be hired by the hour, day or week, and can be a good way to tour a town or area. Your choice may range from a new, imported mountain bike (*vélo tout terrain* in French, or VTT) to ancient, single-gear, steel roadsters.

Away from tourist areas, it's almost always possible to find locals willing to rent their bicycles for the day; good places to enquire include the market or your hotel. Costs range from US$1 to US$10 per day, depending on the bicycle and the area. Remember to always check the roadworthiness of your bicycle, especially if you're heading off-road.

The flat roads of Burkina Faso are particularly good for cycling – they even have their own cycling event, the annual Tour de Faso. The best cycling is around Banfora in the country's southwest; cycling tours are possible around the

otherworldly Sindou Peaks. For mountain biking, try the northern coast of São Tomé on São Tomé & Príncipe.

Desert Expeditions

For many travellers, West Africa means the Sahara, and deep desert expeditions used to be among the region's most rewarding activities. The security situation means that desert expeditions into the Sahara were not safe at the time of research.

Diving & Snorkelling

Cabo Verde is the best place in West Africa to go diving and snorkelling amid the dolphins, sharks and even whales, especially off the islands of Boa Vista and Sal. It's possible to take open-water PADI dive courses at both places, although remember that Cabo Verde has no decompression chambers. March to November are the best months.

One emerging diving and snorkelling destination is São Tomé & Príncipe, while there are reasonable diving possibilities off Dakar in Senegal and around the Banana Islands in Sierra Leone.

Fishing

The Atlantic waters off West Africa are some of the world's richest fishing grounds. Sierra Leone in particular is one of the world's most underrated deep-sea fishing destinations, especially off Freetown and Sherbro Island where many individual line-class records were set.

Other deep-sea fishing possibilities exist off the island of Sal in Cabo Verde, in The Gambia, Guinea-Bissau's Arquipélago dos Bijagós, and Dakar and Saly in Senegal.

Lake Ahémé in Benin offers a fascinating insight into traditional fishing techniques, while Mauritania's Port de Pêche is the region's best fishing market and the place to see what the professionals catch.

In São Tomé & Príncipe, **Makaira Lodge** (☎906 5935; www.makaira-adventure.com; Praia Campanha; s/d/tr with half board €135/165/215) is a fantastic safari tent camp on a beautiful remote beach that specialises in deep-sea fishing, particularly for Atlantic blue marlin.

Hiking

There are many spectacular hiking trails in West Africa. The set-up in this region is very different from that in East or Southern Africa and the experience is often less wilderness than a stirring combination of cultural and natural landscapes. There's little in the way of good walking infrastructure, such as detailed maps, marked trails or trail accommodation, and much of the hiking is through populated areas. All of which means that, as long as you don't mind roughing it, hiking can be a great way to interact with the locals: on foot you can meet on more equal terms than staring at each other through the windows of a bush taxi.

As there's very little formal organisation, expect to arrange everything yourself (so bring a good water filter/purifier, for example). Hiring a local guide (either for the entire expedition or from village to village) is usually a good idea. In some places, because of the distances involved, it may also be necessary to use donkeys, hitching or public transport to get around.

Rock Climbing

West Africa has one world-class climbing destination but it remained off limits at the time of research: the area around Hombori in Mali, where some spectacular rock formations rise above the Sahel and attract a small number of serious rock climbers from Europe. Another area with rock-climbing potential is Mali's Falaise de Bandiagara.

Otherwise, well-known 'climbing' destinations such as Mt Cameroon, Cabo Verde's Mt Fogo and Sierra Leone's Mt Bintumani are actually strenuous hikes that involve no technical climbing.

Surfing, Windsurfing & Kitesurfing

West Africa may not be the world's most famous surfing destination, but discerning surfers are rapidly discovering the region's Atlantic coastline, partly for its waves and partly because you may just have the breaks to yourself.

In general terms, the waves off Mauritania, Cabo Verde, Senegal and The Gambia are best during the European winter, while the coast from Sierra Leone to Gabon offers the best conditions during the European summer.

Ghana has at least two beaches that surfers rave about: Busua and Cape Three Points, while the Cabo Verdean island of Sal is also popular. Even less-known, Bureh Beach, close to Freetown in Sierra Leone, has a fine right-handed break during the rainy season, while Robertsport in Liberia has that unmistakeable call of the remote that hard-core surfers love; *Sliding Liberia,* an award-winning documentary on surfing in Liberia, is definitely worth tracking down. Côte d'Ivoire and Dakar in Senegal are other options.

For wider coverage of surfing in the region, check out Low Pressure (www.lowpressure.co.uk).

Cabo Verde is rightly famous for offering some of the best windsurfing in the world. Most of the buzz surrounds the island of Sal but Boa Vista is also fantastic. Kitesurfing is possible at both places and just north of Nouâdhibou in Mauritania. Other windsurfing possibilities exist in Senegal.

Swimming & Water Sports

You could head to a beach resort in Senegal, The Gambia or Cabo Verde, but West Africa's beaches can be much more appealing than this. In fact, the West African coast has everything you dream of in a tropical beach, with pristine sand, swaying palm trees and, in some cases, not another tourist in sight. You just need to know where to look. Stay informed about the potential dangers of swimming at many West African beaches; locals are usually the best source of information.

There are plenty of water-borne activities (including sailing and other boat hire) in tourist areas such as The Gambia's Atlantic coast or Senegal's Petite Côte. For a less touristy feel, Busua, in Ghana, offers both jet-skiing and sea-kayaking, while jet-skiing can also be arranged on the more placid waters of Lake Bosumtwe.

Children

Children's first impressions of the continent are likely to be the warmth and friendliness of the people. Indeed, many West Africans have grown up in large families and children help open doors to closer contact with local people, who are generally friendly, helpful and protective towards children. In short, travelling with children in West Africa, while not without its challenges, adds a whole new dimension to your journey.

Practicalities

In West African countries with a mainstream tourism industry (eg Senegal and The Gambia), some package-tour hotels cater for families with children and, in large cities, top-end hotels usually have rooms with three or four beds for only slightly more than a double. Alternatively, arranging an extra bed or mattress is generally easy and inexpensive. You'll almost certainly want something with a private bathroom and hot water, thereby precluding most budget accommodation.

Despite such exceptions, there are very few child-oriented facilities in the region. In most hotels there are generally no discounts for children. Likewise, on public transport, if you want a seat it has to be paid for. Most local children travel for free on buses but spend the whole journey on their parent's lap.

In addition to the length and discomfort involved in road journeys, possible concerns include the scarcity of medical facilities, especially outside major cities, and the difficulty of finding clean, decent bathrooms outside of midrange and top-end hotels. Canned baby food, powdered milk and sometimes also baby cereal (usually with sugar in it), disposable nappies, wipes and other items are available in most capitals, but not everywhere, and they can be expensive. It's best to avoid feeding your children street food.

There are other factors to bear in mind when travelling with kids. The rainy season may mean that temperatures are lower, but the risks of malaria and other mosquito-borne diseases are higher. At all times, bring mosquito nets along for your children and ensure they sleep under them. Bring child-friendly mosquito repellent and long-sleeved shirts and trousers.

For more information and hints on travelling with children, Lonely Planet's *Travel with Children* is highly recommended.

Sights & Activities

The specific highlights kids are sure to enjoy include the otherworldly villages and festivals of Koutammakou (the Tamberma Valley, Togo), the stilt villages of Ganvié, Benin, a trip down the Niger River and the beaches, castles and markets all along the West African coast. The thrill of a West African 'safari' to see elephants, gorillas, turtles or other mammals will surely be another highlight.

Electricity

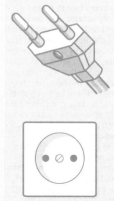

24V/50Hz   220V/230V/50Hz

TEN WEST AFRICA BOOKS FOR KIDS

Start searching for children's books on West Africa and you'll quickly discover a whole library of everything from folk tales to simply told histories that you never knew existed. Aimed at children learning about the diverse peoples of the region, the *Heritage Library of African Peoples: West Africa* is an excellent series. Otherwise, here are some of our favourites:

➡ *The Adventures of Spider: West African Folktales* by Joyce Cooper Arkhurst (suitable for four to eight years)

➡ *The Fire Children: A West African Folk Tale* by Eric Maddern (four to eight years)

➡ *Why Mosquitoes Buzz in People's Ears: A West African Tale* by Verna Aardema (four to eight years)

➡ *The Hatseller and the Monkeys* by Baba Wague Diakite (four to eight years)

➡ *Sundiata: The Lion King of Mali* by David Wisniewski (four to eight years)

➡ *Traditional Stories from West Africa* by Robert Hull (seven to 11 years)

➡ *The Cow-Tail Switch and Other West African Stories* by Harold Courlander (nine to 12 years)

➡ *Indigenous Peoples of Africa – West Africa* by Tony Zurlo (nine to 12 years)

➡ *Ancient West African Kingdoms: Ghana, Mali and Songhai* by Mary Quigley (10 to 14 years)

➡ *Tales from West Africa* by Martin Bennett (mixed ages)

Embassies & Consulates

It's important to realise what your own embassy can and can't do to help if you get into trouble. Remember that you are bound by the laws of the country you are in and this is very much the approach your embassy will take. Your embassy will not be sympathetic if you end up in jail after committing a crime locally, even if such actions are legal in your own country.

In genuine emergencies you might get some assistance, but only if other channels have been exhausted. For example, if you need to get home urgently, a free ticket home is extremely unlikely – the embassy would expect you to have insurance. If you have all your money and documents stolen, it might assist with getting a new passport, but a loan for onward travel will be out of the question.

Note that in some parts of Africa, countries are represented by an 'honorary consul' who is not a full-time diplomat but usually an expatriate with limited (and rarely visa- or passport-issuing) duties. If your country does not have an embassy in a particular country, another embassy will likely be designated to look after your interests (eg Canadian embassies often have an 'Australian interests' section).

Etiquette

Although West Africa is changing, social mores remain conservative. Most locals don't expect you to know all of the rules and will forgive any faux pas. Even so, please keep in mind the following guidelines:

➡ **Attitude** If you're in a frustrating situation, be patient, friendly and considerate. A confrontational attitude can easily inflame the situation (especially when dealing with police officers and immigration officials) and offend local sensibilities.

➡ **Islam** Be respectful of Islamic traditions and don't wear revealing clothing; loose, lightweight clothing is preferable.

➡ **PDAs** Public displays of affection are usually inappropriate, especially in Muslim areas.

➡ **Photography** Always ask permission to photograph people.

➡ **Conversation topics** Avoid vocal criticism of the government or country; the former could get your friends in trouble and many West Africans take the latter personally.

GLBTI Travellers

Homosexuality is explicitly illegal in 10 out of West Africa's 21 countries; the exceptions are Benin, Burkina Faso, Cabo Verde, Côte d'Ivoire, Equatorial Guinea, Guinea-Bissau, Mali, Niger and São Tomé & Príncipe, although remember that even in these countries laws relating to 'offending public morals' may serve a similar purpose. Maximum legal penalties for homosexual acts range from the death penalty in Mauritania and possibly Nigeria, and life imprisonment in The Gambia, to lesser penalties elsewhere.

Regardless of the legality, however, all countries in West Africa are conservative in their attitudes towards gays and lesbians, and gay sexual relationships are taboo and are either extremely rare or conducted in the utmost secrecy. In most places, discretion is key and public displays of affection should be avoided as a means of showing sensitivity to local feelings, advice that applies to homosexual and heterosexual couples.

In the hotels of some countries (eg Guinea and Sierra Leone), same-sex couples, regardless of whether they are indeed a 'couple', will most likely be refused permission to share a room.

Resources

➡ **Afriboyz** (www.afriboyz.com/Homosexuality-in-Africa.html) Worth checking out for (often-dated) links to gay issues around the continent.

➡ **David Travel** (www.davidtravel.com) A US-based tour company offering specialist tours for gay men and women.

➡ **Global Gayz** (www.globalgayz.com/africa) Links to information about the situation for gays and lesbians in most African countries.

➡ **ILGA** (www.ilga.org) Another good resource with information for many West African countries.

Internet Access

High-speed wireless access, or wi-fi, is increasingly the norm across the region, particularly in top-end and many midrange hotels, and in larger towns and cities. Wi-fi access in such places is

FRENCH KEYBOARDS

Many internet cafes in Francophone West Africa have 'French' keyboards, which can slow you down when typing if you're not used to them. Happily, though, some are loaded with English-language settings. To 'Anglicise' a keyboard, look for a 'Fr' icon on the bottom right of the screen, and scroll up to click on 'En'.

sometimes (but not always) free.

Internet cafes are found throughout West Africa and there's usually at least one in every large or medium-sized town. Rates vary but you'll rarely pay more than €1 or US$1 for an hour online. That said, few Internet cafes last the distance these days and wi-fi connections are likely to be far more widespread and useful.

Legal Matters

Although the legal situation varies from country to country, the following guidelines apply across the region:

➡ Drugs are illegal in West Africa, penalties are stiff and prisons are deeply unpleasant. Don't think about bringing anything over the borders or buying it while you're here.

➡ Police, military and other officials are generally polite and on their best behaviour, although petty corruption by local officials and police officers does occur. In your dealings with officialdom, you should always make every effort to be patient and polite in return.

➡ Always carry your passport with you in a secure location inaccessible to pickpockets and keep a photocopy of the main pages (ie the pages with your photo ID and entry stamp or visa) at your hotel.

➡ Homosexual acts are illegal in most countries in the region.

➡ Avoid taking photos of government buildings, bridges, train stations and other landmarks that suspicious officials may deem to be a security risk.

➡ If you find yourself arrested and in prison, you will most likely be granted a single phone call to your embassy, who may be able to arrange a lawyer.

Maps

The regularly updated Michelin map *Africa: North and West* (sheet No 741, formerly No 153, then 953, then 971; scale 1:4,000,000) is one of the best and most detailed, and something of a classic. The map excludes the southernmost portion of Cameroon, as well as Equatorial Guinea, Gabon, the Republic of Congo and São Tomé & Príncipe. For those countries you'll need *Africa Central & South and Madagascar* (No 746; scale 1:4,000,000).

Worth noting are the maps produced by the Institut Géographique National (IGN). The Pays et Villes du Monde series (1:1,000,000) and the more recent IGN Carte Touristique (1:2,000,000) have country maps, which are excellent and available for most countries in West Africa.

To try and track down these and other West Africa maps, your first stop should be Stanfords (www. stanfords.co.uk), the world's largest supplier of maps. They have stores in London, Manchester and Bristol in the UK.

In France, IGN (www.ign.fr) sells its sheet maps at stores in Paris and Dijon.

For GPS electronic maps, try Tracks4Africa (www. tracks4africa.co.za).

Money
ATMs & Eftpos

ATMs are found in most major West African towns and cities. In theory they accept credit and debit cards from banks with reciprocal agreements. In almost all cases, Visa is the most widely accepted credit/debit card at most ATMs, with MasterCard increasingly (but far from universally) possible. Remember that ATMs often go out of service and sometimes run out of money.

There are no internationally connected ATMs in São Tomé & Príncipe.

Whenever you do use an ATM, expect to be slugged with prohibitive bank fees from your bank back home (€15 to €20 is not unusual for a CFA200,000 transaction). For this reason, always take out the maximum the ATM allows.

Black Market

It can sometimes be best to change your money through unofficial sources such as money changers, supermarkets and other businesses, either for convenience (they keep longer hours than banks) or to get a better-than-official exchange rate. In CFA-zone countries, exchange-rate considerations rarely apply because local currency is easily converted and the rate is pegged to the euro, although Abidjan in Côte d'Ivoire has a thriving US-dollar black market. Unofficial money changers are also tolerated by the authorities in some border areas, where there are rarely banks.

Although you may have no choice at a border crossing, the general rule throughout West Africa is to only change money on the street when absolutely necessary. The chances of getting ripped off are high, and even if the money changer is honest, you don't know who's watching from the other side of the street. Even at borders, be alert, as changers are notorious for pulling all sorts of stunts with bad rates and folded notes.

In countries with a real black market (eg Guinea and Nigeria), where you can get considerably more for your money, don't forget that this is against the law. What's more, dealers often work with corrupt police officers and can trap you in a set-up where you may be 'arrested', shaken down and eventually lose all your money.

Cash

Cash is easily the most convenient way to carry your money as it's always the easiest to change. Remember, however, that it cannot be replaced if lost or stolen, even by insurance companies.

In CFA-zone countries, the best currency to travel with is definitely the euro. Other major international currencies such as the US dollar and the UK pound can be changed in capital cities and tourist areas, but at less-favourable rates. In the non-CFA countries, the best currency to travel with is US dollars, with euros and UK pounds sometimes accepted in larger cities.

Whatever currency you decide on, take a mixture of high and low denominations. Rates are better for high denominations (ie €50, €100, US$50 or US$100). Note that the USA changed the design of the US$100 bill in the mid-1990s and old-style US$100 notes are not accepted at some places, especially those that don't have a light machine for checking watermarks. To be sure, try to bring US dollar notes (especially US$100) from 2006 or later.

You may also need some small amounts if you're about to leave the region, or a certain country, and only need to change a small amount. Also, a supply of small denomination cash notes (eg US$1 and US$5 or the euro equivalent) can come in handy for cases when change is unavailable.

In addition to your main travel funds, carry an additional stash of cash with you, preferably kept separate from the rest of your cash and travellers cheques. This will serve as a contingency fund for emergencies.

Unless you're relying on ATMs, try to anticipate your needs and change enough in advance to cover yourself on weekends and during non-banking hours. If you do get stuck outside banking hours, you can try changing money at top-end hotels or tour companies, although rates are likely to be poor. Another option, and much better than changing on the street, is to ask discreetly at a shop selling imported items. 'The banks are closed, do you know anyone who can help me...?' is a better approach than 'Do you want to change money?'.

Credit & Debit Cards

Although things are changing slowly and the situation varies from country to country, you can rarely use a credit card to pay for items, and such occasions are limited to top-end hotels and restaurants, car-rental companies and air tickets; an extra commission is often attached, usually ranging from 3% to 15%. Visa is the most widely accepted card, followed a distant second by MasterCard; credit cards are of especially limited use in Sierra Leone, Guinea-Bissau and Liberia, and you should be wary of using them in Nigeria.

Watching a person put your card through the electronic credit-card machine (as opposed to letting them do it out of sight) is a good idea to ensure you don't receive unwanted bills back home.

NINETEEN COUNTRIES, 12 CURRENCIES

The difficulties of juggling the currencies of the 19 countries in West Africa is ameliorated by the fact that eight countries (Benin, Burkina Faso, Côte d'Ivoire, Guinea-Bissau, Mali, Niger, Senegal and Togo) use the West African CFA (Communauté Financière Africaine) franc, which can be used (or exchanged for local currency) in some other countries, such as The Gambia and Ghana. Many people will also accept it as valid currency, especially in taxis or at market stalls in The Gambia and Guinea.

Two countries (Cameroon and Equatorial Guinea) use the Central African CFA franc. You can't make payments with Central African CFA in the West African CFA zone or vice versa.

Both versions of the CFA are fixed against (and supported by) the euro at a rate of 655.957:1, making it a 'hard' currency. One result of this arrangement is that most banks change euros into CFA without charging a fee or commission. That said, at hotels and foreign exchange bureaux, expect rates of 650 or lower, and plan on paying commissions when changing euro (or any other currency) travellers cheques into CFA.

In recent years, the political leaders of The Gambia, Ghana, Guinea, Nigeria and Sierra Leone – the majority of West Africa's non-CFA block – have spoken of moving towards their own common currency, to be known as the 'eco', which would later merge with the CFA and thereby create a single currency throughout most of West Africa. Don't expect this to happen in a hurry, and it may not happen at all. In the meantime, countries outside the CFA zone each have their own individual currencies.

EXCHANGE RATES AT A GLANCE

COUNTRY	US$1	C$1	A$1	NZ$1	€1	UK£1	¥100
Benin (CFA)	600	440	452	415	656	774	538
Burkina Faso (CFA	600	440	452	415	656	774	538
Cabo Verde (escudo; CVE)	104	74	76	70	110	131	91
Cameroon (CFA)	600	440	452	415	656	774	538
Côte d'Ivoire (CFA)	600	440	452	415	656	774	538
Equatorial Guinea (CFA)	600	440	452	415	656	774	538
The Gambia (dalasi; D)	45	33	34	31	50	59	41
Ghana (cedi; C)	4.1	3	3.1	2.8	4.5	5.3	3.7
Guinea (Guinean fran; GF)	9125	6670	6870	6310	9954	11,768	8160
Guinea-Bissau (CFA)	600	440	452	415	656	774	538
Liberia (Liberian dollar; L$)	94	69	71	65	102	121	84
Mali (CFA)	600	440	452	415	656	774	538
Mauritania (ouguiya; UM)	359	263	271	285	392	464	322
Niger (CFA)	600	440	452	415	656	774	538
Nigeria (naira; N)	305	223	230	211	333	394	273
Sao Tome & Principe (dobra; Db)	22,480	16,440	16,930	15,550	24,530	28,990	20,110
Senegal (CFA)	600	440	452	415	656	774	538
Sierra Leone (Leone; Le)	7525	5502	5667	5207	8210	9704	6732
Togo (CFA)	600	440	452	415	656	774	538

DIRECTORY A-Z MONEY

International Transfers

Western Union Money Transfer has representatives in just about every West African country, usually as part of local banks or post offices.

International bank-to-bank money transfers may save you from carrying large amounts of money, but are best used only as a last resort. Transfers can take three to four days, and sometimes several weeks, to clear. If you do need to transfer money, ask your forwarding bank to send you separate confirmation with full details, including the routing or transfer number, account and branch numbers, and address and telephone contacts. With this, you can then go to the recipient bank with proof that your money has been sent.

Most countries will only give you cash in local currency.

Money Changers

The main places to change money are banks and foreign-exchange bureaux. Where they exist, forex bureaux are often more efficient than banks, usually offer slightly higher rates and are open longer hours, though many don't accept travellers cheques. Charges and commissions vary, with some banks and forex bureaux charging a flat fee, and others a percentage commission; some charge both a fee and a commission. The bank or forex bureau with the higher commission may also offer a higher exchange rate though, so you could still be better off.

Apart from export restrictions, exchanging CFA

francs in countries outside the region is nearly impossible, except in France. In most countries in the CFA zone, it's relatively easy to change remaining CFA francs into euros, but difficult to change CFA francs to dollars. On leaving non-CFA countries, it's usually not possible to reconvert local currency into foreign currency; you can usually change back to CFA francs in The Gambia and Guinea, where it's relatively straightforward, although rates are low. Try and come to an arrangement with other travellers if you think you're going to be caught with a surfeit of local cash.

Also, note that if you're travelling between the West African and Central African CFA zones (eg from Niger to Cameroon), it's easy to change CFA notes of one zone for those of the other at banks, but more difficult to change coins.

Tipping

→ **Hotels** Tips for porters and other staff are expected in fancy hotels; no such expectation in a cheap hotel.

→ **Restaurants** Tips of 10% are expected at better restaurants, although check whether service is included in the bill. At basic restaurants no tips are expected.

→ **Taxis** Locals seldom tip in private taxis, but drivers expect well-heeled travellers to tip around 10%. On short trips, loose change is sufficient.

Travellers Cheques

Well-known brands of travellers cheques are better as they're more likely to be recognised by bank staff. Amex, followed by Visa and Thomas Cook/MasterCard, are the most widely accepted, and some banks will take only one of these three. Most banks require you to show your original purchase receipts in order to change travellers cheques, so it's essential to bring these. Carry them with you (separately from your cheques), but also leave a copy at home, as well as elsewhere in your luggage, in case the original receipts or the cheques themselves are stolen.

Opening Hours

Standard opening hours vary from country to country. As a general rule, the working week runs from Monday to Friday; some shops and tourism-related businesses sometimes open on Saturdays, either all day or just in the morning. In some predominantly Muslim countries, some businesses may close on Friday (either all day or just in the morning), and instead open on Sunday.

Post

Postal services are moderately reliable in most West African capitals and cities. In rural areas, though, service can range from slow to nonexistent.

Letters sent from a major capital take about a week to 10 days to reach most of Europe, and at least two weeks to reach North America or Australasia, although it's sometimes much longer. For more speed and certainty, a few countries have 'express' services, but the main alternative (though expensive) is a courier service. DHL (www.dhl.com), for example, has offices in most West African capitals.

Telephone

Telephone connections to places outside West Africa are reasonably good, as the transmission is sometimes via satellite. Calls between African countries, however, are often relayed on landlines or through Europe, which means the reception is frequently bad – assuming you can get a call through in the first place. Things are improving, but slowly.

The best places to make international calls (unless you have a fast internet connection and telephone through Skype or other software from your laptop or, less privately, at an internet cafe) are at government telephone offices or private telecentres, which you'll find in most towns. International calls using local mobile SIM cards can also work out cheaper than landlines.

Costs for international calls and faxes to Europe, the USA or Australasia start at about US$1 per minute, with a few countries offering reduced rates at night and on weekends.

Dial-direct or 'home-direct' numbers are available from a few countries. With these, you dial an operator in your home country who can reverse the charges, or charge the call to a phone-company charge card or your home number. These home-direct numbers are toll free, but if you are using a phone booth you may need a coin or phonecard to connect. Check with your phone company for access numbers and a list of countries where they have home-direct numbers.

Mobile Phones

Mobile (cell) phones are everywhere in West Africa. In most countries, local SIM cards are readily available from street vendors in any town reached by mobile coverage; top-up cards are similarly widely available. If you prefer not to use your own phone, or your mobile hasn't been 'unlocked' as is the case with many US mobile phones, cheap mobile phones (as little as US$20) can be purchased in capital cities and most larger towns. International calls using a local SIM card often work out cheaper than calling from landlines. Although mobile coverage is usually restricted to urban settlements, coverage is expanding all the time.

A European or North American mobile phone will probably have reception in most West African countries, whereby your carrier's local partner will allow you to receive and send text messages, as well as phone calls, although making calls can be extremely expensive. Remember that if someone calls your mobile phone while you're in West Africa, you may pay the bulk of the charge. In some cases, a local SIM card purchased in one country may also work in other West African countries where that carrier operates; Orange is one carrier that operates in a number of countries in the region and may offer such a service.

Time

Burkina Faso, Côte d'Ivoire, The Gambia, Ghana, Guinea, Guinea-Bissau, Liberia, Mali, Mauritania, São Tomé & Príncipe, Senegal, Sierra Leone and Togo are on GMT/UTC. Cabo Verde is one hour behind. Benin, Cameroon, Equatorial Guinea, Gabon, Niger, Nigeria and the Republic of Congo are one hour ahead.

Toilets

There are two main types of toilet: Western sit-down, with a bowl and seat; and African squat, with a hole in the ground. Standards vary tremendously, from pristine to those that leave little to the imagination as to the health or otherwise of the previous occupant.

In rural areas, squat toilets are built over a deep hole in the ground. These are called 'long drops', and the waste matter just fades away naturally, as long as the hole isn't filled with too much other rubbish (such as paper or synthetic materials, including tampons). Even some Western toilets aren't plumbed in, but just balanced over a long drop. In our experience, a noncontact hole in the ground is better than a filthy bowl to hover over any day.

Tourist Information

With just a handful of exceptions, West Africa's tourism authorities are not geared up for tourism, and there are few tourist offices abroad. Some countries run small tourist offices at their embassies, which may be helpful for getting moderately useful brochures or general travel information.

Once in West Africa, some countries have Ministry of Tourism information offices but, apart from offering a few old brochures, they're unlikely to be of much assistance. Otherwise, you'll usually have more success enquiring with staff at tour companies or hotels.

Travellers with Disabilities

West Africa has very few facilities for the disabled. This, combined with weak infrastructure in the region, can make travel difficult, although it's not impossible. Few hotels have lifts (and those that do are generally expensive hotels), streets may be either badly potholed or else unpaved, footpaths are few and far between, and ramps and other things to ease access are often nonexistent. While accommodation at many budget hotels is on the ground floor, bathroom access can be difficult, and doors are not always wide enough for wheelchairs. Such difficulties are only partly counterbalanced by the fact that West Africans are usually very accommodating and willing to offer whatever assistance they can, as long as they understand what you need.

As for transport, most taxis in the region are small sedans, and buses are not wheelchair equipped. Minibuses and larger 4WD vehicles can usually be arranged through car-rental agencies in major towns and cities, although this will be pricey.

In general, travel and access will probably be easiest in places with relatively good tourism infrastructure, such as some of the coastal areas of Senegal and The Gambia. As far as we are aware, there are no facilities in the region specifically aimed at blind travellers.

Organisations & Resources

Download Lonely Planet's free Accessible Travel guide from http://lptravel.to/AccessibleTravel.

Before setting out for West Africa, travellers with disabilities should consider contacting one of the recommended organisations that may be able to help with advice and assistance.

➡ **Access-Able Travel Source** (www.access-able.com) A US-based site providing information on disabled-friendly tours and hotels.

➡ **Accessible Travel & Leisure** (www.accessibletravel.co.uk) Claims to be the biggest UK travel agent dealing with travel for people with a disability, and encourages independent travel.

➡ **Mobility International USA** (www.miusa.org) In the US, it advises disabled travellers on mobility issues; it primarily runs educational exchange programs, and some include African travel.

➡ **Society for Accessible Travel & Hospitality** (www.sath.org) In the US; offers assistance and advice.

➡ **Tourism for All** (www.tourismforall.org.uk) A useful UK resource on making travel accessible for everyone.

Visas

The general rule for West Africa is to get your visas before leaving home. They're rarely issued at land borders and only occasionally at airports. If you're flying from outside Africa, many airlines won't let you on board without a visa.

Obtaining Visas

Visa agencies are worth considering if you need visas to several countries before you leave or if there's no relevant embassy in your country. For longer trips or more flexibility, it's possible to obtain most of your visas in the region as you go, although this requires some advance planning and careful checking of the location of embassies for the countries in question – most West African countries have insufficient resources to maintain expensive embassies in many countries.

Visa fees average between US$20 and US$50 (Nigerian visas can cost as much as £250!), depending on where you apply, your nationality and whether you're asking for multiple- or single-entry visas. Always check the visa's validity length and its start date when deciding where to make your application. When applying for a visa, you may have to show proof that you intend to leave the country (eg an air ticket) or that you have enough funds to support yourself during your visit.

Most visa applications require between two and four identical passport photos, either black and white or colour. Inexpensive photo shops are found throughout the region, and rural areas sometimes have a village photographer who can do the job for you.

In Equatorial Guinea, you will also need a tourist permit in addition to your visa.

Visa des Pays de l'Entente

The Visa des Pays de l'Entente is a multicountry visa that covers travel in Benin, Burkina Faso, Côte d'Ivoire, Niger and Togo. If you've never heard of it, don't be surprised – it's so poorly publicised that most travellers never learn of its existence. Implementation of this relatively new visa is also still patchy, which significantly diminishes its appeal. In remote border crossings there is also the danger that officials won't recognise the visa and will force travellers to purchase a new individual country visa.

Before you go rushing off to your nearest West African embassy to ask for this visa, you need to learn how it works. For a start, it is only obtainable *within* these five West African countries, which means that you must initially obtain a visa for the first of these countries and, once there, apply at the immigration or visa extension office (or neighbouring country's embassy) in the capital city. To get the Visa des Pays de l'Entente, which is valid for two months, you'll need to take along CFA15,000 to CFA25,000 depending on the country, and up to two passport photos. It usually takes 24 to 72 hours for the visa to be issued.

Although the Visa des Pays de l'Entente may work out to be more convenient in some cases, it's worth remembering that it's only valid for one entry into each country: ideal for overlanders, less so for those who plan to visit countries more than once.

Volunteering

There are quite a large number of volunteers in West Africa, and it's a great way to reduce the ecological footprint of your trip and even make a contribution to local communities. It's also an amazing forum for self-exploration, especially if you touch a few lives and make friends along the way.

Keep in mind that there is no such thing as a perfect volunteer placement. Generally speaking, you'll get as much out of a program as you're willing to put into it; the vast majority of volunteers in West Africa walk away all the better for the experience.

Ghana in particular has numerous volunteering possibilities.

International Organisations

The following international organisations are good places to start gathering information on volunteering, although they won't necessarily always have projects on the go in West Africa.

African Impact (www.african impact.com)

African Volunteer Network (www.african-volunteer.net)

Australian Volunteers International (www.australianvolun teers.com)

Coordinating Committee for International Voluntary Service (ccivs.org)

Earthwatch (www.earthwatch. org)

Frontier Conservation Expeditions (www.frontier.ac.uk)

Idealist (www.idealist.org)

International Citizen Service (ICS; www.volunteerics.org)

International Volunteer Programs Association (www. volunteerinternational.org)

Peace Corps (www.peacecorps. gov)

Step Together Volunteering (www.step-together.org.uk)

UN Volunteers (www.unv.org)

Volunteer Abroad (www.go-abroad.com/volunteer-abroad)

Volunteer Service Abroad (www.vsa.org.nz)

VSO (www.vso.org.uk)

Worldwide Experience (www. worldwideexperience.com)

Local Organisations

Some local NGOs and community projects accept walk-in volunteers, although it's usually a better idea to contact them in advance to discuss opportunities and what they require. Some possibilities include:

Centre de Conservation pour Chimpanzés (www.projetpri mates.com/chimpanzee-con servation-center; Somoria; GFr50,000) Guinea

Federação das ONGs em São Tomé e Príncipe (☏222 7552;

www.facebook.com/pages/Fed
eração-das-ONG-em-São-Tomé-
e-Príncipe/249383918425584)
São Tomé & Príncipe

MARAPA (www.marapa.org) São
Tomé & Príncipe

**Max Planck Institute of
Evolutionary Anthropology**
(Loango Gorilla Programme;
www.eva.mpg.de/primat/
research-groups/chimpanzees/
field-sites/loango-ape-project.
html; per person CFA300,000)
Gabon

SOS Tartarugas (www.sostar
tarugas.org) Cabo Verde

SenExperience+ (www.senexpe
rienceplus.com) Senegal

Women Travellers

When travelling in West
Africa – solo or with other
women – you're unlikely to
encounter any more diffi-
culties than you would elsewhere in Africa. Our female
writers have travelled for
extended periods (including
solo travel) and/or lived in
West Africa, usually without
incident, and most did their
research travelling alone.

Hints

Although women will un-
doubtedly attract more attention than men, more often
than not you'll meet only
warmth and hospitality, and
find that you receive kindness and special treatment
that you wouldn't be shown if
you were a man. While you're
likely to hear some horror
stories from expats who may
be appalled at the idea of
solo female travel, it's worth
remembering that the inci-
dence of rape or other real
harm is extremely rare.

It's important to not let
these concerns ruin your
trip. Remember that some
sections of the region, such
as parts of the Sahel, are
wonderfully hassle free. You'll
also have the opportunity to
meet local women, some-
thing that few male travellers
have the chance to do on the
same terms. Good places to
try include tourist offices,
government departments
or even your hotel, where at
least some of the staff are
likely to be formally educated young to middle-aged
women. In rural areas, starting points include female
teachers at a local school, or
staff at a health centre where
language barriers are less
likely to be a problem.

That said, it's inevitable
that you'll attract some unwanted attention. Here are a
few tips:

➡ Dress modestly. This is the
most successful strategy for
minimising unasked-for male
attention. Wear trousers or a
long skirt, and a conservative
top with sleeves. Tucking
your hair under a cap or
tying it back, especially if it's
blonde, sometimes helps.
Exposing your midriff is
rarely a good idea.

➡ Use common sense. Trust
your instincts and take the
usual precautions when out.
For example, if possible,
avoid going out alone in the
evenings, particularly on
foot. Avoid isolated areas,
roadways and beaches
during both day and evening
hours, and be cautious on
beaches, many of which
can become deserted very
quickly. Throughout the
region, hitching alone is not
recommended.

➡ Don't worry about being
rude, and don't feel the need
to explain yourself. If you
try to start explaining why
you don't want to meet for a
drink/go to a nightclub/get
married on the spot, it may
be interpreted as flirting.

➡ Ignore hissing, calls of
'chérie', or whatever. If
you respond, it may be
interpreted as a lead on.

➡ Wear a wedding ring
or carry photos of 'your'
children, which will make
you appear less 'available' in
most places.

➡ Avoid direct eye contact
with local men; dark
sunglasses help. There are,
however, times when a cold
glare is an effective riposte to
an unwanted suitor.

➡ On public transport, sit
next to a woman if possible.

➡ If you need help (eg
directions), ask a woman
first, although local women
are less likely than men to
have had an education that
included learning English.

➡ Go to the nearest public
place, such as the lobby
of a hotel, to get rid of any
hangers-on. If they persist,
asking the receptionist to call
the police usually frightens
them off.

Tampons & Sanitary Pads

Tampons (imported from
Europe) are available from
pharmacies or large su-
permarkets in capital cities
throughout West Africa, and
occasionally in other large
towns. Elsewhere, the only
choice is likely to be sanitary
pads so you may want to
bring an emergency supply.

Transport

GETTING THERE & AWAY

West Africa is reasonably well-connected to the rest of the world by air, most commonly through Casablanca, Addis Ababa, Johannesburg or Europe. Arriving by land is possible but complex, while travelling by sea is extremely rare.

Flights, cars and tours can be booked online at lonelyplanet.com/bookings.

Entering West Africa

Entering West Africa varies from country to country but is generally hassle free, provided you have all your documents in order. Countries with more difficult visa processes include Gabon, Equatorial Guinea and São Tomé & Príncipe.

Air

There are direct flights from Europe into every West African capital, although very few airlines fly into Bissau (Guinea-Bissau), Freetown (Sierra Leone), Monrovia (Liberia) and São Tomé & Príncipe. Most of the best connections between Europe and sub-Saharan West Africa are via Casablanca with Royal Air Maroc. It's also relatively easy to fly into West Africa from North Africa and the Middle East, with a handful of airlines offering services from elsewhere in Africa. If you're travelling from Australia, Canada or the USA, you'll usually need to connect to a flight from Europe, the Middle East or South Africa.

Airports

International airports with the greatest number of incoming flights (and the best onward connections) include:

Douala International Airport (☎2 33 42 35 77; 10km west of Douala), Cameroon

Félix Houphouët-Boigny International Airport (Port Bouet Airport; www.aeria-ci.com; Port-Bouët), Abidjan, Côte d'Ivoire

Kotoka International Airport (www.gacl.com.gh), Accra, Ghana

Léopold Sédar Senghor International Airport (DKR;☎24hr info line 33 869 5050; www.aeroport-dakar.com), Dakar, Senegal

Murtala Muhammed International Airport (www.lagosairport.net), Lagos, Nigeria

The following are also international airports:

➧ **Aéroport international de Bamako** (www.aeroportbamako.com), Mali

Aéroport International de Cotonou Cadjéhoun (www.aeroport-cotonou.com), Cotonou, Benin

Aéroport International de Ouagadougou (☎25 30 65 15;

CLIMATE CHANGE & TRAVEL

Every form of transport that relies on carbon-based fuel generates CO_2, the main cause of human-induced climate change. Modern travel is dependent on aeroplanes, which might use less fuel per kilometre per person than most cars but travel much greater distances. The altitude at which aircraft emit gases (including CO_2) and particles also contributes to their climate change impact. Many websites offer 'carbon calculators' that allow people to estimate the carbon emissions generated by their journey and, for those who wish to do so, to offset the impact of the greenhouse gases emitted with contributions to portfolios of climate-friendly initiatives throughout the world. Lonely Planet offsets the carbon footprint of all staff and author travel.

www.aeroport-ouagadougou.
com), Burkina Faso

Banjul International Airport
(BLJ; ☑4473000; www.banju-
lairport.com), The Gambia

Conakry International Airport
(www.aeroport-conakry.com),
Guinea

**Diori Hamani International
Airport**, Niamey, Niger

Lungi International Airport
(☑099 714421), Freetown,
Sierra Leone

Malabo International Airport
(Santa Isabel Airport; ☑222 091
554; adge@malabo.aero; 9km
west of Malabo city centre),
Equatorial Guinea

**Nelson Mandela International
Airport** (www.asa.cv/aeroportos/
aeroporto-da-praia; Praia) and
**Amílcar Cabral International
Airport** (www.asa.cv/aeroportos/
aeroporto-internacional-amilcar-
cabral; Sal), Cabo Verde

Nouakchott and **Nouâdhibou**,
Mauritania

**Osvaldo Vieira Interna-
tional Airport** (OXB), Bissau,
Guinea-Bissau

Port Harcourt, Nigeria

Roberts International Airport
(ROB; Robertsfield), Monrovia,
Liberia

São Tomé, São Tomé & Príncipe

**Yaoundé Nsimalen Interna-
tional Airport**, Cameroon

Airlines

Dozens of airlines fly into
West Africa from elsewhere
in Africa, as well as the Middle East and Europe. The
most important ones include:

Air France (www.airfrance.com)

British Airways (www.britishair
ways.com)

Emirates (www.emirates.com)

Ethiopian Airlines (www.ethiopi
anairlines.com)

Iberia (www.iberia.com)

Kenya Airways (www.kenya-air
ways.com)

KLM Royal Dutch Airlines
(www.klm.com)

Lufthansa (www.lufthansa.com)

Royal Air Maroc (www.royalair-
maroc.com)

South African Airways (www.
flysaa.com)

TACV (www.flytacv.com)

TAP Air Portugal (www.flytap.
com)

Tickets

Buying cheap air tickets in
West Africa is a challenge.
Usually the best deal you
can get is an airline's official
excursion fare, and there's no
discount on single tickets unless you qualify for a 'youth'
(under 26, sometimes 23) or
'student' rate. In cities that
handle plenty of international
traffic, such as Dakar or
Abidjan, cheaper tickets are
easier to come by from travel
agents; in Bissau or Monrovia
you won't have much choice
about fares or airlines.

Charter flights are worth
considering as they're generally direct and cheaper
than scheduled flights. Some
charter flights come as part
of a package that includes
accommodation and other
services, but most charter
companies sell 'flight only'
tickets. These are most often
possible for flights to/from
The Gambia and Senegal.

Departure Tax

The situation varies from
country to country, but departure tax is usually included in the price of tickets.

Land

If you're travelling overland
to West Africa independently
– whether cycling, driving
your own car or taking
public transport – you can
approach the region from
three main directions: from
the north, across the Sahara;
from the south and south-
east, through the countries
bordering eastern Cameroon
or Republic of Congo; or
from the east, through Chad.
There is no regular, scheduled public transport along
any of these routes and all
are major undertakings.

Border Crossings

If you're coming from
the north, the main
border-crossing point into
sub-Saharan West Africa
from Morocco and the western Sahara is just north of
Nouâdhibou. In theory, there
are also crossings at Bordj
Mokhtar (Algeria/Mali),
Assamakka (Algeria/Niger)
and Tumu (Libya/Niger), but
these were either closed or
downright dangerous at the
time of research.

If you come into West Africa from the south or east, the
border-crossing points are at
Garoua-Boulaï or Kenzou (for
the Central African Republic),
although security is dire on
the CAR side of the border at
the time of research. There
are crossings between Cameroon and Chad at Kousséri,
Bongor or Léré (for Chad),
but northern Cameroon is
currently off-limits due to the
Boko Haram insurgency and
the dangers of kidnapping. In
more peaceful times, another
option would be to take the
long way around, crossing the
border on the northern side
of Lake Chad on the route to
Nguigmi (Niger). Remember
that very few travellers use
these routes and they are
currently unsafe.

Car

Anyone planning to take their
own vehicle to West Africa
should check in advance
what spare parts and petrol
are likely to be available.

A number of documents
are also required:

Carnet A *carnet de passage*
is like a passport for your car,
a booklet that is stamped on
arrival and departure from a
country to ensure that you
export the vehicle again after
you've imported it.

Green card Issued by insurers.
Insurance for some countries is
only obtainable at the border.
Check with your insurance company or automobile association
before leaving home.

**International Driving Permit
(IDP)** Although most foreign

licences are acceptable in West African countries, an IDP issued by your local automobile association is highly recommended.

Vehicle registration documents Carrying all ownership papers is a must.

CARNETS

A *carnet de passage* is like a passport for your car, a booklet that is stamped on arrival and departure from a country to ensure that you export the vehicle again after you've imported it. It's usually issued by an automobile association in the country where the vehicle is registered. Most countries of West Africa require a carnet although rules change frequently.

The sting in the tail with a carnet is that you usually have to lodge a deposit to secure it. If you default on the carnet – that is, you don't have an export stamp to match the import one – then the country in question can claim your deposit, which can be up to 300% of the new value of the vehicle. You can get around this problem with bank guarantees or carnet insurance, but you still have to fork out in the end if you default.

Should the worst occur and your vehicle is irretrievably damaged in an accident or catastrophic breakdown, you'll have to argue it out with customs officials. Having a vehicle stolen can be even worse, as you may be suspected of having sold it.

The carnet may need to specify any pricey spare parts that you're planning to carry, such as a gearbox, which is designed to prevent any spare-part importation rackets. Contact your local automobile association for details about necessary documentation at least three months in advance.

SHIPPING YOUR VEHICLE

If you want to travel in West Africa using your own car or motorbike, but don't fancy the Saharan crossing, another option is to ship it. The usual way of doing this is to load the car onto a ship in Europe and take it off again at either Dakar or Banjul (Abidjan and Tema, in Ghana, are other options).

➡ Costs vary depending on the size of the vehicle and the final destination, but generally start from around US$1000.

➡ Apart from cost, your biggest problem is likely to be security – many drivers report theft of items from the inside and outside (such as lights and mirrors) of their car. Vehicles are usually left unlocked for the crossing and when in storage at the destination port, so chain or lock all equipment into fixed boxes inside the vehicle.

➡ Getting a vehicle out of port is frequently a nightmare, requiring visits to several different offices where stamps must be obtained and mysterious fees paid at every turn. You could consider using an official handling agent or an unofficial 'fixer' to take your vehicle through all this.

From Chad

Before considering the following, remember that northern Cameroon is curently off-limits due to the Boko Haram insurgency and the dangers of kidnapping.

Between Cameroon and Chad, the main border crossing is between Maroua (Cameroon) and Kousséri, although the actual border is at Nguelé. Corrupt officials abound here. There are also the crossings further south to the towns of Bongor or Léré; the former requires a pirogue (traditional canoe) across the Logone River.

For hard-core travellers, a more arduous (and adventurous) route into West Africa from Chad runs around the top of what's left of Lake Chad between Nguigmi in Niger and the Chadian capital N'Djaména.

From the North – Crossing the Sahara

With rebellion and banditry plaguing northern Mali and northern Niger at the time of research, most trans-Saharan routes have fallen quiet. Apart from entering Mauritania via Morocco and Western Sahara, we are unable to recommend any of the other routes across the Sahara into West Africa. There is no public transport along any of the routes covered here.

Whichever route you take, you'll need to get a thorough update on the security

---

DRIVING TO WEST AFRICA: FURTHER READING

Driving your own car or motorbike to West Africa, and driving off-road within the region, are vast subjects. Two specialist guides that we recommend:

➡ *Adventure Motorcycling Handbook* (1997), by Chris Scott, covers all parts of the world where tar roads end. It contains stacks of good information on the Sahara and West Africa, all combined with humour and personal insights.

➡ *Sahara Overland* (2nd Edition; 2000), by Chris Scott, is the best, most comprehensive book on all aspects of Saharan travel by two or four wheels, with information on established and newer Saharan routes, and more than 100 maps. Chris Scott's highly recommended website, www.sahara-overland.com, has updates of the book, as well as a useful forum.

situation before setting off. Anybody planning to travel in the Sahara should check out the excellent website put together by Chris Scott (www.sahara-overland.com); its forum is particularly useful on which routes are open. Be sure to bring sufficient food, water and warm clothes for the journey.

From Central Africa

There are two main crossing points between Cameroon and the Central African Republic (CAR), but roads that are dire at the best of times are catastrophic in the rainy season. Carefully check the security situation on the CAR side of the border – the country has been at war for much of the past decade.

Sea

For most people, reaching West Africa by sea is not a viable option. The days of working your passage on commercial boats have vanished. Several cargo-shipping companies sail along the West African coast between Europe and South Africa, with a limited number of cabins for public passengers.

Tours

First-time travellers to West Africa may want to consider taking a tour – what you sacrifice in the freedom to go when and where you want, you gain in having someone else take care of all the logistics (such as visas, dealing with officialdom, organising transport and accommodation) that can drive independent travellers to distraction.

Two main options are available: inclusive tours (where you fly to your destination and spend two to three weeks in one or more countries) and overland tours (two- to six-month tours that begin in Europe and travel by land to and around West

Africa). Some overland tours allow you to join for a short section (usually three to five weeks), flying out and back at either end. In addition to the recommended tours, some specialist travel agents also organise tours, as do numerous West African–based agencies, although with these agencies you'll usually need to arrange your own flight into and out of the region.

Inclusive Tours
FRANCE
Explorator (www.explorator.fr)

Pointe-Voyages (www.point-voyages.com)

Terres d'Aventure (www.terdav.com)

ITALY
Antichi Splendori Viaggi (www.antichisplendori.it)

Harmattan Tours (www.harmattan.it)

NETHERLANDS
Sawadee Reizen (www.sawadee.nl)

SPAIN
Viajes Taranna (www.taranna.com)

Viatges Tuareg (www.tuareg viatges.es)

UK
Birdfinders (www.birdfinders.co.uk)

Explore Worldwide (www.explore.co.uk)

From Here 2 Timbuktu (www.fromhere2timbuktu.com)

Imaginative Traveller (www.imaginative-traveller.com)

Limosa Holidays (www.limosa-holidays.co.uk)

Naturetrek (www.naturetrek.co.uk)

Peregrine Adventures (www.peregrineadventures.com)

Rainbow Tours (www.rainbow-tours.co.uk)

Responsible Travel (www.responsibletravel.com)

Songlines Music Travel (www.songlines.co.uk/music-travel)

Undiscovered Destinations (www.undiscovered-destinations.com)

Wildfoot (www.wildfoottravel.com)

USA
Access Africa (www.access africa.com)

Born Free Safaris (www.born freesafaris.com)

Palace Travel (www.palacetravel.com)

Spector Travel (www.spector travel.com)

Wilderness Travel (www.wilder nesstravel.com)

Overland Tours

For these trips, you travel in an 'overland truck' with about 15 to 28 other people, a couple of drivers/leaders, plus tents and other equipment. Food is bought along the way and the group cooks and eats together. Most of the hassles (such as border crossings) are taken care of by the leader. Disadvantages include a fixed itinerary and the possibility of spending a long time with other people in relatively close confines. That said, overland truck tours are extremely popular.

The overland-tour market is dominated by British companies, although passengers come from many parts of the world. Most tours start in London and travel to West Africa via Europe and Morocco. For those with plenty of time, there's also the option to do the West Africa trip as part of a longer trans-Africa trip.

African Trails (www.africantrails.co.uk)

Dragoman (www.dragoman.com)

GETTING AROUND

Air Major capitals are reasonably well connected by flights within West Africa; other smaller capitals may require inconvenient connections. Royal Air Maroc connects most major cities with Casablanca.

Bus & Bush Taxi Often the only option in rural areas, bush taxis in varying stages of disrepair leave when full; buses connect major cities with those of neighbouring countries.

Car Reasonable road infrastructure connects major cities; roads deteriorate elsewhere, and are sometimes impassable after rains.

Train Trains operate in Benin, Burkina Faso, Cameroon, the Republic of Congo, Côte d'Ivoire, Gabon, Ghana, Mali, Mauritania, Nigeria, Senegal and Togo. International services connect Dakar with Bamako, and Ouagadougou with Abidjan.

Air

Travelling by bus, bush taxi and even train are essential parts of the West African experience, but so vast are the distances that a few flights around the region can widen your options considerably if your time is limited. The region has a reasonable network of air routes, with the best connections generally between Francophone countries.

Air safety is a major concern in West Africa and a spate of accidents (especially in Nigeria) means that you should always be wary of the region's local airlines, particularly smaller operators. For more details on the air safety record of individual airlines, visit www.airsafe.com/index.html.

Although the airports in some capital cities are large and cavernous, some smaller West African airports are little more than single-shed terminals. Regardless of the size, don't be surprised if you spend half a day at check-in.

Checking In

In some West African cities, check-in procedures are as much of an adventure as the flight itself. Conakry and Lagos win our vote as the airports with the most disorganised and chaotic check-in procedures, but every traveller probably has their own 'favourites'. The fun starts from the moment you enter the airport building. Underpaid security personnel, in an effort to subsidise their meagre incomes, may view the baggage check procedures as a chance to elicit bribes from tourists. After searching your bag, they might ask what you have for them or, alternatively, try to convince you that you've violated some regulation. Be compliant with requests to open your baggage, be friendly and respectful, smile a lot, and you should soon be on your way. Also remember that, in some cases, officials may search your bag out of genuine curiosity, so put your dirty underwear on top and watch their interest evaporate.

After getting past the initial baggage check, wade into the fray by the check-in counter. While some places have lines, many don't – just a sweaty mass of people, all waving their tickets and talking loudly to a rather beleaguered-looking check-in clerk.

The West African answer to this situation is the 'fixer' – enterprising locals who make their living by getting people smoothly checked in and through other formalities such as customs and airport tax, all for fees ranging from a dollar or two up to about US$10. Without the services of a fixer, the best strategy for avoiding the chaotic scene is to arrive early at the airport.

Once you have your boarding pass in hand, there's usually a second luggage inspection as you pass from the check-in terminal to the waiting area. Then it's just a matter of waiting, and often waiting far longer than you planned.

There is one exception to the general chaos of checking in, at least if you're flying Air France. In most West African capitals where Air France has late-night departures for Paris, the airline allows a morning check-in (either at a central Air France office or, less conveniently, at the airport itself).

Airlines in West Africa

West African airlines come and go with disturbing regularity.

➡ **Air Burkina** (www.air-burkina.com) A reasonably extensive West African service as well as a domestic Ouagadougou–Bobo-Dioulasso service.

➡ **ASKY** (www.flyasky.com) Regional airline based in Lomé and with one of the region's most extensive networks.

➡ **Elysian Airlines** (www.elysianairlines.com) Domestic Liberian, Cameroonian and some wider West African routes.

➡ **Royal Air Maroc** (www.royalairmaroc.com) Has the most extensive regional network.

➡ **TACV** (www.flytacv.com) Connects Praia (Cabo Verde) to Dakar on the mainland, from where they also operate a small range of services to neighbouring countries. Some Nigerian airlines also fly between Nigeria and other West African countries.

Reputable travel agents throughout the region can also sometimes find tickets for international airlines, as they hop between West African cities as part of their intercontinental routes.

Tickets

Long distances, high fuel costs and a state of budgetary crisis among most regional airlines ensure that fares within West Africa don't come cheap. Flying from Dakar (Senegal) to Abidjan (Côte d'Ivoire), for example, can cost the equivalent of flying halfway across the USA. Return fares are usually double the one-way fares, though less expensive excursion fares are occasionally available, as are youth or student fares.

Once you've bought your ticket, reconfirm your reservation several times at least, especially if the airline you're flying with has a less-than-stellar reputation for reliability. After the flight, if you checked in luggage, hold on to your baggage claim ticket until you've exited the baggage claim area at your destination, as you'll often be required to show it.

Bicycle

A small but growing number of travellers visit West Africa on bicycle. As long as you have sufficient time, a sturdy bike, are ready to be self-sufficient and possess a willingness to rough it, cycling is an excellent way to get to know the region. You'll end up staying in small towns and villages, interact more with the local people without vehicle windows and other barriers between you, and eat West African food more frequently.

Wherever you go, you'll be met with great local curiosity (as well as much goodwill). As in most places in the world, don't leave your bike unattended for any lengthy period of time unless it's locked, and try to secure the main removable pieces. Taking your bike into your hotel room, should you decide to take a break from camping, is generally no problem. If you're camping near settlements in rural areas, ask the village headman each night where you can stay. Even if you don't have a tent, he'll find you somewhere to sleep.

Where to Cycle

Because of the distances involved, you'll need to plan your food and water needs in advance, and pay careful attention to choosing a route in order to avoid long stretches of semidesert, areas with no villages or heavily travelled roads. In general, cycling is best well away from urban areas, and in the early morning and late afternoon hours. When calculating your daily distances, plan on taking a break during the hottest, midday period, and don't count on covering as much territory each day as you might in a northern European climate.

The most popular long-haul cycling routes are:

➡ Burkina Faso to Ghana, Benin and Togo

➡ Within Senegal

➡ Benin to Côte d'Ivoire

When to Cycle

The best time to cycle is in the cooler, dry period from mid-October to February. Even so, you'll need to work out a way to carry at least 4L of water, and you'll also need to carry a water filter and purifier. If you get tired, or simply want to cut out the boring bits, bikes can easily be carried on bush taxis, though you'll want to carry some rags to wrap around the gearing for protection. You'll need to pay a luggage fee for this, but it shouldn't be more than one-third to one-half the price of the passenger fare.

Few cyclists make it down to Equatorial Guinea, but the best time to cycle ihere is the dry season, which runs roughly from June to September or October.

Equipment

Mountain bikes are most suitable for cycling in West Africa and will give you the greatest flexibility in setting your route. While heavy, single-speed bicycles can be rented in many towns (and occasionally mountain bikes), they're not good for anything other than short, local rides, so you should bring your own bicycle into the region if you plan on riding extended distances. To rent a bike locally, ask staff at hotels, or enquire at bicycle-repair stands (every town market has one).

Apart from water, your main concern will be motorists. Cyclists are regarded as third-class citizens in West Africa, so make sure you know what's coming up behind you and be prepared to take evasive action, as local cyclists are often forced to do. A small rear-view mirror is well worth considering.

You'll need to carry sufficient spare parts and be proficient at repairs; punctures, in particular, will be frequent. Take at least four spare inner tubes, some tyre repair material and a spare tyre. Consider the number of tube patches you might need, square it, and pack those too. Some people don't like them but we've found inner-tube protectors indispensable for minimising punctures.

Transporting Your Bicycle

If you're bringing your bike with you on the plane to West Africa, some airlines ask that you partially dismantle it and put the pieces in a large bag or box. Bike boxes are available at some airports. Otherwise, you can arrange one in advance with your local bicycle shop. To fit it in the box, you'll usually need to take off (or turn) the handlebars, pedals and seat, and will need to deflate the tyres.

Some airlines don't charge, while others (including many charter airlines) levy an extra fee – usually around US$50 to US$100 – because bike boxes are not standard size.

Some airlines are willing to take your bike 'as is' – you can just wheel it to the check-in desk – although you'll still need to partially deflate the tyres and tie the handlebars into the frame. Check with the airline in advance about their regulations.

Useful Resources

Bicycle Africa (www.ibike. org/bikeafrica) Part of the International Bicycle Fund, it's a low-budget, socially conscious organisation that arranges tours in some West African countries, provides fact sheets and posts letters from travellers who've travelled by bike in the area.

Cyclists' Touring Club (CTC; ☑01483-238337; www.ctc.org. uk) A UK-based organisation that offers tips and information sheets on cycling in different parts of the world.

Boat

At several points along the West African coast you can travel by boat, either on a large passenger vessel or by local canoe. Some of the local canoe trips are definitely of the informal variety, and many are dangerous. Countries where ferries provide an important means of coastal transport include Cabo Verde, Senegal, Sierra Leone, Liberia and Guinea-Bissau.

Unsafe speedboats also make the trip. Places where you can cross international borders by boat are by barge from Guinea to Maliand, and possibly by ferry between Conakry (Guinea) and Freetown (Sierra Leone). At the time of research, ferries between Limbe (Cameroon) and Calabar (Nigeria) were not functioning.

Ferry services also operate between Malabo and Bata in Equatorial Guinea, and between the main islands of São Tomé & Príncipe; the last are unsafe.

On most major rivers in the region, pirogues, pinasses (larger motorised boats, carrying cargo and anything from 10 to 100 passengers) and/or public ferries serve towns and villages along the way, and can be an excellent way to see the country. Some involve a simple river crossing, others can be a longer expedition where you sleep by the riverbank.

Riverboat options include those along the Gambia and Senegal Rivers. Remember that many such journeys are only possible at certain times of the year (usually August to December) when water levels are still high enough after the rains.

Whether you're renting a pirogue or pinasse, or taking a public ferry, check what food and water is included in the price you pay; it's always worth taking more just in case. On some journeys you'll be able to buy snacks and fruit along the way. Also, bring something to protect yourself from the sun, as few boats have any shade, and something to waterproof your gear. Avoid getting on boats that are overloaded, or setting off when the weather is bad, especially on sea routes in coastal areas.

Bus & Bush Taxi

The most common forms of public transport in West Africa are bus (car in some Francophone countries) and bush taxi (taxi brousse). Buses may be run by state-owned or private companies; bush taxis are always private, although the driver is rarely the owner of the vehicle. Vehicles are usually located at a bus and bush taxi park, called gare routière or sometimes autogare in Francophone countries, 'garage', 'lorry park' or 'motor park' in English-speaking countries, and paragem in Portuguese-speaking countries. Most large cities have several gares routières, one for each main direction or destination, often located on the road out of town headed in that direction.

In some countries, buses are common for intercity routes and bush taxis are hard to find; in other countries it's the reverse. Either way, travel generally costs between US$1.50 and US$2.50 per 100km. On routes between countries,

fares can be higher because drivers have to pay additional fees (official and unofficial) to cross the border. You can save a bit of money by taking one vehicle to the border and then another on the other side, but this prolongs the trip considerably.

In many countries, transport fares are fixed by the government, so the only way the bush taxi drivers can earn a bit more is to charge for luggage. Local people accept this, so travellers should too, unless of course it's unreasonable. The fee for a medium-sized rucksack is around 10% of the fare. Small bags will be less and are often not charged at all. If you think you're being overcharged, ask other passengers, out of earshot of the driver. Once you know the proper rate, bargaining will be easy and the price should soon fall.

Bus

Long-distance buses (sometimes called a 'big bus' or grand car, to distinguish it from a minibus) vary in size – from 35 to 70 seats – and services vary between countries and areas. On the main routes buses are good quality, with a reliable service and fixed departure times (although arrival times may be more fluid depending on anything from checkpoints and breakdowns to the number of towns they stop in along the way).

On quiet roads in rural areas, buses may be decrepit, and may frequently break down, and stop regularly. These buses have no timetable and usually go when full or when the driver feels like it. They are usually overcrowded, in contrast with some of the better lines on major routes, where the one-person-per-seat rule is usually respected. Generally, buses are cheaper than bush taxis for a comparable route and are usually quicker.

You may arrange a long ride by bus (or bush taxi) and find yourself transferring to another vehicle somewhere along the way. There's no need to pay more – your driver pays your fare directly to the driver of the next vehicle – but it can mean long waits while the arrangements are made.

RESERVATIONS

You can reserve in advance on some main-route buses, which is advisable. In some countries you book a place but not a specific seat. Just before the bus leaves, names are called out in the order that tickets were bought, and you get on and choose the seat you want. Seats to the front tend to be better ventilated and more comfortable. If you suffer from motion sickness, try to get a seat towards the front or in the middle. Whichever end of the bus you sit in, it's worth trying to get a seat on the side that will be away from

direct sunlight for most of the journey.

Bush Taxi

A bush taxi (known as a tro-tro in Ghana) is effectively a small bus. Almost without exception, bush taxis leave when full, not according to any recognisable timetable. As soon as one car leaves, the next one starts to fill. Depending on the popularity of the route, the car may take half an hour or several days to fill. Either way, drivers jealously guard their car's place in the queue.

There are three main types of bush taxi in West Africa: minibus, Peugeot taxi and pick-up.

Car & Motorcycle
Driving Licences

To drive a car or ride a motorbike in West Africa you'll need a driving licence and,

ideally, an International Driving Permit (IDP). If you intend to hire a car, you will usually need both. IDPs are easy and cheap to get in your home country – they're usually issued by major motoring associations, such as the AA in Britain – and are useful if you're driving in countries where your own licence may not be recognised (officially or unofficially). They have the added advantage of being written in several languages, with a photo and many stamps, and so look more impressive when presented to car-rental clerks or policemen at road blocks.

Fuel

The quality, availability and price of fuel (petrol and diesel – called essence and gasoil, respectively, in the Francophone countries, and gasolina and diesel, or sometimes gasóleo, in former Portuguese colonies)

BUSH TAXI TRICKS

Early customers can choose where to sit. Latecomers get no choice and are assigned to the least comfortable seats – usually at the back, where the seating is cramped and stuffy, seat springs work their way into any orifice and window-winders jam into knees. If you have a choice, the best seats are those in the front, near the window. Some travellers prefer the very front, though you're first in line if there's a collision. Better is the row behind the driver, near a window (ideally one that works), and preferably on the side with more shade during the journey.

If a group of passengers has been waiting a long time, and there are only two or three seats to fill, they may club together and pay extra so as to get moving. If you do this, don't expect a discount because you're saving the driver the hassle of looking for other passengers – time ain't money in Africa. If you pick up someone along the way, however, the fare they pay goes to the passengers who bought the seats, not to the driver.

By far the best time to catch bush taxis is early in the morning; after that, you may have difficulty finding vehicles on many routes. Sometimes, however, departures are determined by market days, in which case afternoon may be best.

If a bush taxi looks like it's going to get uncomfortably full, you can always buy two seats for yourself – it's simply double the price. Likewise, if you want to charter the whole car, take the price of one seat and multiply it by the number available. You can either hire a city taxi or a bush taxi (although in most places, city taxis won't have the necessary paperwork for long-distance routes), or ask around at your hotel and arrange something privately.

The price you pay will have to be worth the driver taking it out of public service for the day. If you want a deal including petrol, he'll reduce the speed to a slow trot and complain every time you take a detour. A fixed daily rate for the car, while you pay extra for fuel, is easier to arrange. Finding a car with a working petrol gauge may be tricky, but you can work on the theory that the tank will be empty when you start and, if you allow for 10km per litre on reasonable roads (more on bad roads), you should be OK.

ROAD DISTANCES (KM)

	Abidjan (Côte d'Ivoire)	Accra (Ghana)	Bamako (Mali)	Banjul (The Gambia)	Bata (Equatorial Guinea)	Bissau (Guinea-Bissau)	Conakry (Guinea)	Cotonou (Benin)	Dakar (Senegal)	Freetown (Sierra Leone)	Lagos (Nigeria)	Lomé (Togo)	Monrovia (Liberia)	Niamey (Niger)	Nouakchott (Mauritania)	Ouagadougou (Burkina Faso)
Accra (Ghana)	560															
Bamako (Mali)	1160	1710														
Banjul (The Gambia)	2490	3210	1340													
Bata (Equatorial Guinea)	2,719	2190	3570	4830												
Bissau (Guinea-Bissau)	2180	2900	1460	310	4830											
Conakry (Guinea)	1700	2260	920	1230	4340	980										
Cotonou (Benin)	910	360	2020	3360	1850	3110	2610									
Dakar (Senegal)	2790	3350	1420	300	4890	585	1530	3360								
Freetown (Sierra Leone)	1590	2090	1210	1440	4220	1190	320	2440	1740							
Lagos (Nigeria)	1030	480	2140	3480	1740	3230	2730	120	3560	2560						
Lomé (Togo)	760	200	1870	3220	2000	2970	2460	160	3290	2290	280					
Monrovia (Liberia)	1020	1520	1040	1860	3730	1610	740	1870	2160	570	1990	1720				
Niamey (Niger)	1570	1390	1410	2750	2660	2880	2320	1040	2740	2900	1160	1190	2330			
Nouakchott (Mauritania)	2800	3360	1650	870	4940	1180	2100	3670	570	2320	3790	3560	2730	3050		
Ouagadougou (Burkina Faso)	1070	970	900	2240	2685	2360	1820	1120	2240	2400	1240	1240	1830	500	2550	
Yaoundé (Cameroon)	2650	2100	3760	4410	530	4160	4350	1740	4670	4120	1620	1620	3610	2090	5240	2860

varies greatly throughout the region. Where taxation, subsidies or currency rates make petrol cheaper in one country than in its neighbour, you'll inevitably find traders who've carried large drums across the border to sell 'black market' fuel at the roadside. However, watch out for fuel sold in plastic bags or small containers along the roadside. While sometimes it's fine, it's often diluted with water or kerosene. Don't expect to find unleaded petrol beyond major cities and even there it may be scarce.

Insurance

➡ Insurance is compulsory in most West African countries.

➡ Given the large number of minor accidents, not to mention major ones, fully comprehensive insurance is strongly advised, both for your own and any rental vehicle.

➡ Always check with your insurer whether you're covered for the countries you intend to visit and whether third-party cover is included.

➡ Car-hire companies customarily supply insurance, but check the cover and conditions carefully.

➡ Make certain that you're covered for off-piste travel, as well as travel between countries (if you're planning cross-border excursions).

➡ A locally acquired motorcycle licence is not valid under some policies.

➡ In the event of an accident, make sure you submit the accident report as soon as possible to the insurance company or, if hiring, the car-hire company.

Rental

There are car-rental agencies in most capital cities and tourist areas. Most international companies (Hertz, Avis, etc) are represented, plus smaller independent operators, but renting is invariably expensive – you can easily spend in one day what you'd pay for a week's rental in Europe or the USA. If the small operators charge less, it's usually because the vehicles are older and sometimes not well maintained, and corners can be cut on insurance, but it can also simply be because their costs are lower and they can do a better deal. If you have the time, check around for bargains. You will need to put down a large deposit (credit cards are usually, but not always, good for this).

It's very unlikely you'll be allowed to take a rental car across a border, but if you are (for example, from The Gambia into Senegal) make sure the paperwork is valid.

If you're uncertain about driving, most companies provide a chauffeur at very little extra cost and, with many, a chauffeur is mandatory. In many cases it's cheaper to go with a chauffeur as you will pay less for insurance.

It's also prudent, as getting stuck on your own is no fun and chauffeurs generally know the intricacies of checkpoint etiquette.

MOPEDS & MOTORCYCLES

In tourist areas, such as The Gambia and Senegal, and in some parts of Burkina Faso, it's possible to hire mopeds and motorbikes. In most other countries there is no formal rental available, but if you want to hire a motorbike (and know how to ride one) you can arrange something by asking at an auto-parts shop or repair yard, or by asking at the reception of your hotel. You can often be put in touch with someone who doesn't mind earning some extra cash by renting out their wheels for a day or two. Remember, though, that matters such as insurance will be easily overlooked, which is fine until you have an accident and find yourself liable for all bills. Also, if you do this, be sure to check out the motorbike in advance to ensure it's in acceptable mechanical condition.

Road Rules

Traffic drives on the right throughout West Africa (as in continental Europe and the USA), even in countries that have a British colonial heritage (such as The Gambia).

Road Safety

Road safety is probably your biggest safety risk in West Africa. Bush taxi drivers, in particular, race along at hair-raising speeds, and overtake blind, in order to reach their destination before another car can get in front of them in the queue for the return journey. Drivers can be sleepy from a long day, and drink-driving is a problem. Travelling early in the morning is one step you can take to cut the risk, as drivers are fresher and roads less travelled. Avoid night travel at all costs.

If you are in a vehicle and feel unsafe, and if it's a heavily travelled route, you can take your chances and get out at a major station to switch to another car (though don't expect a refund, and the second vehicle may not be much better). You can complain about dangerous driving, but this usually doesn't have any effect and, unless things are really out of control, you'll seldom get support from other passengers. Saying that you're feeling sick seems to get better results. Drivers are often quite considerate to ill or infirm passengers and, in any case, seem to care more about keeping vomit off their seats than about dying under the wheels of an oncoming lorry. You might be able to rally other passengers to your side this way as well. Most locals take a stoic approach to the situation, with many viewing accidents as a matter of the will of God or Allah. Drivers seem to discredit the idea that accidents are in any way related to vehicle speed or condition, or to wild driving practices.

Spare Parts

African mechanics are masters of ingenuity, using endlessly recycled parts to coax life out of ageing machines that would have long ago been consigned to the scrap heap in the West. That said, they're often unable to help with newer-model vehicles – for these, either bring your own spare parts, or check with your manufacturer for a list of accredited parts suppliers in West Africa. Be warned, however, that there may be very few (or none at all) of the latter.

Hitching

As in any other part of the world, hitching and accepting lifts in West Africa is never entirely safe, and we don't recommend it. Travellers who decide to hitch should understand that they are taking a small but potentially serious risk. If you're planning to travel this way, take advice from other hitchers (locals or travellers) first. Hitching in pairs is obviously safer, while hitching through less-salubrious suburbs, especially at night, is asking for trouble. Throughout most of the region, women should avoid hitching alone.

In many countries, as you venture further into rural areas, however, the frequency of buses or bush taxis drops, sometimes to nothing. Then the only way around is to ride on local trucks, as the locals do. A 'fare' is payable to the driver, so in cases like this the line between hitching and public transport is blurred – but if it's the only way to get around, you don't have a choice anyway. Usually you'll be riding on top of the cargo – it may be cotton or rice in sacks, which are quite comfy, but it might be logs or oil drums, which aren't.

If you want to hitch because there's no public transport leaving imminently from the *gare routière*, you'll normally have to go well beyond the town limits, as bush taxi drivers may take umbrage at other vehicles 'stealing' their customers. Even so, you'll probably still have to pay for your lift – but at least you'll get moving more quickly.

Hitching in the Western sense (ie because you don't want to get the bus or, more specifically, because you don't want to pay) is also possible but may take a long time. The only people giving free lifts are likely to be foreign expatriates or the occasional well-off local (very few West Africans own a car). Remember, however, that most people with space in their car want payment – usually on a par with what a bus would have cost.

Local Transport

For getting around cities and larger towns, you'll generally have a choice of bus (capital cities only) and a range of taxis.

Bus

➡ Within some capital cities, you may find well-developed city-bus and minibus networks connecting the city centre and suburbs. In most other cities, it's minibuses only.

➡ In general, city buses travel along set routes, while minibuses may detour a little more.

Taxi

MOTORCYCLE TAXI

In many countries, motorcycle taxis (moto-taxis or motos) are used. While they're often cheaper than shared taxis and handy for zipping around, safety can be an issue. If you have a choice, it's usually better to pay slightly more and go with a regular shared taxi.

PRIVATE TAXI

Only in the bigger cities, such as Dakar, Abidjan and Ouagadougou, do taxis have meters (compteurs). Otherwise, bargaining is required or you'll be given the legally fixed rate. In any case, determine the fare before getting into the taxi. The fare from

most airports into town is fixed, but some drivers (in Dakar, for example) will try to charge at least double this. In places like Bamako, it costs up to 50% more to go into town from the airport than it does to go the other way. The price always includes luggage unless you have a particularly bulky item. Also, fares invariably go up at night, and sometimes even in rainy weather.

If the city you're exploring is spread out and you've limited time, or if you're likely to be jumping in and out of taxis, consider renting a taxi by the hour or day. It will probably cost you less (anywhere from about US$20 to US$50 per day), and if the car breaks down it will be the driver's problem.

SHARED TAXI

Many cities have shared taxis that will stop and pick up more passengers even if they already have somebody inside; you pay just for one seat. Some run on fixed routes and are effectively a bus, only quicker and more comfortable. Others go wherever the first passenger wants to go, and other people will only be picked up if

they're going in the same direction. They normally shout the name of the suburb or a landmark they're heading for as the taxi goes past. In some places, it's common for the waiting passengers to call out the name of their destination or point in the desired direction as the taxi passes by.

Once you've got the hang of the shared taxi system, it's quick and inexpensive, and an excellent way to get around cities – and also a good way to experience local life. It's also one of West Africa's great bargains, as fares seldom exceed US$0.50. It's always worth checking the fare before you get in the car though, as they're not always fixed, and meters don't apply to shared trips. If you're the first person in the taxi, make it clear that you're expecting the driver to pick up others and that you don't want a private hire (déplacement, depo, 'charter' or 'town trip') all to yourself.

Train

There are railways in Mauritania, Senegal, Mali, Côte d'Ivoire, Ghana, Burkina Faso, Togo, Nigeria and Cameroon. Most services run only within the country of operation, but there are international services, notably between Dakar and Bamako, and, depending on the security situation in Côte d'Ivoire, between Ouagadougou and Abidjan.

Some trains are relatively comfortable, with 1st-class coaches that may have air-conditioning. Some also have sleeping compartments with two or four bunks. Other services are 2nd or 3rd class only and conditions can be uncomfortable, with no lights, no toilets and no glass in the windows (which equals no fun on long night journeys). Some trains have a restaurant on board, and you can usually buy things to eat and drink at stations along the way.

WEST AFRICA'S TOP TRAIN RIDES

Taking a long-distance West African train is the ultimate road movie with all the region's colours, smells and improbabilities of life writ large. More than a form of transport, West African trains are like moving cities, a stage for street performers, marketplaces and prayer halls. And, like most forms of transport in West Africa, you'll have plenty of time to contemplate the experience, whether waiting on a platform for your train to appear a mere 12 hours late or stopped on remote rails in the middle of nowhere for no apparent reason. But for all their faults (and there are many) the trains work and are an essential part of the West African experience. Our favourites:

➡ Zouérat to Nouâdhibou, Mauritania – one of the great train experiences of the world on the longest train in the world.

➡ Dakar to Bamako – at once endlessly fascinating and interminable (up to 40 hours).

Health

As long as you stay up to date with your vaccinations and take basic preventive measures, you'd have to be pretty unlucky to succumb to most of the health hazards we mention. Africa certainly has an impressive selection of tropical diseases on offer, but you're more likely to get a bout of diarrhoea (in fact, you should bank on it), a cold or an infected mosquito bite than an exotic disease such as sleeping sickness. When it comes to injuries (as opposed to illness), the most likely reason for needing medical help in West Africa is as a result of road accidents – vehicles are rarely well maintained, the roads are potholed and poorly lit, and drink-driving is common.

Before You Go

Planning & Preparation

A little planning before departure, particularly for pre-existing illnesses, will save you a lot of trouble later. Before a long trip get a check-up from your dentist, and from your doctor if you have any regular medication or a chronic illness, such as high blood pressure or asthma. You should also organise spare contact lenses and glasses (and take your optical prescription with you), get a first aid and medical kit together, and arrange necessary vaccinations.

It's tempting to leave it all to the last minute – don't! Many vaccines don't take effect until two weeks after you've been immunised, so visit a doctor four to eight weeks before departure. Ask your doctor for an International Certificate of Vaccination (otherwise known as the yellow booklet or *livre jaune*), which will list all the vaccinations you've received. This is mandatory for the African countries that require proof of yellow-fever vaccination upon entry, but it's a good idea to carry it anyway wherever you travel in case you require medical treatment or encounter troublesome border officials.

Travellers can register with the **International Association for Medical Advice to Travellers** (www.iamat.org). Its website can help travellers find a doctor who has recognised training. Those heading off to very remote areas might like to do a first-aid course (contact the Red Cross or St John Ambulance) or attend a remote medicine first-aid course, such as that offered by the **Royal Geographical Society** (www.wildernessmedicaltraining.co.uk).

If you are bringing medications with you, carry them in their original containers, clearly labelled. A signed and dated letter from your physician describing all medical conditions and medications, including generic names, is also a good idea. If carrying syringes or needles, be sure to have a physician's letter documenting their medical necessity.

Insurance

Find out in advance whether your insurance plan will make payments to providers or will reimburse you later for overseas health expenditures (in many countries doctors expect payment in cash). It's vital to ensure that your travel insurance will cover the emergency transport required to get you to a hospital in a major city, to better facilities elsewhere in Africa, or all the way home by air and with a medical attendant if necessary. Not all insurance covers this, so check the contract carefully. If you need medical help, your insurance company might be able to help locate the nearest hospital or clinic, or you can ask at your hotel. In an emergency, contact your embassy or consulate.

The **African Medical and Research Foundation** (www.amref.org) provides an air-evacuation service in medical emergencies in some African countries, as well as air-ambulance transfers between medical facilities. Money paid by members to their flying doctor service entitles you to air-ambulance evacuation, and the funds go into providing grass-roots medical assistance for local people.

Recommended Vaccinations

The **World Health Organization** (www.who.int/en) recommends that all travellers be covered for diphtheria, tetanus, measles, mumps, rubella and polio, as well as for hepatitis B, regardless of their destination. Planning to travel is a great time to ensure that all routine vaccination cover is complete. The consequences of these diseases can be severe, and outbreaks do occur.

According to the **Centers for Disease Control and Prevention** (wwwnc.cdc.gov/travel), the following vaccinations are recommended for all parts of Africa: hepatitis A, hepatitis B, meningococcal meningitis, rabies and typhoid, and boosters for tetanus, diphtheria and measles. Yellow-fever vaccination is not necessarily recommended for all parts of West Africa,

although the certificate is an entry requirement for many countries.

Medical Checklist

It is a very good idea to carry a medical and first aid kit with you, to help yourself in the case of minor illness or injury. Following is a list of items you should consider packing.

⇒ Acetaminophen (paracetamol) or aspirin

⇒ Acetazolamide (Diamox) for altitude sickness (prescription only)

⇒ Adhesive or paper tape

⇒ Antibacterial ointment (prescription only) for cuts and abrasions (eg Bactroban)

⇒ Antibiotics (prescription only), eg ciprofloxacin (Ciproxin) or norfloxacin (Utinor)

⇒ Anti-diarrhoeal drugs (eg loperamide)

⇒ Antihistamines (for hay fever and allergic reactions)

⇒ Anti-inflammatory drugs (eg ibuprofen)

⇒ Anti-malaria pills

⇒ Bandages, gauze, gauze rolls

⇒ DEET-containing insect repellent for the skin

⇒ Digital thermometer

⇒ Iodine tablets (for water purification)

⇒ Oral rehydration salts

⇒ Permethrin-containing insect spray for clothing, tents and bed nets

⇒ Pocket knife

⇒ Prickly-heat powder for heat rashes

⇒ Scissors, safety pins, tweezers

⇒ Sterile needles, syringes and fluids if travelling to remote areas

⇒ Steroid cream or hydrocortisone cream (for allergic rashes)

⇒ Sun block

If you are travelling through a malarial area – particularly an area where falciparum malaria predominates – consider taking a self-diagnostic kit that can identify malaria in the blood from a finger prick.

Websites

There is a wealth of travel-health advice on the internet. **Lonely Planet** (www.lonelyplanet.com) is a good place to start. The **World Health Organization** publishes the helpful *International Travel and Health*, available free at www.who.int/ith. Other useful websites include **MD Travel Health** (www.mdtravelhealth.com) and **Fit for Travel** (www.fitfortravel.scot.nhs.uk).

Official government travel health websites:

Australia (smartraveller.gov.au/guide/all-travellers/health/Pages/default.aspx)

Canada (www.hc-sc.gc.ca/index_e.html)

UK (www.gov.uk/foreign-travel-advice)

USA (www.nc.cdc.gov/travel)

MANDATORY YELLOW FEVER VACCINATION

⇒ **North Africa** Not mandatory for any of North Africa, but Algeria, Libya and Tunisia require evidence of yellow-fever vaccination if entering from an infected country. It is recommended for travellers to Sudan, and might be given to unvaccinated travellers leaving the country.

⇒ **Central Africa** Mandatory in Central African Republic (CAR) and the Democratic Republic of the Congo, and recommended in Chad.

⇒ **West Africa** Mandatory in Benin, Burkina Faso, Cameroon, Côte d'Ivoire, Equatorial Guinea, Gabon, Ghana, Liberia, Mali, Niger, the Republic of Congo, São Tomé & Príncipe and Togo, and recommended for The Gambia, Guinea, Guinea-Bissau, Mauritania, Nigeria, Senegal and Sierra Leone.

⇒ **East Africa** Mandatory in Rwanda; it is advised for Burundi, Ethiopia, Kenya, Somalia, Tanzania and Uganda.

⇒ **Southern Africa** Not mandatory for entry into any countries of Southern Africa, although it is necessary if entering from an infected country.

Further Reading

➡ *A Comprehensive Guide to Wilderness and Travel Medicine* (1998) by Eric A Weiss

➡ *The Essential Guide to Travel Health* (2009) by Jane Wilson-Howarth

➡ *Healthy Travel Africa* (2000) by Isabelle Young

➡ *How to Stay Healthy Abroad* (2002) by Richard Dawood

➡ *Travel in Health* (1994) by Graham Fry

➡ *Lonely Planet's Travel with Children* (2015) by Sophie Caupeil et al

In West Africa

Availability & Cost of Health Care

Health care in West Africa is varied: it can be excellent in the major cities, which generally have well-trained doctors and nurses, but it is often patchy off the beaten track. Medicine and even sterile dressings and intravenous fluids might need to be purchased from a local pharmacy by patients or their relatives. The standard of dental care is equally variable, and there is an increased risk of hepatitis B and HIV transmission via poorly sterilised equipment. By and large, public hospitals in Africa offer the cheapest service, but will have the least up-to-date equipment and medications; mission hospitals (where donations are the usual form of payment) often have more reasonable facilities; and private hospitals and clinics are more expensive but tend to have more advanced drugs and equipment and better-trained medical staff.

Most drugs can be purchased over the counter in West Africa, without a prescription. Many drugs for sale in West Africa might be ineffective: they might be counterfeit or might not

have been stored under the right conditions. The most common examples of counterfeit drugs are malaria tablets and expensive antibiotics, such as ciprofloxacin. Most drugs are available in capital cities, but remote villages will be lucky to have a couple of paracetamol tablets. It is recommended that all drugs for chronic diseases be brought from home. Also, the availability and efficacy of condoms cannot be relied on – bring contraception. Condoms bought in West Africa might not be of the same quality as in Europe or Australia, and they might not have been correctly stored.

There is a high risk of contracting HIV from infected blood if you receive a blood transfusion in West Africa. To minimise this, seek out treatment in reputable clinics. If you have any doubts, the **Blood Care Foundation** (www.bloodcare.org.uk) is a useful source of safe, screened blood, which can be transported to any part of the world within 24 hours.

The cost of health care might seem cheap compared to its cost in developed countries, but good care and drugs might not be available. Evacuation to good medical care (within West Africa or to your own country) can be very expensive. Unfortunately, adequate health care is available only to very few West Africans.

Infectious Diseases

It's a formidable list for West Africa, but, as we say, a few precautions go a long way...

CHOLERA

Although small outbreaks can occur, cholera is usually only a problem during natural or human-made disasters. Travellers are rarely affected. It is caused by a bacteria and spread via contaminated drinking water. The main symptom is profuse, watery diarrhoea, which causes debilitation if fluids are not

replaced quickly. An oral cholera vaccine is available, but it is not particularly effective. Most cases of cholera could be avoided by making sure you drink clean water and by avoiding potentially contaminated food. Treatment is by fluid replacement (orally or via a drip), but sometimes antibiotics are needed. Self-treatment is not advised.

DENGUE FEVER

Found in Senegal, Burkina Faso, Guinea, and some parts of East and Southern Africa, dengue fever (also called 'breakbone fever') is spread by mosquito bites. It causes a feverish illness with headache and muscle pains similar to those experienced with a bad, prolonged attack of influenza. There might be a rash. Self-treatment: paracetamol and rest. In rare cases in Africa this becomes Severe Dengue Fever, with worsening symptoms including vomiting, rapid breathing and abdominal pain. Seek medical help as this can be fatal.

DIPTHERIA

Spread through close respiratory contact, diphtheria is found in all of Africa. It usually causes a temperature and a severe sore throat. Sometimes a membrane forms across the throat, and a tracheostomy is needed to prevent suffocation. Vaccination is recommended for those likely to be in close contact with the local population in infected areas. More important for long stays than for short-term trips, the vaccine is given as an injection alone or with tetanus, and lasts 10 years.

FILARIASIS

Tiny worms migrating in the lymphatic system cause filariasis. It is found in most of West, Central, East and Southern Africa, and in Sudan in North Africa. A bite from an infected mosquito

Malarial Risk in Africa

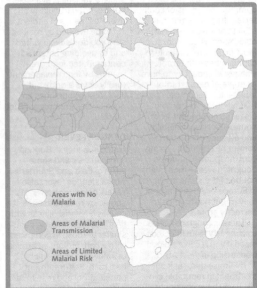

Areas with No
Malaria

Areas of Malarial
Transmission

Areas of Limited
Malarial Risk

spreads the infection. Symptoms include itching and swelling of the legs and/or genitalia. Treatment is available.

HEPATITIS A

Found in all of Africa, hepatitis A is spread through contaminated food (particularly shellfish) and water. It causes jaundice and is rarely fatal, but can cause prolonged lethargy and delayed recovery. If you've had hepatitis A, you shouldn't drink alcohol for up to six months after, but once you've recovered, there won't be any long-term problems. The first symptoms include dark urine and a yellow colour to the whites of the eyes. Sometimes a fever and abdominal pain might occur. Hepatitis A vaccine (Avaxim, VAQTA, Havrix) is given as an injection: a single dose will give protection for a year, and a booster after a year gives 10-year protection. Hepatitis A and typhoid vaccines can also be given as a single-dose vaccine (Hepatyrix or Viatim).

HEPATITIS B

Spread through infected blood, contaminated needles and sexual intercourse, Hepatitis B is found in Africa. It can be spread from an infected mother to the baby in childbirth. It affects the liver, causing jaundice and occasionally liver failure. Most people recover completely, but some might be chronic carriers of the virus, which can lead eventually to cirrhosis or liver cancer. Those visiting high-risk areas for long periods or with increased social or occupational risk should be immunised. Many countries now give Hepatitis B as part of the routine childhood vaccination. It is given singly or can be given at the same time as Hepatitis A (Hepatyrix).

A course of vaccinations will give protection for at least five years. It can be given over four weeks or six months.

HIV & AIDS

Human immunodeficiency virus (HIV), the virus that causes acquired immune deficiency syndrome (AIDS), is a huge problem in Africa but is most acutely felt in sub-Saharan Africa. The virus is spread through infected blood and blood products, by sexual intercourse with an infected partner, and from an infected mother to her baby during childbirth and breastfeeding. It can be spread through 'blood to blood' contacts, such as with contaminated instruments during medical, dental, acupuncture and other body-piercing procedures, and through sharing intravenous needles. At present there is no cure; medication that might keep the disease under control is available, but these drugs are too expensive for the overwhelming majority of Africans, and are not readily available for travellers either. If you think you might have been infected with HIV, a blood test is necessary; a three-month gap after exposure and before testing is required to allow antibodies to appear in the blood.

LEPTOSPIROSIS

This is found in West and Southern Africa; in Chad and the Democratic Republic of the Congo in Central Africa; in Algeria, Morocco and Sudan in North Africa; and in Ethiopia and Somalia in East Africa. It is spread through the excreta of infected rodents, especially rats. It can cause hepatitis and renal failure, which might be fatal. It is unusual for travellers to be affected unless they're living in poor sanitary conditions. It causes a fever and sometimes jaundice.

MALARIA

Malaria is a widespread risk in West Africa and the risk of catching it should be taken seriously. The disease is caused by a parasite in the bloodstream spread via the bite of the female Anopheles mosquito. There are several types of malaria. Infection rates vary with season and climate, so check out the situation before departure. Several different drugs are used to prevent malaria, and new ones are in the pipeline. Up-to-date advice from a travel health clinic is essential as some medication is more suitable for some travellers than others (eg people with epilepsy should avoid mefloquine, and doxycycline should not be taken by pregnant women or children aged under 12).

The early stages of malaria include headaches, fevers, generalised aches and pains, and malaise, which could be mistaken for flu. Other symptoms can include abdominal pain, diarrhoea and a cough. Anyone who develops a fever in a malarial area should assume malarial infection until a blood test proves negative, even if you have been taking antimalarial medication. If not treated, the next stage could develop within 24 hours, particularly if falciparum malaria is the parasite: jaundice, then reduced consciousness and coma (also known as cerebral malaria), followed by death. Treatment in hospital is essential, and the death rate might still be as high as 10% even in the best intensive-care facilities.

Many travellers think that malaria is a mild illness, and that taking antimalarial drugs causes more illness through side effects than actually getting malaria. This is unfortunately not true. If you decide against antimalarial drugs, you must understand the risks, and be obsessive about avoiding mosquito bites. Use nets and insect repellent, and report any fever or flulike symptoms to a doctor as soon as possible. Some people advocate homeopathic preparations against malaria, such as Demal200, but as yet there is no conclusive evidence that this is effective, and

many homeopaths do not recommend their use.

Malaria in pregnancy frequently results in miscarriage or premature labour, and the risks to both mother and foetus during pregnancy are considerable. Travel throughout the region when pregnant should be carefully considered. Adults who have survived childhood malaria have developed immunity and usually only develop mild cases of malaria; most Western travellers have no immunity at all. Immunity wanes after 18 months of nonexposure, so even if you have had malaria in the past and used to live in a malaria-prone area, you might no longer be immune.

MENINGOCOCCAL MENINGITIS

Meningococcal infection is spread through close respiratory contact and is more likely in crowded situations, such as dormitories, buses and clubs. Infection is uncommon in travellers. Vaccination is recommended for long stays and is especially important towards the end of the dry season, which varies across the continent.

Symptoms include a fever, severe headache, neck stiffness and a red rash. Immediate medical treatment is necessary.

The ACWY vaccine is recommended for all travellers in sub-Saharan Africa. This vaccine is different from the meningococcal meningitis C vaccine given to children and adolescents in some countries; it is safe to be given both types of vaccine.

ONCHOCERCIASIS

Also known as 'river blindness', this is caused by the larvae of a tiny worm, which is spread by the bite of a small fly. The earliest sign of infection is intensely itchy, red, sore eyes. Travellers are rarely severely affected. Treatment in a specialised clinic is curative.

POLIOMYELITIS

Polio is generally spread through contaminated food and water. The vaccine is one of those given in childhood and should be boosted every 10 years, either orally (a drop on the tongue) or as an injection. Polio can be carried asymptomatically (ie showing no symptoms) and

---

THE ANTIMALARIAL A TO D

A – Awareness of the risk. No medication is totally effective, but protection of up to 95% is achievable with most drugs, as long as other measures have been taken.

B – Bites: avoid at all costs. Sleep in a screened room, use a mosquito spray or coils, sleep under a permethrin-impregnated net. Cover up at night with long trousers and long sleeves, preferably with permethrin-treated clothing. Apply appropriate repellent to all areas of exposed skin in the evenings.

C – Chemical prevention (ie antimalarial drugs). These are usually required in malarial areas. Expert advice is needed as resistance patterns can change, and new drugs are in development. Not all antimalarial drugs are suitable for everyone. Most antimalarial drugs need to be started at least a week in advance and continued for four weeks after the last possible exposure to malaria.

D – Diagnosis. If you have a fever or flu-like illness within a year of travel to a malarial area, malaria is a possibility, and immediate medical attention is necessary.

could cause a transient fever. In rare cases it causes weakness or paralysis of one or more muscles, which might be permanent. Niger and and Nigeria have both suffered recent outbreaks.

RABIES

Rabies is spread by receiving the bites or licks of an infected animal on broken skin. It's fatal once the clinical symptoms start (which might be up to several months after the injury), so post-bite vaccination should be given as soon as possible. Post-bite vaccination (whether or not you've been vaccinated before the bite) prevents the virus from spreading to the central nervous system. Animal handlers should be vaccinated, as should those travelling to remote areas where a source of post-bite vaccine is not available within 24 hours. Three preventative injections are needed in a month. If you have not been vaccinated you will need a course of five injections starting 24 hours or as soon as possible after the injury. If you have been vaccinated, you will need fewer post-bite injections and will have more time to seek medical aid.

SCHISTOSOMIASIS

Also called bilharzia, this disease is spread by flukes that are carried by a species of freshwater snail. The flukes are carried inside the snail, which then sheds them into slow-moving or still water. The parasites penetrate human skin during paddling or swimming and then migrate to the bladder or bowel. They are passed out via stools or urine and can contaminate fresh water, where the cycle starts again. Avoid paddling or swimming in suspect freshwater lakes or slow-running rivers. There may be no symptoms or there may be a transient fever and rash, and advanced cases can have blood in the

stool or in the urine. A blood test can detect antibodies if you have been exposed, and treatment is then possible in travel- or infectious-disease clinics. If not treated, the infection can cause kidney failure or permanent bowel damage. It isn't possible for you to infect others.

TUBERCULOSIS (TB)

TB is spread through close respiratory contact and occasionally through infected milk or milk products. BCG (Bacille Calmette-Guérin) vaccination is recommended for those likely to be mixing closely with the local population, although it gives only moderate protection against TB. It is more important for long stays than for short-term stays. Inoculation with the BCG vaccine is not available in all countries. It is given routinely to many children in developing countries. The vaccination causes a small, permanent scar at the injection site and is usually given in a specialised chest clinic. It is a live vaccine and should not be given to pregnant women or immunocompromised individuals.

TB can be asymptomatic, only being picked up on a routine chest X-ray. Alternatively, it can cause a cough, weight loss or fever, sometimes months or even years after exposure.

TYPHOID

This is spread through food or water contaminated by infected human faeces. The first symptom is usually a fever or a pink rash on the abdomen. Sometimes septicaemia (blood poisoning) can occur. A typhoid vaccine (typhim Vi, typherix) will give protection for three years. In some countries, the oral vaccine Vivotif is also available. Antibiotics are usually given as treatment, and death is rare unless septicaemia occurs.

TRYPANOSOMIASIS

Spread via the bite of the tsetse fly, trypanosomiasis, also called 'sleeping sickness', causes a headache, fever and eventually coma. There is an effective treatment.

YELLOW FEVER

Travellers should carry a certificate as evidence of vaccination if they have recently been in an infected country, to avoid any possible difficulties with immigration. For a full list of these countries visit the websites of WHO (www.who. int/en) or the Centers for Disease Control and Prevention (wwwnc.cdc.gov/travel). There is always the possibility that a traveller without a legally required, up-to-date certificate will be vaccinated and detained in isolation at the port of arrival for up to 10 days, or possibly repatriated.

Yellow fever is spread by infected mosquitoes. Symptoms range from a flu-like illness to severe hepatitis (liver inflammation), jaundice and death. The yellow-fever vaccination must be given at a designated clinic and is valid for 10 years. It is a live vaccine and must not be given to immunocompromised or pregnant travellers.

Traveller's Diarrhoea

It's not inevitable that you will get diarrhoea while travelling in Africa, but it's certainly likely. Diarrhoea is the most common travel-related illness – figures suggest that at least half of all travellers to Africa will get diarrhoea at some stage. Sometimes dietary changes, such as increased spices or oils, are the cause. To help prevent diarrhoea, avoid tap water unless you're sure it's safe to drink. You should only eat cooked or peeled fresh fruits or vegetables, and be wary of dairy products that might contain unpasteurised milk. Although freshly cooked food can often be a safe option, plates or serving utensils might be dirty, so you should be very selective when eating food from street vendors (make sure that cooked food is piping hot all the way through). If you develop diarrhoea, be sure to drink plenty of fluids, preferably an oral rehydration solution containing water, and some salt and sugar. A few loose stools don't require treatment, but if you start having more than four or five a day you should start taking an antibiotic (often a quinoline drug, such as ciprofloxacin or norfloxacin) and an anti-diarrhoeal agent (such as loperamide) if you are not within easy reach of a toilet. If diarrhoea is bloody, persists for over 72 hours or is accompanied by fever, shaking, chills or severe abdominal pain, you should seek medical attention.

Yellow Fever Risk in Africa

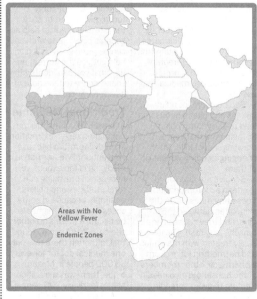

Areas with No Yellow Fever

Endemic Zones

AMOEBIC DYSENTERY

Contracted by eating contaminated food and water, amoebic dysentery causes blood and mucus in the faeces. It can be relatively mild and tends to come on gradually, but seek medical advice if you think you have the illness, as it won't clear up without treatment (which is with specific antibiotics).

GIARDIASIS

Like amoebic dysentery, this is caused by ingesting contaminated food or water. The illness appears a week or more after you have been exposed to the parasite. Giardiasis might cause only a short-lived bout of traveller's diarrhoea, but it can cause persistent diarrhoea. Seek medical advice if you suspect you have giardiasis, but if you are in a remote area you could start a course of antibiotics.

Environmental Hazards

HEAT EXHAUSTION

This condition occurs following heavy sweating and excessive fluid loss with inadequate replacement of fluids and salt, and is common in hot climates when taking exercise before full acclimatisation. Symptoms include headache, dizziness and tiredness. Dehydration is happening by the time you feel thirsty – aim to drink sufficient water to produce pale, diluted urine. Treatment involves fluid replacement with water and/or fruit juice, and cooling by cold water and fans. The treatment of the salt-loss component consists of consuming salty fluids, as in soup, and adding a bit more salt to food than usual.

HEATSTROKE

Heat exhaustion is a precursor to the much more serious heatstroke. In this case there is damage to the sweating mechanism, with an excessive rise in body temperature; irrational and hyperactive behaviour; and eventually loss of consciousness and death. Rapid cooling by spraying the body with water and fanning is best. Emergency fluid and electrolyte replacement is required by intravenous drip.

INSECT BITES & STINGS

Mosquitoes might not always carry malaria or dengue fever, but they (and other insects) can cause irritation and infected bites. To avoid these, take the same precautions as you would for avoiding malaria. Use DEET-based insect repellents. Excellent clothing treatments are also available; mosquitos that land on treated clothing will die.

Bee and wasp stings cause real problems only to those who have a severe allergy to the stings (anaphylaxis). If you are one of these people, carry an EpiPen – an adrenaline (epinephrine) injection, which you can give yourself. This could save your life.

Sandflies are found around the beaches. They usually only cause a nasty, itchy bite but can carry a rare skin disorder called cutaneous leishmaniasis. Prevention of bites with DEET-based repellents is sensible.

Scorpions are frequently found in arid or dry climates. They have a painful sting that is sometimes life-threatening. If stung by a scorpion, seek immediate medical assistance.

Bed bugs are found in hostels and cheap hotels and lead to itchy, lumpy bites. Spraying the mattress with crawling-insect killer after changing bedding will get rid of them.

Scabies are also found in cheap accommodation. These tiny mites live in the skin, often between the fingers, and they cause an intensely itchy rash. The itch is easily treated with malathion and permethrin lotion from a pharmacy; other members of the household also need treating to avoid spreading scabies, even if they do not show any symptoms.

In Gabon and neighbouring countries, the fourou is tiny insect you can neither see nor hear: it bites between 5pm and 6.30pm, is not deterred by anti-mosquito spray and can fly straight through mosquito nets. It leaves very itchy red welts on the skin.

SNAKE BITES

Avoid getting bitten! Don't walk barefoot, or stick your hand into holes or cracks. However, 50% of those bitten by venomous snakes are not actually injected with poison. If bitten by a snake, do not panic. Immobilise the bitten limb with a splint (such as a stick) and apply a bandage over the site with firm pressure (similar to bandaging a sprain). Do not apply a tourniquet, or cut or suck the bite. Get medical help as soon as possible so antivenin can be given if needed. It will help get you the correct antivenin if you can identify the snake, so try to take note of its appearance.

Traditional Medicine

At least 80% of the African population relies on traditional medicine, often because conventional Western-style medicine is too expensive, because of prevailing cultural attitudes and beliefs, or simply because in some cases it works. It might also be because there's no other choice: a WHO survey found that, although there was only one medical doctor for every 50,000 people in Mozambique, there was a traditional healer for every 200 people.

Although some African remedies seem to work on malaria, sickle cell anaemia, high blood pressure and some AIDS symptoms, most African healers learn their art by apprenticeship, so education (and consequently application of knowledge) is inconsistent and unregulated. Conventionally trained physicians in South Africa, for example, angrily describe how their AIDS patients die of kidney failure because a *sangoma* (traditional healer) has given them an enema containing an essence made from powerful roots. Likewise, when traditional healers administer 'injections' with porcupine quills, knives or dirty razor blades, diseases are often spread or created rather than cured.

Rather than attempting to stamp out traditional practices, or pretend they aren't happening, a positive step taken by some African countries is the regulation of traditional medicine by creating healers' associations and offering courses on such topics as sanitary practices. It remains unlikely in the short term that even a basic level of conventional Western-style medicine will be made available to all the people of Africa (even though the cost of doing so is less than the annual military budget of some Western countries). Traditional medicine, on the other hand, will almost certainly continue to be practised widely throughout the continent.

In Transit

Deep Vein Thrombosis (DVT)

Blood clots can form in the legs during flights, chiefly because of prolonged immobility. This formation of clots is known as deep vein thrombosis (DVT), and the longer the flight, the greater the risk. Although most blood clots are reabsorbed uneventfully, some might break off and travel through the blood vessels to the lungs, where they could cause life-threatening complications.

The chief symptom of DVT is swelling or pain of the foot, ankle or calf, usually but not always on just one side. When a blood clot travels to the lungs, it could cause chest pain and breathing difficulty. Travellers with any of these symptoms should immediately seek medical attention.

To prevent the development of DVT on flights you should walk about the cabin, perform isometric compressions of the leg muscles (ie contract the leg muscles

TAP WATER

Never drink tap water unless it has been boiled, filtered or chemically disinfected (eg with iodine tablets).

Also, never drink from streams, rivers or lakes. It's best to avoid drinking from pumps and wells – some do bring pure water to the surface, but the presence of animals can contaminate supplies.

while sitting), drink plenty of fluids, and avoid alcohol.

Jet Lag & Motion Sickness

If you're crossing more than five time zones you could suffer jet lag, resulting in insomnia, fatigue, malaise or nausea. To avoid jet lag drink plenty of (nonalcoholic) fluids and eat light meals. Upon arrival, get exposure to natural sunlight and readjust your schedule (for meals, sleep, etc) as soon as possible.

Antihistamines such as dimenhydrinate (Dramamine) and meclizine (Antivert, Bonine) are usually the first choice for treating motion sickness. The main side effect of these drugs is drowsiness. A herbal alternative is ginger (in the form of ginger tea, ginger biscuits or crystallised ginger), which works like a charm for some people.

Language

West Africa's myriad ethnic groups speak several hundred local languages, many sub-divided into numerous distinct dialects. The people of Nigeria – West Africa's most populous country – speak at least 350 languages and dialects, while even tiny Guinea-Bissau (population just over one million) has around 20 languages.

Consequently, common languages are essential, and several are used. These may be the language of the largest group in a particular area. For example, Hausa has spread out from its northern Nigerian heartland to become widely understood as a trading language in the eastern parts of West Africa. Two other regional lingua francas are Wolof and Yoruba, and we've included the basics of all three in this chapter. In some areas, the lingua franca is a creole – a combination of native African and imported European languages.

All of the countries covered in this book have one of the following languages as official language: English (Cameroon, the Gambia, Ghana, Liberia, Nigeria and Sierra Leone), French (Benin, Burkina Faso, Cameroon, Côte d'Ivoire, Guinea, Mali, Niger, Senegal and Togo), Portuguese (Cape Verde and Guinea-Bissau) or Arabic (Mauritania and Morocco). These languages are also included in this chapter, so you'll be able to get by and be understood across West Africa. See the relevant destination chapter for a list of African languages also spoken in each country.

WANT MORE?

For in-depth language information and handy phrases, check out Lonely Planet's *Africa phrasebook*, *French phrasebook*, *Moroccan ArabicpPhrasebook* and *Portuguese p hrasebook*. You'll find them at **shop.lonelyplanet.com**, or you can buy Lonely Planet's iPhone phrasebooks at the Apple App Store.

ARABIC

The following phrases are in MSA (Modern Standard Arabic), which is the official language of the Arab world, used in schools, administration and the media. Note, though, that there are significant differences between MSA and the colloquial Arabic varieties, which are spoken in different countries but have no official written form: the Moroccan Arabic variety is known as Darija, and the dialect spoken in Mauritania is called Hassaniyya.

Arabic script is written from right to left. Read our coloured pronunciation guides as if they were English and you should be understood. Note that a is pronounced as in 'act', aa as the 'a' in 'father', aw as in 'law', ay as in 'say', ee as in 'see', i as in 'hit', oo as in 'zoo', u as in 'put', gh is a throaty sound, r is rolled, dh is pronounced as in 'that', th as in 'thin' and kh as the 'ch' in the Scottish *loch*. The apostrophe (') indicates the glottal stop (like the pause in the middle of 'uh-oh'). The stressed syllables are indicated with italics. Masculine and feminine options are indicated with 'm' and 'f' respectively.

Basics

Hello.	السلام عليكم.	as·sa·*laa*·mu 'a·*lay*·kum
Goodbye.	إلى اللقاء.	'i·laa al·li·*kaa*'
Yes.	نعم.	na·'am
No.	لا.	laa
Excuse me.	عفواً.	'af·wan
Sorry.	أسف.	*aa*·sif (m)
	أسفة.	*aa*·si·fa (f)
Please.	لو سمحتَ.	law sa·*mah*·ta (m)
	لو سمحتِ.	law sa·*mah*·ti (f)
Thank you.	شكراً.	*shuk*·ran

How are you?

كيف حالك؟	*kay*·fa *haa*·lu·ka (m)
كيف حالك؟	*kay*·fa *haa*·lu·ki (f)

Fine, thanks. And you?

بخير شكراً. bi-*khay*-rin shuk-ran

وأنتَ/أنتِ؟ wa-'an-ta/wa-'an-ti (m/f)

What's your name?

ما اسمكَ؟ maa 'is-mu-ka (m)

ما اسمكِ؟ maa 'is-mu-ki (f)

My name is ...

اسمي ... 'is-mee ...

Do you speak English?

هل تتكلَّم/ hal ta-ta-*kal*-la-mu/

تتكلّمينَ ta-ta-kal-la-*mee*-na

الإنجليزيّة؟ al-'inj-lee-*zee*-ya (m/f)

I don't understand.

أنا لا أفهم. 'a-naa laa 'af-ham

Accommodation

Where's a ...? أين أجدُ ...؟ 'ay-na 'a-ji-du ...

campsite مخيم mu-*khay*-yam

guesthouse بيت للضيوف bayt li-du-*yoof*

hotel فندق *fun*-duk

youth hostel فندق شباب *fun*-duk sha-*baab*

Do you have a ... room? هل عندكم hal 'in-da-kum

غرفة ...؟ *ghur*-fa-tun ...

single بسرير bi-sa-*ree*-rin

منفردٍ *mun*-fa-rid

double بسريرٍ bi-sa-*ree*-rin

مزدوّج muz-*daw*-waj

How much is it per ...? كم ثمنه kam tha-ma-nu-hu

لِ ...؟ li ...

night ليلةٍ واحدة *lay*-la-tin waa-hid

person شخصٍ واحدة *shakh*-sin waa-hid

Eating & Drinking

Can you recommend a ...? هل يمكنكَ أن hal yum-*ki*-nu-ka 'an

توصي ...؟ too-*see*-ya ... (m)

هل يمكنكِ أن hal yum-ki-nu-ki 'an

توصي ...؟ too-*see* ... (f)

cafe مقهىً mak-han

restaurant مطعمّ mat-'am

What would you recommend?

ماذا توصي؟ maa-dhaa too-see (m)

ماذا توصينَ؟ maa-dhaa too-see-na (f)

What's the local speciality?

ما الوجبة الخاصّة maa al-*waj*-ba-tul *khaa*-sa

لهذه المنطقة؟ li-*haa*-dhi-hil *man*-ta-ka

Do you have vegetarian food?

هل لديكم hal la-*day*-ku-mu

طعامٌ نباتيّ؟ ta-'aa-mun na-*baa*-tee

I'd like the ..., please. أريد .... 'u-*ree*-du ...

لو سمحتَ. law sa-*mah*-ta

bill الحساب hi-*saab*

menu قائمة kaa-'i-ma-tu

الطعام at-ta-'aam

beer بيرة *bee*-ra

bottle زجاجة zu-*jaa*-ja

breakfast فطور fu-*toor*

coffee قهوة *kah*-wa

cold باردة baa-rid/baa-ri-da (m/f)

cup فنجان fin-*jaan*

dinner عشاء 'a-*shaa*'

drink مشروب mash-*roob*

fish سمك *sa*-mak

food طعام ta-*'aam*

fork شوكة *shaw*-ka

fruit فاكهة *faa*-ki-ha

glass كأس ka's

hot حار/حارة haar/*haa*-ra (m/f)

(orange) juice عصير 'a-*see*-ru

(برتقال) (bur-tu-*kaal*)

knife سكين sik-*keen*

lunch غداء gha-*daa*'

market سوق sook

meat لحم lahm

milk حليب ha-*leeb*

mineral water مياه معدنية mi-*yaah* ma'-da-*nee*-ya

plate صحن sahn

spoon ملعقة *mal*-'a-ka

vegetable خضراوات khud-raa-*waat*

water ماء maa'

wine نبيذ na-*beedh*

with مع ma-'a

without بدون bi-*doo*-ni

Emergencies

Help! ساعدني! saa-'i-du-nee (m)

ساعديني! saa-'i-*dee*-nee (f)

Go away! اتركني! 'it-*ruk*-nee (m)

اتركيني! 'it-ru-*kee*-nee (f)

Call ...! اتّصلْ بـ ...! 'it-*ta*-sil bi ... (m)

اتّصلي بـ ...! 'it-*ta*-si-lee bi ... (f)

a doctor طبيب ta-*beeb*

the police الشرطة ash-*shur*-ta

Where are the toilets?

أينَ دورات المياه؟ 'ay-na daw-*raa*-tul mee-*yaah*

Numbers – Arabic

1	١	واحد	waa·hid
2	٢	اثنان	'ith·naan
3	٣	ثلاثة	tha·laa·tha
4	٤	أربعة	'ar·ba·a
5	٥	خمسة	kham·sa
6	٦	ستة	sit·ta
7	٧	سبعة	sab·'a
8	٨	ثمانية	tha·maa·ni·ya
9	٩	تسعة	tis·'a
10	١٠	عشرة	'a·sha·ra
20	٢٠	عشرون	'ish·roon
30	٣٠	ثلاثون	tha·laa·thoon
40	٤٠	أربعون	'ar·ba·'oon
50	٥٠	خمسون	kham·soon
60	٦٠	ستون	sit·toon
70	٧٠	سبعون	sab·'oon
80	٨٠	ثمانون	tha·maa·noon
90	٩٠	تسعون	tis·'oon
100	١٠٠	مائة	mi·'a
1000	١٠٠٠	ألف	'alf

Note that Arabic numerals, unlike letters, are written from left to right.

I'm lost.

أنا ضائع. *'a·naa daa·'i'* (m)

أنا ضائعة. *'a·naa daa·'i·'a* (f)

I'm sick.

أنا مريض. *'a·naa ma·reed*

Shopping & Services

I'm looking for ...

أبحث عن ... *'ab·ha·thu 'an ...*

Can I look at it?

هل يمكنني أن أراه؟ *hal yum·ki·nu·nee 'an 'a·raa·hu*

Do you have any others?

هل عندك غيره؟ *hal 'in·da·kum ghay·ru·hu*

How much is it?

كم سعره؟ *kam si'·ru·hu*

That's too expensive.

هذا غال جداً. *haa·dhaa ghaa·lin jid·dan*

There's a mistake in the bill.

في خطأ في الحساب. *fee kha·ta' feel hi·saab*

Where's an ATM?

أين جهاز الصرافة؟ *'ay·na ji·haaz as·sar·raa·fa*

Time & Dates

What time is it?

كم الساعة الآن؟ *kam as·saa·'a·tul 'aan*

It's (two) o'clock.

الساعة(الثانية). *as·saa·'a tu (ath·thaa·nee·ya)*

Half past (two).

(الثانية) *(ath·thaa·nee·ya·tu)*
والنصف. *wan·nus·fu*

morning	صباح	sa·baah
afternoon	بعد الظهر	ba·'da adh·dhuh·ri
evening	مساء	ma·saa'
yesterday	أمس	'am·si
today	اليوم	al·yawm
tomorrow	غداً	gha·dan

Monday	يوم الاثنين	yawm al·'ith·nayn
Tuesday	يوم الثلاثاء	yawm ath·thu·laa·thaa'
Wednesday	يوم الأربعاء	yawm al·'ar·bi·'aa
Thursday	يوم الخميس	yawm al·kha·mees
Friday	يوم الجمعة	yawm al·jum·'a
Saturday	يوم السبت	yawm as·sabt
Sunday	يوم الأحد	yawm al·'a·had

Transport & Directions

Is this the ... هل هذا الـ ... *hal haa·dhaa al ...*
to (...)? إلى (...)؟ *'i·laa (...)*

boat	سفينة	sa·fee·na
bus	باص	baas
plane	طائرة	taa·'i·ra
train	قطار	ki·taar

What time's في أيّ ساعة *fee 'ay·yee saa·'a·tin*
the ... bus? يغادر الباص *yu·ghaa·di·ru al·baas*
  الـ ...؟ *al ...*

first	أوّل	'aw·wal
last	آخر	'aa·khir

One ... ticket, ... تذكرة *tadh·ka·ra·tu ...*
please. واحدة، لو سمحت. *waa·hi·da law sa·mah·ta*

one-way	ذهاب فقط	dha·haa·bu fa·kat
return	ذهاب	dha·haa·bu
	وإياب	wa·'ee·yaab

How much is it to ...?

كم الأجرة إلى ...؟ *kam al·'uj·ra·ti 'i·laa ...*

Please take me to (this address).

أوصلني عند *'aw·sal·nee 'ind*
(هذا العنوان) *(haa·dhaa al·'un·waan)*
لو سمحت. *law sa·mah·ta*

Where's the (market)?
أين الـ (سوق)؟   'ay·na al (sook)

Can you show me (on the map)?
هل يمكنك أن   hal yum·ki·nu·ka 'an
توضح لي   tu·wad·da·ha lee
(على الخريطة)؟   ('a·laa al·kha·ree·ta) (m)

هل يمكنك أن   hal yum·ki·nu·ki 'an
توضحي لي   tu·wad·da·hee lee
(على الخريطة)؟   ('a·laa al·kha·ree·ta) (f)

What's the address?
ما هو العنوان؟   maa hu·wa al·'un·waan

FRENCH

The sounds used in spoken French can almost all be found in English. There are a couple of exceptions: nasal vowels (represented in our pronunciation guides by o or u followed by an almost inaudible nasal consonant sound m, n or ng), the 'funny' u (ew in our guides) and the deep-in-the-throat r. Bearing these few points in mind and reading our pronunciation guides below as if they were English, you won't have problems being understood. Note that syllables are for the most part equally stressed in French.

Masculine and feminine forms of words are provided in the following phrases where relevant, indicated with 'm' and 'f' respectively.

Basics

Hello.	Bonjour.	bon·zhoor
Goodbye.	Au revoir.	o·rer·vwa
Excuse me.	Excusez-moi.	ek·skew·zay·mwa
Sorry.	Pardon.	par·don
Yes.	Oui.	wee
No.	Non.	non
Please.	S'il vous plaît.	seel voo play
Thank you.	Merci.	mair·see
You're welcome.	De rien.	der ree·en

How are you?
Comment allez-vous?   ko·mon ta·lay·voo

Fine, and you?
Bien, merci. Et vous?   byun mair·see ay voo

My name is ...
Je m'appelle ...   zher ma·pel ...

What's your name?
Comment vous appelez-vous?   ko·mon voo·za·play voo

Do you speak English?
Parlez-vous anglais?   par·lay·voo ong·glay

I don't understand.
Je ne comprends pas.   zher ner kom·pron pa

Accommodation

campsite	camping	kom·peeng
guesthouse	pension	pon·syon
hotel	hôtel	o·tel
youth hostel	auberge de jeunesse	o·berzh der zher·nes
a ... room	une chambre ...	ewn shom·brer ...
double	avec un grand lit	a·vek un gron lee
single	à un lit	a un lee

How much is it per night/person?
Quel est le prix   kel ay ler pree
par nuit/personne?   par nwee/per·son

Is breakfast included?
Est-ce que le petit   es·ker ler per·tee
déjeuner est inclus?   day·zher·nay ayt en·klew

Eating & Drinking

Can I see the menu, please?
Est-ce que je peux voir   es·ker zher per vwar
la carte, s'il vous plaît?   la kart seel voo play

What would you recommend?
Qu'est-ce que vous   kes·ker voo
conseillez?   kon·say·yay

I'm a vegetarian.
Je suis végétarien/   zher swee vay·zhay·ta·ryun/
végétarienne. (m/f)   vay·zhay·ta·ryen

I don't eat ...
Je ne mange pas ...   zher ner monzh pa ...

Cheers!
Santé!   son·tay

Please bring the bill.
Apportez-moi   a·por·tay·mwa
l'addition,   la·dee·syon
s'il vous plaît.   seel voo play

beer	bière	bee·yair
bottle	bouteille	boo·tay
bread	pain	pun
breakfast	petit déjeuner	per·tee day·zher·nay
cheese	fromage	fro·mazh
coffee	café	ka·fay
cold	froid	frwa
dinner	dîner	dee·nay
dish	plat	pla
egg	œuf	erf
food	nourriture	noo·ree·tewr
fork	fourchette	foor·shet

glass	*verre*	vair
grocery store	*épicerie*	ay·pees·ree
hot	*chaud*	sho
(orange) juice	*jus (d'orange)*	zhew (do·ronzh)
knife	*couteau*	koo·to
local speciality	*spécialité locale*	spay·sya·lee·tay lo·kal
lunch	*déjeuner*	day·zher·nay
main course	*plat principal*	pla prun·see·pal
market	*marché*	mar·shay
milk	*lait*	lay
plate	*assiette*	a·syet
red wine	*vin rouge*	vun roozh
rice	*riz*	ree
salt	*sel*	sel
spoon	*cuillère*	kwee·yair
sugar	*sucre*	sew·krer
tea	*thé*	tay
vegetable	*légume*	lay·gewm
(mineral) water	*eau (minérale)*	o (mee·nay·ral)
white wine	*vin blanc*	vun blong
with/without	*avec/sans*	a·vek/son

Emergencies

Help!
Au secours! — o skoor

I'm lost.
Je suis perdu/perdue. — zhe swee·pair·dew (m/f)

Leave me alone!
Fichez-moi la paix! — fee·shay·mwa la pay

Call a doctor.
Appelez un médecin. — a·play un mayd·sun

Call the police.
Appelez la police. — a·play la po·lees

I'm ill.
Je suis malade. — zher swee ma·lad

I'm allergic to ...
Je suis allergique à ... — zher swee za·lair·zheek a ...

Where are the toilets?
Où sont les toilettes? — oo son lay twa·let

Shopping & Services

I'd like to buy ...
Je voudrais acheter ... — zher voo·dray ash·tay ...

Can I look at it?
Est-ce que je peux le voir? — es·ker zher per ler vwar

Numbers – French

1	*un*	un
2	*deux*	der
3	*trois*	trwa
4	*quatre*	ka·trer
5	*cinq*	sungk
6	*six*	sees
7	*sept*	set
8	*huit*	weet
9	*neuf*	nerf
10	*dix*	dees
20	*vingt*	vung
30	*trente*	tront
40	*quarante*	ka·ront
50	*cinquante*	sung·kont
60	*soixante*	swa·sont
70	*soixante-dix*	swa·son·dees
80	*quatre-vingts*	ka·trer·vung
90	*quatre-vingt-dix*	ka·trer·vung·dees
100	*cent*	son
1000	*mille*	meel

How much is it?
C'est combien? — say kom·byun

It's too expensive.
C'est trop cher. — say tro shair

Can you lower the price?
Vous pouvez baisser le prix? — voo poo·vay bay·say ler pree

ATM	*guichet automatique de banque*	gee·shay o·to·ma·teek der bonk
internet cafe	*cybercafé*	see·bair·ka·fay
post office	*bureau de poste*	bew·ro der post
tourist office	*office de tourisme*	o·fees der too·rees·mer

Time & Dates

What time is it?
Quelle heure est-il? — kel er ay til

It's (eight) o'clock.
Il est (huit) heures. — il ay (weet) er

It's half past (10).
Il est (dix) heures et demie. — il ay (deez) er ay day·mee

morning	*matin*	ma·tun
afternoon	*après-midi*	a·pray·mee·dee
evening	*soir*	swar

yesterday	hier	yair
today	aujourd'hui	o·zhoor·dwee
tomorrow	demain	der·mun

Monday	lundi	lun·dee
Tuesday	mardi	mar·dee
Wednesday	mercredi	mair·krer·dee
Thursday	jeudi	zher·dee
Friday	vendredi	von·drer·dee
Saturday	samedi	sam·dee
Sunday	dimanche	dee·monsh

Transport & Directions

boat	bateau	ba·to
bus	bus	bews
plane	avion	a·vyon
train	train	trun

a ... ticket	un billet ...	un bee·yay ...
one-way	simple	sum·pler
return	aller et retour	a·lay ay rer·toor

I want to go to ...
Je voudrais aller à ...   zher voo·dray a·lay a ...

At what time does it leave/arrive?
À quelle heure est-ce   a kel er es
qu'il part/arrive?   kil par/a·reev

Does it stop at ...?
Est-ce qu'il s'arrête à ...?   es·kil sa·ret a ...

Can you tell me when we get to ...?
Pouvez-vous me dire   poo·vay·voo mer deer
quand nous arrivons à ...?   kon noo za·ree·von a ...

I want to get off here.
Je veux descendre   zher ver day·son·drer
ici.   ee·see

Where's ...?
Où est ...?   oo ay ...

What's the address?
Quelle est l'adresse?   kel ay la·dres

Can you show me (on the map)?
Pouvez-vous   poo·vay·voo
m'indiquer   mun·dee·kay
(sur la carte)?   (sewr la kart)

PORTUGUESE

Most sounds in Portuguese are also found in English. The exceptions are the nasal vowels (represented in our pronunciation guides by ng after the vowel), which are pronounced as if you're trying to make the sound through your nose; and the strongly rolled r (repre-sented by rr in our pronunciation guides). Also note that the symbol zh sounds like the 's' in 'pleasure'. The stressed syllables are indicated with italics.

Masculine and feminine forms of words are provided in the following phrases where relevant, indicated with 'm' and 'f' respectively.

Basics

Hello.	Olá.	o·laa
Goodbye.	Adeus.	a·de·oosh
Excuse me.	Faz favor.	faash fa·vor
Sorry.	Desculpe.	desh·kool·pe
Yes.	Sim.	seeng
No.	Não.	nowng
Please.	Por favor.	poor fa·vor
Thank you.	Obrigado.	o·bree·gaa·doo (m)
	Obrigada.	o·bree·gaa·da (f)
You're welcome.	De nada.	de naa·da

How are you?
Como está?   ko·moo shtaa

Fine, and you?
Bem, e você?   beng e vo·se

What's your name?
Qual é o seu nome?   kwaal e oo se·oo no·me

My name is ...
O meu nome é ...   oo me·oo no·me e ...

Do you speak English?
Fala inglês?   faa·la eeng·glesh

I don't understand.
Não entendo.   nowng eng·teng·doo

Accommodation

campsite	parque de campismo	paar·ke de kang·peezh·moo
guesthouse	casa de hóspedes	kaa·za de osh·pe·desh
hotel	hotel	o·tel
youth hostel	pousada de juventude	poh·zaa·da de zhoo·veng·too·de

Do you have a single/double room?
Tem um quarto de   teng oong kwaar·too de
solteiro/casal?   sol·tay·roo/ka·zal

How much is it per night/person?
Quanto custa   kwang·too koosh·ta
por noite/pessoa?   poor noy·te/pe·so·a

Is breakfast included?
Inclui o pequeno   eeng·kloo·ee oo pe·ke·noo
almoço?   aal·mo·soo

LANGUAGE PORTUGUESE

Eating & Drinking

I'd like (the menu).
Queria (um menu).   ke·*ree*·a (oong me·*noo*)

What would you recommend?
O que é que   oo ke e ke
recomenda?   rre·koo·*meng*·da

I don't eat ...
Eu não como ...   e·oo nowng ko·moo ...

Cheers!
Saúde!   sa·oo·de

Please bring the bill.
Pode-me trazer a conta.   po·de·me tra·zer a *kong*·ta

beer	cerveja	ser·ve·zha
bottle	garrafa	ga·rraa·fa
bread	pão	powng
breakfast	pequeno almoço	pe·ke·noo aal·mo·soo
cheese	queijo	kay·zhoo
coffee	café	ka·fe
cold	frio	free·oo
dinner	jantar	zhang·taar
egg	ovo	o·voo
food	comida	koo·mee·da
fork	garfo	gar·foo
fruit	fruta	froo·ta
glass	copo	ko·poo
hot (warm)	quente	keng·te
juice	sumo	soo·moo
knife	faca	faa·ka
lunch	almoço	aal·mo·soo
main course	prato principal	praa·too preeng·see·paal
market	mercado	mer·kaa·doo
milk	leite	lay·te
plate	prato	praa·too
red wine	vinho tinto	vee·nyoo teeng·too
restaurant	restaurante	rresh·tow·rang·te
rice	arroz	a·rrosh
salt	sal	saal
spicy	picante	pee·kang·te
spoon	colher	koo·lyer
sugar	açúcar	a·soo·kar
tea	chá	shaa
vegetable	hortaliça	or·ta·lee·sa
vegetarian food	comida vegetariana	koo·mee·da ve·zhe·ta·ree·aa·na
(mineral) water	água (mineral)	aa·gwa (mee·ne·raal)

white wine	vinho branco	vee·nyoo brang·koo
with	com	kong
without	sem	seng

Emergencies

Help!
Socorro!   soo·ko·rroo

Go away!
Vá-se embora!   vaa·se eng·bo·ra

Call ...!	Chame ...!	shaa·me ...
a doctor	um médico	oong me·dee·koo
the police	a polícia	a poo·lee·sya

I'm lost.
Estou perdido.   shtoh per·dee·doo (m)
Estou perdida.   shtoh per·dee·da (f)

I'm ill.
Estou doente.   shtoh doo·eng·te

Where is the toilet?
Onde é a casa de   ong·de e a kaa·za de
banho?   ba·nyoo

Shopping & Services

I'd like to buy ...
Queria comprar ...   ke·ree·a kong·praar ...

Can I look at it?
Posso ver?   po·soo ver

How much is it?
Quanto custa?   kwang·too koosh·ta

It's too expensive.
Está muito caro.   shtaa mweeng·too kaa·roo

Can you lower the price?
Pode baixar o preço?   po·de bai·shaar oo pre·soo

ATM	caixa automático	kai·sha ow·too·maa·tee·koo
internet cafe	café da internet	ka·fe da eeng·ter·ne·te
post office	correio	koo·rray·oo
tourist office	escritório de turismo	shkree·to·ryoo de too·reezh·moo

Time & Dates

What time is it?
Que horas são?   kee o·rash sowng

It's (10) o'clock.
São (dez) horas.   sowng (desh) o·rash

Half past (10).
(Dez) e meia.   (desh) e may·a

Numbers – Portuguese

1	um	oong
2	dois	doysh
3	três	tresh
4	quatro	kwaa·troo
5	cinco	seeng·koo
6	seis	saysh
7	sete	se·te
8	oito	oy·too
9	nove	no·ve
10	dez	desh
20	vinte	veeng·te
30	trinta	treeng·ta
40	quarenta	kwa·reng·ta
50	cinquenta	seeng·kweng·ta
60	sessenta	se·seng·ta
70	setenta	se·teng·ta
80	oitenta	oy·teng·ta
90	noventa	no·veng·ta
100	cem	seng
1000	mil	meel

morning	manhã	ma·nyang
afternoon	tarde	taar·de
evening	noite	noy·te
yesterday	ontem	ong·teng
today	hoje	o·zhe
tomorrow	amanhã	aa·ma·nyang

Monday	segunda-feira	se·goong·da·fay·ra
Tuesday	terça-feira	ter·sa·fay·ra
Wednesday	quarta-feira	kwaar·ta·fay·ra
Thursday	quinta-feira	keeng·ta·fay·ra
Friday	sexta-feira	saysh·ta·fay·ra
Saturday	sábado	saa·ba·doo
Sunday	domingo	doo·meeng·goo

Transport & Directions

boat	barco	baar·koo
bus	autocarro	ow·to·kaa·roo
plane	avião	a·vee·owng
train	comboio	kong·boy·oo

... ticket	um bilhete de ...	oong bee·lye·te de ...
one-way	ida	ee·da
return	ida e volta	ee·da ee vol·ta

I want to go to ...
Queria ir a ...   ke·ree·a eer a ...

What time does it leave/arrive?
A que horas sai/chega?   a ke o·rash sai/she·ga

Does it stop at ...?
Pára em ...?   paa·ra eng ...

Please tell me when we get to ...
Por favor avise-me   poor fa·vor a·vee·ze·me
quando chegarmos   kwang·doo she·gaar·moosh
a ...   a ...

Please stop here.
Por favor pare aqui.   poor fa·vor paa·re a·kee

Where's (the station)?
Onde é (a estação)?   ong·de e (a shta·sowng)

What's the address?
Qual é o endereço?   kwaal e oo eng·de·re·soo

Can you show me (on the map)?
Pode-me mostrar   po·de·me moosh·traar
(no mapa)?   (noo maa·pa)

HAUSA

As one of the lingua francas of West Africa, Hausa is spoken by around 40 million people. For over half of these, Hausa is their first language. Most native speakers live in northern Nigeria and southern Niger, where Hausa is one of the national languages. It's also spoken in parts of Benin, Burkina Faso, Cameroon, Côte d'Ivoire and Ghana. In the past Hausa was written in a modified form of Arabic script, but since the early 19th century a slightly modified Roman alphabet is its official written form.

Hausa's glottalised consonants, represented in our pronunciation guides by an apostrophe after the letter (b', d', k', ts' and y'), are produced by tightening and releasing the space between the vocal cords; note that the sounds b' and d' have an extra twist – instead of breathing out, you breathe in. The apostrophe before a vowel (as in a'a) indicates a glottal stop (like the pause in 'uh-oh').

Hello.	Sannu.	san·nu
Goodbye.	Sai wani lokaci.	say wa·ni law·ka·chee
Yes.	I.	ee
No.	A'a.	a'a
Please.	Don Allah.	don al·laa
Thank you.	Na gode.	naa gaw·dey
Sorry.	Yi hak'uri.	yi ha·k'u·ree
Help!	Taimake ni!	tai·ma·kyey ni

Do you speak English?
Kana/Kina jin   ka·naa/ki·naa jin
turanci? (m/f)   too·ran·chee

I don't understand.
Ban gane ba. — ban gaa·ney ba

How much is it?
Kud'insa nawa ne? — ku·d'in·sa na·wa ney

Where are the toilets?
Ina ban d'aki yake? — i·naa ban d'aa·kee yak·yey

1	*d'aya*	d'a·ya
2	*biyu*	bi·yu
3	*uku*	u·ku
4	*hud'u*	hu·d'u
5	*biyar*	bi·yar
6	*shida*	shi·da
7	*bakwai*	bak·wai
8	*takwas*	tak·was
9	*tara*	ta·ra
10	*goma*	gaw·ma

WOLOF

Wolof is the lingua franca of Senegal (particularly the area north and east of Dakar and along the coast) and Gambia (the western regions), where it's spoken by about 80 percent of the population (eight million people) as a first or second language. It's also spoken on a smaller scale in the neighbouring countries of Mauritania, Mali and Guinea.

Note that in our pronunciation guides, the stressed syllables are in italics. Also, uh is pronounced as the 'a' in 'ago', kh as the 'ch' in the Scottish *loch* and r is trilled.

Hello.	*Salaam aleekum.*	sa·*laam* a·*ley*·kum
Goodbye.	*Mangi dem.*	*maan*·gee dem
Yes.	*Waaw.*	waaw
No.	*Déedéet.*	*dey*·deyt
Please.	*Bu la neexee.*	boo la *ney*·khey
Thank you.	*Jërejëf.*	je·re·jef
Sorry.	*Baal ma.*	baal ma
Help!	*Wóoy!*	wohy

Do you speak English?
Ndax dégg nga angale? — ndakh deg nguh *an*·ga·ley

I don't understand.
Dégguma. — deg·goo·ma

How much is it?
Ñaata lay jar? — nyaa·ta lai jar

Where are the toilets?
Ana wanag wi? — a·na wa·nak wee

1	*benn*	ben
2	*ñaar*	nyaar

3	*ñett*	nyet
4	*ñeent*	nyeynt
5	*juróom*	joo·rohm
6	*juróom benn*	joo·rohm ben
7	*juróom ñaar*	joo·rohm nyaar
8	*juróom ñett*	joo·rohm nyet
9	*juróom ñeent*	joo·rohm nyeynt
10	*fukk*	fuk

YORUBA

Yoruba is one of the main lingua francas in the eastern part of West Africa and is spoken by around 25 million people. It is primarily used as a first language in southwestern Nigeria. There are also Yoruba speakers in Benin and eastern Togo, and a variety of the language is spoken in Sierra Leone.

Yoruba's nasal vowels, indicated in our pronunciation guides with ng after the vowel, are pronounced as if you're trying to force the sound through the nose.

Hello.	*Pèlé o.*	kpe·le o
Goodbye.	*Ó dàbò.*	oh da·bo
Yes.	*Béèni.*	be·e·ni
No.	*Béèkó.*	be·e·ko
Please.	*Jòwó.*	jo·wo
Thank you.	*Oṣé.*	oh·shay
Sorry.	*Má bìínú.*	ma bi·i·nu
Help!	*Ẹ ràn mí lówó ọ!*	e rang mi lo·wo o

Do you speak English?
Ṣé o ń ṣo gèésì? — shay o n so ge·e·si

I don't understand.
Èmi kò gbó. — ay·mi koh gbo

How much is it?
Èló ni? — ay·loh ni

Where are the toilets?
Ibo ni ilé ìgbònṣè wà? — i·boh ni i·lay i·gbong·se wa

1	*òkan*	o·kang
2	*èjì*	ay·ji
3	*èta*	e·ta
4	*èrin*	e·ring
5	*àrun*	a·rung
6	*èfà*	e·fa
7	*èje*	ay·jay
8	*èjo*	e·jo
9	*èsan*	e·sang
10	*ẹ̀wá*	e·wa

GLOSSARY

The following is a list of words and acronyms used in this book that you are likely to come across in West Africa.

achaba – motorcycle taxi (northern Nigeria); see also *okada*

adinkra – handmade printed cloth from Ghana worn primarily by the Ashanti

Afrique Occidentale Française – see *French West Africa*

Afrobeat – a fusion of African music, jazz and soul originated and popularised by Fela Kuti of Nigeria; along with *juju* it's the most popular music in Nigeria

Akan – a major group of peoples along the south coast of West Africa; includes the Ashanti and Fanti peoples

akpeteshie – palm wine

akuaba – Ashanti carved figure

aluguer – for hire (sign in minibus)

Asantehene – the king or su-preme ruler of the Ashanti people

Ashanti – the largest tribal group in Ghana, concentrated around Kumasi

auberge – used in West Africa to mean any small hotel

autogare – see *gare routière*

bacalau – salted flakes of cod

bâché – covered pick-up ('ute') used as a basic bush taxi

balafon – xylophone

Bambara – Mali's major ethnic group found in the centre and south and famous for its wooden carvings

banco – bank; clay or mud used for building

Baoulé – an Akan-speaking people from Côte d'Ivoire with strong animist beliefs

Bobo – animist people of west-ern Burkina Faso and southern Mali, famous for their mask traditions

bogolan cloth – often simply called mud-cloth, this is cotton cloth with designs painted on

using various types of mud for colour; made by the Bambara of Mali but found throughout the region

boubou – the common name for the elaborate robe-like outfit worn by men and women

boukarous – open-sided, circular mud huts

brake – see *Peugeot taxi*

Bundu – Krio word for 'secret society'; used in Liberia and in certain parts of Sierra Leone and Côte d'Ivoire; includes the Poro society for men and the Sande for women; in Sierra Leone, the women's secret society is spelled Bondo

Burkinabé – adjective for Burkina Faso

bush taxi – along with buses, this is the most common form of public transport in West Africa; there are three main types of bush taxi: Peugeot taxi, minibus and pick-up (*bâché*)

buvette – refreshment stall

cadeau – gift, tip, bribe or handout, see also *dash*

campement – loosely trans-lated as 'hostel', 'inn' or 'lodge', but it's not a camping ground (ie a place for tents, although some *campements* allow you to pitch tents); traditionally, *campements* offer simple accommodation

canoa – motor-canoe

car – large bus, see also *minicar*

car rapide – minibus, usually used in cities; often decrepit, may be fast or very slow

carnet – document required if you are bringing a car into most countries of the region

carrefour – literally 'cross-roads', but also used to mean meeting place

carte jaune – vaccination certificate

case – hut

case à impluvium – huge round hut with a hole in the roof to collect rainwater

CFA – the West African franc (used in Benin, Burkina Faso,

Côte d'Ivoire, Guinea-Bissau, Mali, Niger, Senegal and Togo) or Central African franc (Cameroon)

cidade – city

cinq-cent-quatre – 504; see *Peugeot taxi*

climatisée – air-conditioned; often shortened to 'clim'

coladeiras – old-style music; romantic, typically sentimental upbeat love songs

commissariat – police station

compteur – meter in taxi

correios – post office

couchette – sleeping berth on a train

croix d'Agadez – Tuareg talisman that protects its wearer from the 'evil eye'

Dan – an animist people living in western Côte d'Ivoire and Liberia with strong mask traditions

Dahomey – pre-independence name of Benin

dash – bribe or tip (noun); also used as a verb, 'You dash me something...'

déplacement – a taxi or boat that you 'charter' for yourself

djembe – type of drum

Dogon – people found in Mali, east of Mopti; famous for their cliff dwellings, cosmology and arts

durbar – ceremony or celebra-tion, usually involving a cavalry parade, found, for example, in the Muslim northern Nigerian states

Ecowas – Economic Commu-nity of West African States

Eid al-Fitr – feast to celebrate the end of Ramadan

Eid al-Kabir – see *Tabaski*

Empire of Ghana – one of the great Sahel empires that flourished in the 8th to 11th centuries AD and covered much of present-day Mali and parts of Senegal

Empire of Mali – Islamic Sahel empire that was at its peak in the 14th century, covering the region between present-day Senegal and Niger

essence – petrol (gas) for car

Ewe – Forest-dwelling people of Ghana and Togo

fado – haunting melancholy blues-style Portuguese music

fanals – large lanterns; also the processions during which the lanterns are carried through the streets

Fanti – part of the Akan group of people based along the coast in southwest Ghana and Côte d'Ivoire; traditionally fishing people and farmers

fête – festival

fêtes des masques – ceremony with masks

fiche – form (to complete)

Foulbé – see *Fula*

French West Africa – area of West and Central Africa acquired by France at the Berlin Conference in 1884–85 which divided Africa up between the European powers; 'Afrique Occidentale Française' in French

Fula – a people spread widely through West Africa, mostly nomadic cattle herders; also known as 'Fulani', 'Peul' or 'Foulbé'

fula-fula – converted truck or pick-up; rural public transport

funaná – distinctive fast-paced music with a Latin rhythm that's great for dancing; usually features players on the accordion and tapping with metal

gara – a thin cotton material, tie-dyed or stamp-printed, with bright colours and bold patterns

garage – bush taxi and bus park

gare lagunaire – lagoon ferry terminal

gare maritime – ferry terminal

gare routière – bus and bush-taxi station, also called 'gare voiture' or 'autogare'

gare voiture – see *gare routière*

gasoil – diesel fuel

gelli-gelli – minibus in The Gambia

gendarmerie – police station/post

gîte – used interchangeably in West Africa with *auberge* and *campement*

Gold Coast – pre-independence name for modern state of Ghana

Grain Coast – old name for Liberia

griot – traditional caste of musicians or praise singers; many of West Africa's music stars come from *griot* families

Hausa – people originally from northern Nigeria and southern Niger, mostly farmers and traders

highlife – a style of music, originating in Ghana, combining West African and Western influences

hôtel de ville – town hall

ibeji – Yoruba carved twin figures

IDP – International Driving Permit

Igbo – one of the three major peoples in Nigeria, concentrated predominantly in the southeast

IGN – Institut Géographique National

immeuble – large building, for example, office block

impluvium – large round traditional house with roof constructed to collect rain water in central tank or bowl

insha'allah – God willing, ie hopefully (Arabic, but used by Muslims in Africa)

jardim – garden

jeli – see *griot*

juju – the music style characterised by tight vocal harmonies and sophisticated guitar work, backed by traditional drums and percussion; very popular in southern Nigeria, especially with the Yoruba; see also *voodoo*

kente cloth – made with finely woven cotton, and sometimes silk, by Ghana's Ashanti people

Kingdom of Benin – one of the great West African kingdoms (13th to 19th centuries); based in Nigeria around Benin City and famous for its bronze or brass

kora – harp-like musical instrument with over 20 strings

Lobi – people based in southwest Burkina Faso and northern Côte d'Ivoire, famous for their figurative sculpture and compounds known as *soukala*

lorry park – see *motor park*

luttes – traditional wrestling matches

macaco – monkey; a popular meat dish in upcountry Guinea-Bissau

mairie – town hall; mayor's office

maison d'hôte – small hotel or guesthouse

makossa – Cameroonian musical form that fuses Highlife and soul

malafa – crinkly voile material worn as a veil by women in Mauritania

Malinké – Guinea's major ethnic group, also found in southern Mali, northwestern Côte d'Ivoire and eastern Senegal; closely related to the Bambara and famous for founding the Empire of Mali; also related to the Mandinka

Mandinka – people based in central and northern Gambia and Senegal; also the name of their language, which is closely related to Malinké; both Malinké and Mandinka are part of the wider Manding group

maquis – rustic open-air restaurant; traditionally open only at night

marché – market

mbalax – percussion-driven, Senegalese dance music

mercado – market

minicar – minibus

Moors – also called 'Maurs'; the predominant nomadic people of Mauritania, now also well known as merchants and found scattered over French-speaking West Africa

mornas – old-style music; mournful and sad, similar to the Portuguese *fado* style from whence they may have originated

Moro-Naba – the king of the Mossi people

Mossi – the people who occupy the central area of Burkina Faso

485

LANGUAGE GLOSSARY

and comprise about half the population of that country

motor park – bus and bush-taxi park (English-speaking countries); also called 'lorry park'

moto-taxi – motorcycle taxi

Mourides – the most powerful of the Islamic brotherhoods in Senegal

mud-cloth – see *bogolan cloth*

oba – a Yoruba chief or king

occasion – a lift or place in a car or bus (often shortened to 'occas')

okada – motorcycle taxi

oni – chief priest

orchestra – in West Africa, this means a group playing popular music

paillote – a thatched sun shelter (usually on a beach or around an open-air bar-restaurant)

palava – meeting place

paletuviers – mangroves

pam-pah – large cargo/passenger boats (Sierra Leone)

paragem – bus and bush-taxi park

patron – owner, boss

pensão – hotel or guesthouse

pension – simple hotel or hostel, or 'board'

Peugeot taxi – one of the main types of bush taxi; also called *brake, cinq-cent-quatre,* 'Peugeot 504' or *sept place*

Peul – see *Fula*

pinasse – large *pirogue*, usually used on rivers, for hauling people and cargo

pirogue – traditional canoe, either a small dugout or large, narrow sea-going wooden fishing boat

pharmacie de garde – all-night pharmacy

piste – track or dirt road

poda-poda – minibus

posuban – ensemble of statues representing a proverb or event in Fanti culture

pousada – guesthouse

praça – park or square

praia – beach

préfecture – police headquarters

PTT – post (and often telephone) office in Francophone countries

Ramadan – Muslim month of fasting

residencial – guest house

rond-point – roundabout

rua – street

Sahel – dry semi-desert and savannah area south of the Sahara desert; most of Senegal, The Gambia, Mali, Burkina Faso and Niger; the name means 'coast' in Arabic

Scramble for Africa – term used for the land-grabbing frenzy in the 1880s by the European powers in which France, Britain and Germany laid claim to various parts of the continent

Senoufo – a strongly animist people straddling Côte d'Ivoire, Burkina Faso and Mali

sept place – Peugeot taxi seven-seater (usually carrying up to 12 people)

sharia – Muslim law

Songhaï – ethnic group located primarily in northeastern Mali and western Niger along the Niger River; also Empire of Songhaï which ruled the Sahel with its heyday in the 15th century

soukala – a castle-like housing compound of the Lobi tribe found in the Bouna area of southern Burkina Faso

spirale antimostique – mosquito coil

sûreté – police station

syndicat d'initiative – tourist information office

Tabaski – Eid al-Kabir; also known as the Great Feast, this is the most important celebration throughout West Africa

taguelmoust – shawl or scarf worn as headgear by Tuareg men

tama – hand-held drum

tata somba – a castle-like house of the Batammariba tribe who live in northwestern Benin and Togo

taxi brousse – bush taxi

taxi-course – shared taxi (in cities)

taxi-moto – see *moto-taxi*

télécentre – privately run telecommunications centres

tikit – traditional thatched stone hut used as accommodation in Mauritania

toca-toca – small minibus in Bissau

totem – used in traditional religions, similar to a fetish

town trip – private hire (taxi)

tro-tro – a minibus or pick-up

Tuareg – nomadic descendants of the North African Berbers; found all over the Sahara, especially in Mali, Niger and southern Algeria

voodoo – the worship of spirits with supernatural powers widely practised in southern Benin and Togo; also called *juju*

vu gbe – **talking drums**

wassoulou – singing style made famous by Mali's Oumou Sangaré

Wolof – Senegal's major ethnic group; also found in The Gambia

woro-woro – minibus

Yoruba – a major ethnic group concentrated in southwestern Nigeria

zemi-john – motorcycle-taxi

Behind the Scenes

SEND US YOUR FEEDBACK

We love to hear from travellers – your comments keep us on our toes and help make our books better. Our well-travelled team reads every word on what you loved or loathed about this book. Although we cannot reply individually to your submissions, we always guarantee that your feedback goes straight to the appropriate authors, in time for the next edition. Each person who sends us information is thanked in the next edition – the most useful submissions are rewarded with a selection of digital PDF chapters.

Visit **lonelyplanet.com/contact** to submit your updates and suggestions or to ask for help. Our award-winning website also features inspirational travel stories, news and discussions.

Note: We may edit, reproduce and incorporate your comments in Lonely Planet products such as guidebooks, websites and digital products, so let us know if you don't want your comments reproduced or your name acknowledged. For a copy of our privacy policy visit lonelyplanet.com/privacy.

OUR READERS

Many thanks to the travellers who used the last edition and wrote to us with helpful hints, useful advice and interesting anecdotes:

Alex Wharton, Andrew Anderson, Anna Maedl, Ask Gudmundsen, Daniel Herszberg, Dimitrije Wentner, Flavia Robin, Jaime Diniz, Jeroen van der Hof, Jon Wisloff, Jonathan Fowle, Karen Kort, Karin Torsdotter, Lesley Wieme, Luke Edwards, Mickaël Tricot, Mikkel Christensen, Monique Teggelove, Nathan Nlanc, Peter Shortall, Rhia Haywood , Samuel Akologo, Santiago Ormeno, Sofie Nielsen, Yvonne & Lex Warners,

WRITER THANKS

Anthony Ham

Sincere thanks to Matt Phillips, my editor and wise Africa hand, for letting me roam across the continent in person and in print. Huge thanks also to the numerous writers who contributed to this edition.

Stuart Butler

First and foremost I must thank my wife, Heather, and children, Jake and Grace, for their patience and understanding while I was away in Guinea. Thanks to Patrick Madelaine for the car and Bouba for driving. Big thanks to Christelle Colin and team for a great weekend with the chimps. Thank you to Ismaël for the hospitality. Finally, thanks to the *guerisseur* for making the magic spell for my children – they loved it!

Michael Grosberg

In Guinea-Bissau, thanks to Adlino Costa for sharing his insights about his homeland; Daniel da Silva for his good-natured help; Mario for getting me to the islands; Solange and Alain on Rubane for their hospitality and assistance when sick; and to the Swiss travellers with whom I shared a beautiful Thanksgiving lunch and who picked me up when sick on the beach after hippo spotting on Orango. And my baby Rosie for her wonderful homecoming hugs. In Mauritania, my gratitude goes to Theresa Eno, Sidi Boidaha, Jimmy Baum, Adam Janssen, Isabelle and Frederic, and Betsy Freeman.

Nana Luckham

Thanks to all who helped me along the way, including Joe Addo, Aboubacar Diédhiou, Melvin Kraan, Richard at the Sleepy Hippo Hotel, Geoffrey Awoonor-Renner at Visit Sierra Leone for his invaluable advice, Fritz and Angela for their company on the road in Sierra Leone, Tapsir and Hannah for their hospitality in Freetown, Elizabeth Yirenchi, George Tenkorang and Zena Ampofo-Tenkorang for putting me up in Accra, Patrick Smith at Africa Confidential for useful pre-departure advice as always, and Yaa Yeboah and Benjamin Swift for minding the fort at home.

Vesna Maric

I would like to thank Matt Phillips for commissioning me for the project. Additional thanks go to Pascale and Charlotte in Abidjan, Ali in Burkina Faso, and Cheryl in Grand Bassam.

Helen Ranger

In Equatorial Guinea, thanks to Ambassador Crisantos Obama Ondo in Morocco who encouraged my trip to his country. In Malabo, Ángel Vañó shared his kaleidoscopic knowledge of Equatorial Guinea with great enthusiasm. To the local inhabitants who were astonished to see a tourist, thank you for a fascinating experience. May you see many more.

Caroline Sieg

Thanks to Myriam and Glenn in Cotonou for being such amazing hosts and travel buddies and for getting me sorted when my phone was stolen on Day 2. I owe you both massive beers in Munich. Special thanks to Lara for the pre-trip Liberia info and for being a voice on the phone when I most needed it. Big *bisou* to Lawrence for all the picnic supplies and last but not least, thanks to my Fatima for the endless supply of information and suggestions.

Helena Smith

Thanks for pre-trip help to Ranx, Segun, Alastair and Helen and Cordelia. In Cameroon: Caesar for excellent driving, Agatha and Ashwu in Limbe, Cyril in Buea for his kind invitation, Ismael in Foumban, Kelvin from Bamenda and Chris in Yaoundé. In Nigeria: Bikiya, Toba, Odunola and Leke for the warmest Lagos welcome, our friends Chike and Edet at Bogobiri, Kunle and his wife at the Jazz Hole, Boma for taking us to the Shrine, Rasheed for fantastic driving, Nike and her team, Doyin for a gracious Yoruba welcome, Puja and Philip in Benin and Zac in Calabar. And to Art, for bringing a guitar and an open heart to Africa.

Regis St Louis

Countless guides, drivers, boat captains, innkeepers and many others helped along the way – and I am deeply grateful to the warmhearted people in West Africa. Special thanks go to Adama Ba, whose driving skills, humor and patience made the Senegambia journey a success. In Cabo Verde, thanks to Erick on Brava, Fatima on Fogo, Guillaume on Santo Antão, and Carolyn, Ismael and Bemvindo on Maio. Thanks to the support of Cassandra and daughters Magdalena and Genevieve, who make this whole endeavour worthwhile.

Paul Stiles

My great thanks to Matt for this terrific assignment, to Diogo and Luis for helping steer me through the country, and to the many guides I met along the way, particularly Armando, Helton, Yves, Ruben, and Ramos. No leve leve allowed! As usual, I must also thank Sarah for taking care of the home front while I was away, not to mention putting up that São Tomé wood carving in the kitchen.

ACKNOWLEDGEMENTS

Climate map data adapted from Peel MC, Finlayson BL & McMahon TA (2007) 'Updated World Map of the Köppen-Geiger Climate Classification', Hydrology and Earth System Sciences, 11, 163344.

Cover photograph: Basketry market near Thies, Senegal, Tuul and Bruno Morandi/Getty ©

THIS BOOK

This 9th edition of Lonely Planet's West Africa guidebook was researched and written by Anthony Ham, Stuart Butler, Michael Grosberg, Nana Luckham, Vesna Maric, Helen Ranger, Caroline Sieg, Helena Smith, Paul Stiles and Regis St Louis. The previous edition was written by Anthony Ham, Jean-Bernard Carillet, Paul Clammer, Emilie Filou, Nana Luckham, Tom Masters, Anja Mutić, Caroline Sieg, Kate Thomas and Vanessa Wruble. This guidebook was produced by the following:

Destination Editor Matt Phillips

Product Editors Bruce Evans, Sandie Kestell

Senior Cartographer Diana Von Holdt

Book Designer Gwen Cotter

Assisting Editors Imogen Bannister, Janice Bird, Nigel Chin, Melanie Dankel, Andrea Dobbin, Samantha Forge, Carly Hall, Ali Lemer, Jodie Martire, Lou McGregor, Monique Perrin, Gabrielle Stefanos, Fionnuala Twomey, Simon Williamson

Assisting Cartographers Rachel Imeson, James Leversha

Assisting Book Designer Ania Bartoszek

Cover Researcher Naomi Parker

Thanks to Lauren O'Connell

Index

NOTES

Map Legend

Sights
- Beach
- Bird Sanctuary
- Buddhist
- Castle/Palace
- Christian
- Confucian
- Hindu
- Islamic
- Jain
- Jewish
- Monument
- Museum/Gallery/Historic Building
- Ruin
- Shinto
- Sikh
- Taoist
- Winery/Vineyard
- Zoo/Wildlife Sanctuary
- Other Sight

Activities, Courses & Tours
- Bodysurfing
- Diving
- Canoeing/Kayaking
- Course/Tour
- Sento Hot Baths/Onsen
- Skiing
- Snorkelling
- Surfing
- Swimming/Pool
- Walking
- Windsurfing
- Other Activity

Sleeping
- Sleeping
- Camping

Eating
- Eating

Drinking & Nightlife
- Drinking & Nightlife
- Cafe

Entertainment
- Entertainment

Shopping
- Shopping

Information
- Bank
- Embassy/Consulate
- Hospital/Medical
- Internet
- Police
- Post Office
- Telephone
- Toilet
- Tourist Information
- Other Information

Geographic
- Beach
- Gate
- Hut/Shelter
- Lighthouse
- Lookout
- Mountain/Volcano
- Oasis
- Park
- Pass
- Picnic Area
- Waterfall

Population
- Capital (National)
- Capital (State/Province)
- City/Large Town
- Town/Village

Transport
- Airport
- Border crossing
- Bus
- Cable car/Funicular
- Cycling
- Ferry
- Metro station
- Monorail
- Parking
- Petrol station
- Subway station
- Taxi
- Train station/Railway
- Tram
- Underground station
- Other Transport

Note: Not all symbols displayed above appear on the maps in this book

Routes
- Tollway
- Freeway
- Primary
- Secondary
- Tertiary
- Lane
- Unsealed road
- Road under construction
- Plaza/Mall
- Steps
- Tunnel
- Pedestrian overpass
- Walking Tour
- Walking Tour detour
- Path/Walking Trail

Boundaries
- International
- State/Province
- Disputed
- Regional/Suburb
- Marine Park
- Cliff
- Wall

Hydrography
- River, Creek
- Intermittent River
- Canal
- Water
- Dry/Salt/Intermittent Lake
- Reef

Areas
- Airport/Runway
- Beach/Desert
- Cemetery (Christian)
- Cemetery (Other)
- Glacier
- Mudflat
- Park/Forest
- Sight (Building)
- Sportsground
- Swamp/Mangrove

Helen Ranger

Equatorial Guinea Although born and brought up in the UK, Helen left in her early twenties to explore other shores. Cape Town was her home for many years but she now lives in Fez, Morocco. She has contributed to Lonely Planet's *Fez Encounter, South Africa, Lesotho & Swaziland, Cape Town, Africa* and *Morocco* guides. Follow her on Twitter: @helenranger @fezriads @conciergmorocco and on Instagram: helenranger and conciergemorocco.

Caroline Sieg

Benin, Liberia, Togo Caroline began her career producing foreign-language textbooks before hopping over to travel publishing, first as a travel editor at Frommer's Travel in the US and later as a commissioning editor at Lonely Planet in London. She then managed and curated digital marketing content for diverse brands including Travelzoo and Art Basel. She's written about destinations across the globe. For Lonely Planet she's covered the US, Africa and Europe.

Helena Smith

Cameroon, Nigeria Helena is an award-winning writer and photographer covering travel and food – she has written guidebooks on destinations from Fiji to northern Norway. Helena is from Scotland but was partly brought up in Malawi, so Africa always feels like home. She also enjoys global travel in her multicultural home borough of Hackney and wrote, photographed and published *Inside Hackney,* the first guide to the borough (insidehackney.com).

Regis St Louis

Cabo Verde, The Gambia, Senegal Regis grew up in a small town in the American Midwest and developed an early fascination with foreign dialects and world cultures. Regis has contributed to more than 50 Lonely Planet titles, covering destinations across six continents. His travels have taken him from the mountains of Kamchatka to remote island villages in Melanesia, and to many grand urban landscapes. When not on the road, he lives in New Orleans. Follow him on www.instagram.com/regisstlouis.

Paul Stiles

São Tomé & Príncipe When he was 21, Paul bought an old motorcycle in London and drove it to Tunisia. That did it for him. Since then he has explored around 60 countries, and covered many adventure destinations for Lonely Planet, including Morocco, Madagascar, São Tomé & Príncipe, Indonesia, the Philippines, Hawaii, Maui, and Kaua'i. In all things, he tries to follow the rocking chair rule: when making key life decisions, assume the perspective of an elderly person sitting in a rocking chair. Because some day that will be you.

OUR STORY

A beat-up old car, a few dollars in the pocket and a sense of adventure. In 1972 that's all Tony and Maureen Wheeler needed for the trip of a lifetime – across Europe and Asia overland to Australia. It took several months, and at the end – broke but inspired – they sat at their kitchen table writing and stapling together their first travel guide, *Across Asia on the Cheap*. Within a week they'd sold 1500 copies. Lonely Planet was born.

Today, Lonely Planet has offices in Franklin, London, Melbourne, Oakland, Dublin, Beijing and Delhi, with more than 600 staff and writers. We share Tony's belief that 'a great guidebook should do three things: inform, educate and amuse'.

OUR WRITERS

Anthony Ham

Plan, Understand, Survival Guide Anthony is a freelance writer and photographer who specialises in Spain, East and Southern Africa, the Arctic and the Middle East. When he's not writing for Lonely Planet, Anthony writes about and photographs Spain, Africa and the Middle East for newspapers and magazines in Australia, the UK and US.

Stuart Butler

Guinea, Mali, Nigeria Stuart's earliest travel writing was all based on surfing and exploring little-known coastlines for waves. Today, as well as guidebooks, Stuart writes often about conservation and environmental issues (mainly in eastern and southern Africa), wildlife watching and hiking. He also works as a photographer and was a finalist in both the 2015 and 2016 Travel Photographer of the Year Awards. His website is at www.stuartbutlerjournalist.com.

Michael Grosberg

Guinea-Bissau, Mauritania Michael has worked on over 45 Lonely Planet guidebooks. Prior to his freelance writing career, other international work included development on the island of Rota in the western Pacific; South Africa where he investigated and wrote about political violence and helped train newly elected government representatives; and Quito, Ecuador, teaching.

Nana Luckham

Ghana, Sierra Leone Nana began writing about travel in 2006, after several years working as a United Nations press officer in New York. She has been all over the world for Lonely Planet including to Malawi, Zambia, Algeria, South Africa, Fiji and Tuvalu. She has also written features for lonelyplanet.com and for other leading publications. Currently based in London, she's lived in New York, France, Ghana, Zimbabwe, Tanzania and Australia.

Vesna Maric

Burkina Faso, Côte d'Ivoire Vesna has been a Lonely Planet author for over a decade, covering places as far and wide as Bolivia, Algeria, Sicily, Cyprus, Barcelona, London and Croatia, among others. Her latest work has been updating the Burkina Faso and Ivory Coast chapters for the West Africa and Africa guides.

OVER PAGE MORE WRITERS

Published by Lonely Planet Global Limited
CRN 554153
9th edition – Sep 2017
ISBN 978 1 78657 042 0
© Lonely Planet 2017   Photographs © as indicated 2017
10 9 8 7 6 5 4 3 2 1
Printed in China